INTERNATIONAL HANDBOOK OF HOUSING POLICIES AND PRACTICES

International Handbook of Housing Policies and Practices

Edited by **Willem van Vliet—**

Foreword by
WILLIAM MICHELSON

GREENWOOD PRESS

New York • Westport, Connecticut • London

Library of Congress Cataloging-in-Publication Data

International handbook of housing policies and practices / edited by
    Willem van Vliet ; foreword by William Michelson.
        p.   cm.
    Includes indexes.
    ISBN 0–313–25427–3 (lib. bdg. : alk. paper)
    1. Housing policy.   2. Housing—Finance.   I. Van Vliet, Willem.
HD7287.I523   1990
363.5′8—dc19   88–34733

British Library Cataloguing in Publication Data is available.

Library of Congress Catalog Card Number: 88–34733
ISBN: 0–313–25427–3

First published in 1990

Greenwood Press, 88 Post Road West, Westport, CT 06881
An imprint of Greenwood Publishing Group, Inc.

Printed in the United States of America

The paper used in this book complies with the
Permanent Paper Standard issued by the National
Information Standards Organization (Z39.48–1984).

10 9 8 7 6 5 4 3 2 1

Contents

Figures

Tables

Foreword

WILLIAM MICHELSON

This handbook is not only a report but a resource. It does indeed report a wide range of housing considerations and information from twenty-three nations and, in so doing, provides a unique service. Beyond that, a book like this on the great extent of variation in form, organization, financing, policy concerns, and more transcends limitations to thinking based on what "has been" and presents more chance to consider what "might be."

Although housing itself is a universal need, its provision has been unusually decentralized. Most builders deal with only small segments of local markets. Very few participate in national markets and fewer yet do so internationally. Thus, few individuals or corporate entities have been in a position to view the "big picture" of housing. Housing literature mirrors this circumstance.

The practical forces that constrain housing provision are similarly limiting in reach. While there is some technological basis for factory-built housing, units are not typically mass-produced like automobiles. Many considerations in the housing market are local. For example, estimating demand, financing land development, land-use regulation, building permits, and pricing require local knowledge and contact, although such efforts are certainly stimulated, constrained, or channelled by national policies. International architectural fads and policy programs do have some cross-national presence. However, these have been found fraught with dysfunctional consequences when used indiscriminately in different cultures and settings.

Hence, despite the universal need for housing, the actual objectives underlying the creation of tangible housing units may vary widely in the absence of international or national consensus on why housing should be built and the forms and pricing it should have. It is here that the gap between formal policies at higher levels and the incentives that precipitate local production in reality may be great.

Thus, a book like this is valuable because it serves as a report on the wide-ranging considerations and practices attached to housing in various kinds of political jurisdictions around the world. However, a unique purpose is served, too. Professor Van Vliet— has organized the work of the knowledgeable contributors so as to cover, wherever possible, similar aspects of housing. Hence, beyond the obvious value of the national analyses and the editor's broader analysis of cross-cutting issues, the book presents the reader with a de facto matrix of information on many aspects of housing across the twenty-three nations. Therefore, the book is also a considerable resource to those interested in testing out for themselves the concomitants and implications of their own hunches and theories. Thus, this book is a major contribution at more than one level of housing analysis.

Acknowledgments

This project was initiated in 1985 at the suggestion of Mary Sive, then editor, social and behavioral sciences, at Greenwood Press. She was succeeded by Loomis Mayer who was very helpful throughout and patiently understanding when completion of the manuscript was delayed.

During the several years that the book was being prepared, the authors showed great responsiveness, making time to accommodate a shared chapter format that frequently asked for the gathering and compiling of hard-to-access information as well as the development of new lines of analysis. In addition, they responsibly incorporated one or more rounds of editorial feedback in writing the final version of their chapters. For assistance in this process, thanks are due to the Editorial Advisory Board. Its members gave generously of their time and made thoughtful comments to aid in the preparation of specific chapters.

Skilled secretarial help was provided by Lorraine Self, Lori Dewender, and Marcia Van Camp. Xirun Liu was indispensible in the composition of the tables. At Greenwood Press, Brian Dietz and Alicia S. Merritt proved to be extremely reliable and professional production editors. Raymond G. Studer, dean of the College of Environmental Design, University of Colorado, Boulder, gave much appreciated support to activities related to the production of this book.

Introduction

LARRY S. BOURNE

ON THE CONTEXT AND CONTENT OF HOUSING

Housing issues and policy problems are both universal and inherently specific to a given time and place. On the one hand, all countries, rich and poor, capitalist and socialist, developed and developing, are wrestling with their own housing problems and with the everyday mechanics of housing supply and regulation. The specific problems vary immensely from country to country, and most certainly the policy instruments and institutions chosen to address those problems vary. Nonetheless, there is a universal concern for the provision of adequate and affordable shelter within reasonably comfortable and supportive living environments.

On the other hand, as the chapters in this volume amply demonstrate, our definitions of housing problems and our approaches to housing policies are firmly embedded in particular national and cultural contexts. They mirror the dominant economic, political, and social conditions within each nation–state and in the numerous regions and constituencies that make up that nation. To be more precise, in most modern societies housing is not simply an object but is an integral component in the nation's financial system, its social structure, and its political and policy-making apparatus. Housing is also highly sensitive to policy decisions made in other economic and social sectors that typically do not have housing as one of their objectives. These linkages may be defined as constituting the external relations or the external context of housing. In most instances these relationships also outline a condition of dependence in which the housing sector is assigned a relatively low priority on the national political agenda.

A few simple examples of these external relations will suffice to make the point. The housing sector, directly in the capitalist world and indirectly in centrally planned and developing economies, is heavily and increasingly dependent on the cost and availability of credit, for purposes of both production and consumption. As a consequence, housing is now integrated into national and international capital markets. Its sensitivity to credit, in turn, renders it especially vulnerable to fluctuations in interest rates and to the whims of government in setting tax and fiscal policies. Furthermore, and despite their disclaimers, governments in market economies frequently use the housing sector in an attempt to dampen cyclical swings in the national economy and particularly to reduce fluctuations in employment rates, wages, and investment levels. In the socialist world, housing is often used as an instrument for achieving specific planning objectives in terms of economic and territorial development. Although the approach varies, the result is essentially the same: the housing sector is one small appendage to a much larger macroeconomic system.

For all political systems, and regardless of the mechanisms employed for housing provision, housing is invariably the unintended recipient, or victim, of policy shifts in other sectors, policies that also have differential impacts among localities. Most governments, for example, have experimented with spatial policies designed to influence the location of industry and regional economic development, the distribution of population and employment, and national transportation facilities. All governments have explicit aspatial policies with respect to national defense, immigration, health, the organization of administrative services, trade and tariffs, and social welfare, to name but a few, all of which impact on housing in some way.

In each case, these nonhousing policies, however well intentioned, act to redistribute the demand and need for housing and to restructure the matching of existing supply to that demand. In market economies such policy changes are seldom explicitly linked to the housing requirements of the population. Some of these impacts are immediate and obvious, such as the effect of a change in the taxation of capital gains on home ownership and the viability of the private rental industry. Others are less obvious and of longer-term importance, as in the case of favoring expressway construction over public transit. In centrally planned economies, in contrast, the housing sector has been used intentionally as a vehicle for implementing other policy goals, such as in facilitating large-scale industrial development or by restricting access to housing in order to control the migration of population and thus to limit the growth of the major urban areas. Third World countries, depending on their particular ideology, follow one or other of these courses, or both.

In both capitalist and socialist examples, however, the dependency status of the housing sector is evident. In the former instance the housing sector is called on to pick up the debris left by the market or by other policy initiatives, often reflected in a very inequitable distribution of housing resources. In the latter case housing is part of the advance guard for other agencies and purposes of central government. The result is typically an absolute shortage of housing and a lower overall level of housing quality. Third World countries tend to display both characteristics in varying blends.

To reiterate, such nonhousing policies, in combination, may have more substantial impacts on the housing sector than the labeled or explicit housing policies. These impacts, largely unintended and implicit, have been defined by some observers as a nation's "real" housing policy. All too often housing researchers focus their attention exclusively on the impacts of explicit policies, ignoring the much larger roles of other policies. Admittedly, it is not an easy assignment to attempt an assessment of the housing impacts of such a large and complex set of policies. In some instances the outcomes are simply not measurable or may not be apparent for some decades. Nevertheless, it is usually a mistake to attribute observed changes in housing conditions exclusively to specific housing policy initiatives apart from events in other national sectors.

LIVING WITH UNCERTAINTY

Assessing the contribution to the measurement of housing progress of shifts in the demand side of the housing equation is especially difficult. Most countries in the industrialized world have witnessed dramatic changes in their demographic structures, life-styles, and household-income profiles since 1945. Living arrangements, and thus housing demand, have been altered accordingly. Who would have anticipated the baby boom of the 1950s and 1960s and the marriage bust of the 1970s and 1980s? Or the shrinkage of average household size and the rapid rise in the proportion of one-person households? How far will this social process, which effectively partitions the units of housing demand into smaller and smaller units, go? We might also turn this question around. What role does the availability of an abundant supply of housing play in facilitating new household formation? Clearly, the supply and demand components in any housing system must be treated as part of the same equation, but each component also has its own internal dynamic.

Adding to the uncertainties posed by social and demographic change are the difficult problems involved in interpreting some of the standard indices used to measure current housing conditions. What, for example, does a low rental-vacancy rate imply? A shortage of dwelling units in the rental sector perhaps? Or, conversely, it could suggest that proportionally more households have been able to establish separate living quarters than was the case previously because their incomes are higher and because the stock is available. Or does it suggest a shortage not in rental housing but elsewhere in the housing stock, such as in the owner-occupied sector or in public housing? Similar alternative interpretations may be applied to a range of other indices, such as an increase in prices and in the proportion of household income spent on housing (the affordability and quality problem). The point is that we cannot simply accept standard housing indices at face value without at least exploring the varied factors underlying changes in those indices.

HOUSING, LAND, AND THE LOCAL STATE

To complicate further the life of the housing analyst, the actual delivery of dwelling units, or, more broadly, the provision of housing services, in fact takes place within particular localities and indeed on specific sites. This, in turn, ties housing and people to land; to local social networks, employment, and environmental characteristics; and, finally, to a local political state. Typically, urban land and the infrastructure services necessary for the construction and subsequent occupancy of housing are provided by local or regional municipalities or their agents. Although national governments may provide the financial resources and set the overall regulatory framework for housing provision and exchange, local authorities are usually the final intervening authority between capital and consumers. These governments implement building codes, establish zoning and subdivision controls, specify occupancy standards, grant planning permission, and provide public services. Although the provision of these services is increasingly being shifted into the private sector, the local state still sets the regulatory environment.

One obvious result of these linkages is to confirm that housing is dependent on the joint decisions of central and local government authorities as well as on fluctuations in national and local market conditions. The fact that these conditions, and the criteria on which decisions by the nation–state and local governments are made, are often out of phase, if not in conflict, poses a set of basic conundrums for those who face the task of designing means of providing adequate housing for all members of society. A parallel source of uncertainty and conflict arises in the interface between public and private agents of housing provision. In market economies, the dominant role of the private sector continues, but it now operates within an increasingly complex institutional framework established by different levels of government. In centrally planned economies, the central role of the state is clear, but increasingly, the private sector is assuming a significant mandate in housing supply.

TOWARD COMPARATIVE RESEARCH

These conundrums, although daunting, are at least suggestive of some of the potential benefits of comparative research. One obvious benefit is that a greater awareness of the varied experiences of other societies, cultures, and jurisdictions in dealing with such policy conundrums facilitates a more informed assessment of our own national experience and priorities. How have other countries dealt with the increasing financial needs of the housing sector? How do they regulate demand? How have housing conditions changed over the post–World War II period, and which social groups and localities have benefited most? What policy initiatives have proven to be successful, under what circumstances, and why?

It is usually not practical to transfer policy instruments and plans directly from one political context to another. The principal reason is that institutions and, more importantly, institutional networks seldom work the same way in different political and cultural circumstances. Nor is it possible to replicate the social conditions prevailing in one place and during the period when a policy was introduced in another place and at another time.

Nevertheless, the results of those policy experiments do offer valuable lessons, both positive and negative, and pose basic questions that are of immediate relevance in other jurisdictions. For example, we are now aware that certain types of housing design, notably the high-rise built form, are not suitable for many kinds of households. Furthermore, it has become obvious (at times painfully obvious) that massive and homogeneous housing developments serving to concentrate large numbers of disadvantaged households in small areas often lead to an intensification of existing levels of social pathology and a rapid deterioration in housing quality. We are also aware of the importance of providing social support services in conjunction with a physical stock of housing for those households with special needs as part of a comprehensive housing bundle.

More generally, the evidence is now clear that policymakers who insist on tinkering with one part of the housing system—regardless of whether it is a market system or a state-owned system—without a reasonably solid understanding of how that system works will usually succeed only in making matters worse. Similarly, we are also asking questions about old standards, such as the merits of imposing uniform housing standards on all households, regardless of their preferences and the diversity of environments in which they live. Standards are socially defined but are applied to individual households and groups of households living in particular localities. They must be a part of the decision-making process.

A second benefit deriving from comparative research is more sobering. For readers of this handbook it will be immediately apparent that there are no complete or simple solutions to contemporary housing problems. The problems that housing policy is directed at are continually shifting in terms of their origin, content, and location. Governments also tend to redefine the issues as social attitudes (e.g., to home ownership) and circumstances (e.g., demographic structure) shift and to suit their own immediate political purposes (e.g., getting elected). As a result, policy initiatives tend to lurch from crisis to crisis and then are almost as quickly forgotten. In many countries housing policies seem to be chaotic precisely because they are continually revised. The half-life of an explicit housing policy, at least in North America, might be about two years.

Housing problems also seem to exhibit an inherent tendency to disappear and then reappear but usually in different forms. For instance, in the industrialized countries we may appear to have eliminated one problem, such as a lack of indoor plumbing facilities or physical overcrowding, only to create new ones, such as affordability or homelessness, in the process. Here we can see how easily housing problems can be transformed from one base or scale of reference to another while retaining some of the previous sources and directions of inequality in terms of differential access to housing services. Yet there is also a more practical lesson. As the traditional and largely quantitative and physical criteria used to measure housing progress are gradually replaced by qualitative and socially conditioned criteria, which are inherently more complex and subjective, the identification of the housing problem itself becomes more uncertain and more vulnerable to redefinition.

Another obvious reason for the continual redefinition of housing problems and policy priorities is the ambiguity attached to the varied and often contradictory roles that housing serves in contemporary societies. Is it strictly a physical box or a market commodity, a shelter from the elements or a tax shelter, a factor in consumption or a unit of production? Or is it a merit good, a social service, and an integral part of a nation's social welfare net? Housing cannot be expected to fill all of these roles simultaneously.

This ambiguity, in turn, raises further questions about the entire process of housing supply and the means of distributing housing resources to people. How much housing in total does a country need? What proportion of national wealth should be directed to that sector? Is there any limit to the latent demand for housing? What modes of production and which systems of allocating housing are most efficient and equitable? Is a trade-off inevitable between efficiency, in maximizing output in the housing sector, and equity, when the latter includes both vertical equity (among social classes) and spatial equity (among communities and places)? Who should design and regulate those systems and how? What should be the balance between public and private roles in housing provision, between individual choice and collective responsibility, and among the different levels of government that are all legitimate actors in the housing system?

Each political state must also address the basic contradictions inherent in its own system of allocating housing. For instance, in centrally planned economies housing is allocated, in theory at least, according to collective social goals and needs, but the actual assignment is based on individual households and dwelling units. In market economies, on the other hand, the allocation mechanism is based largely on individual preferences, tastes, and income, but the market never assigns individuals to units, only classes of individuals. How is it possible to reconcile individual and collective goals and needs?

These are the kinds of questions that one might also address to the contributions in this volume as one form of comparing national housing experiences. There is little doubt that housing conditions for most of the population have improved dramatically in almost all countries since 1945. This is perhaps the most obvious conclusion from an analysis of postwar housing progress. Nevertheless, and although standards and expectations with respect to housing differ, there is also no doubt that serious problems remain. No political system or any system of housing provision can claim to have solved these problems. In some countries, notably in the Third World but also in most centrally planned economies, those problems still reflect an absolute shortfall in housing supply and unacceptably low levels of physical construction and environmental quality. In the industrialized market economies the issues that are now of prominent concern relate to high prices, to the inequitable distribution of housing resources, and to the persistence of unequal levels of access to housing opportunities among classes, social groups, and localities. Supply shortages and high prices are both in effect techniques for rationing consumption; unfortunately, they are both inequitable.

THE SEARCH FOR SOLUTIONS

There are, as a result, only partial and incremental solutions to contemporary housing problems. Preferably, and guided by some concept or goal of social justice, we should concentrate our efforts on those policy initiatives that offer the most benefits to the largest number of society's least fortunate members. The homeless, the sick, the working poor, and the socially and physically handicapped are obvious examples of those who have often been left behind in the postwar emphasis on demonstrating housing progress through the use of aggregate indices.

All countries, of whatever political orientation, will continue to face difficult questions in the formulation of housing policies that are both sensitive to varied needs and efficient with respect to attaining national goals. Specifically, they will have to face the increasing dependence of the housing sector on an external and volatile contextual environment. The context will often determine the content of the housing sector. The apparent conflicts between the goals of national policies and locality-specific land-use planning and development practices, not to mention the ambiguous roles that housing serves in the fabric of contemporary society, will further complicate the formulation and implementation of housing policies. Further progress in housing quality will require not only greater coordination between different levels of government but also formal partnerships between those public and private agencies involved in housing provision. The national reports in this volume serve to emphasize the importance of these concerns and the varied routes that it is possible to follow in the search for answers.

INTERNATIONAL HANDBOOK
OF HOUSING POLICIES
AND PRACTICES

1

Cross-National Housing Research: Analytical and Substantive Issues

WILLEM VAN VLIET—

Introduction
The Purpose of This Book
The Purpose of This Chapter
Cross-National Housing Research
  Reasons for Cross-National Comparison
Cross-National Comparison as an Analytic Strategy
  Difficulties in Cross-National Research
  Countries Covered in This Book
Trends in Construction and Conditions
  Capitalist Nations
  Socialist Nations
  Third World Nations
Policies
  Antecedents
  Context
Major Issues
  Self-Help
  Building Standards
  Institutional Organization and Resourcing
  Site Planning and Hazard Mitigation
  Shortages

INTRODUCTION

The 1980s have shown a resurgence of research on housing. In many countries, interest in the implications of significant national policy shifts has sparked a spate of studies. An increasing number of these studies appear to have an international orientation. Several recent collections contain contributions from different countries that are organized around broad themes such as public housing (Prak and Priemus 1985), self-help housing (Ward 1982; Skinner and Rodell 1983; Patton 1987), residential segregation (Peach et al. 1982; Huttman, Blauw, and Saltman 1990), and fiscal austerity (Van Vliet— 1987b) or are focused on a certain geographical area (e.g., Morrison and Gutkind 1982; Wynn 1984; Ha 1987; Sillince 1989; Stren and White 1989) or on segments of the population such as the elderly, the homeless, or women (Moser and Peake 1987; Van Vliet— 1989). This and similar work approaches issues from disparate national angles, sequentially, one by one. It often provides useful insights that may set a context for the initiation of analysis across nations. However, its isolated individual treatment fails to converge on comparative and integral consideration of the issues in a truly cross-national manner.

Genuine cross-national housing research is relatively rare. Various studies, however, have selected uniform aspects of housing and compared them across two or more countries. A number of these studies rely on available data, making statistical comparisons of, for example, the average number of persons per room, the average number of rooms per dwelling, the percentage of dwellings with piped water and flush toilets, per capita housing production, private home-ownership rates, and so forth (e.g., Economic Commission for Europe 1986; Barnett, Groth, and Ungson 1985). Studies of this type may provide useful descriptive background reports. However, the information is often of limited use, first, because it is frequently dated and, second, because the categories selected for comparison tend to be either not strictly comparable or too broad to be meaningful. Furthermore, the presentation of data in these studies typically lacks a historical perspective and is devoid of an empirical context and a theoretical framework that would direct their interpretation, outline implications for policy, and identify directions for future cross-national research.

A different type of comparative work has investigated specific housing themes, explicitly focusing on its occurrence or functioning in two or more countries.

For example, Stephen Mayo (1986) has systematically evaluated the efficiency of producer- and consumer-oriented housing-subsidy programs in the United States and the Federal Republic of Germany (see also Mayo and Barnbrook 1985; see Mandelker 1973 for an earlier U.S.-Britain comparison and Oxley 1987 for a discussion of housing allowances in Western Europe). Graham Hallett (1988) and his colleagues have studied land policies and markets as factors shaping housing and urban development in the U.S., Britain, the Federal Republic of Germany, France, the Netherlands, and Yugoslavia. Topics examined by others include housing provision (Harloe and Martens 1985; Ambrose and Barlow 1987), housing for the elderly (Heumann and Boldy 1982; Butler 1986), homelessness (Daly 1988), private rental housing (Harloe 1985), home ownership (Harris and Hamnett 1987), housing cooperatives (Clapham and Kintrea 1987), tenure conversion (Lundqvist 1986), housing obsolescence (Nesslein 1988c), the sale of public housing (Howenstine 1985), affordability (Thorns 1988), mortgage markets (Boleat 1984; Ball, Martens and Harloe 1986; Roistacher 1987), and various aspects of housing in the Third World (e.g., Gilbert and Ward 1985; Wells 1986).

An example of a broader perspective is B. Headey's (1978) comparative study of housing conditions and policies in Sweden, Britain, and the United States, countries that he identified as having embraced distinctly different approaches to housing provision, focusing on what he termed, respectively, comprehensive planning, social welfare, and stimulating private enterprise. This work, like the book by David Donnison and C. Ungerson (1982), is heavily oriented to (objectives of) public policy, which, in line with functionalist assumptions, is seen as intervention by a "benevolent" state in response to perceived needs on a path of societal progress (Marcuse 1982; Harloe and Martens 1984). Imperfect conditions tend to be viewed as either remnants of the past or outcomes of deficient policy implementation rather than a reflection of conflicting claims inherent in the system of housing provision. There is little or no concern with the dynamics among and divergent interests of stakeholder groups in the production and distribution of housing and its associated infrastructure.

Another example of cross-national housing research is Chester McGuire's (1981) analysis of housing production, finance, and consumption in selected countries across the world. His approach concentrates on economic factors, the conceptualization of which is in terms of structural features with scant attention given to interactions with their political and cultural context.

A contrasting approach is illustrated in recent work by Harvey Molotch and Serena Vicari (1988) who explore how economic and political institutions intermesh differently in producing built environments in the U.S., Japan, and Italy. Although all three are capitalist systems, these countries differ significantly in terms of local/national government relations, the significance and quality of political party systems, the nature of citizen activism, and the roles played by parochial business and national industrial elites. In the United States local growth coalitions dominate and national government intervention is minimal, whereas

in Japan national government is a powerful actor working in tandem with con-
glomerate firms to shape local development, and in Italy, political parties wield
legislative and bureaucratic power with considerable influence in, for example,
setting rent levels and controlling land uses. In all three countries there are
entrepreneurs who help shape the built environment as they seek to develop and
trade it for private profit. However, the tangible outcomes of their actions diverge
according to the particular contexts within which they operate.

Michael Ball, Michael Harloe, and Maartje Martens (1988) cover a somewhat
larger range of countries and restrict their focus to offer more in-depth, inter-
disciplinary treatment of historically patterned forms of housing provision and
the dynamic interrelationships between the institutional actors implicated in the
processes of housing production, exchange, finance, and consumption.

THE PURPOSE OF THIS BOOK

This book is set up somewhat differently than are the studies just mentioned.
It brings together chapters on housing in selected countries around the world.
In comparison with other existing publications that are oriented predominantly
or exclusively toward either capitalist industrialized nations (e.g., Headey 1978;
Pugh 1980; McGuire 1981; Van Vliet—, Huttman, and Fava 1985; Ball, Harloe,
and Martens 1988; Hallett 1988) or Third World countries (e.g., Morrison and
Gutkind 1982; Gilbert and Ward 1985; Skinner and Rodell 1983; Patton 1987),
the twenty-three countries included here display relatively greater diversity with
respect to important economic, political, demographic, geographic, and cultural
characteristics (see below). It would be difficult for one person to develop the
expertise required for comprehensive and in-depth treatment of any combination
of such varied situations as are represented. It would take not only a theoretical
framework to identify the salient issues and guide their comparative analysis but
also a detailed knowledge and understanding of locally specific circumstances
and the different historical processes associated with them.

Considering these challenges and in view of a decision, explained later, to
include nevertheless a broad array of countries, a different approach was chosen.
Accordingly, each of the following chapters was written by one or more acknowledged authorities whose expertise emphasizes, but is not limited to, the
country covered. In addition, each chapter was especially prepared according to
a common format, intended to facilitate cross-national comparison. Together
these chapters constitute a handbook on housing that was produced to serve
several purposes.

First, each chapter presents for an individual country statistical data on a
variety of housing aspects such as construction rates, housing standards, and
tenure distributions. To the extent that data were available, developments in the
years following World War II are brought out, with an emphasis on the most
recent period. Authors also review basic components and operations of national
housing systems, including, for example, the role of major actors in the financing,

construction, and distribution of housing. It was thought that these types of descriptive information would be useful for gaining a basic knowledge of housing conditions and trends in these countries and for acquiring an understanding of the organization of the systems underlying them.

In addition, based on this foundation, the authors provide coverage that is more analytical. The focus and orientation of these analyses were in part guided by the authors' perceptions of what appeared to be salient in each individual case. However, the analyses were also directed by various questions derived from the shared chapter format, intended to elucidate, for example, the antecedents of housing policy formulation, its usage as a tool to attain other national objectives, the interactions between the public and private sector, major issues such as affordability of and inequities in housing, and prospective developments.

The combination of factual documentation and analytical insights, grounded in the relevant literature, should provide readers with a good overview of the current state of housing in the countries included in this volume. As is appropriate for a handbook, each chapter also contains suggestions for further reading. Moreover, Appendix B lists the names and addresses of organizations, institutes, and agencies that can be contacted to obtain additional information. In this sense, this publication should be useful as a reference work on housing in selected countries worldwide.

The production of this volume was also undertaken with another objective in mind, namely, to make available to housing researchers a sourcebook that can be used to conduct cross-national housing analyses. Although there are obvious limitations in this regard, it is important to underline this book's potential for such analyses. The material in this book lends itself to cross-national examination of a variety of questions, several of which are suggested by this chapter. Hellmut Wollmann and Wolfgang Jaedicke (1989), for example, used preliminary chapter versions to compare the differential evolution of social housing in Britain, the Federal Republic of Germany, Italy, and the Netherlands. It is possible as well to use countries not included here as test cases for hypotheses that can be derived from the analyses that follow. Studies of housing in countries not represented here can also generate hypotheses that can be examined against the evidence presented in this book. Such cross-national analyses help establish the generalizability and validity of observations obtained from the study of single nations, thereby advancing the state of housing theory and strengthening recommendations for policy.

THE PURPOSE OF THIS CHAPTER

This chapter highlights, brings together, and interprets aspects of housing treated more fully in later chapters.[1] Owing to space limitations, not all important issues can be included here, and coverage of those selected can only be cursory, pointing to common trends, identifying salient characteristics, and drawing out comparisons, without treating any of them in great detail, to develop a context for more in-depth examination of specific issues deferred to other places. The purpose of this chapter is not to present a summary of each chapter. Rather, it draws on chapters, as appropriate, to explore broader questions that cut across individual countries. These questions roughly follow the format adopted for coverage of individual countries, reflected in the outline preceding each chapter. They concern trends in housing construction and conditions, the antecedents and contexts of housing policy, and major housing issues that currently confront many countries worldwide. Interwoven with the many considerations brought to bear with respect to these concerns are several familiar themes recurring in the housing literature. Examples of such themes are the distinction between the provision of housing as a product and a process (Turner 1976), the importance of quantitative versus qualitative aspects of housing, the treatment of housing as a social entitlement or an economic commodity, and the broader issue of housing as an instrument to redistribute wealth. It is impossible in this chapter to raise all of the relevant questions, let alone answer them. However, it is hoped that by adopting the approach just sketched, this chapter will suggest directions for and encourage the use by others of the material in this book for further cross-national analyses of housing. Much has been written about the value of such cross-national comparisons, but it is useful at this point to consider briefly the reasons for undertaking such studies, the available approaches, and the difficulties associated with them.

CROSS-NATIONAL HOUSING RESEARCH

In spite of improved transportation technologies and the advent of modern communication media, facilitating contact among researchers and permitting the almost instantaneous transmission of information from one part of the world to another, several studies indicate that spatial proximity still significantly shapes interactions among academic researchers (Blaivas, Kochen, and Crickman 1981; Line 1981; Van Vliet— 1983a). Notwithstanding documented internationalization of social science research (see, for example, Evan 1975), in comparison with their counterparts in the physical sciences, social scientists remain fairly parochial in their outlook and activities. Svein Kyvik (1988) has offered several reasons for this ethnocentrism, such as the geographic context of social science research, the availability of suitable publication outlets, and the disciplinary reward system. In the U.S. context, Michael Armer and Allen Grimshaw (1973) have pointed to the limited availability of resources for research, concern with scientific status, and political isolationism as factors that have hindered cross-national research in the past. In addition, it would appear that the subject matter of the social sciences is inherently more particularistic than that of the physical sciences. This is not the place to join the more general debate on social science methodology and related epistemological postulates of positivism and critical theory. However, questions arise as to the comparative method in cross-national social science research on housing. What types of approaches are available?

What are their merits? What kinds of difficulties are associated with their use? Before turning to these questions, it is appropriate to review briefly the suggested benefits of cross-national research.

Reasons for Cross-National Comparison

Cross-national studies tend to assume the advantages of cross-national comparison as a given, supposedly obvious to the reader, without explicitly stating the reason(s) for adopting this approach. There can be, in fact, various reasons for undertaking cross-national comparisons.

The literature is dominated by studies prompted primarily by a concern with policy-relevant issues. Their approach is typically descriptive as it aims to uncover and learn from the experiences of other nations (e.g., Howenstine 1985). The underlying rationale is to assess a given national housing policy in light of alternative policies pursued elsewhere (Masser 1981). The focus of this type of research is dictated by pragmatic considerations—"where the shoe pinches." Extant problems—for example, deterioration of central cities, limited availability of housing finance, shrinking rental housing stock—precipitate an interest in how other countries have addressed similar issues. Ensuing work attempts to develop grounds for (re)formulating relevant policies and programs.

Another type of cross-national housing research is less concerned with substance. Instead it seeks to advance the development of appropriate methods (e.g., Annez and Wheaton 1984). There is also cross-national methodological research that is more generic but whose applications can also include housing (e.g., Elder 1976; Kuechler 1987; Lonner and Berry 1986; Ragin 1987). Of course, these two types of cross-national research are not mutually exclusive. The difference is sometimes one of emphasis, and ideally they reinforce each other.

A third type of cross-national housing research is motivated by a desire to elucidate theoretical questions. Applied, policy-oriented studies tend to give issues "serial treatment" (Walton 1981) that identifies similarities and differences among countries without addressing the underlying reasons. The more theoretical analyses go beyond this and seek to explain the patterns found to exist in terms of one or more models (Pickvance 1986). Cross-national analyses advance the state of theory by helping establish the generalizability and the validity of observations obtained from the study of single nations. They force us to take account of cross-national differences, otherwise not uncovered. The discovery of such discrepancies may lead to the reformulation of theory on a more general level, capable of explaining similarities as well as differences between nations; it may also lead to the specification of conditions under which more curtailed theories apply to the implicated relationships (compare Kohn 1987). It is beyond the scope of this chapter to review the development of theory in cross-national housing research (we return to it briefly in the conclusion of this chapter). It is in order, however, to underline its importance as housing evolves in large part in institutional contexts that are significantly structured by decidedly national characteristics (compare Friedmann 1967). Variation in such contexts is more easily observed and its implications for housing are more readily understood in research that includes a range of countries. Therefore, this book covers a broad international spectrum (see below).

Having briefly outlined substantive, methodological and theoretical functions of cross-national housing research—functions that are potentially mutually enriching—we now turn to some observations about cross-national comparison as an analytic strategy.

CROSS-NATIONAL COMPARISON AS AN ANALYTIC STRATEGY

Any analysis, even in its simplest form, involves comparison. Statistical analyses aim to predict the comparative value of particular variables on the basis of relationships that have been empirically ascertained or simulated. Theoretical analyses seek to explain observed or presumed outcomes by reference to the comparative contributions of causative processes that produce those outcomes. Although there are significant differences between statistical prediction and theoretical explanation, both types of analysis rely on comparison. What is of interest then is not the use of comparative analysis per se, but the appropriateness of a focus on nations as units of analysis in such comparisons.

National boundaries delimit and reflect distinct societies created by historic interactions between particular combinations of social, political, cultural, and economic factors. These factors have produced distinctly national housing systems through the enactment of national legislation, the establishment of national institutions, the formulation of national policy, the application of national resources, the implementation of national programs, and so forth. Nations are, therefore, a relevant (albeit not the only) context for investigating housing systems to the extent and in the ways that variations in housing policies and practices are systematically related to variations in national characteristics, although the potential value of cross-national comparison should not obscure the need to look as well beyond national aggregates at internal variations and their associated antecedents.[2]

It is far easier to establish nations as legitimate units of analysis in housing research than it is to identify theoretically appropriate models needed to guide such analysis. The literature offers a number of useful discussions of theoretical perspectives that can provide direction for cross-national analyses. Many are formulated without specific reference to housing, although they are frequently pertinent in that connection. For example, John Williamson's (1987) study of the physical quality of life in developing nations attempts to explain observed variation by theoretical perspectives that direct attention to conflict, dependency, and other factors that are equally relevant in the context of housing (see also Chase-Dunn 1982; Form 1979). Such perspectives are indispensible in directing cross-national analysis. However, what is meant here by the need for "theoretically appropriate models'' is not the need for models that contribute appropriate theory, although important of themselves, but the need for models appropriate to the development of theory. Such models have been advanced from various different perspectives (Armer and Grimshaw 1973; Przeworski and Teune 1970), and several of them have emerged within a framework of urban research (e.g., Abu-Lughod 1976; Walton 1981). The best discussion in the present context is perhaps provided by Pickvance (1986) in an article that distinguished between three approaches to comparative analysis. The first approach entails a (two-variable) single model; for example, the spread of private home ownership as a function of the expansion of effective consumer demand. The second approach uses linked submodels. As an example, Pickvance discusses work by Mullins (1981) that seeks to explain differences in owner occupation and state provision of urban infrastructure in relation to different forms and requirements of private capital accumulation characteristic of, respectively, industrial, mercantile, and corporate capitalism. The third approach to comparative analysis relies on the use of diverse models. It involves consideration of different causative dynamics producing parallel outcomes. This approach recognizes that similar conditions may result from different factors. An example would be an explanation of private home-ownership rates that posits a positive relationship to the level of long-term, stable household earnings in advanced capitalist countries and a negative relationship to the scale of house building by the state in socialist nations. Another example of this approach would be the occurrence of inequalities in access to housing, seen in market economies as a reflection of differential ability to pay and in centrally planned economies as a reflection of differentially privileged positioning in bureaucratic allocation.

Pickvance (1986) argues persuasively that all three approaches have a place in comparative analysis, but that the approaches using linked submodels and diverse models need proper recognition. These last two approaches more explicitly direct attention to the possibility of plural causation. Their focus challenges convergence theories, pervading much of the research on urban development and housing, and is inclusive of a broader array of potentially relevant explanatory factors.

As mentioned, one of the intended functions of this book is the provision of source material on housing that lends itself to cross-national analysis. Countries were selected with a view to allowing examination of issues using variously appropriate approaches as just outlined. Accordingly, as a later section makes clear, the countries covered in subsequent chapters span a broad spectrum. The representation of countries with such widely varied characteristics orients study of dissimilar housing systems to the express consideration of historically unique circumstances that explain divergent outcomes.

On the other hand, countries were also selected so as to permit examination of similar housing situations in light of broadly shared structural regularities transcending historical differences between nations (compare Kohn 1987). Accordingly, where possible and appropriate, the discussion of substantive aspects of housing in this chapter is organized into three global categories: market-oriented capitalist nations (including welfare states as well as countries more strongly oriented to private profit seeking), socialist nations with comprehensive central planning, and nations in the Third World. This distinction is not to deny the important variations that exist within each of these categories, nor the combinations found among them, but it takes general principles of economic organization, political ideology, resource base, level of technological development, and demographic trends as rudimentary initial building blocks in the construction of a broadly descriptive classificatory framework. Against this background, theoretical formulations, appropriate to the question at hand, can be brought to bear in guiding transtaxonomic analyses of specific issues.

Difficulties in Cross-National Research

Cross-national comparison of housing systems is fraught with numerous difficulties. The hindrances are of various types, and the literature contains ample discussion of them (see, for example, Armer and Grimshaw 1973; Masotti and Walton 1976; George 1986; Williams 1984; Lisle 1985; Bourne 1986). Among them are practical problems having to do with impediments in the operational mechanics of conducting cross-national research as well as threats to the validity of its results arising from conceptual pitfalls. The former include, for example, obstacles to obtaining the funds needed to sustain complex international projects, relevant background knowledge, linguistic competence, and organizational infrastructure. Illustrative in this connection is the experience of the Vienna Centre for Research and Documentation in the Social Sciences (Charvat, Stamatiou, and Villain-Gandossi 1988). Regarding conceptual hazards, the earlier discussion already made mention of the implications of adopting one rather than another analytical approach to delineate classes of relevant variables to be included in the examination of particular issues. Decisions at this level act, for example, to establish or sever linkages between the question under consideration and its broader institutional context. They also impinge at a level of greater specificity on choices regarding the most appropriate methods of data collection.

Once collected, cross-national data require cautious interpretation. Comparisons between countries frequently have to contend with different accounting procedures and possibly nonequivalent measures (Smelser 1976). For example, nations vary greatly in their definition of what constitutes a room. In the Federal Republic of Germany and Norway, rooms with a floor space of less than 6 square meters are not counted as rooms, whereas the Swedes disregard rooms with a floor space of less than 7 square meters and not receiving daylight. In Japan, kitchens with a floor space of less than 5 square meters do not qualify as rooms; in Ireland the cut-off point for kitchens is 10 square meters, and in France it is 12, whereas in Canada only bedrooms are counted and kitchens (as well as living rooms) are excluded altogether (U.N. Department of International Economic and Social Affairs 1980). Whether or not kitchens are counted as rooms may modify the national average number of rooms by as much as 20 to 35 percent (Economic Commission for Europe 1985b). Likewise, classification criteria for urban places are known to differ from one country to another (Simmons and Bourne 1978). As a final example, the low proportion of women in the economically active population of less developed countries similarly does not reflect the frequent and central involvement of women in the informal economy.

National characteristics may also conceal important differences within any given country. Readers will notice that many chapters in this book contain examples of interregional disparities in housing quality, a reflection of unequal distributions of economic and political power, unbalanced technological development, and uneven availability of resources and labor skills. There are other examples of housing inequalities within nations like the association between tenure status and regressive subsidies that reinforce existing patterns of socio-economic stratification. As discussed later, such inequalities are found in market-oriented housing systems as well as in those that are centrally planned, through different modalities to be sure, but nevertheless resulting in similar outcomes.

Countries Covered in This Book

As noted, there are important differences between the countries covered in this book. Table 1.1 shows selected demographic characteristics related to housing need. It includes countries with a relatively small population such as Singapore (2.6 million), Israel (4.3 million), Cuba (10 million), and Hungary (10.7 million), as well as China whose mere population size (more than 1 billion) creates problems of its own in housing provision. The proportion of the urban population ranges from 100 percent in Singapore and 92 percent in Britain to 30 percent in Pakistan and 20 percent in Kenya. The population growth rate for the 1985–1990 period is estimated to be 4.1 percent in Kenya, the highest in the world, and −0.2 percent in the Federal Republic of Germany. Also factors related to the formation and maintenance of households vary greatly. The fifteen- to twenty-four-year-old age cohort, always generating an important new housing demand, is more than 22 percent of the total population in Cuba and is relatively large in Third World countries generally. Marital dissolution, another factor contributing to household formation and housing demand, is about 20 times higher in the United States than in Italy, Brazil, and Mexico, countries where predominantly Roman Catholic religious institutions are a powerful force opposed to divorce.

Selected economic characteristics, shown in table 1.2, also reveal important national differences. In 1985 the per capita Gross National Product (GNP) ranged from 310 U.S. dollars in China to $16,690 in the United States. The proportion of economically active males varied between 60 percent in Singapore and Japan and 43 percent in Mexico; the rate of participation in the labor force by women was 45 percent in Poland but only 6 percent in Egypt. The relative contributions of the agricultural and industrial sectors to the GNP similarly vary. Countries

Table 1.1
Selected Demographic Characteristics of the Countries Covered in This Book

Country	Population Size 1985 (x 1,000)	Urban Population 1985 (%)	Population Growth Rate 1985-1990(%)
WESTERN AND SOUTHERN EUROPE			
Great Britain	56,125	92	.1
FGR	60,877	86	-.2
The Netherlands	14,500	89	.5
Italy	57,300	67	.1
EASTERN EUROPE			
Soviet Union	278,618	66	1.0
Hungary	10,697	56	0.0
Poland	37,187	61	.9
NORTH AMERICA			
Canada	25,426	76	1.1
United States	238,020	74	.9
CENTRAL AMERICA AND THE CARIBBEAN			
Cuba	10,038	72	.6
Mexico	78,996	70	2.6
SOUTH AMERICA			
Brazil	135,564	73	2.2
Colombia	28,714	67	2.1
MIDDLE EAST			
Egypt	46,909	46	2.4
Israel	4,252	90	1.8
AFRICA			
Kenya	20,600	20	4.1
Ghana	13,588	32	3.2
South Africa	32,392	56	2.5
ASIA			
Singapore	2,559	100	1.2
China	1,059,521	29	1.2
Japan	120,742	77	.7
Pakistan	100,380	30	3.1
OCEANIA			
Australia	15,698	86	1.3

Sources: United Nations Fund for Population Activities, 1986; United Nations, 1987.

Note: NA = not available.

[1]1984

Population Density per sq. km.(1985)	Life Expectancy at birth(1985)	Population 15-24 as % of total(1985)	Population 60+ as % of total(1985)	Divorces per 1,000 of population(1985)
228	74	16.3	20.2	2.89[1]
246	74	16.5	19.7	2.14
355	76	17.2	16.8	2.35
189	75	15.5	18.7	.29
12	71	16.0	13.1	3.39[1]
116	70	12.5	18.3	2.69
120	71	14.2	14.0	1.32
3	76	17.1	14.1	2.75
25	74	16.7	16.1	4.96
88	73	22.4	11.1	2.89
40	66	21.0	4.3	.35
16	63	20.3	6.6	.23[1]
25	64	21.8	5.9	NA
47	58	19.8	6.7	NA
207	74	16.9	11.9	1.18
35	53	18.9	3.0	NA
57	52	18.9	2.0	NA
27	54	19.3	6.2	NA
4,427	71	20.4	7.7	.93
111	68	21.9	8.0	NA
323	77	14.2	14.3	1.49[1]
126	50	20.7	4.5	NA
2	75	17.1	14.2	2.76[1]

Table 1.2
Selected Economic Characteristics of Countries Covered in This Book

Country	Economically Active Population		Agriculture	
	Males (%)	Females (%)	as % of EAP*	as % of GNP**
WESTERN AND SOUTHERN EUROPE				
Great Britain	59[5]	36[5]	2.5[5]	2[9]
FGR	59[5]	34[9]	5.1[9]	2[10]
The Netherlands	54[9]	26[9]	5.0[9]	4[10]
Italy	55[10]	27[10]	11.1[10]	6[10]
EASTERN EUROPE				
Soviet Union	47.3[10]		20.0[8]	20[8]
Hungary	54[10]	41[10]	22.1[6]	13[8]
Poland	57[4]	45[4]	34.6[1]	18[8]
NORTH AMERICA				
Canada	59[6]	40[6]	4.4[8]	3[8]
United States	57[7]	40[7]	3.4[7]	2[7]
CENTRAL AMERICA AND THE CARIBBEAN				
Cuba	47[2]	12[2]	NA	10[8]
Mexico	43[3]	12[3]	40.9[2]	8[8]
SOUTH AMERICA				
Brazil	54[5]	20[5]	29.9[5]	10[7]
Colombia	50[5]	16[5]	28.5[5]	19[8]
MIDDLE EAST				
Egypt	48[5]	6[5]	40.2[5]	19[5]
Israel	43[10]	25[10]	5.4[10]	6[10]
AFRICA				
Kenya	52[2]	26[2]	NA	28[7]
Ghana	44[2]	31[2]	NA	59[9]
South Africa	50[2]	25[2]	NA	4[8]
ASIA				
Singapore	60[7]	34[7]	1.0[7]	1[8]
China	57[2]	36[2]	NA	45[8]
Japan	60[7]	37[7]	9.5[7]	3[8]
Pakistan	52[8]	8[8]	50.3[8]	22[8]
OCEANIA				
Australia	57[6]	35[6]	6.5[8]	4[7]

Sources: United Nations, 1986, 1987; World Bank, 1987.

Note: NA = not available.

[1]1974   [4]1978   [7]1982   [10]1985
[2]1975   [5]1980   [8]1983
[3]1976   [6]1981   [9]1984

*EAP = Economically Active Population.
**GNP = Gross National Product.

Industry		GNP**
as % of EAP*	as % of GNP**	per capita 1985 (in US $)

28.9[5]	30[9]	8,460
34.2[9]	32[9]	10,940
19.7[10]	26[5]	9,290
32.0[10]	33[10]	6,520
38.0[10]	46[8]	NA
33.0[6]	38[8]	2,150[8]
30.2[1]	50[8]	2,130[8]
17.3[8]	25[8]	13,680
22.9[7]	28[7]	16,690
NA	32[8]	1,910[8]
19.6[2]	35[8]	2,080
17.2[5]	27[7]	1,640
14.5[5]	26[8]	1,320
14.9[5]	30[5]	610
23.3[10]	21[10]	4,990
NA	13[7]	290
NA	4[9]	380
NA	40[8]	2,010
30.4[7]	27[8]	7,420
NA	42[8]	310
24.7[7]	34[8]	11,300
14.8[8]	21[8]	380
22.3[8]	28[7]	10,830

also differ significantly in the ways and extent that they rely in their economic functioning on private profit-oriented market mechanisms and planned intervention by central authorities.

Nor are the systems of political decision making alike. Included are single-party systems (e.g., Singapore) and nations with severe restrictions on or repression of activities by parties opposing the authorities in power (e.g., USSR),[3] including the virtually complete oppression of public dissent (e.g., South Africa). At the other end of the spectrum are countries whose political praxis is historically rooted in the forging of coalitions of multiple parties with competing interests (e.g., the Netherlands). Some countries show a record of institutional stability and continuity of policy, others are characterized by frequent changes of government and drastic policy shifts.

There are also variations in the regulatory empowerment and resource-allocation capabilities of different levels of government. In the Netherlands, local government plays an important role in housing provision; in Israel it does not. The national government in Great Britain operates differently from the one in Canada that is federally based and whose powers of intervention in the production and consumption of housing are constitutionally limited inasmuch as the British North America Act gave the provinces control over property and civil rights (Belec 1984). The regional authorities in Britain are appointed and serve an administrative function, whereas the states in the United States and Australia have elected political decision-making entities with considerable jurisdictional autonomy and responsibility in housing; in Singapore there is no intermediate or local level of government at all. Clearly, these different configurations preclude facile cross-national generalization about the role of the state in housing provision (see Gans 1984; Paris forthcoming).

Coverage of individual countries varies as the salience of issues varies from country to country. For example, as shown later, in some countries there still exists an absolute shortage of dwelling units, but in other countries there is a housing surplus, and it is affordability rather than availability that is problematic. Similarly, there are countries where national government plays an active and direct role in the financing, construction, distribution, and management of housing, whereas in other countries national government, for lack of resources, political will, or other reasons, assumes very limited responsibility, leaving housing by and large to private market forces that it may selectively and indirectly influence by, for example, the provision of construction incentives, the abatement of development fees, or lower taxation. The treatment of individual countries reflects these and other differences in national features.

Variation in the coverage of countries also occurs because of differences in the availability of information from statistical sources as well as previous research. As a result, to a certain degree, the national housing profiles mirror unique circumstances and national idiosyncrasies. However, as noted, the authors use a shared descriptive and analytical framework to facilitate an examination of similarities as well as differences.

The remainder of this chapter is oriented mostly to the substance of housing. It examines similarities and differences among the countries that are covered in subsequent chapters and explores possible underlying reasons. The discussion is divided into three main sections: (1) trends in construction and conditions, (2) policies, and (3) major issues. The conclusion briefly considers the need for theory development in future cross-national housing research.

TRENDS IN CONSTRUCTION AND CONDITIONS

Following World War II, a severe shortage of dwellings characterized the housing situation of many countries. War ravages had destroyed significant proportions of the housing stock, particularly in European cities. According to a recent Soviet report (Vladimirov 1985, 38), almost 50 percent of the housing stock in the USSR was destroyed, and more than 25 million people were left homeless. In what is at present the German Democratic Republic (GDR), 620,000 dwellings had been entirely destroyed and another 200,000 had been damaged; more than 50 percent of the inner-city housing stock had been lost (Rueschemeyer 1989). In the area that now forms the Federal Republic of Germany, one out of every five dwellings was lost. In Poland, where housing conditions were among the worst of any European country during the prewar period, a comparable proportion of the total and 60 percent of the urban housing stock had been devastated. All countries directly impacted by the war experienced acute and unprecedented shortfalls.

The housing deficits had been created not only by the reduced stock (chiefly in European countries) but also by large construction backlogs that had emerged as national productive capacities had been diverted to the war effort. Returning demobilized military personnel forming new households often presented an additional, pent-up demand for housing. Sizable refugee and immigrant flows further augmented housing needs in some countries. Most countries continued to face a strong demand for housing as a result of natural population growth and accelerated household formation associated with demographic trends such as a steady decline (until recently) in home-leaving age and increased longevity. Housing demand was propelled as well by sustained urbanization of employment and population and increased affluence, although these developments obviously proceeded from various baseline conditions and operated at an uneven pace across different countries.

A number of countries also experienced consequences of decolonization. In France and Britain, for example, this meant an influx of minority populations, presenting an additional demand for housing and posing a previously little-known challenge of ethnic integration. On the other hand, the newly politically independent nations found themselves economically highly dependent and left with the vestiges of colonial housing delivery systems geared to the affluent only. Having neither an institutional apparatus, nor policies, nor resources, these countries were ill prepared to address the housing needs of very large majorities of their populations, which were growing at a very high rate, particularly in cities, as a result of tremendous rural-urban migration.

Capitalist Nations

Generally, industrialized capitalist nations experienced vigorous economic growth for at least two decades following the end of the war. The rising prosperity contributed to the high rates of residential construction typical of this period, tending to reach their peak in the early and mid–1970s. As a result, by the end of that decade absolute housing shortages had been eliminated or much diminished in most of these countries. As we will see later, at that time affordability of housing became a growing concern. During the 1980s, construction output declined in many capitalist countries. Sources of private capital identified alternative investment opportunities with higher yields and public authorities increasingly withdrew from the provision of housing under pressures of economic recession combined with fiscal austerity and conservative political ideologies (Van Vliet— 1987b).

Parallel with their relative success in addressing quantitative aspects of their housing problems, capitalist nations managed to improve the quality of their housing stock. There were, for example, impressive and very widespread increases in the proportion of dwellings with electricity, running water, flush toilet, shower or bath, and central heating. The average floor area of dwellings also rose greatly. The average number of rooms did increase as well. Levels of crowding dropped. Individual country chapters that follow provide detailed information documenting this progress. As shown later, during the late 1980s, this long-term trend to improvement appears to have tapered off and even reversed itself as repair and maintenance problems associated with an aging housing stock began to require increasing attention. At this time a marked policy shift, first apparent in Western European countries, has taken place, away from new construction and emphasizing urban rehabilitation (see below).

An exception to the pattern just sketched is that found in Japan, a country that, following World War II, developed into a capitalist superpower founded on a philosophy of virtually unbridled "free" enterprise embraced by the conservative parties continuously in power since 1947. Meteoric economic growth supported rates of residential construction which during their peak (1975–1984) exceeded those ever attained by other countries, so that the quantitative housing problem has been solved. However, the quality of housing has not improved as fast as in Western capitalist countries; in 1988 almost 25 percent of Japan's housing stock did not meet space standards, lacked minimum facilities, or was in need of major repair.

A common characteristic of residential construction in many capitalist countries is that it is typically undertaken by firms and technologies that are considered small and backward by standards of other manufacturing sectors. Although there is a tendency to increases in scale, small enterprises still abound. In 1982, 92 percent of the construction firms in the United States employed twenty or fewer people. Comparable figures in Western Europe were 82 percent in the Federal Republic of Germany (1987), 88 percent in the Netherlands (1985), and 96 percent in Britain (1985); in Scandinavian countries the proportion ranged between 80 percent in Finland (1984) and 96 percent in Denmark (1984). In Canada new housing also tends to be constructed by numerous small firms, typically producing fewer than ten units per year. Likewise, the Australian residential construction industry is still highly fragmented with about 20,000 companies that in 1984–1985 averaged three employees (including working proprietors) who produced on average eight dwellings per year. A notable development in the last country is the significant intermediary role played by Japanese construction and property development companies in converting transnational capital, mobilized by global financiers, into urban and regional infrastructure. Attracted by profit opportunities created by rivalry among individual commonwealth states competing for foreign investment, these Japanese firms have now moved into speculative real-estate transactions. Out of a concern for inflationary effects on house prices the federal government has sought to curtail the scope of operations of foreign capital in the housing market, making it impossible in September 1987 to sell houses to foreigners (Rimmer 1989).

Table 1.3 shows the organization of construction activity in selected countries in 1985. In Western countries there is a predominance of small firms and a concentration of construction employees in small firms that expectedly contribute proportionately less to output value.

There is also another perspective on the perceived backwardness of the residential construction industry in advanced capitalist countries. Michael Ball (1988), for example, has argued that the particular nature of the organization of housing construction in these countries is in many ways a functional adaptation to the environment within which builders operate. Increased fragmentation of demand (locationally and by dwelling type), rising real interest rates, a shift toward renovation and repair away from new building, expansion of private ownership, and greater market volatility have combined to create conditions to which builders have reacted by increasing their production flexibility (Ball 1988:170). Fordism (Florida and Feldman 1988)—the organization and technology of mass production—is ill suited to respond to sharp fluctuations in building demand. Moreover, conventional approaches have incorporated modern tools, new building materials, and innovative construction techniques.

Another factor to be considered is the way in which labor management is facilitated by arrangements that rely heavily on subcontracting, non-union employees, and (im)migrant workers. An analysis of construction in and development of Sydney, Australia, by Short (1988) reveals a significant union role coinciding with a property boom during a period of intense construction activity,

Table 1.3
Organization of the Construction Industry in Selected Countries, 1987

Country	Construction Firms by Size			Employees by Firm Size			Value of Output by Firm Size		
	up to 5 employees	6 to 19 employees	500 + employees	up to 5 employees	6 to 19 employees	500 + employees	up to 5 employees	6 to 19 employees	500 + employees
Eastern Europe									
GDR	[— 29	.8]	39.1	[—	.2]	83.0	[—	.2]	86.9
Hungary	[.01	.04]	9.3	[1.9	]	68.0	[2.2	]	73.0
Poland	[	.001]	28.8	[	.001]	73.2	[	.001]	76.3
Bulgaria	[	.001]	95.5	[	.001]	99.6	[	.001]	86.9
Scandinavia									
Finland[1]	41.0	39.0	NA	3.0	12.1	40.9	2.8	11.6	44.6
Denmark[3]	68.7	26.8	.05	24.0	37.5	.04	NA	NA	NA
Norway[2]	68.0	23.3	.009	18.0	24.7	9.0	15.4	21.9	12.4
Sweden[3]	70.4	17.3	.003	17.6	13.5	36.5	16.7	8.2	47.5
Western Europe									
France[4]	NA	42.2	.8	NA	14.2	24.6	NA	10.4	27.1
FGR[5]	[81.8	]	.1	[32.3	]	7.4	[27.6	]	8.5
Netherlands[3]	75.4	12.8	.15	25.5	15.5	8.0	19.7	13.5	11.0
Great Britain[6]	85.5	10.9	.09	13.6	18.7	24.1	19.1	16.2	26.9
U.S.A.[7]	62.4	29.2	.001	12.0	25.4	11.0	9.5	22.6	14.2

Source: Economic Commission for Europe, 1988.

Note: Firms by number of employees, number of employees by size of firm, and value of output by size of firm (as % of total); NA = not available.

[1] 1984 data; smallest categories: up to 4 employees and 5–19 employees.
[2] 1986 data.
[3] 1986 data; smallest categories: 2–9 employees and 10–19 employees.
[4] 1984 data; firms with 1–10 employees not included; smallest category: 11–19 employees.
[5] 1985 data; smallest categories: up to 9 employees and 10–19 employees.
[6] 1985 data.
[7] 1982 data.

and Michelson (1976, 21–23) has pointed to the part played by Swedish construction unions in removing a government quota on *småhus* (detached dwellings and town houses) and reversing the "inevitable" trend of high-rise building during the 1970s. However, such union influence is not common in the highly fragmented building industries found in capitalist countries.

Other aspects of construction activity show considerable differences among capitalist countries. The approach to housing provision in, for example, the United States, Canada, Australia, and Japan has relied heavily on "free" market mechanisms driven by private profit seeking, where price of the supply is a function of the demand's ability to pay. A fundamental assumption underlying this approach has been that those unable to compete for the more desirable stock occupy units that "filter down" as more affluent households move into new housing of higher standards. Chapters in this book make clear that these housing markets have not, in fact, been free markets at all. Governments in these countries have intervened in significant though mostly indirect ways, helping shape the rules of the game and supporting some players, commonly the ones who needed it least, a great deal more than others (by, for example, regressive tax expenditures).

Marked distortions have also occurred as a result of discrimination, in part reflecting the "risk aversiveness" of (systems driven by) private investors motivated by profit seeking. In the United States such discriminatory practices were legally mandated until 1950, as the federal government insisted upon them as a prerequisite to housing aid. The Federal Housing Administration's official manuals cautioned against "infiltration of inharmonious racial and national groups," "a lower class of inhabitants," or the "presence of incompatible racial elements" in new neighborhoods. Zoning was advocated as a device for exclusion, and the use was urged of a racial covenant (prepared by FHA itself) with a space left blank for the prohibited races and religions, to be filled in by the builder as occasion required (Abrams 1965, 61). Although made illegal in 1968 by Congress and the Supreme Court, discriminatory practices can still be observed in the United States today, not only on the basis of race but also against women (for example, in mortgage lending) and families with children who at present find themselves excluded from one out of every four rental units (Marans and Colten 1985; see also Ritzdorf 1986 and later discussion). When housing finally does filter down, it is often dilapidated and in deteriorated neighborhoods (Fainstein 1980).

Although the private profit motive propels housing provision in all capitalist systems, there are considerable differences among capitalist countries in, for example, the places where investments enter the system, the ways in which private funds are channeled once they are in the system, and the arrangements under which profits exit (see Ambrose and Barlow 1987 for a useful discussion). These differences have multiple, complex antecedents and reflect the different roles played by the state.[4]

In Scandinavia and Western Europe national government emerged from World

War II with a legitimate and active responsibility in spheres of collective welfare (Flora and Heidenheimer 1981). This responsibility derived in part from traditional legacies. Additionally important was the collapse of private markets. In the context of more encompassing recovery programs, government stepped in to infuse much-needed finance capital. These efforts were buttressed by the Marshall Plan, which was consolidated in the more broadly oriented Organization for European Economic Cooperation, superseded in 1961 by the more expansive Organization for Economic Cooperation and Development (OECD). Furthermore, for reasons that cannot be detailed here, political constituencies in many European countries were better positioned to extract government commitment to public concerns such as education, health, and housing than was the case in the United States, Canada, and Australia.

A basic premise underlying government involvement in European welfare states has been that private profit-oriented "free" market mechanisms cannot address the needs of economically disadvantaged population groups that are unable to articulate an effective market demand.[5] Notwithstanding distinct differences among individual welfare states, the role of their national governments explicitly included the direct or indirect provision of housing.

Accordingly, one finds, historically, considerable differences between the investment sources of construction activity in welfare states and so-called free market economies. In the latter, subsidized housing in general and public housing in particular have represented a small and usually declining proportion of new construction in the postwar period. In the United States the construction of public housing never constituted more than a fraction of total new building nationwide. The ratio over private units dropped from 0.025 in 1965 to an even more minuscule 0.002 in 1985 (Pit and Van Vliet— 1988). In 1989 public housing accommodated about 1.5 percent of the U.S. population. In Canada, public housing accounted for 0.7 percent of new residential construction between 1949 and 1963. By the late 1980s, it made up 2 percent of that country's housing stock, bringing the total share of social (including nonprofit) housing to 4 percent. In Australia, public housing hovered around 5 percent of all units for most of the postwar period, standing at 7 percent in 1986. Japan is another country with a record of comparatively little government intervention in housing on behalf of economically disadvantaged groups. In 1983 its proportion of public housing reached a historic high of 7.6 percent, but since then budgetary allotments for public housing have declined. Dwellings provided by employers, another form of housing subsidy in Japan, decreased from 7 percent of the national stock in 1963 to 4.2 percent in 1988.

In contrast, subsidized and public housing, through various modalities, came to represent significant proportions of the housing stock in welfare states. For example, in the Netherlands, 44 percent of the housing stock in 1987 consisted of rental dwellings in the social sector of which 84 percent was owned by housing associations and 16 percent by municipalities or other public bodies. Britain expanded its public rental housing from 18 percent of the total stock in 1951 to

31 percent in 1981, and in 1987, after years of unremitting privatization (see, e.g., Crook 1986), the share of this sector still stood at 25.9 percent. In 1980, 20 percent of the Danish housing stock consisted of subsidized rental dwellings. In 1985 Swedish public housing comprised more than 20 percent of the stock, and about another 15 percent consisted of cooperative housing (The Swedish Institute 1987; Lindberg and Karlberg 1988). In France, the proportion of low and moderately priced housing (*habitation à loyer modéré*) was 16 percent in 1981 (Ghorra-Gobin 1983, 47). In the Federal Republic of Germany, 20 percent of the housing stock in 1984 fell into the social sector; of this proportion, 80 percent comprised rental dwellings, of which 62.5 percent was owned by non-profit organizations.

The share of social housing in welfare states, as just described, reflects *past* performance. There is considerable divergence among welfare states in their *present* policy orientations regarding social housing. In Britain and the Federal Republic of Germany, for example, commitment by the national government to social housing has been significantly reduced; this is much less the case in the Netherlands, whereas in Italy current developments show increased government intervention (see also Harloe 1988). Many capitalist countries also face a crisis in private rental housing, including diminished availability, affordability problems, and lack of maintenance (see below). Table 1.4, which summarizes tenure differences in housing stock composition of selected countries, reflects patterns of national intervention as well as assistance by lower levels of government.

Differences in physical and locational characteristics of housing, in part, parallel the distinction between welfare states and nations whose economies are more private-profit oriented. In the latter, incentives for and constraints on residential construction combined with widespread consumer preference to produce extensive low-density neighborhoods, commonly on the periphery of established urban centers, featuring a predominance of detached dwellings and often excluding nonresidential land uses. In welfare states like those mentioned earlier, consumers' attitudes had traditionally been more accepting of higher density housing to start out with, and preferences for single-family dwellings did not materialize as extensively, in part owing to lower levels of affluence; more importantly, government tended to undertake and regulate residential construction more in an overall context of land-use planning, which generally did not favor low-density residential development. Welfare states also had to consider investment of their more limited resources in terms of cost-effectiveness vis-à-vis its other domains of responsibility such as education, health care, and military defense. Accordingly, one finds less suburban sprawl in welfare states and, as a rule, residential development tends to be contained in planned entities, at higher densities, comparatively better served by public transportation and more mixed with nonresidential land uses (see Popenoe 1985).

As stressed before, it is important to bear in mind that general trends and characteristics, as just described and indeed throughout this section, are just that:

Table 1.4
Housing Tenures as a Proportion of Occupied Dwellings in Countries Covered in This Book (In Percentages)

Country	Privately Owned	Private Rental	Public Rental	Other Social Rental	Other Tenures
WESTERN AND SOUTHERN EUROPE					
Great Britain (1987)	64.1	7.5[4]	25.9	2.5	
FGR (1984)	42.0	38.0		20.0	
The Netherlands (1987)	43.0	12.0	7.0	37.0	1.0
Italy (1981)	65.9	29.7	5.6		5.6
EASTERN EUROPE					
Soviet Union (1985)[1]	22.0	NA	NA	NA	NA
Hungary (1984)	73.7	1.4	24.9		
Poland	NA	NA	NA	NA	NA
NORTH AMERICA					
Canada (1986)	63.0	33.0	2.0	2.0	
United States (1988)	64.0	31.0	2.0		3.0
CENTRAL AMERICA AND THE CARIBBEAN					
Cuba (1988)	80.0				20.0
Mexico (1985)	67.0	NA	NA	NA	NA
SOUTH AMERICA					
Brazil (1984)	63.4	22.3			14.3
Colombia (1973)	54.8	32.0			13.2
MIDDLE EAST					
Egypt	NA	NA	NA	NA	NA
Israel (1983)	73.0	11.0	12.0	1.0	3.0
AFRICA					
Kenya	NA	NA	NA	NA	NA
Ghana (1986)	[80.0]		NA	NA	NA
South Africa (1970)[2]	49/22/33	[	49/73/61	]	2/5/6
ASIA					
Singapore (1988)	[15.0]		17.0		68.0[3]
China (1985)	13.0	2.5	84.0		
Japan (1983)	62.3	24.9	7.6		5.2
Pakistan (1980)	78.4	7.0	.7		13.9
OCEANIA					
Australia (1986)	70.0	19.0	7.0		4.0

Source: Various national census publications.

[1]Urban areas only.

[2]Urban areas only: Whites/Coloreds/Indians. Data on blacks not available. Data from the 1980 census not shown because of serious inaccuracies.

[3]Housing Development Board units purchased by occupants.

[4]Includes other tenures.

general trends. They do not reveal, for example, important variations of housing quality; nor do they show the differential housing benefits bestowed by government on different population groups. Such internal differences may give rise to problems, and we will return to several of them when reviewing major housing issues.

Socialist Nations

In centrally planned socialist economies, a major premise of societal organization is that the state distributes costs and benefits, resulting from national functioning and development, equally among all population segments. According to this egalitarian ideology, the state must maintain full administrative control over rationally conducted planning, production, management, and consumption processes.

In line with these normative principles, residential construction in the East Bloc countries following World War II had to be and with notable exceptions (e.g., in rural areas) was indeed undertaken by the state. This approach to the problem of building the urgently required new urban units presented national authorities with a dilemma: On the one hand, political ideology demanded universal provision of housing by the state against low cost for its citizens (typically 15 to 20 percent of what their capitalist counterparts are expected to pay); on the other hand, economic realities demanded that financial, material, and human resources would be committed to productive investments with higher returns, chiefly in the heavy manufacturing sectors.

In this trade-off, the latter generally received priority. As a result, residential construction in the centrally planned economies of Eastern Europe reflects compromises in terms of quantity as well as quality; it also contains concessions to alternative instrumentalities that do not fit the official ideological mold (e.g., co-ops and even private sector arrangements) but that have nevertheless been tolerated (see, e.g., Hegedüs 1987), albeit it inconsistently, at least in part because they help alleviate industrial production problems associated with shortages of worker housing.

Historical data on housing in Eastern European nations tend to be sparse, particularly for the USSR. The available information sketches a mixed picture. Table 1.5 shows that annual housing output of the USSR (7.5 units per 1,000 of population in 1986), Hungary (1985: 6.8), and Poland (1985: 5.1) is as high as or higher than it is in many industrialized capitalist countries.

A simple comparison of residential construction rates, however, is of limited value. Such comparisons can easily lead to misinterpretation, because they reveal nothing about demand. A low rate may be more than adequate in a country where past building has already satisfied demand, whereas a relatively high rate may still be insufficient in another country where supply has never caught up with demand. A ratio of housing stock over population (table 1.5) correlates very imperfectly with demand for new housing, because it does not reflect, for

Table 1.5
Residential Construction and Housing Stock in Selected Countries, 1987 (Per 1,000 of Population)

Capitalist Nations	New Construction	Stock
Belgium	2.6[1]	405[2]
Italy	2.7	402[3]
Sweden	3.7	NA
Great Britain	3.8[2]	399[1]
FGR[1]	4.1	448
France[1]	5.3	451
Denmark[1]	5.6	448
Norway	6.7	417
The Netherlands	7.9	381
USA	6.9	419
Canada[1]	7.5	366
Australia[1]	8.8	324
Japan	10.0[3]	332[4]

Socialist Nations		
Romania	4.6[2]	NA
Poland	4.9	292
Hungary	5.4	370
Czechoslovakia	5.5	373
Yugoslavia[1]	5.6	297
Bulgaria	7.1	364
USSR	7.5[1]	272[5]
GDR	12.9	419

Sources: Economic Commission for Europe, 1988; various national census publications.

Note: NA = not available.

[1]1986   [4]1983
[2]1985   [5]1980
[3]1984

example, demographic trends or the quality of the stock; nor does it take account of culturally specific housing norms or possible incongruities between supply and demand in terms of dwelling characteristics versus household requirements (e.g., qua space, location, or price).

Unfortunately, housing systems in centrally planned economies, by their very nature, restrict the ways and extent that demand for housing is articulated. Hence statements about (relationships between) housing (supply and) demand in countries such as the USSR, Poland, and Hungary are necessarily construed from proxy measures. However, such indicators show that by the late 1980s, all three of these countries still faced, in varying degrees, absolute housing deficits, contrary to most capitalist countries where questions of affordability, equity considerations, and renewed concerns about quality had taken precedence over quantitative aspects.

The USSR is the only European nation not to furnish data on households and dwelling units to the *U.N. Statistical Yearbook*. However, its annual housing production falls far short of the units needed by households newly formed by marriage (see table 6.3). A number of such households will occupy units that have become vacant in the extant stock, although this effect is at least partially offset by additional demand generated by divorces (the Soviet rate is among the highest in the world) and units lost to the stock. Although the precise dimensions of the Soviet housing deficit are hard to gauge, there is no doubt that a severe shortage of dwellings persists. In 1986, according to official sources, about 20 percent of the population still lived communally, meaning that two or more households shared a single (apartment) dwelling (see also Andrusz 1984; Alexeev 1988a).

Bronislaw Misztal, in chapter 8, used government statistics and information compiled by the Solidarity movement to estimate that of the 5 million people seeking housing in Poland in 1987, 52 percent were unwillingly "doubling up" with other households, and the rest lived under very difficult or substandard circumstances. Also in Hungary demand still exceeds supply in both the state and the private sector, particularly in Budapest, which houses about 20 percent of the nation's population (see also Dániel 1985 and Baross 1987). However, its production targets are met more effectively, and there seems to have been relatively more progress as, for example, the average number of persons per dwelling dropped from 3.73 in 1949 (comparable to 3.75 for Poland in 1950) to 2.77 in 1986, clearly below the Polish level in 1985 (3.16) and not much higher than that of 2.65 in the Netherlands in 1986.

Assessments of housing conditions in these Eastern European countries vary according to the frame of reference that is used. In comparison with conditions found in capitalist countries, measures of availability and quality of housing clearly indicate lesser achievements. For example, in 1986, 27 percent of Hungarian dwellings lacked a bathroom, compared with 13 percent in Italy (1981), 5 percent in the Netherlands (1981), 1.7 percent in Britain (1981), and 1 percent in Australia (1976). Also, living space in Soviet apartments averaged only 56 square meters in 1988, compared with 82 square meters in the Federal Republic of Germany (1982), 90 square meters in Japan (1988), 152 square meters in the United States (1985), and 159 square meters in Australia (1981). Indeed, current Soviet law prohibits families from occupying dwellings that exceed 60 square meters (Alexeev 1988b). Similarly, in 1976 the average number of persons per room in the USSR was 1.7 (Andrusz 1984, 179); in 1986, it was 1.26 in Hungary, and Misztal estimates the Polish 1985 figure around 2. Corresponding figures for Western capitalist countries are less than one-half. For example, in Canada it was 0.48 in 1986 (the 1976 average was 0.57); in Australia it was 0.54 in 1981 (the 1976 average was 0.57). Even in Italy, where between 1971 and 1981 about 30 percent of new construction was illegal (*abusivismo edilizio*) and often nonconforming to prevailing standards, the average number of persons per room dropped from 0.85 in 1971 to 0.64 in 1981. Table 1.6 shows density levels and living space in the countries covered in this book.

However, housing norms are in large part culture bound and historically derived. Consider, for example, the case of household density, one of the more widely researched issues in the field of housing. At what level does a given ratio of persons per room become unacceptable? What adverse effects are demonstrable when this threshold, if indeed it exists, is exceeded? Our best answer is: it depends. It depends on cultural context, for example, as shown by comparative studies (e.g., Schmitt 1963). Within any given culture it depends on temporal considerations, both in a historical sense, as household densities once considered normal decline concomitant to income gains and heightened expectations, as well as in the life cycle of individual households, which may accept otherwise unreasonable densities in the prospect of impending improvement of their situation (see Michelson 1980).

In this perspective, Eastern European countries appear to have made great strides. In 1986 about one out of every five households living by necessity communally with other households might have seemed a rather dismal situation from, for example, a Western European viewpoint, but in the USSR it certainly was a vast improvement over 1960 when 40 percent of all households were living under such arrangements. Similarly, today virtually all dwellings in North America are equipped with flush toilets, and the proportion of Hungarian dwellings with this amenity, 66 percent in 1986, seems low in comparison but represents a tremendous advance over the 14 percent of 1949.

In building activities, a very large majority of residential construction in the centrally planned economies of Eastern Europe has been undertaken by the state apparatus (see table 1.3). A major exception is construction in rural areas and in many small towns where self-help practices, similar to those found in the Third World, have been dominant. There is also a small but growing amount of conventional private sector building. In urban areas, extensive bureaucracies have typically adopted standardized industrial technologies, using prefabricated components in the building of multistory complexes. Gregory Andrusz (1984)

Table 1.6
Density Levels and Living Space in Countries Covered in This Book

Country	Average Number of			Average Size of Dwelling (m²)	Living Space per Capita (m²)
	Rooms per Dwelling	Persons Per dwelling	Persons Per room		
WESTERN AND SOUTHERN EUROPE					
Great Britain (1985)	4.92	2.56	.52	NA	NA
FGR (1987)	NA	2.3	NA	82[3]	35
The Netherlands (1986)	5.0	2.65	.58	NA	NA
Italy (1986)	4.0[3]	2.58[3]	.64[3]	86[3]	31
EASTERN EUROPE					
Soviet Union (1987)[g]	NA	NA	NA	56[e]	15
Hungary (1984)	2.2	2.77	1.3	65	23.5
Poland (1985)	3.3	3.49	2.0	NA	NA
NORTH AMERICA					
Canada (1986)	5.7	2.7	.48	113[a]	NA
United States (1985)	5.3	2.5	.47	152	60.8
CENTRAL AMERICA AND THE CARIBBEAN					
Cuba (1981)	4.08	4.23	1.03	NA	NA
Mexico (1985)	NA	5.35	NA	NA	NA
SOUTH AMERICA					
Brazil (1984)	5.0[4]	4.3	.8	NA	NA
Colombia (1980)	3.0	6.6	2.2	42	6.4
MIDDLE EAST					
Egypt (1986)	NA	NA	1.9	NA	NA
Israel (1983)	3.0	3.43	1.2	127[e]	NA
AFRICA					
Kenya	NA	NA	NA	NA	NA
Ghana (1988)	5.6[2]	10.11[2]	1.8[2]	52	5.2
South Africa (1970)[f]	4.3/2.4/3.4	3.8/6.9/7.6	.75/2.0/1.9	NA	NA
ASIA					
Singapore (1983)	NA	4.8	NA	32-155	7.9-38.7
China (1986)[b]	2.23/5.27[c]	3.87/5.12[d]	1.7/1.0	NA	6.66/14.7[1]
Japan (1988)	4.87	3.20	.66	90	28.1
Pakistan (1980)	2.0	6.7	3.5	NA	NA
OCEANIA					
Australia (1981)	5.5	3.0[h]	.54	159	53

Sources: Various national census publications.

Note: NA = not available.

[1] 1985   [3] 1981
[2] 1984   [4] 1980

[a] Average floor area of new houses financed under the NHA.
[b] Urban/rural.
[c] Rooms per household.
[d] Persons per household.
[e] Average for units completed in 1987.
[f] Urban areas only: Whites/Coloreds/Indians. Data on blacks not available. Data from 1980 census not shown because of serious inaccuracies.
[g] Urban areas.
[h] Private sector.

has reviewed the organizational deficiencies of the Soviet system and the attempts to deal with them, and in this book Misztal describes inefficiency in Poland where in 1986, in spite of acute housing shortages, only 62 percent of productive capacities was used (see also Misztal and Misztal 1987, 199). In Hungary 36 percent of all units completed during the 1976–1980 period had been constructed in the state sector. However, in 1986–1987 the state's share in new building had declined sharply to 12 percent, although the state building society, OTB, was given a more significant role in mortgage financing to facilitate private building and ownership. This trend of privatization, most pronounced in Hungary but also observed in several other Eastern European countries (Van Vliet— forthcoming), has had implications for the massive institutions established by the state during the 1960s to produce large high-rise complexes. The organizational inflexibility of these large corporations and the rigidity of their technological infrastructure have hampered their ability to adjust to the changed circumstances, and, as in the USSR and Poland, they operate inefficiently. In the GDR, production of housing is almost completely industrialized, using prefabricated components. This mode of construction rose from 49 percent of completed dwellings in 1960 to 84 percent in 1974 to 96 percent in 1988. In the process, efficiency did increase, as the number of working hours to complete one unit declined from 2,000 in 1950 to 600 at present (Rueschemeyer 1989).

Housing tenure patterns in Eastern European countries vary considerably between urban and rural areas. In the latter, most or all housing is self-built so that there is a very high proportion of private homeowners. In contrast, in large cities in particular, much urban housing has been built or redistributed by the state, and in addition, various cooperative and nonprofit arrangements are found. Tenure patterns also vary from country to country. For example, private ownership rates in Czechoslovakia (1980: 46.3 percent) and the GDR (1981: 47.9 percent) are much lower than in Hungary (1984: 73.7 percent) and Bulgaria (1980: 77 percent; see Economic Commission for Europe 1986). These rates tend to be higher than those found in the more industrialized capitalist countries where they range from a low of 42 percent (1984) in the Federal Republic of Germany; (29.7 percent in Switzerland in 1980; ibid.) to a high of 70 percent (1986) in Australia (see table 1.4). However, although the past twenty years show a stable or increasing private home-ownership rate in capitalist countries, Eastern European countries tend to show a decline, particularly the GDR (from 62.1 percent in 1971 to 47.9 percent in 1981). Hungary is an exception where privatization has resulted in an increase in private home ownership from 66.5 percent in 1970 to 73.7 percent in 1984 (see also Lowe and Tosics 1988).

Third World Nations

The Third World includes countries with diverse political economies. Some, like Pakistan, Thailand, Brazil, and Ghana, contain many of the elements of capitalist "laissez-faire" market systems; others, like Cuba, Vietnam, and China, display features prominent in centrally planned socialist systems. However, among the common characteristics that tend to set Third World nations apart are a low level of industrial development, an inadequate organizational and physical infrastructure, a position of high economic dependency, a large low-income population, formidable population growth, and massive urbanization (see table 1.1). Some countries fit this profile better than others, and the differences between Third World countries are as important as the elements they share in common (Van Vliet— 1987a).

Information on housing in Third World nations is typically fragmented and incomplete. This situation is in part a reflection of the relatively low priority that Third World countries generally accord to housing in their overall scheme of national development (see below). If data on housing are collected, it is usually on a local basis rather than nationwide. By the time they become available, they have often been overtaken by subsequent developments. Residential construction frequently takes place in an irregular and piecemeal manner and without systematic monitoring. Much building also occurs illegally, without legal title or permit and in contravention of prevailing building codes, zoning ordinances, and land-use plans. As a result, the volume of officially authorized construction may seriously underrepresent the number of units actually constructed. For example, in Colombia more than one-half of all urban dwellings have been built illegally, and in Egypt illegal construction has been estimated to account for as much as 75 to 90 percent of all new building. Nevertheless, the information available from disparate sources is often consistent and combines to form a general picture.

Rapid household formation during the postwar period and its concentration in urban centers, particularly as a result of rural-urban migration, presented a challenge to housing provision that few countries have been able to meet effectively. Typically, squatters have undertaken "self-help" building in response to the inability of the public and private sectors to deal effectively with the overwhelming demand for housing in cities. Spontaneous settlements of different types have sprung up in the Near East, Far East, Africa, and South and Central America. Known as *favelas* (Brazil), *tugurios* (El Salvador), *barridas* (Peru), *barrios piratas* (Colombia), *callampas* (Chili), *ranchos* (Venezuela), *colonias populares* (Mexico), *djugis* (India), *katchi abadis* (Pakistan), *bidonvilles* (former French colonies), *gecekondu* (Turkey), *panjachon* (Korea), and *barongs-barongs* (Philippines), they frequently house a large proportion of the urban population: for example, according to current U.N. estimates, 32 percent in Rio de Janeiro, 33 percent in Lima, 37 percent in Karachi and Kuala Lumpur, 40 percent in Manila, 50 percent in Lusaka and Mexico City, 59 percent in Bogotá, 70 percent in Casablanca, and 85 percent in Addis Ababa.

These settlements are commonly located on land that is inexpensive because it is unsuitable for profitable development, often in remote locations on the urban fringe from where access to employment and community facilities is difficult.

However, there are also significant differences among these spontaneous settlements, for example, with respect to physical infrastructure, legality of land tenure
and construction, and use of building materials, as well as availability of educational opportunities, health care, and jobs (Lim 1987; Van Vliet— 1987a).

Few Third World countries have been able to develop effective national strategies to cope with the housing emergencies with which they have been faced.
In most of these countries, there is little or no realistic prospect that formal
housing provision, either through the state or through the private sector, will
eliminate the severe shortages that exist. These shortages are reflected in density
levels that are much higher than those found in the capitalist and socialist countries reviewed earlier (see table 1.6).

The housing shortages of most Third World nations are exacerbated by the
pervasive lack of basic amenities and poor quality of dwellings. For example,
20 percent of Colombia's households are estimated to live under substandard
conditions. In 1980 more than 50 percent of the housing in Pakistan had been
built with unbaked bricks or with mud as a binding agent. In 1984 almost one
out of every ten houses in Brazil was not made out of durable materials. In 1985
one out of every five houses in Mexico had been constructed with mud brick.
In most countries, also, the provision of water, electricity, and sewerage facilities
is far from ubiquitous. For example, in 1984, 21 percent of all dwellings in
Brazil lacked electricity, 38 percent did not have piped water, and 52 percent
were not connected with a sewer system or septic tank. In 1985, 24 percent of
Mexican dwellings lacked water supply, and 34 percent did not have drainage.

Housing conditions are very similar in most other Third World countries,
although there are notable exceptions like Singapore and Cuba. There are, however, important variations within countries. Especially discrepant is the inferior
quality of rural housing compared with that of urban housing, save only for
density levels, which tend to be lower in rural areas. There are also differences
reflecting social hierarchies where positions of privilege may derive from tribal
lineage, ethnic origin, caste membership, or economic class.

In spite of the constant burden of extraordinary demand for housing, in the
context of still more pressing requirements of national development, many Third
World countries have nevertheless recorded relative improvements in their housing situation. Such progress is amply documented in chapters in this book and
elsewhere in the literature. For example, household densities have declined in
many countries and per capita living space has gone up. In Mexico the average
number of people per dwelling dropped from 5.82 in 1970 to 5.35 in 1980. In
Brazil, during the same period, it declined from 5.3 to 4.7 (4.3 in 1984). In
China urban residents nearly doubled their living space between 1977 (3.6 square
meters per capita) and 1985 (6.7 square meters). Other available indicators of
density, such as average number of people per room and number of rooms per
dwelling, show similar improvements. Among the countries covered in this book,
Pakistan is an exception, where the average number of persons per dwelling
increased from 5.1 in 1961 to 6.7 in 1981. However, in that country, too, there

have been improvements in, for example, the proportion of houses connected to electricity, water mains, and sewer systems. In many countries, there has also been an increase in the proportion of houses constructed of durable materials. Tables 12.1 and 13.3 through 13.6 in this volume attest to the great strides made in these regards by, respectively, Mexico and Brazil. Again, it is important to bear in mind that these advances reflect aggregate statistics that obscure important intranational differences. For example, in chapter 17, Kinuthia Macharia sets forth how low-income households in Kenya have often moved from bad housing during colonial times (rooms of 10 by 10 feet, or about 9 square meters) to worse housing today (makeshift carton structures), whereas people in public office have bettered their housing, a number of them benefiting from arrangements ostensibly targeted at low-income groups.

To sum up, the volume of residential construction in Third World countries falls far short of the demand for housing. There are no signs that this situation will change any time soon. Neither the public nor the private sector has managed to provide a sufficient number of decent and affordable dwellings (exceptions are discussed below). In most Third World countries, low-income households, forming a large population majority, have been left with no alternative but to "self-help." They have done so in various ways (often including subcontracting), and government responses have ranged from the bulldozer approach to the provision of infrastructural supports (see below). The quality of housing in the Third World also compares unfavorably with that in industrialized capitalist and socialist countries, although during recent decades, conditions have drastically improved in a relative sense. However, as Peter Ward notes for Mexico, many Third World countries have "run fast to stand still," since in *absolute* terms their housing problems have worsened. For example, in Mexico the number of dwellings without drainage *in*creased from 4.8 million in 1970 to 6.3 million in 1985, even though as a proportion of the total housing stock such dwellings *de*creased during that same period from 59 to 44 percent (table 12.1). Likewise, in China, the number of urban households with insufficient floor space *in*creased from 6.9 million in 1978 to 7.5 million in 1982 while the proportion of such households *de*creased from 35.8 to 31.3 percent (Lee 1988, 389).

Paths to Success. It is worth noting the different experience and relatively more successful housing record of several other Third World countries. Hong Kong evolved under a British colonial administration from entrepôt trade to manufacturing and emerged as a leading financial center in Asia on the foundation of a capitalist market economy. During the 1950s Hong Kong's population more than doubled. Government, which owns much of the land, embarked on a public housing program that in 1987 housed about 44 percent of the population, mostly concentrated in new towns (Fong and Yeh 1987, 34).

Singapore shares many of these traits, including also a small but densely populated land area, but it has a sovereign government with socialist origins that is highly autocratic and that interferes more heavily in many spheres of life.

After 1959, in a short time, the Singaporean government transformed the former British colony, then dominated by squatter settlements and traditional *kampongs*, into a modern city-state that in 1989 housed more than 80 percent of the population in publicly constructed high-rise buildings, as in Hong Kong, often clustered in new towns.

Israel, although not itself among Third World countries, experienced many of the problems attendant upon these countries, including nation building and a fivefold population increase since the state's inception in 1948, in part caused by considerable immigration from North Africa and the Middle East. As in Hong Kong and Singapore, population and land area are small. The government is based on a parliamentary democracy that mixes socialist principles with increasingly influential capitalist formulas and that has benefited from capable elites and a large inflow of foreign capital owing to *Wiedergutmachung* payments, contributions from diaspora communities and, more recently, U.S. aid. Public sector building, facilitated by public ownership of much of the land, accounted for about 80 percent of all units completed during the initial decade of nationhood, declining subsequently as shortages diminished (table 16.1). As in Hong Kong and Singapore, much of the public building has been concentrated in newly developed towns that in 1989 contained about 18 percent of the population.

Cuba is another country with a relatively successful housing record, and it, too, has relied heavily on government to provide the housing needed, contributing 42 percent of total new construction from 1986 to 1988. Socialist principles, guiding societal organization since the 1959 revolution, have not consolidated residential construction in a large state bureaucracy, as in most East Bloc countries. Instead, a much more decentralized approach has been developed, including local government initiative, support for self-building by the popular sector, and various mechanisms structured around the workplace, most notably the so-called microbrigades. The effective use of workplaces as sources of building activity contrasts with the unplanned construction initiated by employers in Poland (Misztal and Misztal 1987) and Hungary (Pickvance 1989). Relatively isolated economically, Cuba has benefited from a significant infusion of Soviet aid.

Like Cuba, China conforms to a socialist model, put in place with the 1949 Communist revolution. However, whereas Cuba's population numbers only about 9 million and is already highly urbanized (72 percent), China's population exceeds 1 billion, and only 29 percent is urbanized. In 1984, public housing accounted for 83 percent of China's urban stock, and while its standards appear to be lower than those in the countries just mentioned (Carlson 1988), extensive squatter settlements, characteristic of most Third World countries, are conspicuously absent (Ma 1981). Housing production has reached record levels (Carlson 1987), and until Summer 1989, there was increasing experimentation with market principles to create housing finance capital and to overcome inefficiencies in housing allocation and land-use planning (Carlson 1986; Badcock 1986).

Finally, Saudi Arabia is a feudal monarchy, ruled by strict adherence to Islamic traditions, which experienced a serious housing deficit and skyrocketing housing costs from 1975 to 1985, as rural migrants flocked to the cities and an influx of foreign workers added more than 1 million to its population of 8 million to 9 million people. During that period, the shortage was alleviated as direct public construction accounted for 26 percent of all new building, and private construction under heavily subsidized arrangements amounted to 53 percent, with the remaining 21 percent built under government requirement by major development project contractors for their employees. Such construction output was made possible by a sevenfold increase in national revenues resulting from petroleum exports, which provided the country with unparalleled resources for housing provision, including precast concrete components imported from the Netherlands (Tuncalp 1987, 351).

It behooves to be curious about the ingredients that go into the success stories of these countries. What underlying factor(s) can explain their accomplishments? The summary portrayals, just given, indicate that these countries differ in major ways but share in common that key housing functions have been fulfilled by the central government. This observation might lead one to conclude that the nation–state is a cardinal element in effective housing provision. However, nation–states are not uniform, nor do they operate in a vacuum. They do not act as neutral arbiters to further "the public interest" (Harloe and Martens 1984). Central government in these countries is constituted very differently, its political accountability varies greatly, and it operates according to widely divergent ideological principles in radically different economic contexts.

Also, intervention by central government is not in and of itself sufficient to guarantee successful provision of decent and affordable housing. The experience of Brazil is a case in point. In this country, a military regime founded the National Housing Bank (BNH) in 1964. The dictatorship vested this institution with far-reaching authority. Its financial foundation was a system of voluntary and forced savings, not unlike that adopted by Singapore. It became the second largest bank in the country and an international model that before its bankruptcy in 1986 made possible the production of 4.4 million dwellings. However, as detailed in chapter 13 and elsewhere (e.g., Valladares 1985; see also Batley 1988), the BNH's primary responsibility for low-income households was perverted as middle- and upper-income strata became the chief beneficiaries of its policies and programs. Likewise, in South Africa, extensive government intervention in housing is explicitly directed by the ways and extent that it serves to implement *apartheid* policies rather than by intent to meet housing needs per se (see chapter 19; Soussan 1984; Parnell 1988). A final example is afforded by Chile, which during the Allende presidency (1971–1973) achieved record housing production as public construction rose to 75 percent of all residential building and government action greatly increased in related matters such as land development and financing. This episode ended abruptly when domestic opposition, backed by foreign capitalist sources, machinated a coup d'état, putting into place a military dictatorship, headed by General Pinochet, which lowered the public sector contribution to 13 percent of residential construction (average, 1974–1985) and left the country with a steadily growing housing deficit (Kusnetzoff 1987). These examples from Brazil, South Africa, and Chile illustrate how a variety of factors may interact with or intervene in government provision of housing; whether purposely or not, such factors can significantly affect the production and distribution of housing.

What, then, are we to make of these observations? First, it appears that the central government has played a pivotal role in these cases where Third World countries managed to respond relatively effectively to the housing crises with which they were confronted. Second, although state intervention may have been a necessary condition for success, it has not been a sufficient condition. Rather, the central government has functioned as an instrumentality to effectuate housing provision. The modes and outcomes of its intervention have interacted with an array of contextual factors. Third, in line with the manifold configurations, intervention by the central government has been multimodal and has taken a variety of forms, including institution building, devising and underwriting of financing schemes, land transactions, infrastructure development, direct construction of units for rent or sale, object and subject subsidies, tenure legalization, incentives for private sector construction, and regulatory mechanisms. Fourth, not readily apparent from the terse sketches given here, in none of these countries has the solving of housing problems been the sole or even chief objective. Housing policies were often subservient and sometimes owed their relative success to other national policies (see below). This linkage is evident, for example, in Singapore and Hong Kong, where economic modernization, to be competitive on world markets, required on the one hand maintenance of low wages and on the other hand the provision of (low-cost) urban housing for the new working class. Prevailing political conditions and the generation of housing finance through mechanisms connected with employment were important contributing factors in this regard. Fifth, there is no Open Sesame that unfailingly brings success. There is no single model that describes the diverse housing experiences of these countries, and there is no simple formula that captures the contrasting elements that are variously present, such as small versus large populations, small versus large land areas, capitalist versus socialist ideologies, scarce versus abundant financial resources, little versus highly urbanized settlement patterns, and so forth. In each case, the particulars of housing demand and supply and their dynamics have historically evolved in singular ways, requiring commensurately unique responses. The lack of a ready recipe notwithstanding, certain ingredients may well lend themselves to usage elsewhere. However, their adoption should be carefully considered in view of their suitability in the context of locally specific circumstances.[6]

POLICIES

Public policies are plans for undertaking or refraining from action regarding a collective objective.[7] As such, analysis of housing policies is of little value. Frequently, policy objectives are purposely formulated in vague terms (e.g., a decent home and suitable living environment for every American family in the U.S. Housing Act of 1949). This lack of specificity makes it difficult or impossible to ascertain progress toward or attainment of the objective and hence hold actors accountable for their actions. Because of political opposition, deficient resources, bureaucratic fragmentation, and countless other reasons, policies are often not implemented, and if they are, it is not uncommon to find that they had unintended outcomes or unforeseen side effects. Harloe and Martens (1984) have pointed out the limitations of comparative housing research that concerns itself with policies disjunct from markets. It can be stated more broadly that housing policies are of interest only in connection with their antecedents, their concurrent context, and their implications. It is far beyond the scope of this chapter to address these aspects of housing policy in a comparative cross-national perspective. The discussion here is restricted to some remarks on policy antecedents and context. A later section will concern itself with a number of policy implications that have emerged as major issues.

Antecedents

Housing policies have numerous nationally distinct antecedents that in and of themselves appear to be neither necessary nor sufficient to bring about a given result. National affluence is conducive to the production of good quality housing but does not guarantee it is provided to population groups that are less well off. For example, the United States has a proportionately larger population that is homeless or living under substandard conditions than various European countries with lower GNP per capita ratios. The same observation holds for cultural values. A cross-national public opinion poll, conducted in 1985–1986, confirmed the common U.S. lack of enthusiasm for government intervention regarding an array of concerns. According to 25 percent of the U.S. sample, the provision of adequate housing is an essential responsibility of government, a percentage lower than that in any of the seven European countries included in the study (Smith 1987, 119). However, in Italy, where the highest percentage (69 percent) was recorded, government housing policy until the 1980s had been less interventionist than in any of the other six European nations where there were less marked preferences for making housing provision an essential government responsibility.[8]

Recognizing the difficulty of explaining housing differences in the face of a complex matrix of antecedents, Coralie Bryant and Louise White (1976, 83) have offered an explanation that views factors such as economic resources and cultural values as elements constituting a "strategic situation" that expressly also includes government policy, to which "groups" then respond, resulting in housing that reflects actions that these groups choose to pursue in light of the options seen to be afforded by the "strategic situation" in which they find themselves. However, it should be clear that policies do not generate their own objectives. This may seem so obvious a point as not to merit mention. Nevertheless, numerous policy analyses accept a policy's objectives as a given, without examination of why, how, and by whom they were formulated. Sometimes policy objectives are linked to political parties. However, such parties are merely an organizational articulation of constituent interests that tend to remain obscure. Such a focus also precludes consideration of powerful nonpolitical arenas that may promote policy. Equally important are mechanisms responsible for the nonformulation of policy, preventing issues from ever entering onto the public agenda, processes that are comparable to what political scientists have described as "mobilization of bias" (Bachrach and Baratz 1970). In this connection, it is useful to point out that governments may pursue policies that obviate the need for any involvement on their part. An example is the deliberate policy by which the Swedish government has relegated the issue of tenant influence in rental housing to landlord and tenant associations in order that the (private) parties involved negotiate an agreement (Lundqvist 1988; see also note 8).

The position taken here contrasts with that adopted by Bryant and White (1976, 90) who followed T. Lowi (1972) when arguing that "policies determine politics." Thus they stated that a government chooses a policy the implementation of which then presents opportunities for potential groups that are seen to behave rationally in response to perceived trade-offs between costs and benefits. Bryant and White attempted to substantiate this argument in a comparison of the differential housing subsidy policies in Britain and the United States. In Britain subsidies have been directed foremost at consumers; in the United States producers have commonly been targeted. Therefore, according to this reasoning, the British system provided incentives for action by housing consumers who have organized themselves in tenant cooperatives, housing associations, squatter movements, and the like. The U.S. system, on the other hand, offered rewards for producer groups that have in turn responded to become the recipients of these benefits.

These observations about the beneficiaries of British and U.S. housing subsidies are, by and large, correct. There is also no question that once subsidies of a given type were made available, eligible groups have undertaken steps necessary to obtain and, if possible, enhance those benefits. However, the view that interest groups respond only to policies ignores the point made earlier, namely, that policies do not generate their own objectives. As noted and abundantly illustrated by chapters in this book, the nation–state is not a neutral arbiter acting in a vacuum in "the public interest." Its often contradictory actions and policies reflect a balance of unequal power between contending forces. Predomination of capitalist interests in the outcomes of these struggles is likely in capitalist systems but not certain and remains an empirical question, more so in differently constituted housing systems where leverage in conflict derives less from accumulation of private capital.

Context

In overall schemes of national development, housing competes for finance, scarce materials, and skilled labor with other concerns that are often viewed as being more important. Military expenditures frequently take precedence. In addition, housing is typically not considered to be a productive investment. This is particularly so in socialist countries whose ideologies stipulate housing as an entitlement, commonly limiting households' housing expenditures to less than 5 percent of income, so that cost recovery is extremely slow (in China in 1985: 200 years). Additional operating and maintenance costs further augment the constant flow of required public investments. Hence in these systems scarce national resources have typically been committed more heavily to the manufacturing sector for greater returns. In general, education and medical services are also given priority, particularly in the Third World. Apart from political and humanitarian reasons, improving education prepares the population for more productive participation in the labor force, thus accelerating economic growth. Medical services are similarly seen as contributing to the enhanced quality and output of productive activity (Barkin 1985). In addition, housing resources in Third World countries are severely constrained by their dependency on foreign capital (see below).

The importance of contextual factors is underlined further by the frequent usage of housing as a tool to advance other policy objectives. Foremost among these external objectives are those that are economic. For example, in capitalist economies, returns on investments by profit-motivated private investors are a systemic requisite. Following World War II, such systems put into place policies to create, strengthen, and direct consumer demand in order to absorb rejuvenated productive capacities. Residential construction and private home ownership were prominent features in this scheme. In the United States President Truman, in his message to Congress of September 1945, explicitly stated that "the largest single opportunity for the rapid post-war expansion of private investment and employment lies in the field of housing" (see note 26 in chapter 10). This statement echoed earlier comments made by President F. D. Roosevelt, also cited by P. Marcuse, who defended the government's establishment of the Homeowners Loan Corporation in 1933, intended to protect private mortgage lending institutions against widespread foreclosures, by asserting that "the broad interests of the nation require that special safeguards should be thrown around home ownership as a guarantee of social and economic stability." Similarly, during the 1930s, the Central Mortgage Bank in Canada was conceived of as state intervention necessary to rescue the national credit system whose collapse was feared when mortgage default became widespread, in particular among debt-ridden wheat farmers in the prairie provinces who experienced serious crop failure; this initiation of finance capital management laid the basis for postwar housing actions (Belec 1984). Notable differences with the United States and Canada notwithstanding, also Western European countries in various ways incorporated housing policies into their postwar economic development (Ball, Harloe, and Martens 1988), recognizing that housing investments, amounting to a significant proportion of GNP, have many backward and forward linkages that create important multiplier effects. Among them is the rapid expansion of "home-and-garden" and "do-it-yourself" industries in most Western countries. Residential construction is, therefore, a potentially powerful lever to regulate levels of inflation and (un)employment (see also Economic Commission for Europe 1985b).

Housing has also been an instrument in various population-related policies. Dominant among them have been plans for (re)distribution of the population. Examples include Britain, the Netherlands, Sweden, Israel, Egypt, Singapore, Hong Kong, India, Cuba, Nicaragua, and China. Such plans have often been elaborated as part of broader strategies for urban and regional development in conjunction with measures to stimulate economic growth. Objectives in this connection have been, for example, to curtail adverse effects of overurbanization, to protect agricultural land, to reduce regional disparities, and to enhance military defense capabilities. Toward these ends, housing has been built in new towns and growth pole settlements. In a somewhat different vein, using regulatory mechanisms, the USSR and, in an earlier period, China have imposed stringent limitations on residential mobility to restrict access to and demands on urban infrastructure, whereas South Africa has implemented what have been euphemistically termed "influx controls" to enforce *apartheid* policy (chapter 19; Tomlinson 1988). Other examples in this connection are the Tanzanian rural settlement policy during the 1970s to form communal *ujamaa* villages and the current Romanian policy of wholesale resettlement of entire ethnic village populations into urban mass housing. The degree of success of such efforts mirrors in large part the range of alternative options open to the targeted populations (e.g., Van Vliet— 1985).

Another objective of population policy has been the integration of diverse population groups via the allocation of housing in projects, neighborhoods, and towns that were to become "microcosms" of society at large. In the United States, there were limited experiments with racial integration in public housing during the 1950s (e.g., Deutsch and Collins 1951) and later the new town of Reston, Virginia, included a deliberate private sector attempt to attain social integration (Fava 1987). The defiance by the city council of Yonkers, New York, of a federally ordered desegregation plan calling for the construction of several hundred low- and middle-income housing units in predominantly white neighborhoods, gaining widespread publicity in 1988 (e.g., Magnuson 1988), is but a symptomatic illustration of the limited national success of efforts at residential integration in the United States. New towns in Britain typically involved the development of neighborhood units (Perry 1939) with a socially balanced population (Mann 1958). The approach has been criticized on ideological grounds, because it would dilute the resource mobilization capabilities of the working class (Dennis 1958; Isaacs 1948), and empirically, B. J. Heraud (1968) found a process of neighborhood rehomogenization as "birds of a feather flocked together," exercising self-selection through residential choice.

In Israel, housing and neighborhood planning have been used intentionally to further the social integration of the veteran population with immigrants of many different national and cultural backgrounds (e.g., Marans 1978). Its experience holds a lesson regarding the role of spatial scale in these processes but also illustrates the limitations of residential integration when it is not linked to economic integration (see also Boeschenstein 1971; and Vischer 1986).

Singapore is a multi-ethnic society where government has sought to end intercommunal strife by dispersal and relocation of residents in troubled areas, clearing their previous neighborhoods in the process. As J. John Palen points out in chapter 20, the privilege of such renewal was often bestowed first on neighborhoods with a history of opposing the government. In this case, social control has become a dominant concern, illustrated further by the management practices of the powerful Housing and Development Board, which has, for example, banned independent resident organizations in the more than 80 percent of the national housing stock for which it is responsible.

Apart from the genocidal deurbanization of perceived dissenters in Kampuchea, Cambodia, by the Khmer Rouge, perhaps the strongest postwar expression of intent to control, shown in housing patterns, is found in South Africa, where housing is both a tool and a reflection of *apartheid* policy (see chapter 19). The use of housing to exercise social control in more subtle ways has been extensively discussed in the literature on private home ownership in capitalist countries. The argument that homeowners develop a stake in the existing system and, therefore, will favor the status quo and vote conservatively is persuasive on the face of it, but the empirical evidence is mixed (see, e.g., Pratt 1986). Moreover, it has been well documented that in many countries there are substantial numbers of homeowners who have low incomes, live in deteriorated housing, and would stand to gain from a change in circumstances. Furthermore, in centrally planned economies, private homeowners frequently find their housing aspirations frustrated by the existing system and in spite of their relative affluence, or perhaps owing to it, tend to favor change toward less restrictive arrangements. However, on a more general level it is clear that the provision of housing involves distribution of scarce resources, to various groups through various ways, with the potential to obtain social consent. Analyses in later chapters and elsewhere leave no doubt that such considerations and intent play a role in the allocation of housing benefits in capitalist systems as well as socialist systems.

Finally, housing in any given country may also be influenced by the foreign policies of other countries. A clear example of this is the Alliance for Progress. Launched during the early 1960s by President Kennedy to counteract the potential spread of the Cuban revolution, it provided Latin American countries with development aid that helped raise their levels of housing construction. Restrictive international lending practices have converse impacts (see below).

MAJOR ISSUES

Any review of major housing issues condensed in a short chapter section must be brief and incomplete. Readers are referred to the chapters that follow for fuller coverage. However, the housing issues selected here do represent major concerns not limited to any single country and currently facing many nations across the world. The issues most germane to the situation of Third World countries are discussed first.

Self-Help

Government response to spontaneous or self-help housing in the Third World has taken different forms. In Brazil, for example, repressive military regimes undertook complete eradication, *remocão*, of squatter settlements, whereas that country's more populist administrations favored programs to upgrade them, *urbanizacão* (Valladares 1985). Chapters in this volume reveal comparable fluctuations in government responses in other countries (see also Patton 1987). However, increasingly, governments tend to view spontaneous building less as a problem and more as a solution that they actively seek to support. Such sponsorship is also a function of the prevailing approaches of institutions and agencies like the World Bank, the U.N. Human Settlements Center, and U.S. AID (Sumka 1987). Although these sponsors vary in the roles they accord to the private versus the public sector, they favor supported self-help and propagate site-and-services schemes and slum upgrading through a variety of mechanisms (e.g., Struyk 1982).

Opinions differ about the nature and distribution of costs and benefits associated with self-help practices (e.g., Burgess 1982; Turner 1982). Consider, for example, legalization of land tenure. Many squatters live on land that was illegally invaded or subdivided. It has been argued that the threat of eviction discourages residents from investments to upgrade their dwelling. Granting a legal title or lease would provide security of tenure and, thence, stimulate initiatives to better housing conditions. The empirical evidence is mixed, partially because legalization often is part of a more encompassing program that also integrates infrastructural improvements so that the precise significance of legalization per se remains unclear (see Varley [1987] for a good discussion). Moreover, de facto tenure security perceived by residents may be more important than de jure tenure security, which, it has been suggested, may displace squatters because it imposes new financial burdens on them and incorporates their plots into the competitive land market, driving up prices (e.g., Burgess 1985). The contrary experience of Cuba (see chapter 11) and Nicaragua (Mathéy forthcoming) suggests that such outcomes would depend on the contextual factors surrounding tenure legalization. The issue illustrates the ongoing debate about self-help efforts. In the field, this debate translates into a dilemma for activists who see self-help as the only practicable general strategy for a temporary solution, even though it may make the patterns of socioeconomic stratification they oppose more permanent (Betancur 1987).

Building Standards

A recurring theme in much of the Third World housing literature is the use of excessively high building standards. Often derived from Western norms and promulgated under previous colonial administrations, their feasibility is hampered by practical constraints related to scarcity of funds and materials, lack of skilled labor, and logistical impediments. The chapters on Egypt and Ghana, for example, mention the difficulty of importing cement. In Kenya, building codes require that urban dwellings should contain at least two rooms made of permanent materials with a kitchen and a bathroom. The problem with such high standards is that the numbers of conforming units that can be built fall far short of what could be achieved under more realistic standards. Moreover, their price puts them beyond the reach of all but privileged minorities. The affordability implication of Third World housing standards finds a parallel in exclusionary zoning practices in the United States that stipulate minimum lot sizes and other requirements that effectively exclude low-income populations. Likewise, in gentrifying neighborhoods, strict enforcement of building codes may result in displacement of incumbent low-income populations. Another example is HUD's regulations regarding its funding of "substantial rehabilitation" of rental units. Requirements of a separate bathroom, kitchen, and other features result in costs that effectively preclude the renovation of single-room occupancy units to accommodate low-income renters.

In the context of Third World development John F. C. Turner (1976) has made a useful distinction between prescriptive planning, which sets minimum standards, spelling out what *must* be done, and proscriptive planning, which sets limits, specifying what *may* be done, suggesting the latter as the more appropriate approach. The counterproductive effects of minimum standards are now increasingly recognized (e.g., Mayo, Malpezzi, and Gross 1986). However, ill-adapted standards exist not only with respect to physical construction but also regarding type of design, which is frequently insensitive to user needs (e.g., Brolin 1972; Grenell 1972; Waltz 1989). Salient in this connection as well is the insistence on unique occupancy, i.e., one household per dwelling unit (Lim 1987).

Institutional Organization and Resourcing

The provision of a sufficient number of decent and affordable housing units in any country requires efficient organization of institutions that, singly or in combination, through direct or indirect means, ensure effective and comprehensive functioning of the housing system. The diverse experiences of countries with relatively good housing records indicate that successful institutional organization of housing can take various forms. However, most of these countries have a central organization, such as a national housing or mortgage bank, with authority to regulate and supervise the supply of housing finance, the conditions of lending, the provision of technical assistance, and the like. Many have also created special institutions with schemes designed primarily to generate housing finance capital, such as the savings and loan associations in the United States, the building societies in Britain and Australia, and the *Bausparkasse* in the Federal Republic of Germany. In each case financing, a crucial aspect of housing provision, has been integrally tied into the broader economy through instrumentalities involving voluntary or compulsory private savings, public revenues, and employer contributions.

The institutional organization of housing provision presupposes institutional functioning in other societal sectors to make such interdependency possible. For various reasons, institution building in many Third World countries is fragmented and inadequate. At the local level, abuses of devolved power are worst when the operating agency has no finance-raising ability (Amos 1984). But problems of institutional organization are not found only in the Third World. The bankruptcy of the Brazilian National Housing Bank, for example, has a counterpart in major crises and scandals that have recently besieged the institutional organization of housing in Italy, the Federal Republic of Germany, and the Netherlands. In the United States, a 1989 audit of the FHA revealed a loss of 4 to 5 billion dollars owing to mismanagement. Further, former Reagan administration officials have been found to benefit handsomely from favoritism in HUD's co-insurance and moderate rehabilitation programs, intended to aid low- and moderate-income households. These multibillion dollar fiascoes came on the heels of a crisis in the savings-and-loan industry, resulting from a combination of poor judgment and outright fraud, made possible by deregulation (see Roistacher forthcoming and below). The unprecedented bailout by government is estimated by the GAO to cost taxpayers between 325 and 500 billion dollars.

It remains to be demonstrated that enhancing the income-generating capabilities of housing is an apposite basis for progress, as Douglas McCallum and Stan Benjamin (1985) have suggested for Third World countries, for in resultant markets some groups are likely to benefit at the expense of others. More important constraints on housing resources in Third World countries derive from the very high economic dependency on more industrialized, commonly capitalist countries and organizations. According to World Debt Tables released by the World Bank in December 1988, the gap between poor and rich countries continues to grow.

Poorer countries are transferring their wealth at unprecedented levels. For example, it is estimated that in 1988 the seventeen most highly indebted Third World countries gave more affluent countries and multinational lending institutions U.S. $31.1 billion more than they received, triple the amount in 1983. Problems related to this dependency are reflected and perpetuated by international lending practices that serve to increase export opportunities for lending countries while augmenting the debt service burden of Third World countries. In Latin America, for example, external debt service as a percentage of exported goods and services increased from 27 percent in 1975 to 65 percent in 1983 (Dewitt 1987, 283). The economic development of Third World countries is further undermined by influential growth forecasts issued by the World Bank and U.N. agencies. A recent review of such forecasts found them to be systematically biased, exaggerating the growth potential and locomotive effect of industrialized countries (Cole 1989). Apart from other factors, in view of these realities and considering the priorities of alternative national investments mentioned earlier, Third World housing problems are unlikely to be solved until more equitable economic and geopolitical arrangements emerge.

Site Planning and Hazard Mitigation

Earlier, it was noted that squatter settlements are commonly located on land that is cheap because it is unsuitable for profitable development. A common ecological characteristic is their siting on steep hillsides, dry riverbeds, and other areas liable to natural hazards. Considering also the generally low structural quality of construction, calamities are bound to occur—and they do. The earthquakes that struck Santiago and other Chilean cities (March 1985), Mexico City (September of the same year), and San Salvador (October 1986) are but three examples of such disasters. Large-scale flooding, cyclones, sudden volcanic eruptions, and mudslides happen almost regularly with enormous loss of life and material damage and destruction, leaving homeless populations that number often in the tens or even hundreds of thousands.[9] Demographic data indicate that during the past twenty-five years there has been an increase of 100 million in the population of the urban poor living in extremely disaster-prone areas (Havlick 1986, 11). There is a paucity of documentation on responses to the housing crises caused by catastrophic events (e.g., Alexander 1984; Breshna 1988). Furthermore, planning to mitigate these hazards is typically absent or poorly developed, and implementation is still in its infancy. Given the better protection of more affluent population groups and their minimal role in housing provision for the poor, conditional foreign assistance may form the most effective incentive for greater commitment to preventative site planning.

Shortages

As noted, in most Third World countries and centrally planned socialist nations, absolute housing shortages persist, that is, households outnumber dwellings. In some cases, the shortage is getting worse. In most industrialized capitalist countries, absolute housing shortages have been eliminated. Frequently, they have been overtaken by shortages relative to characteristics of need. Thus it is possible to find high vacancy rates in one region and overcrowding in another because people gravitate toward job opportunities in the latter, whereas they leave the former when it is economically depressed. It is also possible to find vacancies and homelessness in the same area, when house prices and rents are beyond the reach of those in need of housing. Apart from aspects of location and cost, housing may be in short supply because the available stock does not match household requirements in terms of tenure, size, or type.

Relative housing shortages have gained in significance as a result of recent economic and demographic trends. High rates of capital mobility have contributed to a restructuring of employment. Disinvestment (for example, in the steel industry in the United States) has caused sometimes massive local unemployment and lateral diversification has redistributed job opportunities spatially and shifted them from one employment sector to another with concomitant incongruities between labor and housing markets. Likewise, changes in household composition have generated a demand for housing that has not been satisfactorily met. Significant in this connection is the widespread increase in single-parent households. Most of them are headed by women; a majority of them have low incomes. Their difficulties in finding suitable and moderately priced housing in supportive neighborhoods have been well documented (Ahrentzen 1985; Smith and Thompson 1987). The rise in elderly populations also presents a significant housing challenge to which different countries are adopting different approaches. In the United States, for example, a very large majority lives in a variety of "ordinary" household configurations (e.g., with spouse, alone, with children), and a very small minority lives in federally assisted housing, institutional environments, and retirement communities. In Scandinavia and Western Europe alternative living arrangements are much more common, spanning the entire spectrum from independent living through a graduated array of supportive settings to full-time care facilities (Heumann and Boldy 1982; Butler 1986). In Singapore the government, attempting to minimize its responsibilities, offers incentives to restore traditional practices of dependent elderly living with their children. In China, filial care for the elderly also still prevails, but economic modernization and the one-child-per-family policy increasingly focus attention on needed changes in the relationship between the family and the state (Streib 1987). Since 1978, reforms in this connection have included a dramatic increase in the number of homes for the childless elderly in rural areas (*jing lao yuan*) and greatly expanded voluntary nursing services (*bao hu zu*) for in-home care of the childless elderly by neighborhood resident committees in urban areas (Olson 1988). In Japan economic and social trends also combine to reduce support for arrangements under which the elderly are cared for by family members, although in the 1980s about 70 percent of people aged sixty or older still lived with their children (Kamo 1988). In the United States the corresponding figure is only about 15 percent and, unlike in the countries just mentioned, government attempts to develop alternative housing for the elderly based on greater involvement by family members are constrained by the absence of a strong cultural tradition in this regard. Indeed, it has been suggested that the economic restructuring, social and spatial mobility, and demographic change characteristic of market economies necessitate centralized state-administered approaches to security schemes for the elderly in Western countries (Myles 1988). Housing for the elderly is without question an issue that can benefit from cross-national research.

A final shortage to be mentioned here is relative to tenure. Most notable in this context is, first, the lack of affordable and appropriate housing to accommodate private home ownership, which many governments seek to expand and to which, surveys show, many households aspire (Fleming and Nellis 1987). There is also an emerging crisis in rental housing. In Britain, the private rental sector declined from 51 percent in 1951 to 20 percent in 1971 to 10 percent in 1986. Attempts to stem this demise have focused on the removal of present rent controls and the substitution of free market conditions. Government policy proposals along these lines have been criticized, however, for failing to take into account the needs and characteristics of the population groups dependent on private rental housing and for not addressing issues of distributive justice and economic feasibility (Ivatts 1988; Crook forthcoming). Although the decline of the private rental sector has been most precipitous and remains problematic in Britain (Kleinman forthcoming), the stock of private rental housing has shrunk in virtually all industrialized capitalist countries (Howenstine 1981). In the Federal Republic of Germany, the national government ceased subsidizing the construction of rental units in 1986; it is estimated that as much as 50 percent of the stock of subsidized rental housing existing in 1984 will be lost as government offers incentives to private investors for accelerated repayment of conditionally favored loans, thus shortening the period during which such rental units are protected from market forces (Krätke 1989). The United States faces a similar situation (see below). The malaise is not universal as shown, for example, in the Netherlands, but the concern is widespread (see Harloe 1985 for a good analysis of recent trends in private rental housing in the United States, Britain, the Federal Republic of Germany, France, the Netherlands and Denmark).

Quality and Rehabilitation

Although much improved in recent decades, in most Third World countries the quality of much of the housing stock is still poor by current Western standards. Today, slum clearance has been abandoned almost everywhere. At best, it displaced the problems; more often than not it exacerbated them. Current efforts are increasingly directed at supporting upgrading by residents. Such support is not restricted to dwelling structures only but extends itself to infrastructural improvements such as the installation of electricity and sewer systems and the provision of health services.

The East Bloc countries also still face problems of housing quality. Contributing to these problems is a housing stock, part of which is still lacking basic amenities such as flush toilet and shower and part of which was built to low standards, with poor workmanship and inadequate quality control. Soviet government expends as much as 40 percent of its housing budget on modernization, renovation, maintenance, and management (Vladimirov 1985, 39), and there are none of the decrepit and insalubrious slums found in many U.S. cities. However, rents paid by tenants in Soviet public housing cover less than one-third of maintenance costs and contribute nothing to capital repairs.[10] In the German Democratic Republic rents paid by tenants also amount to only one-third of operating costs (Staemmler 1984, 237). In addition to lack of funds, there is a shortage of skilled labor to undertake maintenance, repair, and renovation. Such work suffers from low prestige, thus holding little attraction for qualified workers. Furthermore, the large building corporations are oriented first to new construction. Nevertheless, in Eastern Europe housing deterioration is a growing concern, and increasing attention is being given to renovation of the older stock as part of broader programs for the rehabilitation of run-down inner-city neighborhoods (Economic Commission for Europe 1983).

An earlier part of this chapter described impressive improvements in housing quality in many capitalist countries following World War II, even though this spread of progress has been unequal. In industrialized capitalist countries where quantitative housing deficits have been largely eliminated, policy priorities have shifted to renovation of the existing stock and rehabilitation of deteriorating neighborhoods, most but not all of which are found in inner-city areas. The magnitude of these problems in financial terms is considerable.

The 1981 House Condition Survey in Britain indicated that the total cost (at 1981 prices) of carrying out all necessary repairs on the English housing stock, without modernization, would be £35.4 billion, more than one-half of it for owner-occupied housing. According to more recent data, the figure for repairing and modernizing just public housing in England, Wales, and Scotland would be £25 billion, and it has been estimated that the backlog of disrepair in this sector is growing by £900 million per year. In the Netherlands, results from a 1985 survey of the national housing stock produced estimates of repair costs ranging from 20 billion to 25 billion U.S. dollars (excluding modernization), about 40 percent of which would be for owner-occupied housing. However, average repair costs per dwelling were by far the highest for private rental units (see table 4.6).

Although cost estimates are not as readily available, repair of a deteriorating housing stock is a growing concern in most other European countries as well (Economic Commission for Europe 1981, 1983). In Italy, it is considered a key housing problem that affects especially private rental housing and historic urban districts. In the Federal Republic of Germany, policies since the 1970s have emphasized urban rehabilitation. The focus of these efforts, there and elsewhere, is not exclusively on the older stock but includes also multistory complexes built after World War II. These estates were often constructed with inferior materials and techniques liable to cause problems. These problems have frequently been exacerbated by poor design and inaccessible location, which made these estates less popular still and led to a spiral of rising vacancy and vandalism rates. In Australia, Canada, and the United States as well as in Scandinavia and many Western European countries (Britain, the Netherlands, Sweden, Denmark), high-rise buildings were strongly criticized during the 1970s or officially declared an inappropriate housing type for families with children (Van Vliet— 1983b). The case of Pruitt Igoe (e.g., Yancey 1971)—a design award winning, high-rise public housing project in St. Louis, Missouri (USA), dynamited less than twenty years after the first tenants moved in—has many parallels in other countries. The application of social science research methods to study user needs has since resulted in the formulation of (for various reasons only occasionally implemented) guidelines for planning and design of housing environments that are more congruent with the lifestyle requirements of particular population groups (e.g., Cooper Marcus 1975; Cooper Marcus and Sarkissian 1986; Newman 1980). Design principles as embodied by the notion of "defensible space" (Newman 1972) were specifically intended to induce in residents a greater sense of responsibility to each other and their immediate environment in order to increase security, improve upkeep, and reduce vandalism. Their success has been found to be contingent on a variety of factors, including characteristics of the social environment and bureaucratic as well as political processes surrounding the design process. Adopting a very different approach, some countries have tried to reduce problems by privatization of maintenance and management (Ditkovski and Van Vliet— 1984; Werczberger forthcoming).

Housing deficiencies are often reflected in residents' perceptions. In 1983 about 10 percent of all homeowners in the United States rated their dwellings as being of poor or only fair quality, and a similar proportion so evaluated the quality of their neighborhoods; this rather bleak assessment corresponded to objective conditions and was found more than twice as frequently among black homeowners and was four times more prevalent among black renters (Van Vliet— 1988b). A 1985 survey produced similar results (U.S. Bureau of the Census 1988). In Japan the proportion of the population dissatisfied with housing conditions climbed from 35 percent in 1973 to 52 percent in 1988.

The reasons for the greater emphasis given to renovation and rehabilitation in industrialized capitalist nations reflect several developments. First, the reduction or elimination of absolute housing shortages freed up resources previously committed to new construction. However, although it may have facilitated rehabilitation policies, this factor in itself did not cause them. The need for repair and rehabilitation also became increasingly apparent, as deferred maintenance of aging dwellings added to the urgency and scale of the problems. However, the manifest nature of housing problems has rarely been a cause for action either. Additional factors include popular response in many cities in the United States and Europe (in spite of important differences) to previous approaches to urban renewal, which emphasized clearance over renovation, and a reappraisal of city environments. This reevaluation has occurred not only among gentrifiers with an appreciation of the cultural and economic benefits associated with owning housing in urban neighborhoods compatible with the life-style of young upwardly mobile professionals. Private investors have also recognized selected urban neighborhoods as a source of profit. This recognition has been aided further by lucrative incentives offered by policies aimed at privatization of urban renewal and rehabilitation (Thomas 1986; Brindley and Stoker 1987; 1988). This trend is reinforced by the devolving of traditionally national responsibilities to local government that, having inadequate resources, seeks and anticipates additional revenues through urban upgrading and favors private ventures or private-public partnerships to that end (Catanese 1984; Law 1988). These processes have been found to displace incumbent populations, resulting as well in new residential patterns along demographic, socioeconomic, and tenure lines (Palen 1988; Chambers and Gray, forthcoming).

Affordability

In most Third World countries the enormous demand for housing in the face of limited supply and multiple constraints on new residential construction make availability of dwellings a more immediate housing concern than affordability. Nevertheless, units intendedly produced for low-income groups are frequently not affordable for the targeted households (see below). This problem relates, in part, to speculative practices in land and housing markets and to the adoption of high building standards, both of which drive up housing prices. Chapters in this book provide ample illustration of the ensuing affordability problems. For example, in Karachi, Pakistan, in the early 1980s, two-room public housing units, built for low-income households, cost U.S. $3,800 when 80 percent of these households earned less than U.S. $58 per month and spent 70 percent of this income on food and clothing and had no access to mortgage loans. In Egypt 25 percent of an average family income buys only 3.7 square meters of living space per capita. In many Third World countries, there is also widespread and frequent misappropriation of subsidized housing, ostensibly built for low-income groups, by more powerful political and economic interests.

A variety of approaches to increase affordability have been proposed and implemented. They include site-and-services and "wet-core" schemes, lowering of building standards, subsidization of land costs or construction materials, gratis technical assistance, and rent control. Loans are typically limited in value, if they are at all available; in case they are, squatters are frequently not accepted as creditworthy, even though their incomes from vending, hawking, petty trading, and other jobs in the informal sector may be higher than those of eligible public employees (see, for example, Asiama 1985 and Teilhet-Waldorf and Waldorf 1983 for, respectively, Accra, Ghana, and Bangkok, Thailand).

In a number of countries, squatters have organized informal savings and credit associations to finance major housing expenditures by members on a rotating basis. In Pakistan, such arrangements are known as *bisis*. In Egypt, they are called *gam' iyyat*, run by women who also take responsibility for the management of land-purchase transactions, payment of registration fees, obtaining building permits, and so on (El-Messiri 1985; Wikan 1985). There have also been attempts to exploit the income-generating potential of housing, for example, by encouraging low-income owners to rent out part of their dwelling (see McCallum and Benjamin 1985). It is clear, however, that all of these approaches are constrained, first, by the heavy dependence of Third World nations on their creditors and, second, by arrangements and processes outside housing that perpetuate existing intranational inequities.

In socialist countries, housing is a legislated entitlement, and affordability is not a problem for residents in dwellings provided via the state. Their housing costs are typically less than 5 percent of household income.[11] However, affordability may become an issue inasmuch as bribes and under-the-table payments are necessary to obtain housing or trade dwellings in the second economy (see, e.g., Morton 1980, 1985; Alexeev 1988c). Housing in the private sector tends to be extremely expensive; in the early 1980s the average price per square meter of new residential construction in Poland, for example, ranged between U.S. $200 and $300, comparable to prices in Western Europe, while the median salary of Polish workers was much lower. The affordability of private home ownership is limited further by the severely restricted availability of funds for mortgage loans. In Hungary (an exception in this regard) housing construction has shifted in recent years from the public to the private sector, more than in any other Eastern European country. Necessary mortgage loans are provided by the state building society, OTB, which has just increased its interest rate from 3.0 to 19.5 percent under pressure from the International Monetary Fund. Although repayment conditions were somewhat adjusted, there is no question that housing costs in Hungary, at least in urban areas, are a growing problem, also because the price of construction materials for self-built housing has increased considerably. Recent indications clearly point to an affordability issue similarly emerging from a privatization trend in Poland. Nevertheless, certainly in comparison to capitalist countries, affordability is as a rule not a serious housing problem in most socialist nations.

In capitalist countries, the price of housing is, by the very nature of their political economy, more a function of private profit-oriented market forces than it is in socialist countries. However, there are considerable differences among capitalist countries. In welfare states, housing is commonly recognized as a right. For example, in the Netherlands, the provision of adequate housing is a responsibility of central government anchored in (Article 22 of) the national constitution and legislated into a local function by various national housing acts. Everyone reaching age eighteen is entitled to request a dwelling through the municipal housing distribution authority (the actual allocation of a dwelling depends on local circumstances and the applicant's ranking according to a point system based on need). This acceptance of housing as an entitlement has also formed the basis for legislation that limits tenants' rental expenditures (see table 4.12). Sweden operates according to similar principles (Appelbaum 1985; Nord forthcoming), as do other European welfare states, although the specific approaches to make housing affordable have varied considerably (see, for example, Wynn 1984, Oxley 1987; Ball, Harloe, and Martens 1988).

The articulation of affordability objectives, however, does not guarantee their attainment. Indeed, it is clear from the chapters in this book and elsewhere in the literature (e.g., Friedrichs 1988) that also in Western Europe and Scandinavia housing affordability may be problematic; it is particularly so for segments of the population such as ethnic minorities, young people, single-parent families, and the unemployed and elderly living in rural areas and inner-city neighborhoods. Although in different degrees and not to the same extent as in the United States, these countries also have growing homeless populations.

In the Federal Republic of Germany, the proportion of households paying more than 25 percent of their income on housing, a commonly accepted standard, increased from 18.1 percent in 1978 to 23.4 percent in 1982. The construction of social housing has dropped steadily: from 6.7 (per 1,000 of population) in 1950, to 5.9 in 1960, 2.7 in 1970, 1.6 in 1980, and 0.7 in 1987 (table 3.4). It has been estimated that about one-half of the stock of subsidized rental housing will be lost by 1994 if current developments continue unchanged. In Italy, the illegal construction of dwellings, in large part a response to the failure in housing provision by the public and private sectors, is far from a residual phenomenon. Attempts by Italy's government to expand private home ownership further have run afoul of the inability of low-income households to bear the costs associated with owning a home. The same situation exists in Britain (Fleming and Nellis 1987; Crook 1986a, 1986b) where the national government has proposed the wholesale transfer to private corporations of public housing estates occupied by residents unable to exercise their right to buy their units even under deep government discounts (or unwilling to be lured more permanently into stigmatized housing that has often remained unsold as the least desirable stock). Statistics indicate the growing affordability problems among British homeowners: mortgage defaults went up by 800 percent between 1979, the year before enactment of the "Right to Buy," and 1986; during the same period, arrears increased by 400 percent, in addition to a rise in forced sales. Similar trends have been observed for France, the Federal Republic of Germany, the Netherlands, and Denmark (Ball, Harloe, and Martens 1988, 165).

In the United States the question is not *whether* there is a problem of housing affordability but *for whom* it is a problem. There is, for example, a growing problem of home-ownership affordability among younger age groups. Reversing a long trend of steady increases, between 1976 and 1984, in the twenty-five to twenty-nine age group, the proportion of owners declined from 43.6 to 38.4 percent; in the thirty to thirty-four age group, it went down from 62.3 to 54.4 percent (Van Vliet— 1988a). Between 1980 and 1988 the average age of first-time buyers rose from 28 to 32. The median proportion of income spent on housing by homeowners with mortgages increased between 1974 and 1985 from 17 to 21 percent. Those paying more than 35 percent of their income increased from 8 to 15 percent during this period, while those paying less than 25 percent decreased from 69 to 53 percent (U.S. Bureau of the Census 1988). The percentage of loans ninety days or more past due increased by 45 percent between 1977 and 1989; the initiation of foreclosures on conventional loans rose by 100 percent (National Association of Home Builders 1989). Since the early 1970s, the gap between median income and median sales price of new as well as existing dwellings has widened very significantly (Van Vliet— 1988a, 334). The National Association of Realtors and the National Association of Home Builders construct affordability indices that capture the relationship between household income and housing costs for, respectively, existing and new homes. Figures in both categories show a clear decrease in affordability of home ownership since the mid–1970s.[12]

Housing costs, however, are not a growing problem just for owners. The median rent-to-income ratio increased from 23 percent in 1975 to 27 percent in 1985. This ratio is higher among minorities. In 1985, more than 39 percent of Hispanics and blacks paid more than 35 percent of their income on rent; 25 and 15 percent paid more than 50 and 70 percent of their income on rent, respectively. Renters below the poverty level paid on average 65 percent of their income on housing (U.S. Bureau of the Census 1988). Among households with incomes of 80 percent or less of the local area's median family income, the proportion of those with a rent burden of more than 30 percent of income increased between 1975 and 1983 from 54 to 64 percent. During the same period, the proportion with a rent burden of more than 50 percent increased from 38 to 49 percent among households with less than one-half of their area's median family income (Hartman 1988). As in the Federal Republic of Germany, the U.S. federal subsidization of rental housing provision has frequently required owners to rent their units for a limited period to households below certain income ceilings. These requirements are now expiring. As a result, by 1997 as much as 50 percent of these units for low- and moderate-income households may be converted to the private market (Appelbaum and Dreier forthcoming; Roistacher forthcoming).

Canada is among the most affluent countries worldwide, and a large majority of its population can afford to live in housing of good quality. Nevertheless, substantial numbers of households do not share in this good fortune and face high housing costs. Although the proportion of private home ownership has remained fairly stable around 62 percent during the past twenty years (table 9.4), home ownership has become much more expensive. For example, in Toronto, the average price of a home increased between 1972 and 1987 from 32 to 50 percent of median family income. Although differential increases in house prices are associated with different home-ownership patterns in Toronto, Montreal, and Vancouver, in each of these cities the poor and self-employed have been most affected by increased ownership costs (Harris 1986). Canadian renters have more serious problems of housing affordability. They face a declining supply and increasing costs. In Toronto, for example, 11,000 rental units were lost between

1976 and 1985 due to conversion, redevelopment, and demolition. In 1987 the vacancy rate on the rental market was only 0.3 percent, and waiting lists for social housing were long and expanding. In 1976, 23 percent of all renter households paid more than 30 percent of their income on rent; in 1986 it was 27 percent (Hulchanski 1988, 13). There is also an increasing problem of homelessness (Oberlander and Fallick 1987; Daly 1988).

In Australia, since 1970 housing costs have in general not greatly increased relative to average earnings. The rent index, in fact, rose less than the index of average earnings (table 24.7). However, housing costs are problematic for a growing minority that includes, particularly, single-parent households, the unemployed, and aboriginal households. In Melbourne, the proportion of sold detached houses affordable at 25 percent of household income declined from 75 percent in 1968 to 18 percent in 1982 (for apartments it decreased from 82 percent to 37 percent; King 1987, 289). It has become increasingly difficult to accumulate the money required for a down payment (Thorns 1988). Since 1972, the average period to accumulate the necessary savings has more than tripled for single-income families and more than doubled for dual-earner families. Furthermore, the supply of public housing is inadequate (Paris, Williams, and Stimson 1985), and private rental housing of good quality is often not available or affordable for those in need of it (Paris 1984; Watson and Coleman 1986).

In Japan housing is generally considered expensive. For example, taking differences in floor space into account, the ratio of housing price over annual household income is 2.5 to 2.7 times higher than it is in the United States (Horioka 1988a). The relatively high cost of Japanese housing derives in large part from high land prices. The price of land is mostly a function of competition between market forces in which commercial entrepreneurs and speculators dominate over residential developers. As a result, land prices have escalated, showing sharp increases, in particular since the early 1970s (see figure 22.1). From 1950 to 1988 the increase in the average house price has greatly outpaced the increase in average income. As in Israel, it is customary in Japan for first-time home buyers to get financial help from relatives (Horioka 1988b). The government has also targeted support at first-time buyers (Donnison and Hoshnino 1988), and in comparison with their counterparts in other advanced capitalist countries, Japanese homeowners and renters are spending a modest proportion of their income on housing: in 1986, 12 and 11 percent, respectively. Nevertheless, in recent years housing costs in both tenure forms have been increasing while the proportion of employer-provided housing is on the decline and eligibility criteria for public housing are being tightened (figure 22.2).

This discussion can only briefly mention some of the major correlates and antecedents of the affordability problem. Martens (1988, ch. 4) has described the breakdown of conventional housing-finance circuits as a recent development affecting mortgage-lending practices with potentially significant (yet so far little documented) impacts on the affordability of private home ownership. These specialized circuits had traditionally been dominant in the generation and flow of housing capital and had received government protection, insulating them from investment risks faced by lenders in the general market. During the recent period, this protection has been severely eroded in many countries as financial markets have been deregulated and competition among lending institutions has greatly increased (e.g., Roistacher 1987; Florida 1986). In the United States this development was first embodied in the Depository Institutions Deregulation and Monetary Control Act of 1980 (Kane 1984; see also Guttentag 1984; Kaufman 1984; and *Housing and Mortgage Market Review*, various issues). Specialized mortgage lenders also had to adjust to rising and volatile interest rates (particularly during the 1970s and early 1980s). This change most affected institutions that had traditionally offered long-term fixed interest rate loans (Martens 1988, 145–46).

To be competitive with other lending institutions, previously excluded from housing finance, traditional residential mortgage lenders have invested heavily in branching networks, advertising campaigns, and new technologies, the costs of which have been passed on to borrowers. Their more diversified portfolios have also opened up opportunities for investment alternatives more profitable than housing finance. This expansion is likely to exacerbate lending practices that restrict access by households most in need of and least able to afford loans.

The precise relationships between deregulation and affordability are hard to disentangle. Like other developments with clearer effects on housing affordability—in particular, higher real interest rates, tax reforms, budget cutbacks, a shift from object to subject subsidies, and changes in the investment climate—they should be seen against the background of trends in the general economy such as increased mobility of capital, industrial disinvestment, and lateral diversification, which produce a broader class of problems with ramifications for the affordability of housing. Particularly salient is the persistence of conjunctural and the increase in structural unemployment, particularly among the young generations. Some analysts, like David Macarov (1988), have concluded that the unemployment pattern that has emerged is not a temporary aberration—one that can be remedied by policies and will disappear in an economic upswing—but is a permanent feature inherent in the development of industrialized market economies. Should these analyses prove to be correct, the affordability problem will likely worsen given the documented close linkage between housing and labor markets and careers (e.g., Murphy and Sullivan 1986; Hughes and McCormick 1987; Forrest and Murie 1987b) and the absence of alternative arrangements to produce or redistribute income. An illustration of this point is provided by a recent U.S. study that showed how deregulatory trends exacerbated regional economic difficulties. Delinquent homeowners were found to be less successful in negotiating forbearance with their lenders in the type of nonlocal, competitive secondary mortgage markets that have developed under deregulation than homeowners with locally held mortgages (Heisler and Hoffman 1987). Tightened operating rules imposed upon the U.S. savings-and-loans, following their debacle under deregulation, and mandated mergers will have mixed effects.

Initially at least, the release of large numbers of foreclosed properties on the market is likely to offset a decline in affordability that may result from a decrease in lending institutions.

Responses to recent housing affordability problems have been diverse and have occurred at various levels. Here it is possible to refer only briefly to a few points. The response of homeowners has included deferred maintenance in order to apply money thus saved toward repayment of mortgage loans. There also has been a significant increase in dual-earner households, since a second income has frequently become a necessity in qualifying for and repaying a loan (Myers 1985; Wulff 1982). In the United States a second income accounted in 1987 for more than 10 percent of total household income for about 68 percent of all first-time buyers consisting of households with two adults; for about one-third of them it contributed between 40 and 50 percent of total household income (U.S. League of Savings Institutions 1988).

A general response on the part of mortgage lenders has been a liberalization of loan policies. Innovative schemes introduced in this connection have been described by, for example, D. C. Thorns (1988) and Robert Carter (forthcoming). To promote the production of low-cost housing, governments may extend tax credits to suitable investors, as done in the United States under provisions of the 1986 Tax Reform Act for rental housing at a maximum of $10 billion over three years.

At the local level, public funds are increasingly used as leverage in complicated patchworks of public-private partnerships. There is also a growing practice of linking permits for urban development to the provision of housing for low- and moderate-income households (see Goetz 1989 for an example in San Francisco, and Ehrlich and Dreier 1988 for the evolution of this practice in Boston). Such linkage policies can help produce low-cost housing for owners as well as renters, although their contribution to solving the overall problem of housing affordability remains very minor. Indeed, it is unrealistic to expect local solutions to housing problems whose local manifestation is anchored in national and even international processes.

Governments in many countries have also introduced a variety of rent-allowance schemes to reduce tenants' rising housing costs (see, e.g., Howenstine 1986). Questions remain about this approach. For example, one question concerns the limited take-up of rent allowances when a stigma is attached to claiming them or when people are unaware of them or put off by complex regulations or bureaucratic procedures (Harloe 1985). It also remains to be demonstrated that demand-oriented subsidies can take the place of subsidies directed at the supply side and can stimulate investment in and production of sufficient numbers of suitable dwellings. The results of several simulation studies remain inconclusive, and to date, there has been no systematic attempt to examine the elasticity of producer responses empirically (Oxley 1987).

Furthermore, the costs of automatic entitlements such as rent allowances are much harder to predict and control than capped production expenditures. Consequently, allowance programs have increased sharply in size. In the Netherlands, the number of recipients increased by more than 100 percent between 1977 and 1986, and the total sum of disbursements during that period rose by 150 percent (table 4.9).[13] In Britain, the government's housing budget, on the face of it, appears to have declined from a figure indexed at 100 in 1979–1980 to 64 estimated for 1988–1989. However, alternative computations by Ray Forrest and Alan Murie (1987) show how the seeming reduction in housing expenditure of £1,318 million between 1979–1980 and 1984–1985 was, actually, more than offset by the increase of £2,020 in housing benefits (which are disguised as social security expenditures). Total housing expenditures show much more significant increases still when also tax expenditures such as mortgage interest deductions from taxable income are added. In this light, Forrest and Murie (1987) concluded that, notwithstanding the government's privatization policies and apparent budget cutbacks, public housing expenditure has, in fact, not been reduced but rather reoriented toward consumers of housing within a framework that strongly favors private home ownership. This observation brings up the more general point of equity in the distribution of housing benefits to which we turn next.

Inequities, Discrimination, and Polarization

In this chapter, we have signaled various housing problems such as absolute shortages, qualitative deficiencies, and affordability. Conceivably, these problems might be more or less evenly or randomly distributed across a population; in reality, they are not. It is possible, for example, to find comparable households with unequal access to housing opportunities or living under comparable conditions, yet paying different rents. Such imbalances are imbedded in broader patterns of societal stratification that cannot be discussed here. This brief review is restricted to inequities that originate or manifest themselves in the realm of housing, acknowledging that processes and outcomes in this sphere are inextricably and very significantly interwoven with inequities in, for example, education and employment.

In housing, as elsewhere, inequities result mostly from discriminatory rather than inadvertent practices. Officially, discrimination exists when actions and decisions disfavor individuals who qualify for equal treatment according to formal norms. However, this view of discrimination is overly restrictive since formal norms themselves are discriminatory when they diverge from standards derived from the social ethics of universal justice and fairness. Discrimination may be based on prejudice, an attitude dominated by emotional and stereotypical elements. However, it may also be based on apparently rational judgment, as explained later. Either way, discrimination leads to inequities—a distribution of benefits and costs that diverges from what is legitimately just.[14] Cedric Pugh (1980) states as a defining characteristic of inequities that they "occur for arbitrary reasons.'' However, evidence, presented in this book and elsewhere, suggests that inequities arise *systematically* (rather than arbitrarily) from structural patterns of normative, utilitarian, and coercive power. Discrimination occurs when such power is (ab)used without legitimate criteria.

Discrimination may be historical with carry-over effects that perpetuate inequities in the present, for example, through intergenerational transfer of property wealth (see Forrest and Murie 1989 for a thoughtful discussion), but much of it is current. Discrimination occurs in all stages of the housing process—design, construction, distribution, management, exchange, and demolition. Discrimination can be direct and personal, as by realtors or landlords, or it can be more subtle, obscured by complex regulations and bureaucratic institutions.

Third World. Discrimination is found in many countries, including those in the Third World. For example, in Egypt after 1973, 60 percent of all heavily subsidized, public housing units were reserved for army personnel and government employees, irrespective of income. In Colombia the *Corporaciones de Ahorro y Vivienda*, private sector housing finance corporations, supply 70 percent of the capital for residential construction, and it has been estimated that 70 percent of its loans have been issued to private developers building for the affluent, 30 percent to high- and middle-income buyers, and none at all to low-income households. In Ghana, squatters employed in the informal sector find themselves barred from mortgage loans available to government employees with lower incomes, and a program granting public land against a nominal fee benefits senior civil servants, army personnel, and university staff. In Brazil, the National Housing Bank diverted funds intended to finance low-cost public housing and in part obtained from savings of the working class toward real-estate speculation and the construction of middle-class and luxury housing. From 1964 through 1985, 87 percent of Brazil's housing expenditures were targeted at the wealthiest 17 percent of the population. In Mexico housing-assistance programs have also frequently not reached those most in need of them. In chapter 12 Peter Ward describes favored access to housing by employees in government, the military, and strategic industries, such as the railway and state-owned oil company, that had powerful lobbies as labor unions or welfare agencies that did not cover the poorest households relegated to shelter in the popular sector. In Karachi, Pakistan, 25 percent of the population—high- and middle-income groups—have received about 64 percent of the available housing resources. In Kenya, Egypt, and indeed throughout much of the Third World, evidence shows that site-and-services schemes frequently do not benefit the low-income households for whom they are intended (e.g., Macharia 1985; Soliman 1988; Nientied and Van der Linden 1988). In China the deprivatization that followed the 1949 revolution facilitated a more equitable redistribution of housing resources. A recent analysis, however, shows the emergence of new patterns of inequity in that country (Lee 1988). First, most of the state's housing investment (83 percent in 1982) benefits employees of state-owned enterprises. These subsidies reinforce already existing inequities, for workers in state-owned enterprises are already privileged in terms of income, welfare services, and job security. A second source of inequity is the rent-subsidy system. Such subsidies are distributed not according to the financial needs of households but according to the size of their dwelling. The larger the living area, the larger the subsidy, so that, for example, a household of four living in an apartment of 40 square meters will receive twice the subsidy available to a household of the same size living in an apartment of 20 square meters. This subsidization scheme further accentuates the privileged position of state employees since they live in larger dwellings (11 square meters of living space per capita versus 9.8 for workers in collectively owned enterprises). If the recent introduction of market principles into the Chinese economy (also observed in the housing sector) endures, it may compensate for or exacerbate existing inequities. Pressures for change are likely to mount only if political reforms are articulated in conjunction with the economic restructuring.

Socialist Countries. The situation in China illustrates that inequities can be found in housing systems modeled according to socialist principles of egalitarianism. Further evidence for housing inequities in such systems is provided by the experiences of Hungary, Poland, and the USSR. Zsuzsa Dániel (1985) examined the results of a household budget survey, conducted in Hungary, to compare the housing subsidies provided by the state to households in various income groups. Her findings showed that households in the lowest income groups received the smallest subsidies, both as a proportion of their income and as an absolute amount, leading her to conclude that the distribution of housing benefits increased rather than reduced inequities. This conclusion is in line with observations by Ivan Szelenyi (1983, 1987) regarding the preferential treatment accorded to occupants of high-ranking positions in the social hierarchies of Eastern European countries, such as the leading intelligentsia, the party elite, and top officers in the military and security forces. In this volume, Misztal reveals how nonmanual workers in Poland have been able to circumvent regulations and how households' housing standards tend to mirror their place in the stratification of Polish society.

Michael Alexeev (1988a) has estimated that, at least in the Soviet Union, payments made in the second (quasi-legal) economy largely offset the redistributive effects of subsidization of more affluent households. Using data from a survey of recent Soviet (urban) emigrés in the United States, he found that bribes, side payments, and cooperative-apartment purchases alter the original pattern of subsidization. It is unclear to what extent these distortive processes occur in other Eastern European countries where housing supply and demand are governed by somewhat different conditions. However, although the leverage of a second income in the redistribution of state-owned housing in the USSR may modify existing inequities, it does not eliminate them and indeed may simply replace them with inequities generated through the operation of underground market forces. The latter possibility is suggested by a recent analysis of similar "back-door" deals in China (Fung 1987). This study concluded that the favors exchanged between sellers and buyers to gain preferential access to rationed goods (whose prices are controlled by the state at below-market levels) are available only to well-placed individuals in the distribution channels for such goods and to officials who control access to positional advantages. Such exchange practices illegally divert scarce resources, thereby sabotaging attempts to achieve their equitable distribution, undermining government integrity, and hindering rational economic development.

Capitalist Countries. The potential for discrimination and attendant inequities becomes magnified in capitalist market systems. Such markets are driven by private investors who seek to maximize their profit and minimize their risk. Since housing is treated as an economic commodity rather than a social entitlement, this profit orientation and risk aversiveness logically leads to housing markets that discriminate against or exclude households that produce relatively low returns on investment or constitute a negative investment risk—typically, low-income groups, ethnic or racial minorities, and women. Thus discrimination, including that based on prejudice, is often presented under the veil of rational market behavior.

As stressed earlier, there are great differences among capitalist countries. A recent survey, conducted in sixteen countries, showed that 72 percent of the U.S. sample considered individual freedom more important than equality (defined as the absence of underprivileged people and lack of social class differences), whereas respondents in European countries, in varying degrees, placed greater value on equality (Heald 1988, 77). Different governments have shaped the "free" interplay of market forces in different ways, often assuming the role of active participant, sometimes to provide for those unable to compete in the housing market, other times to accelerate the capitalist engine (i.e., to help maximize capital accumulation by private investors). As shown earlier, European welfare states have undertaken to establish significant social housing sectors for low-income groups. There is, however, increasing evidence of inequities and discrimination along ethnic and racial lines (e.g., Schwartz 1984; Commission for Racial Equality 1987; Wuertz and Van der Pennen 1987). Racial discrimination in housing is seen in its most extreme form in the Republic of South Africa's official policy of "separate development."

Although discrimination in housing transactions is illegal in the United States, it has not been defined in specific terms in the law or in the court beyond the case specifics. Nor has the Department of Housing and Urban Development (HUD) issued pertinent regulations under the law. It remains unclear, therefore, what does and what does not constitute illegal housing discrimination, other than the most blatant situations. Based on an examination of experiences of comparable black and white home seekers with the same housing agent, a 1977 HUD study of 1,600 cases, conducted in forty cities nationwide, concluded that black prospective buyers going to four housing agents would encounter discrimination 48 percent of the time (not counting racial steering) and black renters 72 percent of the time (Pearce 1988). According to a fair housing audit conducted in Boston in 1981, black housing seekers were told about 30 percent fewer available housing units than whites (Yinger 1986). Discrimination on racial and ethnic grounds continues into the present (see, e.g., Goering 1986; Schuman and Bobo 1988).

There is also widespread discrimination against women. Women make up one-half of the world's population, are responsible for two-thirds of all hours worked, yet are counted as only one-third of the labor force, receive 10 percent of earnings and own one percent of property. In the United States examples of such discriminatory practices are provided by the frequent experiences of women who want to buy a home and have difficulty getting a mortgage because lending institutions consider them a poor investment risk (Card 1980; Shalala and McGeorge 1981), and in the rental sector there are women without any realistic housing alternatives who are victims of sexual harassment by landlords against whom they are reluctant to press charges for fear of eviction (Cahan 1987; Fuentes and Miller 1989). In addition, women are greatly underrepresented in the design professions and in the decision-making contexts that surround the production of the built environment (Wekerle, Peterson, and Morley 1980; Van Vliet— 1989b).

Families with children are another population group in the United States that encounters discrimination, particularly in the rental sector. A recent nationwide survey showed that 25 percent of all rental units exclude families with children, and another 50 percent restrict families with children (Marans and Colten 1985). These restrictive rental practices are increasing and in addition to exclusionary zoning practiced to establish and maintain "adults only" communities (Calvan 1979; Ritzdorf 1986). Few states or cities prohibit discrimination against families with children as part of their fair housing policy. Continuation of such discrimination, combined with a shrinking supply of low-income housing, falling family incomes among the poor, and cuts in federal housing assistance have made families with children the fastest growing segment of the homeless population (Edelman and Mihaly 1989). The effectiveness of a federal anti-discrimination law, enacted late in 1988, remains yet to be demonstrated.

An important source of housing inequity in the United States is the highly regressive nature of housing subsidies. In 1984 households earning more than U.S. $50,000 received, on average, U.S. $1,824 in combined direct and indirect subsidies; households with incomes under U.S. $10,000 got less than one-third of that amount: U.S. $576 (table 10.11). In Canada, similar disparities exist. In 1984 the average benefit from housing tax expenditures for Canadian households with incomes of Can. $100,000 and over was Can. $6,753; for those earning less than Can. $5,000 it was only Can. $32 (Hulchanski and Drover 1987).

There is another important dimension of inequity in housing benefits, in the United States and many other capitalist countries, namely, their differential distribution across tenure forms. Typically, government expenditures have heavily favored owners over renters. The principal form of owner subsidization has come through the deduction of interest on mortgage loans from taxable income. These foregone revenues often do not show up in housing budgets. However, if included, they amount in fact to very large tax expenditures. Additional benefits frequently accrue to owners through several other ways, including exemption from tax on imputed net rent and capital gains realized in the sale of a dwelling, the possibility to write off property taxes and home repair or improvement expenses, preferential tax treatment of savings for home purchase, discounts given in the sale of public housing, and below-market interest rates on government mortgages.[15]

In the United States these tax losses totaled more than $52 billion in 1988 alone (Roistacher forthcoming), more than all of the housing assistance paid over more than fifty years, since the inception of public housing in 1937 through 1989 under programs of the Department of Housing and Urban Development. R. G. Dowler (1983) has estimated that in 1979, 80 percent of all federal housing subsidies in Canada benefited homeowners (even when counting credits and tax concessions to private developers as renter subsidies), about 75 percent of which was in the form of foregone revenues. In fiscal year 1984–1985, tenants in Australian public housing received U.S. $24.02 per capita in commonwealth assistance; this was more than the U.S. $10.94 received by tenants in the private rental sector but clearly less than the U.S. $27.20 allocated to first-time buyers (in direct outlays) and paling in comparison to the U.S. $121.18 per capita additional assistance for homeowners. In 1984–1985, a little over 73 percent of all housing assistance in Australia was for owners. Similar patterns can be observed in other countries (see, for example, tables 3.6, 4.9, 4.10, 10.7, 24.3; see also Roistacher forthcoming and tables 2.1–2.3 in Forrest and Murie 1987).

The benefits thus extended to owners are inequitable (and economically ill-advised but politically expedient) because owners tend to be better off financially than renters. In the United States in 1987, the median income of renters was 54.8 percent of that of owners (U.S. Bureau of the Census 1989, 441). This difference in income between owners and renters is found not only in the United States. In Canada in 1986 the poverty rate among renters was 36.8 percent, almost four times higher than among owners (9.4 percent; table 9.6). The same pattern is found in Europe. In Britain in 1985 the median income of tenants in public and private rental housing was, respectively, 59 percent and 69.4 percent of that of owners (table 2.3). In the Netherlands in 1986 the median disposable income of renters was 78.3 percent of that of owners (tables 4.13 and 4.14). The situation in Japan is not very different: in 1986 the average income of renters was 63.5 percent of that of owners (tables 22.5 and 22.6). What we see then is that in general renters have lower incomes than owners, hence are more in need of financial assistance, yet receive much smaller subsidies.

The approaches through which governments have sought to encourage private home ownership vary somewhat from country to country and so do the mechanisms through which inequities are effectuated. For example, Canadian homeowners are not allowed to deduct mortgage interest payments from taxable income, and those in Japan were permitted to do so only as of January 1988 with several limiting conditions, whereas in Australia mortgage interest deductions have been gradually phased out. In the Netherlands and Sweden, imputed net rental income is added to the taxable income of owner–occupiers, but in

Britain, Australia, and Canada it is not. The particular mix of political, economic, and cultural factors leading to the widespread favoring of private home ownership, as well as the intensity, historical timing, and effectiveness of its promotion by government, also differ from country to country. Discussion of these aspects is beyond the scope of this chapter. Here it suffices to underline the pervasiveness of inequitable distributions of benefits between owners and renters.

It is important to add that inequities also occur within tenures. Tax relief formulas for homeowners, for example, are almost without exception highly regressive, so the more expensive the home, the larger the subsidy. In 1984 households earning U.S. $50,000 or more per year made up less than 10 percent of all households in the United States, yet received nearly one-third of all housing subsidies, almost all of it for owners (table 10.11). Owners of more expensive homes also tend to benefit more from house price inflation; although the evidence regarding differential appreciation rates across property value categories is mixed, owners of more expensive homes will capitalize on larger absolute gains unless there is a significantly inverse deceleration of house price inflation.

Inequities are found in the rental sector as well where they may result from historic cost pricing, which makes newly built dwellings more expensive than older dwellings of similar quality. Inequities can also occur when degressive capital subsidies are used in the construction of rental dwellings so that rent levels increase over time to exceed those in newer dwellings of comparable or higher quality (see Friedrichs 1988 for an example in the Federal Republic of Germany).

Polarization. The persistence of inequitable processes in housing contributes to an intensification of existing disparities. This polarization is particularly evident along socioeconomic lines across tenures. For example, in Britain, the difference in median income between economically active owner–occupiers and public housing tenants increased from 24 percent in 1972 to 41 percent in 1985. Between 1967 and 1980, the proportion of public housing tenants among welfare recipients increased from 45 to 61 percent, and that of homeowners rose only slightly from 17 to 19 percent. In the United States, the median income of renters as a percent of that of owners in 1986 dollars declined from 64 percent in 1967, to 55 percent in 1977, to 48 percent in 1987. From 1984 to 1987, poverty-level households among renters increased by 300,000, but decreased among owners by 500,000 (Apgar 1988). Between 1976 and 1984, ownership fluctuated around 65 percent for households and 72 percent for families, but it increased in older age groups, whereas it decreased in younger age groups that have lower incomes (Van Vliet— 1988a). Similarly, in Canada the national rate of home ownership in 1981 was up by 0.6 percent compared to 1967, obscuring a 19 percent decline in ownership among households in the lowest income quintile and a 10 percent increase in the highest income quintile. Thus although overall home-ownership rates may remain stable, there are significant changes in *whom* the owners are (Hulchanski and Drover 1987).

Consequently, in many countries, there is a residualization of the rental sector in general and of the subsidized rental stock in particular. Rental housing is increasingly occupied by those unable to afford home ownership, disenfranchised population groups such as ethnic and racial minorities, single-parent families, the unemployed, and others with low incomes. These households are typically marginal to economic and political processes and tend to live in housing that is physically inferior and socially stigmatized, bypassed as less desirable by conversion, gentrification, and public sale (Flynn 1986). The pattern in many countries thus shows increasing socioeconomic segregation across tenure lines with ownership as the preferred tenure, unavailable to those with lower incomes (e.g., Bentham 1986).

This process of polarization has greatly intensified as a function of both the privatization and decentralization of housing, involving a shift of traditionally state responsibilities in housing from, respectively, the public to the private sector and from the national to lower levels of government. These trends can be observed in many capitalist countries, including European welfare states, but also in a number of socialist economies, and many Third World countries (see, for example, Tosics 1987; Mandic forthcoming; Hegedüs and Tosics forthcoming; Lee 1988; and Lim and Moore 1989; also the chapters in this volume). There are significant differences in the ways and the extent that privatization and decentralization manifest themselves and in the forces behind these processes (Van Vliet— forthcoming). However, a common outcome is a deterioration of the housing situation of disadvantaged households. Although distributions of (dis)advantage overlap with tenure forms, they do not coincide with them, for example. In capitalist countries there are growing numbers of homeowners who experience severe financial hardship and live under substandard conditions, whereas in the East Bloc it is households that have neither access to state housing nor resources to buy or self-build that are worst off.

It remains to be seen how these developments will play out. It is apparent, however, that they contain growing contradictions. Central among these contradictions is the pursuit of policies that rely on private sector initiatives to provide housing for all but the poorest population when the market is less able or willing to produce the required supply at prices that are generally affordable than would have been the case in the 1960s and early 1970s, ironically, a period when consumer spending power was rising faster and social housing provision was more accepted. Subsidizing the private sector to stimulate production is generally not the most cost-effective approach to the provision of low-cost housing and would also run counter to the intended reduction in government expenditure. Although widely practiced, housing tax expenditures are not an efficient policy measure to promote an expansion of home ownership either, since they fail to benefit those low-income households that prefer home ownership but cannot afford acquisition and subsequent ownership costs (Wood 1988). Also, shifting the burden of providing low-income housing to local government assumes a redistribution of income that exceeds the capacities of local jurisdictions and has been found to produce fiscal strain (Roistacher forthcoming). Harloe (1988) offers a useful brief discussion of several of these contradictions. Other contradictions occur in socialist countries that introduce market principles into housing provision while lacking essential requisites for their effective implementation (e.g., private capital and institutional mechanisms such as mortgage banks and real estate firms). Relevant questions in this connection cannot be engaged further here, but readers will find that a number of them are addressed by others elsewhere in this book in the context of developments in individual countries.

CONCLUSION

It is impossible to do justice in a single chapter to the complexity of the diverse housing systems in the countries included in this book. The purpose here, however, was not to provide comprehensive coverage. An all-embracing review would not appear to be very fruitful, whether undertaken with as great a number of countries as possible or with a view to including every possible aspect of housing. There is little value in such broad-ranging summaries, and readers are referred to the chapters that follow for fuller treatment of individual countries. Nor is there much value in the undirected amassing of more and more information on housing. To be sure, information for particular analyses is sometimes wanting. However, leaving aside the specific information required for ad hoc policy decisions and furnished by applied research, it is theoretical frameworks that help identify such lacunae. The primary challenge for housing research, therefore, is not to generate more data; it is to formulate more theory.

The field of housing research has been firmly established (Van Vliet— 1987c). Appendix A in this book lists many journals that are exclusively or significantly devoted to the publication of housing studies. Appendix B contains the names and addresses of numerous organizations, institutes, and agencies whose function it is to generate, analyze, and disseminate information on housing. Each year, the results of hundreds of new studies become available. In short, there is an astounding amount of information on housing already. Theory is what there is very little of. Theory will help convert available descriptive material into analytical categories and order them within more encompassing frameworks that articulate causative processes to explain the variability of outcomes. Theory is also necessary to understand how accumulated studies contradict, corroborate, and supplement each other, to direct appropriate research designs for additional data collection, and to inform successful housing policies and practices.

Recent indications point to an increasing interest in the development and testing of theory regarding housing and the production of the built environment more generally (Michelson and Van Vliet— forthcoming). Space limitations do not allow discussion or elaboration of this work. However, the chapters that follow have been structured to facilitate examination of the applicability of such theoretical perspectives by readers of this book. Although it is only appropriate to be extremely modest about its contribution to the vast and immensely complex field of housing research, it is important not to overlook this book's potential utility in that respect. This volume is the product of an effort whose total value was intended to be more than the sum of its parts. In this sense, this is indeed a handbook meant to be useful as a tool in further cross-national housing analyses. This chapter has identified a number of cross-national similarities and differences, salient trends, and major issues in housing and has explored their antecedents in order to suggest possibilities for and stimulate such analyses.

NOTES

1. Unless otherwise referenced, source material for this chapter comes from the remainder of this volume. Thanks are due to Sylvia F. Fava, Yozsef Hegedüs, Michael Harloe, Elizabeth Huttman, William Michelson, and Elizabeth Roistacher for their comments on various parts of an earlier draft.

2. Indeed, cross-national comparison of intranational variations should clarify which of such variations are nationally unique and which are transnational, that is, attributable to broader underlying factors, found in more than one country.

3. This statement applies to most East Bloc nations for most of the post–World War II period during which present housing conditions were largely effectuated. However, recently there have been signs of change. In the current spirit of *glasnost* and *perestroika*, *Izvestia*, the official Soviet government newspaper, recognized in 1987 that homelessness is a real problem in the USSR. Similarly, in April 1989, the Polish government legalized the Solidarity movement—which has persistently raised housing and urban problems as salient national concerns and which is likely to play a significant role in defining future policy priorities—and in Hungary a reform movement is rapidly gaining strength and certain to bring about important changes modelled after Western European systems. Processes of privatization, observed in these countries, also point to a significant relinquishing of the reins of state control.

4. The terms (central) *government* and (nation) *state* are used interchangeably in this chapter.

5. Nor were such mechanisms seen as effective regarding collective aspects of housing—the tissues that tie individual dwellings into a wider community and broader urban fabric through the provision of neighborhood facilities and the interwoven development of physical, economic, social, and cultural infrastructure. A recent economic analysis of the basic premises of the welfare state model regarding housing is offered by Nesslein (1988a) who suggests elsewhere (1988b) that the success of the Scandinavian countries and the Netherlands in providing good housing affordable to low-income households is based on a redistribution of private income rather than a reduction of national housing costs.

6. Space limitations permit only one example here, land tenure. It has been argued that public ownership of land keeps construction costs down by controlling market speculation that would inflate land prices. Such cost containment, however, is not automatic, as demonstrated by Hong Kong, where the government auctions off land it owns to generate revenue. It has done little to curtail speculative practices in the land market because doing so would reduce income from its land sales, which amounted to 20 percent of total revenues in 1979–1981 (Fong and Yeh 1987, 33). At the same time, however, such practices have fueled increases in rents and housing costs. On the other hand, just

as public ownership of land per se is not necessarily a positive factor, private land ownership is not inevitably an impediment, as shown by aggressive acquisitions conducted in Singapore and judicious use of regulation and taxation instruments in various other countries (see, for example, Hallett 1988).

7. Although public policies can be conceived of at different levels of aggregation, the discussion here is restricted to aspects of national policies.

8. Government (in)action in Italy before the 1980s, however, has impacted on housing in that country in at least two major ways: first, the government's imposition of strict rent controls amounted, in effect, to subsidization of tenants by landlords (and contributed to current problems arising from extensive maintenance neglect and a diminished private rental sector); second, the government has been lax in regulating building and planning and in enforcing existing standards, particularly in the South, permitting extensive illegal construction practices to satisfy the housing need that would otherwise have gone unmet and would have required that the government become involved.

9. Fire is another hazard related to poor site planning. For example, the Christmas Eve fire of 1953 in a high-density Hong Kong squatter settlement in Kowloon left 53,000 people homeless (Havlick 1986:7).

10. Recognizing this problem, the Central Committee of the Communist party proposed in April 1986 that payment for housing should be closely linked to "size and quality of space occupied." At present, no information is available on the implementation of this proposal.

11. This low-cost recovery creates problems of its own that governments in the East Bloc countries, China (until recently), and Cuba are seeking to overcome in experiments with privatization (Van Vliet— forthcoming).

12. There are other signs of growing housing affordability problems in the United States, including higher estimates of households "doubling up" and the increase in the "new" homeless (Stefl 1987), which are not exclusively tied to affordability of ownership and also related to factors other than housing (see, for example, Wolch, Dear, and Akita 1988).

13. In deviation from a common pattern, building subsidies for rental dwellings increased even more (by 300 percent).

14. The distinction between vertical equity (*between* social strata) and horizontal equity (*within* social strata) cannot be elaborated here but is implied in the following discussion.

15. Owners also benefit significantly from house-price increases that have historically outpaced the general rate of inflation, providing capital gains that have exceeded those yielded by conventional investment sources available to renters.

REFERENCES

Abrams, Charles. 1965. *The City Is the Frontier*. New York: Harper & Row.

Abu-Lughod, Janet. 1976. "The Legitimacy of Comparisons in Comparative Urban Studies: A Theoretical Position and Application to North African Cities." Chapter 2 in *The City in Comparative Perspective: Cross-National Research and New Directions in Theory*, edited by John Walton and Louis H. Masotti. New York: Sage.

Ahrentzen, Sherry. 1985. "Residential Fit and Mobility Among Low-Income, Female-Headed Family Households in the United States. In *Housing Needs and Policy Approaches; Trends in Thirteen Countries*, edited by Willem van Vliet—, Elizabeth Huttman, and Sylvia F. Fava, 71–87. Durham, N.C.: Duke University Press.

Alexander, David. 1984. "Housing Crisis after Natural Disaster: The Aftermath of the November 1980 Southern Italian Earthquake." *Geoforum* 15, no. 4:489–516.

Alexeev, Michael. 1988a. "The Effect of Housing Allocation on Social Inequality: A Soviet Perspective." *Journal of Comparative Economics* 12:228–34.

———. 1988b. "La répartition des logements en U.R.S.S. et les facteurs qui l'influencent." *Revue d'études comparatives est-ouest* 19, no. 1:5–36.

———. 1988c. "Market vs. Rationing: The Case of Soviet Housing." *The Review of Economics and Statistics* 70, no. 3:414–20.

Ambrose, Peter, and James Barlow. 1987. "Housing Provision and House Building in Western Europe: Increasing Expenditure, Declining Output?" In *Housing Markets and Policies under Fiscal Austerity*, edited by W. van Vliet—, 111–26. Westport, Conn.: Greenwood Press.

Amos, Francis J. C. 1984. "Political and Administrative Factors in Low-Income Housing." Chapter 9 in *Low-income Housing in the Developing World*, edited by G. K. Payne. New York: Wiley.

Andrusz, Gregory D. 1984. *Housing and Urban Development in the USSR*. Albany, N.Y.: State University of New York Press.

Annez, Philippe, and William C. Wheaton. 1984. "Economic Development and the Housing Sector: A Cross-National Model." *Economic Development and Cultural Change*, pp. 749–66.

Apgar, William C. 1988. "The Nation's Housing: A Review of Past Trends and Future Prospects for Housing in America." Cambridge, Mass.: MIT Center for Real Estate Development, MIT Housing Policy Project HP#1.

Appelbaum, Richard P. 1985. "Swedish Housing in the Postwar Period." *Urban Affairs Quarterly* 21, no. 2:221–44.

Appelbaum, Richard P., and Peter Dreier. Forthcoming. "The Deregulation of Rental Housing: Recent Developments in the United States." Chapter 6 in *The Deregulation of Housing*, edited by W. van Vliet— and J. van Weesep. Newbury Park, Calif.: Sage.

Armer, Michael, and Allen D. Grimshaw, eds. 1973. *Comparative Social Research: Methodological Problems and Strategies*. New York: Wiley.

Asiama, S. 1985. "The Rich Slum-Dweller: A Problem of Unequal Access." *International Labour Review* 124 (May-June): 353–61.

Bachrach, P., and S. M. Baratz. 1970. "Decisions and Non-Decisions: An Analytical Framework." In *The Structure of Community Power*, edited by M. Aiken and P. Mott, 308–20. New York: Random House.

Badcock, Blair. 1986. "Land and Housing Policy in Chinese Urban Development, 1976–86." *Planning Perspectives* 1:147–70.

Ball, Michael. 1988. "The International Restructuring of Housing Production." In *Housing and Social Change in Europe and the USA*, edited by Michael Ball, Michael Harloe and Maartje Martens, 169–98. London: Routledge.

Ball, Michael, Michael Harloe, and Maartje Martens. 1988. *Housing and Social Change in Europe and the U.S.A.* New York: Routledge.

Ball, Michael, Maartje Martens, and Michael Harloe. 1986. "Mortgage Finance and Owner Occupation in Britain and West Germany." *Progress in Planning* 26, no. 3: 185–260.

Barkin, D. 1985. "Housing and National Development." *Trialog, Zeitschrift für das Planen und Bauen in der Dritten Welt*, no. 6 (Summer): 6–7.

Barnett, Teresa, Alexander J. Groth, and Christopher Ungson. 1985. "East-West Housing Policies: Some Contrasts and Implications." In *Public Policy across Nations: Social Welfare in Industrial Settings*, edited by Alexander J. Groth and Larry L. Wade, 129–50. London: JAI Press.

Baross, Paul. 1987. "Managing the Housing Queue in Hungary." *Habitat International* 11, no. 2:161–75.

Batley, R. 1988. "National Housing Banks in India and Brazil." *Third World Planning Review* 10, no. 2:203–8.

Belec, John. 1984. "Origins of State Housing Policy in Canada: The Case of the Central Mortgage Bank." *Canadian Geographer* 29, no. 4:377–82.

Bentham, Graham. 1986. "Socio-Tenurial Polarization in the United Kingdom, 1953–83: The Income Evidence." *Urban Studies* 2:157–62.

Betancur, John J. 1987. "Spontaneous Settlement Housing in Latin America: A Critical Examination." *Environment and Behavior* 19, no. 3:286–310.

Blaivas, A., M. Kochen, and R. Crickman. 1981. "Geographic Patterns of Choice Among Peers." *Social Science Information Studies* 1:283–95.

Boeschenstein, W. 1971. "The Design of Socially Mixed Housing." *Journal of the American Institute of Planners* 37, no.5: 311–18.

Boleat, Mark. 1984. *National Housing Finance Systems: A Comparative Study*. London: Routledge Chapman & Hall.

Bourne, L. S. 1986. "Urban Policy Research in Comparative Perspective: Some Pitfalls and Potentials." *Tijdschrift voor Economische en Sociale Geografie* 77, no. 3:163–68.

Breshna, Abdullah. 1988. "Shelter for the Homeless After a Flood Disaster: Practical Experience in S. W. Afghanistan." *Geography, Planning & Development* 12, no. 3:203–08.

Brindley, Tim, and Gerry Stoker. 1987. "The Privatization of Housing Renewal: Dilemmas and Contradictions in British Urban Policy." In *Housing Markets and Policies under Fiscal Austerity*, edited by W. van Vliet—, 33–47. Westport, Conn.: Greenwood Press.

————. 1988. "Housing Renewal Policy in the 1980s—The Scope and Limitations of Privatisation." *Local Government Studies* 14, no. 5:45–68.

Brolin, B. C. 1972. "Chandigarh Was Planned by Experts, but Something Has Gone Wrong." *Smithsonian* 3, no. 3:56–63.

Bryant, Coralie, and Louise G. White. 1976. "Housing Policies and Comparative Urban Politics." In *The City in Comparative Perspective*, edited by John Walton and Louis H. Masotti, 81–95. New York: Sage.

Burgess, R. 1982. "Self-Help Housing Advocacy: A Curious Form of Radicalism." A Critique of the Work of John F. C. Turner. Chapter 3 in *Self-Help Housing: A Critique*, edited by P. Ward. London: Mansell.

————. 1985. "The Limits of State Self-Help Housing Programmes." *Development and Change* 16, no. 2:271–312.

Butler, Alan. 1986. "Housing and the Elderly in Europe." *Social Policy and Administration* 20, no. 2:136–52.

Cahan, Regina. 1987. "Home Is No Haven: An Analysis of Sexual Harassment in Housing." *Wisconsin Law Review* 6:1061–97.

Calvan, R. 1979. "Children and Families—The Latest Victims of Exclusionary Land Use Practices." *Challenge* 10, no. 11:26–28.

Card, Emily. 1980. "Women, Housing Access, and Mortgage Credit." *Signs: Journal of Women in Culture and Society* 5, no. 3 (Spring):215–19. Supplement.

Carlson, Eric. 1986. *Housing Finance Development in China: An Overview of Issues and Prospects.* Chicago, Ill.: International Union of Building Societies and Savings Associations.

———. 1987. "China Achieves Record Housing." *Habitat International* 11, no. 4:47–67.

———. 1988. "Housing Conditions in the People's Republic." *Journal of Property Management* (May/June).

Carmon, Naomi, and Moshe (Morris) Hill. 1988. "Neighborhood Rehabilitation Without Relocation or Gentrification." *Journal of the American Planning Association* 54, no. 4:470–81.

Carter, Robert A. Forthcoming. "Mortgage-Backed Securities, Inflation Adjusted Mortgages, and Real Rate Funding: Recent Initiatives in Housing Finance in Australia." Chapter 11 in *The Deregulation of Housing*, edited by W. van Vliet— and J. van Weesep. Newbury Park, Calif.: Sage.

Catanese, A. J. 1984. *The Politics of Planning and Development.* Beverly Hills, Calif.: Sage.

Chambers, D. and F. G. Gray. Forthcoming. "Housing Renewal in Britain: The Declining Role of the State." In *The Deregulation of Housing*, edited by Willem van Vliet— and Jan van Weesep. Newbury Park, Calif.: Sage.

Charvát, F., W. Stamatiou, and Ch. Villain-Gandossi (eds.). 1988. *International Co-operation in the Social Sciences. 25 Years of Vienna Centre Experience.* Vienna: European Coordination Centre for Research and Documentation in the Social Sciences.

Chase-Dunn, Christopher K. 1982. "The Uses of Formal Comparative Research on Dependency Theory and the World-System Perspective." In *The New International Economy*, edited by Harry Makler, Alberto Martinelli, and Neil Smelser. 117–37. London: Sage.

Clapham, D., and K. Kintrea. 1987. "Importing Housing Policy: Housing Cooperatives in Britain and Scandinavia." *Housing Studies* 3, no. 3:158.

Cole, S. 1989. "World Bank Forecasts and Planning in the Third World." *Environment and Planning A* 21:175–96.

Commission for Racial Equality. 1987. *Living in Terror: A Report on Racial Violence and Harassment in Housing.* London.

Cooper Marcus, Clare. 1975. *Easter Hill Village.* New York City: The Free Press.

Cooper Marcus, Clare, and Wendy Sarkissian. 1986. *Housing As If People Mattered: Site Design Guidelines for Medium-Density Family Housing.* Berkeley and Los Angeles, Calif.: University of California Press.

Crook, A.D.H. 1986a. "Privatisation of Housing and the Impact of the Conservative Government's Initiatives on Low-Cost Homeownership and Private Renting Between 1979 and 1984 in England and Wales: 2. Implementation of Low-Cost Homeownership Policy." *Environment and Planning A* 18, no. 8:827–35.

———. 1986b. "Privatisation of Housing and the Impact of the Conservative Government's Initiatives on Low-Cost Homeownership and Private Renting Between 1979 and 1984 in England and Wales: 3. Impact and Evaluation of Low-Cost Homeownership Policy." *Environment and Planning A* 18, no. 8:901–11.

———. Forthcoming. "Deregulation of Private Rented Housing in Britain: Investors'

Responses to Government Housing Policy." In *The Deregulation of Housing*, edited by Willem van Vliet— and Jan van Weesep. Newbury Park, Calif.: Sage.

———. 1986c. "Privatisation of Housing and the Impact of the Conservative Government's Initiatives on Low-Cost Homeownership and Private Renting between 1979 and 1984 in England and Wales: 4. Private Renting." *Environment and Planning A* 18, no. 8:1029–37.

Daly, G. 1988. *A Comparative Assessment of Programs Dealing with the Homeless Population in the United States, Canada, and Britain*. Ottawa: Canada Mortgage and Housing Corporation.

Dániel, Zsuzsa. 1985. "The Effect of Housing Allocation on Social Inequality in Hungary." *Journal of Comparative Economics* 9:391–409.

Dennis, N. 1958. "The Popularity of the Neighborhood Unit Idea." *Sociological Review* 6:191–206.

Deutsch, M., and M. Evans Collins. 1951. *Inter-racial Housing: A Psychological Evaluation of a Social Experiment*. Minneapolis: University of Minnesota.

Dewitt, R. Peter. 1987. "Policy Directions in International Lending, 1961–1984: The Case of the Inter-American Development Bank." *The Journal of Developing Areas* 21:277–84.

Ditkovsky, Orit, and Willem van Vliet—. 1984. "Housing Tenure and Community Participation." *Ekistics* 307:345–48.

Donnison, David, and Shinya Hoshino. 1988. "Formulating the Japanese Housing Problem." *Housing Studies* 3, no. 3: 190–95.

Donnison, D., and C. Ungerson. 1982. *Housing Policy*. Harmondsworth, Eng.: Penguin Books.

Dowler, R. G. 1983. *Housing and Related Tax Expenditures: An Overview and Evaluation*. Major Report No. 22. Toronto: Centre for Urban and Community Studies, University of Toronto.

Economic Commission for Europe. 1981. *La rénovation urbaine et la qualité de la vie*. Geneva.

———. 1983. *The Improvement of Housing and Its Surroundings*. Geneva.

———. 1985a. *Forecasting and Programming of Housing*. Geneva.

———. 1985b. *Relationship between Housing and the National Economy*. Geneva.

———. 1986. *Human Settlements Situation in the ECE Region around 1980*. Geneva.

———. 1988. *Annual Bulletin of Housing and Building Statistics for Europe, 1980–1987*. Geneva.

Edelman, Marian Wright, and Lisa Mihaly. 1989. "Homeless Families and the Housing Crisis in the United States." *Children and Youth Services Review* 11:91–108.

Ehrlich, B., and P. Dreier. 1988. "Downtown Development and Urban Reform: The Politics of Boston's Linkage Policy." Paper. Boston: Boston Redevelopment Authority.

Elder, Joseph W. 1976. "Comparative Cross-National Methodology." In *Annual Review of Sociology*, vol. 2, edited by Alex Inkeles, 209–30. Palo Alto, Calif.: Annual Reviews, Inc.

El-Messiri, Sawsan. 1985. "The Squatters' Perspective of Housing: An Egyptian View." In *Housing Needs and Policy Approaches*, edited by W. van Vliet—, E. Huttman, and A.S.F. Fava, 256–70. Durham, N.C.: Duke University Press.

Evan, William M. 1975. "The International Sociological Association and the Internationalization of Sociology." *International Social Science Journal* 27:385–93.

Fainstein, S. S. 1980. "American Policy for Housing and Community Development: A Comparative Examination." In *Housing Policy for the 1980s*, edited by R. Montgomery and D. R. Marshall, 215–29. Lexington, Mass.: D. C. Heath.

Fava, Sylvia F. 1987. "Diversity in New Communities: A Case Study of Reston, VA, at Age 20." In *Housing and Neighborhoods: Theoretical and Empirical Contributions*, edited by Willem van Vliet—, Harvey Choldin, William Michelson, and David Popenoe, 139–54. Westport, Conn.: Greenwood Press.

Fleming, Michael C., and Joseph G. Nellis. 1987. "Fiscal Austerity and the Expansion of Home Ownership in the United Kingdom." In *Housing Markets and Policies under Fiscal Austerity*, edited by W. van Vliet—, 129–44. Westport, Conn.: Greenwood Press.

Flora, Peter, and Arnold J. Heidenheimer, eds. 1981. *The Development of Welfare States in Europe and America*. New Brunswick, N.J.: Transaction Books.

Florida, Richard L. 1986. "The Political Economy of Financial Deregulation and the Reorganization of Housing Finance in the United States." *International Journal of Urban and Regional Research* 10, no. 2:207–31.

Florida, Richard L., and M.M.A. Feldman. 1988. "Housing is US Fordism." *International Journal of Urban and Regional Research*. 12, no. 2: 187–210.

Flynn, Rob. 1988. "Political Acquiescence, Privatisation and Residualisation in British Housing Policy." *Journal of Social Policy* 17, no. 3:289–312.

Fong, Peter K. W., and Anthony G. O. Yeh. 1987. "Hong Kong." In *Housing Policy and Practice in Asia*, edited by Seong-Kyu Ha, 12–47. London: Croom Helm.

Form, William H. 1979. "Comparative Industrial Sociology and the Convergency Hypothesis." In *Annual Review of Sociology*, vol. 5, edited by Alex Inkeles, 1–25. Palo Alto, Calif.: Annual Reviews, Inc.

Forrest, Ray, and Alan Murie. 1987a. "Fiscal Reorientation, Centralization, and the Privatization of Council Housing." In *Housing Markets and Policies under Fiscal Austerity*, edited by Willem van Vliet—, 15–31. Westport, Conn.: Greenwood Press.

———. 1987b. "The Affluent Home Owner: Labour Market Position and the Shaping of Housing Histories." *The Sociological Review* 35, no. 2:370–403.

———. 1989. "Differential Accumulation: Wealth, Inheritance and Housing Policy Reconsidered." *Policy and Politics* 17, no. 1:25–39.

Friedmann, J. 1967. "The Institutional Context." In *Action Under Planning: The Guidance of Economic Development*, edited by B. M. Gross. New York: McGraw Hill.

Friedrichs, J. 1988. "Large New Housing Estates: The Crisis of Affordable Housing." In *Affordable Housing and the Homeless*, edited by J. Friedrichs, 89–102. Berlin and New York: De Gruyter.

Fuentes, Annette, and Madelyn Miller. 1989. "Unreasonable Access: Sexual Harassment Comes Home." In *Women, Housing, and Community*, edited by Willem van Vliet—, 153–59. Aldershot, Eng.: Avebury.

Fung, K. K. 1987. "Surplus Seeking and Rent Seeking through Back-Door Deals in Mainland China." *American Journal of Economics and Sociology* 46, no. 3:299–317.

Gans, Herbert J. 1984. "American Urban Theories and Urban Areas: Some Observations on Contemporary Ecological and Marxist Paradigms." In *Cities in Recession:*

Critical Responses to the Urban Policies of the New Right, edited by I. Szeleny, 279–308. Beverly Hills, Calif.: Sage.

George, Janet E. G. 1986. "Comparative Social Research: Issues in Comparability." *Acta Sociologica* 29, no. 2:167–70.

Ghorra-Gobin, Cynthia. 1983. "The Subsidized Housing System in France." *Planning and Administration* 10, no. 1:47–56.

Gilbert, A., and P. Ward. 1985. *Housing, the State, and the Poor: Policy and Practice in Three Latin American Cities*. Cambridge: Cambridge University Press.

Goering, John M. 1986. *Housing Desegregation and Federal Policy*. Chapel Hill, N.C.: University of North Carolina Press.

Goetz, E. 1989. "Office-Housing Linkage in San Francisco." *Journal of the American Planning Association* 55, no. 1 (Winter):66–77.

Grenell, P. 1972. "Planning for Invisible People: Some Consequences of Bureaucratic Values and Practices." In *Freedom to Build*, edited by J. Turner et al., 95–121. New York: Macmillan.

Guttentag, Jack M. 1984. "Recent Changes in the Primary Home Mortgage Market." *Housing Finance Review* (July):221–54.

Ha, Seong-Kyu, ed. 1987. *Housing Policy and Practice in Asia*. London: Croom Helm.

Hallett, Graham (ed). 1988. *Land and Housing Policies in Europe and the USA: A Comparative Analysis*. London: Routledge.

Harloe, Michael. 1985. *Private Rented Housing in the United States and Europe*. New York: St. Martin's Press.

———. 1988. "The Changing Role of Social Rented Housing." In *Housing and Social Change in Europe and the USA*, by Michael Ball, Michael Harloe, and Maartje Martens, 41–86. London and New York: Routledge.

Harloe, Michael, and Maartje Martens. 1984. "Comparative Housing Research." *Journal of Social Policy* 13:255–77.

———. 1985. "The Restructuring of Housing Provision in Britain and the Netherlands." *Environment and Planning A* 17:1063–87.

Harris, Richard. 1986. "Boom and Bust: The Effects of House Price Inflation on Home-ownership Patterns in Montreal, Toronto, and Vancouver." *The Canadian Geographer* 30, no. 4:302–15.

Harris, Richard, and Chris Hamnett. 1987. "The Myth of the Promised Land: The Social Diffusion of Home Ownership in Britain and North America." *Annals of the Association of American Geographers* 77, no. 2:173–90.

Hartman, Chester. 1988. "Affordability of Housing." In *Handbook of Housing and the Built Environment in the United States*, edited by Elizabeth Huttman and Willem van Vliet—, 111–29. Westport, Conn.: Greenwood Press.

Havlick, Spenser W. 1986. "Building for Calamity: Third World Cities at Risk." *Environment* 28, no. 9:6–15.

Headey, B. 1978. *Housing Policy in the Developed Economy: The United Kingdom, Sweden, and the United States*. London: Croom Helm.

Heald, Gordon. 1988. "A Comparison between American, European, and Japanese Values." In *Values*, edited by Brenda Almond and Bryan Wilson, 75–90. Atlantic Heights, N.J.: Humanities Press International.

Hegedüs, Jozsef. 1987. "Reconsidering the Role of the State and the Market in Socialist Housing Systems." *International Journal of Urban and Regional Research* 11, no. 1:79–97.

Hegedüs, Jozsef, and Ivan Tosics. Forthcoming. "Filtering and Innovation in Hungarian Housing." In *The Deregulation of Housing*, edited by Willem van Vliet— and Jan van Weesep. Newbury Park, Calif.: Sage.

Heisler, Barbara S., and Lily M. Hoffman. 1987. "Keeping a Home: Changing Mortgage Markets and Regional Economic Distress." *Sociological Focus* 20, no. 3:227–41.

Heraud, B. J. 1968. "Social Class and the New Towns." *Urban Studies* 5, no. 1:33–58.

Heumann, Leonard, and Duncan Boldy. 1982. *"Housing for the Elderly: Planning and Policy Formulation in Western Europe and North America."* London: Croom Helm.

Horioka, Charles Yuji. 1988a. "Saving for Housing Purchase in Japan." *Journal of the Japanese and International Economies* 2, no. 3:351–84.

———. 1988b. "Tenure Choice and Housing Demand in Japan." *Journal of Urban Economics* 24, no. 3:289–309.

Housing and Mortgage Market Review (New York: Salomon Brothers). Various Issues.

Howenstine, E. Jay. 1981. *Private Rental Housing in Industrialized Countries*. Washington, D.C.: Department of Housing and Urban Development, Office of Policy Development and Research.

———. 1983. *Attacking Housing Costs: Foreign Policies and Problems*. Rutgers, N.J.: Center for Urban Policy Research.

———. 1985. "Selling Public Housing to Individuals and Cooperatives: Lessons from Foreign Experience." *Urban Law and Policy* 7, no. 1:1–31.

———. 1986. *Housing Vouchers: An International Analysis*. New Brunswick, NJ: Center for Urban Policy Research.

Hughes, Gordon, and Barry McCormick. 1987. "Housing Markets, Unemployment and Labour Market Flexibility in the UK." *European Economic Review* 31:615–45.

Hulchanski, J. D. 1988. *Do All Canadians Have a Right to Housing*? UBC Planning Papers. Vancouver: School of Community and Regional Planning, University of British Columbia.

Hulchanski, J. David and Glenn Drover. 1987. "Housing Subsidies in a Period of Restraint: The Canadian Experience." In *Housing Markets and Policies under Fiscal Austerity*, edited by Willem van Vliet—, 51–70. Westport, Conn.: Greenwood Press.

Huttman, Elizabeth, Wim Blauw, and Juliet Saltman, eds. 1990. *Urban Housing Segregation of Minorities in the U.S. and Western Europe*. Durham, N.C.: Duke University Press.

Isaacs, R. R. 1948. "The Neighborhood Theory: An Analysis of Its Adequacy." *Journal of the American Institute of Planners* 14, no. 2:15–23.

Ivatts, John. December 1988. "Rented Housing and Market Rents: A Social Policy Critique." *Social Policy and Administration* 22, no. 3:197–209.

Kamo, Yoshinori. June 1988. "A Note on Elderly Living Arrangements in Japan and the United States." *Research on Aging* 10, no. 2:297–305.

Kane, Edward J. 1984. "Change and Progress in Contemporary Mortgage Markets." *Housing Finance Review* 3, no. 3:257–82.

Kaufman, George G. 1984. "The Role of Traditional Mortgage Lenders in Future Mortgage Lending: Problems and Prospects." *Housing Finance Review* (July):285–315.

King, Ross. 1987. "Monopoly Rent, Residential Differentiation, and the Second Global Crisis of Capitalism—The Case of Melbourne." *Progress in Planning* 28:195–298.

Kleinman, M. Forthcoming. "New Approaches to Financing Rented Housing in Britain." In *The Deregulation of Housing*, edited by Willem van Vliet— and Jan van Weesep. Newbury Park, Calif.: Sage.

Kohn, M. L. 1987. "Cross-National Research as an Analytic Strategy." *American Sociological Review* 52, no. 6:713–31.

Krätke, Stefan. 1989. "The Future of Social Housing." *International Journal of Urban and Regional Research* 13, no. 2: 282–303.

Kuechler, Manfred. 1987. "The Utility of Surveys for Cross-National Research." *Social Science Research* 16:229–44.

Kusnetzoff, Fernando. 1987. "Urban and Housing Policies under Chile's Military Dictatorship, 1973–1985." *Latin American Perspectives* 53, no. 14:157–86.

Kyvik, Svein. 1988. "Internationality of the Social Sciences: The Norwegian Case." *International Social Science Journal* 40, no. 1:163–72.

Law, C. M. 1988. "Public-Private Partnership in Urban Revitalization in Britain." *Regional Studies* 22, no. 5:446–52.

Lee, Yok-shiu F. 1988. "The Urban Housing Problem in China." *China Quarterly* 115:387–407.

Lim, Gill-Chin. 1987. "Housing Policies for the Urban Poor in Developing Countries." *American Planning Association Journal* 53, no. 2 (Spring):176–85.

Lim, Gill-Chin, and R. J. Moore. 1989. "Privatization in Developing Countries: Ideal and Reality." *International Journal of Public Administration* 12, no. 1:137–62.

Lindberg, Göran, and Björn Karlberg. 1988. "Decentralisation in the Public Housing Sector in Sweden." *Scandinavian Journal of Housing and Planning Research 5*, pp. 1–15.

Line, M. 1981. "The Structure of Social Science Literature as Shown by a Large-Scale Citation Analysis." *Social Science Information Studies* 1:67–87.

Lisle, Edmond A. 1985. "Validation in the Social Sciences by International Comparison." *International Social Science Journal* 37, no. 1:21–29.

Lonner, Walter J., and John W. Berry, eds. 1986. *Field Methods in Cross-Cultural Research*. Cross-Cultural Research and Methodology Series, volume 8.

Lowe, Stuart, and Ivan Tosics. 1988. "The Social Use of Market Processes in British and Hungarian Housing Policies." *Housing Studies* 3, no. 3:159–71.

Lowi, T. 1972. "Four Systems of Policy, Politics, and Choice." *Public Administration Review* (July, August).

Lundqvist, L. 1986. *Housing Policy and Equality: A Comparative Study of Tenure Conversions and Their Effects*. London: Croom Helm.

———. 1988. *Housing Policy and Tenure in Sweden: The Quest for Neutrality*. Aldershot, Eng.: Gower/Avebury.

Ma, Laurence J.C. 1981. "Urban Housing Supply in the People's Republic of China." Pp. 222–59 in *Urban Development in Modern China*, edited by L.J.C. Ma and E. W. Hanten. Boulder, Colo.: Westview Press.

Macarov, David. 1988. "Quitting Time: The End of Work." *International Journal of Sociology and Social Policy* 8, nos. 2, 3, 4. Special issue.

Macharia, K. 1985. "Low Income Housing in Kenya: The View from the Bottom." *International Journal of Urban and Regional Research* 9, no. 3: 405–19.

Magnuson, Ed. 1988. "A House Divided: Yonkers, N.Y. Becomes a Symbol of White Resistance to Integration." *Time* 132, no. 7 (August 15): 14–15.

Mandelker, Daniel R. 1973. *Housing Subsidies in the U.S. and England*. Indianapolis, Ind.: Bobbs-Merrill.

———. 1987. "Making Difficult Choices for Lower Income Housing Subsidies." *Urban Law and Policy* 8:191–204.

Mandic, Srna. Forthcoming. "Housing Provision in Yugoslavia: Changing Roles of the State, Market and Informal Sector." In *The Deregulation of Housing*, edited by Willem van Vliet— and Jan van Weesep. Newbury Park, Calif.: Sage.

Mann, P. H. 1958. "The Socially Balanced Neighborhood Unit." *Town Planning Review* (July):91–97.

Marans, R. W. 1978. "Kiryath Gat, Israel: A New Town." In *The Role of Housing in Promoting Social Integration*, 79–125. New York: United Nations, Department of Economics and Social Affairs.

Marans, R. W., and M. E. Colten. 1985. U.S. Rental Housing Policies Affecting Families with Children: Hard Times for Youth. In *Housing Needs and Policy Approaches: Trends in 13 Countries*, edited by W. van Vliet—, E. Huttman, and S. Fava, 41–58. Durham, N.C.: Duke University Press.

Marcuse, P. 1982. "Building Housing Theory: Some Notes on Recent Work." *International Journal of Urban and Regional Research* 6, no. 1:115–20.

Martens, Maartje. 1988. "The Revolution in Mortgage Finance." In *Housing and Social Change in Europe and the USA*, by Michael Ball, Michael Harloe, and Maartje Martens, 130–68. London and New York: Routledge.

Masotti, Louis H., and John Walton. 1976. "Comparative Urban Research: The Logic of Comparisons and the Nature of Urbanism." In *The City in Comparative Perspective*, edited by John Walton and Louis H. Masotti, 1–15. New York: Sage.

Masser, Ian. 1981. *Comparative Planning Studies: A Critical Review*, TRP 33. Sheffield, England: University of Sheffield, Department of Town and Regional Planning, Faculty of Architectural Studies.

Mathéy, Kosta. Forthcoming. "The Development of New Housing Policies in Nicaragua." In *The Deregulation of Housing*, edited by Willem van Vliet— and Jan van Weesep. Newbury Park, Calif.: Sage.

Mayo, Stephen K. 1986. "Sources of Inefficiency in Subsidized Housing Programs: A Comparison of U.S. and German Experience." *Journal of Urban Economics* 20:229–49.

Mayo, Stephen K., and Jörn Barnbrook. 1985. "Rental Housing Subsidy Programs in West Germany and the United States: A Comparative Program Evaluation." In *U.S. and West German Housing Markets*, edited by Konrad Stahl and Raymond J. Struyk, 115–54. Berlin: Springer.

Mayo, Stephen K., S. Malpezzi, and D. Gross. 1986. "Shelter Strategies for the Urban Poor in Developing Countries." *Research Observer* 1:183–203.

McCallum, Douglas, and Stan Benjamin. 1985. "Low-Income Urban Housing in the Third World: Broadening the Economic Perspective." *Urban Studies* 22:277–87.

McGuire, Chester C. 1981. *International Housing Policies: A Comparative Analysis*. Toronto: Lexington Books.

Michelson, William. 1976. "Reversing the 'Inevitable' Trend: High-Rise Housing in Sweden and Denmark." Research Paper No. 79, University of Toronto, Centre for Urban and Community Studies.

————. 1980. "Long and Short-Range Criteria for Housing Choice and Environmental Behavior." *Journal of Social Issues* 36, no. 3:135–49.

Michelson, William, and W. van Vliet—. Forthcoming. "Social Theory and the Built Environment." In *The Handbook of Environmental Sociology*, edited by W. Michelson and R. Dunlap. Westport, Conn.: Greenwood Press.

Misztal, Bronislaw, and Barbara A. Misztal. 1987. "Scarce State Resources and Unrestrained Processes in the Socialist City: The Case of Housing." In *Housing Markets and Policies under Fiscal Austerity*, edited by W. van Vliet—, 191–202. Westport, Conn.: Greenwood Press.

Molotch, Harvey, and Serena Vicari. 1988. "Three Ways to Build: The Development Process in the United States, Japan, and Italy." *Urban Affairs Quarterly* 24, no. 2:188–214.

Morrison, W. K., and P. C. Gutkind, eds. 1982. *Housing the Urban Poor in Africa*. Syracuse, N.Y.: Syracuse University Foreign Comp.

Morton, Henry. 1980. "Who Gets What, When, and How? Housing in the Soviet Union." *Soviet Studies* 32:235–59.

————. 1985. "The Housing Game." *The Wilson Quarterly* (Autumn):61–74.

Moser, Caroline, and Linda Peake, eds. 1987. *Women, Human Settlements, and Housing*. London: Routledge.

Mullins, P. 1981. "Theoretical Perspectives on Australian Urbanization. I. Material Components in the Reproduction of Australian Labour Power." *Australian and New Zealand Journal of Sociology* 17:65–76.

Murphy, M. J., and O. Sullivan. 1986. "Unemployment, Housing, and Household Structure among Young Adults." *Journal of Social Policy* 15, no. 2:205–22.

Myers, D. M. 1985. "Wives' Earnings and Rising Costs of Homeownership." *Social Science Quarterly* 66, no. 2:319–29.

Myles, John. 1988. "Social Security and Support of the Elderly: The Western Experience." *Journal of Aging Studies* 2, no. 4:321–37.

National Association of Home Builders. 1989. *National Delinquency Survey* (Mortgage Bankers Association). Washington, D.C.: Economics, Mortgage Finance and Housing Policy Division.

Nesslein, Thomas S. 1988a. "Housing: The Market Versus the Welfare State Model Revisited." *Urban Studies* 25:95–108.

————. 1988b. "Housing in the Welfare State: Have Government Interventions Raised Housing Investment and Lowered Housing Costs?" *Urban Affairs Quarterly* 24, no. 2:295–314.

————. 1988c. "Urban Decay and the Premature Obsolescence of Housing: A Cross-Country Examination of the Basic Economic Determinants." *Scandinavian Journal of Housing and Planning Research* 5.

Newman, Oscar. 1972. *Defensible Space*. New York: Macmillan.

————. 1980. *Community of Interest*. Garden City, N.Y.: Anchor Press/Doubleday.

Nientied, P., and Jan van der Linden. 1988. "The 'New' Policy Approach to Housing: A Review of the Literature." *Public Administration and Development* 8:233–40.

Nord, Lars. Forthcoming. "National Housing Policy and Local Politics in Sweden." In *The Deregulation of Housing*, edited by William van Vliet— and Jan van Weesep. Newbury Park, Calif.: Sage.

Oberlander, H. P., and A. L. Fallick. 1987. *Shelter or Homes? The Search for Solutions to Homelessness in Canada.* Vancouver: University of British Columbia, Centre for Human Settlements.

Olson, Philip. 1988. "Modernization in the People's Republic of China: The Politicization of the Elderly." *The Sociological Quarterly* 29, no. 2:241–62.

Oxley, Michael J. 1987. "The Aims and Effects of Housing Allowances in Western Europe." In *Housing Markets and Policies under Fiscal Austerity*, edited by W. van Vliet—, 165–78. Westport, Conn.: Greenwood Press.

Palen, J. John. 1988. "Gentrification, Revitalization and Displacement." In *Handbook of Housing and the Built Environment in the U.S.*, edited by Elizabeth Huttman and Willem van Vliet—, 417–31. Westport, Conn.: Greenwood Press.

Paris, Chris. 1984. "Private Rental Housing in Australia." *Environment and Planning A* 16:1079–98.

———. Forthcoming. "Local Government, the State and Housing Provision: Lessons from Australia." In *The Deregulation of Housing*, edited by W. van Vliet— and J. van Weesep. Newbury Park, Calif.: Sage.

Paris, Chris, Peter Williams, and Bob Stimson. 1985. "From Public Housing to Welfare Housing." *Australian Journal of Social Issues* 20, no. 2:105–17.

Parnell, Susan. 1988. "Public Housing as a Device for White Residential Segregation in Johannesburg." *Urban Geography* 9, no. 6:584–602.

Patton, Carl V., ed. 1987. *Spontaneous Shelter: International Perspectives and Prospects.* Philadelphia: Temple University Press.

Peach, C. et al., eds. 1982. *Ethnic Segregation in Cities.* Athens: University of Georgia Press.

Pearce, Diana. 1988. "Minorities and Housing Discrimination." In *Handbook of Housing and the Built Environment in the United States*, edited by Elizabeth Huttman and Willem van Vliet—, 301–12. Westport, Conn.: Greenwood Press.

Perry, C. A. 1939. "The Neighborhood Formula." In *Urban Housing*, edited by W.L.C. Wheaton et al., 94–109. New York: Free Press (1966).

Pickvance, C. G. 1986. "Comparative Urban Analysis and Assumptions About Causality." *International Journal of Urban and Regional Research* 10, no. 2:162–84.

———. 1988. "Employers, Labour Markets, and Redistribution under State Socialism: An Interpretation of Housing Policy in Hungary, 1960–1983." *Sociology* 22, no. 2:193–214.

Pit, Fenna, and Willem van Vliet—. 1988. "Public Housing in the United States." In *Handbook of Housing and the Built Environment in the United States*, edited by Elizabeth Huttman and Willem van Vliet—, 199–223. Westport, Conn.: Greenwood Press.

Popenoe, D. 1985. *Private Pleasure, Public Plight: American Metropolitan Community Life in Comparative Perspective.* New Brunswick, N.J.: Transaction.

Prak, Niels L., and Hugo Priemus, eds. 1985. *Post-War Public Housing in Trouble.* Delft, the Netherlands: Delft University Press.

Pratt, Geraldine. 1986. "Housing Tenure and Social Cleavages in Urban Canada." *Annals of the Association of American Geographers* 76, no. 3:366–80.

Przeworski, Adam, and Henry Teune. 1970. *The Logic of Comparative Social Inquiry.* New York: Wiley-Interscience.

Pugh, Cedric. 1980. *Housing in Capitalist Societies.* Aldershot, Eng.: Gower Press.

Ragin, Charles C. 1987. *The Comparative Method: Moving Beyond Qualitative and Quantitative Strategies.* Berkeley: University of California Press.

Rimmer, Peter J. 1989. "Japanese Construction Contractors and the Australian States: Another Round of Interstate Rivalry." *International Journal of Urban and Regional Research* 12, no. 3:404–24.

Ritzdorf, Marsha. 1986. "Adults Only: Children and American City Planning." *Children's Environments Quarterly* 3, no. 4:26–33.

Roistacher, Elizabeth A. 1987. "The Rise of Competitive Mortgage Markets in the United States and Britain." In *Housing Markets and Policies under Fiscal Austerity*, edited by W. van Vliet—, 91–110. Westport, Conn.: Greenwood Press.

———. Forthcoming. "Housing Finance and Housing Policy in the United States: Legacies of the Reagan Era." In *The Deregulation of Housing*, edited by Willem van Vliet— and Jan van Weesep. Newbury Park, Calif.: Sage.

Rueschemeyer, M. 1989. "New Towns in the German Democratic Republic." *International Journal of Sociology* 18, no. 4:117–43.

Schmitt, R. C. 1963. "Implications of Density in Hong Kong." *Journal of the American Institute of Planners* 24:210–17.

Schuman, Howard, and Lawrence Bobo. 1988. "Survey-based Experiments on White Racial Attitudes Toward Residential Integration." *American Journal of Sociology* 94, no. 2:273–99.

Schwartz, Nathan H. 1984. "Race and the Allocation of Public Housing in Great Britain: The Autonomy of the Local State." *Comparative Politics* 16, no. 2:205–22.

Shalala, Donna E., and Jo Ann McGeorge. 1981. "The Women and Mortgage Credit Project: A Government Response to the Housing Problems of Women." In *Building for Women*, edited by Suzanne Keller, 39–43. Lexington, Mass.: Lexington Books, D. C. Heath.

Short, J. R. 1988. "Construction Workers and the City: 1. Analysis." *Environment and Planning A* 20:719–32.

Sillince, John A. A., ed. 1989. *Housing in Eastern Europe and the Soviet Union*. London: Croom-Helm.

Simmons, James W., and Larry S. Bourne, eds. 1978. "Defining Urban Places: Differing Concepts of the Urban System." In *Systems of Cities: Readings on Structure, Growth, and Policy*, 28–41. New York: Oxford University Press.

Skinner, R. J., and M. J. Rodell. 1983. *People, Poverty, and Shelter; Problems of Self-Help Housing in the Third World*. London: Methuen.

Smelser, N. J. 1976. *Comparative Methods in the Social Sciences*. Englewood Cliffs, N.J.: Prentice-Hall.

Smith, Rebecca L., and C. Lee Thomson. 1987. "Restricted Housing Markets for Female-Headed Households in U.S. Metropolitan Areas." In *Housing and Neighborhoods; Theoretical and Empirical Contributions*, edited by Willem van Vliet—, Harvey Choldin, William Michelson, and David Popenoe, 279–90. Westport, Conn.: Greenwood Press.

Smith, Tom W. 1987. "The Polls—A Report: The Welfare State in Cross-National Perspective." *Public Opinion Quarterly* 51:404–21.

Soliman, Ahmed. 1988. "Housing the Urban Poor in Egypt: A Critique of Present Policies." *Interntional Journal of Jurban and Regional Research* 12, no. 1:65–86.

Soussan, J. 1984. "Recent Trends in South African Housing Policy." *Area* 16, no. 3:201–7.

Staemmler, Gerlind. 1984. "East Germany." In *Housing in Europe*, edited by Martin Wynn, 220–46. London: Croom Helm.

Stefl, Mary E. 1987. "The New Homeless: A National Perspective." In *The Homeless in Contemporary Society*, edited by Richard D. Bingham, Roy E. Green, and Sammis B. White, 46–63. Newbury Park, Calif.: Sage.

Streib, Gordon F. 1987. "Old Age in Sociocultural Context: China and the United States." *Journal of Aging Studies* 1, no. 2:95–112.

Stren, R., and R. White (eds.). 1989. *African Cities in Crisis: Managing Rapid Urban Growth*. Boulder, Colo.: Westview Press.

Struyk, Raymond J. 1982. "Upgrading Existing Dwellings: An Element in the Housing Strategies of Developing Countries." *The Journal of Developing Areas* 17:67–75.

Sumka, Howard J. 1987. "Shelter Policy and Planning in Developing Countries; Introduction." *American Planning Association Journal* 53, no. 2 (Spring):171–75.

Swanstrom, Todd. 1989. "No Room at the Inn: Housing Policy and the Homeless." *Washington University Journal of Urban and Contemporary Law* 35:81–105.

The Swedish Institute. 1987. "Housing and Housing Policy in Sweden." Report. Stockholm, August.

Szelenyi, Ivan. 1983. *Urban Inequalities under State Socialism*. Oxford: Oxford University Press.

———. 1987. "Housing Inequalities and Occupational Segregation in Socialist Cities." *International Journal of Urban and Regional Research* 11, no. 1:1–8.

Teilhet-Waldorf, S., and W. H. Waldorf. 1983. "Earnings of Self-Employed in an Informal Sector: A Case Study of Bangkok." *Economic Development and Cultural Change* (April):587–607.

Thomas, D. A. 1986. *Housing and Urban Renewal: Residential Decay and Revitalization in the Private Sector*. London: George Allen and Unwin.

Thorns, D. C. 1988. "New Solutions to Old Problems: Housing Affordability and Access within Australia and New Zealand." *Environment and Planning A* 20:71–82.

Tomlinson, Richard. 1988. "South Africa's Urban Policy: A New Form of Influx Control." *Urban Affairs Quarterly* 23, no. 4:487–510.

Tosics, Ivan. 1987. "Privatization in Housing Policy: The Case of Western Countries and That of Hungary." *International Journal of Urban and Regional Research* 11, no.1:61–78.

Tuncalp, Secil. 1987. "The Housing Programme in Saudi Arabia." *Town Planning Review* 9, no. 4:345–59.

Turner, John F. C. 1976. *Housing by People: Towards Autonomy in Building Environments*. New York: Pantheon Books.

Turner, John F. C. 1982. "Issues in Self-Help and Self-Managed Housing." Chapter 4 in *Self-Help Housing: A Critique*, edited by P. Ward. London: Mansell.

U.N. Department of International Economic and Social Affairs. 1980. *Compendium of Social Statistics: 1977*. Statistical Papers, Series K. No. 4. New York: United Nations.

U.N. Fund for Population Activities. 1986. *Assistance and Population Data*. New York.

United Nations. 1986. *World Statistics in Brief*. 10th ed. Statistical Papers, Series V, No. 10. New York: U.N. Department of International Economic and Social Affairs, Statistical Office.

————. 1987. *1985 Demographic Yearbook*. New York: U.N. Department of International Economic and Social Affairs, Statistical Office.

U.S. Bureau of the Census. 1988. *American Housing Survey for the United States in 1985*. Current Housing Reports H-150-85. Washington, D.C.

U.S. Bureau of the Census. 1989. *Statistical Abstract of the United States: 1989*. 109th ed. Washington, D.C.

U.S. League of Savings Institutions. 1988. *Homeownership: A Decade of Change*. Chicago.

Valladares, Licia. 1985. "Popular Housing in Brazil: A Review." In *Housing Needs and Policy Approaches Trends in Thirteen Countries*, edited by W. van Vliet—, Elizabeth Huttman, and Sylvia F. Fava, 222–36. Durham, N.C.: Duke University Press.

Van Vliet—, Willem. 1983a. "The Study of Scientific Communities: Bringing Space Back In?" *Social Science Information Studies* 3:135–45.

————. 1983b. "Families in Apartment Buildings: Sad Storeys for Children?" *Environment and Behavior* 15, no. 2:211–34.

————. 1985. "Housing Policy as a Planning Tool." *Urban Studies* 22:105–17.

————. 1987a. "Housing in the Third World." *Environment and Behavior* 19, no. 3:267–85.

————, ed. 1987b. *Housing Markets and Policies under Fiscal Austerity*. Westport, Conn.: Greenwood Press.

————. 1987c. "Introduction: Some Comments on Recent and Current Research." Introduction to *Housing and Neighborhoods: Theoretical and Empirical Contributions*, edited by Willem van Vliet—, Harvey Choldin, William Michelson, and David Popenoe, 1–15. Westport, Conn.: Greenwood Press.

————. 1988a. "The Housing and Living Arrangements of Young People in the United States." In *Handbook of Housing and the Built Environment in the United States*, edited by Elizabeth Huttman and Willem van Vliet—, 313–45. Westport, Conn.: Greenwood Press.

————. 1988b. "Prospects and Issues in U.S. Housing: A Comment." In *Handbook of Housing and the Built Environment in the United States*, edited by Elizabeth Huttman and Willem van Vliet—, 455–460. Westport, Conn.: Greenwood Press.

————. 1989. "Communities and Built Environments Supporting Women's Changing Roles." Chapter 1 in *Women, Housing and Community*, edited by Willem van Vliet—. Aldershot, England: Avebury.

————. Forthcoming. "Privatization and Decentralization of Housing and Urban Development." Chapter 1 in *The Deregulation of Housing*, edited by W. van Vliet—and J. van Weesep. Newbury Park, Calif.: Sage.

Van Vliet—, Willem, Elizabeth Huttman, and Sylvia F. Fava, eds. 1985. *Housing Needs and Policy Approaches: Trends in Thirteen Countries*. Durham, N.C.: Duke University Press.

Varley, Ann. 1987. "The Relationship between Tenure Legalization and Housing Improvements: Evidence from Mexico City." *Development and Change* 18:463–81.

Vischer, Jacqueline, C. 1986. "The Complexity of Designing for Social Mix: An Evaluation of Site-Planning Principles." *Journal of Architectural and Planning Research* 3:15–31.

Vladimirov, M.P.L. 1985. "La rénovation urbaine et al qualité de la vie." In ECE/HBP/31, Commission Economique pour l'Europe, 38–39. New York: United Nations.

Walton, John. 1981. "Comparative Urban Studies." *International Journal of Comparative Sociology* 22, nos. 1–2:22–39.

Waltz, S. E. 1989. "Women's Housing Needs in the Arab Cultural Context of Tunisia." In *Women, Housing and Community*, edited by W. van Vliet—, 171–85. Aldershot, Eng.: Gower Press.

Wang, L. H., and Anthony G. O. Yeh. 1987. "Public Housing-Led New Town Development." *Town Planning Review* 9, no. 1:41–63.

Ward, P., ed. 1982. *Self-Help Housing: A Critique*. London: Mansell.

Watson, Sophie, and Lisa Coleman. 1986. "Housing, Demographic Change, and the Private Rental Sector." *Australian Journal of Social Issues* 21, no. 1:16–27.

Wekerle, Gerda R., Rebecca Peterson and David Morley, eds. 1980. *New Space for Women*. Boulder, Colo.: Westview Press.

Wells, Jill. 1986. *The Construction Industry in Developing Countries: Alternative Strategies for Development*. Beckenham, Eng.: Croom Helm.

Werczberger, Elia. Forthcoming. "The Privatization of Public Housing in Israel." In *The Deregulation of Housing*, edited by Willem van Vliet— and Jan van Weesep. Newbury Park, Calif.: Sage.

Wikan, U. 1985. "Living Conditions among Cairo's Poor—A View from Below." *The Middle East* 39 (Winter): 7–26.

Williams, R. H. 1984. "Cross-National Research: Translating Theory into Practice." *Environment and Planning B: Planning and Design* 11:149–61.

Williamson, John B. 1987. "Social Security and Physical Quality of Life in Developing Nations: A Cross-National Analysis." *Social Indicators Research* 19:205–27.

Wolch, Jennifer R., Michael Dear, and Andrea Akita. 1988. "Explaining Homelessness." *Journal of the American Planning Association* (Autumn):443–53.

Wollmann, Hellmut, and Wolfgang Jaedicke. 1989. "The Rise and Fall of Public and Social Housing." *Tijdschrift voor Economische en Sociale Geografie* 80, no. 2:82–88.

Wood, Gavin A. 1988. "Housing Tax Expenditures in OECD Countries: Economic Impacts and Prospects for Reform." *Policy and Politics* 16, no. 4:235–50.

World Bank. 1987. *World Development Report, 1987*. New York: Oxford University Press.

Wuertz, Karen, and Ton Van der Pennen. 1987. "Participation by Ethnic Minorities in Urban Renewal in the Netherlands." Chapter 7 in *Housing and Neighborhoods: Theoretical and Empirical Contributions*, edited by Willem van Vliet—, Harvey Choldin, William Michelson, and David Popenoe. Westport, Conn.: Greenwood Press.

Wulff, Maryann. 1982. "The Two-Income Household: Relative Contribution of Earners to Housing Costs." *Urban Studies* 19 (October): 343–50.

Wynn, M., ed. 1984. *Housing in Europe*. New York: St. Martin's Press.

Yancey, W. L. 1971. "Architecture, Interaction and Social Control." *Environment and Behavior* 3, no. 1:3–21.

Yinger, John. 1986. "Measuring Racial Discrimination with Fair Housing Audits: Caught in the Act." *The American Economic Review* 76, no. 5:881–93.

I

WESTERN AND SOUTHERN EUROPE

2

Great Britain

MICHAEL HARLOE

Britain is a relatively small and densely populated country (56 million people, 0.24 million square kilometers) whose population has been growing slowly in the postwar period. Unlike several other Western European countries, Britain has had a fairly balanced inflow and outflow of population in recent decades, although immigration from the Caribbean and the Indian subcontinent occurred on a substantial scale in the 1950s and 1960s. Uniquely among the world's nations, the process of urbanization was virtually complete by 1900, and by this date some cities, notably London, had already begun to decentralize. Since 1945 all major urban centers have lost population, at first to their suburbs and lately to the surrounding countryside. More than other countries in Western Europe, Britain has experienced many of the aspects of inner-city decline that have been common in the United States, although the scale and intensity of the problems are far less.

Britain's economic fortunes have been in decline for much of this century, but immediately after World War II its inhabitants still had relatively high per capita incomes. However, unlike other Western European countries such as West Germany and France, Britain made little effort to restructure and modernize the economy. As a consequence, by the 1960s it was already becoming one of the poorer advanced industrial economies, a process that continued in subsequent decades. The onset of recession and deindustrialization in the midseventies had a particularly severe impact. In the early 1980s the true level of unemployment probably went above 4 million although toward the end of the decade it was slowly declining.

The country is a representative democracy with a unitary state and a constitutional monarchy. Unlike the United States, in Britain there is no separation of the legislature and the executive; the majority party in the House of Commons forms the executive, which is headed by a prime minister and cabinet of departmental ministers. There is a fully professional civil service, although a very few political appointees act as ministerial advisors. There is a two-tier system of local government that consists of directly elected councillors and a professional staff. Local government in Britain has less freedom of action than in some other countries; its powers are defined by the national legislature, and it has become highly dependent on central government grants, its other main source of revenue being local property taxation (rates). Postwar politics has been dominated by the two major parties, the Conservatives and Labour, although there is a center party, since 1988 called the Social and Liberal Democrats. In Scotland, Wales, and Northern Ireland there are also regionally based parties, but they have held real political power only in Northern Ireland. Between 1964 and 1979 the Labour party governed for all but four years. Between 1979 and 1987, however, the Conservatives won three successive election victories, and Margaret Thatcher became the longest serving prime minister of the century.

POSTWAR TRENDS IN HOUSING CONDITIONS AND CONSTRUCTION

Areas and Statistics

Some important divisions within the nation affect housing conditions, policies, and administration. What is commonly referred to as Britain is more properly the United Kingdom of Great Britain and Northern Ireland, and Great Britain consists of England, Wales, and Scotland. Many housing statistics (including census data) are presented separately for three areas—England and Wales, Scotland, and Northern Ireland (in 1987 these areas contained 88 percent, 9 percent, and 3 percent of the U.K. population, respectively). Others are collected for Great Britain and very few for the United Kingdom. Much housing legislation and policy implementation are specific to these three areas, too, although the Scottish and Northern Irish legislation often follows that for England and Wales in general outline. The implications of these variations of legislation and policy for housing—and this account oversimplifies them—cannot be dealt with in this chapter. Therefore, most of the statistical material presented here will refer either to England and Wales or to Great Britain, and the discussion of policies will refer to England and Wales.

A second issue concerns the availability of statistics. Census data are readily available, the first postwar census being taken in 1951 and decennially thereafter. But the amount of census information relevant to housing has always been limited, although it has improved over time. For example, detailed information by tenure divisions has been collected only since 1961. Moreover, before the 1960s there were relatively few other sources of information on housing, although details of household expenditures on housing were collected from the midfifties onwards, and there are data on house building. In the sixties and seventies there were a number of special surveys (such as the 1978 *National Housing and Dwelling Survey*), and several survey series began, including irregularly repeated *House Condition Surveys* and annual *General Household Surveys*. In addition, nongovernmental bodies began to collect useful housing-related data.

What follows reflects these limitations. The development of housing in the early postwar period can only be sketched in; more can be said about developments in the last quarter of a century. But the most frustrating limitation is the lack of some key information on developments in the 1980s, during which time important changes have occurred in housing. In part this is because the last census was in 1981, but also there has been a reduction in official research and data collection since 1979.

Trends in Basic Conditions Since 1951

In the early postwar period there was an absolute shortage of housing (table 2.1). This was a situation that had existed, although on a declining scale, at least since the Industrial Revolution. It was exacerbated by wartime damage and losses and the high rates of household formation after 1945. Despite a major building effort by the first postwar Labour government, the problem still remained when that government left office in 1951. Indeed, the new Conservative administration had, as one of its key election pledges, the promise to construct more housing.

It took until the early sixties to achieve a crude surplus of housing (table 2.1). But despite the continuation of a trend to smaller households since then, the problem of an absolute national shortage of housing has not returned (although shortages of affordable and decent housing for disadvantaged groups have remained). The figures given for overcrowding in table 2.1 reflect this progress from shortage to crude surplus. The years since 1951 have also seen a massive improvement in housing amenities. Table 2.1 shows one indicator of this: the numbers of households without a fixed bath fell from almost 5 million in 1951 to just over 300,000 in 1981. In addition, by 1984, 97 percent of households in Great Britain had sole use of a bath or shower, and the same percentage had the sole use of an inside toilet. The proportion of households with central heating rose from 35 percent in 1971 to 66 percent in 1984. However, despite these massive improvements in housing conditions, there are now signs that the economic austerity, which began in the mid–1970s and which has been accompanied by large reductions in public investment in housing production, has resulted in a slowing down of this housing progress and even its reversal in some respects. One potent indicator comes from the latest of a series of official *Housing Conditions Surveys* that assesses levels of unfitness (a statutorily defined measure of extreme housing dilapidation), lack of amenities, and disrepair. For many years each successive survey showed reductions in all of these problems, but the 1981 survey showed either an increase or no more than a stabilization of the levels of unfitness and an increase in the number of properties suffering from serious disrepair (there is some dispute about just how the unfitness figures should be interpreted, but on either basis of interpretation previous progress with reducing unfitness had ended).

The Changing Pattern of Tenures

The most dramatic single change in postwar housing relates to the pattern of tenures. Table 2.2 outlines these changes. In 1951 the majority tenure was private rental, as it had been since the nineteenth century, although it had been in decline since World War I. Public rental housing had begun to expand in the interwar period, initially serving the better-off working class but by the 1930s being developed in association with the clearance of inner-city slums and the rehousing

Table 2.1
Trends in Housing Conditions, England and Wales, 1951–1981

Year	Stock (x1,000)	Households (x1,000)	Surplus/Deficit (x1,000)	Average Household Size (x1,000)	Overcrowding %	Lacking Amenities (x1,000)
1951	12,389	13,118	-729	3.33	5.1	4,850
1961	14,646	14,724	-78	3.14	2.8	3,221
1971	17,024	16,779	+245	2.95	1.4	1,443
1981	19,250	18,242	+1,008	2.69	0.6	333

Source: Census reports 1951–1981.

Notes: Overcrowding is defined as 1.5 or more persons per room. *Lacking amenities* means without a fixed bath or shower.

Table 2.2
The Changing Pattern of Tenures, Great Britain, 1951–1986

Tenure	1951	1961	1971	1981	1986
Owner occupied	31%	42%	50%	56%	63%
Public rented	18	26	30	31	27
Private rented	51	32	20	13	10

Sources: Census reports, various years; *Housing and Construction Statistics*, various years.

Notes: The figures are for percentage of households; the figures for the private rented sector include housing association tenancies (despite the fact that this is normally regarded as a form of public housing). The percentage of housing association tenancies in the above figures for the private rented sector was below 1 percent before 1971; by 1986 it amounted to 2.5 percent.

of their low-income populations. Owner occupation (as home ownership is referred to in Britain) began to develop rapidly in the 1930s, mainly as housing for white-collar workers in the expanding economy of southern England. The first postwar Labour government was committed to a massive expansion of public housing, and this continued, although on a diminishing scale after 1953–1954, under successive governments into the 1970s. After the return of a Conservative government in 1951 increasing emphasis was put on encouraging owner occupation, and this drive has continued under all successive administrations. Favorable subsidy regimes for owner occupation (and, for many years, for public housing) and the continuation of forms of rent control have resulted in the virtual extinction of the private landlord, so private renting is now concentrated in the larger urban housing markets and certain special locations such as seaside resorts and university towns.

However, a new phase of more radical change in this long-term pattern is now underway. As table 2.2 shows, in the 1980s the proportion of public housing has, for the first time in British housing history, begun to decline, and this trend seems likely to continue. Major changes have occurred in government housing policy since the return of the first Thatcher government in 1979. Subsidies for new public housing have been sharply reduced, and there has been a program of sales of existing public housing to its tenants. Following the reelection of the Conservatives in 1987, a new phase in the drive toward the complete privatization of housing has begun; this involves the transfer of public housing to private landlords, nonprofit housing associations and tenant cooperatives, and an attempt to revive new building by private landlords (almost no new private rental housing has been built since the 1930s). The government's intention is that those who cannot afford owner occupation or who do not want to live in this tenure will resort to a revitalized private rental sector.

A Profile of the Main Tenures

A profile of the main housing tenures is given in table 2.3; other figures, not presented here, for homeowners with a mortgage show that access to ownership, aided by the liberalization of loan conditions over time, is extensive even among those under twenty-five years of age. The low proportion of the elderly who are owners reflects the conditions of the earlier postwar years when home ownership was less extensive. In contrast, there is a high proportion of the elderly in both forms of rental housing; this again reflects these earlier conditions when a majority of working-class households rented rather than owned. The age distribution of households in the small remaining private rental sector is bipolar, both the young and, to a lesser degree, the elderly being overrepresented. However, these two sections of the population live in two very different types of private rental housing. The young households mainly live in furnished accommodations, much of them consisting of small-sized converted apartments or rooms with shared facilities. This type of accommodation—despite the existence in theory of some controls on rents and security often let on a free-market basis—still provides an important source of low-quality, poor-value-for-the-money, but reasonably accessible accommodations for newly formed households in urban areas. The elderly in contrast mainly live in the remnants of the older established unfurnished private rental sector, in houses rather than apartments, with more space but few amenities. More of this type of accommodations is still subject to a form of rent control and legally guaranteed security of tenure.[1]

The rest of table 2.3 reflects these differences. Thus the data for the socioeconomic composition of tenants and owners show not only, as might be expected, that a high proportion of "higher" white-collar groups are homeowners but also that ownership is significant further down the social structure among "lower" white-collar and skilled working-class households. Over time ownership has spread to large sections of the working class; for example, between 1961 and 1981 the share of skilled manual workers who were homeowners rose from 37 to 56 percent; in comparison, the share among employers and managers rose from 67 to 82 percent. In sharp contrast, the public sector serves the less-skilled working class and contains a high proportion of economically inactive heads of household, some of them are elderly, but public housing also contains concentrations of the unemployed, single-parent families, and others dependent on social security benefits. In fact, until the fifties there was a far less skewed distribution of households in public housing, but the expansion of home ownership, together with the collapse of private renting (which housed many on the lowest incomes), has resulted in a growing polarization, in terms of incomes and socioeconomic composition, between the two main tenures (see Hamnett 1983; Murie 1983; Forrest and Murie 1983; Robinson and O'Sullivan 1983). It is this trend that has given rise to recent concern about the "marginalization" or "residualization" of public housing and its possible reduction to welfare housing on the U.S. model.

Table 2.3
Tenure Profiles, Great Britain, 1985 (In Percentages unless Otherwise Stated)

	Owner	Private rented	Public rented	All tenures
Age				
under 25	2	15	5	5
25-9	8	11	7	8
30-44	34	21	19	28
45-64	34	24	33	33
65 on	21	29	36	27
SEG				
1	26	18	2	18
2	16	17	7	13
3	23	14	21	22
4	8	14	19	12
5	27	38	51	35
Median Income	183	127	108	160
House	93	57	60	79
Apartment	7	41	40	20
Other	0	2	0	1
Sole Bath	99	86	99	98
Sole WC	100	91	99	98
pre 1919	26	51	5	22
post 1965	28	12	34	29

Source: *General Household Survey*, 1985.

Notes: Socio-Economic Group (SEG) Key: 1—professional/employer/manager; 2—other white collar and service; 3—skilled manual; 4—un/semiskilled manual; 5—not economically active. Percentages may not add up to 100 due to rounding. Income data are for household heads.

The gap between those who own and those who live in public housing has worsened in the past decades (table 2.3); for example, in 1985 the median income of local authority tenant heads of household who were economically active was 41 percent less than the owner-occupier median. In 1972 the disparity was only 24 percent. Moreover, the local authority sector now accommodates a far higher proportion of the economically inactive than it did in the early seventies, and the decline in the share of the economically active in this tenure has been at a far faster rate than the decline in the owner-occupier sector. One indicator of this change is the shift in the proportions of Supplementary Benefit (welfare payment) recipients in these two tenures over time. In 1967, 17 percent were homeowners and 45 percent local authority tenants; by 1980 the figures were 19 and 61 percent, respectively.

The socioeconomic group data for private rental housing again reflect its dual character, acting as initial housing for a high proportion of white-collar workers, most of whom become homeowners after a few years, as well as for a considerable number of elderly low-income households, most of whom are tenants of many years standing. Disaggregated data not shown here also show that the incomes of the elderly tenants in private rented housing are close to those of public housing tenants, whereas the median income of the younger households in the furnished subsector is closer to that of homeowners.

Recent comparable data on housing costs in relation to incomes are not available. But household expenditures are available, although there are problems in computing homeowner payments because mortgage payments are being used to purchase a capital asset as well as to buy shelter (the following data are based, for homeowners, on the somewhat shaky construct of "gross imputed rents," not mortgage repayments). In 1985 the proportion of the total household gross expenditure on all housing averaged 18 percent; those buying on a mortgage and in the unfurnished private rental sector paid 17 percent; council tenants paid 20.5 percent; and tenants in furnished rental accommodations paid 22 percent. These gross figures include local taxes but not utilities. However, the pattern changes when account is taken of certain deductions from the gross payments, in particular the income-related housing benefit in the rental sectors. Thus the net expenditure on all housing averaged 16 percent; those buying on a mortgage paid 16.5 percent; and tenants in private furnished rentals paid 19 percent. But tenants of unfurnished private rentals only paid 13 percent and council tenants just over 11 percent. As these figures reveal, income-related housing subsidies virtually halve the housing-payments burden for council tenants.

As the figures in table 2.3 show, Britain is essentially a nation of house rather than apartment dwellers (roughly a fifth of these houses are single-family "detached" houses, and the rest split evenly between duplexes—"semidetached"— and row or "terrace" houses). But about a third of the public housing stock is apartments, concentrated in the larger cities, and the private rental sector has a similar proportion. In this latter case, as noted above, the split reflects the division between furnished and unfurnished accommodations.

The data for provision of facilities illustrate that a high basic level of amenities has been achieved, although there are still major deficiencies in the private rental stock that was mainly built before 1919. But these data are somewhat misleading for, although they show that over a quarter of the owner-occupied stock and a third of the public housing has been built since 1965, and hence has good amenities, they do not reveal the disrepair that has been spreading, even in housing that has been built relatively recently. The 1981 *House Condition Survey* showed a substantial growth of major disrepair and unfitness in owner-occupied housing. In an era of economic austerity and with an aging stock and population, many homeowners have been forced to cut back on essential maintenance. A similarly serious situation exists in the public sector where the cuts in public expenditures in recent years have added to a longer-term legacy of inadequate maintenance and refurbishment. Particularly serious problems exist on some of the projects that were built in the fifties and sixties using industrialized techniques. Some of this housing began to exhibit major problems after a few years due to inadequate design and materials and poor planning, construction, and mainte-nance. The physical conditions of some of these projects, many of which are high rise and high density, are exacerbated by their lack of "defensible space," by vandalism, by boarded up apartments that have deteriorated so much that they are unlettable, and by other symptoms of a complex combination of physical and social pathologies. (Note, however, that not *all* industrially built high-rise projects are so problematic, nor are these severe conditions only restricted to housing of this type). According to official figures, in 1983 about 300,000 units of public housing came into the severely problem-ridden category; more than 75 percent of them were located in London and the major metropolitan centers.

On the basis of the figures in the 1981 *House Condition Survey*, the total cost at 1981 prices of carrying out all of the necessary repairs (without modernization) on the English housing stock would be £35.4 billion; more than half of this would have to be spent on owner-occupied housing. More recently, local au-thorities' representatives have estimated that the total cost of repairing and mod-ernizing the public sector stock in England, Wales, and Scotland would be up to £25 billion (cited in Cantle 1986). It also has been officially estimated that the backlog of disrepair in public housing is growing by £900 million per annum (Audit Commission 1985, 26). This enormous problem is the main reason that an increasing proportion of the reducing amount that the government now allows local authorities to spend on housing capital investment is being used for the repair and upgrading of the existing stock, not new building.

Housing Deprivation

Some indication has already been given of the incidence of housing depri-vation. It remains here to add some brief comments on specific groups that suffer from poor housing conditions. In general, the single, elderly, low-income, and larger households are most likely to be in poor housing conditions, and, conversely, high proportions of all households living in such accommodations fall into these groups. However, it is true that the postwar expansion of public housing has weakened the link between low incomes and social disadvantage, on the one hand, and poor housing conditions, on the other hand, which is at its strongest in private housing markets. But the development of major defects in public housing and government policies to privatize much of this housing and reduce investment in the rest now seem likely to reverse this progress.

The problems faced by specific groups experiencing housing deprivation differ somewhat. Thus large families, not surprisingly, are particularly liable to suffer from overcrowding, and this is likely to persist for many years since the opportunity to move to larger accommodations is limited. Research has shown the serious consequences of overcrowding on health and child development in such households.

Another deprived group is young single people who often find access to reasonable housing beyond their means (and who tend to be excluded by the administrative rules of access from public housing). Often they are forced to share private rental accommodations with poor facilities. This may be only a relatively temporary state, although the growth of very high levels of youth unemployment in recent years has exacerbated the problem. For those who leave school without adequate qualifications, the prospects are now for long-term unemployment and the reductions in public housing activity may mean that they have to live for many years in poor and insecure private rental housing.

In the past twenty-five years there has been a rapid growth of single-parent families (mainly female headed). Such households have high priority for admittance to public housing, but there are a significant proportion in the private rental sector living in overcrowded and poor conditions. The position of the children of families living in such accommodations (which otherwise now includes mainly households without children) is particularly serious since research has shown that such housing can have a very serious effect on their development.

A fourth major group consists of ethnic minorities. The two main minority groupings in Britain (although there are many others besides) were established by the mass migrations in the postwar period from the Caribbean and the Asian subcontinent (India, Pakistan, and Bangladesh). These migrants initially settled in poor-quality inner-city rental housing, but more recently a high proportion of those who migrated from the Caribbean and their children have filtered into public housing, whereas a high proportion of those who migrated from Asia have become homeowners; many have bought poor-quality ex-private rental housing in declining urban areas. There is considerable evidence of racial discrimination limiting access to decent and affordable housing for both groups. For example, public housing allocation processes are often discriminatory, with more restrictions on entry and a high proportion of blacks being allocated to the worst parts of this stock. Many who have bought have been steered by realtors and others toward dilapidated inner-city housing. But the effects of direct housing-related discrimination are also bound up with the consequences of discrimination and disadvantage in education and employment that result in high levels of poverty among ethnic minorities. This in itself leads to restricted access to decent and affordable housing.

The growing number of homeless households has been an issue for housing campaigners since the early 1960s, leading in 1977 to legislation that placed a duty on local housing authorities to provide accommodations for some categories of the homeless, mainly families with children, the elderly, and the disabled. Satisfactory statistics on the homeless do not exist, but the number of households applying to local authorities as homeless and the number provided with accommodations are known. Between 1978 and 1979 and 1985 and 1986 applications in England and Wales rose from around 130,000 per annum to almost 190,000 and the number rehoused from about 56,000 to 85,000. The problem is particularly acute in London, where housing costs are extremely high and there is an acute shortage of lower-income housing in the public and private sectors. A study published in 1986 found that, since 1970, the number rehoused as homeless in London had risen by 700 percent (Greater London Council 1986a). Nationally, about half of those accepted as homeless are immediately rehoused in public housing, often in the poorer and less popular parts of this stock. The rest are forced to live in a variety of temporary accommodations such as hostels and bed and breakfast "hotels," often in extremely overcrowded and even dangerous conditions, while waiting for permanent rehousing in the public sector. In London about two-thirds of accepted applicants are first accommodated in this unsatisfactory way. About a third of those homeless households who are rehoused have been evicted by friends or relatives with whom they have been "doubling up"; about 20 percent have been evicted or otherwise lost private rental accommodations, and a similar proportion have lost their housing after the breakdown of a relationship with a partner. These reasons for homelessness have not changed much in their incidence over time, but homelessness due to mortgage default has increased rapidly since the late 1970s, up from 6 percent in 1978 to 13 percent by 1985.

Women feature prominently in several of the groups discussed above, particularly among the homeless and in single-parent households. But the elderly are a more separate group. Their needs have grown as the proportions of the elderly and now of the very elderly in the population have risen rapidly. Few of them who worked in manual or even "junior" white-collar jobs have occupational pensions. Many are dependent on social security payments, which are barely above poverty-line levels. In recent years considerable effort has been put into building public housing for some of the elderly, although there is fierce debate about whether this is the best way of using limited resources. Despite this new building, the elderly still, on average, live in poorer housing conditions than the population as a whole.

Construction and Improvement

Most of the public sector housing has been built by local councils, but the output of nonprofit housing associations expanded in the 1970s, and in the 1980s half or more of the reducing annual production of public sector housing has come from this source. Despite this, the associations still only own about 2.5 percent of the British housing stock, or about 8 percent of the public housing stock. House-building rates per thousand population have been low in international terms, certainly in comparison with much of Western Europe and the United States. However, Britain's population has been growing slowly, and its urbanization was completed long before the postwar period. (Figure 2.1 shows details of the post-war output of new housing for the private sector (almost entirely for owner occupation) and the public sector.)

There have been several phases of development of building activity:

1945–1951. This was a period of postwar reconstruction under a Labour government. A high priority was given to public housing, and private output was restricted. But the postwar economic crisis meant that total output was also restricted and was far below outstanding demand. House-building rates increased slowly to just over 4 per 1,000 of the population.

1951–1964. This was a period of Conservative government. After an initial and rapid expansion of public housing, the longer-term strategy was to restrict public housing construction to provide for households relocating from urban slum-clearance schemes and other "special needs" and to encourage new housing for home ownership. At the end of this period there was some reconsideration of policy and an increase in public building. House-building rates reflected these changes, falling from 6.9 per 1,000 of the population in 1954 to just over 5 by the late 1950s and then increasing to just under 6 by the early 1960s.

1964–1970. A returning Labour government pledged to expand housing output to 500,000 per year but was committed to the expansion of both the public and the private sectors. Output peaked in the late sixties but then began to collapse as the first real effects of Britain's poor postwar economic record and rapid inflation led the government to slash public expenditures. By 1968 the house-building rate was 7.6 per 1,000 population, the highest yet achieved in the postwar years, but it then began to fall sharply.

1970–1974. A Conservative government was committed to deep cuts in new public housing and the promotion of the private sector. But the removal of credit and banking restrictions led to a short-lived property boom and then a disastrous collapse that for a time threatened banking stability. Private output collapsed in 1974, when only 4.8 units per 1,000 of the population were being completed.

1974–1979. This was something of a rerun of the history of the 1960s Labour administration but at lower overall levels of output. Labour came to power and promised to increase public and private investment in housing, but after an initial surge by 1975—under the impact of the growing world economic crisis as well as Britain's own special problems—sharp cuts were made in public expenditures,

Figure 2.1
Output of Social Rented and All Housing, England and Wales, 1945–1985

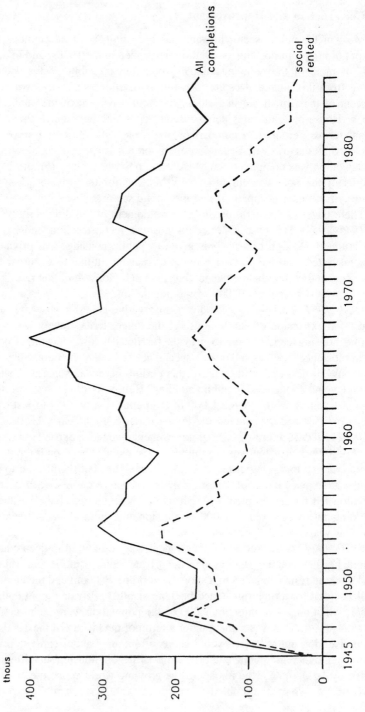

Source: Housing and Construction Statistics, various years.

and output later began to fall in the private sector. After a brief rally in the mid–seventies the house-building rate had fallen to 4.3 per 1,000 of the population by 1979.

1979–present. The election of the Thatcher government, coinciding with the world recession, resulted not only in the severest slump yet seen in the postwar private housing market but also, by 1986, in the lowest number of peacetime public house-building completions since 1925. There was a slow recovery of private housing after the depths of the recession in the early 1980s, although it remains far below the level that it reached in the 1960s and early 1970s. In terms of output per 1,000 of the population, the levels in the 1980s were far lower than they had been since the immediate aftermath of World War II, down to only 3.1 in 1982 with only a modest recovery since then.

In the decade or so after World War II, policies focused almost entirely on new additions to the housing stock in order to eliminate the crude shortage of dwellings. But by the mid–fifties the government had returned to the large-scale clearance of the many thousands of Victorian slum properties that still existed, especially in the major cities. Mass slum clearance had begun in the 1930s but had been interrupted by the war. The annual numbers of slums demolished rose almost threefold between the mid–fifties and the late sixties to peak at around 70,000 per annum. Since the early seventies clearances have fallen away sharply, reaching around 20,000 per year by the mid–eighties.

By the mid–sixties the policy of mass clearances was coming under increasing scrutiny, and more emphasis began to be placed on the improvement of defective property. There were several reasons for this switch. By this date most of the very worst property had been eradicated, so potentially improvable housing was beginning to be demolished. In addition, increasing proportions of this property were owner occupied rather than rented, and so opposition to its loss mounted. Also, there were criticisms of the disruptive effects of large-scale clearance and belief that improvement would be quicker and cheaper. In addition, as the local authority stock began to age there was a need to begin improvements in this sector.

Modest grants for improvement had been available since 1949 (and since 1926 in rural areas). But even following additional legislation in 1954, only about 30,000 houses a year benefited in the 1950s. After the introduction of a new grant for the installation of standard amenities in 1959, the average rate of take up quadrupled in the early sixties but then began to tail off. Between 1969 and 1974 new policies were introduced to encourage improvement, and local authorities began to promote area-improvement schemes as well as greatly increasing investment in the renovation of their own stock. The numbers of houses improved rose from just over 100,000 in 1969 to 361,000 in 1973. For the first time grants that were wholly for repairs also became available.

However, improvement expenditures were among the earliest victims of the cutbacks in public expenditures that occurred from the midseventies onwards, and by the late seventies grant approvals fell again to their levels of a decade earlier. In the early eighties new legislation and, for a brief period, government encouragement led to a revival in grant-aided improvement but to nowhere near the level of the early seventies. Moreover, the rising disrepair that the 1981 House Condition Survey had identified led many commentators to wonder whether the late twentieth century might see a return to the era of mass slum housing that barely 20 years earlier has seemed to be no more than a rapidly disappearing memory of the Victorian age.

In recent years the government has been reluctant to make any estimate of future housing needs and the output required to meet them. The last official figures date from 1977. However, these data were updated by two academics in 1982 (Fleming and Nellis 1982). The results of their work suggested that around 300,000 units a year needed to be added to the stock in Great Britain to meet current housing demand. In fact, average annual net stock gain up to the mid–1980s was about half this level. Average annual new-housing completions between 1981 and 1986 were 191,000 units. Moreover, instead of a projected net gain of 20,000 houses per year in the existing stock resulting from the rehabilitation of previously unfit housing (as had been anticipated by the government in 1977), in the late 1970s and early 1980s there was a net loss of about 30,000 per year (Thomas 1986, 30). The record is unlikely to have improved since then.

HOUSING FINANCE

Private Housing

Most of the private housing is financed with mortgage loans. Traditionally, these loans were repaid on the annuity principle, but recently, an increasing proportion have been linked to insurance policies that, at maturity, are sufficient to retire the loan principal (until 1983 they attracted tax benefits). Throughout most of the postwar period home lending was dominated by the building societies, the British equivalent of the U.S. thrifts. These formally nonprofit, mutual organizations collected funds from individual savers, so-called retail funds, and lent them to home buyers. Loans typically are for up to twenty-five years and up to 90 percent or more of the property price. For many years virtually all mortgages have been at a variable interest rate, so the societies avoided the problem of disintermediation that has plagued the U.S. thrifts (although with the recent growth of finance obtained from the capital markets—see below—some development of fixed-interest medium-term loans is now being seen). But just as in the United States, in Britain dramatic changes in mortgage finance have occurred in the 1980s with considerable deregulation of this formerly protected circuit of finance. Banks and other financial intermediaries have entered the market with aggressive lending policies, and the building societies have been forced to adapt, abandoning restrictive practices, such as a long-standing interest-rate cartel. By the mid–1980s these new lenders had taken about 20–30 percent of the market, often lending on terms that were far more liberal than had hitherto been common. These changes have brought about an acceleration of basically defensive mergers by the building societies, which, in 1986, also obtained new legal powers to move into a range of other financial and housing activities. In 1988, following the removal of the last legal restrictions, the societies were allowed to convert from mutual entities to public limited companies providing a wide range of financial services. Within a few days of the announcement of these changes the second largest society announced that it would make this move in 1989; others are likely to follow its example.

An important consequence of the expansion of home ownership in recent years and house-price inflation is that the retail savings market can no longer supply all of the funds that are required for house purchase. Accordingly, in the early 1980s the building societies began to obtain "wholesale" funds, that is, funds raised on the money and capital markets. In 1981 only just over 1 percent of their funds were obtained in this way. By 1986, the figure was about a third. The mid–eighties has also seen the start of a secondary mortgage market—previously unknown in Britain—and the first issues of mortgage-backed securities. These changes have resulted in a greater availability of housing loans and an ending of mortgage queues, which were necessary from time to time when most of the finance came from the retail sector (given that the societies were often reluctant to raise their borrowing and lending rates to increase the inflow of funds when they lagged behind demand—sometimes because of political pressures on them not to do so). But the real cost of mortgage finance has risen sharply since the suppliers of funds are no longer willing to accept the low or even negative real rates of return that they encountered in the inflationary seventies. In the eighties nominal mortgage interest rates have ranged between 10 and 14 percent at a time when the rate of inflation has been falling—to below 5 percent by 1987. This has had serious consequences for the affordability of home ownership, which is discussed below.

Public Sector

Construction in the public sector has normally been financed by loans raised on the private capital and money markets. The terms of the loan repayments vary, although new building has been amortized over sixty years. The funds come from each local authority's general loans pool, which consists of many individual medium- and short-term loans. For many years there were no significant central government controls on public housing capital expenditures, although there was some control of rates of building through, in particular, changes in the subsidies that were available for every house built. However, the economic crisis of the mid–seventies resulted in controls being imposed by the then Labour government, which later became highly restrictive. Since the early eighties, as the levels of permitted new capital spending have been slashed, local authorities have been allowed to use a (reducing) proportion of the recipients from the sale of council houses for additional capital expenditures. In fact, new authorizations (net of the reuse of receipts) fell from about £2.8 billion at the end of the 1970s to about £1.3 billion by 1987–1988. By the latter date, as noted above, much of this was used for renovation of the existing stock as well as some building of special needs housing, for example, for the elderly (some authorities built only sheltered housing for the elderly, in part because this was not subject to the council house-sales legislation that they opposed). At the same time, reflecting its ideological preferences, the government, within a declining overall level of capital authorizations, increased the share devoted to the construction and re-habilitation of rental housing by nonprofit housing associations, up from about 15 percent of net new capital expenditures in 1979–1980 to almost 50 percent from 1982–1983 onwards.

The current expenditure of the local housing authorities is paid for by a mixture of charges (mainly rents), subsidies from the central government, and local (property) taxes. In addition, since 1980 councils also have been able to bank the capital proceeds from council housing sales and use the interest on these accounts to offset some current housing expenditures. In recent years local authority rents have risen sharply, subsidies have been reduced or eliminated, and in some areas the rent income now not only pays for most of the local authority's housing activities but subsidizes other locally provided services, too, a situation that many tenants object to.[2] These changes have dramatically altered the pattern of local housing finance. In 1977–1978 just over 40 percent of local housing expenditures were covered by rents and a similar proportion by central government subsidies. Around 10 percent was paid out of local taxes, and the balance came from other miscellaneous sources. By 1983–1984 rents covered 55 percent, but the central government contribution was only 16 percent. Local taxes still contributed 10 percent and "other income"—now mainly the interest on council house sales—a similar proportion (Leather and Murie 1986, 51).

As far as private rental housing is concerned, as has already been noted, there has been little new building since the war (although some private tenants do live in post-war housing, it is unlikely to have been built initially for rental). Insofar as landlords do buy existing housing and require capital for repairs and improvement, they have to borrow from banks and other institutions on normal commercial terms. However, in 1987–1988 a series of measures was announced by the government, including generous tax allowances for new construction, which were aimed at reviving investment in private rental housing. It will be some years before the real significance of these changes can be assessed.

Housing Costs and Incomes

Figure 2.2 shows changes in the retail price index (RPI) and various indices of housing costs for the period 1975–1987. In the latter part of the 1970s housing costs rose more or less in line with the general consumer price index, but since then, despite some fluctuations, the overall trend of homeowner mortgage payments had been sharply upwards while rents in the public sector have increased

Figure 2.2
Indices of Housing Costs, Great Britain, 1975–1987

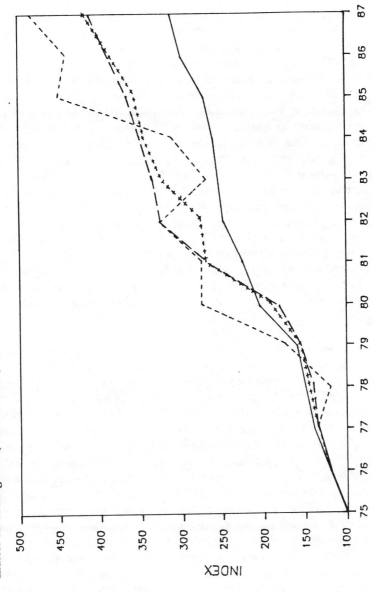

Sources: Annual Abstract of Statistics; CIPFA Housing Rents Statistics, various years.

Note: All figures are for Great Britain except council rents, which are for England and Wales.

much more rapidly than the RPI in the early 1980s. The increase in private rents has been more in line with the general rate of price rises (but see below).

Home-ownership costs have been particularly affected by the much higher real interest rates now charged for home loans, a consequence of the changes in the mortgage market discussed earlier. Between 1980 and 1986 the ratio of the average loan made to first-time buyers to their average annual incomes rose from 1.67 to 2.03, the latter figure being higher than at any time since the short-lived property boom of the early seventies. Moreover, the average percentage of the price of properties advanced on mortgages to first-time buyers rose to a historic high of just over 86 percent by 1986. Demand for home ownership has been sustained only by a considerable liberalization of lending terms, as well as by a switch to smaller properties—especially by first-time buyers. The situation is most acute in the relatively prosperous south of Britain, where house-price rises have greatly outstripped increases in earnings. By 1986 one large building society found that the average home buyer in the Southeast of England would have to find 5.2 times his or her annual income to buy the average priced house, although in the economically depressed North of England the multiple was only just over 3.0. Nationally, the price-earnings ratio has been climbing throughout the 1980s, although at 3.58 in the first quarter of 1987 it was still a good way below the extraordinary levels of well over 4.00, that it reached in the frenzied property boom of the early seventies. But there has been a widening divergence between house prices in the prosperous southern regions and in the areas of high unemployment and low wages elsewhere. In the South especially, in an increasing number of households home ownership can be afforded only if two or more earners are working and contributing to the loan repayments. In fact, house prices and the rate of house-price increase are now so high in the Southeast region that they are a serious disincentive to those not already in the regional housing market moving there to take up employment (and others are reluctant to move out of this market for employment reasons for fear that, should they wish to return later, they will be unable to do so). Nationally, there are startling differences in value for money in housing. For example, in 1987 the average price of all houses mortgaged by the building society referred to above was £43,350. For this price a purchaser could buy a modern three- or four-bedroom detached house in the North of England but only a one-bedroom converted (rather than purpose-built) apartment in an old building in London—and this only in a few of the least desirable areas of this city. (Converted apartments are units created by the subdivision of formerly single-family housing, usually of considerably lower quality than units purposely built as apartments.)

Rents in the public sector are set administratively. The rents of most housing-association tenancies are set on the so-called "fair-rent" basis that applies to some private rented tenancies (see below). Central government subsidies meet the difference between these rent levels and what the associations require to meet their expenses. From the start, the levels of council house rents were set independently by each local housing authority, taking into account the level of central government subsidy and additional subsidy that the locality wanted to make from local taxation and subject only to the general legislative provision that they should be "reasonable." There was always a wide variation in what tenants were charged and what contribution was made from local taxes. Since the late 1950s local authorities have charged pooled rents.[3] This means that rather than relate rents to the actual costs of debt servicing for each individual unit (which would result in very low rents on older property, built when costs were much lower, and very high rents on new properties, that is, relating rents to historic costs), "profits" are made by charging higher-than-cost rents on the older units and using the surplus to reduce the rents of newer units.

However, this local autonomy was breached by the 1970–1974 Conservative government, which was determined to cut subsidies and raise rents by removing the power of local authorities to set rents and link them instead to the arrangements for rent setting in the private sector. The change led to considerable political conflict, and the legislation was repealed by the following Labour government in 1975. By the end of the seventies the central government adopted a new mechanism to control rent levels. It was invented by the same Labour government but was enacted and then used to raise rents sharply by the new Conservative government after 1980.

The new law allowed the local authorities to retain their legal responsibility for rent setting, but the government assumed that there would be a certain level of rent rises when calculating the amount of subsidy payable to each authority. Local authorities were therefore forced to raise rents or to risk running large deficits on their council housing operations, deficits that would have to be met by big increases in local taxes. This latter option was, however, limited by further legislation that penalized local authorities if their local taxes were raised above specified limits. These were the reasons for the sharp increases in the level of council house rents in the early 1980s as shown in figure 2.2. In fact, between 1979 and 1982 average local authority housing rents rose by 110 percent, far faster than general prices, which increased by 55 percent in the same period. Since the latter date, rents (to 1986) have increased by only about 21 percent, in line with increases in prices during that period. The reason for this change is that as subsidies were reduced and rents increased, more and more councils were no longer in receipt of any subsidy, so the government lost the lever it had used to enforce further rapid rent increases. It could have legislated to maintain these increases at their earlier rate, but it probably has not done so because of the consequences in inflating the level of subsidies it pays to individual low-income tenants in the form of income-related housing allowances. (This point is discussed below.)

The arrangements for rent determination in the private rental sector are varied and complex. Until the late fifties on all but newly built property (of which there was very little) rents were essentially frozen at their 1939 levels, and some of them had been controlled (but subject to a few increases) since the first rent controls were introduced in 1915 as a wartime emergency measure. In 1957 the

Conservative government passed a much opposed law that would, over a period of years, have decontrolled all rents and returned them to free-market levels. This encouraged tenant harassment and illegal eviction and was repealed when Labour was returned to office in 1964. It was replaced by a system of so-called fair rents (supposed to be the rent that would be set in conditions in which there was no undue scarcity of accommodations to rent) determined by independent, publicly appointed rent officers.

This system never applied to all tenancies, and although it continued in much-amended form into the 1980s, many private sector rents were by then fixed, legally or as a consequence of evasions of the controls, on a free-market basis. So official statistics for "fair rents" refer only to a minority of lettings now occurring. This particularly applies to the furnished subsector; a higher proportion of tenants in the unfurnished subsector have "fair" rents, and rents are negatively correlated with the degree of control. In 1983 average rents in the furnished subsector were 50 percent higher than in the unfurnished subsector. Despite this, tenants in the former accommodations have less space and more sharing of amenities than those in the latter subsector. In fact, a substantial proportion of those in the furnished subsector pay over 25 percent of their income in rent (23 percent in 1979, compared with only 2 percent in the unfurnished subsector— unfortunately, more recent figures at this level of detail are not available). In hard-pressed urban housing markets, especially London, very few new tenancies are now subject to effective controls on rents or security of tenure, and a survey in 1983 showed that the rent per room for such a tenancy was over 300 percent higher than the average rent per room for a "fair rent" tenancy (Greater London Council 1986b). Interestingly, surveys of landlords' rates of return show that they are around 4–6 percent of capital values for "fair rented" tenancies outside areas where there is excess demand but only 2–3 percent in London where, as noted above, house prices are very high. So the rates of return on free-market rentals in the capital city probably range from 5 to 10 percent.

HOUSING INSTITUTIONS AND ORGANIZATIONS

Some details have already been provided concerning the various housing institutions and organizations; what follows supplements this account.

Central Government

The principal ministry responsible for housing policy in England (and related matters such as land-use planning) is the Department of the Environment (separate ministries are responsible for Scotland, Wales, and Northern Ireland). In Britain's unitary system of government national housing policies and the supporting legislation are determined by the central government. There is extensive legislation covering public and private housing, but the implementation of this legislation is mainly the responsibility of other bodies.

Local Housing Authorities

Britain has a two-tier system of elected local government. In England and Wales housing responsibilities are located with the second-tier district councils (a broadly similar system applies in Scotland; in Northern Ireland housing is controlled by the central government, and a nonelected body appointed by government exercises many of the powers and duties devolved to district councils elsewhere). Housing is one of the main responsibilities of the district councils. In 1985 there were about 400 local housing authorities in Britain with an average housing stock of about 12,000, but there is a very wide variation around this average. Thus a 1985 study of housing management in England and Wales showed that there were 12 small authorities each with a stock of less than 4,000 dwellings, a further 108 with an average stock of 4,000–8,000, and 129 with 10,000 units or more—of which 20 manage more than 40,000 properties each (Audit Commission 1986, 12, 15–16).

Within the councils the main responsibility for housing is exercised by committees of local councillors served by professionally staffed housing departments, but other departments are often involved in matters such as the control of housing conditions in the private sector and the design, planning, and construction of public housing. Local authorities have by law a general duty to be concerned with housing conditions in their areas, but they are also limited by the doctrine of *ultra vires* (that is, they may only do what is specifically permitted in the various national housing and other relevant laws). Some of these powers and duties are mandatory, but most are discretionary, so there is a considerable variation in the extent to which the councils are active in housing matters. In general, Labour-controlled councils have been more active than Conservative (or other) controlled councils especially in relation to public housing.

Housing Associations

The housing associations are nonprofit bodies that have mainly been providing an alternative form of subsidized rental housing targeted at lower-income households. Their origins are in the attempts in the latter part of the nineteenth century to provide a solution to the low-income housing problem by charitable effort. But they began to develop on a major scale only after 1974, when they first obtained major government subsidies, especially in inner cities where they bought up dilapidated private rental property and renovated it. They are scrutinized and funded via a "quango," the Housing Corporation, whose board is appointed by the government. The associations are run by boards of mainly nonelected "notables" (there is also a small but growing cooperative housing sector). The larger associations have professional staffs, but many of the smaller ones do not. In 1984 there were about 4,400 associations (including some that for various reasons, are not subject to the Housing Corporation). More than 80 percent of them owned less than 250 units, and only 5 percent owned more than 100. Less than

100 associations own two-thirds of the total housing-association stock. Moreover, only about 550 associations were involved in development activity in 1985–1986 on a significant scale.

Private Landlords

Traditionally, much of the private rental sector was owned by small landlords, as in many other countries. There were larger landlords too; for example, many insurance companies owned extensive stocks, especially of the up-market variety. But by the 1980s almost all of the larger landlords had sold off their housing, often to owner-occupiers, as the differential between vacant possession and tenanted values made this an economically rational strategy. Many landlords, especially those providing unfurnished housing, have inherited their property from relatives; many are now elderly and are themselves on fairly low incomes. Most have little inclination or the resources to upgrade their property. A lot of private rental housing has been demolished in slum-clearance schemes (especially in the 1950s and 1960s), sold off—to the sitting tenants or with vacant possession, or taken over by local authorities and housing associations for renovation and reletting as public housing. This may change as a consequence of new policies toward the sector that the government announced in 1987 (see below).

House Builders

In the past some public housing was constructed by the local authorities' own building organizations, but they have been run down in recent years and now mainly concentrate on repairs and maintenance work. Most public housing has been built by large-scale private contractors. As the demand for building has shifted from the public to the private sector these firms have developed their speculative house-building operations (as in the United States but unlike much of the rest of Western Europe, little commissioned building occurs in Britain except at the very top end of the market). As elsewhere, there are a large number of medium and small builders in Britain, although the former have been declining rapidly in recent years. The small firms tend to concentrate on repair, maintenance, and improvement work. Contrary to the popular image of a technologically backward industry, there has been rapid change in recent years, although the development of industrialized methods in the fifties and sixties (mainly in public housing) and of timber-framed construction in the seventies (in public and private housing) both ran into severe difficulties. Many of the large firms that increasingly dominate housing production are now subsidiaries of larger, nonhousing companies. They are not only able to employ the new technologies but also can put considerable resources into marketing their products as well as retaining the large land banks that are necessary to ensure continuity of production. At the same time labor organization has been undergoing rapid change, both in terms of the way in which the building process is arranged and how labor is employed. There has been an extensive growth of subcontracting and self-employment in the industry and a serious decline in the training of the necessary skills; these trends have been accentuated by the depressed levels of house building in the 1980s, during which time building workers have suffered very high rates of unemployment.

Building Societies

Reference has already been made to the role of the building societies. They have a unique legal status as mutual institutions and are exempt from many of the controls that govern other financial institutions. Their origins lie in the eighteenth century when special forms of friendly societies were formed to collect members' subscriptions and build houses for them. In the nineteenth century this type of society was gradually superseded by the modern form of building society in which there is no necessary link between investors and borrowers. Until recently, the societies had to use most of their funds for lending on a first mortgage to private individuals for house purchase or improvement. Any surplus from their operations is added to reserves rather than being distributed to "shareholders" (i.e., investors each of which can own only one share per society). The societies have benefited from various forms of tax relief, although such relief has been eroded in recent years. The societies are formally run by boards of directors elected by their members (i.e., by those who deposit funds with the societies, not those who borrow from them). In fact, their directorates are largely self-perpetuating, and most policy is made by their paid professional managers. There has been acute competition in recent years for new deposits, both among the societies and with other financial institutions such as the banks. This has driven up the interest rates offered to depositors and paid by borrowers. It has also involved considerable investment in new technology, advertising, and branch offices and the expansion into a range of other financial services such as the provision of cash dispensers, travelers checks, and, now, with the aid of the new legislation, consumer loans. It is likely that before long the largest societies will renounce their special legal status as nonprofits and become fully fledged commercial banking and financial services operations. These changes have resulted in an accelerating degree of concentration since the smaller societies are unable to compete and are forced to merge with larger bodies. Thus the number of societies was halved, from 782 to 382, between 1953 and 1975 and reduced by well over half again, down to only 148 by 1986. As of 1986 the largest 5 societies controlled 57 percent of all building-society assets and the largest 10 just under 80 percent. The biggest societies are financial giants, controlling more assets than the main commercial banks.

Although the role of the banks and some other financial intermediaries has greatly expanded in recent years, it is still minor in relation to their share of the stock of outstanding mortgage loans. For many years local authorities also lent considerable sums for private house purchases, and they still have the power to do so. Most of their loans were aimed at assisting moderate-income buyers and were often concentrated in areas of older housing that the building societies were reluctant to lend on. But since the expenditure cuts that began in the later 1970s, councils have been running down their home-loan portfolios, although they still, by law, must if requested provide mortgages for ex-tenants who are buying their council houses. However, many tenant purchasers prefer to obtain private sector mortgages.

HOUSING SUBSIDIES AND ALLOCATION

Subsidies

There are two main and long-established subsidies for homeowners. They are mortgage-interest tax relief and exemption from the capital gains tax that is payable on other appreciating assets. Tax relief may be claimed on the first £30,000 of housing loans and at the individual's marginal income tax rate (in 1988 most earners paid 25 percent after certain allowances, but the highest marginal rate was 40 percent). Until 1988 the £30,000 limit applied to individuals and married couples, so two or more unmarried earners could join together to buy a house, each claiming the maximum tax relief. This became especially significant in the high-cost housing markets of southern England. However, in 1988 this loophole was abolished. Now the limit for tax relief applies to the property. At the same time, tax relief on loans for improvement was abolished. There has been much criticism of these subsidies, which are regressive with respect to income. The only significant modification to this regressivity is that, since 1967, mortgagors who do not pay tax have had their interest payments reduced by an amount equivalent to what they would have received had they been taxpayers. To date none of the major political parties is prepared to legislate for the reform of owner-occupier tax reliefs since this is widely regarded as a path to political suicide.

There are also a range of government grants, as discussed earlier, administered by the local authorities, available for the repair and improvement of private housing. In some areas these grants have been used by gentrifying speculators who buy up older rented housing, remove (by fair means or foul) their tenants, and improve the property for resale to homeowners (grants are also available for private landlords, but relatively few have used them).

Since the passage of legislation in 1980 that forced councils to sell off their public housing to those tenants who wanted to buy, there has been a further major subsidy to private housing in the form of extensive sales-price discounts (up to 70 percent depending on the length of tenancy and the type of unit). In recent years the increases in house prices along with the much higher interest rates and the general expansion of home ownership have led to a rapid escalation of the costs to the government of the two main forms of tax relief for home ownership; these tax losses amounted to about £6.5 billion in 1985–1986. Public spending on tax relief in 1979–1980 was about one-third the level of expenditure on the public sector (excluding the cost of individual housing allowances but including improvement grants that also mainly benefit homeowners), but by the mid–1980s it had exceeded the latter level, a position that was exacerbated by the sharp reductions in public sector subsidies over this period as well as the rise in interest rates and house prices that automatically inflated the levels of tax relief. In addition, between 1980 and 1983 about £2.9 billion of additional subsidies went to home ownership in the form of discounts of council house sales.

Public Sector Subsidies

The public sector subsidies have a much more complicated history. Until the 1960s the government paid a fixed annual amount to local councils for each new house they built in order to reduce the annual debt charges. The size of the subsidy varied according to the particular housing act under which the houses were constructed. However, as interest rates rose to unprecedentedly high levels in the 1960s, new construction was subsidized by payments that reduced the effective interest rate on the construction loans (but it was still a fixed subsidy thereafter). These arrangements were changed in the early 1970s, and again in mid-decade. In addition to receiving these building subsidies local authorities received specific subsidies for other activities such as the acquisition and im-provement of formerly privately owned housing. In 1980 these specific subsidies were abolished to be replaced by a single subsidy, based on a formula set by government. Essentially, the subsidy now covers the difference between the annual increases in loan charges on the local authorities' housing investment plus other costs (such as repairs, maintenance, management, and administration) and the sum that the government assumes can be raised locally. This "local contribution" comes mainly from public housing rents. This subsidy formula is the mechanism described earlier that the government used to force up the levels of rents in the early 1980s and which has resulted in many authorities no longer receiving any subsidy.

In addition, local authorities have always been able to make extra contributions to the costs of running their housing operations from local property taxation— until now the sole form of local taxation but due to be replaced by a form of poll tax in the early 1990s. For many years local authorities were legally required to make such a contribution. Since the mid–fifties it has been discretionary— and has declined in importance. Under proposals announced in 1987 it will no longer be permissible, at least with respect to subsidizing the costs of operating council housing.

Housing associations are subsidized in a different way, by means of capital grants to reduce the initial cost of building plus annual grants to meet any remaining deficit in the costs of their operations. Apart from their eligibility for the various forms of renovation or repair grants noted above, private landlords have not received direct subsidies in the postwar period. Moreover, unlike many other businesses, they have been unable to set depreciation against income for taxation purposes, although they can offset certain expenses including interest payments on loans. This adverse tax treatment has been a source of continued complaints from landlords' organizations. As mentioned earlier, tax assistance for new building was made available on closely controlled terms for some landlords from 1988.

When council housing began, the only subsidies available to the local authorities were the construction-linked payments noted above plus the contributions from local taxation, but from the 1930s councils were able to pool rents and to operate differential (i.e., income-related) rent schemes. From the mid–1950s, with encouragement from a government that wanted to economize on central subsidies, increasing numbers of local authorities pooled rents and provided individual rent allowances for low-income households. A national scheme of rent allowances was introduced in the early 1970s, in conjunction with the reforms in local housing finance, already mentioned, which aimed to increase rents and reduce subsidies. The scheme was soon made applicable to most private rental housing as well; the admissible rent for the purposes of the scheme was the "fair rent" applicable to the accommodation or an estimate of it when no "fair rent" was officially registered. Along with this system of allowances there was a long-standing separate system of housing payments made by the government to social security beneficiaries (social security is nationally determined) as well as a locally administered but nationally determined system to reduce payments of local taxation (rates) by low-income households.

In 1982 these various schemes were unified in a single system of Housing Benefit, which is administered by the local authorities but paid for out of the national social security rather than the housing budget. The scheme is administratively very complex, and the change was accompanied by confusion and conflict (as some beneficiaries lost out under the new system while others gained). As subsidies for public housing authorities have declined, unemployment (in the early eighties) has increased, and rents have been driven up, the costs of the Housing Benefit scheme have risen sharply. Indeed, one reason that, after the early eighties, the government did not press ahead with further rapid rent increases relates to the declining level of net savings in public expenditures actually achieved by higher rents and higher housing benefit payouts. Even by 1980 it was calculated that for every increase of £1 in rental income for public housing an extra 40p had to be paid out in benefits.

By the mid–1980s on many public housing projects 60–70 percent of the tenants were receiving housing benefits. The total cost of the pre–1983 allowances (excluding payments through the social security system) rose by about 250 percent between 1976 and 1983, to just under £1 billion. Between 1984, when the new scheme was fully operational, and 1986 the costs rose by almost 25 percent to over £4 billion (this total, however, includes the payments to social security recipients). Taken together with the reductions in subsidies to local housing authorities, there has therefore been a massive switch of emphasis from support for new housing investment toward consumer subsidies (note, too, that the subsidies for owner occupation mainly involve support for housing exchange rather than investment in new or improved housing). As the costs of the allowances rose, however, the government began to make changes in its provisions to reduce eligibility and restrain individual levels of payment. This, together with the fact that an estimated 25–30 percent of those who are potentially eligible do not make a claim, means that many low-income households have suffered growing hardship because of the rapid increases in rents and local taxes.

Allocation and Related Issues

Access to private housing is mainly determined by ability to pay. The key gatekeepers for home ownership are the institutions that provide mortgage finance. There is evidence that some of them have discriminated against ethnic minorities and women, and, as already noted, realtors have steered black home seekers away from certain areas, but their role has probably been less significant than in the United States. Levels of ethnic segregation anyway are rarely as high in Britain as they are in many areas of the United States. Private landlords are often highly discriminatory in their choice of tenants, not only on ethnic grounds but also, for example, by discriminating against families with children. But in such a fragmented sector it is difficult to discern any clear overall patterns. Discrimination in housing on grounds of race is in fact illegal, although enforcement of the law is very weak.

The rules for allocation of public housing are matters for local determination and, in the case of housing associations, by these organizations themselves. However, local authorities are under a legal duty to offer accommodations to households displaced by slum clearance (which they also carry out). In the 1950s and 1960s this was an important factor in housing allocation. However, due to the removal of the worst Victorian slums, a major switch from demolition to rehabilitation in older housing, and the more recent public expenditure cuts, slum clearance fell from a peak annual rate of about 60,000 in the early 1960s to less than 10,000 in England and Wales in 1985–1986. Its place as a major source of demand for rehousing has been taken by the increasing numbers of homeless households whom local authorities are obliged to rehouse.

Most other households are selected for rehousing from the waiting lists that are kept by every local housing authority. In the past many authorities favored "date order" schemes; that is, people were rehoused as property became available on the basis of their length of time on the list. Nowadays more authorities favor "point schemes"; applicants are awarded "points" according to the degree of severity of their existing housing conditions (mainly overcrowding and lack of amenities) with perhaps some small allowance for the length of time they have been on the waiting list. Urgent medical cases may also receive rehousing priority, and there may be special, separate schemes for particular groups such as the elderly and, occasionally, the young.

In general, families with children and the elderly have a much higher priority for rehousing than single people of below retirement age, childless couples, or other adult households. In 1985–1986, 62 percent of all new lettings in England were to households on the waiting list, 22 percent to the homeless, and 16 percent to other categories. The proportion going to the homeless has been rising, thus increasing the time that most other applicants have to wait. This situation has been made worse by the reduction in new building that has occurred as well as the loss of relets due to council house sales (over a million were sold between 1979 and 1986, although the rate peaked in 1983 and has since been declining— this amounts to about 15 percent of the total council stock as of 1981). There is considerable evidence of racial discrimination in letting, as mentioned earlier, and many authorities also have tended to concentrate "problem families" in particular sections of the housing stock, thus often exacerbating their difficulties and the deterioration of these housing areas. In general, the allocation procedures of the housing associations are similar to those of the local authorities, although they are not under a legal duty to house the homeless, ex-slum dwellers, or any other specific type of needy household.

CURRENT PROBLEMS, POLICIES, AND FUTURE PROSPECTS

The postwar period has seen an immense improvement in British housing conditions. Initially, it was the expansion of public housing that spearheaded this development; later a major role was also taken by new building for home ownership and, from the late sixties onwards, the improvement of older private housing, often involving tenure conversion from rental to ownership.

In many Western European countries there have been strong links between housing policy and wider economic policies. For example, in the Netherlands, France, and West Germany, especially in the period until the 1960s, housing policies were strongly influenced by the postwar reconstruction and modernization of their economies. In the case of West Germany, there was also a strong desire to secure the political and social order against possible challenge from within and without the new state. The encouragement of small-scale property capital was seen as having a central role in achieving this objective. These broader economic and political goals were less evident in Britain. No very special effort was made to restructure the economy after the war, although a certain amount of housing was provided in conjunction with a policy of building new towns, some of which were intended to provide growth poles in areas of the country that had been economically depressed in the interwar period. Housing investment also has been used occasionally as an economic regulator. More often it has been reduced in response to macroeconomic problems.

Housing policies, however, have not simply, or even to a predominant degree, been a response to housing needs, except perhaps in the period from 1945 to the mid–1950s and again briefly in the early years of the Labour governments in the 1960s and 1970s. As in the United States, in Britain the private housing industry has increasingly dominated housing production and exchange. Speculative house building and private mortgage finance developed rapidly from the 1950s in ways that were very similar to those occurring in the United States. In contrast, in many other European countries, this rise to dominance of the private housing industry took longer and faced more difficulties. This growth in private housing activity has provided a major stimulus for a wide range of consumer-goods industries; for example, do-it-yourself stores and garden centers have been among the most rapidly growing commercial enterprises in the past twenty years, and this expansion is directly linked to the growth in home ownership. In addition, the building societies have become some of the most powerful financial institutions in the country, challenging the major commercial banks. This struggle is about to be taken a step further as the larger societies convert from mutual institutions limited to lending for house purchase to major general-purpose financial institutions; some of them now have the resources to take over commercial banks, and they are also expanding within the housing market, for example, by buying up chains of real estate agencies.

So the private housing market has a powerful influence on housing policies. But political support for home ownership has been ideologically driven as well. The Conservative party in particular has always believed in the value of the ''property-owning democracy''; its commitment to large-scale public housing was never permanent but inspired by temporary circumstances, for example, the need to reduce the absolute housing shortage after the war and before the private market had revived and the need to complete slum clearance in the 1950s and 1960s. Labour's strong commitment to social housing lasted as long as this tenure provided necessary housing for its core supporters, the more skilled and often unionized working class. But as this group began to move into home ownership in the 1950s and 1960s the Labour party also shifted toward increasingly strong support for private housing and began to accept that public housing would, in the future, be confined to a supplementary role, housing those who could not afford home ownership. In the first instance this was probably simply a recognition that continued coolness to home ownership was becoming electorally damaging; later there was a perceptible shift in ideological priorities. Interestingly, Labour has gone through a similar set of changes in the 1980s. Initially, it strongly opposed the forced sale of council housing, but after it lost a second election in 1983 it reluctantly accepted that the policy was popular with many of its former supporters. By the 1987 general election Labour had fully endorsed the sales policy and, more generally, accepted large parts of the Conservative critique of the faults of council housing, providing only a rather weak Parliamentary opposition to the new proposals introduced after this election to break up large-scale holdings of public housing.

So the expansion of home ownership has been aided by both major political parties. Their attitudes to rental housing, especially in the 1940s and 1950s, differed more significantly, Labour being for public housing and the Conservatives being ideologically inclined toward the private landlord. However, in practice for much of the time, whether the Conservatives or Labour was in power, the expansion of public housing continued, and little or nothing was done to stem the decline of private rental housing. Subsidies greatly assisted the development of mass home ownership and public housing while private rented housing got virtually no support. It was this differential financial treatment, not just the persistence of rent and security controls, that made private renting a "poor relation" in the British housing system. The growth of home ownership was underpinned by the years of full employment and rising real incomes, lasting until the late 1970s.

Since then both the political and the economic situation has altered radically. Although those in employment have continued in most cases to benefit from rising real incomes, unemployment had increased rapidly to well over 3 million (and probably nearer 4 million if the effect of "adjustments" in the way in which official figures are now calculated is discounted) in the early 1980s and had only begun to dip below this level in 1987. There was also a big increase in the proportion of the elderly in the population in the 1960s and 1970s. Therefore, there was a growing mass of the population dependent on state benefits as their only source of income. Most required access to subsidized rental housing if they were to achieve better housing conditions, or indeed any housing in some cases, as the rise in homelessness illustrates. Unemployment was especially high in major inner-city areas, among young households who were newly entering the housing market, and among ethnic minorities.

At the same time the developments in mortgage finance discussed earlier have meant that even those who have entered the private housing market now find housing less affordable. There are various indicators of this problem; for example, the number of mortgage defaults increased by about 800 percent between 1979 and 1986 and late payments by about 400 percent, and there are many more "forced sales" to avoid default or arrears (although this is as yet not a serious problem for the financial institutions concerned). Another indicator of rising affordability problems is the already mentioned growth of the necessity for more than one earner to contribute to mortgage repayments and a shift in new building toward smaller houses and apartments (some of which reflects the changed demographic composition of the population, but not all). The liberalization of mortgage lending rules that has occurred (increases in the proportion of the house price that will be lent and increases in the ratio of the sum borrowed to the borrower's annual income) are also responses to the affordability problem. Finally, as the data on house conditions illustrated, disinvestment in the existing stock is leading to an increase in defective accommodation, reversing the long-term trend toward better-quality housing.

Not all of these changes are well recognized by politicians, or by the general public—most of whom remain reasonably well housed at costs they can afford.

It is the changes in housing policies that have received far more attention. Here there has been a radical break with the basic approach to housing that, despite some differences, the main political parties have accepted in previous decades— the approach based on a mixture of public and private provision. The reduction in state support for public housing began in earnest under the 1974–1979 Labour government. However, these cuts were made out of (presumed) necessity rather than conviction. In contrast, the post–1979 cuts have been made out of conviction and in accordance with a distinctively different conception of the state's role in housing provision from that accepted by the Labour party or, in essence, by previous Conservative governments. Although the government's policies have evolved over time in ever more radical directions, the general objective has been to disengage the state (including local government) from the direct provision of housing, to encourage more home ownership and, in theory at least, to reduce subsidies.[4] In fact, in the first two Thatcher governments (1979–1987), while subsidies for public housing were severely reduced, those for private housing continued to increase and were added to by the council house sales discounts. At the same time, while public housing rents were raised and some cuts were made in the conditions for the receipt of the Housing Benefit, the costs of this escalated. Small steps were taken in the early 1980s, mainly involving changes in regulatory legislation, to encourage private rental housing investment, but these steps were almost wholly ineffective. More significantly, there were some small-scale experiments in which public housing projects were sold off to private developers for refurbishment and reletting or sale to homeowners. Most of these projects were among the 300,000 or so "hard-to-let" units. There were also some pilot schemes aimed at improving the management and physical conditions in other parts of this stock (and more generally in the public sector). These plans involved decentralized management (the inflexibility of large-scale bureaucratic local housing departments has been a target for much criticism) and occasionally the transfer of some management responsibilities to tenant cooperatives.

The sales of council housing and the cuts in new building reduced the share of public housing in the total stock by about 5 percent between 1979 and 1987. But, as already noted, even with the extensive discounts for tenant purchasers, sales decreased after 1983. The problem for the government was that there was a limit to how far its privatization strategy could be pushed, given that fewer and fewer of the remaining tenants could afford to buy even with the discounts. So in 1987 the government introduced new legislation that aims at a far more radical alteration of the rental housing market. Now it seems to be accepted that *some* households will always want or need to rent (perhaps around 30 percent). So the basic objective of the new policy is to replace the public rental sector as the houser of lower-income households by a combination of the private rental sector, housing associations, tenant cooperatives, and private "housing trusts."

Principal features of this new legislation include the following:

- a right for the public sector tenants to "opt out" of public sector management in favor of a new landlord or by forming a tenant cooperative. It seems likely that government will find a way to put considerable pressure on tenants to make this seem an attractive option;
- the establishment of "housing action trusts" by the government to take over areas of run-down local authority housing, improving it, and then selling it to new owners;
- decontrol of the rents of new lettings by private landlords and measures that will probably remove most of the long-term security of tenure that some tenants have enjoyed in the past; and
- decontrol of new housing association rents as well as new arrangements that will provide shallower subsidies for the associations to build higher-income rental property with a greater degree of private capital involvement.

The government also proposed to remove the right of councils to make contributions to the cost of public housing from local taxation. According to the government statement on the new policies, in the future

there will no longer be the same presumption that the local authority itself should take direct action to meet new or increasing demands. The future role of local authorities will essentially be a strategic one identifying housing needs and demands, encouraging innovative methods of provision by other bodies to meet such needs, maximizing the use of private finance, and encouraging the new interest in the revival of the independent rented sector. (Secretaries of State for the Environment and Wales 1987, 14)

It remains to be seen just how far this intention of virtually eliminating the public role in the direct provision of lower income housing will go. Already in 1987 it was clear that some new development of unsubsidized or, more likely, shallowly subsidized rental housing would occur, especially in London and the South of England, where significant numbers of younger middle-income households could no longer afford to buy. But even by the mid–1970s more than 50 percent of public housing tenants were below what has conventionally been accepted as the poverty line. By 1987, in a time of mass unemployment and following the loss of many better-off households from the sector via council house sales, this proportion had risen to 63 percent. So the new strategy will be crucially dependent for its success on the level of subsidies that the government is willing to provide (and the extent to which lower-income households can be forced to accept increasingly onerous housing-cost burdens).

There was no indication that the government, while introducing its new legislation, was prepared for a major increase in housing subsidies, and it appeared to believe that private money would substitute for reduced public finance for housing investment. Ironically, a strategy of switching from the public to the private sector is much *less* viable in the 1980s that it would have been in previous years, when there was full employment and rising real incomes for all but a small fraction of the population and when the cost of capital for housing was far less than in this decade. One solution would be to redistribute the subsidies radically from home ownership to the support of the "new" rental sector via, for example, a single means-tested housing allowance, covering homeowners and renters. However, this has many technical problems, and it would probably be more feasible to have a new more-limited subsidy system for lower-income home buyers and new entrants to the housing market. But in a country where two-thirds of the population live in their own homes (or are at least buying them), despite the fact that many do badly as a result of the present regressive tax subsidies, few major politicians are prepared to contemplate such reforms and certainly not the Thatcher government.

Responses to the changes in housing policy that have occurred since 1979 have been muted. After initial opposition, the Labour party rapidly accepted the principle of council house sales. In addition, it has been unable to arouse much public support for its opposition to other aspects of the Conservatives "privatization" of public housing, nor has it managed to make much critical impact over issues such as the new deterioration of the housing stock, the rising level of homelessness, or the affordability problems for many would-be home buyers. In the 1987 General Election campaign the Labour party put forward a program for housing that did contain some limited evidence of fresh thinking. The centerpiece of the program was a major increase in housing investment, but there was little said about how this program was to be paid for. One obvious possibility was a radical reform of the present home-ownership subsidies, but here Labour remained trapped within the conventional wisdom regarding the unacceptability of any such reforms to the electorate, so the sections of Labour's policy document dealing with finance were anodyne.

More extensive proposals for reform came from two reports published in 1986 by blue-ribbon commissions. The first, "British Housing," was chaired by the Duke of Edinburgh; the second, established by the Archbishop of Canterbury, was concerned more broadly with issues relevant to the problems of inner cities, including housing. Both reports called for a radical restructuring of housing finance. Neither has made much political impact, although certain proposals put forward by the Duke's commission relating to the breakup of the local authority housing stock and the revitalization of the private rental sector proved to be very much in line with current government thinking anyway (private sector interests were strongly represented on this commission, and they had a big influence on its recommendations).

Several groups campaign on behalf of the homeless and badly housed; many of them originate from the period of grass-roots political activism that occurred in the 1960s and early 1970s. Their influence on housing policies has waned since then. In part this is a reflection of the generally more conservative political culture of the 1980s, but there are also particular reasons why campaigns for housing reform now arouse less response than issues such as those relating to education or health services. In Britain most education and health care is provided through state-run and -financed services. This has never been the case in housing where a majority of the population has always been dependent on the private market, formerly on private rental housing and now on home ownership. But from World War I to the late 1950s at least there was major support for the expansion of public housing from large sections of the organized working class. This found expression through the trade unions to which many of these workers belonged and through their political expression, the Labour party. But the expansion of home ownership has meant that many of the types of household that either lived in or hoped to live in public housing in the early postwar years now either live in, or aspire to live in, their own homes. As already noted, there has been an increasing concentration of low-income households in council housing. Much of this population is outside the labor market and is not engaged in trade union or Labour party activity. As a consequence, they have a weak political voice. It is this combination of political and economic (and, indeed, social) disadvantage that some recent housing researchers have been referring to when they suggest that public housing is becoming a form of "residual" provision, housing an increasingly "marginalized" population, that is, a population that is marginal to the requirements of the contemporary British economy and to the mainstream of its politics.

British housing markets and policies are now in a period of substantial restructuring. The political and economic landscape has been altered by developments such as the massive deindustrialization that has occurred in the past few years and the accompanying growth of poverty and unemployment and by the end of the postwar political consensus on the main outlines of the welfare state. All of this makes any firm predictions about what the next few years will bring a risky business. Recent housing policies have been driven more by ideological imperatives than by rational analysis of what is required to resolve problems such as deteriorating stock, homelessness, or the affordability of home ownership. Those on the Center or Left of politics who always argued for a "mixed economy" in housing, based on the private market but with state involvement to ensure greater equality in housing than the market alone can provide, have been relegated to the sidelines in the contemporary politics of housing. They have as yet not been able to mount any convincing counterproposals to the current policy directions followed by the government. A very few analysts of housing markets and policies now argue (as do their counterparts in countries such as the United States and West Germany) that far more radical change is necessary if decent and affordable housing for all is to be made a reality. Some of them also argue that the private market in housing is now built on foundations (for example, in relation to the new structures of housing finance) that are extremely fragile. But although the market continues to provide reasonable housing conditions for the majority of the population, it is unlikely that much political support will be mobilized for the sort of changes that the radical reformers advocate. However, as the government's new policies are implemented over the next few years the ability of the market to deliver may be crucially tested.

Meanwhile, the housing agenda continues to be dominated by the broader political, social, and economic objectives of the government—rather than any narrower concern with problems such as housing decay or affordability. It is often not recognized, even in Britain, that the sale of council housing has been the largest element in the government's program of privatizing state assets, and the new proposals to dispose of local authority housing to private landlords will take this process a step further. For some time, but especially since the mid–1980s, it has become clear that the Thatcher government has been embarked on a fundamental effort to weaken permanently and, it hopes, eventually to eradicate the last bases of support for the blend of the mixed economy with a fairly extensive "welfare state" that dominated British society and politics from 1945 to the late 1970s. Privatization is much more than simply a way of saving on public expenditure and raising money to reduce the public sector borrowing requirement. It is also aimed at creating a much wider spread of small-scale property and capital ownership among the population, increasing the recourse to private welfare linked to the ability to pay and reducing the state role, and reshaping state institutions so that their collectivist objectives are replaced by a commitment to fostering these other objectives. Politically, the objective is to exclude permanently the Labour party and all those who espouse collectivism from government or at least from the opportunity to implement such policies. In the aftermath of her third election victory in 1987 Margaret Thatcher was open in stating these aims, and the new housing policies have subsequently been accompanied by further privatizations, increased controls over local government finance, and moves to begin the breakup of the National Health Service and state provided education.

The British housing system has several characteristics that may hold lessons for other nations. Its private housing industry is highly developed, and home ownership is even today more extensive than in closely comparable nations in Western Europe. It has put a good deal of effort into housing improvement, and the scope and limits of these policies would merit close study by those who are trying to deal with aging housing stocks. In addition, it still has the largest public housing sector of any Western nation, and both the problems and the many achievements of this means of providing social housing are of considerable interest. However, during the next few years, the key developments to follow will undoubtedly be those that are linked to the government's current attempt to replace social housing by forms of private sector renting. In several respects these initiatives mark a reversion to late-Victorian "solutions" to the problem of lower-income housing, in the era before public housing was politically acceptable. Then much (misplaced) reliance was put on the ability of the private rental market and of "5 percent philanthropy" to solve the "housing question." The government's proposals for the breakup of public housing and its disposal to a mix of commercial and limited profit landlords, nonprofit housing associations, and cooperatives looks familiar to those with a long view of British housing history. Moreover, the proposed new role for local housing authorities, regulating but not intervening directly in the lower-income housing provision, also has nineteenth-century parallels. From the 1840s to the early 1900s the major emphasis in British housing legislation was on just such a regulative role. Although the limitations of this approach were evident well before 1914, it took the social, economic, and political crisis of the war years to bring about a definitive shift in policy direction. This process was sustained by the exigencies of the interwar period and then World War II and the postwar housing shortages. Further housing historians may identify the 1970s and 1980s as a period when a new social and economic crisis led to a radical shift away from the politics of the mixed economy and the welfare state, and with it the onset of a new Victorian age in housing, to accompany the rebirth of those "Victorian values" that Margaret Thatcher, in a famous speech, committed herself to fostering.

Alternatively, the ability of the private market to deliver lower-income housing without massive and continuing state support may be tested and found wanting, as it was in Victorian Britain. However, the political consequences of such failure will not necessarily lead to a reversion to the status quo ante. Provided that the majority of the population remains reasonably well housed, the living conditions of the poor—increasingly marginal to the labor market and with little organized political voice—may remain a topic of limited governmental concern. In this respect Britain's housing future may now be converging with that of the United States and other postindustrial societies.

NOTES

1. There is a third subsector, not discussed in this chapter. It involves tenancies held in connection with employment. Here rents are often low or nonexistent, being a part of the remuneration for the job. The largest group of such tenancies consists of farm workers' housing.

2. Until 1972 local authority housing could not be run at a "profit." Between 1972 and 1975 "profits" could be made, but a proportion of them had to be remitted to the national exchequer. Then, between 1975 and 1980, the nonprofit rule was reinstated. Since 1980 "profits" have again been allowed, but now all of them are retained locally, thus reducing the property taxes paid by all local taxpayers, including local authority tenants. These shifts in policy have coincided with moves away from and back to purely cost-covering rent regimes.

3. Local authorities were first allowed to pool rents in 1935. However, little use was made of this facility until the mid–fifties. At this time the Conservative government began to cut back on housing subsidies, and the cross-subsidy that pooling allows helped achieve this objective.

4. Paradoxically, this supposed disengagement has in practice involved several measures that have greatly increased central government controls over the local authorities— for example, regarding levels of housing investment, rents, and local taxation and the policy of forced council house sales.

REFERENCES

Audit Commission for for Local Authorities in England and Wales, The. 1985. *Capital Expenditure Controls in Local Government in England*. London: Her Majesty's Stationery Office.

————. 1986. *Managing the Crisis in Council Housing*. London: Her Majesty's Stationery Office.

Cantle, Ted. 1986. "The Deterioration of Public Sector Housing." In *The Housing Crisis*, edited by P. Malpass, 57–85. London: Croom Helm.

Fleming, Michael C., and Joseph G. Nellis. 1982. "A New Housing Crisis?" *Lloyds Bank Review* 144:38–53.

Forrest, Ray, and Alan Murie. 1983. "Residualization and Council Housing: Aspects of the Changing Social Relations of Housing Tenure." *Journal of Social Policy* 12, no. 4:453–68.

Greater London Council, The. 1986a. *Homelessness in London: A Statement and Recommendations by the Research Team*. London.

————. 1986b. *Private Tenants in London: The GLC Survey 1983–4*. London.

Hamnett, Chris. 1983. "Split City." *Roof* (July–August): 13–14.

Leather, Philip, and Alan Murie. 1986. "The Decline in Public Expenditure." In *The Housing Crisis*, edited by P. Malpass, 24–56. London: Croom Helm.

Murie, Alan. 1983. *Housing Inequality and Deprivation*. London: Heinemann.

Robinson, Ray, and Tony O'Sullivan. 1983. "Housing Tenure Polarisation: Some Empirical Evidence." *Housing Review* (July–August):116–17.

Secretaries of State for the Environment and Wales, The. 1987. *Housing: The Government's Proposals*. Cm 214. London: Her Majesty's Stationery Office.

Thomas, Andrew D. 1986. *Housing and Urban Renewal*. London: Alan & Unwin.

FURTHER READING

The decennial population census contains much information on the housing stock and its occupants but no data on costs and incomes. The key volume from the last census is Office of Population Censuses and Surveys, *Census 1981, Housing and Households, England and Wales* (London: Her Majesty's Stationery Office, 1983). This also has an index of housing-related data contained in other volumes of the census reports. Other important government surveys include the *General Household Survey* and the *Family Expenditure Survey*, both published regularly by Her Majesty's Stationery Office. Of more historic interest now is Department of the Environment, *National Dwelling and Housing Survey* (London: Her Majesty's Stationery Office, 1979). Very useful historical data and history are also found in Department of the Environment, *Housing Policy Technical Volume, Parts I–III* (London: Her Majesty's Stationery Office, 1977). The department also brings together a wide range of data in its *Housing and Construction Statistics*, published annually by Her Majesty's Stationery Office. Finally, there is Alan Clinton, *Housing Statistics: A Guide to Sources* (London: Institute of Housing, 1986) obtainable from the Institute at Angel House, White Lion Square, London N1.

Useful data and articles on matters relating to the building societies and owner occupation can be found in the quarterly *BSA Bulletin*, published by the Building Societies Association (3 Savile Row, London W1X 1AF), and in bulletins from some of the major building societies (for example, Nationwide Anglia Building Society, Chesterfield House, Bloomsbury Way, London WC1V 6PW). The local authority finance officers' professional body publishes statistics on many aspects of local authority housing finance including rents and homelessness (Chartered Institute of Public Finance and Accountancy, 3 Robert Street, London WC2).

The following books contain full accounts of the long-term development of the major tenures: Stephen Merrett, *State Housing in Britain* (1979), and his *Owner Occupation in*

Britain (1982), both published by Routledge & Kegan Paul (London and Boston); and Michael Harloe, *Private Rented Housing in the United States and Europe* (London: Croom Helm; New York: St. Martin's Press, 1985). Michael Ball, *Housing Policy and Economic Power* (London and New York: Methuen, 1983), is an important analysis of home ownership in the context of the house-building industry. A slightly dry but full discussion of urban renewal policy is Andrew Thomas, *Housing and Urban Renewal* (London and Boston: Allen & Unwin, 1986).

Many recent publications deal with the contemporary housing situation. Among the most enlightening are Peter Malpass, *The Housing Crisis* (London: Croom Helm, 1986); Peter Malpass and Alan Murie, *Housing Policy and Practice* (London: Macmillan, 1987); this one also contains useful detail on the policy-making; David Clapham and John English, eds., *Public Housing: Current Trends and Future Developments* (London: Croom Helm, 1987); Christine Whitehead and Mark Kleinman, *Private Rented Housing in the 1980s and 1990s* (Cambridge, Eng.: Granta Editions, 1986); and Anne Power, *Property before People* (London and Boston: Allen & Unwin, 1987), the history of local authority housing management and much on the contemporary problems of management and of the severely deteriorated public housing estates.

The best recent discussion of housing deprivation is in Alan Murie, *Housing Inequality and Deprivation* (London: Heinemann Educational Books, 1983). On ethnic minorities, the key source is Colin Brown, *Black and White Britain* (Aldershot, Eng.: Gower, 1985); and on women and housing, Sophie Watson with Helen Austerberry, *Housing and Homelessness: A Feminist Perspective* (London: Routledge & Kegan Paul, 1986). There are chapters on the housing of the young and of the elderly in Malpass, *The Housing Crisis*. A survey on state of homelessness and related policy issues can be found in the chapter by Bob Widdowson, in *Year Book of Social Policy, 1986–7*, edited by Maria Brenton and Clare Ungerson, pp. 215–230 (Harlow, Eng.: Longman, 1987).

There are many important but more specialized studies on some of the topics mentioned in the chapter, as well as on some that there was not space to include. Among them are John Doling and Mary Davies, *Public Control of Privately Rented Housing* (Aldershot, Eng.: Gower, 1984), on "fair rents"; Doreen Massey and Alejandrina Catalano, *Capital and Land* (London: Edward Arnold, 1978), on landownership, dated but still useful; Michael Dunn, Marilyn Rawson, and Alan Rodgers, *Rural Housing: Competition and Choice* (London and Boston: Allen & Unwin, 1981), a topic on which little is published; Valerie Karn, Jim Kemeny, and Peter Williams, *Home Ownership in the Inner City: Salvation or Despair?* (Aldershot, Eng.: Gower, 1985), an important study of low-income owner occupation; John Ermisch, *Housing Finance: Who Gains?* (London: Policy Studies Institute, 1984); Jeff Henderson and Valerie Karn, *Race, Class, and State Housing* (Aldershot, Eng.: Gower, 1987), on racism in council housing allocation; and Peter Ambrose, *Whatever Happened to Planning?* (London and New York: Methuen, 1986), on land-use planning.

The recent blue-ribbon commission reports referred to in the chapter are Inquiry into British Housing, *Report* (London: National Federation of Housing Associations, 1985); and Archbishop of Canterbury's Commission on Urban Priority Areas, *Faith in the City* (London: Church House Publishing, 1985). The Labour party's recent proposals are found in The Labour Party, *Homes for the Future* (London, 1985). A discussion of all of these reports is in an essay by Michael Harloe in Brenton and Ungerson, *Year Book of Social Policy*, pp. 196–214. The government's 1987 proposals for housing reform are contained in *Housing: The Government's Proposals*, Cm 214 (London: Her Majesty's Stationery

Office, 1987). For a radical alternative, see Michael Ball, *Home Ownership: A Suitable Case for Reform* (London: Shelter Publication, 1986).

It has not been possible in this chapter to discuss the earlier history of housing in Britain (but see Merrett, *State Housing*; and Harloe, *Private Rented Housing*). Two standard works are Enid Gauldie, *Cruel Habitations* (London: Allen & Unwin, 1974), covers 1780–1914; and John Burnett, *A Social History of Housing, 1815–1985* (London: Methuen, 1986). In recent years there also have been several excellent monographs including Mark Swenarton, *Homes Fit for Heroes* (London: Heinemann Educational Books, 1981), on early council housing; David Englander, *Landlord and Tenant in Urban Britain, 1838–1918* (Oxford: Clarendon Press, 1983); Martin Daunton, *House and Home in the Victorian City* (London: Edward Arnold, 1983); a collection edited by Daunton, *Councillors and Tenants* (Leicester, Eng.: Leicester University Press, 1984), on local authority housing in the interwar period; and Patrick Dunleavy, *The Politics of Mass Housing in Britain, 1945–75* (Oxford: Clarendon Press, 1981), mainly on high-rise, industrially built council housing. Finally, there is a detailed account of housing history to be found in Alan Holmans, *Housing Policy in Britain: A History* (London: Croom Helm, 1987); the author is the chief economic adviser to the Department of the Environment.

There are few well-researched studies of British housing in an international context. Readers might like to try the book by Harloe on private rental housing noted above; see also Michael Ball, Michael Harloe, and Maartje Martens, *Housing and Social Change in Europe and the USA* (London and New York: Routledge, 1988); Peter Dickens, Simon Duncan, Mark Goodwin, and Fred Gray, *Housing, States, and Localities* (London and New York: Methuen, 1985), on Britain and Sweden; and Roger Duclaud-Williams, *The Politics of Housing in Britain and France* (London: Heinemann, 1978).

Two of the best housing journals are *Roof* (bimonthly), published by the main campaigning body for the homeless and badly housed, but it covers all housing issues (obtainable from Shelter, 88 Old Street, London EC1V 9HU); Shelter also publishes many other relevant books and papers; and *Housing Studies* (quarterly from Longman, Fourth Avenue, Harlow, Essex CM19 5AA). Academic papers occur in the latter journal and also a range of other journals such as *Journal of Social Policy*, *International Journal of Urban and Regional Research*, *Policy and Politics*, and *Urban Studies*. There are also three major academic research centres that publish much on housing. They are the School for Advanced Urban Studies (University of Bristol); Centre for Urban and Regional Studies (University of Birmingham), and Centre for Housing Research (University of Glasgow). A comprehensive housing bibliography is produced by the Birmingham Centre, and the Library of the Department of the Environment (2 Marsham Street, London SW1) also produces various specialist bibliographies.

3

Federal Republic of Germany

WOLFGANG JAEDICKE AND HELLMUT WOLLMANN

References

Further Reading

TRENDS IN HOUSING CONDITIONS AND CONSTRUCTION: 1945–1988

In 1945, after World War II, Germany suffered from a dramatic shortage of housing; 2.3 million dwelling units out of an entire stock of 10.5 million units on the territory of what became the Federal Republic of Germany had been destroyed or severely damaged. The big cities had been most disastrously hit. In cities like Cologne, Hamburg, Hannover, and Dortmund, nearly 50 percent of the dwelling units had been destroyed. During the war years housing construction had been almost completely discontinued. The postwar emergency was still aggravated by the fact that millions of expellees and refugees from the Eastern provinces poured into the Western part of Germany occupied by the Western powers. In sum, in 1950 the Federal Republic of Germany (FRG) was short 4.8 million dwelling units (Schulz 1986, 157; von Beyme 1987, 36–43). Quantitatively, the housing supply was in as poor a condition as it had been around the turn of the century.[1] (See table 3.1.)

This urgent housing shortage was successfully combatted in the 1950s, 1960s, and early 1970s through enormous construction activities (see table 3.2).[2] In the peak year of 1973, more than 700,000 new dwelling units were constructed. By comparison, in the 1920s, during the Weimar period, the volume of newly constructed dwelling units never went beyond 320,000 units a year in the entire Reich (Blumenroth 1975, 213).

The need for construction of housing units remained high even after the war destruction had been overcome. Between 1950 and 1970 the population of the FRG grew from about 50 million to about 60 million people, particularly due

Table 3.1
Number of Dwellings per 1,000 Inhabitants, Federal Republic of Germany, 1880–1980

Year	Dwelling Units
1880	214
1890	216
1900	219
1910	222
1920	222
1930	243
1940	263
1950	214
1960	291
1970	341
1980	412

Source: Federal Statistical Office.

Table 3.2
Housing Construction, Federal Republic of Germany, 1950–1988

Year	Number of Newly Constructed Dwelling Units	Per 1,000 Inhabitants
1950	363,300	7.6
1955	562,610	8.5
1960	574.402	10.5
1965	591,916	10.0
1970	478,050	7.9
1975	436,829	7.1
1980	388,904	6.3
1985	312,124	5.1
1986	251,940	4.1
1988	208,344	3.4
1950-1988	18,597,590	

Source: Federal Statistical Office.

to the postwar baby boom and the steady stream of people that left the Communist German Democratic Republic until the Berlin Wall was erected by the East German government to stop this exodus. In the 1960s and 1970s the FRG witnessed a considerable influx of migrant workers. The number of foreign nationals increased from 3.0 million in 1970 to 4.5 million in 1980. The demand was additionally fed by the general trend of the population to form smaller households. In 1960 the households consisting of one or two persons still made up about 30 percent out of 13.3 million households. By 1982 this percentage had doubled, amounting to 60 percent out of 23.2 million households.

On the average, households have become smaller, while dwelling units have become larger. The quality of housing has clearly improved too. In 1982 two-thirds of the housing stock were equipped with bath and central heating. Only 10 percent were without bath and toilet. (See table 3.3.)

In terms of supporting housing construction through public subsidies, the promotion of owner-occupied housing has been given a high priority almost since the beginning of housing policy after 1945. Although the percentage of owner-occupied housing has markedly increased over the years, the majority of the households still lives in rental units. Households living in their own housing belong, by and large, to higher-income groups and enjoy more living space than renter households (see Deutsches Institut für Wirtschaftsforschung 1986).

Since the mid–1970s the construction of new housing has drastically receded. In 1987, not more than 217,000 new dwelling units were constructed. This reduction has been particularly marked in rental housing in multiple unit structures, which was the main field of construction in the 1950s and 1960s. In 1986,

Table 3.3
Selected Characteristics of the Housing Stock, Federal Republic of Germany, 1960–1982

Year	Number of Inhabited Dwellings in 1,000	Average Size of Dwelling in m² (1)	Percentage of Dwellings With Bath and Central Heating	Percentage of Rental Dwellings
1960	14,334	68	10	
1965	17,814	69	22	65
1972	20,633	74	42	64
1978	22,254	81	59	62
1980	22,801	82	62	61
1982	23,233	82	66	60

Source: Federal Statistical Office.

(1) Size of all inhabited rooms including kitchen, bathroom, and hall.

only 86,000 new dwelling units were built in multiple unit structures, out of which 42,000 were rentals.

Since 1950 more than 17 million dwelling units have been constructed in the Federal Republic of Germany. This high production output has been achieved by a construction industry that is still marked by the dominance of small firms. In 1982 four out of five firms had fewer than twenty employees (see Heuer et al. 1985, 373).

HOUSING MARKETS AND POLICY ORIENTATIONS

During the entire period of rapid industrialization and urbanization that took place in the last third of the nineteenth century, "Manchester Liberalism" prevailed in the housing field (Niethammer 1979; Wollmann 1983, 1985). During World War I a deep breach was made in the then dominant free-market doctrine when rent control and tenure security for rental housing were introduced. In the aftermath of the revolution of November 1918 that led to the creation of the Weimar Republic, there was a short period in which the socialization of the housing stock as well as of other branches of the national economy was heatedly debated. But such revolutionary or reformist blueprints did not materialize. The housing economy continued to be essentially a private market operation.

Yet the emergence of the welfare state that marked the change from the Bismarck Reich to the Weimar Republic was manifested in important advances in housing policies, changing the "rules of the game" for the private housing market in a crucial way. Within this new understanding of the welfare state, government on the federal, state, and local levels was seen to be responsible for providing the population with adequate housing. It is true, the sector within which government started to construct and run housing of its own, such as housing for public employees, remained minimal. Yet government began to interfere with the operation of the private housing market particularly in two dimensions. On the one hand, welfare-state legislation invaded the free-market discretion of landlords in order to improve the status of renters (e.g., rent control). On the other hand, government stepped up subsidy programs to give incentives for private investors in housing.

Although there have been considerable changes both in the housing economy and in the housing-policy field during the past sixty years, striking continuities can be noted (Schulz 1986, 162; Wollman and Jaedicke 1989). Today the housing market still is one of the markets in which government interference and regulation are particularly extensive.

Housing Provision

Not-for-Profit Housing Associations. The first not-for-profit housing associations (*gemeinnützige Wohnungsunternehmen*) were established about 100 years ago. These housing corporations experienced an enormous expansion when, in the 1920s, they were viewed and also used by government as the main addressees and also instruments of governmental housing policies. According to the understanding that inspired the establishment of such corporations, they did not seek profit but saw their main goal in providing low-income households with adequate housing, voluntarily committing themselves to follow "charitable" rules. The term *not-for-profit* is misleading since these enterprises could and even should make a profit to invest in additional housing construction (see Jenkis 1973).

In 1930 the operation of not-for-profit housing associations was finally regulated by legislation: Their scope of activities was defined and limited to provide small housing units (*Kleinwohnungen*), preventing them from building luxurious flats. The associations are subject to a limited dividend rule (4 percent of the invested capital). In the calculation of the rents they are held not to exceed the cost for building, maintaining, and managing the dwelling units (cost-based rent, or *Kostenmiete*). In turn, the not-for-profit housing associations are exempt from income, property, and business tax.

Historically, there are two groups of not-for-profit housing associations: co-operatives (*Genossenschaften*) and stock corporations (*Kapitalgesellschaften*). The cooperatives are collectively owned by the renters. In 1986 about 1 million dwelling units belonged to them. Regarding the stock companies, different owner groups can be distinguished, such as private enterprises, trade unions (until the collapse of the corporation Neue Heimat [see below]), the federal railroad service, and the federal postal service. The most important segment of the not-for-profit stock corporations, however, is owned by local authorities (municipal housing corporations). In total, the stock corporations possess about 2.3 million rental dwelling units.

Between 1950 and 1985 the not-for-profit housing associations constructed 3.7 million dwelling units, of which 2.8 million were rentals. They were hit most severely by the recession in housing construction that occurred in the mid–1970s. The number of newly built housing units dropped by 58 percent from 1976 to 1986 while the entire housing construction fell by only 36 percent in this period (Gesamtverband gemeinnütziger Wohnungsunternehmen 1986, 1987).

Social Housing. Public subsidies for housing construction originated in the 1920s. Because of rent control provisions that had been introduced during World War I and that were resorted to also during the Weimar period, rents were held on a comparatively low level (Winkler 1985, 382–84). The low rents, hardly promising profitable investment in housing, and the general shortage of capital led to a situation in which sizable public subsidies were held to be necessary for stimulating private investors to get involved in housing construction, whereby the incentives were targeted mainly at not-for-profit housing associations. The financial resources for these loans were procured through a "house interest tax" (*Hauszinssteuer*), a kind of tax on the existing housing stock paid by homeowners and landlords (see Witt 1979). After World War II a similar situation prevailed.

The very shortage of capital made it impossible to rely on the "market forces" for coping with the glaring housing shortage. Thus, again, large-scale public funding was pumped into housing construction. Under the Federal Housing Construction Act, from 1950 rental units as well as owner-occupied dwellings were subsidized. The ground rule of social housing subsidies (*sozialer Wohnungsbau*) consists of a kind of barter between government and private investors: while private investors receive a subsidy from government, they commit themselves to accept certain "strings attached" (Winter 1981). Among these strings are guidelines regarding the size, equipment, and so on of dwellings and a mechanism of regulated rents and selling prices. In addition, social housing units are allowed to be sold or rented only to households within a certain income level.

For a better understanding of the institutional setting in which housing policies developed after World War II, some remarks on the constitutional and intergovernmental fabric should be helpful. The question as to which level of government has the responsibility and the jurisdiction for housing policies has long been a bone of contention between the federal and the state (*Länder*) levels. The states maintained that it was in their power to make the substantial decisions on housing subsidies, notwithstanding the federal government's power to pass housing legislation, including the subsidy formula, and to contribute handsomely to the system of housing subsidies (see Scharpf, Reissert, and Schnabel 1976, 187; Jaedicke and Wollmann 1983). So despite the heavy federal outlays in housing subsidies, particularly in the immediate postwar years, the states jealously insisted on preserving considerable discretion in the actual spending of the matching-grant money, eager to reduce or avoid the red tape of federal guidelines. Similarly, local government exercises considerable influence on the kind of housing projects for which public subsidies are used. Besides providing subsidies of their own (see Grüner, Jaedicke, and Ruhland 1988), the municipalies may resort to land-use planning as a powerful way to promote and influence social housing construction.

Right after the war, in the 1950s, the public subsidies consisted mainly of public loans to private investors including not-for-profit housing associations. This changed in the late 1960s when public loans were increasingly replaced by private capital market loans. Under these changed circumstances, the public subsidy was meant to assist the private investor in paying the interests. This subsidy was tailored on a degressive formula, so that the rents for this type of social housing were subject to built-in increases.

In total, between 1950 and 1988, more than 7.74 million social housing dwellings were constructed (see table 3.4). The public subsidy reached its peak in the 1950s and in the early 1960s. Since then, the volume of subsidized housing construction has almost continuously decreased from year to year. The construction of rental dwellings that had been given priority in the early period was particularly hit by this decrease. For about ten years, owner-occupied dwelling units had represented the largest share in the new social housing construction.

Table 3.4

Social Housing Construction, Federal Republic of Germany, 1950–1988

Year	Number of Social Housing Units	Per 1,000 Inhabitants	Percentage of Rental Units
1950	319,350	6.7	
1955	341,407	6.5	
1960	326,663	5.9	71
1965	209,271	3.5	69
1970	165,135	2.7	69
1975	153,989	2.5	53
1980	91,175	1.6	41
1985	68,952	1.1	44
1986	52,066	0.8	31
1988	40,859	0.7	34
1950-1988	7,744,831		

Source: Federal Statistical Office.

Table 3.5

Average Total Costs for Social Housing Units, Federal Republic of Germany, 1971–1985 (In Deutschmarks)

Year	Owner-Occupied One Family Unit	Rental Unit
1971	136,620	76,720
1975	208,300	110,430
1980	292,630	172,660
1985	336,840	203,820

Source: Federal Statistical Office.

But in 1986 the federal government decided to limit its subsidies to owner-occupied housing. So subsidization of and support for the construction of social rental housing was left to the states and the local authorities.[3]

The sharp decrease in the volume of social housing construction certainly has to do with the fact that housing policy has been losing attention and importance on the political agenda. At the same time, it is due to the steep rise of construction costs. Between 1971 and 1985 the construction costs for social housing dwellings more than doubled (see table 3.5). Correspondingly, the subsidy for every new social housing unit increased. On the average, the subsidy for a rental unit is larger than for an owner-occupied unit, so subsidizing owner-occupied housing appears to be more "economical" for government.

Tax Benefits. Traditionally, tax benefits for would-be housing investors loom large in the collection of housing policies in Germany. The property tax, for instance, is reduced for new construction for the duration of ten years. This tax incentive is meant to reach a wide spectrum of the population. To dwellings that exceed a certain size (for instance, 108 square meters in the case of rental dwellings), this tax benefit, hence, does not apply.

Owner-occupied housing is also subsidized through income tax rebates. Yet, unlike the case in other countries, in the FRG mortgage interest cannot be deducted. Instead, 5 percent of the building costs or of the purchase amount may be deducted from the income liable to taxation for the duration of eight years. The deduction must not exceed 15,000 deutschmarks a year. For each child the owner is granted a further tax rebate of 600 deutschmarks (B. Meyer 1986).

Similarly, public incentives for "saving for building" (*Bausparen*) serve primarily the cause of owner-occupied housing. The "Saving for Building Banks" (*Bausparkassen*) play a major role in financing housing construction in Germany, as far as owner-occupied housing is concerned. These banks collect savings and provide the saver, after a number of years, with loans earmarked for housing construction. On the one hand, the banks pay only small interest on the deposits. On the other hand, because of this, the banks can provide building loans with low interest, largely independent of the ups and downs of the general money market (see Heuer et al. 1985, 406–8). Payments to "saving for building" deposits can be deducted from the income liable to be taxed. Within a certain income ceiling, a direct public subsidy can be claimed instead of the tax benefit.

Subsidizing the Rehabilitation of Housing. In the 1950s and 1960s housing policy in the FRG was dominated by the goal of new construction. In the 1970s the preservation and "upgrading" of the old housing became an additional goal (see tables 3.6 and 3.7). There are several reasons for this policy shift. First, rehabilitation of the old housing stock and urban renewal were given increased attention as a field in which, in a period of economic slump, public incentives were able to produce sizable leverage and "pump-priming" effects. Second, the shift reflects an important value change. People who had fled the core cities to become "suburbanites" started to reappraise the merits of downtown living. The historical old quarters that had survived wartime bombing (and postwar "bulldozer" renewal) were rediscovered in their charm, comparing favorably to the "faceless" architecture of high-rise buildings on the outskirts of the cities. Third, in line with this trend, many municipalities started to upgrade worn-down quarters to make them attractive again to households with higher income. In sum, the federal government as well as state and local governments inaugurated a multitude of subsidy programs meant to promote the rehabilitation and modernization of old stock housing. As the costs threatened to drive up rents in old stock housing, the public subsidies were, at least in part, meant to forestall steep

Table 3.6
Subsidies for Housing, Federal Republic of Germany, 1986

Subsidies	Total	Federal		State and Local [1]	
	(in Million Deutschmark)	Million Deutschmark	%	Million Deutschmark	%
Direct Financial Assistance	12,021	5,273	44	6,748	56
among this:					
Social Housing	6,719	2,219	33	4,500	67
"Saving for Building"	968	968	100	0	0
Rehabilitation	951	101	11	850	89
Housing Allowances	3,359	1,961	58	1,398	42
Tax Benefits	8,663	3,192	37	5,471	63
among this:					
Owner Occupied Housing	6,036	2,567	43	3,469	57
"Saving for Building"	640	272	43	368	57
Rehabilitation	630	269	43	361	57
Property Tax Rebates	1,060	0	0	1,060	100
Not-For-Profit Assoc.	239	67	28	172	72
Total of Subsidies	20,684	8,465	41	12,219	59

Sources: Bundesregierung, 1987; state budgets, 1988.

(1) Not including local financial assistance for social housing and rehabilitation.

rent increases that would have accelerated the process of "gentrification" already well on its way. In the 1980s subsidy schemes were tried out to promote rehabilitation and modernization through renters' self-help.

Housing Allowances. Traditionally, housing policies in Germany have pursued the goal of promoting housing construction through supply-side subsidies, that is, through producer-oriented incentives (see Mayo and Barnbrock 1985). Strategies to promote housing construction through demand-side, that is, consumer-oriented, subsidies, operating via transfer payments to renters, are more recent. In Germany, housing allowances (*Wohngeld*) were introduced in the 1960s to cushion the effect of the abolishment of rent control and of the "liberalization" of the rent law that was carried through by the Christian Democrat-led federal government from 1960 onward. The housing allowances can be claimed by households within certain income categories that vary with family size. It is true also that homeowners may receive housing allowances. But 95 percent of the recipients are renters. Since their inauguration, the housing allowances have become an important transfer payment for a growing number of households. The number of recipients increased from 400,000 in 1965 to 1.5 million in 1984 (Bundesregierung 1985).

Table 3.7
Subsidies for Housing, Federal Republic of Germany, 1974–1986

Subsidies	1974		1980		1986	
	in billion Deutschmark	% of total subsidies	in billion Deutschmark	% of total subsidies	in billion Deutschmark	in % of subsidies
Social housing	3.8	30	5.2	30	6.7	32
Tax benefits for owner-occupied housing	1.7	14	4.1	24	6.0	29
Housing allowances	1.6	13	2.1	12	3.4	16
"Saving for building"	3.7	29	2.6	15	1.6	8
Rehabilitation	0.3	2	1.3	8	1.6	8
Other tax rebates	1.5	12	1.8	11	1.3	6
Total of subsidies	12.6	100	17.1	100	20.7	100

Sources: Deutsches Institut für Wirtschaftsforschung, 1980; Bundesregierung, 1987; state budgets, 1976, 1982, 1988.

The Public Subsidy Budget. The attempt at calculating all public financial resources that are directed at improving the provision of housing is facing considerable difficulties (see Deutsches Institut für Wirtschaftsforschung 1980).

First, subsidies are partially handed out as grants and are partially given as loans. Second, the volume of subsidies provided through tax benefits can be at best roughly estimated.

In 1986 the total of public subsidies—direct subsidies as well as tax benefits—for housing amounted to about 21 billion deutschmarks (1.1 percent of the gross national product or about 339 deutschmarks per capita), of which about 41 percent came from the federal budget. Subsidies for social housing and rehabilitation as well as several tax benefits are primarily financed by state and local government (see table 3.6).

The relative importance of the different housing-policy instruments has changed since the mid–1970s, as table 3.7 shows. It is true that social housing subsidies have maintained their share of about one-third of the housing-policy outlays between 1974 and 1986. In contrast, the importance of tax benefits for owner-occupied housing as well as of housing allowances has increased markedly. This trend is likely to continue in the foreseeable future.

Allocation Mechanisms

In the period immediately following the end of World War II, private landlords were practically stripped of their property rights in terms of managing their rentals. The ceiling and development of rents in private housing were politically determined. Municipal housing agencies resumed the task of distributing available living space to people seeking shelter. These components of public interference were abolished step by step during the 1950s and the early 1960s.

In the late 1960s the pendulum swung back again. When the Social Democrat-led Social-Liberal Coalition replaced the former Christian Democrat-led government coalition on the federal level in 1969, one of its early measures was directed at strengthening public intervention in the housing economy again in order to counteract the wave of rent hikes that had swept the demand-ridden big-city housing markets. The regulatory changes introduced in 1971 reduced the right of landlords to give renters notice and spelled out a tight procedure for raising the rent. Thus the position of renters was clearly strengthened. With small modifications, these regulatory provisions are still in effect today.

Contract. In principle, it follows from the market economy that it is up to the landlords to decide to whom to rent. Social housing units are an exception to this rule. They can be rented only to households whose income is within the limits spelled out in the Second Federal Housing Construction Act of 1956 (for example, an annual gross income of 47,800 deutschmarks for a household of four persons in 1988). In areas of urgent demand for housing the landlord is obliged to rent social housing units only to households that are proposed by the municipal housing agency. Furthermore, additional "strings attached" may be agreed upon between the housing investor and the public agencies during the application and allocation of the subsidy. In such cases, the municipal housing agency may have the right to nominate families with many children or with disabled persons as candidates for a rental contract.

Rent. When a new rental contract is made, the rent to be paid is a matter of agreement between the two parties. A statutory protection of the renter against being overcharged is offered by a clause in the Penal Code penalizing usury. In reality, this clause has little relevance.

The landlord is subjected to some legal provisions for raising the rent within a valid contract. He is bound to prove that the rent he wants to draw corresponds with rents already paid for comparable housing units in the locality.

The setting of rents in social housing units follows a different principle. In social housing the rents cannot be freely settled between the parties. Instead, they are calculated on the basis of the current costs of the apartment (cost-based rent, or *Kostenmiete*). "Current costs" are those necessary for the operation of the dwelling (administration, repair, current fees, and so on) and for covering the interest payments on loans for the investment. Strictly speaking, the rent level in social housing units is, to a large extent, politically regulated. The states and—in the case of additional municipal funding—the municipalities determine the conditions of housing subsidies, thus also determining, for all practical purposes, the rent level. Not-for-profit housing associations traditionally find themselves in a particular situation insofar as their entire stock (that is, not only the housing built with social housing subsidies) is guided by the rule that the rent exacted from the renters must not exceed the cost-based rent.

Renter-Protection Law. The landlord's right to give notice to the renter has been curtailed considerably. By and large, notice can be given to the renter only under two conditions: first, if the renter violated the rent contract and, second, if the landlord actually needs the apartment for himself. In the latter case, the landlord carries the burden of proof. But, in a 1989 ruling, the Constitutional Court clearly "softened" the renter-protecting thrust of this provision.

MAJOR PROBLEMS AND FUTURE DEVELOPMENTS

Housing Demand

In the 1980s the housing provision in the Federal Republic of Germany has been, in general, quantitatively as well as qualitatively, better than previously in German history. Since about 1984, there has been increasing talk about the problem of vacancies. In fact, a number of factors and developments should be taken into account that result in an ambivalent assessment of the situation marked, with regional and social differences by overdemand (particularly on the part of low-income or no-income households), on the one hand, and by oversupply (on the part of overpriced and ill-located dwellings), on the other hand.

In the long run, the general demand for housing will fall, because the German population is expected to decrease dramatically after the year 2000. Yet until then the number of households will still increase, because there is a clear trend toward the one-person or two-person household notwithstanding the "value change" that is expressed by the fact that particularly young people prefer to share large dwellings (Gesamtverband gemeinnütziger Wohnungsunternehmen 1987, 15–20; Berndt 1988).

The pattern of spatial distribution of people and jobs that we have known from the beginning of industrialization and urbanization has basically changed (Häussermann and Siebel 1988, 22–32). Since the 1960s the core cities have been losing population to the neighboring suburban areas. As a result of the structural change, particularly in industrial production, the number of employees has been declining in core cities since the mid–1970s.

Do these developments and changes mean that the provision of housing may be left to "the market," because, in the future, an oversupply of housing appears to be more likely than an overdemand? Could and should housing policy be further deregulated and its instruments be dismantled?

A number of considerations caution against such conclusions. Too often in the past overall assessments and interpretations have proven to be wrong or at least rash. In the mid–1970s there was already a period in which the talk about the well-balanced housing market was predominant. Only a few years later, since about 1979, the discussion about housing policy stood under a completely different leitmotif. All of a sudden it was conventional wisdom that there was a "new housing emergency" (neue Wohnungsnot) particularly in the big cities (see Deutscher Stätetag 1980). About five years later increasing vacancies were discussed as a severe problem by politicians and experts. Most recently, new bottlenecks in the housing supply are being hinted at. One of the main reasons for this new housing shortage lies in the stream of immigrants of German descent that comes from East European countries, particularly the Soviet Union and Poland, amounting to 200,000 persons in 1988 and to 350,000 in 1989. These ups and downs of the issue cycle should be a warning against rash conclusions, all the more so as the movements of the issue cycle have undoubtedly much to do with prevailing political and economic interests and their ability to push their view and position onto the agenda of public discussion and discourse.

A careful analysis of the situation should depart from the insight that there is not "one" housing market but rather a multitude of regionally, sectorally, and socially differentiated submarkets. Thus housing supply in the FRG shows important regional differences. In areas in which the economic development is promising and attractive to people seeking jobs, there is an overdemand for housing. This holds particularly true for cities in the South of the FRG like Munich and Stuttgart. But in regions with economic problems and mass unemployment and left by people seeking jobs elsewhere, there is much less "purchasing power" and demand for housing at least in the middle and upper price segments of the market.

In the 1980s the rents have risen at a higher rate then general living expenses.

In 1978 the renter households, on the average, had to spend about 15.5 percent of their net income on rent (not including heating). In 1982 this percentage increased to 17. The share of households that have to spend more than a quarter of their net income on rent increased from 18.1 percent in 1978 to 23.4 percent in 1982 (Deutsches Institut für Wirtschaftsforschung 1986; see also von Lüde 1986). It is particularly the low-income and no-income households that suffer most from these rent burdens. Their number is bound to increase as a result of mass unemployment. So the development of West German housing markets is marked by an increasing polarization. On the one hand, the majority of households maintain or even improve their housing situation. On the other hand, low-income households find it increasingly difficult to find affordable housing.

Shrinking Social Housing Stock

The situation for low-income and no-income groups may be additionally aggravated by the fact that the number of social housing dwellings will decline dramatically (see Wollmann and Jaedicke 1989). The "strings attached" to social housing rentals are in effect only as long as these units are subject to the subsidy and "barter" formula. This period ends when the loans are finally and totally paid back by the investor. The elapsing of the "strings attached" will become critical in the near future, particularly because the public loans that went into the social housing rental stock in the 1950s and 1960s are about to be completely paid back by the investors, thus terminating the period during which the investors were obliged to rent these dwellings to low-income households within a regulated rent formula. When these dwellings cease to be social housing rentals, landlords are free to pick the renters and to get a rent as high as the market will yield.

This process of social housing rentals "falling out" of the market was, in the past, accelerated by public incentives to motivate private investors to pay back the loans earlier than were set out in the subsidy contract. According to a recent estimate, out of the 4 million social housing rentals still available in 1984 (16 percent of the total housing stock; see figure 3.1) about one-half will be turned over to the private market by 1995. The number of newly constructed dwellings will be far from making good this loss. For a housing policy meant to assist low-income households in finding adequate and affordable housing, this development is downright agonizing because the old stock of social housing rentals has a much lower rent level than that built more recently.

Apart from the problems that come from the erosion of low-rent rental housing, there are additional problems stemming from the fact that, through its eligibility rules, social housing rentals gave a chance to get adequate housing to groups that, independent of their "purchasing power," have had specific difficulties in finding adequate housing in the private housing market. Foreign workers and their families and single mothers with children loom large among those discriminated-against groups. These households often have been assisted in finding an apartment by municipal housing agencies that could resort to their right

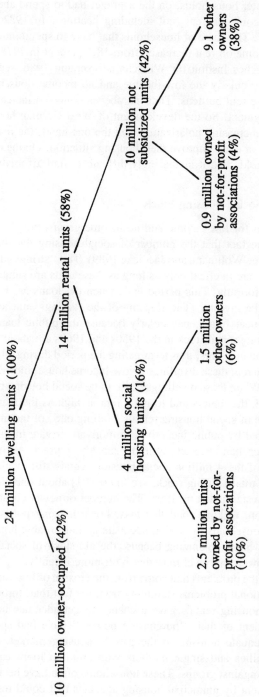

Figure 3.1
Housing Stock in the Federal Republic of Germany, 1984

24 million dwelling units (100%)

10 million owner-occupied (42%)

14 million rental units (58%)

4 million social housing units (16%)

10 million not subsidized units (42%)

2.5 million units owned by not-for-profit associations (10%)

1.5 million other owners (6%)

0.9 million owned by not-for-profit associations (4%)

9.1 other owners (38%)

Sources: Gewos, 1984, 49; Gesamtverband gemeinnütziger Wohnungsunternehmen, 1987, 162.

to nominate needy households as renters in social housing rentals. The smaller the number of social housing rentals, the fewer the possibilities of municipal authorities to provide discriminated-against households with adequate housing.

To some degree the housing stock owned by the not-for-profit housing associations could replace the shrinking social housing stock. Yet the traditional legal scheme of not-for-profit housing will be abolished by 1990.

There are good reasons to maintain that governmental interference in the housing market still is and will continue to be necessary for social policy considerations. As was argued above, there are still glaring market imbalances, if the multitude of regional, sectoral, and social "submarkets" are taken into account. To counteract these market distortions for the sake of the economically, socially, and ethnically discriminated-against groups still is and remains a crucial challenge for public housing policies.

Yet one should not ignore the shortcomings that the historically grown system of housing policy concepts and instruments revealed vis-à-vis changing policy contexts and changing social demands.

Distributional Effects

The subsidy system, from its very beginning, was designed to evoke and promote maximum new-construction output. Its distributional effects and distortions, latent or manifest, were largely neglected. So to expand new housing production, housing policy was targeted at social and income groups that were not strictly dependent on public subsidies in making their investment. An analysis of the entire subsidy budget, encompassing both direct subsidies and tax benefits, reveals that it is particularly the middle-income and high-income households that take a lion's share of this budget (see Ulbrich 1980; Füllenkemper 1982; Behnken 1982). The main reason is that owner-occupied housing is predominantly subsidized through tax write-offs. Since a percentage of the construction costs or selling prices is deducted from the income subject to taxation, those homeowners that have the highest income and, hence, are exposed to the highest tax rate are receiving the highest subsidies.

Shortcomings of Social Housing

Even the distributional effects of the direct subsidies in social housing are dubious. It is true that only households up to a certain income level are admitted as renters in social rental housing. Thus higher income groups are excluded from these moderate rental units. However, there is again a "bias in the system" in favor of middle-income households because landlords, in having to choose among "eligible" would-be renters, tend to prefer families with middle-class-type stable incomes over poor and needy families. Furthermore, income criteria for eligibility are checked only once, namely, before the household moves into the premises. There is no legal way to make renters move out of their social rental dwelling if their income in time rises above the eligibility line. The existence of these "misallocatees" certainly plays an important role in preventing the social housing compounds from deteriorating into ghettolike quarters as happened to public housing in the United States. Nevertheless, it is a serious shortcoming because a considerable number of those who are really needy remain locked out of social housing. Some state governments have authorized large cities to collect a special charge on "misallocatees" amounting to an extra rent on top of the cost-based rent.

Another shortcoming of social housing is that rents may differ largely from compound to compound or even from building to building, because they are calculated on the basis of the construction costs of the particular building in the specific year. Thus independent of the quality of the building and of the dwellings, rents in social housing buildings erected in the 1950s and 1960s are much lower than those that were constructed more recently. In addition, the changes in the subsidy modalities led to different rent levels. For instance, the subsidy modality introduced in the late 1960s has resulted in yearly rent increases that, in part, push the rent level of social housing above the level on the "free" housing market. It is particularly in high-rise housing complexes of these subsidy "age groups" that dwellings are vacant.

Since the 1970s the distributional bias and distortion of the housing subsidy system has increased further, although the most urgent housing shortage that might dictate output-oriented subsidy strategies had been long overcome at that point, and the time had come for a more social policy-oriented reappraisal and retargeting of housing subsidies. As was critically said regarding development since the 1970s, "housing policy has ceased to provide a safety net for low-income people and has turned, instead, into an instrument to assist the high-income households" (Jordan 1981, 797).

The Decline of the Not-for-Profit Sector

There has been a long debate over the years about whether the not-for-profit housing associations still perform a role and function differently from the housing corporations operating on the "free" housing market and whether this role still justifies their special status, particularly their tax benefits (see Peters 1984, 345–88). The big stock corporations especially have been criticized and attacked for having practically forgotten their social commitment and for behaving, instead, like full-fledged profit-seeking private enterprises. Some critics, departing from neoliberal concepts, have concluded that the tax privilege enjoyed by not-for-profit corporations is a historical relic that should be abolished (see Unabhängige Kommission 1985; Hamer 1985).

Such criticism is substantiated to some extent by the experiences renters have with these housing corporations. Often renters complain about high rents and a bureaucratic attitude that ignores their wishes. Similar criticism is voiced by municipal housing agencies that have a hard time activating even those housing corporations of which the cities are the sole or the majority shareholder. In trying to provide needy households with adequate housing or just shelter, municipalities find it difficult to get corporations to cooperate (Weinberger 1982). The corporations are frequently reluctant to accommodate what are often pejoratively called "problem cases"; instead, they prefer to choose renters with a stable income and a middle-class profile. Yet it should be added that the record of private housing corporations is far worse. If the municipalities do have a chance to find help in their housing policies, it is with the not-for-profit sector of the housing economy (see Krischausky and Mackscheidt 1984).

A more optimistic and hopeful view is often voiced with regard to the cooperatives that traditionally constitute the second branch of the not-for-profit housing economy. Ideally operating on the principles of self-determination and self-help, the cooperatives may offer a promising choice and alternative compared to anonymous and expensive living in high-rise and large-scale housing complexes. Yet the empirical evidence about how, in reality, cooperatives usually operate is sobering (see Wollmann 1987). They have largely lost their historically grown specific features. As a rule, the members of cooperatives perceive themselves and behave like "normal" renters. Self-help is all but marginal. The cooperatives often act in a "closed-shop" fashion, eager to maintain and prolong the privileges of their long-standing members, on the one hand, and to keep out newcomers, particularly "problem cases," on the other hand.

The decline of the not-for-profit housing associations in general and eclipse of the cooperatives in particular may, at least in part, be traced to the 1930s, when the Nazis undertook to destroy the not-for-profit housing associations as independent political entities (Novy and Uhlig 1983, 162). During the Weimar period, the not-for-profit housing associations were thriving in a social and cultural context and were rooted particularly in the socialist and catholic labor movement. They not only constructed and managed housing units but also established and maintained educational and cultural facilities, such as evening schools, libraries, kindergartens, and civic centers. Being suspicious and disdainful of such quasi-autonomous activities, the Nazis enacted provisions through which the housing associations were forbidden to perform any activities outside the mere operation of housing construction and management. As a result, the cultural and political identity of the not-for-profit housing sector was dealt a blow from which it never recovered.

For different reasons, the socioeconomic development of postwar Germany appears to have exacerbated this erosion of a historical identity and pattern. The labor and the trade union movements did not see any reason for reactivating the historical ideas of such corporations, cooperatives, and "settlements" as nuclei of cultural and political identity. The dominant economic order based on the "economic man" appeared so successful that any alternative in terms of cooperative ownership or not-for-profit rules of action appeared to be doomed to failure or oblivion.

The discussion about the future course and cause of the not-for-profit housing sector was overshadowed, in the last years, by the scandal around the trade union-owned mammoth corporation Neue Heimat. With a stock of 300,000 dwellings Neue Heimat was the largest housing corporation in the FRG. Entrepreneurial miscalculations and mismanagement resulted in heavy financial losses in the late 1970s and in the 1980s. In addition, a group of top managers had enriched themselves at the corporation's expense. At first, Neue Heimat tried to overcome its financial crisis by selling part of its housing stock. Finally, the trade unions decided to give up completely their financial engagement in housing. After a bizarre episode in which the trade unions attempted to sell the entire corporation to a bread producer, they tried to sell the housing stock of Neue Heimat, piece by piece, to other not-for-profit corporations and to the states.

To mobilize the financial resources necessary for covering the enormous losses incurred by the Neue Heimat housing corporation, the trade unions, in dramatic moves, saw themselves forced to sell a major bank (Bank für Gemeinwirtschaft) as well as a large insurance company (Volksfürsorge). They had been operating these enterprises as flagships in their ambition to pursue and practice principles of a "public-oriented economy" (*Gemeinwirtschaft*) as a complement and corrective to the capitalist economy.

As far as the future role of the not-for-profit housing sector as an actor and instrument of housing policy is concerned, two major contradictory courses of action took shape within the ruling Christian-Liberal coalition during the past few years.

On the one hand, there were advocates for even strengthening the role and responsibility of the not-for-profit housing associations with regard to providing low-income households with adequate housing. A proposal coming out of the Federal Ministry of Housing suggested that housing associations should commit themselves through contracts with the municipalities to rent their dwellings to the "problem households" of the housing market. Although according to this concept, the housing economy at large should be further deregulated, the not-for-profit associations should strengthen their social policy role in the housing field. As a "reward" for shouldering this task, their traditional tax benefits should be preserved. While the municipalities and a number of academics (see Krischausky and Mackscheidt 1984) supported this scheme, the not-for-profit housing sector was explicitly against it, rejecting the idea of becoming a kind of housing policy stopgap.

On the other hand, there has been a debate for years about abolishing the not-for-profit housing sector altogether. This position was voiced and pushed particularly by advocates eager to strike out any deviation from the free-market principle. During the entire period in which the Federal Ministry of Housing pursued its aforementioned proposal, this course did not have a chance to succeed. The situation changed dramatically in the summer and fall of 1987 when the details of the planned tax reform were discussed within the Christian-Liberal coalition. At that point the free-market advocates gained the support of the taxation experts who were eager to abolish the tax benefits of the not-for-profit housing associations in their drive to cut off tax benefits wherever possible. Without any further discussion with experts or with the not-for-profit housing sector itself and taking the federal minister of housing virtually by surprise, the governmental tax-reform group decided to terminate the tax benefit formula traditionally underlying the not-for-profit housing sector. In the future, the tax benefits shall be granted only to the cooperatives renting dwellings to their members. In June 1988 such a bill was passed by the federal legislature, thus abolishing the time-honored not-for-profit status of the housing associations, turning their housing stock, as far as it is not subject to social housing regulations, over to the "free" rental market.

PROSPECTS: THE END OF HOUSING POLICY?

Housing policy in Germany has been marked by a striking continuity. From the beginning, it has mainly aimed at stimulating the construction of new housing. Through "strings attached" to the subsidies given to the investors, it was intended to achieve the construction of dwelling units that, on the one hand, met certain quality standards for the sake of "broad segments of the population" and, on the other hand, were available at moderate rents.

The main instruments of housing policy in Germany have traditionally been the following:

- First, a rent law with renter-protection clauses: This was based on the assumption that a legal provision that would give the landlord complete discretion in making contractual arrangements would work to the detriment of the renter. The most important elements of the present rent law are provisions through which the right of the landlord to give notice to the renter is legally limited and rent increases are narrowly circumscribed.

- Second, the stimulation of the construction of new social housing dwellings via subsidies: This was based on a kind of "barter logic" in which the private investor receives public subsidies in exchange for "strings attached," particularly with regard to rent level and eligibility of renters.

- Third, the existence of not-for-profit housing associations historically operating on an understanding that is also marked by a kind of "barter logic": These associations are benefiting from a number of tax exemptions and commit themselves, in turn, to pay a limited dividend (4 percent) on the shares and to calculate the rents on the basis of the current operational costs of the dwelling units (cost-based rent).

The second and the third of the traditional pillars of a social policy-oriented housing policy will continue to crumble in the years to come. The social housing stock will dwindle due to the continuous elapse of the "strings attached." Few new social housing rentals will be built. Furthermore, the not-for-profit housing associations, hitherto operating under the traditional not-for-profit rules that require them to base rents on cost, will be able to operate in a market-oriented manner—particularly with regard to fixing the rents—after 1990 when the historical not-for-profit scheme will elapse, as decided by recent federal legislation. Both developments will further diminish the stock of rentals "earmarked" for social policy goals. Only the renter-protecting components of the rent-law and the housing allowance scheme will remain as social policy-oriented instruments of housing policy.

Why is it that the main pillars of a socially targeted housing policy are about to be erased with surprisingly little public controversy and without loud protest of the parties concerned? To grasp this, it should be helpful to have a second look at the two basic concepts that have been rivals from the very beginning of the formulation of housing policy after World War II (for more detail, see Jaedicke and Wollmann 1988).

On the one hand, there was the free-market position voiced by the Christian Democrats and the Liberals. With regard to the housing sector, the free-market position, while grudgingly accepting that massive state intervention was temporarily necessary vis-à-vis the unprecedented housing shortage, urged to return the housing sector to the free-market mechanisms and to terminate state interference as soon as possible. The free-market advocates are convinced that it is only through the demand and supply operation of a free market that the housing problems, also of the low-income groups, can be solved, at least in the long run.

But this belief in the free market is not without modifications. Certain renter-protection clauses in the rent law are often accepted. As far as publicly subsidizing the housing sector is concerned, free-market advocates prefer the housing allowance given to the renter over the direct subsidy given to the investor, arguing that the housing allowance can be better targeted and tailored on the concrete financial needs of the renter.

In addition to the free-market stance, the Christian Democrats have been staunch protagonists of the idea that as many households as possible should live in their own homes. In the 1950s, when the Cold War climaxed, the concept of widespread home ownership had a strong ideological underpinning, as it was meant to make people, by acquiring real estate and, hence, "having a stake," immune to communism (see Wandersleb 1959, 14). As time went on, this strategy was guided by the political calculation that homeowners would develop a political leaning toward the conservative and liberal cause. Thus one of the main goals of the subsidy system that was developed in the 1950s and 1960s under Christian Democratic leadership was to stimulate and financially assist owner-occupied housing. To promote this goal quantitatively, the homeowner-oriented subsidies were designed in an across-the-board fashion, indiscriminately granting the subsidy also to the well-to-do who could have afforded to acquire a home without the subsidy (for a rare position that, consistent with a pure free-market stand, pleads for discontinuing such a general subsidy for homeowners, see Biedenkopf and Miegel 1978).

On the other hand, from the concept of an active welfare state propagated and shared particularly by the Social Democrats, it was concluded that the state should intervene in the market, not only in a temporary but in a permanent fashion, to correct malfunctions. The basic assumptions underlying this position are that, taking the specific features of the "commodity" housing and dwelling, the market will not be able to provide the population, particularly the low-income groups, with adequate housing, certainly not in the short run and probably not even in the long run. So it is a crucial task and responsibility of an active welfare state to counteract the "social blindness" of the market forces. For achieving this, the Social Democrats saw an important instrument in the creation of a "second housing market" that was capable of complementing and also correcting the "free" housing market by providing dwellings especially for low-income households. Within this concept, the main agents carrying this "second housing market" were seen in the not-for-profit housing associations. For the Social Democrats the promotion of social housing rentals was the focus of their housing policy. Although they did not reject the idea of promoting private home ownership, they kept arguing that to fulfil the housing demands in large-scale fashion, the construction of new rentals should be primarily pushed.

When the Christian-Liberal government under Adenauer resorted to massive public interference with the housing market, its understanding was that these interventions should be temporary and limited. In fact, the government, already during the early 1950s, proceeded to reintroduce the rules of the free market by lifting rent control. Yet when the Social Democratic-led coalition took over in 1969, the concept and instruments of public intervention were sharpened again. This was effected particularly by amending the rent law to strengthen the position of the renter. Another important course of action was seen in stepping up the subsidy programs for social housing construction.

The proponents of a housing policy that is based on the catchwords *less state* and *more market* gradually began to achieve their political breakthrough in the mid–1970s, that is, still during the Social-Liberal coalition and before the change of government to the Christian-Liberal coalition in 1982. Since the mid–1970s the federal government started to withdraw from the housing policy field. There were certain financial reasons for this retreat. But it was also facilitated by political disillusionment that spread as the shortcomings, distortions, and problems of the historically grown and politically implemented system of housing-policy concepts and instruments became increasingly visible. These shortcomings and deficits were eagerly taken up and expounded by neoliberal positions that increasingly gained ground in politics as well as in academia. Aided by powerful interest groups like the well-organized National Association of Real Estate and Homeowners, the gist of this neoliberal choir was that these deficits were caused "not by market failures, but by policy failures" (Eekhoff 1981, 461; see also Biedenkopf and Miegel 1978; D. Meyer 1986).

In a balanced judgment, it probably would have to be said that the current and foreseeable problems in the housing area stem both from market failures and policy failures in a peculiar mix. Designed under the conditions of the postwar situation marked by an unparalleled housing shortage, the entire subsidy system was tailored primarily to construct new housing in as massive a scale as possible. The production output that was achieved is impressive. Yet the housing-policy agenda should have been rewritten at the latest in the 1970s to revamp the entire subsidy system, making it socially more targeted and concentrating the subsidy budget to assist those in finding adequate housing who really needed it. These necessary changes, which would have had to include also the subsidies for owner-occupied housing, were not tackled because of political and administrative inertia and the power play of vested interests.

NOTES

1. The information that can be drawn from the official statistics with regard to the housing stock is woefully inadequate. It is true that there are detailed data on the construction of new housing, but for all of the rest, the data are strikingly poor. The main reason is that the last general census on buildings and dwellings took place in 1968. There were partial censuses in 1972, 1978, 1980, and 1982, but because different indicators and methods were used, the data are only partially comparable. The results from the General Census that was finally carried out in 1987 will not be available before 1989.

The data used in this chapter are based on publications by the Federal Statistical Office, if not marked otherwise.

2. This chapter deals only with housing policy in the Federal Republic of Germany. For a comparison between the FRG and the German Democratic Republic, also in the housing policy field, see Jenkis (1976), Melzer (1983), and von Beyme (1987).

3. Responding to a mounting housing shortage, exacerbated by the unprecedented influx of immigrants of German descent (*Aussiedler*) from Eastern European countries since the mid–1980s, the federal government, in 1989, again reversed its hosing policy course and launched a new subsidy program for social rental hosing.

REFERENCES

Behnken, Renate. 1982. *Soziale Gerechtigkeit und Wohnungspolitik. Eine empirische Verteilungsanalyse für die Bundesrepublik Deutschland*. Berlin: Duncker and Humblot.

Berndt, Holger. 1988. "Perspektiven des Wohnungsmarktes." *Bundesbaublatt* 37:14–18.

Biedenkopf, Kurt, and Meinhard Miegel. 1978. *Wohnungsbau am Wendepunkt*. Stuttgart: Bonn aktuell.

Blumenroth, Ulrich. 1975. *Deutsche Wohnungspolitik seit der Reichsgründung*. Münster: Institut für Wohnungs- und Siedlungswesen.

Bundesregierung. 1985. *Wohngeld- und Mietenbericht 1985*. Bonn: Deutscher Bundestag, Drucksache 10/3222, April 19.

Deutscher Städtetag. 1980. *Neue Wohnungsnot in unseren Städten*. Stuttgart: Kohlhammer.

Deutsches Institut für Wirtschaftsforschung. 1980. "Keine Neuorientierung der Wohnungsbauförderung." *DIW-Wochenbericht* 47:517–25.

———. 1986. "Zur Entwicklung der Mietbelastung privater Haushalte." *DIW-Wochenbericht* 53:45–52.

Eekhoff, Johann. 1981. "Wohnungspolitik in der Sozialen Marktwirtschaft." In *Zukunftsprobleme der sozialen Marktwirtschaft*, edited by Otmar Issing, 455–79. Berlin: Duncker and Humblot.

Füllenkemper, Horst. 1982. *Wirkungsanalyse der Wohnungspolitik in der Bundesrepublik Deutschland*. Münster: Institut für Wohnungs- und Siedlungswesen.

Gesamtverband gemeinnütziger Wohnungsunternehmen. 1986. *Der lange Weg. Positionen der gemeinnützigen Wohnungswirtschaft*. Köln.

———. 1987. *Wohnungswirtschaftliches Jahrbuch, 1987/88*. Hamburg: Hammonia.

Gewos. 1984. *Wohnungspolitik im Spannungsfeld der Anforderungen von Staat und Bewohnern*. Bonn.

Grüner, Hans, Wolfgang Jaedicke, and Kurt Ruhland. 1988. "Rote Politik im schwarzen Rathaus? Bestimmungsfaktoren der wohnungspolitischen Ausgaben bundesdeutscher Grossstädte." *Politische Vierteljahresschrift* 29:42–57.

Hamer, Eberhard. 1985. *Mittelstand und Wohnungswirtschaft*. Minden, West Ger.: Philler.

Häussermann, Hartmut, and Water Siebel. 1988. *Neue Urbanität*. Frankfurt: Suhrkamp.

Heuer, Jürgen H. B., Lidwina Kühne-Büning, Volker Nordalm, and Marlis Drevermann. 1985. *Lehrbuch der Wohnungswirtschaft*. Frankfurt: Knapp.

Jaedicke, Wolfgang, and Hellmut Wollmann. 1983. Wohnungsbauförderung im Bundesländervergleich: Macht Landespolitik einen Unterschied?" *Bauwelt* 74:437–45.

———. 1989. "Wohnungspolitik zwischen Staatsintervention und Markt." In *Politik in der Bundesrepublik*, edited by Klaus von Beyme and Manfred Schmidt. Opladen, West Ger.: Westdeutscher Verlag.

Jenkis, Helmut W. 1973. *Ursprung und Entwicklung der gemeinnützigen Wohnungswirtschaft*. Hamburg: Hammonia.

———. 1976. *Wohnungswirtschaft und Wohnungspolitik in beiden deutschen Staaten*. Hamburg: Hammonia.

Jordan, Jörg. 1981. "Überlegungen zur Wohnungsbaupolitik, 1981." *Die neue Gesellschaft* 28:796–802.

Krischausky, D., and Klaus Mackscheidt. 1984. *Wohnungsgemeinnützigkeit: Zwischen bedarfswirtschaftlicher Tradition und wohnungspolitischer Neuorientierung*. Köln: Heymann.

Mayo, Stephen K., and Jörn Barnbrock. 1985. "Rental Housing Subsidy Programs in West Germany and the United States: A comparative program evaluation." In *U.S. and West German Housing Markets*, edited by Konrad Stahl and Raymond J. Struyk, 115–54. Berlin: Springer.

Melzer, Manfred. 1983. *Wohnungsbau und Wohnungsversorgung in beiden deutschen Staaten—ein Vergleich*. Berlin: Duncker and Humblot.

Meyer, Bernd. 1986. *Die Neuregelung der steuerrechtlichen Förderung selbstgenutzten Wohneigentums nach dem Wohneigentumsförderungsgesetz*. Berlin: Erich Schmidt.

Meyer, Dirk. 1986. "Staatsversagen im Wohnungsmarkt?" *Archiv für Kommunalwissenschaften* 25:200–218.

Niethammer, Lutz. 1979. "Ein langer Marsch durch die Institutionen. Zur Vorgeschichte des preussischen Wohnungsgesetzes von 1918." In *Wohnen im Wandel*, edited by Lutz Niethammer, 363–86. Wuppertal, West Ger.: Peter Hammer.

Novy, Klaus, and Günther Uhlig. 1983. "Wohnungsbaugenossenschaften ohne Genossenschaftskultur?'' In *Genossenschafts-Bewegung: Zur Geschichte der Wohnreform*, edited by Klaus Novy, 153–63. Berlin: Transit.

Peters, Karl-Heinz. 1984. *Wohnungspolitik am Scheideweg.* Berlin: Duncker und Humblot.

Scharpf, Fritz W., Bernd Reissert, and Fritz Schnabel. 1976. *Politikverflechtung.* Kronberg, West Ger.: Scriptor.

Schulz, Günther. 1986. "Kontinuitäten und Brüche in der Wohnungspolitik von der Weimarer Zeit bis zur Bundesrepublik." In *Stadtwachstum, Industrialisierung, sozialer Wandel—Beiträge zur Erforschung der Urbanisierung im 19. und 20. Jahrhundert*, edited by Hans-Jürgen Teuteberg, 135–73. Berlin: Duncker and Humblot.

Ulbrich, Rudi. 1980. *Verteilungswirkungen des Förderungssystems für den Wohnungsbau.* Bonn: Bundesministerium für Raumordnung, Bauwesen and Städtebau.

Unabhängige Kommission. 1985. *Gutachten zur Prüfung der steuerlichen Regelungen für gemeinnützige Wohnungs- und Siedlungsunternehmen.* Bonn: Bundesministerium de Finanzen.

von Beyme, Klaus. 1987. *Die Wiederaufbau. Architektur und Städtebaupolitik in den beiden deutschen Staaten.* Munich: Piper.

von Lüde, Rolf. 1986. "Liberalisierung des Wohnungswesens als Abkehr von einer sozialverpflichteten Wohnungspolitik." In *Neue alte Ungleichheiten*, edited by Hans-Werner Franz, Willfried Kruse und Hans-Günter Rolff, 171–95. Opladen, West Ger.: Westdeutscher Verlag.

Wandersleb, Hermann. 1959. "Entwicklungstendenzen im Wohnungsbau in der Bundesrepublik Deutschland." In *Beiträge zur Theorie und Praxis des Wohnungsbaues, Festschrift für A. Knoblauch*, 7–25. Bonn: Domus.

Weinberger, Bruno. 1982. "Kommunen und Gemeinnützige in einem Boot." *Der Städtetag* 35:691–95.

Winkler, Heinricht August. 1985. *Von der Revolution zur Stabilisierung. Arbeiter und Arbeiterbewegung in der Weimarer Republik.* Berlin and Bonn: J. H. W. Dietz Nachfahren.

Winter, Gerd. 1981. "Soziale Wohnungspolitik als Wirtschafts- und Sozialpolitik." *Leviathan* 9:87–119.

Witt, Peter-Christian. 1979. "Inflation, Wohnungszwangswirtschaft und Hauszinssteuer." In *Wohnen im Wandel*, edited by Lutz Niethammer, 385–407. Wuppertal, West Ger.: Peter Hammer.

Wollmann, Hellmut. 1983. "Entwicklungslinien kommunaler Wohnungspolitik—eine wohnungspolitikgeschichtliche Skizze." In *Kommunale Wohnungspolitik*, edited by Adalbert Evers, Hans-Georg Lange, and Hellmut Wollmann, 92–106. Basel: Birkhäuser.

———. 1985. "Housing policy: Between State Intervention and the Market." In *Policy and Politics in the Federal Republic of Germany*, edited by Klaus von Beyme and Manfred G. Schmidt, 132–55. Hants, U.K.: Gower.

———. 1987. "Schlussfolgerungen—Empfehlungen—Forderungen." In *Wohnungsversorgung und Wohnungspolitik in der Grossstadtregion*, edited by Heik Afheldt, Walter Siebel, and Thomas Sieverts, 331–63. Gerlingen, West Ger.: Bleicher.

Wollmann, Hellmut, and Wolfgang Jaedicke. 1989. "The Rise and Fall of Public and Social Housing." *Tijdschrift voor Economische en Sociale Geografie* 80, no. 2: 82–88.

FURTHER READING

Becker, Ruth. "Grundzüge der Wohnungspolitik in der BRD seit 1949." *Arch+* 19, no. 57–58 (1981): 64–68.

Böhle, Thomas. "Die Erhaltung preisgünstigen Wohnraums als Leitlinie Kommunaler Wohnungspolitik." *Der Städtetag* 40 (1987): 401–4.

Brech, Joachim, ed. *Wohnen zur Miete.* Weinheim, West Ger.: Beltz, 1981.

Bundesregierung. *11. Subventionsbericht.* Bonn: Deutscher Bundestag, Drucksache 11/1378, November, 1987.

Dangschat, J. Friedrichs J. et al. *Gentrification in Hamburg.* GSS-Series. Vol. 8. Hamburg: GSS, University of Hamburg, 1988.

Dörhöfer, Kerstin. *Erscheinungen und Determinanten staatlich gelenkter Wohnungsversorgung in der Bundesrepublik Deutschland.* Berlin: Technische Universität, 1978.

Eekhoff, Johann. *Wohnungs- und Bodenmarkt.* Tübingen: Mohr, 1987.

Friedrichs, Jürgen. "Urban Renewal Policies and Back-to-the City Migration." *American Planning Association Journal* 70–79 (Winter 1987).

Fuhrich, Manfred. *Wohnungsversorgung als sozialer Auftrag.* Berlin: Technische Universität, 1984.

————. *Sicherung des Sozialmietwohnungsbestandes.* Frankfurt: Haag and Herchen, 1986.

Hallett, G. *Housing and Land Policies in West Germany and Britain.* London: MacMillan, 1977.

Häring, Dieter. *Zur Geschichte und Wirkung staatlicher Interventionen im Wohnungssektor.* Hamburg: Christians, 1974.

Hecht, Michael. *Subventionsformen in der Wohnungswirtschaft.* Munich: V. Florenz, 1978.

Ipsen, Detlev, Herbert Glasauer, and Vera Lasch. *Markt und Raum. Die Verteilungswirkungen wohnungspolitischer Subventionsformen im städtischen Raum.* Frankfurt: Campus, 1986.

Jenkis, Helmut. *Die Gemeinnützige Wohnungswirtschaft zwischen Markt und Sozialbindung.* Berlin: Duncker & Humblot, 1985.

————. "Reform oder Abschaffung des Wohnungsgemeinnützigkeitsgesetzes?" *Zeitschrift für öffentliche und gemeinwirtschaftliche Unternehmen* 9 (1986):14–23, 155–68.

Kennedy, Declan. "West Germany." Chapter 3 in *Housing in Europe*, edited by Martin Wynn. London/Canberra: Croom Helm, 1984.

Kornemann, Rolf. "Der Wohnungs- und Städtebau in den Regierungserklärungen." *Der langfristige Kredit* 27 (1981): 534–41, 565–69.

Krätke, Stefan, Renate Hirsch-Borst, and Fritz Schmoll. *Zwischen Selbsthilfe und Staatsbürokratie.* Hamburg: VSA, 1984.

Marcuse, Peter. "Determinants of State Housing Policies: West Germany and the United States." In *Urban Policy under Capitalism*, edited by S. Fainstein and N. Fainstein, 83–115. Beverly Hills, Calif.: Sage, 1982.

Novy, Klaus. "Weg mit der Gemeinwirtschaft". *Bauwelt* 76 (1985): 1940–41.

Novy, Klaus, and Günther Uhlig. "Zur Organisationsdynamik wohnungspolitischer Selbsthilfeinitiativen—Eine Probemskizze zur Geschichte lokaler Wohnungspolitik in Deutschland." In *Kommunale Wohnungspolitik*, edited by Adalbert Evers,

Hans-Georg Lange, and Hellmut Wollmann, 335–54. Basel, Boston, and Stuttgart: Birkhäuser, 1983.

Pergande, Hans-Günther, and Jürgen Pergande. "Die Gesetzgebung auf dem Gebiete des Wohnungswesens und Städtebaus." In *50 Jahre im Dienste der Bau- und Wohnungswirtschaft*, edited by Deutsche Bau- und Bodenbank, 13–209. Frankfurt, 1973.

Schneider, Dieter. *Selbsthilfe, Staatshilfe, Selbstverwaltung. Ein Streifzug durch Theorie und Praxis der Wohnungspolitik*. Frankfurt: Nassauische Heimstätte, 1973.

Schneider, Hans K., and Rolf Kornemann. *Soziale Wohnungsmarktwirtschaft*. Bonn: Eichholz, 1977.

Westphal, Helmut. "Die Filtering-Theorie des Wohnungsmarktes und aktuelle Probleme der Wohnungspolitik." *Leviathan* 6 (1978): 536–57.

Wild, T., ed. "Residential Environments in West German Inner Cities in Trevor." *Urban and Rural Change in West Germany*. London: Croom Helm, 1983.

Wullkopf, Uwe. "Ist ein Abbau sozialer Disparitäten in der Wohnungsversorgung noch lohnendes Ziel der Wohnungspolitik." In *Wohnungspolitik am Ende?* edited by Institut Wohnen und Umwelt, 9–20. Opladen, West Ger.: Westdeutscher Verlag, 1981.

———. "Wohnungsbau und Wohnungspolitik in der Bundesrepublik." *Aus Politik und Zeitgeschichte* 32, no. 10 (1982): 11–25.

4

The Netherlands

HUGO PRIEMUS

Housing in the Netherlands in the eighties is largely determined by factors outside housing. At the beginning of the decade the Netherlands was afflicted by a severe economic recession. Unemployment soared, incomes fell, interest rates went up, and the state's financing deficit grew. The owner-occupier sector collapsed and the government stepped up the building program in the rented sector to ensure continuity in house building. Unemployment in the construction industry could not be allowed to increase further.

All of this led to a high expenditure on the housing budget. The extensive building programs in the recent past have brought with them long-term subsidy obligations. Now that the economy is growing again, the economic prospects are reasonably favorable, and the interest rates have decreased, pressure is being exerted from all sides to economize on the housing budget. As equilibrium has been attained in parts of the housing market, a restriction of housing subsidies also seems a sound course to follow. However, for the future it is not clear where this course will lead. Will the present policy structure be largely maintained, or will we see a dismantling of the greater part of the instruments now applicable: building subsidies, housing allowances, rent policy, dynamic costing, house-building programming, housing distribution? The discussions on the housing policy to be pursued are dominated by buzz words like *liberalization, deregulation, decentralization,* and *privatization.* On the other hand, housing associations, builders, and other participants in the market urgently call for policy continuity. New construction will decline in the nineties. Housing-stock policy will grow in importance. Parts of the housing market will probably be liberalized more or less. In other parts policy will perhaps be intensified. Partially in the light of a parliamentary inquiry into building subsidies (occasioned by a sensational fraud case; Priemus 1987), housing policy is now being fundamentally reconsidered. In 1988 a government memorandum on housing policy in the nineties was announced (Heerma 1988; 1989). In the Netherlands housing is at the crossroads (see also Van Weesep 1986b; Van der Schaar 1987).

TRENDS IN BASIC CONDITIONS UNDERLYING THE HOUSING SITUATION

Demographic Conditions

After World War II the Dutch population underwent rapid growth. (The growth of the population in the period 1977–1986, divided into birth, death, immigration, and emigration, is shown in table 4.1.) The birth rates in the fifties and sixties were exceptionally high; mortality rates, on the contrary, were very low. The natural growth was further intensified by a number of (unplanned) immigration waves; above all, in 1946 there was an influx of people who settled in the Netherlands from the former colony of Indonesia, which became independent in 1947. Since about 1965, but above all in the seventies, many "guest workers" left a number of Mediterranean countries to come to work in the Netherlands.

Before 1975 (the start of the independence of Surinam, a former colony), a large part of the population of that country migrated to the Netherlands. This led to the immigration peak of 127,000 in 1975. The "guest workers" were followed after a number of years by the remaining members of the family (family reunion); this, in addition to the continuing immigration from Surinam, explains the immigration peak in 1979–1980 (see figure 4.1).

In the fifties active attempts were made to encourage emigration. The effects of this emigration policy time after time were cancelled out by the effects of immigration. Only in the period 1982–1984 was the migration balance practically in equilibrium. The immigration led not only to an additional population increase but also to a gradual development of the Netherlands into a multiracial society. As a result of the increasing pressure of applicants for asylum, immigration has been increasing again in recent years. On January 1, 1986, 3.8 percent of the Dutch population consisted of non-Dutch nationals; many allochthons (e.g., those from Surinam) possess Dutch nationality. In the cities in particular we see concentrations of foreigners, in a number of districts with relatively unfavorable housing conditions, of up to 25 percent and more.

Since 1968 the birth rates have fallen strongly, as a result, among other things, of the wide distribution of contraceptives and the growth in the number of employed women. In recent years the birth rates have been extremely low. Since 1983 a slight increase in the birth rates can be observed.

According to the most recent population forecast of the Central Bureau of Statistics (1986, middle variant), the population, which as of January 1, 1986, amounted to 14,529,000, will have grown to 15,588,000 by the year 2000. Thereafter, the population growth will continue somewhat to 15,750,000 in the year 2005 and then contract to 14,599,000 in the year 2035. The number of households will continue to increase after the year 2005 and ultimately more or less stabilize. As a result of the low birth rates in the seventies and eighties, the growth in the number of households, in particular after 1990, will be modest. The households on average will be smaller and older than today, with a marked increase in the proportion of single persons in particular.

Uncertain factors continue to be not only the future development of the birth rates (in the years to come the birth rate could rise again) but also the development of immigration (increasing pressure of the number of applicants for asylum or immigrants from the Netherlands Antilles and/or South Africa in connection with possible political developments). Finally, the Netherlands, too, will have to wait and see what the development of euthanasia will be, to what extent major causes of death such as cancer and cardiovascular disease will increase or decrease, and the extent to which the spread of aids (now as yet limited) will proceed to assume dramatic forms and leave behind demographic traces. The official population forecast does not base itself on such (not impossible) surprises.

All in all a certain demographic stagnation is expected in the decades to come and bound up with this a stagnating development in the demand for housing. The same period will see the occurrence of three interrelated trends: "ungreening" (a drop in the percentage of young people), "greying" (an increase in the percentage of elderly people above the age of sixty-five), and "silvering" (an increase in the percentage of old people above the age of eighty).

The proportion of persons who are dependent on the income of others will increase in the future, above all as a result of this aging. On balance, the need for full or partial care will also increase as a result of the increasing greying.

All in all, the prospect of an increasing differentiation in kinds of households

Table 4.1
Demographic Indicators, the Netherlands, 1977–1986

Demographic Indicators		1977	1978	1979
1.	Birth rate (per 1,000 inh.)	12.5	12.6	12.5
2.	Death rate (per 1,000 inh.)	7.9	8.2	8.0
3.	Natural growth (1-2) (per 1,000 inh.)	4.6	4.4	4.5
4.	Number of births (x 1,000)	173	176	175
5.	Number of deaths (x 1,000)	110	114	113
6.	Natural growth (4-5) (x 1,000)	63	61	62
7.	Immigration (x 1,000)	84	89	105
8.	Emigration (x 1,000)	61	61	60
9.	Net migration (7-8)	23	28	45
10.	Growth of population* (x 1,000)	83	88	105
11.	Population (x 1,000)	13,814	13,898	13,986
12.	# of households (x 1,000)	4,752	4,839	4,911

Source: Central Bureau of Statistics.

ªIncludes balance of administrative corrections.

1980	1981	1982	1983	1984	1985	1986
12.8	12.5	12.0	11.8	12.1	12.3	12.7
8.1	8.1	8.2	8.2	8.3	8.5	8.6
4.7	4.4	3.8	3.6	3.8	3.8	4.1
181	179	172	170	174	178	185
114	116	117	118	120	123	125
67	63	55	52	54	55	59
112	80	71	67	67	79	87
59	63	67	61	59	55	55
53	17	3	6	7	24	32
118	77	54	55	59	76	86
14,091	14,209	14,286	14,340	14,395	14,454	14,529
5,006	5,105	5,215	5,321	5,420	5,522	5,620

Figure 4.1
Share of Gross Housing Costs in the Consumer Expenditures of Families, by Real Per Capita Consumer
Expenditures, the Netherlands, 1950–1982 (1950 = 100)

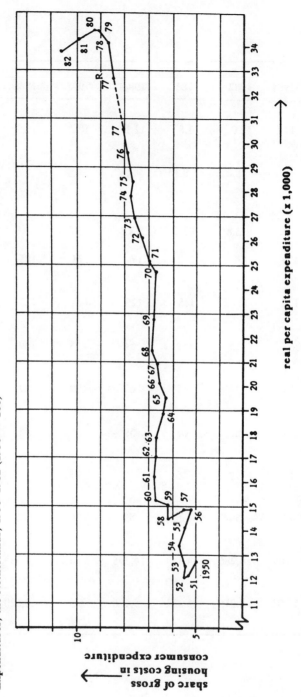

Source: Central Bureau of Statistics (CBS), *Nationale Rekeningen,* various years.

seems the most probable: there will be increasing differences in age (young, middle aged, old), in household size (growing numbers of single persons), in ethnicity (growing number of foreigners, mixed marriages), by number of incomes (nonearners, single earners, and several earners), and—partially in connection with the last category—by household income. This expected increase in household differentiation provides housing and housing policy with new challenges.

Economic Conditions

In the fifties and sixties the Netherlands experienced an unprecedentedly strong economic growth; unemployment occurred to only a limited extent. On the contrary, as a result of strain on the labor market, wages came under pressure. A greater supply of labor as the result of the immigration of foreign workers brought only partial relief. After 1970 inflation was fanned: 4.5 percent in 1970, 8 percent in 1971, to 10 percent and more in 1974 and 1975. The first oil crisis, in 1973, marked a sharp recession. In the seventies unemployment grew, assuming dramatic forms after 1978 (second oil crisis), with a peak of 820,000 (about 18 percent) jobless in 1984 (table 4.2).

The second oil crisis in 1978 led to a decline in real national income in 1980–1982. Since then a recovery has occurred. After the inflation in the seventies, the eighties brought from 1986 onwards a limited deflation. The principal economic indicators in the period 1977–1987 are surveyed in table 4.2.

Labor costs per unit of product, a strategic factor in particular for the international competitive position of the Netherlands, still rose strongly in the seventies; after 1982 a stabilization fortunately occurred, the years 1987 and above all 1984 even displaying a fall in costs.

The volume of production by firms and the volume of consumption increased identically in the period under review: the recession in the years 1980–1984 stands out clearly. Since 1985 both production and consumption have been growing by 2.0–2.5 percent per year. In the development of the volume of investment we see the usual cyclical movement in intensified form. The years 1980 and 1981 in particular were low points.

For the demand side of the housing market the development of purchasing power is of great importance. Real disposable income fell in the period 1980–1984. Only recently has disposable income been increasing again, by 2–3 percent per year.

Employment likewise fell in the period 1980–1984 and has been recovering since then only very gradually. Following the peak year of 1980, employment is still some 150,000 jobs lower today. Unemployment has been increasing since the sixties. Since 1980 the increase in registered unemployment may be described as dramatic. No wonder that the government could not accept a sharp decline in house building in that year. After unemployment had reached a peak of 820,000 in 1984 and a possible figure of 1 million was already being mentioned, a decline

Table 4.2
Economic Indicators, the Netherlands, 1977–1987

Percent change, compared with previous year	1977	1978	1979	1980
GNP real national income	3	2.5	0	-0.5
Price index private consumption	6	4.5	4.5	7
Labour productivity in firms	3	2.5	0.7	0.5
Labour costs per unit product	4	3	3.5	4
Production volume of firms	3	2.5	2	1
Volume of private consumption	5	4	2	-0.5
Volume of investments of firms (excl. housing)	18	6	2	-7
Real disposable income (modal income)	2.5	3	1.7	-1 to-1.5
Levels per year				
Employment (x 1,000 years)	4,662	4,681	4,767	4,796
Registered unemployment (x 1,000 persons)	204	206	210	248
Savings (1)	14.6	13.4	12.5	11.5
Public financing deficit (1)	3.6	4.5	5.5	7.2
Tax rate (1)	31.4	31.9	31.0	31.4
Social security premium rate (1)	19.8	20.1	19.8	20.2

Source: Central Planning Bureau, Macro-economic Investigations.

(1) As a percentage of net national income, market price.

1981	1982	1983	1984	1985	1986	1987
-2	-1	0.5	2.5	3	2.75	0.75
6.5	5.5	3	2.5	2.5	0.25	-0.5
0.5	1	3.5	3	1.25	0.75	1
1	4.5	0.5	-5.5	1.5	2.5	0
-1.5	-2	1	2.5	2.5	2.75	2
-2.5	-1.5	0.5	-0.5	2	3	2.75
-12	-2	1.5	4	12.75	12	4
-3 to-2	-1.5	-3	-0.5	2.25	3.5	2.25
4,742	4,619	4,525	4,511	4,589	4,670	4,704
385	655	801	822	761	711	680
11.5	11.5	11.5	14.5	15.5	15	14.5
9.1	10.1	10.7	9.1	7.1	6.3	7.3
29.8	29.3	28.5	27.6	27.4	28.7	29.8
20.9	22.1	24.6	23.2	22.9	21.8	22.4

set in, partially through changes in the definition. Nevertheless, measured by general standards unemployment still remains unacceptably high.

After a lower figure in the period 1980–1983 the savings ratio has stabilized at a value of 14–15 percent. The burden of taxes and social security contributions is at a fairly stable level of upwards of 50 percent. Although the government is aiming at a reduction of this burden, there is as yet nothing to be seen of a declining trend. That declining trend does exist with regard to the financing deficit of the authorities, which rose between 1977 and 1983 from 3.5 percent to 10.7 percent and since then has fallen to approximately 7 percent.

The general picture is clear. At the beginning of the eighties a serious economic recession manifested itself, which was halted around 1984. Since then unemployment has fallen, real national income has been increasing again, investments are recovering, and purchasing power has been picking up again, all this in a slightly deflationary situation. The forecasts for economic development in the years to come now proceed from an economic growth of 2 percent per year.

The Netherlands has a very open economy and is therefore largely dependent for the development of its prosperity on international developments. The country now exports natural gas to a value of many billion guilders per year. The price of the natural gas is linked to that of crude oil. The recent fall in oil prices has had negative effects on the economic development of the Netherlands and notably on the budgetary situation of the central government. In 1986 the export price of natural gas fell by 30 percent; the export volume fell in that year by 17 percent. Natural gas profits result in considerable income for the central government. The Netherlands has an interest in high energy prices. The rise in natural gas prices after 1973 (the first oil crisis) and 1978 (the second oil crisis) led to a sharp increase in heating costs. The result was an extra rise in living costs, a reduction in the size of new dwellings, and greater emphasis on the improvement of the energy quality of dwellings. Now that natural gas prices have fallen, the volume of retrofitted insulation work has fallen again.

The socioeconomic inequalities between different regions are relatively small. The country may be largely regarded as one urban field. The Randstad is, in this context, the center of economic activity (Rotterdam as the world's first port, Amsterdam as sociocultural and financial center, with Schiphol airport and a large seaport, The Hague as center of government, and Utrecht at the junction of railways and road links). But the position of the provinces of Gelderland, North Brabant, and Limburg, where industry is vigorously developing, is also very favorable. The most disquieting situation is encountered in the three northern provinces (Groningen, Friesland, Drenthe), which are in an isolated location, and in the less attractive parts of the cities.

In the seventies house-building programming played an essential part in physical planning policy (among other things, by the allocation of growth poles in the surroundings of the cities to counter urban sprawl). For the years to come the function of house building for physical planning will lose importance. The expansion of the growth poles will gradually be reduced in this process.

The fourth Physical Planning Memorandum has recently been published, with as a principal theme the strengthening of the economic potential of the Netherlands, the emphasis falling on the Randstad, on the international position of the Netherlands ("gateway to Europe"), and on the possible development of the infrastructure (e.g., a high-speed train link with other European countries). The former stress on promotion of the more peripheral regions, such as the North of the country, has receded entirely into the background.

Administrative Conditions

The Netherlands is a parliamentary democracy, governed by changing coalitions. There is a political party on a denominational basis (CDA), a social-democratic party (PvdA), and a (smaller) liberal-conservative party (VVD). In the period 1973–1977 a denominational-socialist coalition ran the country, laying the foundations for the present rules in the field of housing. The Rent and Subsidy Policy Memorandum, 1974, introduced dynamic costing and a rent-adjustment policy in conformity with market principles and covering all rented dwellings. Dynamic costing (which applied until 1988) means that in the staggering of income and expenditures over a certain period, allowance is made for rising returns from rent and rising operating expenses. As a consequence, the cost-price-based rent is not constant for fifty years (as in traditional costing) but is lower at the start, and then it rises during the total operating period. A mixed system of building subsidies and housing allowances in the rented sector, a system with premiums to encourage owner occupancy (notably via the promotion of new construction), and far-reaching rent protection were continued in 1974 and more firmly anchored in the policy. In parts of the country (above all the Randstad) dwellings are still subject to a distribution mechanism strongly influenced by the authorities.

Since 1977 the Netherlands has been governed by a coalition of the CDA and VVD, with the responsibility for housing policy always in CDA hands. Since the end of the seventies efforts have been made to decentralize housing and urban-renewal policy. The traditionally highly centralized house-building programming has been replaced by a procedure in which local authorities make their wishes and claims known. Through this system the government can make better allowance for specific local circumstances and plan when allocating quotas. Since January 1, 1988, a more decentralized subsidy policy has also been introduced in the social rented sector: the Standard Cost System (discussed later).

In the past ten years the need for cuts in government expenditures has become increasingly cogent. The financing deficit increased steadily in the seventies (table 4.2), reaching a record height of 10.7 percent of net national income in 1983. This deficit leads to high interest charges and is regarded as too high by the government. Nor does housing policy escape cuts. Until 1984 housing expenditure grew, both absolutely and as a percentage of national income. In recent years "rethinking memoranda" have been published per policy sector, indicating how substantial economies can be made on the respective budgets.

There is a strong tendency to curb the growth of government expenditures, partially because there is a desire to reconsider government tasks. However, the opposite is also true. Because the government wants to economize, the established policy has suffered. In particular, "open-ended arrangements" are strongly criticized by the Ministry of Finance. Buzz words in this context are *deregulation*, *privatization*, and *cutting back government services*. Housing does not escape this discussion either. Above all, now that the most acute housing shortages have been overcome and the interest rate is relatively low, some doubt the utility of extensive building subsidies and the need for detailed regulations.

In 1986 a parliamentary inquiry into building subsidies got under way (see Priemus 1987), an in-depth investigation by a parliamentary commission that has questioned more than seventy witnesses under oath. The inquiry was occasioned by the suspicion that in some cases investors had received too much building subsidy. In the background of the initiative, unanimously adopted by the Second Chamber of Parliament, the idea was probably entertained that an in-depth investigation could help to find new bases for housing policy. The mass media (television, radio, newspapers) devoted considerable attention to the public hearings of the Inquiry Commission. Its report was critical of the government's control over housing subsidies, precipitating the resignation of the minister of housing. His successor issued a "Memorandum on Housing Policy in the 1990s" (Heerma 1988), which generated widespread debate. The memorandum implies a structural decline in state housing expenditures during the 1990s. Policy will be directed at increasing the autonomy of the non-profit rental sector and decentralization. Private home ownership is to be increased from 42 to 55 percent in the year 2000. In general, the new approach means less government involvement and more reliance on market mechanisms. Nevertheless, central responsibilities for housing will remain those of the national government. Individual rent subsidies will be maintained. Dynamic cost pricing will be eliminated. If interest rates remain low and the expected economic growth is realized, rents will rise faster than incomes, so that object subsidies would be reduced. The new policy will promote the sale of social housing, but it will not introduce the "Right to Buy" as in Britain. Although the priority of housing has declined on the political agenda for the 1990s, there are grounds for some optimism regarding prospective developments.

THE ROLE OF HOUSING INSTITUTIONS AND ORGANIZATIONS

Under the Constitution the central government in the Netherlands has accepted general responsibility for the quality of housing. However, the primary responsibility is vested in the local authorities. The Netherlands is divided into twelve provinces and about eight hundred local authorities.

In the programming of house building the central government, provinces, and local authorities all play a role. In the programming procedure a distinction is made between a rising and falling cycle. In the rising cycle the municipalities formulate their plans and requirements. They are collected and considered by the Provincial Housing Committee. The provincial plans are then considered by the Government Committee for Housing. Partially on the basis of these signals, but above all on the strength of budgetary possibilities and limitations, the minister of housing, physical planning, and the environment compiles every year a Multiyear Housebuilding Plan with a currency of five years, of which the program for the first year is binding. As soon as this plan has been adopted by Parliament, the various categories of the subsidy quotas are distributed among the provinces, which in turn distribute them among the local authorities. Of the total annual programs, 80–90 percent have been subsidized until recently. Now the share of non-subsidized new dwellings is about 40 percent. The programs for subsidized dwelling improvement are also included in this procedure.

The subsidy policy has of old been centralized. Until recently, the central government granted subsidies directly to both tenants and landlords. The granting of individual rent subsidies is still centralized. Since January 1, 1988, the granting of building subsidies has operated via local authorities, in which budgets are assigned as part of the Standard Cost System. Operating subsidies are given by the central government via local authorities to landlords.

Rent policy, too, is a centralized matter in the Netherlands. Under the Housing Rental Act (1979) Parliament establishes every year the rent trend that is obligatory during the first five years for subsidized new construction and dwellings improved with a subsidy. For the rest, the rent trend applies if the old rent is in accordance with the quality. To arrive at rent adjustment differing from the rent trend there is room for negotiation between tenant and landlord, with a dwelling evaluation system as the basis.

The financing of housing derives in the main from four sources. In the past about one-third of house building has been financed via government loans. In effect from January 1, 1988, this arrangement has completely ceased to exist. A second source of financing is provided by the institutional investors, who not only build for themselves but also finance house building in the nonprofit rented sector. In the owner-occupied sector financing by mortgage banks and general banks, which also grant mortgage loans, is of importance. In the owner-occupied sector some 80 percent of the dwellings are financed wholly or partially by a mortgage. The last source (of modest size) is formed by homeowners' own money.

Housing-distribution policy (Housing Distribution Act, 1947) is, above all, a matter for local authorities. In those parts of the country where the Distribution Act applies, a residence permit is required. Prospective residents are given a permit if they satisfy certain priority criteria. There is often a form of cooperation between local authorities and housing associations in the distribution of scarce accommodation.

When strategic matters are involved (such as amendments of the law) the minister of housing has to consult the Housing Advisory Council, a broadly constituted advisory body of involved parties and experts.

The initiative for house building projects is taken by the following:

- Development companies or building contractors, who institute on a commercial basis housing projects, for both owner occupancy and for rent, that they do not operate themselves

- Institutional investors (pensions funds and insurance companies) that have dwellings for rent built to operate them on a commercial basis

- Housing associations and municipal housing companies that have dwellings built in the nonprofit rented sector that they operate themselves; in general, housing associations have priority in this over municipal housing companies

- In relatively exceptional cases: development of one's own dwelling by (usually prosperous) private persons

Vital to the system of Dutch housing are the housing associations, which under the 1901 Housing Act are regarded by the state as "authorized institutions," active "solely in the interests of housing" and financially supported by the authorities. The housing associations are regulated by public law and supervised by the authorities, but they are and remain private institutions: in about three quarters of the cases they have the legal status of an association and in the other cases they form a foundation. Through their private nature and their independence from local government the housing associations in the Netherlands have been less troubled by bureaucratization than those in some other countries in Western Europe.

HOUSING MARKETS AND POLICY ORIENTATIONS

Size and Composition of the Housing Stock

Table 4.3 presents a number of indicators giving an impression of the development of the housing stock in the period 1977–1986.

The Dutch housing stock is managed by three categories of owners:

1. Owner-occupiers, whereby the percentage of housing cooperatives (unlike, for instance, the Scandinavian countries) is negligible

2. Commercial landlords, whereby in the prewar stock the percentage of the individual private landlords and small operating companies is large, and in the postwar stock the percentage of pension funds and insurance companies is large

3. Nonprofit landlords, with a modest participation by local authorities and a dominating market share of the housing associations

Between 1976 and 1986 the housing stock grew from 4,480,000 to 5,483,000, a growth of 1 million dwellings in ten years. In the second half of the seventies

Table 4.3
Housing Stock Indicators, the Netherlands, 1977–1986

Indicators	1977	1978	1979	1980	1981	1982	1983	1984	1985	1986
Size of housing stock										
(x 1,000 dwellings)	4,578	4,672	4,747	4,850	4,957	5,072	5,178	5,289	5,384	5,483
(per 1,000 of population)	331	336	339	344	349	355	361	367	372	377
Owner occupied dwellings (%)	42	42	43	43	42	41	41	42	43	43
Rented dwellings, owned by housing associations (%)	-	-	-	32	31	34	35	34	34	36
Rented dwellings, owned by municipalities or other public bodies (%)	-	-	-	9	8	9	9	8	8	7
Privately rented dwellings (%)	-	-	-	15	17	14	14	13	14	13
Average number of inhabitants per dwelling	3.01	2.98	2.95	2.92	2.87	2.82	2.77	2.73	2.70	2.65
Vacancy rate (%)	1.9	2.0	2.0	2.2	2.2	2.3	2.3	2.3	2.4	2.3
average rent in the stock (guilders/month)	217	227	244	264	289	317	346	363	377	389

Sources: National Rayon Onderzoek (NRO), 1981–1985; Central Bureau of Statistics, 1977–1980, 1986.

Table 4.4
Distribution of the Housing Stock, by Year of Construction, the Netherlands, December 31, 1984

Year of Construction	%
before 1906	9.1
1906–1930	12.8
1931–1944	8.0
1945–1959	15.4
1960–1970	22.8
1971–1980	23.1
1981 and later	8.8
N (100%)	5,289,000

Source: Ministry of Housing.

the proportion of owner-occupied dwellings increased from 41 to 43 percent. In the first half of the eighties this proportion remained practically constant. In this period the proportion of housing association dwellings grew from 32 to 36 percent. The share of local authorities fell from 9 percent to 7 percent and that of private dwellings fell on balance from 15 to 13 percent; within this the proportion of private institutions (notably institutional investors) rose and that of private persons fell. The degree of occupancy fell in ten years from more than 3 to 2.7. The percentage of vacancy increased somewhat, from 1.9 to 2.3. Around 1980 vacancy was strongly concentrated in new construction (above all dwellings for owner occupancy) and since then has shifted primarily toward rented dwellings in the stock.

Rents in the stock rose considerably as a result of nationally applicable trend rent increases determined by Parliament, rent harmonization (departure from the trend in connection with extra or deficient quality), housing improvement, and new construction. In 1977 the average level was upwards of 200 guilders (about 100 U.S. dollars); in 1982 an average of 300 guilders (about 150 U.S. dollars) was already clearly being exceeded, and in 1986 an average of 389 guilders (about 195 U.S. dollars) was reached.

As of December 31, 1984, the distribution of the housing stock by year of construction was as follows (see table 4.4): Of the whole housing stock, 29.9 percent had at that time been built before 1945 and 68.1 percent before 1970. Incidentally, in the cities the proportion of prewar dwellings is much greater than average.

In October 1981 the occupied dwellings could be differentiated by a number of characteristics (see table 4.5). The proportion of apartments was 31.7 percent. In the rented sector this figure was more than 48 percent and in the owner-

Table 4.5
Occupied Dwellings, by Selected Characteristics, the Netherlands, October 1981

Characteristics	Total	Owner-occupied dwellings	Rented dwelling by sector			
			Total	Non-commer-cial(2)	Commer-cial(2)	Un-known
Dwellings (x 1,000)	4,940.5	2,064.7	2,875.8	1,918.0	850.8	106.9
Number of rooms						
3	12.3%	4.1%	18.3%	15.8%	22.1%	31.1%
4	16.0	10.3	20.1	19.1	22.5	19.7
5	37.9	35.0	39.9	45.3	29.6	23.8
6	23.8	33.0	17.2	17.3	17.5	13.1
7	10.0	17.5	4.6	2.5	8.4	12.4
Type of building						
Single-family house	68.3%	91.1%	51.9%	55.4%	44.2%	49.6%
Apartment, etc.	31.7	8.9	48.1	44.6	55.8	50.5
Facilities						
With bathroom	95.9%	97.4%	94.8%	97.0%	90.2%	92.7%
With central heating	66.1	76.0	59.0	64.2	46.6	63.8

Source: Housing Demand Survey (WBO), 1981.

(1) Housing association, local authority, and so on.
(2) Private bodies and persons.

occupied sector not more than 9 percent. Of all dwellings, 12.3 percent had three rooms (including kitchen) or fewer (0.5 percent: 1 room; 2.6 percent: 2 rooms; 9.2 percent: 3 rooms). The average number of rooms in the stock was 5.05. Of all occupied dwellings, 4.1 percent had no bathroom and 33.9 percent no central heating.

Construction Quality

In 1985 an extensive investigation was performed into the constructional quality of the housing stock: Table 4.6 gives a survey of the quality arrears by tenure. In the whole stock, the costs of alleviating deficiencies are estimated at a total of 40–50 billion guilders (about 20–25 billion U.S. dollars). This amount does not include aspects relating to amenities (absence of a toilet, rooms too small, absence of balconies and so on).

The housing association dwellings have relative low average repair costs. The average in the owner-occupied sector is identical to that for the institutional investors. The average of private rented dwellings is more than twice as high: 14,600 guilders per dwelling.

The differences in repair costs are bound up with tenure status (professional investors versus often not very professional private landlords) and above all with differences in year of construction (investors: primarily postwar; private landlords: primarily prewar). Unfortunately, in a number of published Qualitative Housing Registration tables the private rented dwellings and the investors' dwellings have been taken together. This applies for instance to table 4.7, which shows the relationship between repair costs per dwelling, tenure and year of construction.

Quality deficiencies are highly concentrated in the prewar stock. Owner-occupied dwellings from before 1945 have average repair costs of 12,500 guilders per dwelling. In the private rented sector from before 1945 the costs are 16,400 guilders per dwelling. In each of the three separate tenure categories it is roughly correct that the repair costs per dwelling constructed before 1945 are twice as high as those constructed between 1945 and 1959, which in turn are twice those for dwellings built after 1959. Within each construction period the repair costs are always highest in the private rented sector and lowest in the owner-occupied sector. The differences in repair costs between construction periods are, however, much greater than those, within a given construction period, between tenure categories. The identification of extensive quality arrears (moisture, cracks, deficient paintwork, wood rot, and so on) has reinforced the increasing priority of subsidy schemes for dwelling improvement.

Production

A further insight into characteristics of the annual production in the past ten years can be seen in table 4.8. The number of new dwellings initially fell to

Table 4.6
Repair Costs, by Tenure, the Netherlands, 1985

Ownership	Total repair costs (billions of guilders)	Average repair costs per dwelling (x 1,000 guilders)
owner-occupier	15.6	7.1
housing association	8.3	5.4
local authority	3.5	8.8
private landlord	7.5	14.6
institutional investor (pension fund, insurance company)	3.9	7.1
Total (excl. VAT)	38.8	7.5

Source: Qualitative Housing Research (KWO).
Note: VAT = Value Added Tax.

Table 4.7
Repair Costs, by Tenure and Age of Dwelling, the Netherlands, 1985

Ownership category	Year of construction	Total repair costs (billions of guilders)	Average repair costs per dwelling (x 1,000 guilders)
housing associations and local authorities	before 1945	3.6	14.7
	1945–59	3.4	7.3
	after 1959	4.8	3.9
private landlords and institutional investors	before 1945	9.0	16.4
	1945–49	0.7	8.2
	after 1959	1.7	4.1
owner-occupiers	before 1945	10.0	12.5
	1945–49	1.8	6.7
	after 1959	3.8	3.4
Total		38.8	7.5

Source: Qualitative Housing Research (KWO).

88,000 in 1979. When the owner-occupied sector collapsed and employment in the construction industry proceeded to rise, the government encouraged the construction of dwellings for rent. This encouragement was so successful that after 1979 total production increased to 123,000 dwellings in 1982. Since then a gradual decline has set in. It is striking that the number of dwellings demolished annually has been falling since 1980: from 15,000 to 10,000 in 1985. This figure is generally regarded as too low.

Building costs increased very strongly every year in the second half of the seventies. In 1980 an overcapacity began to manifest itself, partially through the limited activity in the industrial building sector. Many building firms were bankrupted, and unemployment in building soared (from 16,000 in 1979 to 121,000 in 1983). Competition became fiercer. Building costs fell by a few percent in the period 1982–1985. Recently, building costs have started to increase again, and since 1983 unemployment in the construction industry has continued to fall.

In the development of the building-plus-land costs of dwellings built with government loans, privately financed dwellings for rent, and subsidized dwellings for owner occupancy, we see the same trend: increases up to 1981 or 1982 and then a pronounced decline. This is also reflected in the trend in the rents of new social housing. They increased to 438 guilders per month in 1981, after which a decline set in. Since 1984 rents for new construction have been rising again, partially through measures to curb expenditures on building subsidies.

The increase in the percentage of apartments in new construction is striking. This percentage rose from 20 in 1979 to 37 in 1984. The reason for this is probably the increase in the number of dwellings for rent since 1979, the rise in the number of small dwellings, and the concentration of building activities in the built-up area (urban renewal, urban concentration). In the sixties and the first half of the seventies the Netherlands experienced a real wave of high-rise construction, often with estates having ten to sixteen stories. These often massive high-rise estates usually proved unpopular among the residents and furthermore involve high operating costs. For the residents the price-quality ratio of these high-rise buildings is in general unfavorable, and the management also encounters operating problems precisely in this sector. Apartment blocks built in the eighties are often limited to three or four stories, usually without a lift (to save costs) and often fitting in with the height of older urban buildings.

Financial Data

The statutory rent increases in 1977 were still 7 percent (inflation). As a result of extra rent adjustments in connection with extra quality in the stock (rent harmonization) the actual rent increases were on average ever higher. Gradually, the rent increases in the period under review fell to 2 percent in 1986 and 1987. Mortgage interest reached a peak in 1981 (nearly 13 percent) and then fell to about 7 percent in 1986. Further drops are expected. Partially as a result of this,

Table 4.8
Housing Production Indicators, the Netherlands, 1977–1986

Production Indicators	1977	1978	1979
Number of dwellings completed (x 1,000)	111	106	88
Number of dwellings demolished (x 1,000)	15	13	14
Net growth of the housing stock (1-2)	96	92	74
% change in building costs (incl. VAT)	9.4	9.5	9.5
Building and land costs of publicly financed dwellings (x 1,000 guilders)	85	94	104
Building and land costs of privately financed, subsidized rented dwellings (x 1,000 guilders)	87	97	110
Building and land costs of subsidized owner-occupied dwellings (x 1,000 guilders)	116	129	138
Owner-occupied dwellings (% of housing production)	54	61	64
Initial rent of publicly financed dwellings (guilders/month)	359	408	416
% multi-family dwellings (2)	23	20	20
% small dwellings (1-4 rooms kitchen included) (2)	24	21	21
Registered unemployment in the building industry (1). (x 1,000 persons)	20	16	16

Sources: (1) Ministry of Social Affairs and Employment; (2) P.J.C. van der Hoek, Studie rapport, *Nieuwbouwprogrammering, 1986* (Study report, Programming of New Construction, 1986) (The Hague: Housing Ministry, 1987).

Note: VAT = Value Added Tax.

1980	1981	1982	1983	1984	1985	1986
114	118	123	111	113	98	103
15	14	13	11	12	10	12
99	104	111	100	101	88	92
7.9	3.1	-2.0	-0.7	-0.3	-1.0	2.5
111	114	109	109	110	108	109
136	136	140	131	122	123	115
130	142	143	143	137	138	-
56	40	28	33	38	44	47
425	438	418	415	429	433	455
21	26	31	36	37	31	27
24	29	33	38	42	35	-
32	65	108	121	110	89	69

Table 4.9
Housing Finance Indicators, the Netherlands, 1977–1986

Finance Indicator	1977	1978	1979
% rent increase (national trend)	7	7	5
Mortgage interest (%)	8.92	8.61	9.64
Number of recipients of housing allowances (x 1,000)	357	384	395
Expenditure of Ministry of Housing (draft budget, x billion guilders)	7.4	8.3	9.1
Total public expenditure on housing (draft budget, x billion guilders)	6.4	7.0	7.6
Public housing expenditure as a % of total public expenditure, draft budget	7.99	7.55	8.04
Housing allowances for tenants (x billion guilders)	0.6	0.7	0.8
Building subsidies for rented dwellings (x billion guilders)	1.8	2.1	2.2
Return on dynamic cost price	8.13	7.80	8.79
Return on government loans	7.93	7.74	8.84

Sources: (1) Ministry of Housing; (2) National Bank of the Netherlands.

[a]After 1984: with tax and premium overhead.
[b]Provisional figure.

1980	1981	1982	1983	1984	1985	1986	Source
6	6	6/4	5	3	3	2	VROM(1)
11.39	12.71	11.05	9.13	8.99	8.36	7.26	DNB(2)
418	456	530	629	635	715	7.78	VROM(1)
10.1	11.3	12.0	14.0	16.2	16.6	16.4	VROM(1)
8.6	9.8	10.3	11.8	· 14.0	14.9	14.6	VROM(1)
8.19	9.54	8.30	9.27	9.9	-	-	VROM(1)
0.9	1.1	1.3	1.5	1.9	1.6	1.5	a
2.2	2.4	2.5	3.0	3.9	4.8	5.9	b
10.26	11.64	10.59	8.58	8.70	7.57	6.93	b
10.17	11.56	9.93	8.24	7.44	7.32	-	

the owner-occupied sector is being stimulated. (See table 4.9 for key financial data with regarding to housing.)

After a drastic expansion of the scheme in 1975, the number of recipients of individual rent subsidy steadily increased. When incomes began to fall, the growth of the number of recipients of a subsidy after 1980 accelerated perceptibly. Through the adjustment of the scheme and later as the result of a more favorable development of incomes, the growth rate slackened, but this subsidy scheme still displays an expansive development.

The budget of the Ministry of Housing has been growing steadily since 1977. Not until 1986 did we see a slight decline. As a percentage of total government expenditures, there was an increase in housing expenditures from 1978 to 1984. Since then a decline has set in. In absolute terms housing expenditures rose until 1985. Setting the pace within the housing budget is the expenditure on housing allowances and building subsidies. Spending on housing allowances grew year after year. Not until 1985 did a decrease in the draft budget follow, but this is something of an optical illusion. The tax and premium overheads formerly included in the individual housing subsidy expenditure were kept outside the budget of the Ministry of Housing after 1984. The growth of the pure expenditure on housing allowances slowed down but has not been halted. Expenditures on building subsidies also increased, at first less quickly than that on housing allowances, but during the period 1977–1985 the increase was nevertheless just as great. In 1977 expenditures on building subsidies were three times as great as on housing allowances; we see the same ratio in 1985.

For the financing of the subsidized rented sector the return on the dynamic cost price is important. This return is in general somewhat higher than that on government loans. Precisely when the production of subsidized dwellings for rent was the highest (1980–1982) the returns were the highest. In 1980 an attractive subsidy scheme was introduced that tempted investors back to the house-building market. Through the high return rates this scheme was disproportionately expensive for the state.

Expenditures on rent subsidies pale in significance compared to the tax relief that owner–occupiers enjoy. On balance, 2.6 billion guilders (approximately 1.3 billion U.S. dollars) was deducted from income in 1975. By 1981 that amount had risen to 9.1 billion guilders (more than 4.5 billion U.S. dollars). The latter sum meant a loss of revenue of some 4 billion guilders (2 billion U.S. dollars), a sum that is higher than the subsidies on rented dwellings (See table 4.10.).

For a long time the share of housing costs increased as a part of total consumer expenditures (figure 4.1). There are striking increases in 1950–1952 (Korea crisis), 1956–1960 (restriction on spending), and 1978–1982 (second oil crisis). In recent years the housing costs/income ratio has risen with unprecedented rapidity, whereas consumer spending has fallen (see Van Fulpen, Van der Schaar, and Priemus 1983). The average housing costs/income ratio rose between 1977 and 1981 (table 4.11) and this rise continued after 1981. The lower the income, the higher the ratio.

Table 4.10

Tax on Imputed Rent and Deduction for Mortgage Interest, the Netherlands, 1975, 1977, 1979, 1981

	Tax on imputed rent		Interest deduction	
Year	(x 1,000)	Total amount (millions of guilders)	(x 1,000)	Total amount (millions of guilders)
1975	1,383	786	949	3,335
1977	1,560	1,256	1,114	5,629
1979	1,732	1,705	1,293	8,654
1981	1,700	1,850	1,417	11,000

Source: Central Bureau of Statistics (CBS), Income Tax Statistics, various years.

The same figures for owner–occupiers and renters are given separately in table 4.12. The ratios are much higher for owner–occupiers than for renters. Above all, in the first income quartile, the ratio for owner–occupiers rose strongly between 1977 and 1981 (crisis on the owner-occupied market). Although their ratio is very high, their actual expenditures can be fairly low, if they have paid off their mortgage wholly or largely. In the rented sector we see the increasing effect of the individual rent subsidy, especially in the first income quartile. Between 1977 and 1981 the ratio in the rented sector has remained about the same: the effect of the high interest rate in this period was shouldered entirely by the state, which strongly increased building subsidies in the rented sector. Since 1982 housing costs for renters have increased considerably more quickly than those of owner–occupiers.

The development of housing costs since 1982 is broken down into the rented and owner-occupied sectors in tables 4.13 and 4.14. In the rented sector housing costs increased sharply between 1982 and 1985. Through a fall in energy costs the burden of housing costs was alleviated after 1986. The remaining budget fell between 1982 and 1985, rising after that.

In the owner-occupied sector housing costs remained practically constant between 1982 and 1985. In this period, the remaining budget decreased much less for owners than for renters. After 1985 the remaining budget increased for owner–occupiers as well. After 1985 owner–occupiers also profited from a fall in energy prices.

Demand and Building Programs

The Bureau for Strategic Market Research (1985) has estimated the development of housing demand in the years to come, partially on the strength of demographic and economic forecasts. The principal data are given in table 4.15.

A distinction has been made between a variant with 1 percent economic growth

Table 4.11
Gross and Net Housing Cost/Income Ratios, by Income Quartile, All Households, the Netherlands, 1977 and 1981

		1st quartile	2nd quartile	3rd quartile	4th quartile	total
1977	gross	21.0	14.2	13.6	12.8	15.3
	net	19.4	13.8	13.5	12.8	14.8
1981	gross	23.5	17.4	15.4	13.6	17.5
	net	21.4	16.8	15.3	13.6	16.8

Source: Van der Schaar, 1986.
Note: Gross is before deduction of mortgage interest, including rent subsidy; Net is after deduction of mortgage interest, including rent subsidy.

Table 4.12
Gross and Net Housing Cost/Income Ratios, by Income Quartile, Owner–Occupiers and Renters, the Netherlands, 1977 and 1981

	1st quartile	2nd quartile	3rd quartile	4th quartile	total
1977 (owner-occupiers)	23.4	18.1	17.1	15.3	17.6
1981 (owner-occupiers)	33.3	23.9	19.6	16.4	21.5
1977 (tenants)					
gross	20.2	12.4	10.9	9.4	13.8
net	18.0	11.8	10.8	9.4	13.0
1981 (tenants)					
gross	20.4	13.7	12.3	9.5	14.8
net	17.6	12.9	12.1	9.4	13.6

Source: Van der Schaar, 1986.

183

Table 4.13
Development of Housing Costs in the Rented Sector, the Netherlands, 1982–1987

Disposable income (guilders)	(1)
Basic rent	(2)
Individual rent subsidy	(3)
Net rent	(2)-(3)
Energy costs	(4)
Charges	(5)
Remaining budget	(1)-(2)+(3)-(4)-(5)

and one with 2 percent economic growth. The development is the same in both variants. Until 1995 building will decline very gradually. After that year it will fall strongly to about 60,000 dwellings per year in the period 1995–2000.

The Multiyear Housebuilding Plan, 1988–1992, presents the government's most recent view with regard to the pursued trend of housing production. The following shifts are envisaged:

• Declining new production

• Declining proportion of the social rented sector

• Increasing volume of subsidized dwelling improvement

• Increasing proportion of improvements in the postwar housing stock

It is striking that for the period 1988–1992 an annually unchanging program is envisaged. Policy adjustments are concentrated almost entirely in the transition between 1987 and 1988: a strong increase in the free sector, a decrease in the social rented sector (where since January 1, 1988, public loans have disappeared entirely), and a restriction of the premium owner-occupied sector. The 1987–1992 new construction program in accordance with the Multiyear House-Building Plan, 1987–1991 (Brokx 1986), and the Multiyear House-Building Plan, 1988–1992 (Heerma 1987), is shown in table 4.16.

The dwelling-improvement program for 1987–1992 (Brokx 1986; Heerma 1987) comprises 69,400 subsidized dwelling improvements in 1987, 71,600 programmed dwelling improvements in 1988 (of which 57,600 are subsidized), and 79,100 subsidized dwelling improvements in 1989, increasing to 92,400 subsidized dwelling improvements in 1992. For 1988, 14,000 unsubsidized dwelling improvements are envisaged in order to skim off from housing asso-

1-1-1982	1-4-1985	1-4-1986	1-4-1987
2,205	2,207	2,253	2,298
229	389	401	412
20	31	32	33
279	358	369	379
205	232	241	193
30	33	34	34
1,691	1,584	1,609	1,692

Source: Woonlastensignalering (signalling of housing costs), Second Chamber, 1986–1987, 119,823, no. 1.

ciations and other nonprofit landlords financial gains that came about through the accelerated repayment of expensive loans by these landlords in past years.

In general, the aim is a steady increase in private dwelling improvement in the prewar housing stock and an increase in postwar dwelling improvement in both the social and the private rented sector. For the improvement of owner-occupied dwellings, national terms of reference are absent. Expressed in numbers of dwellings, the number of subsidized dwelling improvements will be higher from 1990 onwards than the number of subsidized new dwellings.

MAJOR PROBLEMS AND PROSPECTIVE DEVELOPMENTS

The results are now becoming available from the most recent Housing Demand Survey, which was held in 1985. Housing shortages are greater than was formerly assumed. The shortage increased dramatically in 1987 from 60,000 to 127,000. Individualization is making more progress in the Netherlands than one appears to realize. The strong economic recession at the beginning of the eighties was accompanied by a dramatic collapse of the owner-occupied sector. After a rapid increase in the second half of the seventies, the prices of dwellings for owner occupancy fell sharply. The proportion of newly built dwellings in that category declined strongly. Now that economic prospects are reasonably favorable, interest rates have fallen sharply, and prices for aspiring buyers have reached an attractive level, the owner-occupied sector is picking up again. For years to come an increasing percentage of owner-occupied dwellings in new construction is expected, together with a growing number of conversion of rented dwellings in the stock into condominiums, above all in the cities (Maas 1984; Van Weesep and Maas 1984; Maas and Van Weesep 1986; Van Weesep 1986a).

Table 4.14
Development of Housing Costs in the Owner–Occupied Sector, the Netherlands, 1982–1986

		1-1-1982	1-4-1985	1-4-1986
Net imputed costs (guilders)		580	557	562
Disposable income	(1)	2,702	2,789	2,879
Net owner's cost on a cash basis	(2)	393	439	423
Energy costs	(3)	229	275	284
Charges	(4)	40	44	45
Remaining budget	(1)-(2)-(3)-(4)	2,040	2,031	2,127

Source: Woonlastensignalering, Second Chamber, 1986–1987, 19,823, no. 1.

Table 4.15
Required House-Building Production, the Netherlands, 1985–2000 (x 1,000 Dwellings)

Year	Expansion demand	Replacement demand	Growth in dwelling reserve	Making up arrears	Total
		1% variant			
85–90	74.2	15	1.8	5.6	96.6
90–95	64.6	18	1.6	5.6	89.8
95–00	46.6	18	1.2	–	65.8
		2% variant			
85–90	78.6	15	1.9	5.6	101.1
90–95	69.0	18	1.7	5.6	94.3
95–00	50.4	18	1.2	–	69.6

Source: Bureau for Strategic Market Research, 1985.

The expected economic growth also means that the demands the occupants will make of their dwellings will probably increase. Against this background, the authorities will see themselves obliged in the years to come to introduce further cuts. It is expected that the share of the social rented sector will fall further, that the financing of this sector will be taken over entirely by the private capital market, and, furthermore, that the free sector will flourish again.

A drawback to the expected economic growth is the expected increase in building and land costs. In recent years inflation has been very low in the Netherlands; it is expected that in the years to come inflation could flare up to some extent.

At present the private sector has access to a generous supply of capital. Nevertheless, sticking points appear to exist for the private financing of housing, since it is not clear to what extent the risks for the providers of capital are limited by government guarantees. There is considerable pressure from the private sector to liberalize housing gradually: abolition of housing distribution rules, freer determination of rents, and abolition of the leasehold. This liberalization applies not only to rent-adjustment policy and housing-distribution policy but also to house-building programming and subsidy policy. Dynamic cost pricing has been eliminated recently for new dwellings. The investors now receive a fixed contribution with a relatively short currency. Some experts even call for a complete abolition of building subsidies. As a result of the fall in interest rates the expenditure on building subsidies for new dwellings is, in any case, dropping not inconsiderably.

At the end of 1985 the "Rethinking of Rent and Subsidy Policies in the

Table 4.16
New Construction Program in Accordance with the Multiyear House-Building
Plan, the Netherlands, 1987–1991 and 1988–1992

Construction Sector	1987-1991		1988-1992
	1987	1988	1988-1992 per annum
Social rented sector	36,000	31,000	29,500
Market sector with premium	35,000	35,000	29,000
- premium rented	9,000	9,000	9,000
- premium owner-occupied	26,000	26,000	20,000
Free sector with non-recurrent contribution	20,000	20,000	21,000
Total subsidized new construction	91,000	86,000	79,500
Unsubsidized sector	7,000	8,000	15,000
Total new construction	98,000	94,000	94,500

Source: Ministry of Housing.

Nineties'' memorandum was published, in which are outlined the possibilities and consequences of spending cuts of 20 percent and more for housing. Five variants for cutbacks were worked out: cuts on subject subsidies or building subsidies, mixed variant, encouragement of filtering, a mild liberalization variant, and the sweeping liberalization variant.

Partially on the strength of this exercise it was laid down in the Coalition Agreement of the second Lubbers Cabinet (1986–1989/90) that over a four-year period spending cuts of 1.5 billion guilders had to be made on housing. This is being done above all by a decrease in the proportion of social housing and savings on building subsidies. Various quarters advocate an increase in the controllability of the expenditure and contraction of the subsidy period per dwelling. Above all, the rising subsidies per dwelling, which are now inherent in dynamic costing, meet with many objections. Little if any thought is given to an increase in costs for owner–occupiers.

In the rules for improvement subsidies in the rented sector, the government loans for the improvement of prewar social housing have been done away with, whereas the subsidies for the improvement of postwar dwellings have been raised. The problems of the improvement of postwar dwellings have become the focus of considerable attention. A growing number of postwar housing estates have been the subject of publicity through structural letting problems, in some cases in relation to design and constructional faults. In some cases the demolition of such estates is even being considered (Prak and Priemus 1985).

The government is according high priority to the promotion of urban renewal. Since the adoption on January 1, 1985, of the Town and Village Renewal Act, every year the sum of nearly 1 billion guilders (about 500 million U.S. dollars) is distributed among local authorities and the provinces, which have the free disposition of these budgets, provided that spending of the funds serves the interests of urban renewal. Upon the introduction of this act more than twenty separate subsidy schemes were incorporated into the urban renewal budget. In this way the tackling of urban renewal has made a strong contribution to the decentralization of policy that the government is pursuing. The improvement of owner-occupied dwellings is subsidized by local authorities from moneys supplied by the urban renewal fund.

A major change in rent and subsidy policy is the proposed introduction (in effect since January 1, 1988) of the Standard Cost System. In this system the subsidy is linked to what the authorities regard as acceptable building-plus-land costs and the size of the dwelling. The acceptable building-plus-land costs consist of acceptable land costs and standard building costs. In addition, there are costs connected with the location that do not lead to higher quality. These (standardized) location costs are fully subsidized. If the building costs rise above the level of standard building costs and location costs, extra costs come about. Since it is assumed that these extra costs lead to extra quality, they are not subsidized. These costs must be passed on to the tenant to cover them or be borne by the landlord. The larger local authorities are assigned annual budgets on the basis of the permitted house-building programs for location costs and subsidies to be paid. The local authority can, within strict limiting conditions, adjust the subsidy amounts to some extent so that some scope is created for local considerations (flexibility).

A remarkable development is the preparation of the Building Decree. At present, the technical building standards are formulated by local authorities in a municipal building code. The Association of Netherlands Local Authorities has been endeavoring for years to promote as much standardization as possible by publishing a Model Building Code, which in general is followed by local authorities. As part of the policy deregulation, efforts are being made to arrive at a national standard, laid down in the Building Decree, in which in particular the amenities standards are simplified to give the designer and the principal more freedom. However, many fear that introduction of the Building Decree, in combination with the repeated spending cuts, will lead to considerable deterioration in the quality of new construction. However, introduction of the Building Decree is being seized as an opportunity to raise the standards regarding the required thermal insulation drastically. Considerable attention is being devoted to increasing the energy efficiency of new and existing dwellings.

To meet the housing demands of the elderly, the young, the handicapped, students, and foreigners, the general subsidy regime is applied as much as possible. The starting point is that building is done to meet demand and that there is no discrimination in housing distribution. In general, this point of departure is put into practice reasonably well. A specific subsidy scheme has been developed for the adaptation of dwellings to the special requirements of the handicapped.

In the cities housing shortages persist. It is there, above all, that the demand of young people is concentrated. They have to turn in particular to the informal part of the housing market like many squatters in Amsterdam and Nijmegen. The policy of building special small dwellings for young people, pursued since 1975, has largely failed. These housing units often proved too expensive, were sometimes poorly located, and now often have to contend with operating problems.

Government policy is aimed at encouraging the elderly to live independently. Additional old people's homes are being built only in exceptional cases; the emphasis is on the renovation of these homes and on promoting support services for old people, as a result of which the elderly can continue to live independently as long as possible. Through the expected greying of the population, and notably the increase in the percentage of very old people, the problems of the housing and care of the elderly are becoming of increasing interest. In view of this expected greying of the population, building for the elderly seems to be one of the key tasks for the nineties.

For years to come the following developments appear to be of strategic importance:

- continuous pressure on the national budget to implement cuts, also in housing; in times of high interest rates, housing expenditures may nevertheless increase again;

- in connection with this, a gradual withdrawal of the authorities from parts of the housing market, whereby participants in the market are left more freedom (partial liberalization); this liberalization trend will alternate with periods of reregulation;

- attempts to decentralize housing policy, which will prove only partially successful;

- gradually declining new construction and a steadily growing emphasis on maintenance and improvements of the stock;

- strong growth of the problems of decay, management, improvement, and restructuring of parts of the postwar stock (above all, high-rise estates in the nonprofit rented sector);

- increasing automation in the development and management of dwellings;

- strengthening of housing consumer organizations, in both the rented and the owner-occupied sector;

- growing importance of the accommodation of the elderly and the need to alleviate the need for care of some of these elderly persons in relation to their housing situation; and

- structural growth of home ownership, in the cities especially in the form of condominiums.

REFERENCES

Brokx, G. Ph. 1986. *Meerjarenplan woningbouw, 1987–1991* (Multiyear House-Building Plan, 1987–1991). The Hague: Government Publishing Office.

Bureau for Strategic Market Research. 1985. *Toetsing en actualisering trendrapport volkshuisvesting* (Testing and Updating of the Housing Trend Report). The Hague: Ministry of Housing, January.

Heerma, E. 1987. *Meerjarenplan Woningbouw, 1988–1992* (Multiyear House-Building Plan, 1988–1992). The Hague: Government Publishing House.

———. 1988. *Ontwerpnota Volkshuisvesting in de Jaren Negentig.* (Draft Memorandum). The Hague: Staatsuitgeverÿ.

———. 1989. *Nota Volkshuisvesting in de Jaren Negentig.* Final Memorandum. The Hague: Staatsuitgeverÿ.

Maas, M. W. A. 1984. "Condominium Conversion In Prewar Neighborhoods: An Urban Transformation Process in Dutch Cities." *Tijdschrift voor Economische en Sociale Geografie* 75:36–45.

Maas, M. W. A., and J. van Weesep. 1986. "The Condominium: An Option for When the Chips are Down." *Netherlands Journal of Housing and Environmental Research* 1:27–41.

Prak, N. L., and H. Priemus, eds. 1985. *Post-war Public Housing in Trouble.* Delft: Delft University Press.

Priemus, H. 1987. "Housing Subsidies in the Netherlands: Origins of a Parliamentary Inquiry." *International Journal of Urban and Regional Research* 11, no. 3 (September): 417–20.

Van der Schaar, J. 1986. *De huisvestingssituatie in Nederland, 1900–1982* (The Housing Situation in the Netherlands, 1900–1982). Delft: Delft University Press.

———. 1987. *Groei en bloei van het Nederlandse volkshuisvestings-beleid* (The Growth and Flourishing of Dutch Housing Policy). Delft: Delft University Press.

Van Fulpen, J. A., J. van der Schaar, and H. Priemus, eds. 1983. *Who Will Pay the Housing Bill in the Eighties?* Delft: Delft University Press.

Van Weesep, J. 1986a. "Condominium: A New Housing Sector in the Netherlands." Dissertation, Rijksuniversiteit, Utrecht.

———. 1986b. "Dutch Housing: Recent Developments and Policy Issues." *Housing Studies* 1:61–66.

Van Weesep, J., and M. W. A. Maas. 1984. "Housing Policy and Conversion to Condominiums in the Netherlands." *Environment and Planning, A,* 16:1149–61.

FURTHER READING

Boelhouwer, P. M., and J. van Weesep. "Financial Repercussions of the Sale of Public Housing in the Netherlands." *Housing Studies* 3, no. 3 (1988):183–89.

Cruijsen, H. "Bevolkingsprognose voor Nederland, 1986–2035" (Population Forecast for the Netherlands, 1986–2035). *CBS Maandstatistiek Bevolking*, no. 2 (1987):15–21.

Deurloo, M. C., W. A. V. Clark, and F. M. Dieleman. "Tenure Choice in the Dutch Housing Market." *Environment and Planning A* 19 (1987):763–81.

Dieleman, F. M. "The Future of Dutch Housing—a Review and Interpretation of the Recent Literature." *Tijdschrift voor Economische en Sociale Geografie* 77, no. 5 (1986):336–45.

Dieleman, F. M., and J. van Weesep. "Housing Under Fire: Budget Cuts, Policy Adjustments and Market Changes." *Tijdschrift voor Economische en Sociale Geografie* 77 (1986):310–15.

Draaisma, J., and P. van Hoogstraten. "The squatter movement in Amsterdam." *International Journal of Urban and Regional Research* 7, no. 3 (1983): 406–16.

Everaers, P. C. J., and W. A. V. Clark. "Policy and Mobility in Dutch Housing Market Contexts: The Influence of National and Local Policies on Intra- and Inter-City Mobility." *Tijdschrift voor Economische en Sociale Geografie* 75, no. 4 (1984):242–48.

Flynn, Rob. "Cutback Contradictions in Dutch Housing Policy." *Journal of Social Policy* 15, no. 2 (1986):223–36.

———. "The Mediation of Bureaucratic-Professional Influence: Decentralization in Dutch Housing Policy." *Political Studies* 34 (1986):607–19.

Gale, Dennis E. "Urban Revitalization in Paris, Stockholm and Amsterdam: A View from the United States." *Research in Urban Economics* 5 (1985):173–92.

Levine, Myron A., and Jan van Weesep. "The Changing Nature of Dutch Urban Planning." *Journal of the American Planning Association* 54, no. 3 (1988):315–24.

Linde, M. A. J., F. M. Dieleman, and W. A. V. Clark. "Starters in the Dutch Housing Market." *Tijdschrift voor Economiche en Sociale Geografie* 77, no. 4 (1986):243–50.

Machielse, E. C. M. "The Multiformity of Neighborhood Revitalization in the Netherlands." Chapter 4 in *Housing and Neighborhoods*, edited by Willem van Vliet—, Harvey Choldin, William Michelson, and David Popenoe. Westport, CT: Greenwood Press, 1987.

Ministry of Finance. *Heroverweging 1985, Huur- en subsidiebeleid in de '90-er jaren* (Rethinking 1985, Rent and Subsidy Policy in the Nineties). Subreport no. 78. The Hague: Ministry of Finance, 1985.

Priemus, H. "Economic and Demographic Stagnation, Housing and Housing Policy: The Case of the Netherlands (1974–1984)," *Housing Studies* 2, no. 1 (1987):17–27.

Rima, Annemarie, Leo van Wissen, and Peter Nijkamp. "A Dynamic Household Model for the Housing Market of Amsterdam." *Geographical Analysis* 19, no. 3 (1987):233–42.

Van der Laan, Lambert. "Residential Migrations and Spatial Policies in Mixed Economies, a Case Study of the Dutch Randstad." *Trans. Inst. Br. Geogr.* N. S. 12 (1987):84–96.

Van Fulpen, J. A. "An Analysis of the Housing Market in the Netherlands." *Urban Studies* 25 (1988):190–203.

———. *Volkshuisvesting in demografisch en economisch perspectief* (Housing in a De-

mographic and Economic Perspective). Sociale en Culturele Studies no. 8. The
Hague: Government Publishing Office, 1985.

Van Kempen, Eva. "High-Rise Estates and the Concentration of Poverty." Chapter 12
in *Housing and Neighborhoods*, edited by Willem van Vliet—, Harvey Choldin,
William Michelson, and David Popenoe. Westport, CT: Greenwood Press, 1987.

Van Weesep, J. "Intervention in the Netherlands: Urban Housing Policy and Market
Response." *Urban Affairs Quarterly* 19 (1984):329–53.

Van Weesep, Jan, and Peter J. Boelhouwer. "The Sale of Public Housing and the Social
Structure of Neighborhoods." *Built Environment* 14, nos. 3, 4 (1988): 145-54.
Special theme issue on "Social Housing," guest edited by Frans Dieleman and
Hugo Priemus.

Verhoef, R., and R. F. J. Tas. "Demografie van de niet-Nederlandse bevolking in Nederland, 1985" (Demography of the Non-Dutch Population in the Netherlands,
1985). *CBS Maandstatistiek Bevolking*, no. 3 (1987):23–35.

Warringa, R. *Kwalitatieve Woningregistratie: Drie steekproeven* (Qualitative Housing
Registration: Three Samples). The Hague: Ministry of Housing, 1985.

The Netherlands Journal of Housing and Environmental Research frequently
includes articles on Dutch housing.

5

Italy

ANTONIO TOSI

HOUSING TRENDS AND POLICIES: SOME PRELIMINARY REMARKS

The trends in housing conditions and construction delineate two distinct periods in the past decades of housing history in Italy—two periods that can to some extent be associated with two phases in the country's development. The 1950s and the early 1960s signaled Italy's "economic miracle" that saw a surge in industrialization and demographic development, a hefty exodus from the less-

Table 5.1
Increases in Population and Housing Stock, by Region, Italy, 1951–1981

	Increases in Thousands			Percentages of Total Increases		
	1951-61	1961-71	1971-81	1951-61	1961-71	1971-81
Population						
Metropolitan areas	2,677	3,041	1,040	89.1	85.0	40.2
North-West	1,191	1,315	177	39.7	36.7	6.8
Rest of Italy	1,486	1,726	863	49.5	48.2	43.4
Urban areas	1,036	1,392	1,451	34.5	38.9	56.2
Rural areas	-710	-854	93	-23.6	-23.9	3.6
Total	3,003	3,579	2,587	100.0	100.0	100.0

Number of Rooms

Metropolitan areas	4,680	6,425	6,949	46.0	39.4	28.0
North–West	1,752	2,247	1,872	17.2	13.8	7.6
Rest of Italy	2,928	4,178	5,077	28.7	25.6	20.5
Urban areas	4,230	7,306	11,983	41.5	44.8	48.4
Rural areas	1,275	2,575	5,852	12.5	15.8	23.6
Total	10,185	16,306	24,784	100.0	100.0	100.0

Sources: Istituto Centrale, 1981; Consiglio Nazionale, 1986.

developed areas, and the growth of the metropolitan areas in northern and central Italy. This phase of general expansion extended into the 1960s. The most telling factor was the intense migration, mostly flowing from the agricultural regions (especially those in the South) toward the Northwest corner of the country where most of the industrial growth was actually taking place (Ferracuti and Marcelloni 1982).

The tide began to turn at the end of the 1960s. The first signs of recession and a falloff in demographic growth began to appear, and changes in settlement trends likewise manifested themselves, gathering momentum during the 1970s. In fact, the expansion of the metropolitan areas declined, and the growth in population shifted to the smaller cities and to rural areas—mainly in the Northeast and the central belt of the country where a new type of industrialization was beginning to take hold, based on the small firm and on what came to be dubbed "informal economy" (Consiglio Nazionale 1986; see also Dandri 1978).

The variations that took place in the geographical distribution of the country's population are the main features of the framework, which served as a backdrop to the evolution of housing conditions and construction (table 5.1). Along with the redistribution of the population across the country, there was an intensive continuous period of new house building, from after the war to the 1970s. The sharp upturn in housing stock figures between 1951 and 1981 was accompanied by a parallel rise in stock quality and housing conditions. A further key element was the leap in home ownership (tables 5.2 and 5.3). Toward the close of the 1970s, new house building began to slacken. Since 1982 there has been a manifest drop in construction figures. Over the same period, while construction declined, rehabilitation activities showed an upswing (Centro Ricerche 1987). The new trend ushered in a corresponding tightening of the private rental situation (see Centro Studi 1986).

The picture that can be drawn is similar to that which has characterized housing history in other developed nations during the same period. The same data also suggest, however, the existence of important distinctive characteristics. One is given by the importance and complexity of regional differentiations, which goes beyond the historical juxtaposition of North versus South, reflecting on the one hand the traditional geographic divisions of the country and on the other hand recent changing trends in overall settlement patterns. Another is the importance of noninstitutional or "informal" aspects of production, of which illegal construction practices are a manifestation (table 5.3).

For the purpose of interpretation, however, the most interesting aspects are concerned with policies. Until the seventies, the dominant view describing "the Italian model" of housing policies had emphasized different specific characteristics. The image given (even if questionable on various aspects) had been one of nondiscriminating policies, based on indirect intervention and support to the private sector and oriented toward the increase of home ownership, more so than had been witnessed in other countries. This model was defined in terms of its distance from the comprehensive state-involvement models tied to the welfare state that had taken root in Northern European countries. Thus the accent was

Table 5.2
Evolution of Housing Stock and Population, Italy, 1951–1981 (In Thousands)

	1951	1961	1971	1981
Population	47,516	50,624	54,137	56,557
Households	11,814	13,747	15,981	18,632
Rooms	37,342	47,528	63,834	88,618
Dwellings	11,411	14,214	17,434	21,937
occupied	10,756	13,032	15,301	17,572
non-occupied (a)	655	1,182	2,133	4,365
Population/rooms difference	-10,084	-3,096	+9,697	+32,061
Persons per room	1.27	1.06	0.85	0.64
Owner-occupied dwellings: % of housing stock	40.1	45.3	49.8	59.1

Source: Istituto Centrale 1981, 1985.

(a) Unoccupied dwellings, dwellings occupied temporarily for study or work, and second homes.

usually placed, by those studying the "Italian model," on the inadequacy of direct intervention and of state housing and on the nonplanning nature of the interventions. In general, further emphasis was placed on the inadequate productivity of public intervention, due to its complexity and fragmentation and to the rigidity of the administrative procedures. Associated with these latter points, an emphasis was placed on the inadequate social effectiveness of the policies, even though the total volume of state interventions was considerable (see Ferracuti and Marcelloni 1982).

Shortly afterwards, the scene changed. Given the altered political situation that marked the end of the 1970s and the urgency of new problems such as those related to the rehabilitation of historical centers, new demand for public services, and environmental quality (Padovani 1984), a series of institutional reforms were introduced: in this way the model appeared to come closer to the comprehensive state-involvement type. As we shall see, a significant consequence of this was the high level of direct public intervention during the 1980s, when elsewhere the state was actually pulling out of housing.

After the 1970s new problems appeared. Another element highlighted by the data is the persistence of differences and imbalances in housing conditions. Growth and improvement trends in housing stock have indeed resulted in a

Table 5.3

Selected Housing Indicators, by Region, Italy, 1971–1981

Characteristics	Year	North	Center	South	ITALY
Number of households (x 1,000)	1981	9,130	3,577	5,925	18,632
Number of dwellings (x 1,000)	1971	8,551	3,314	5,569	17,434
	1981	10,481	4,163	7,293	21,937
Housing stock: % change 1971–81		+22.6	+25.6	+30.9	+25.8
Non-occupied dwellings(a): % of total dwellings	1971	11.2	13.6	13.1	12.2
	1981	17.4	19.5	23.6	19.9
House-sharing: % of total families	1981	7.9	13.5	12.4	10.0
Dwellings with bathroom: % of total dwellings	1971	71.4	76.0	47.0	64.5
	1981	89.9	92.3	77.6	86.5

Rented stock: % of total occupied dwellings	1981	38.4	35.3	28.3	35.3
Illegal construction: % of housing stock	1981	7.7	14.2	18.0	12.3
Public housing stock: % of total occupied dwellings	1980	5.4	6.0	5.8	5.7
% of total rented dwellings	1980	14.1	17.0	20.5	16.0
Applications for public housing per 1,000 households, 1979-80		22.7	30.1	40.2	29.8
% Assignments against total of applications		9.3	6.7	4.9	6.9

Sources: Centro Studi, 1985; Associazione Nazionale, 1987.

(a) Unoccupied dwellings, dwellings occupied temporarily, and second homes.

general improvement in housing conditions. Group and regional-level analysis, however, shows the presence of sizable areas of unsatisfied needs (see table 5.3). This is not a residual phenomenon. As we shall see later, the new "housing stresses" are to some extent linked to new phenomena such as the reduction in the rental housing stock and the increase in the actual cost of housing; they are also linked to new development trends, such as the deurbanization processes and the crisis of the metropolitan centers. For this reason we might reasonably talk in terms of the emergence of a new "housing question."

INSTITUTIONS AND INSTITUTIONAL MEANS

According to institutional definitions, financial support for "public interest housing" (*Edilizia residenziale pubblica*) is twofold. On the one hand, the public housing provision, supported by direct capital investment, is designed for rental accommodations for low-income citizens.[1] In this case (*Edilizia sovvenzionata*), housing is completely state subsidized and directly built and managed by public authorities (and in some cases by municipalities). In the following discussion, the term *(low-rent) public housing* applies to fully subsidized housing directly provided by the state, which is the main component of direct public intervention and has now become a substantial portion of all financial support of "public interest housing" (Comitato 1987).

On the other hand, financial support has been provided for housing for owner occupation, through various forms of grants and loans, available to builders and buyers (primarily when organized as housing cooperatives) (*Edilizia agevolata*). Until recently, the overwhelming majority of partial financial aid was in the form of low-interest loans and mortgage assistance, managed by special mortgage-loan institutions. In the text "state-aided housing" (and "subsidized private housing") refers to this type of partially subsidized housing, supporting owner occupation (Consiglio Nazionale 1986). In addition to direct financial aid, the private sector (and housing for owner occupation) is supported by "indirect" measures. Historically, tax relief has been by far the most important measure (Mortara 1975; Padovani 1984).[2]

Indirect intervention and housing were often aimed at specific categories of beneficiaries. As a result, today, in the field of subsidized private housing, there are many different institutions, each operating within its own area of responsibility and with specific subsidy mechanisms. As far as public housing is concerned, most programs are developed by a special authority (the IACP: Instituto Autonomo Case Popolari), which operates on a territorial basis and has both planning and management roles. In 1987 the stock of the more than 100 IACPs added up to more than 1 million dwellings, equal to 16.3 percent of the total rented stock. The percentage was higher in many districts and exceeded 20 percent in the smaller county areas (Associazione Nazionale 1987). Although the total proportion was somewhat lower than in other countries in Europe, it was still a sizable quantity of houses. As we shall see, the problems were related rather to the use of this stock: the rationality of the criteria for gaining access to it and the impact of the public investment on the rental market. Here we find the traditional problems of Italian housing policy-making.

Observers of the housing policies in Italy have tended to stress the negative implications of the basic setup of planning tools outlined above. Due to the fragmentation of the interventions and to the complexity and rigidity of the procedures involved, the system seemed unworkable and inadequate when it came to policy implementation. In addition, the social effects of the system have been judged to be inadequate because of its market orientation, the nondiscriminating nature of the interventions, and the absence of a planning dimension (see Ferracuti and Marcelloni 1982).

At the end of the seventies, the institutional framework changed substantially. A series of legislative measures furnished the means for comprehensive state involvement similar to that established in many other European countries. Throughout the same period, group and need-specific measures, similar to those being adopted in other Western countries, were also being adopted in Italy. In its general focus, the redefinition of the institutional framework was an answer to changes in housing needs and demands. It also represented the institutional "final chapter" of the urban social activism of the sixties and seventies and of related changes in attitudes and in political relations. The new housing needs (such as those related to changes in localization patterns, to the crisis in metropolitan growth, and to deurbanization trends) and the new problems (mainly those related to the rehabilitation of historical centers and the reuse of existing stock) were met by the profound inadequacy of a market-oriented model and provided a legislative opening for cultural and political stances that had been developed by the Left for decades (Padovani 1984).[3]

The new legislation that was developed between 1977 and 1978 profoundly renewed at the institutional level the conditions of public intervention. The Land Regulation Act of 1977 set the basis to enable local authorities to plan the development of areas allocated for construction. The "Fair Rent" (*Equo Canone*) Act of 1978 introduced new regulations of the rental market. The Ten-Year Plan for Public Housebuilding (*Piano Decennale*) of 1978 redefined the entire system of public intervention in housing construction and the housing market (see Padovani 1984; Ferracuti and Marcelloni 1982).

The last measure was the most significant of the three. Even though it was aimed at subsidized housing, this law was ambitiously meant to apply to all housing construction. By allocating an exceptional pool of resources and by mobilizing every means of public intervention, the Ten-Year Plan meant to address the problems of a large demand in the social housing sector and in the private ownership sector. Between wholly subsidized housing and state-aided housing the objective was to realize about 100,000 units per year. Long-term planning was introduced and procedures were redefined to shorten the duration and increase the effectiveness of the interventions. All of the principal sources of revenue for housing (workers' contributions, proceeds from public rents, and ad hoc state investments) were thus concentrated into one channel of distribution. To extend public control to the building activity of the private sector, new contractual devices were introduced between private developers and local authorities.[4] There was a clear redefinition of the roles of new and existing authorities and of the relationships between the responsibilities of different levels of government.[5] Local authorities were accorded greater executive power, and the regional authorities received enhanced planning means. Two main planning levels were provided. Regional fund allocation for public interest housing and the determination of housing needs in different areas were the responsibility of the central planning level. Some major objectives were to reduce the program-development time and to concentrate resources on the needier areas. The regional level was entrusted with more specific analogous tasks: the localization of intervention and the selection of the authorities and contractors who were to carry them out. Local administration were made responsible for the acquisition of land and for providing the necessary infrastructures for intervention. Finally, norms were introduced for guiding both private and public rehabilitation and reuse and for strengthening the role of municipalities in this field.

Innovations in the institutional framework continued in the following years with various laws that introduced the concepts of "extraordinary intervention" and "emergency intervention." They were intended to address the particular problems of the evicted, of young couples in search of their first home, of residents of large cities in metropolitan areas, and so on. To increase the speed and efficiency of operations, these interventions enabled additional funds and the introduction of ulterior innovative means and procedures. In those urban areas where housing problems were particularly severe, special funds were assigned and new powers of intervention conferred on municipalities. By means of these laws, the needs of "special" groups began to be the object of special provisions, following a rationale that would subsequently establish itself in Italian housing policies.

State intervention came out of these reforms modified in substantial ways. For the first time the municipalities joined the IACPs as the operators of public housing. For state-aided housing, the innovations were that rehabilitation could now be considered and that—in addition to builders and cooperatives—access to state aid would be opened to the individual citizen. In 1982 a further alternative to state-aided mortgages was introduced by conceding buyers allowances and personal grants (*Buoni casa*).

These innovations modified in a variety of ways the roles and the involvement of the agents of public intervention in housing. At a local level, enactment of subsidized housing now involves three main types of agents, whose responsibilities can be summarized as follows (see Consiglio Nazionale 1986):

- The IACPs: main agents in the field of public housing, their duties include the building of completely subsidized housing units to be assigned to low-income citizens and the management of the housing stock thus realized. The new legislation incorporated the activities of these bodies into the general planning process of public intervention and redefined the role of the IACPs by attributing some of the social housing responsibilities to the municipalities. Of the funds allocated to public housing between 1978 and 1987, 75 percent went to the IACPs.

• The cooperatives: organizations that have the objective of implementing and assigning to their own members units for ownership or rental: with regard to the first objective, which has been their prevalent activity for a long time, they represent the main beneficiary of the funding for state-aided housing (about 50 percent of the financing set aside by the Ten-Year Plan for state-aided housing was reserved to programs promoted by the cooperatives).

• The municipalities: among the traditional agents in the housing field, especially through municipal planning, they have now also become the recipients of funding for state-aided housing in order to develop accommodations to be assigned as rental units. The large municipalities have also been promoters and implementors of the appropriate programs for social housing in metropolitan areas, which have absorbed substantial amounts of "extraordinary" funding (roughly 17 percent of public funds between 1978 and 1987). Furthermore, they have taken on an important role in the control and promotion of rehabilitation activities.

HOUSING MARKETS AND POLICY ORIENTATIONS, 1978–1987

The decline in new house building in Italy occurred with a certain delay compared to the majority of European countries: in the seventies, even if various problems began to appear, construction remained at a sustained level, especially as a result of the contribution of informal construction.

In the eighties, the scenario changed (table 5.4). From 1981 to 1985 investments in housing decreased in real terms by about 9 percent (Centro Studi 1986, 457). Between 1984 and 1987 the number of dwellings completed dropped from about 400,000 to about 300,000 per year (Centro Ricerche 1987).[6] Since then, in spite of state support, construction has not risen again. Among the reasons for this are the overproduction of the past decades and the relative saturation of most of the market. With a percentage of resident owners greater than 60, and with a reduction of buying power among the lower-middle and lower classes, the solvent demand has lessened drastically. During the same time families' propensities toward investments changed. They now had better alternatives (for example, the stock market). The depressed state of the construction sector, however, also reflects the falling demographic trends and a decline in population mobility (Consiglio Nazionale 1986). Along with the crisis came changes in the characteristics of housing production. For example, there were changes in the locales of construction: on the one hand, there was an unmistakable "southern shift" in building activity; on the other hand, a concentration in smaller municipalities (in 1985, 80.5 percent of new dwellings were built in towns numbering less than 20,000 inhabitants) (Centro Studi 1986, 449). As will be seen, all of this has brought penetrating changes in the structure of markets, type of demand,

Table 5.4
Investments in Housing, Italy, 1979–1985

	1979	1980	1981	1982	1983	1984	1985
Investments in housing (in billion lire)	13,723	17,922	22,087	24,785	27,486	30,064	32,349
New construction	7,868	10,302	12,770	14,055	15,307	16,457	17,223
Rehabilitation	5,855	7,620	9,317	10,730	12,179	13,607	15,126
Private Sector	12,845	16,145	19,978	21,954	24,487	26,127	28,144
Public Sector	878	1,777	2,109	2,831	2,999	3,937	4,205

Annual % change	22.6	30.6	23.2	12.2	10.9	10.9	7.6
% Change in real terms	3.0	4.9	0.7	-4.5	-2.4	-0.7	-0.8
Rehabilitation as % of total investments	42.7	42.5	42.2	43.3	44.3	45.3	46.7
Public investments as % of total investments	6.4	6.6	9.5	11.4	10.9	13.1	13.0

Sources: Centro Ricerche, 1987 and Consiglio Nazionale, 1986.

Notes: Current values; 1970 currency equivalents; average exchange rates, 1978: 1,000 lire for 1.17 U.S. dollars; 1985: 1,000 lire for 0.49 U.S. dollars.

and housing conditions. Among the more problematic consequences are the severe reduction of the rental market and the new deterioration in housing conditions of large cities.

Two main elements characterize the turn in the eighties. The first, common to all European countries, is the growth in importance, while new construction decreased, of renewal and rehabilitation. After 1978 investments in rehabilitation, which were about 20 percent of housing investments in the sixties, and 30 percent in the seventies, went regularly beyond 40 percent of all housing investments, and in 1987 they reached 48 percent (Centro Ricerche 1987). The other element to which we shall return—and this is a specific component of the Italian case in the eighties—is the importance of illegal construction activity. The tendency toward a "southern shift" in construction is in large part due to this component (Centro Studi 1985).

Another specific characteristic of the Italian case concerns the role of state intervention in the "crises" of the eighties. In a general situation of slackening investments, there was for several years an increment in public expenditures and construction, especially in large cities: an effect of both the Ten-Year Plan and the laws on "extraordinary" intervention of the early eighties. Between 1980 and 1984, with the whole or partial contribution of the state, about 60,000 dwellings per year were built (Centro Ricerche 1987). This constitutes a sizable production, even if far from the objectives of the Ten-Year Plan. The largest increases were with regard to public housing, both from the municipalities and from the IACPs. Between 1981 and 1984 spending on public housing rose by 30 percent in terms of real money (Centro Studi 1986, 484).

Thus the relative weight of investments activated by public expenditures increased. In the eighties the incidence of public investments—which in the seventies was about 6 percent (Padovani 1984, 263)—grew to a share between 10 and 13 percent of total investments in housing (Centro Studi 1986, 483). For new construction, the percentage reached above 16. The share of subsidized housing is, however, notably higher in large urban areas, where it amounts to average values near or higher than 50 percent of total investments for new construction (Comitato 1987).

In absolute terms, the size of subsidized housing is considerable. From 1978 to 1987 the state allotted—for both new construction and rehabilitation—more than 21,000 billion lire, a figure that places housing among the most significant sectors of state intervention. Of this figure, 18,340 billion was allocated for the financing of public housing. Almost 80 percent of this figure went to finance interventions by the Ten-Year Plan; the rest went to extraordinary and experimental programs (table 5.5).

The boost in public intervention is the most significant element of the new policies. Particularly noteworthy is the direct provision of housing that has received a financial push that has few precedents in Italian housing history. Furthermore, within these policies, the typical measures that have been part of

Table 5.5
Public Expenses for Housing, Italy, 1978–1987

	Allotted Funds (billion Lire)	Utilization up to 1985
Public housing (*Edilizia sovvenzionata*)	18,340	10,503
Ordinary programs (IACPS and municipalities)	14,440	8,478
Extraordinary programs	3,600	2,025
Experimental programs	300	-
State-aided housing (*Edilizia agevolata*)	1,565	854
Individual allowances and grants (*Buoni casa*)	440	28
Land acquisition and infrastructure provision	780	200
Total	21,125	11,585

Source: Comitato, 1987.

"state withdrawal" elsewhere (e.g., the sale of public housing, the increase of public rents, and so on) have been adopted on a very limited scale only.

Yet it is difficult to evaluate at this time the effects of the new policies. In general, the increase in public expenditure should benefit the housing situation. For example, the state has underwritten the decrease in new production, with appreciable results especially in large cities. This has probably mitigated effects of the fall of the rental supply. There are, however, doubts about the overall productivity and social effectiveness of current government intervention (Centro 1986).

Under these conditions the focus of the discussion must move to the type and structure of state involvement. This brings into consideration both traditional and innovative elements of the model of intervention. In the first instance the weight of indirect intervention appears to be still relevant, as well as the implementation deficiency of the intervention system, which also concerns direct intervention. Among the innovative aspects, the central point is the breadth of the "special" or "extraordinary" policies, through which a large part of the social programs of the latter years have passed.

In general terms, these policies shared two types of objectives with European policies of the same period: (a) to maintain access to ownership as the main solution of the housing problem, as had occurred in periods of economic growth; and (b) to redefine the social role of public intervention by more strictly delimiting the groups to which intervention is directed and by reinstating the "promotional" role of the state in the market. In this sense both objectives represent attempts to adapt to new conditions the policy models of the 1950–1960s (Tosi 1984).

The effort to pursue the first objective is immediately apparent. All dispositions in recent years—even the extraordinary ones—imply, more or less strongly, an increase in resident ownership. As we saw, subsidized private housing is supported once more by increasing its funding and bringing innovations to forms of state aid and incentives (for instance, allowances and loan facilities directly offered to individuals). As elsewhere, the success of these efforts has been limited. With the disappearance of the expansionary conditions upon which these policies were traditionally based, adaptations are inevitably insufficient. In any case, the percentage of the population still able to gain ownership has now greatly decreased, and the chances are high that these provisions will have regressive effects by simply multiplying opportunities for middle-income groups.

There appear to be distinctive characteristics with regard to the second objective, the redefinition of public intervention. A first aspect of the problem concerns the possibility for public rental stock to continue to carry out its traditional functions: to meet low-income needs and to bring down the prices in the rental market. From this point of view, the difficulties—which have recently been worsened by the financial and management "crisis" of the IACP (inducing the sale of some public housing)—owe their inadequacy to established elements of the system of intervention. The problems seem to derive more from the inappropriate use of public stock than from the quantitative limits of the same (Associazione Nazionale 1987).

As for the "social" functions of the stock, the problems stem from the definition of the access criteria. The difficulty of controlling the evolution of the relationships between the envisaged conditions for access (i.e., low income, overcrowding, substandard housing, eviction) have meant that the criteria for assigning homes do not always match the hierarchy of needs (Centro Studi 1985). (The proof of this is that the different regional authorities who are required to apply the norms governing access to homes have each drawn up diverse sets of criteria). What is more, the complexity of the controlling mechanism and the inflexibility of the procedures for repossession make it difficult to repossess public housing even when the legal requirements of the occupants are no longer met (Associazione Nazionale 1987).[7] The irrationability of the assignment mechanism and the "immovability" of recipients have often transformed public housing into a sort of protected "reserve" (Centro Studi 1985).

On the whole, the sector covered by public housing has had a strong "social assistance" character, as is indicated by the very low-rent policies of the past fifteen years. This has also curtailed the chances of a strategic use of the public housing stock—the "impermeability" or lack of interchange between the public sector and private housing market has seriously impaired the possibility of using the public stock for holding down prices and for controlling developments of the rental market according to planning criteria (Associazione Nazionale 1987).

The improper use of public housing is nothing other than a blatant aspect of the limits that characterize state intervention. The perception of these defects, after the relative failure of the Ten-Year Plan that was to be the rebirth of public intervention, called into question the entire system of intervention. As elsewhere, the emphasis was placed on the possible regressive effects that even public intervention can have when it uses nonselective means (Consiglio Nazionale 1986).

In addition, a traditional trait was underscored that is related to the social effectiveness of interventions: the barely adequate implementation ability that characterizes the Italian public system. On observing the experience of the past few years, it would appear that public intervention (and direct provision in particular) has a "fixed potential": it seems able to realize only a definite number of dwellings a year, regardless of (though in relative measure to) the size of the financial resources at its disposal. Any normative or financial push would therefore be cut down to size by the implementation ability of the intervention system (Centro Studi 1985). In addition, the complex relations that join expenditure to production procedures create a large time gap between fund allocation and expenditure and between the planning and realization of programs, all of which obviously increase costs and worsen the problem of the social effectiveness of intervention (Centro Studi 1985; see also Comitato 1987).[8]

In regard to state-aided housing, an additional problem is the plurality of jurisdictions and regulating bodies and the variety in the modalities of state aid. The result is that, even under the same conditions, intervention can produce different effects. Furthermore, the task of reconciling the social requisites of qualification and of solvency of the families involved often provokes incongruous effects. In general terms, the problem of mapping the social objectives of intervention onto the ability of families to gain access to mortgage loans remains the big tangle of state-aided housing. The most paradoxical consequence is that families that meet income requirements for obtaining loans often do not have the means to pay them back (Centro Studi 1985, 354).

HOUSING NEEDS AND PROBLEMS IN THE 1980s

If analyzed according to the traditional indicators, national housing conditions have improved enormously from after the war to today. Between 1951 and 1981 there was a shift from 1.27 to 0.64 persons per room. Recently, intensive processes of rehabilitation have produced a noticeable improvement in the housing stock. Between 1971 and 1981, for example, according to census data, "fully serviced dwellings" (i.e., dwellings with main water supply, toilet, and electricity) went from 64.2 to 85.4 percent of the total (Centro Studi 1985, 364).

The data indicate, however, a more complex picture of the present situation. In 1985 the people living in accommodations classified as "overcrowded" (those that have a ratio of rooms per resident of less than 1) are still 20 percent of the population. Twenty-one percent of all occupied dwellings are classified as "deteriorated" (25 percent of those rented) (Consiglio Nazionale 1986, 18). Also, 11.3 percent do not have minimum functional requirements such as water or electricity (Centro Studi 1985, 367). There is evidence that starting in the 1970s the housing situation worsened in various ways. If we consider only the occupied dwellings, the "surplus" of families over the number of dwellings was 679,653 in 1971 and increased to 1,027,512 in 1981.[9] In the meantime, house sharing rose from 7 percent of households in 1971 to about 10 percent in 1981 (see table 5.3). The number of overcrowded dwellings also increased, although slightly (Istituto Centrale 1981). Classified by social groups and geographical areas, the data indicate that the housing problems are indeed socially and geographically differentiated (Istituto Centrale 1985; see also table 5.3). There are no doubts as to where the heavy concentration of problems falls: the low-income strata that rent in a few urban areas. However, the problem is considerably more complex. Actually, the stopping, or the reversal, of the trend of improvement probably indicates the emergence of new terms in the "housing question."

The new housing stress can be related in part to long-term trends. It basically exposes the shortcomings of the "quantitative" approach to the housing question (see Folin 1981) and of using a development model that is prevalently based on nondiscriminating policies and on the heavy support of the private sector and owner occupation. The situation was also aggravated, as we shall see, by changes that have characterized recent years: the fall in investment levels, the shrinking rental market in the large cities, and the overall increased cost of housing. The processes of rehabilitation and gentrification have further aggravated the situation by helping to reduce the rental market and low-cost housing in the cities. It is important, however, also to take into account the more general economic, social, demographic, and territorial transformations that have characterized these years. Clearly, phenomena such as the recession and demographic changes—the increased number of households composed of elderly people or small households—have also played a key role. Since they generate a "weak" demand, or demands that cannot easily be met by the prevalent supply, these changes have laid the foundations for new critical housing situations. However, in the Italian case, in this decade the face of the country has been changed the most by transformations in the social and territorial structure: the crisis of the metropolitan centers, the "peripherization" of development, the decline of interregional migrations, the important growth of "informal" dimensions in the structure of economic and social processes, are all phenomena that have changed and made more complex the lines of differentiation of needs and housing conditions (Tosi 1984; see also Padovani 1984). All of this is easily observable in the present features of the housing market. With the above-mentioned evolutions, the market looks decidedly more segmented and is strongly determined by both local and "informal" factors. As a result, the market seems now characterized by a plurality of rationales, of organizational principles, and agencies (Centro Studi 1985, 370).

The view widely held since the 1970s that the housing problem has been solved for the majority of the population and now concerns only "special" population groups does not seem adequate as a representation of the new terms of the housing question. This view grasps the fact that the new problems are not those of mass housing: the local and "specific" character of the new deprivations and the relationship that exists between particular social groups and the most acute shelter problems. What it does not grasp, however, are the structures and dynamics that constitute the new map of housing stresses; in the measure to which this view suggests that they are "marginal" or "residual" problems, it appears to be an untenable simplification. There is in reality a relative "diffuseness" of the stress.

The low-income populations are obviously the hardest hit by the economic and housing "crisis." But these crises also imply an enlargement of the problems of affordability: elements of stress now concern, selectively, a vast scale of social groups, which also involve portions of the middle class and segments that in the past were thought to be exempt from housing problems, such as owner–occupiers. The extent of unsatisfied needs is greater if one considers the growing inconsistency between the housing stock and the new needs tied to demographic transformations, family structures, and life-styles (Folin 1981). The above-mentioned relationship between the structure of the housing problems and the new trends and developments hint at the nonresidual nature of the question and at the "systemic" character of the new stress.

Representing the new housing question as an ensemble of "special" problems is ideologically functional, but underestimates the diffusiveness of housing stress. Projection of problem fragmentation also denies the interconnections that exist between different problems. The primary defining characteristic of the new housing stress is the increased variation in housing conditions and problems by groups, areas, and market segments, making established analytical schemes of housing differentiation ineffective.

A second qualifying trait is the polarization of housing needs and conditions. On the general map of "diffusive" stress, there appears both a zone of particularly critical housing conditions and another zone of "opulent" levels of consumption (large houses, second houses, and so on) (Padovani 1984). It is possible that the regressive implications of the trends and policies already in place will accentuate the widening of this gap. A series of major problems are connected to these tendencies: problems that correspond to particularly severe stress and problems that the policies seem particularly useless to solve.

Severe Stress

One of the problems is the creation of areas of heavy stress at the point where several factors coexist. These situations correspond in part to those of low income or otherwise underprivileged populations. Even in such areas of problems, the situation is complex. In addition to social class factors, there are differences in access to political and institutional resources (aid and guarantees offered by the state through housing policies and the social security system). It is possible that with the emergence of new areas of poverty, areas of housing poverty will become more consolidated: "blocked" situations, in which the lack of both economic and political resources allows only "marginal" solutions (e.g., house sharing or so-called informal building solutions) (Consiglio Nazionale 1986).

Rental Housing

The deterioration of housing conditions is a phenomenon that has mainly affected rental housing. The problem is linked to the growing tension between supply and demand due to the drastic reduction of (new) supply and to the reduction of rental housing stock, caused by converting the latter into ownership stock or for nonresidential uses. At the same time, rent controls have proved to be ineffective or have even aggravated the situation.

In the short term, two types of events contribute to make the problem explosive: (1) the events of the real estate market that from the end of the 1970s had alienated risk capital from the rental sector and (2) the rental regulations, which had contributed to the disappearance of the rental market in large cities. Between 1978 and 1984 the rental market shrank drastically due to the lack of supply (Centro Studi 1985). Rentals tended to be polarized and to be restricted to very high- or very low-income levels. These data are part of a specific situation characterized by a relatively low incidence of rental housing when compared with that of other European countries. After 1986 families in rental accommodations comprised about 30 percent of the total. The implications are worrisome for two reasons: the concentration of rental housing in the large urban areas (where the incidence is between 50 and 60 percent) and the high percentage of renters in the lowest-income categories (Consiglio Nazionale 1986; Zajczyk 1988).

An additional factor affecting this framework is the 1978 law on fair rents. After decades of rent freezes, the law regulated the criteria for establishing rent levels and for adjustments over time and the duration of the contract or the way in which the owner can ask for repossession. Again, the orientation adopted diverged from that of other European countries: rent levels were determined on the basis of parameters of law, and the owner was guaranteed the right of eviction at each contract expiration. It is precisely these two aspects that are problems in the application of the law, making the rental market situation worse still. Rents fail to follow the movements of the market. The profound difference between rent market values and those defined on the basis of parameters indicated by the law has been instrumental in the disappearance of the market in the large cities and has also fed an "underground" market in which tenants and owners reach compromises and agreements with respect to the rents set by the law. Moreover, the possibilities for the owners to repossess the dwelling at the end of the contract have actually been very scarce: the dearth of available rental stock continues to postpone (by law or by judicial means) the execution of the evictions. Between 1984 and 1986 only 69,500 of 420,000 evictions were actually carried out (Centro Studi 1986, 478). (This is one of the reasons that the percentage of income set aside for the payment of rent in Italy—which increased from 7.4 percent in 1980 to 9.4 percent in 1984—is still far from the European average of 12.5 percent.) But the continual postponement of evictions also helps to curtail the supply of rental accommodations by reducing the advantages for landlords.

The Metropolitan Areas

The principal large cities are the areas of heavy concentration of housing stress. In 1985, 82 percent of the families in substandard housing conditions and 98 percent of the overcrowded dwellings were in large cities (Consiglio Nazionale 1986). This is in part attributable to the percentage of families renting, which is much higher in the large cities. Moreover, the deterioration of the rental housing stock is more marked, and the situation of evictions is more serious. The most severe problems are among the low-income strata. Where maintenance is not compensated for by the rents, the market crisis induces an accelerated process of deterioration and therefore a worsening of living conditions for the needier tenants.

Renewal and Housing Rehabilitation

The deterioration of the housing stock is a key housing problem. An increase in deterioration hits hardest the housing stock in the historic parts of quite a few urban centers—of which Naples and Palermo are the most notorious cases—as well as large sections of rental housing stock. With regard to the last point, there is a tendency to "ghettoize" the remaining rental housing stock: the units in better condition have been conspicuously transferred from rental to ownership or have been "withdrawn" from the residential housing stock (Consiglio Nazionale 1986).

Public intervention has been limited to the development of a few exemplary projects and to financing the private renewal. A large part of this has been, up to now, spontaneous renewal, small-size operations carried out by families, outside any real public control, and aimed above all at improving their functional amenities. This type of renewal has shown itself to be of little productive value: it has had little effect on the rehabilitation of the more dilapidated housing stock

(Centro Studi 1985). The promotion and the control of rehabilitation activities are now major objectives of government orientations.

Illegal Construction Practices

It has been calculated that about 30 percent of the residences built between 1971 and 1984 were produced by "unauthorized" or "irregular" construction (*Abusivismo edilizio*). With regard to the existing stock, they constituted about 18 percent in the South and 12 percent at the national level. Later, the phenomenon spread: for 1984 it is estimated that unauthorized or illegal housing reached 14 percent of the total. After 1984 the phenomenon declined (Centro Studi 1985; Somma 1987).

A short overview of the situation would reveal a very heterogenous gamut of processes and products. Small, compact, self-built buildings are the typical product of *abusivismo* practices that are linked to the satisfaction of primary needs. Second houses in particularly desirable areas are products of what has been defined as "quality *abusivismo*." *Abusivismo* practices for speculative ends are headed by construction firms that develop multistoried buildings or subdivide entire areas which appeal to the small and medium investor, for both primary and vacation uses. "Family *abusivismo*" practices produce a type of house that is adaptable to the changing necessities of the family: as time goes on, floors are added to meet new requirements (Consiglio Nazionale 1986, 167).

Informal housing, which shows differing grades of "irregularities"—where *abusivismo* (unauthorized or illegal construction practices) is the most severe form—is deeply rooted in the housing reality of the country. This does not mean that these are "traditional" or "residual" phenomena: their importance in the housing market—especially in the South, where the growth has been partially supported by salary transfers from migrant workers—has increased in the 1970s, intertwined with the growth of "informalization" that has characterized recent developments in the economy and the society. With the heavy increase and relevance that it had acquired in the 1980s, *abusivismo* has changed connotations: no longer an emergency solution of marginal social groups, it has assumed a widespread character, involving different types of operators and users and covering different levels of supply, demand, and products. In fact, the functions served by *abusivismo*—which often implies self-building practices—are extremely varied: satisfaction of primary needs and speculative dimensions, strategies of family investment, and the quest for flexibility (of the production and of the product) that state and market had not been able to ensure.

The consequences of *abusivismo* practices have been very serious, both in the precariousness of the housing conditions of those living in the illegal stock and in the deterioration of the environment that these practices have caused. The widespread nature of the phenomenon—and the solid interlocking of economic and political interests that have developed around this type of construction on a local level—has made the political treatment of the problem difficult up to now.

The attempts at solutions at the national level and by way of legislation have given, up to now, partial and contradictory results.

PROSPECTIVE DEVELOPMENTS

Demographic changes as the growth of elderly households or the increase in the number of households and the decrease in their size continue to determine new types of demands. The decline in large migrations, in favor of a more selective intraregional mobility, and the strengthening of the processes of "peripherization" will probably continue to influence the geography of production and of demand. There could still be an increase in the concentration of housing development in the smaller council areas, in the South, and in the central and northeastern regions, where this "informal economy" based on smaller businesses has found a fertile seedbed. Changes in the occupational structure, the structuring of localized informal economies, and the persistence of high rates of unemployment contribute to the modification of class configurations and poverty lines and therefore of the relationship between needs and the distribution of housing resources (Tosi 1984). In addition, the growing importance in the "subjective" and "qualitative" dimensions of housing (Centro Studi 1986) means a change in the cultural housing models that involves large strata of the population: generally pushing up the qualitative prerequisites of the housing demand. The spreading of positive attitudes toward housing in historical centers could provide an added thrust to the whole process of rehabilitation.

These factors threaten to increase the incoherence between demand and existing housing stock and accentuate problematic tendencies in housing conditions and needs. For example, the large growth of informal and local dimensions in the production and the market tend to accentuate even more the "dispersion" and the fragmentation of demand and to further confound the lines of differentiation among needs.

The polarization of demand could also become more pronounced. In 1986 the movements in the market were almost totally made up of two types of demand: the first from those who sought to better their present housing status; the second has been called the "emergency market," that is, those who need a house because of something such as eviction, marriage, or transfer to another city (Centro Studi 1986). Behind this second type of demand (one of the principal targets of extraordinary or special measures) there is an area of primary needs that remain largely frustrated. This therefore extends the pressure of the demand on the state: a demand that basically cannot be satisfied in terms of the traditional policies of support for ownership and that tends to increase the masses of contending applicants for public housing.[10]

Policies seem to be oriented in three main directions: (1) the revitalization of the rental market (which includes the redefinition of the role that the state must play with its 1 million dwelling units and the revision of the legislation on fair rents); (2) the promotion of housing rehabilitation and the renewal of the urban and nonurban fabric (which includes the renovation of areas of illegal expansion); (3) the diversification of the interventions, according to the reinstating of policies aimed at special groups, and the redefinition of the criteria of access to the aid offered by the state.

The problems all challenge the organizations and the current means of public intervention. Renewal and rehabilitation expand the field of housing policies, integrating them into the framework of urban and regional planning policies: this implies new modes of operating. The difficulty of state intervention in addressing "localized" needs and problems has been the common experience of these years of special policies. The consolidated means of state intervention seem badly suited for dealing with a fragmented universe of needs. Most of the local-character solutions adopted are a symptom of this inadequacy. However, the difficulties experienced with state intervention in facing the localized stresses constitute a central issue in the debate relative to special policies.

The debate in progress pushes for a revision of the model of state intervention. The accent is placed mainly on the institutional aspects and the means of intervention. It would seem, in fact, necessary to tackle anew the historic problem of the inefficiency of public intervention. In addition, it may be necessary to redefine the institutional framework, after the erosion of that which was adopted in the 1970s (Consiglio Nazionale 1986).

The difficulties are especially large and refer to a historical breakdown of the model. The institutional framework built up in the 1970s was structurally precarious. It was in the 1970s that most structural and ideological preconditions of the models that were established in European housing policies—such as economic expansion and commitment to welfare ideologies—waned (Tosi 1984; see also Folin 1981). There was in particular a weakening of the ideological support for the comprehensive state involvement variants, precisely those adopted in Italy with the laws of the 1970s. The state-involvement model was adopted in Italy just when the preconditions for their functioning were beginning to disappear.

A possible result of the breakdown of the established models might be the return to "residual" conceptions of state intervention: the emphasis on special policies may be one such indication. Extraordinary measures, aimed at special groups and areas, have been important elements of state intervention in the 1980s, so much so that the comprehensive nature of state involvement may, in reality, be an illusion.

The special measures seem the critical point for the interpretation of recent policies. Represented as the means most adapted to confront the new housing problems, these interventions seem strongly questionable from exactly this aspect. Most certainly, the recourse to selective means must be one condition for reaching the redistributive objectives of state intervention, but from this point of view the result of the special policies are doubtful.

The judgment could be different if it took into account the "political" functioning of the special policies. The inadequacy of the view that the housing problems now concern only special groups of the population has already been highlighted as an analytical category. Ostensibly, it is more a political category. One of its functions, often pointed out by observers of housing policies, is the shifting of attention from the causes of the problem to the characteristics of the particular groups that are suffering from it, thus hiding the systemic character of the stress. Another function is the relation between special policies—inasmuch as they select and compartmentalize the needy—and redistribution of housing resources as a means of obtaining social consent. Here the new special provisions appear to be situated within the mainstream of the great tradition of housing policies as integrative policies.

In Italy social consent objectives have always had great weight in determining the type of policies (see Tosi 1984). From this point of view the special measures have strong continuity with tradition: a multiplicity of programs gives privileges, from time to time, to changing beneficiaries among potential recipients, usually the more conflictual ones, almost never those without political voice or leverage.

But the breakdown of the model is also a breakdown of legitimation. Its instability is also a poor functioning of the traditional mechanisms of benefit distribution. It is therefore doubtful whether the integrative processes tied to housing policies can continue to function as they did in the past.

NOTES

1. Until the 1970s a substantial share of public housing was set aside for "redemption" (*Case a riscatto*): the renter could enter ownership according to long-term rent-to-own programs.

2. It was not until the end of the 1970s, with the "fair rent" legislation, that cash subsidies to low-income tenants were made available in any systematic way.

3. Between 1972 and 1975 an average of 660,000 households per year moved, but only a quarter of them went into newly built dwellings (Padovani 1984, 274).

4. Through "special agreements" (*Convenzioni*) the developers were offered incentives (land at low cost and credit or tax benefits) and held to constraints on housing quality and costs (Padovani 1984, 276).

5. In Italy there are four government levels: national, regional, provincial, and municipal. Before the onset of the reforms of the 1970s, the implementation of the housing policies largely drew on decentralized spheres of government, especially local councils, whose housing activities were mainly conducted through municipal urban planning.

6. From 1980 to 1984 the volume of the housing sales shrank by 40 percent (Centro Studi 1986, 462).

7. The frequent inability of the IACP management to carry out checks or apply provisions for repossessing is also due to the considerable social conflict that has colored relations between the IACP management and its tenants throughout the 1970s.

8. In the first eight years of the Ten-Year Plan, only 55 percent of the allotments have been actually used (see table 5.5).

9. In 1981 nonoccupied dwellings were about 20 percent of the total stock. According to National Census classification, *non-occupied dwellings* include also dwellings occupied

temporarily for study or work and second homes (45 percent of all non-occupied dwellings; Zajczyk 1988).

10. The discrepancy between the number of applications for public housing and the number of assignments (see table 5.3) is a clear indicator of the existing pressure. According to estimates, in 1986, 76.5 percent of families had an income low enough to qualify them for access to public housing (Associazione Nazionale 1987).

REFERENCES

Associazione Nazionale Istituti e Consorzi Case Popolari. 1987. "Dossier Informativo." *Edilizia Popolare* 194:8–51.

Centro Ricerche Economiche Sociologiche di Mercato sull'Edilizia. 1987. "Indicatori congiunturali del settore delle abitazioni." *Cresme Notizie* 9:15–42; 10:17–27.

Centro Studi Investimenti Sociali. 1985. *XIX Rapporto sulla Situazione sociale del Paese.* Milano: Angeli.

———. 1988. *XX Rapporto sulla Situazione sociale del Paese.* 1988. Milano: Angeli.

Comitato per l'Edilizia Residenziale. 1987. "L'Edilizia Residenziale Pubblica dal 1978 al 1987." Rome.

Consiglio Nazionale dell'Economia e del Lavoro. 1986. "Schema di Osservazione e Proposte per una Nuova Politica Abitativa." Rome.

Dandri, C. 1978. "The Evolution of the Italian Housing Situation from 1951 to 1978." *Review of the Economic Conditions in Italy* 2–3:137–52.

Ferracuti, Giovanni, and Maurizio Marcelloni. 1982. *La casa. Mercato e programmazione.* Torino: Einaudi.

Folin, Marino. 1981. "Crisis of Public Housing in Europe." In *Krise der Wohnungspolitik*, edited by H. Frank and H. Harms, 75–88. Hamburg: Hochschule fur Bildende Kunste.

Istituto Centrale di Statistica. 1981. *Censimento della Popolazione e delle Abitazioni, 1981.* Rome.

———. 1985. *Annuario Statistico Italiano.* Rome.

Mortara, Carlo Andrea. 1975. "Venti anni di edilizia pubblica in Italia." *Economia pubblica* 2–3:34–51.

Padovani, Liliana. 1984. "Italy." In *Housing in Europe*, edited by M. Wynn, 247–80. London: Croom Helm.

Somma, Paola. 1987. "Freedom to Build in Italy: Participation or Illegality?" *Open House International* 12:64–67.

Tosi, Antonio. 1984. "La politica della casa." In *Welfare State all'Italiana*, edited by U. Ascoli, 239–63. Bari: Laterza.

Zajczyk, Francesca. 1988. "Abitazioni e famiglie." In ISTAT-AIS, *Immagini della società italiana*, 79–103. Rome: ISTAT.

FURTHER READING

Alexander, David. "Housing Crisis After Natural Disaster: The Aftermath of the November 1980 Southern Italian Earthquake." *Geoforum* 15, no. 4 (1984):489–516.

Molotch, Harvey and Serena Vicari. 1988. "Three Ways to Build: The Development Process in the United States, Japan, and Italy." *Urban Affairs Quarterly* 24(2):188–214.

II

EASTERN EUROPE

6

Soviet Union

HENRY W. MORTON

Of all Soviet urban problems, housing remains one of the most intransigent. During his years in power, Stalin (1927–1953) invested heavily in industry but failed to provide the resources to house the millions who left the farms to work in factories. The German invasion of the Soviet Union in 1941 made an already intolerable housing situation even worse. The war caused widespread destruction of the European part of the USSR. According to Soviet figures, 1,710 cities, towns, and urban settlements were fully or partially destroyed. More than 25 million people were left homeless. Leningrad, Kiev, Minsk, Smolensk, and other cities and towns had to be almost completely rebuilt from heaps of broken bricks and rubble. After World War II's devastation, Stalin's low priority for housing continued. In 1950 the estimated living space per person was less than 5 square meters (7 by 7 feet).

Shortly after Stalin's death in 1953, his successsor, N. S. Khrushchev, was determined to eliminate the severe housing shortage. Since 1957 the USSR has built 2 million housing units yearly—a remarkable achievement, even though the size and quality of units until recently were below Western standards. The result of this effort is visible in every city and town, as new housing districts by far outnumber the old. By the mid–1980s the per capita living space in urban areas rose to 9 square meters (10 by 10 feet); in 1950 it was half as much. In spite of these great improvements Soviet citizens still suffer from one of the poorest housing situations of any industrialized nation, principally because so many families still live communally with strangers. In the 1980s about 20 percent of urban households still share apartments and kitchen and bathroom facilities with strangers (*Stroiteln'naia Gazeta*, December 8, 1983). About an additional 5 percent still live in workers' dormitories. Actually, the housing shortage is much greater than the statistics indicate. Large population centers are closed off to migrants to prevent Moscow, Leningrad, Kiev, and other large population areas from becoming overrun by rural and provincial migrants. Exceptions are made for those who have special skills that are needed or those who perform menial tasks, such as dvorniki who clean up public areas in and outside of buildings. To live in any city or town, a resident permit (*propiska*) is required. Without it, one cannot apply for housing.

TRENDS IN HOUSING CONDITIONS AND CONSTRUCTION, 1945–1985

Housing Quality

Urban housing in the USSR is primarily measured by the number of square meters of "living space" and secondarily by the number of persons per room. Living space includes bedrooms and living rooms but not kitchens, bathrooms, corridors, and storage areas. Living space and nonliving-space areas make up the aggregate "useful space" of an apartment; living space is approximately two-thirds of the total. The goal of one person per room has so far not been achieved in many households. Each of the 15 republics in the Soviet Union determines by law the minimum (which is also the maximum) housing standard for its citizens. In the Russian Republic, which is by far the largest in size and population, the lawful amount of living space was 9 square meters (a 10 by 10 foot area) in Moscow in 1985. This is a great improvement over the past several decades, although the Party Program of 1961 promised that twenty years hence every Soviet family would live in its own apartment, a goal that had to be postponed to the year 2000.

In the post–World War II period practically all new apartment buildings were equipped with plumbing, central heating, hot water, bathrooms, and toilets. The proportion of the housing stock that is substandard is not published. The Rural Housing Fund in 1985 totaled 1,511,000 square meters. The average rural resident occupied 15.6 square meters per person and occupied more space than city dwellers but often lacked indoor plumbing and central heating. Rural housing is predominantly privately owned (*Narodnoe Khozaiistvo S.S.S.R.*, Finansy i Statistiki, 1987, p. 509). Housing construction of collective farms showed steady increases from 1961 to 1985, as shown here:

7th Five-Year Plan	1961–1965	5.3 million sq m
8th Five-Year Plan	1966–1970	12.3 million sq m
9th Five-Year Plan	1971–1975	16.7 million sq m
10th Five-Year Plan	1976–1980	22.1 million sq m
11th Five-Year Plan	1981–1985	35.4 million sq m

Source: *Narodnoe Khozaiistvo S.S.S.R. 70*, Moscow, Finansy i Statistiki, 1987.

Tenure

Of the *urban* housing stock in 1985, 77.2 percent belonged to the state (*Narodnoe Khozaiistvo SSSR v 1985*; *Statistical Yearbook* 1986). This consisted of several categories: housing belonging to ministries and other government agencies; that belonging to cities and towns by approximately equal amounts; cooperatives, accounting for 7 percent; and the rest, 22.8 percent, privately owned. Private urban housing construction was not permitted in the Russian Republic in population centers of more than 100,000. In 1985 the Soviet urban population numbered 182,930,000, or 57.7 percent of the total. In three republics urban private housing still consisted of more than 40 percent of the total: Uzbekistan with 41.1 percent, Georgia with 41.3 percent, and Irghizia with 41.1 percent, all in the southern areas of the USSR, in the Caucasus, and in Central Asia. Four other republics had 30 percent or more of private urban housing stock: Azerbaidzhan, 37.7 percent; Belorussia, 33.7 percent; Tadzhikistan, 31.3 percent; and Armenia, 30.1 percent (see table 6.1).

A second home market in owning and renting has been flourishing for years. These are *dachas* (summer houses). They come in all sizes from stately villas

Table 6.1

Percentage of Private Urban Housing in Rank Order, by Republics, USSR, 1985–1986

U.S.S.R.	22.2%	Moldavia	27.8
Uzbekistan	41.5	Turkmenia	27.6
Georgia	41.3	Kazakhstan	26.4
Kirghizia	41.0	Lithuania	21.9
Azerbaidzhan	36.7	Ukraine	19.9
Belorussia	33.7	Estonia	18.4
Tadzhikistan	31.3	Russia	16.9
Armenia	30.0	Latvia	16.1

Source: Narodnoe Khozaiistvo U.S.S.R. v 1985, Moskva, Finansy i Statistiki, 1986, p. 428. (Statistical Yearbook of the USSR, 1986)

with servants for the political, economic, and cultural elites to an overpriced room rented from collective farmers (shared with other tenants) with electricity and running water but often without toilet facilities and costing hundreds of rubles. Legally, the rent is 1.32 rubles per square meter, but that only exists on paper. Despite great demand, the government is not permitting a rapid expansion of summer homes. Buying a *dacha* can be even more difficult than renting one. The market is fierce because so few are for sale. The least expensive is a *khibarka*, a little shack with a small plot that costs about 5,000 to 50,000 or more rubles, but they are scarce. When one buys a house one also buys a plot, although legally the sale of land is not permitted since, in theory, it belongs to the state. The problem then is finding a plot of land to build on. A way around it is to buy a phantom cottage for several thousand rubles. "Once a person buys a house, often one that has collapsed or does not exist, that person gains the use of the land and can build his own dacha" (Morton 1980).

Housing Type

Housing types depend on the size of cities. In communities with a population of less than 100,000, detached housing is still common. In smaller and middle-sized towns five-story walk-up apartment buildings are more prevalent. In large cities, high-rise structures of nine, twelve, fifteen, eighteen, and twenty-two stories predominate, especially in capitals of large republics. Mobile homes are rarely used.

Location

In 1940 the rural population numbered 130,945,000; by 1985 this number had declined to 95,854,000, a reduction of 35,111,000. In 1985 only 35 percent of the population lived in rural designated areas (*Narodnoe Khozaiistvo SSSR v 1985, Statistical Yearbook* 1986). Communities with a population of fewer than 50,000 inhabitants were not listed in the *Statistical Yearbook*. Once a city's limit is reached, often with high-rise housing estates still immediately in sight, one is abruptly thrust into the country. Continuous communities linked one to another in a suburban fringe do not exist. Those who commute do not do so by choice; they are not permitted to reside in Moscow, Leningrad, and other large cities because of the still very severe housing shortage. An estimated 100,000 live illegally in the nation's capital (Morton 1979).

Special Population Groups

There are many thousands of people in the U.S.S.R. who have no definite place of residence or work. They are the homeless, who spend their nights in a variety of places: lofts, basements, heat ducts, cemeteries, train stations, wooden areas, construction sites, buildings that are deserted or undergoing repairs, doorways, freight cars, unguarded industrial plants, abandoned churches, and monasteries. "The vagrants' territory is the whole country, but most are found in the southern provinces, Central Asian Republics and the Far East." The Soviet press has reported extensively on the problems of vagrants, the unemployed, and the homeless. Focusing on Central Asia and Azerbaidzhan in the Caucasus, in Baku 1,500 specialists in various cultural fields and hundreds of physicians were looking for jobs; more than one-third of all college graduates were working in fields outside of their specialization, and many were unemployed (*Sotsialisticheskia Industria*, March 28, 1987).

At the outskirts of Baku, 200,000 lived in shantytowns. Seventy percent of all people on the waiting list for housing worked for the Petroleum, Gas, and Petroleum Refining Ministries (*Sotsialisticheskia Industria*, 1987). They were promised attractive working and housing conditions, but they did not materialize. To provide housing for those on the working list, 1 million square meters of housing will need to be built yearly. Currently, only half of that amount is going up. That is the reason why Baku is surrounded by shantytowns.

Soviet society is aging. More people are retiring than are entering the labor force. The retirement age for women is fifty-five; for men it is sixty. Currently, between one-fifth and one-sixth of the population that lives in the European part of the USSR is of pensioner age. These retirees do not consider leaving Moscow, Leningrad, and other large urban centers to move to the Soviet "sun belt," the Caucasus and Central Asia, for several reasons. Entry into those cities is restricted, and they are as overcrowded as in the North. Moreover, in many instances they would have to lower their living and housing standards, would have to get in line on the waiting list for housing, and, most important, would lose their networks of contacts (which they spent a lifetime developing) to acquire scarce consumer goods and access to officials who can assist in side-stepping bureaucratic red tape (Morton 1984).

Families have become less stable. The divorce rate has tripled since the 1960s; more than 900,000 divorces take place every year. The highest ratio of divorces in 1985 occurred in Leningrad, Odessa, and Riga; the lowest in Erevan, Baku, and Tbilisi in the Caucasus (*Vestnik Statistiki*, no. 11, 1985, p. 67). Divorces are numerous, particularly when the wife is also a wage earner and therefore has financial independence. Overcrowded and cramped housing conditions are also an important factor as are husbands who drink and are unwilling to share domestic chores with their wives. The Soviet working woman has the burden of shopping in long lines after a day's work and then cooking and cleaning for her family. This is called the "second job." Divorces increase the number of children and adolescents living in single-parent households by about 700,000 a year. Victor Prevedentsev, a prominent Soviet demographer, identified "fatherlessness" as one of the most serious problems the USSR faces currently. It is estimated that the total number of fatherless children in the Soviet Union is growing at the rate of 1.5 million every year (*Nedelia*, no. 34, 1987).

The USSR is a multiethnic society that has more than 100 nationalities, who live primarily in their native republics and autonomous areas. Exceptions are the Russians, Ukranians, and Jews who are found in every republic. Nationalities with a population of more than 1 million are listed below:

Russians	137,397,000	Tadzhiki	2,898,000
Ukranians	42,347,000	Lithuanians	2,851,000
Uzbeki	12,356,000	Turks	2,028,000
Belorussians	9,463,000	Germans	1,936,000
Kazaki	6,556,000	Kirgizi	1,906,000
Tatars	6,317,000	Jews	1,811,000
Azerbaidzhni	5,477,000	Chuvashi	1,751,000
Armenians	4,151,000	Dagestini	1,657,000
Georgians	3,571,000	Moldavians	2,968,000

Source: *Narodnoe Khozaiistvo SSSR v 1985*, Moscow, 1986, p. 24.

Construction

Nikita S. Khrushchev, Communist party leader (1954–1964), revolutionized the Soviet housing construction industry. He launched a crash program to overcome the very critical housing shortage in urban areas. To accomplish this goal, he introduced in the mid–1950s story-high, prestressed-concrete, wall-sized panels, which replaced the more expensive and labor-intensive building materials of brick, wood, and steel. This permitted continuous construction even during the long, severe Russian winter. It also greatly reduced the need of skilled labor, which was in very short supply. These prefabricated panels were produced in large building sites, where they were assembled by huge cranes, which placed one panel on top of the other until the building was completed.

The buildings initially ranged from five to nine stories high, in the late 1960s and the 1970s. As the technology progressed, they evolved to heights of eleven, fourteen, eighteen, twenty-two, and twenty-five stories. The highest buildings were reserved hierarchically for capitals of republics (of which there are fifteen). Lower heights were prescribed for large cities with a population of 1 million, of which there were twenty-two in 1985 (Morton 1987).

Generally, the repetitive standard design of newly built apartment buildings "did not meet the expectations of their new tenants in terms of comfort and convenience, although they were eager to move into them, given the still very serious housing shortage" (Andrusz, 1985). A standard complaint was that the apartments had more family members than rooms, that bathrooms and halls were too narrow and lacked storage space for baby carriages and bicycles, and that in their outward appearance the concrete paneled buildings were stereotypically uniform, differing primarily in height but hardly in design from one another.

Finance

Limited sources of funding housing construction in cities and towns originate from government ministries and agencies and other public institutions, such as the Academy of Sciences, the trade unions, and the Armed Forces. Cities and towns also make a lesser contribution in financing housing construction. Numerous communities are still company towns. Their destiny is chiefly in the hands of factory directors belonging to industrial ministries, of which there are about fifty-five. In many instances these directors play an important role in providing the funding for public housing construction and will negotiate with city authorities where these buildings will be sited.

Although Moscow, Leningrad, and republic capitals have greater control over revenue sources and city-planning discretion, even they are still dependent on financing from ministries. This can be a serious constraint on a municipality's ability to plan and improve urban services. But factories belonging to ministries are also in a bind. Managers petition their home ministries for desperately needed funds for housing construction for their workers to prevent rapid labor turnover, which is a very serious problem. But only a few of the many requests a ministry receives can be granted because there are not sufficient funds to go around. The relatively small number of plant managers who do get funding may have to wait for a long time for housing construction to begin, because the demand on builders is much greater than their ability to deliver.

A major reason for the steady increase in housing costs from the sixth Five-Year Plan (1956–1960) of 45.0 billion rubles, to the eleventh Five-Year Plan (1981–1985) of 127.7 billion rubles was the 18 percent increase in unit size, as contemporary Soviet apartments, despite deficiencies in the quality of construction, were improved in design and equipment. They are located in predominantly medium and high-rise structures complete with utilities and contemporary design (see table 6.2).

HOUSING INSTITUTIONS AND MARKET ORIENTATIONS

Government Agencies

The State Committee for Civil Construction (Gosgrazhdanstroi), with its headquarters in Moscow, has affiliates in union republics and in major cities. It is responsible for initiating and coordinating standard designs of different housing types, engages in research and development of prefabricated building materials, calculates the relative costs of 1 square meter of living space for different housing types, and consults with Gosplan (the State Planning Agency) in regard to yearly and five-year national plans for housing construction. Gosgrazhdanstroi reports to its parent organization, Gosstroi (the State Committee for All Construction including the industrial sector).

The State Committee for Civil Construction is responsible for defining the

Table 6.2
Capital Investment in Housing Construction in the Public and Private Sectors, USSR, 1918–1985

		6th 5 Yr. Plan		7th		8th		9th		10th		11th	
1918-40	1940	1956-60	1960	1961-65	1965	1966-70	1970	1971-75	1975	1976-80	1980	1981-85	1985
A. 11.4	1.2	45.2	10.8	52.7	11.2	70.4	15.8	89.1	19.2	101.9	21.1	127.1	28.1
B. 18.4	16.4	23.5	22.7	18.9	17.5	17.7	17.1	15.8	15.0	14.2	14.0	15.1	15.6

Source: Narodnoe Khozaiistvo S.S.S.R. v 1985, Moskva, Finansy i Statistiki, 1986, p. 428. (Statistical Yearbook of the USSR, 1986)

A. Capital investment in housing construction in billion rubles.
B. As a percentage of all capital investments.

principal technical and scientific problems in the area of housing construction and architecture. The committee has seven central scientific research and design institutes and five zonal institutes in Leningrad (the Russian Republic), Kiev (Ukraine), Novosibirsk (Siberia), Tallinn (Estonia), and Tashkent (Central Asia), which study climatic and geographic factors, testing among others the safety of foundations built in permafrost areas and the reinforcing of buildings in seismic areas of Central Asia (Andrusz 1985).

Cooperatives

Housing cooperatives amounted to about 7 percent of the urban housing stock in 1985. There are no statistics in this area, because cooperatives are included, without differentiation, as part of the socialist housing stock. Cooperatives have had an up and down history in Soviet housing, falling in and out of grace. They were established in the early 1920s but were summarily abolished in the late 1930s. Permission to form new construction cooperatives began only in 1964. It usually takes at least two years or more of start-up time before construction can begin. First a board and chairperson must be elected. They are usually middle-level managers or pensioners who have the time available to negotiate with the municipality for the siting of the buildings. This is followed by a lengthy documentation-approval process before construction can begin. Construction workers work reluctantly on cooperative housing projects because they are under the scrutiny of coop members, who oversee the quality of workmanship and watch over their prospective apartments, and for good reason. In new public housing, workers routinely hold up incoming tenants when construction is completed by stealing faucets, doorknobs, and other removable objects (seldom available in stores) and selling them back illegally to new tenants.

The government has an incentive to increase the number of housing cooperatives versus tenant housing, because this will reduce its financial investment in the housing sector. Consequently, in 1982, to spur cooperative construction, the down payment was reduced from 40 to 30 and even 20 percent of the cost, depending on the regional location. The rate is highest in the major cities of the USSR and lowest in Siberia, to attract new settlers there.

A standard three-room cooperative apartment bought in 1976 cost about 12,000 rubles. Ten years later its worth had appreciated to 20,000 rubles. The monthly payment for the mortgage including utilities came to 45 rubles, compared with 10 to 12 rubles for a government apartment of equal size. A cooperative can be inherited by a spouse and children and can be sold with the permission of the coop board (Nedelia, May, 1979, pp. 7–13).

Private Owners

In 1985, 22.8 percent of urban housing was in the private sector (*Narodnoe Khozaiistvo SSSR v 1985*). It was self-financed from savings and money borrowed from families and friends, since loans from the state were not available. This long-standing policy was reversed by the Politburo at its February 1988 meeting (perhaps at Secretary Gorbachev's request), which strongly urged speeding the development of individual housing construction in cities and rural areas:

In many Union republics, territories and provinces . . . not enough attention has been given to the construction of individual homes. Unwarranted restrictions and prohibitions have been established in this area and improper often negative attitude toward people building their own homes is common. Local agencies do not always help people solve problems having to do with the allocation of lots and housing construction. (*Pravda*, March 9, 1988)

Will this be a green light for new private housing construction in cities? Promises were given for the financing and construction and repair of private homes and building materials, which in the past were habitually in short supply, would be available on the market. If those promises are kept, and not sabotaged by bureaucratic interests, this may begin a new era for private home building, even in large cities. This time the expense of home building would primarily be borne by the private sector and not at the government's expense, which is undoubtedly Gorbachev's intent.

Public Renters

Soviet citizens living in urban housing owned by municipalities, factories, and other public institutions pay the lowest rent of any industrialized society. Established in 1928, according to law, the rents may not exceed 13.2 kopeks (cents) per square meter of dwelling space, regardless of location and quality of one's lodging. (Tenants with more than 12 square meters per person pay extra.) Even when the cost of utilities (gas, electric heat, and hot water) are included, the rental cost averages less than 4 percent of a family's monthly budget.

Since rents contribute only 1.3 billion rubles to the maintenance cost of public housing, an annual subsidy of 5 billion rubles is required for the upkeep. Despite the very low housing tariffs, rent dodging by tenants is a serious problem. It costs the city of Moscow about 2 million rubles a year and the Russian Republic tens of millions. Although nonpayment of rents and utilities is prosecutable, judges are reluctant to sentence offenders or to evict them (Radio Liberty Research, August 28, 1985).

MAJOR ISSUES

Maintenance

Rents paid by tenants in public housing cover less than one-third of the maintenance costs and contribute nothing to current capital repairs. Figures available for 1975 indicate that the government subsidized public housing and communal services at a rate of 5 billion rubles and spent an additional 1.4 billion rubles for capital repairs of housing owned by municipalities. These subventions needed to be increased yearly because of the steady growth of the public housing sector, which sinks more deeply in the red every year. Even such large state subsidies were not sufficient to buy the necessary equipment and materials to maintain an ever-growing, but also an aging, housing stock. Even if sufficient funding were available, it is doubtful with a poorly functioning distribution system, characterized by chronic delays and sporadic deliveries, that equipment and materials could be delivered on time.

The repair and maintenance sector, in contrast to that of new housing construction, suffers from low prestige and has difficulty recruiting skilled workers. In the context of a severe labor shortage, the construction industry with its many research institutes is in a much better position to attract qualified personnel (although it, too, suffers from rapid turnovers). It was only in the 1970s that Moscow's housing-repair department was finally given an institute to train its staff. "The repair shortage," so named by frustrated tenants because they cannot get service from the city, forces households to seek out private handymen to do the work (Morton 1984).

Housing Shortages

Soviet citizens suffer from the poorest housing of any industrialized nation principally because so many households still live communally. (A *household* is defined as a married couple, a parental pair with children, a single parent with children, or an individual.) According to *Pravda* (December 2, 1980), about 80 percent of the urban population lived in separate apartments in 1980. This meant that at least 20 percent lived communally. But the report left unsaid that about 5 percent, mostly singles, lived in workers dormitories. The fact that conditions were worse in 1960 when 40 percent of all families lived communally is of little comfort to the large numbers still living in inadequate conditions. A numerical comparison of units to households is crucial in measuring Soviet housing needs, but this information is not published. This statistical gap is not an oversight. *The United Nations Statistical Yearbook* provides such figures for every European country except the USSR.

Since the numerical relationship between households and dwellings is not available, the next best indicator is a comparison between the number of yearly marriages and the number of housing units built. If more housing units are built annually than marriages registered and the country possesses an equal or superior number of dwellings over households, the basis for a good housing situation is present. This does not mean that the nation's housing problem is solved. It does signify, however, that a basic goal has been achieved and that other pressing qualitative concerns can receive higher priority: the size of a dwelling, the facilities with which it is equipped, the desirability of the neighborhood or a

Table 6.3
Housing Units Built, Marriages, and Housing Deficit, USSR, 1980–1985

Year	Housing Units Built	Marriages	Shortage of Units
1980	2,004,000	1,724,600	-720,600
1981	1,997,000	2,788,100	-791,100
1982	2,002,000	2,769,200	-767,200
1983	2,030,000	2,834,800	-804,800
1984	2,008,000	2,634,100	-626,100
1985	1,991,000	2,710,000	-719,000
Total Shortage of Units 1980–1985:			4,428,800

Sources: *Radio Liberty Research Bulletin*, no. 155/86, April 14, 1986, 5; *Nik* 1985, pp. 5, 30.

house, the time it takes to get to and from work, and so on. The tenant's ability to afford comfortable housing, or to bribe state officials to acquire desirable accommodations, is then a primary consideration.

Between 1980 and 1985, a six-year period, 4,430,000 more marriages were formed than housing units built; this did not include the number of divorces that took place during this time, which meant that one ex-spouse needed to find new lodgings but for lack of them may have had to stay with his or her former partner in the same apartment or room. Moscow's housing deficit in 1982 was 43,947 units, and Leningrad's was 26,000 units. Newlyweds, then, have had little chance of moving into their own apartment and may be destined to live with in-laws for decades (see table 6.3).

Bureaucratic Allocation and Corruptive Practices

The urban housing deficit is really much larger than the figures indicate. With a zero vacancy rate in Soviet urban areas, a family's desire to live in an apartment of its own is strictly (if not always successfully) monitored by the authorities. If a family's sanitary norm of 9 square meters of living space per person has been satisfied, getting on the waiting list is virtually impossible except through connections. To discourage new households from forming, singles who wish to live apart from the extended family will frequently be denied a place on the list. Also denied will be the many who have to live beyond the city limit and commute to work. Many of these "suburbanites" are the underprivileged of Soviet society—not necessarily because of low income, although this also can be a factor, but because there are few urban amenities beyond the city limits. To prevent huge influxes of rural migrants, permission to move to large population centers such as Moscow, Leningrad, and Kiev is rarely granted without sponsorship from a governmental agency, even with an apartment to exchange from another city, unless an individual has special skills. Moscow has the severest restrictions of all. Many difficulties have to be overcome, which can take years. A sponsoring agency has to provide an apartment or a room for the newcomer, because residence must be established before a *propiska* (residence certificate) can be issued. Chances of receiving a *propiska* improve if two families of approximately the same size in different cities agree to exchange comparable apartments.

City residents who have a *propiska* but live in cotenancy, subleased apartments, or dormitories and wish to improve their poor housing situation by moving into better quarters are entirely dependent on the housing authorities, who determine waiting-list eligibility. If a family's per capita norm of 9 square meters of living space has been satisfied, permission can be arranged only through connections. Eligibility usually begins with less than 5 or 7 meters, but this differs from locality to locality. Figures are rarely published, but in Moscow, 180,000 families, about 590,000 persons, were on the list in 1974 (Morton 1984).

Individual couples with a residence permit, but with no lease on an apartment or room, have no housing to exchange; they therefore have few options. They can rent a room or an apartment, but that is difficult and expensive because of black-market prices, or they can try to join a construction cooperative, but they are expensive, require a hefty down payment, and take years to build.

To engage in housing exchange, a person must have a room or apartment in his or her name. It can be state or cooperatively owned. In either case, it becomes that person's "working capital" to try to exchange current quarters for more suitable housing. A public housing unit thus becomes a commodity. To succeed in the exchange market, a Soviet citizen needs ingenuity, tenacity, patience, luck, influence, and cash, and it can take years. The Bureau of Housing Exchanges maintains a card file (for a 3 ruble fee per entry) of citizens who wish to exchange their housing. Notices also appear in the *Bulletin for Housing Exchanges*, which most large cities publish. The Moscow edition appears usually biweekly and carries more than 1,000 listings.

Because exchange bureaus provide little help, a lively, open-air "stock market" trading in rooms and apartments operates in all kinds of weather just outside the Central Exchange Bureau's office. In Moscow it is located just off Prospekt Mira, one of the oldest sections in the city. Every Sunday, its most active day, hundreds go there eager to make a deal. Exchanges involving a chain of families are seldom equal. Some will accept a decrease in living space; others will give up a desirable, centrally located district for one that is on the city's outskirts with more rooms. Those who stand to gain from a transaction will privately pay their exchange partners a sum of money mutually agreed upon, based on what the market will bear. Such illegality is winked at by the housing authorities, who will officially approve an exchange as long as the same number of persons exchange roughly similar amounts of space.

Just as the housing market has led to scores of illegal practices in the USSR, so have the *propiska*, the housing-allocation process, and the past restrictions on private home ownership (which may be lifted). Since government officials monopolize the supply of housing, it is understandable that housing bureaucrats will be offered bribes. Persons on the waiting list are tempted to jump the queue, because doing so can reduce their waiting list from ten years or more to zero. But for such an act to succeed, *blat* (influence) or a bribe or both are needed. It is one of the most frequently cited violations in the housing system.

Another common form of corruption occurs when the local party and government officials, plant managers, and other well-placed bureaucrats with connections build and equip oversized homes (far in excess of 60 square meters of living space) on illegally assigned plots, using stolen building materials, state-owned construction machinery, and labor on the public payroll. Sometimes they own several private homes (though only one is legally permitted to each household), while maintaining a state-owned apartment in the city. Thus housing is an integral part of the reward system of the Soviet society. State agencies, holding a monopoly in the distribution of housing, ration out new units on the basis of occupational work and influence—only secondarily on the basis of need. Thus housing is increasingly becoming stratified between haves and have-nots and is also becoming segregated in the cities as different profession groups cluster together in housing complexes financed by ministries, organizations, and unions.

The poorest housing class in the USSR, the "least favored," are the millions clustered beyond the limits of large cities who seek to be let in. In the city, the housing poor are the "less favored" living communally or in dormitories. Possessing a legal right to live in the city, they hope that they will receive an apartment of their own. In the meantime, they can profit from the advantage that city life offers in the form of shopping, medical care, education, and cultural opportunities. Households living in self-contained apartments in newly erected housing districts are much better off. They are the "more favored" even though they are located far from the center. Commuting to work may take an hour by crowded bus or subway, and shopping where they live is difficult. "Most favored" are those families living in their own apartment in or near the center of town. Generally, they are the political, military, security, economic, scientific, cultural, educational, and worker elites. They are the most heavily subsidized because they are paying the same low rent as those living communally. Thus the most advantaged become the beneficiaries of redistributed wealth, which they can pass on to their children.

PROSPECTIVE DEVELOPMENTS

The rate of housing construction in the Soviet Union continues unabated, but is still not enough. In the tenth Five-Year Plan (1981–1985) 22 million square meters of new housing were built and approximately 10 million citizens improved their living conditions. Over several decades, Soviet apartments have become larger in size, though they are still small by Western standards, averaging 56 square meters of living space, and in 1988 the per capita space per person rose to 9 square meters.

However significant the improvements, a very severe housing shortage still remains in practically every city and town. The pledge that every family would live in a separate apartment or home, promised by Party Secretary Nikita S. Khrushchev in 1961, was to be achieved by 1980. That goal had to be postponed, first to 1995, and most recently to the year 2000. The housing situation is particularly bleak for the 20 percent of the population who still live in communal apartments and dormitories; most newlyweds will have to live with their in-laws for many years to come. There is a list of 13 million families in cities and towns who have been waiting to move into separate apartment units, and the overall housing quality of new construction is still unsatisfactory, despite monitoring by special quality control teams.

Future prospects are not very encouraging. According to the party's plan, individual and cooperative housing construction should have increased much more rapidly, at least by 20 percent, and the cooperative sector is still ten years behind schedule. To eliminate the housing shortage 40 million units will have to be built by the year 2000.

Housing is one area in which General Secretary Gorbachev has attempted to demonstrate progress since coming to power in 1985. The annual number of apartments built reached an all time high of 2.7 million units in 1987, although the housing shortage is far from being solved: 3.3 million housing units will need to be built yearly without any loss of the existing housing stock. However, the government's heavy investment in housing construction at present is a positive sign that the housing shortage is finally taken seriously.

REFERENCES

Andrusz, G. D. 1985. *Housing and Urban Development in the U.S.S.R.* Albany: New York State University Press.

Morton, Henry W. 1979. "Housing Policies and Problems of Eastern Europe." *Studies in Comparative Communism* 22, no. 4 (Winter): 300–321.

————. 1980. "Who Gets What, When and How: Housing in the Soviet Union." *Soviet Studies* 22, no. 2: 235–59.

————. "The Housing Game." 1987. *The Wilson Quarterly* 9: 61–74.

————. 1984. "Housing in the Soviet Union." In *The Soviet Union in the 1980s*, edited by Erik P. Hoffman, 76. New York: The Academy of Political Science.

FURTHER READING

Alexeev, Michael. "The Effect of Housing Allocation on Social Inequality: A Soviet Perspective." *Journal of Comparative Economics* 12 (1988): 228–34.

————. "Market vs. Rationing: The Case of Soviet Housing." *The Review of Economics and Statistics* 70, no. 3 (1988): 414–20.

————. "La répartition des logements en U.R.S.S. et les facteurs qui l'influencent." *Revue d'Études Comparatives Est-Ouest* 19, no. 1 (1988): 5–36.

Andreyev, A. *Housing in the USSR Today and Tomorrow*. Moscow: Novosti Press Agency, 1978.

Andrusz, G. D. "The Built Environment in Soviet Theory and Practice." *International Journal of Urban and Regional Research* 11, no. 4 (1987): 478–99.

Barry, D. D. "Soviet Housing Law: The Norms and Their Application." In *Soviet Law After Stalin*, edited by D. D. Barry, 1977.

Bates, A. Allan. "Low Cost Housing in the Soviet Union." In *Industrialized Housing*. Washington, D.C.: U.S. Government Printing Office, 1979, 1–21.

Berg, Voldemar. "The Soviet Urban Housing Problem." *Bulletin, Institute for the Study of the U.S.S.R.*, November 1957.

Block, Alexander. "Soviet Housing—The Historical Aspect: Some Notes on Problems of Policy." *Soviet Studies* 3, no. 1 (July 1951): 1–15.

————. "The Historical Aspect: Some Notes on Problems and Policy—II." *Soviet Studies* 3, no. 3 (January 1952): 229–57.

————. "Soviet Housing—The Historical Aspect: Problems of Amount, Cost, and Quality in Urban Housing—I." *Soviet Studies* 1, no. 3 (January 1954): 246–77.

Cattell, David T. *Leningrad: A Case Study of Soviet Urban Government*. New York: Praeger, 1968.

DiMaio, John, A., Jr. *Soviet Urban Housing Problems*. New York: Praeger, 1974.

Grant, Steven A. *Soviet Housing and Urban Design*. Washington, D.C.: U.S. Department of Housing and Urban Development, 1980.

Hazard, John N. *Soviet Housing Law*. New Haven, Yale University Press, 1939.

Herman, Leon M. "Urbanization and New Housing Construction in the Soviet Union." *The American Journal of Economics and Sociology* 30, no. 2 (April 1971): 203–19.

Kruusvall, J. "Mass Housing and Psychological Research in the Soviet Union." In *Environmental Policy, Assessment and Communication*, edited by D. Canter, M. Drampen, and D. Stea, 147–74. Aldershot, Eng.: Avebury, 1988.

Morton, Henry W. "Soviet Housing." In *Handbook of Soviet Social Science Statistics*, edited by Ellen Mickiewicz, 119–35. New York, The Free Press, 1973.

————. "What Have Soviet Leaders Done about the Housing Crisis?" In *Soviet Politics and Society*, edited by Henry W. Morton and Rudolf L. Tökés, 163–99. New York: Free Press, 1974.

————. "The Leningrad District of Moscow—An Inside Look." *Soviet Studies* 20, no. 2 (1979): 206–18.

————. "Recent Reforms in the Soviet Housing Construction Process." *Soviet Housing and Design*. Washington, D.C., U.S. Government Printing Office, 1980, 3–7.

————. "Housing Quality and Housing Classes in the Soviet Union." In *Quality of Life in the Soviet Union*, edited by Horst Herlemann, 95–115. Boulder: Westview Press, 1987.

Niit, T., M. Heidmets, and J. Kruusvall. "Environmental Psychology in the Soviet Union." In *Handbook of Environmental Psychology*, edited by D. Stokols and I. Altman, 1311–35. New York: Wiley, 1987. This review chapter contains several references to earlier publications on housing.

Sillince, John A. A. *Housing in Eastern Europe and the Soviet Union*. London: Croom Helm, 1989.

Sosnovy, Timothy. *The Housing Problem in the Soviet Union*. Research Program on the USSR. New York, 1954.

———. "Housing Conditions and Urban Development." *New Directions in the Soviet Economy*. Washington, D.C.: Joint Economic Committee, U.S. Congress, 1966, 533–53.

7

Hungary

JOHN A. A. SILLINCE

In 1945 Hungary was still a relatively backward agrarian country whose housing stock was largely in poor condition or damaged by the war. The period until

1960 saw no great improvement in housing conditions. Investment was concentrated in heavy industry in Budapest and the North. The largest number of new dwellings (mostly privately built) was in the villages; yet the village population fell by 11 percent from 1949 to 1960. Despite 100,000 new dwellings in the towns (excluding the capital, Budapest) the number of town inhabitants per dwelling rose by 21 percent as a result of large-scale migration.

Throughout the late 1950s, especially in the Seventh, Eighth, and Ninth Party Congress meetings, there was criticism of the lack of housing in Hungary. In 1960 a fifteen-year housing plan was launched that aimed at 50,000 to 80,000 new dwellings per year, an ambitious increase over the average 26,000 new dwellings per year of the previous eleven years. Moreover, investment funds shifted away from heavy industrial investment toward a geographically more even spread of investments in light industry and infrastructure. Also the difficulty of controlling Budapest's growth was acknowledged—the fifteen-year plan accepted the need for a quarter of a million more dwellings in the capital (i.e., a quarter of all planned provisions).

The target of a million new homes in fifteen years was reached. With demolitions, the total net increase in the period 1960–1975 was 816,000 new homes. Despite this the number of dwellings with no basic amenities fell very slightly, and by 1970 still two-thirds of the nation's housing stock was without basic amenities.

TRENDS IN HOUSING CONDITIONS AND CONSTRUCTION, 1945–1986

Housing Quality

Although the situation is still unsatisfactory, there has been a dramatic improvement between 1949, when 9.2 million people lived in 2.467 million dwellings, and 1986, when 10.64 million people lived in 3.846 million dwellings. This improvement is illustrated in table 7.1.

The largest qualitative advance has occurred since 1966, when demolition rates rose markedly, to a peak in 1976–1980 (99,200 demolished) after which they declined (to 76,000 in 1981–1985) and, when construction rates rose, to a peak in 1976–1980 (452,700 built) after which they declined (to 369,000 in 1981–1985) (Központi 1985a, 8–9).

However, the problem of quality has not been merely due to history before 1945. Much new building until about 1970 was of poor quality. For example, in the period 1961–1965, 37.7 percent of new dwellings were without a bathroom, 71.4 percent without flush toilet, 7.4 percent without electricity, 51.8 percent without water mains, and 80.6 percent without gas mains. The improvement here has been considerable: comparable 1981–1985 figures are 0.8, 1.2, 0, 0.9, and 63.9 percent (Központi 1985a, 12).

There has been a gradual increase in dwelling size, from 52 square meters in

Table 7.1
Housing Quality, Hungary, 1949, 1986

Housing Feature	1949	1986
One-room dwellings	70.5%	19.5%
Two-room dwellings	24.6%	48%
Dwellings without mains water	83%	22.8%
Dwellings without flush toilet	87.4%	34.3%
Dwellings without mains gas	93%	69.8%
Dwellings without Sewerage	NA	21.4%
Dwellings without bathroom	89.9%	27%
Average density (persons per 100 rooms)	265	126
Average density (persons per 100 dwellings)	373	277

Source: Központi, 1985b, p. 277.
Notes: NA = not available; all are figures for January 1, 1986.

1971–1975 to 54 square meters in 1981–1985 for state-built dwellings, and from 69 square meters in 1971–1975 to 80 square meters in 1981–1985 for private sector dwellings. The national average (state and private sectors) has increased from 63 to 74. The Budapest average has increased from 55 to 60. Differences between the two sectors are most marked for dwellings of three or more rooms. For example, in 1981–1985 the average size for the state sector was 32 square meters (one room), 55 (two), 75 (three), and for the private sector it was 38 (one), 63 (two), 102 (three) (Központi 1985a, 15).

The problem of low-housing quality has been more a rural than an urban problem. In 1949 the percentage of dwellings without amenities was 56 in Budapest, 86.4 in the towns, and 97.6 in the villages. Despite subsequent advances, the rural-urban bias still remains. The 1970 figures are 33 for Budapest, 47 for the towns, 67 for the villages (Építésgazdasági 1979; Központi 1978, 8).

Tenure Status

In 1985, 74.5 percent of the dwellings were privately owned. Tables 7.2 and 7.3 show how many new dwellings were constructed in the state and private

Table 7.2

New State and Private Sector Construction of Dwellings, Hungary, 1961–1985

	1961-65	1976-80	1981-85
New state sector	104,100	162,000	81,500
New private sector	178,200	289,000	289,000

Source: Központi, 1985b.

Table 7.3

New Construction of Dwellings in Budapest, Towns, and Villages, Hungary, 1976–1985

	1976-80	1981-85
Budapest	85,600	79,400
Towns	201,500	159,800
Villages	165,600	135,500

Source: Központi, 1982a, 1985a.
Note: With some variations, "towns" are settlements outside Budapest larger than 8,000 population.

sectors in recent years. The fall in construction since 1980 has affected the towns most, then the villages, and Budapest the least.

Government attempts to encourage home ownership since 1970 (by providing cheap mortgages via the state building society and credit company, OTP) have had a large effect (table 7.4). The category of "shared house and freehold flat" is that of ready-built OTP apartments (as well as a preexisting number of old subdivided houses), which spread rapidly. The category "own house" includes inherited, paid-off, and self-built houses. The first three groups (i.e., the private sector) expanded by 34.2 percent (1970–1985) compared with the state sector increase of 17 percent. The table also shows that the number of dwellings in villages decreased (1970–1980). Also, the proportion of state dwellings is highest in Budapest.

Housing Type

In 1985, 34,356 detached houses were built, 47.4 percent of the total number of units constructed (72,506); 56,564 (78.0 percent) of all units were in buildings with four floors or less (including detached houses), 12,312 (17 percent) were in buildings with five to ten floors, and 1,657 (2.2 percent) were in buildings

Table 7.4
Ownership of the Housing Stock, Hungary, 1970, 1980, 1985 (x 1,000)

	1970				1980				1985
	Budapest	Towns	Villages	Total	Budapest	Towns	Villages	Total	
Own house	176	486	1,446	2,108	168	555	1,434	2,157)	
Shared house and freehold flat	34	19	4	58	70	123	17	210)	2,828.5
Self build group	19	29	1	49	61	106	5	173)	
Government and other owners	389	269	161	819	410	347	119	877	958.5
Total	619	804	1611	3,034	709	1,132	1,575	3,417	3,787

Source: Központi, 1982b, 1985b.

with eleven or more floors. Besides these houses, 3,527 holiday homes were built.

Location

In terms of growth rates of settlements of different sizes, it is the towns between 15,000 and 20,000 that have grown the fastest between 1972 and 1982 (93 percent). The next fastest growth has been in the big towns of 100,000 to 500,000 (a growth rate in 1972–1982 of 59.4 percent). The small towns have grown despite low state housing and low infrastructure spending. But they do have a very high investment per head in industrial companies, presumably expanding where labor is most available (Központi 1982c, 205, 207, 209). The large towns have grown fast because of high levels of housing and infrastructure investment.

Special Population Groups

Low-income groups tend to have worse and more expensive accommodations, both in the state and private sectors (Szelenyi 1983, Sillince 1985b; Dániel 1985). Partially because of this, after 1975 special tenants' rebates and preferential mortgages (see below) were made available for families with three or more children. A well-publicized though numerically small number of small, "temporary state" apartments were also made available for young couples. However, these dispensations have slowly been withdrawn in recent years—more emphasis is now placed on the waiting time for the allocation of state apartments. Homelessness and squatting do not occur.

The size and quality of housing increase steadily from the poorest to the richest individuals (table 7.5). (For other predictors of housing size and quality, see Dániel 1985.)

Single parent families are not noticeably worse off—they have accommodations comparable to those of childless couples (table 7.6). Indeed, table 7.6 shows that apartment size and quality are generally distributed appropriately, at least with regard to family status.

Retired people generally have larger and higher-quality dwellings than their incomes would suggest. This is undoubtedly due to low residential mobility (Dániel 1985), rather than to policy.

Construction

New house and apartment building by the state sector is only a fifth of that in the private sector (see table 7.7). Within the private sector, the state building society, OTP, plays a prominent role as lender to individuals. As far as building method is concerned (see table 7.7) most construction using traditional methods is private sector construction.

Table 7.5
Dwelling Amenities, by Individual Monthly Income, Hungary, 1979

	Monthly Income	
Amenities Per 100 households	Less than 8 dollars	More than 56 dollars
Rooms	121.4	228.2
Bathrooms	12.2	73.8
WCs	10.2	71.8
Hot-water facilities	11.2	71.8
Modern Central Heating Systems	2.0	51.5
Telephones	1.0	35.9
Modern dwellings	8.2	41.7

Source: Központi, 1982a, p. 336.

The majority of current construction is dwellings with three or more rooms. In 1985, 56.7 percent had three or more rooms (3.86 per 1,000 population), 36.6 percent had two rooms (2.49 per 1,000), and 6.8 percent had one room (0.46 per 1,000).

About half of all new construction is detached houses (34,356 were built in 1985, a rate of 3.2 per 1,000 population). Very few semidetached new houses are built (only 1,424 in 1985, a rate of 0.13 per 1,000.) Multidwelling buildings (mostly state-sector built) form the other large group—for example, in 1985 there were 25,115 new dwellings grouped together with more than 25 dwellings per building (Központi 1985a, 42).

Finance

The financial changes in recent years can be shown by comparing state and private investment. (An exchange rate of 100 Hungarian forints to one U.S. dollar is assumed. U.S. dollars will be referred to throughout.) In 1976–1980 state housing investment was $751 million (43.3 percent of the total); private housing investment was $984 million (56.7 percent of the total). In 1980–1985 state housing investment was $551 million (24.8 percent of the total), and private housing investment was $1,673 million dollars (75.2 percent of the total). Considering all investment (all sectors) in 1976–1980 total national investment was $10,297 million of which housing was $1,735 million (16.9 percent). By 1980–

Table 7.6
Size and Quality of Housing, by Family Status, Hungary, 1979 (Per 100 Households)

Family Status	Rooms	Bath rooms	WC	Hot Water	Modern Central Heating	Modern Flats
Non-family household	156.3	36.2	36.3	33.1	21.1	17.2
- one individual	152.3	34.9	35.1	31.8	20.3	16.3
- more individuals	181.7	44.1	43.5	40.9	25.8	22.6
One-family household (without relative)	195.7	54.3	49.9	49.8	26.4	29.0
- couple without children	179.9	46.3	42.2	42.2	21.2	30.3
- couple with children	207.3	59.5	54.8	55.1	29.3	28.7
- single parent with children	179.1	48.1	46.9	43.8	26.8	26.1
One-family household (with relative)	230.5	59.5	52.2	53.2	24.0	33.9
- couple without children	214.4	51.7	50.0	48.3	20.0	30.0
- couple with children	235.9	62.2	52.9	54.8	25.3	35.2
Average	194.1	52.0	47.6	47.3	24.8	27.6

Source: Központi, 1982a.

1985 the total national investment was $11,203 million, of which housing was $2,224 million (19.9 percent). This reflects the stability of housing investment relative to the cutbacks in productive investment after 1980. Considering the state housing sector only, where there have been cutbacks, total national state sector investment in 1976–1980 was $9,248 million of which housing was $751 million (8.1 percent). The corresponding figures for 1981–1985 are $939.6 million and $55.1 million (5.9 percent).

In 1985 the average new housing cost was $120 per square meter, an increase of 53.8 percent over 1980. There were regional variations. Budapest was highest at $130 (an increase of 51.2 percent); Györ was lowest at $103 (an increase of 68.8 percent).

The costliest type of dwelling in 1985 was the detached state-built house (neither a local council tenancy nor built by a local council for sale), averaging 98 square meters and costing $18,425 to build. The cheapest was the high-rise apartment bought with an OTP mortgage, averaging 57.2 square meters and costing $6,565 to build.

To buy a dwelling, a person can borrow up to $1,800 from OTP at 2 percent interest per annum over twenty-five years. For sums between $1,800 and $4,000, 4 percent must be paid. Bank loans are available for larger sums, but interest is 8 percent per annum over ten years. For families "in need", OTP gives interest-free mortgages. However, the concept of "in need" has been drastically narrowed since the late 1970s. To buy, rebuild, or extend a family (detached) house, one can borrow, since 1983, up to $900, 70 percent of the purchase price at 3 percent interest per year from OTP. Otherwise, family houses can be financed by OTP with ten-year loans at 8 percent interest a year. An extra $1,400 mortgage is available at 3 percent interest for modernizing central heating (away from oil) and for insulation. To change a one-story house into a two-story house (to encourage the efficient use of land) one can borrow 50 percent of the cost up to $1,400 at 3 percent over twenty-five years and a bank loan up to $500 at 6 percent over ten years. For an extra dormer room (in the attic) the money is available subject to the necessary local council permission. Recently, OTP rates have increased significantly.

THE ROLE OF HOUSING INSTITUTIONS AND ORGANIZATIONS

There are three ways of acquiring home ownership. One can build a house oneself, one can join a housing cooperative, or one can buy a dwelling. In 1985, out of a total of 59,551 private sector completions, 37,675 were self-built, 19,629 were bought, and 2,247 were built by a housing cooperative.

In the vast majority of cases in which one builds oneself, the couple and family members, friends, and neighbors do nearly all of the work. Often a private builder provides an inexpensive overseer role. Dwellings are predominantly simple detached bungalows or two-story dwellings. This method offers maximum choice of dwelling type and involves about a quarter of the cost of buying a ready-made dwelling. Employing a builder to do all of the work speeds up the job but makes it more expensive.

With housing cooperatives, payment is in installments as and when it can be afforded. The person buying can provide all of the labor or pay extra. Some cooperatives allow persons to participate only if they provide the labor themselves. However, a majority provide a cheap shell for the owner to complete.

Ready-built dwellings are provided by local councils (2,936 in 1985) and by OTP (41,082 in 1985). Their number has expanded since the growth in mortgage finance in the seventies.

Besides home ownership, there is a reliance on state-housing provision. In 1985, 8,162 extra local council tenancies were created, and there were 1,858

Table 7.7

Sponsorship and Building Methods of Newly Constructed Dwellings, Hungary, 1981–1985 (Rate per 1,000 Population in Parentheses)

Sponsorship	1985		Yearly Average 1981-85
New council tenancies	8,162	(.77)	9,717
New council built dwellings for sale	2,936	(.28)	4,609
Other new state dwellings	1,858	(.17)	1,971
Total new state sector construction	12,956	(1.22)	16,297
New OTP - built dwellings	18,469	(1.73)	17,631
Other new dwellings using OTP finance	40,102	(3.76)	38,555
Other new dwellings not using OTP	980	(.09)	1,484

250

Total new private sector construction	**59,551**	**(5.59)**	**57,640**
Total new dwelling construction	**72,507**	**(6.8)**	**73,937**
Building Method:			
prefabricated panels	24,144	(2.26)	26,000
concrete cast in situ	4,858	(.42)	4,600
bricks on reinforced concrete frame	1,450	(.14)	2,780
other modern methods	798	(.07)	760
traditional methods	41,619	(3.9)	39,800

Source: Központi, 1985, p. 278.

other new state apartments. This latter group is built for members of the army, police, and so on and are not distributed by local councils. Allocation is by means of a points system, administered by local councils. There is no systematic and accurate information on what the points system involves. Applicants can find out their number of points but cannot find out how the points are given. No systematic study exists, and anyway it is almost certain that the points system regularly changes, as new administrative fashions prevail. In the early to mid-seventies the criteria were heavily weighted toward the needy (the old, those who had not had a workplace and who thus had no workplace pension, large families), but this weighting has been relaxed since then. Having more than two children is almost certainly still the dominant criterion, but it is probably replaced by other conditions such as a reference from the applicant's workplace. Work-places play a complicated role here. For example, some workplaces have allo-cated a housing quote so that applicants with a small number of points who work at such workplaces nevertheless find accommodations. Other workplaces promise housing after a specified period of service, but this has been known not to be honored if the company has no housing available. There are cases cited in the newspapers of special small and temporary accommodations where tenants are promised larger accommodations on condition of having children. Other cases have been cited where the queue can be bypassed on payment of a deposit or on signing a document promising to have children.

The point system is applied not only to council apartments but also to co-operative and OTP apartments. Thus even housing that finally ends up as privately owned passes through some form of state-mediated allocation process. The coun-cils must publish waiting lists with points but do not need to justify the points given. A proportion of council apartments are given to families whose homes have been demolished; such an allocation does not use the points system. Gov-ernment and party officials obtain the best state apartments, and in some instances such apartments are used to induce "key workers" (e.g., doctors, teachers) to migrate to where they are needed. There was some criticism of the lack of equity in the system, and some experimentation in the middle seventies, giving greater weight to "need" in allocation of points. These experiments have receded now following responses, for example, to the spectacle of large families getting good state apartments at low rent and then "selling" them (the exchange price can be half to three-quarters of what the apartment would bring if it were private) and afterwards moving back to cheaper accommodations. Moreover, state pro-vision is declining, and few accommodations are now available for such purposes.

The social function or role of state housing has changed in an important way in the past three decades. Until 1970 state housing was the least expensive and was of the highest quality. But after 1970 the situation changed, and the relative quality of state apartments has fallen.

State apartments have relatively very low rents. Tenants can stay without condition for a lifetime, and the occupancy right can be inherited. The low rents have induced an illegal market to appear—the tenancy right of the apartment is sometimes sold to the highest bidder. For new tenants, payment of a deposit, or "key money," offsets the bargain character of state-built apartments for rent.

The institutional structure of the state building industry has many implications for design, building development, management, and rehabilitation. In the sixties eleven huge building corporations were established to produce factory-built industrialized housing. These firms enjoy a powerful monopoly position. They make a narrow range of products that are difficult or impossible to adapt to nonhigh-rise housing types. Their infrastructure (large cranes, lorries, and so on) are suitable only for high-rise building. They suffer from a problem of overcapacity, created in the sixties when the trend was to have very large plants and companies. In the sixties the idea was to build the majority of apartments with state resources: something like a ratio of 70–80 percent state, 20–30 percent private, was aimed at. This is leading to a problem of overcapacity now that government resources devoted to housing are starting to be reduced (along with greater encouragement of private home ownership and self-building). Because of overcapacity most of these house-building companies are in a position of imbalance. This results in the problems of a lack of new investment and in widening their range of products. These problems are aggravated by the many unskilled workers they employ. Such large numbers cannot easily be diverted to other sectors. They have relatively low efficiency compared to the industrial average. The companies are beset by problems of rising energy and raw material prices. On the other hand, private builders tend to take away the better-trained workers from the state building firms, so that the labour-market position of the large state building firms is not advantageous. It is under these circumstances, understandably, that state building firms try to keep their monopolistic position by lobbying national, county, and city politicians to get more orders and to get the necessary state subsidies. But state resources are limited—often when construction costs rise, local councils respond by cutting back on housing targets rather than by raising the budget allocation. This further aggravates the problem of overcapacity and creates a vicious circle.

The problems of the lack of lower-cost methods of building became strikingly apparent after the shift in the ownership distribution of newly built apartments in the late seventies and early eighties. Experts hoped this would lead to a radical change in the attitude of the big building firms and to a more flexible approach to the needs of potential owners. Although many of them tried to work out new schemes—building terraces, for example—the prices of them could be afforded by only a small minority of potential owners, particularly among those on the waiting lists. The whole procedure tended to prove the relative cheapness of high-rise building and paradoxically led to a reinforcement of the monopoly position of the state building companies. They have been able to dictate freely the architectural and planning solutions because of this monopoly. This is why a nationwide series of television debates on high-rise schemes, on the effect of such environments on people's ways of life, and on escalating housing costs subsided after a promising start in the early eighties. Politicians agreed to further subsidize state building firms and do little to reform them.

These institutional problems underlie many questions associated with urban renewal and rehabilitation. Opinion among architects and planners has followed opinion elsewhere and has become much more favorable toward rehabilitation. But the state building firms have neither the skills nor the interest in such work. Until now rehabilitation, besides that in tourist areas, has remained a political question rather than having a certain future. Renewal is becoming more important—the 1975–1990 housing plan greatly increased the planned demolition rate. Recently, the demolition rate declined due to financial reasons rather than to a rise in the political fortunes of the rehabilitation lobby.

POLICY ORIENTATIONS

Housing policy has been used as an instrument in attaining other policy objectives. It has been intricately connected with the problem of restraining Budapest's growth, the problem of rural depopulation, the problem of rewarding bureaucrats in the state and party organizations, and the problem of low population fertility.

Budapest has had special problems (Sillince 1985a; Hegedüs and Tosics 1983), partially due to the weakness of planning controls over immigration into the capital and partially due to the large housing shortages there. If we consider the proportions of housing shortage calculated from waiting lists for state dwellings, in Budapest it rose from 3 percent in 1960 to 39 percent in 1975, whereas in the towns it was much lower (21 percent in 1960, 25 percent in 1975), and in the villages it fell noticeably (41 percent in 1960, 35 percent in 1975) (Sillince 1985b). In 1975 the estimated housing shortage was still 470,000 of which 65 percent was in Budapest and the towns. Besides stricter measures in Budapest, the current (1975–1990) fifteen-year housing plan envisages much reduced housing investment in the towns to discourage movement away from the rural areas (Építésügyi 1971; Barath 1981). This involves a target housing stock change in 1980–1990 of 21 percent for Budapest (compared with a change of 16 percent in 1970–1980), a target housing stock change in 1980–1990 of 25 percent for the towns (compared with 41 percent for 1970–1980), and a target housing stock change in 1980–1990 of 3 percent for the villages (compared with a negative change in 1970–1980 of −3 percent) (Közpanti 1973, 34; 1982b, 289; Council of Ministers 1975).

There has been a realization that keeping people in the villages prevented the development of further housing problems in the towns. Also, it was found that the average size of a village family was larger than that of a town family (2.95 for Budapest, 3.05 for towns, 3.35 for villages for 1975 [Építésgazdasági 1979, 26]), representing a potential source of further overcrowding in the towns. Moreover, the environmental factors that influenced lower birth rates in the towns were considered detrimental to the national policy of encouraging fertility (Cseh-Szombathy 1979; Gyözöné 1978).

Partially because of Budapest's large size compared with the national population (it has about 20 percent of the population) and partially to spread economic development more equally across the country, a policy of decentralization from Budapest has evolved. The problem of the growth of Budapest has been more complicated than was first realized. The regulations in the fifties and sixties were that those who had worked in the capital for a mimimum of five years or who could show evidence that they had lived there in poor housing for five years had a right to be put on the various Budapest housing waiting lists. The first regulation was frequently circumvented by commuting for a period of five years (often from very far afield or by weekend commuting). The second could be circumvented by getting relatives in the capital to state that one had lived with them. There also were shared private accommodations available—often at exploitative rents. The problem for the planners was that Budapest was one of the engines of economic growth in the fifties and sixties. So the 1960–1975 fifteen-year housing plan accepted this and proposed a quarter of all new provision for Budapest. Attempts were made, therefore, to change the balance away from Budapest by other methods. Expanding Budapest economic enterprises were tempted by government money to set up branches outside the capital. Also, more new towns were designated with special government aid to offset Budapest's hypertrophy slightly and to attract potential migrants away from the capital to other areas.

However in the 1975–1990 housing plan the planned distribution of over-crowding favors Budapest over the villages, a pattern unhelpful to decentralization. For 1990 the planned number of individuals per hundred rooms are: 100 for Budapest, 109–115 for the towns, and 118 for the villages. The 1990 planned numbers of individuals per 100 apartments are 222 for Budapest, 227–228 for the towns, 235 for the villages (Council of Ministers 1975). However, relatively small apartments are now being built in Budapest, an average in 1981 of 57 square meters compared with the national average of 70 square meters; also, only 26.7 percent of 1981 construction in Budapest had three or more rooms, compared with a national average of 45.6 percent, suggesting a less favorable policy toward Budapest (Központi 1982c, 131).

Proposed in the 1975–1990 fifteen-year housing plan is an increase in total housing stock from 3,573,536 to 4,030,000 dwellings, after allowing for demolitions. The total planned new dwellings amount to 1,200,000, of which 550,000–600,000 is the net increase after allowing for demolitions. This represents a rate of 80,000 new dwellings per year, a continuance of the highest rate during the previous fifteen-year-plan period, and a rate of 40,000 demolitions per year, a doubling of the highest previous rate. The 1990 target is likely to be met, although partially because demolitions have proceeded much slower than planned—annual numbers have been falling, and the 1985 figure of 12,490 demolitions was the lowest since 1963.

There are a multitude of often conflicting objectives involved in policy matters. The allocation of state housing is often used as a wage supplement, a reward for political services or for a key worker moving to an unpopular region. A private electrician or plumber can earn $400 per month (in 1985), whereas a company director gets about $200, and a government minister $250; an average party worker at his workplace gets nothing (besides his usual income) for his party activities. Although such examples may not be entirely typical, they do fit in with public perceptions of the rewards of different occupations. One understandable response by government organizations with influence upon housing-allocation decisions is to use housing as a means of attracting and retaining useful personnel. Therefore, the government perceives a need to use housing to compensate for the deficiencies of the system of rewards. Why the system of rewards cannot instead be changed is an interesting political question. But the system has become intolerant of major changes. Also, the allocation of state housing is used to encourage the migration of key workers to less attractive parts of the country. For example, village primary teachers earn only $40 a month and village doctors only $60. C. G. Pickvance (1986) asked interesting questions about employer influence in housing allocation. Also, another objective of state housing is to redistribute incomes and help the needy. Parallel now to similar principles in the private sector is the principle of permanent rights. State apartments can be occupied for life. Occupants other than heads of households acquire the ability to inherit such rights. This principle may conflict with helping the needy. It reduces the turnover of dwellings. There is also the objective of encouraging fertility, but long waiting lists are no great encouragement. The most recent objective is the encouragement of private finance. It conflicts with many previous objectives, for example, helping the needy, giving political rewards, and using housing as a means to redistribute income.

MAJOR PROBLEMS

Quantity

There are essentially two housing markets—the state and the private sectors. Within the state sector there is a chronic housing shortage (Kórnai 1980) characterized by average waiting times that have remained around eight to ten years since the early 1970s. However, some deserving cases receive state housing relatively quickly while others must wait much longer. The private sector is characterized by high prices. Both markets are "imperfect" in that there is friction between buyer and seller: in the state sector those waiting do not know how long they need to wait or whether it is worth their while making alternative arrangements; in the private sector information is not freely available about what is for sale and at what price.

Segregation

The most important question here relates to whether the 300,000 or so Gypsies are forming ghettos as seems to be occurring in District 8 in Budapest. With the exception of the early seventies, Gypsies are usually the least skilled and poorest and are therefore given the worst housing, a policy likely to lead to segregation. Official data do not exist about Gypsies. With regard to social segregation of a more general nature, little is known and then only with regard to Budapest. The motivation for official interest came after Joszefváros (in Budapest) was redeveloped. Partially the interest arose from the renewal versus rehabilitation debate. Several studies were made in the late seventies. One of them (Ekler, Hegedüs, and Tosics 1980) revealed the continuation of outmigration from parts of the central core. Some small subareas showed a loss as high as 25 percent over ten years. Moreover, the pace of outmigration was found to be increasing. Although the overall tendency throughout Greater Budapest was found to be a gradual leveling out of ecological differences in the different social groupings (confirmed for the 1950–1980 period by Sillince 1985a and for Prague between 1930 and 1970 by Musil 1987), many of the older, denser areas were found to show a fall in social status and a rise in average age. This approach to studying ecological differences on a district-by-district basis has been criticized by Csanádi and Ladányi (1985). Their Budapest study argues that the rich may live in good apartments facing the street, and the poor may live in bad apartments facing the back or inner courtyard; both rich and poor may occupy the same street; yet significant segregation is still occurring.

Quality, Residential Satisfaction, and Preferences

The following are the results of a series of sample surveys of 2,500 representative individuals throughout the country in 1970–1976 by the Central Statistical Office (Hoffmann 1981). No matter what their present housing circumstances, the family (detached) house was preferred by all, moderated somewhat by experience in a high-rise apartment. This preference increased with age. Council high-rise apartments were consistently unpopular. Questions on attitudes revealed that people are preoccupied with shortages and the difficulties in getting a dwelling.

Equity

Ivan Szelenyi (1983) has shown how in several socialist countries including Hungary, housing is treated as a kind of wage supplement. For his 1971 case studies of Pecs and Szeged, the best and most subsidized housing, he showed, was administratively allocated to the highest occupational groups. The 1979 national data (Magyar Szocialista Munkáspart 1980) show that among occupational groups, the intelligentsia (nonself-employed and middle class in white-collar occupations) had by far the largest proportion of the best government tenancies (50 percent compared with the average per occupational group of around 20 percent) and the smallest proportion of owned houses (only 34 percent compared with the average of 74 percent). This occupational group comprises key workers who get preferential treatment on waiting lists. It is also concentrated more in Budapest, which has the largest proportion of government tenancies, especially those of high quality.

This occupational link suggests two things. First, there is a significant amount of privileged access in the Hungarian housing market. (See also Konrád and Szelenyi 1971; Szelenyi 1972, 1983. For comparisons with the USSR, see Di Maio 1974; Hoffmann 1981, 77. For further more recent evidence of inequity in Hungarian and other Eastern European housing, see Szelenyi 1987; Ciecho-cinska 1987; Musil 1987; Dangschat 1987; Tosics 1987; and Hegedüs 1987.) Second, despite the widespread popularity of home ownership, an important sector (and that which is highest paid) of the population considers it to be unnecessary. However, this elite preference is shifting toward privately owned apartments. An indication of the good bargain that the (controlled) rental sector represents is given by the fact that between 1954 and 1975, only in three years (1956, 1972, 1973) did income from council-rented property exceed maintenance expenses (Council of Ministers 1975). Another indication is that between 1959 and 1982, 70,000 council dwellings were offered for sale to tenants in Budapest. Only 2,300 were brought by private individuals. However, this situation may be less true for state-built dwellings built since 1970 (see above). In the uncon-trolled sector, there is a small but important sector of illegal tenancies at high rents ($12 a month for one room in Eger in 1983; Falus 1983).

J.A.A. Sillince (1985b, table 9) showed that rents and mortgages are relatively cheaper the higher the person's income. He showed that for the occupational group that rents more than it mortgages (the intelligentsia), a high income is combined with a rent of 4 percent of income. For the occupational group that is most heavily involved in home ownership, the laborers in cooperatives (94 percent home ownership), the necessary mortgage repayment is 9 percent of income. Szelenyi (1983, 59–68) showed similar data for rents and deposits. Mortgages, like rents, are massively subsidized. Thus high-income groups are subsidized more than low-income groups in relative and absolute terms.

In overall terms, the housing of the top occupational group is the best quality on a range of indicators while cooperative laborers are provided with the worst housing (Sillince 1985b, table 10; Központi 1982a, 49).

For those in rented apartments and houses, the intelligentsia, junior nonmanual workers, and foremen have equal quality housing, whereas, again, cooperative laborers occupy the poorest accommodations. For those in mortgaged apartments and houses, the intelligentsia, junior nonmanuals, and the retired occupy the best-quality housing, and manual workers occupy the worst accommodations (Magyar Szocialista Munkáspart 1980). Sillince (1985b, table 11) showed some housing-quality indicators and income for paid-off owners. Some of the poorest families are in the worst accommodations. This is easily understandable—the majority of owned property is rural and of lower quality. For mortgages the picture is not so clear-cut (Sillince 1985b, table 12). There is only a vague association between income and housing quality. Besides amenities within the dwelling, size and number of rooms are other important indicators. Sillince (1985b, table 13) showed that in terms both of numbers of rooms and of density of people per room, the richer families do better than poorer ones. See Dániel (1985) for a parallel investigation.

PROSPECTIVE DEVELOPMENTS

The current high priority of housing policy in Hungary dates from discontent that surfaced after the uprising and political changes of 1956. In the sixties, as a result, a modern, large-scale house-building industry was created. In the seventies volumes were further increased by means of an expansion in mortgage credit. Numbers, size, and quality of dwellings all dramatically increased. But outside the private self-build sector, state officials (mainly in local councils) continued to influence allocation. This led to unequal access: better-off people got the best housing almost free.

This situation was criticized by Szelenyi (1983). He followed market-oriented ideas by Liska (1969) and suggested that the Central Planning Office should cut housing construction and relax controls on private house building. Since those criticisms were written in May 1972, those suggestions have been put into practice (although state rents are still very low). The relative quality of state-built dwellings has fallen. But only 17 percent of families now receive state-built housing, so only a minority of new dwellings are allocated by the state. A far more important recent source of inequality in 1985 is family help in the acquisition of home ownership. It is convenient for the government to overlook this, however, since it wishes to encourage home ownership.

Summarizing the current state of knowledge, it is fair to state that today the fact that Hungarian and other East European housing is inequitably distributed is unquestioned. What is in doubt is (a) whether inequalities are increasing or decreasing and (b) whether (although a purely private sector housing system would lead to the greatest inequalities) a mixed private sector and state sector system reduces the inequalities of a purely state sector system. On (a), there are differences of opinion. Musil (1987) has argued for a trend to greater inequality and has offered data on the 1930–1970 period in Czechoslovakia; Szelényi (1987) has argued that these data and other available East European data were not detailed enough before 1970 to reach a conclusive answer. On (b), with particular regard to Hungary, both Tosics (1987) and Hegedüs (1987) argued that the market cannot counteract inequalities created by state-allocation processes. Instead, they argued for intervention of the society into the state and into the market. Szelenyi, who has argued for the development of a more mixed welfare state economy in Hungary (see Szelenyi and Manchin 1986) commented that this "is an attractive idea (and a very fashionable one in Eastern Europe today) but it has to be further elaborated to be believable" (Szelenyi 1987, 4). The crucial point of disagreement concerns what happened in Hungary during the seventies, Tosics and Hegedüs arguing that state-allocation methods became more egalitarian and Szelenyi arguing that the much larger construction volumes enabled such changes to occur.

Certainly, unequal access to housing is one important measure of inequalities in socialist countries, and Hungary seems to share this problem with other East European countries. Whether more steering toward the market would reduce these inequalities must remain an open question. A much more certain conclusion is that periods of expansion in construction volume as during the seventies allowed experimentation toward greater egalitarianism. The harsher economic climate since 1980, however, has meant that other themes of market orientation have instead been emphasized—the need to make prices reflect costs more faithfully and the encouragement of the already important private sector. The costs of state-built housing construction will continue to be on the political agenda, as they continue to rise. Private house-building firms build three times as many houses per employee than do state house-building firms.

REFERENCES

Barath, E., ed. 1981. *Orszagos Teruletrendezesi Terv Konceptio* (The National Physical Plan). Építésügyi és Városféjlesztési Miniszterium 11. Budapest: Regionalis Irona.

Ciechocinska, M. 1987. "Government Interventions to Balance Housing Supply and Urban Population Growth: The Case of Warsaw." *International Journal of Urban and Regional Research* 11, no. 1:9–26.

Council of Ministers. 1975. *Elóterjesztés a Minisztertanacs részére a lakásépítés és gazdálkodás 1990—ig szolo térvról* (Proposal to the Council of Ministers on House Building and Management until 1990). Budapest.

Csanádi, G., and J. Ladányi. 1985. "Budapest—a városszerkezet történetének es Különbözö társadalmi csoportok városszerkezeti elhelyezkedésének nemökológiai viszgálata" (Budapest: A Nonecological Study of the History of Urban Structure and Ecological Distribution of the Population). Manuscript referred to in Szelényi 1987.

Cseh-Szombathy, L. 1979. *A csaladpolitika célja, tartalmi Kore, eszkoz rendszere* (The Aims of Family Politics and the Maintenance of a Good Proportion in the Means of Production). Tarsadalmi terveszési fuzetek III Köt, 20–21. Budapest: Országos Tervhivatal Tervgazdasági Intézete.

Dangschat, J. 1987. "Sociospatial Disparities in a 'Socialist' City. The Case of Warsaw at the End of the 1970's." *International Journal of Urban and Regional Research* 11, no. 1:37–60.

Dániel, Z. 1985. "The Effect of Housing Allocation on Social Inequality in Hungary." *Journal of Comparative Economics* 9, no. 4:391–409.

Di Maio, A. J. 1974. *Soviet Urban Planning: Problems and Politics.* New York: Praeger.

Ekler, D., J. Hegedüs, and I. Tosics. 1980. *A városépítés alkalmazott társadalmi-gazdasági modelljének elméleti és módszertani kérdései: A városféjlödés társa-*

dalmi-térbeli összefüggései (Socioeconomic Models for Planning: Social and Spatial Considerations). Budapest példáján I és II Kötét (Examples of Budapest, Vols. 1 and 2). Budapest: Budapest Városépítési Tervezö Vallalat (Budapest Town Planning Company).

Építésgazdasági és Szervezési Intézet (Housing Economy and Management Institute). 1979. *Építésgazdasági és Szervézetési* (Housing Economy and Management). 4884/5 Tanulmany. Budapest.

Építésügyi es Városféjlesztési Miniszterium (Ministry of Town Building and Planning). 1971. *Orszagos Településhalozat-Féjlesztési Konceptio* (The National Physical Plan). Budapest.

Falus, G. 1983. "Garzonház Egerben" (Bachelors Plats in Eger). *Népszabadság*, March 26, 3.

Ferge, Z. 1979. *A Society in the Making*. Harmondsworth, Eng.: Penguin.

Gyözöne, K. 1978. *A falusi lakokörnyezet alakulasrol* (The Living Environment of Villages). Budapest: Szövetkezeti Kutató Intézet Közlemények (Cooperative Research Institute Publications).

Hegedüs, J. 1987. "Reconsidering the Roles of the State and the Market in Socialist Housing Systems." *International Journal of Urban and Regional Research* 11, no. 1:79–99. Hoffmann, I. 1981. *Lakáskörülmények* (Housing Circumstances). Budapest: Kossuth Könyvkiádó.

Hegedüs, J., and I. Tosics. 1983. "Housing Classes and Housing Policy: Some Changes in the Budapest Housing Market." *International Journal of Urban and Regional Research* 7, no. 4:467–94.

Hoffmann, I. 1981. *Lakáskörülmények* (Housing Circumstances). Budapest: Kossuth Könyvkiádó.

Konrád, G., and I. Szelenyi. 1971. "A késleltett városfejlödés tarsadalmi konfliktusai" (Social Conflicts Arising from Delayed Urban Development). *Valosag* 15, no. 12:19–35; appeared as "Social Conflicts of Under-Urbanisation." In *Captive Cities*, edited by M. Harloe. New York: Wiley, 1977.

Kórnai, J. 1980. *Economics of Shortage*. Amsterdam: North Holland.

Központi Statisztikai Hivatal (Central Statistical Office). 1973. "Népszamlalás 1970 26 Kötét" (Population Census, 1970). Budapest.

———. 1978. *Lakásépítés és megszünés 1977* (Constructions and Demolitions, 1977). Budapest.

———. 1982a. *Életkörülmények és lakásviszonyok* (Living Conditions and Housing Standards). Budapest.

———. 1982b. *Statisztikai évkönyv, 1981* (Statistical Yearbook, 1981). Budapest.

———. 1982c. *Területi statisztikai évkönyv, 1981* (Regional Statistical Yearbook, 1981). Budapest.

———. 1985a. *Lakásstatisztikai Évkonyv* (Housing Statistics Yearbook). Budapest.

———. 1985b. *Statisztikai Évkonyv* (Statistical Yearbook). Budapest.

Liska, T. 1969. "A bérlakás—Kereskedelem koncepciója" (Ideas on the Market in Tenant's Flats). *Valóság* 1:22–35.

Magyar Szocialista Munkáspart. 1980. *Magyar Szocialista Munkáspart 12 Kongresszusa* (Hungarian Socialist Workers Party 12th Congress). Budapest: Kossuth Könyvkiádó.

Musil, J. 1987. "Housing Policy and the Sociospatial Structure of Cities in a Socialist

262   Eastern Europe

Country—The Example of Prague." *International Journal of Urban and Regional Research* 11, no. 1:27–36.
Pickvance, C. G. 1986. "Economic Organisation and Housing Change in the Pattern of State Socialist Redistribution." Paper presented at the Eleventh World Congress of Sociology, New Delhi, August 18–23, 1986.
Sillince, J.A.A. 1985a. "The Housing Market of the Budapest Urban Region, 1949–1983." *Urban Studies* 22:141–49.
———. 1985b. "Housing as Social Problem versus Housing as a Historical Problem: The Case of Hungary." *Environment and Planning C Government and Policy* 3:299–318.
Szelenyi, I. 1972. "Tarsadalmi struktura és lakásrendszer" (Social Structure and Housing System). Budapest Kandidatus értekezés (doctoral thesis), Karl Marx Egyetem, Budapest.
———. 1983. *Urban Inequalities under State Socialism.* Oxford: Oxford University Press.
———. 1987. "Housing Inequalities and Occupational Segregation in State Socialist Cities: Commentary to the Special Issue of IJURR on East European Cities." *International Journal of Urban and Regional Research* 11, no. 1:1–8.
Szelenyi, I., and R. Manchin. 1986. "Social Policy and State Socialism." In *Stagnation and Renewal in Social Policy*, edited by G. Esping-Anderson, L. Rainwater, and M. Rein, 34–93. White Plains, N.Y.: Sharpe.
Tosics, I. 1987. "Privatisation in Housing Policy: The Case of the Western Countries and That of Hungary." *International Journal of Urban and Regional Research* 11, no. 1:61–78.

FURTHER READING

Barath, E. "Decentralizalasi tendenciak a magyar településhalozat féjlesztéseben a 70-es évtizedben" (Decentralization Tendencies of Hungarian Physical Planning in the 1970s). *Városépítés* 26, no. 2: 26–30.
Baross, Paul. "Managing the Housing Queue in Hungary." *Habitat Intl.* 11, no. 2 (1987): 161–75.
Compton, P. A. "Planning and Spatial Change in Budapest." In *The Socialist City: Spatial Structure and Urban Policy*, edited by R. A. French and F.E.I. Hamilton, 461–92. New York: Wiley, 1979.
Dániel, Z. "Igazságos vagy igazságtalan lakáselosztás" (Just or Unjust Distribution of Dwellings). *Valóság* 4 (1980): 51–73.
Dániel, Z. "A lakasszektor reformja" (The Reform of the Housing Sector). *Valóság* 12 (1981): 1–20.
Dániel, Z. "Public Housing, Personal Income, and Central Redistribution in Hungary." *Acta Oeconomica* 31 (1983): 87–104.
Dienes, L. "The Budapest Agglomeration and Hungarian Industry—A Spatial Dilemma." *Geographical Review* (December 1973): 356–77.
Dolescsko, K. "Hol tart a budapesti lakásgazdalkozas?" (Where Is the Budapest Housing Market?) *Népszabadság*, July 30, 1983, 9.
Hamilton, F.E.I. "Aspects of Spatial Behaviour in Planned Economies." *Papers of the Regional Science Association* 25 (1970): 83–105.

————. "Spatial Structure in East European Cities," In *The Socialist City*, edited by R. A. French and F.E.I. Hamilton, 93–120. London: Wiley, 1979.

Hoffmann, I. "A folyomatos árszinvonal-emelkedés hatása lakásépítésre" (The Impact of the Continuous Price Rise on Housing Construction). *Közgazdasági Szemle* 30 (1983): 608–12.

Hörcher, N., and E. Vajdovich-Visy. *Structural Changes in the Hungarian Settlement Structure*. Budapest Twenty-fifth European Congress of the Regional Science Association proceedings, August 27–30, 1985. Budapest.

Horváth, T. "Morognak a lakók" (The Natives Are Grumbling). *Magyarország* 20 (1983): 35.

Konrad, G., and I. Szelenyi. *Sociological Aspects of the Allocation of Housing*. Budapest: Sociological Research Group, Hungarian Academy of Sciences, 1969.

Kossuth Könyvkiádó. *Az Életszinvonal Alakulasa Magyarországon, 1950–1975*. (The Formation of Living Standards in Hungary, 1950–1975). Budapest: Kossuth Könyvkiádó, 1976.

Kovacs, I. "Development of Living Standards in Hungary from 1975–1983." *Acta Oeconomica* 33 (1984): 155–80.

Központi Statisztikai Hivatal (Central Statistical Office). Ten Yearly. *Népszamlalás*. (Population Census). Budapest.

————. Yearly. *Demográfiai Évkönyv* (Demographic Yearbook). Budapest.

————. Yearly. *Lakásépítés és megszünés* (Constructions and Demolitions). Budapest.

————. Yearly. *Lakásstatisztikai Évkönyv* (Housing Statistics). Budapest.

————. Yearly. *Területi Statisztikai Évkönyv* (Regional Statistical Yearbook). Budapest.

Lowe, Stuart, and Ivan Tosics. "The Social Use of Market Processes in British and Hungarian Housing Policies." *Housing Studies* 3, no. 3 (1988): 159–71.

Magyar Nemzet. "Házépítés sajat eróból?" (How Easy Is It to Build Your Own?) *Magyar Nemzet*, August 7, 1983, 5.

————. "A lakás tulajdonosság Tatabanyában" (Home Ownership in Tatabanya). *Magyar Nemzet*, July 27, 1983, 2.

————. "Peldaul Somogy." (For example, Somogy). *Magyar Nemzet*, July 20, 1983, 3.

————. "Problémák Építöiparnál." (Problems in the Building Industry). *Magyar Nemzet*, August 7, 1983, 1.

Major, Iván. "Housing in Hungary: the Situation During the 1980s" (in French). *Revue d'Etudes Comparatives Est-Ouest* 19, no. 1 (March 1988): 1.

Mihályi, P. "Történeti szempontok a magyarországi lakashiány értékeléséhez" (Historical Viewpoints of Evaluating the Housing Shortage in Hungary). *Valóság* 5 (1977): 1–33.

Népszabadság. "Több ezer új lakás keszül el a fövárosban" (Thousands More New Flats Ready in Budapest). *Népszabadság*, September 2, 1983, 1.

Nök Lapja. "Lakás Lakás" (Flats, Flats). *Nök Lapja* 34, no. 33 (1982): 3–5.

Pickvance, C. G. "Employers, Labour Markets, and Redistribution Under State Socialism: An Interpretation of Housing Policy in Hungary 1960–1983." *Sociology* 22, no. 2 (1988): 193–214.

Szelenyi, I. "Social Conflicts of Underurbanisation." In *Captive Cities*, edited by M. Harloe, 103–29. London: Wiley, 1977.

————. "Social Inequalities in State Socialist Redistributive Economics." *International Journal of Comparative Sociology* 19 (1978): 63–87.

————. "Inequalities and Social Policy under State Socialism." *International Journal of Urban and Regional Research* 6 (1982): 121–27.

Szelenyi, I., and G. Konrád. *Az uj lakótelepek szocialógiai problémái* (Sociological Problems of the New Housing Estates). Budapest: Akademiai Kiado, 1969.

Tomassy, I. "A magánlakásépítés helyzete Nógrád Megyében" (Private House Building in Nograd County). *Városépítés* 19, no. 2 (1983): 8–10.

Varga, E. "A telekalakitasi eljarásrol" (Procedures for the Arrangement of Building Plots). *Városépítés* 19, no. 3, (1983): 31.

8

Poland

BRONISLAW MISZTAL

HOUSING AND THE ECONOMIC CYCLES IN SOCIALIST POLAND

The Polish economy, devastated during World War II, underwent several political reconstructions that, during the past four decades, involved deepening disproportions of growth and led to a series of economic crises, which in turn affected housing policies. All of those processes were initiated in July 1944 when the Provisional Government (PKWN) proclaimed the reconstruction of the national economy. Since 1944 there have been five distinct periods of economic development: reconstruction (1944–1948), forced industrialization (1949–1958), accelerated investment (1959–1969), the second phase of industrialization (1970–1980), and the profound economic crisis (1981–). Economic crises emerged throughout the entire period, namely, in 1948, 1956, 1970, and 1976 and on a continuous basis since 1980.

Looking for a common denominator or for a causal factor that might explain the core features of the socialist path of economic development adopted in Poland, it appears that the unprecedented high proportion of accumulation spending and industrial investments characterized the GNP throughout the four decades.[1] For example, if the four indices were taken as 100 in 1950, their growth in 1970 would be 282 for the GNP, 377 for the accumulation, 481 for the investment spending, and 528 for the industrial investments. The distribution of the GNP was, and still is, determined politically and not economically.

Several economic processes with further political implications resulted from such an economic structure. First, production of the means of production (tools, machinery, etc.) increased on average twice as fast as production of the means of consumption. Second, the agricultural production lagged behind the industrial production; during an extended period (1950–1970) the former was increasinng approximately seven times slower. Third, a higher and still increasing inflation haunted the economy in the 1970s. In the 1980s inflation reached an annual rate of approximately 20 percent. In 1988, inflation in Poland even reached 66 percent due to drastic price increases, with some of the prices (fuel, energy, central heating) affecting directly the cost of housing (price increases varied from 140 to 200 percent; see *The Economist* 1988, 47). Fourth, until the mid–1970s there was a continuous increase in consumption, which started falling in 1977–1978.

These macroeconomic and political processes have had a clear impact on housing policies. They were responsible, first, for the continuous transfer of population to the cities, a transfer that went beyond the cities' capacity to absorb the rural migrants. The cultural differences that underlay the demographic trends (traditionally high rate of natural growth among the rural migrants) have affected the housing situation in both the short and long run. A rapidly increasing rate of natural growth immediately affected the density of urban dwellings, and housing resources that were modestly adequate at the time of settlement fast became insufficient for many of the families. Also, within two decades following World War II the baby boom created a pressure on the housing market, and the state socialist administration was unprepared for this increased demand. The central state was simply too burdened with the problems of industrial development that had to sustain production levels needed to satisfy Poland's international obligations. In this context the supply of housing was considered to be a less urgent task; consequently, the population of Polish towns has grown much faster than the housing stock. The continuous shortage of agrarian products and other consumption goods was such that even during the period of relative affluence (the 1970s), housing had had a relatively peripheral position within the consumption processes, since the increased spending power experienced by some segments of society during this period was directed to goods of immediate consumption rather than the housing market itself.

HOUSING CONDITIONS AND PROBLEMS

The gap between housing needs and resources was not inherent in the socio-economic and political situation of socialist Poland. In the prewar period Poland already was among the countries with the worst housing conditions in Europe with an average occupancy rate of 2.0 and 3.1 persons per room in urban and rural areas, respectively. Housing consisted mostly of small units, with one-room apartments making up 68.9 percent of the urban and 86.7 percent of the rural stock. More than a half of the prewar housing stock did not have any amenities whatsoever, and only 13 percent of urban housing had sewerage (Andrzejewski 1979, 262). Nevertheless, an apartment in the city was a precious commodity, and its value was determined by its size, quality, and location as it is in any other market economy.

Immediately after World War II, when more than 60 percent of the urban stock was destroyed, the housing gap continued to have mostly a physical character, since there was an insufficient number of inhabitable buildings and dwellings for the remnant population. Interestingly, the decrease in the number of units was considerably lower than the decrease in the size of population (21.09 percent and 26.01 percent, respectively), which allowed for immediate and relative improvement of housing conditions, although only in absolute numbers and not in terms of cultural standards. Western readers of the late 1980s might find this hard to believe; one should bear in mind, however, that during World War II more than 6 million Polish people perished (including 2.8 million Jews, who inhabited mostly small towns). Extermination of the population, therefore, created a certain vacuum in the cities, and the survivors experienced some improvement in housing conditions.

Despite Ivan Szelenyi's criticism of the "egalitarian past of state socialism" (1987, 2), the average occupancy rate fell from 2.01 persons per room to 1.67 in the cities and from 3.1 to 2.3 in the rural areas (i.e., by 21.4 and 25.8 percent, respectively; see table 8.1 for full data). Szelenyi, however, was correct in pointing to the fact that such improvements have resulted mostly from the "redistributional activities" of the state and not from the construction of a large volume of new housing. He also hypothesized that such overall improvements do in fact cover up inequalities in access to housing stock of good quality. High-quality housing was, in those early times, already reserved for "the new cadre intelligentsia, . . . the top party and state bureaucrats, high ranking officers in the army and security forces" (1987, 2).

Further improvement in the housing situation in the 1946–1956 period was due to two main factors: intensive rebuilding and reconstruction of destroyed cities and, to a considerable degree, politically motivated large transfers of population.

Table 8.1
Housing Resources and the Population, Poland, 1931–1985

YEAR	POPULATION IN MILLIONS	APARTMENTS IN MILLIONS	HABITABLE ROOMS	AVERAGE ROOM/DWEL	AV. PERSONS/ROOM	AV. PERSON/DWELLING
1931	**8.7** (23.2)	**1.93** (4.47)	**4.2** (7.6)	**2.20** (1.70)	**2.01** (3.10)	**4.42** (5.27)
1946	**7.5** (16.1)	**1.95** (3.1)	**4.5** (7.0)	**2.30** (2.29)	**1.67** (2.30)	**3.84** (5.27)
1950	**9.6** (15.0)	**2.45** (3.40)	**6.0** (7.7)	**2.44** (2.26)	**1.54** (1.95)	**3.75** (4.40)
1960	**14.2** (15.2)	**3.57** (3.46)	**8.9** (8.4)	**2.50** (2.42)	**1.53** (1.80)	**3.82** (4.35)
1970	**17.1** (15.6)	**4.51** (3.58)	**12.5** (10.7)	**2.77** (3.01)	**1.31** (1.43)	**3.62** (4.30)
1974	**18.2** (15.4)	**5.0** (3.55)	**14.3** (11.1)	**2.86** (3.14)	**1.23** (1.36)	**3.51** (4.27)
1975	**19.0** (15.1)	**5.34** (3.71)	**15.4** (11.3)	**2.95** (3.17)	**1.18** (1.32)	**3.49** (4.19)
1978	**20.1** (14.9)	**5.84** (3.68)	**17.6** (11.7)	**3.07** (3.28)	**1.10** (1.25)	**3.37** (4.12)
1980	**20.9** (14.7)	**6.13** (3.66)	**19.1** (12.1)	**3.12** (3.32)	**1.05** (1.20)	**3.28** (3.99)
1984	**22.1** (14.8)	**6.58** (3.67)	**21.2** (12.6)	**3.22** (3.45)	**1.01** (1.16)	**3.27** (4.01)
1985	**22.4** (14.8)	**6.83** (3.83)	**21.7** (13.0)	**3.18** (3.40)	**0.99** (1.13)	**3.16** (3.83)

Sources: Andrzejewski, 1979, p. 265; Rocznik Statystyczny, 1975, 1978, 1980, 1984, 1985.
Note: **Bold faced** urban population; parenthesized: rural population.

The latter involved 16.5 million people, approximately one-third were ethnic Germans forcefully expelled, thus giving the Poles room for resettlement in urban centers in the Western, so-called recovered provinces. The remaining two-thirds were mostly resettlers from the Eastern provinces of Poland, which became part of the Soviet territory following World War II and the arrangements between the superpowers.

Gap between Supply and Demand

This relative improvement in housing conditions immediately after the war and during the following decade did not, however, resolve the housing problem permanently. Macroeconomic and political processes contributed to the gap that existed between the objective and subjective needs of the population on the one hand and the supply of housing stock on the other hand. It is argued here that until the 1970s this gap was mostly physical, that is, in absolute terms people needed more apartments than were actually available. In demand was ''an apartment,'' an independent dwelling unit, no matter how big or small this unit would be or where it would be located or what its technical standard (amenities) would be. At this stage of absolute shortage of housing, people would not be fussy about living conditions: an apartment in a large apartment block, located somewhere in the outskirts of a city in a new housing estate where no shops, schools, roads, parking, and so on would be available, would still be somewhat attractive and, since it was allocated practically cost free to the tenants, they would accept it. Therefore, it is further argued that the physical gap existed as a result of disparity between the objective needs and the supply of housing—a classical form of absolute deprivation.

With the increased restratification of Polish society in the 1970s, the gap became one of dual character: for part of the population—mostly the young, the uneducated, or the poorer segments of society—it was still a problem of getting any housing whatsoever; for other segments—mostly the professional, intelligentsia or well-salaried, skilled workers of the large industrial plants—it was becoming a problem of getting access to socially or culturally adequate housing, that is, either larger or better located apartments or housing of higher technological standards. Therefore, it is also argued here that the mid–1970s saw a transformation of housing demand in Poland from a merely physical gap (absolute deprivation) to a cultural gap between subjective needs and what the market offers (relative deprivation).

Crowding, Space Standards, and Amenities

Because housing is intertwined with political or macrosociological issues, housing quality becomes a complex variable that reflects the structural characteristics of society on the one hand and the spatial characteristics of the national economy on the other hand. Consequently, despite the egalitarian premises of socialism, the quality of housing varies according to class position and place of residence. The quality of housing available to blue-collar workers and to white-collar workers within the same town or region is different, and housing available to members of the same class in various towns or regions differs as well.

One of the features of housing in Poland is "doubling up" with other households. In 1985, for which the most recent and comparable national data exist, there were 7,084,000 households in the cities (10,906,000 total) compared with 6,832,000 occupied apartments (10,666,000 total) (*Rocznik Statystyczny* 1986, 51, 434–35). This gap is even more conspicuous when one compares the size of the urban population (22,096,000; 36,914,000 total) with the 6.8 million apartments available (ibid., 39). This excess of population or households over the available housing stock has an impact on both technical and cultural quality standards: small apartments that have to house two or three households in a two-bedroom, one-bath unit quickly become run down.

The available data on social structure come from the mid–1970s since this was a unique period in which at least some research was done on a national scale. Although at that time approximately 16 percent of all households were doubling up, the proportion of working-class families living in such conditions was higher: 18 percent (Jarosinska and Kulpinska 1977, 142). Data for the peasant population come from the 1960s and indicate that the corresponding proportion was only 13 percent and had a tendency to decrease (Turski 1977, 78). The 1970s saw a considerable construction boom in the countryside, which also experienced a decrease of population (see table 8.1). The occupancy rate, measured by the number of persons per room in a dwelling unit, improved very slowly (from 1.31 in 1970 to 1.10 in 1980 and 0.99 in 1985). The number of people per dwelling improved equally slowly: from 3.62 in 1970 to 3.28 in 1980 and 3.16 in 1985. Therefore, the rate of improvement was approximately 0.02 persons per dwelling per year (see table 8.1 for complete results). One can only hypothesize that these data already reflect considerable social differentiation of living standards experienced by the urban population of Poland in the 1980s. The number of rooms per dwelling still fell in 1985 compared to the number in the preceding year (3.18 against 3.22) and improved fairly slowly from 2.77 in 1970 to 3.12 in 1980 (0.45 rooms per unit improvement during the decade).

Even with those slow improvement trends, manual workers lived under relatively worse conditions. Already in 1974 only 27.3 percent of the manual workers lived in apartments with a low density (one person or less per room) compared with 46.4 percent of the white-collar population. This indicates that the best housing conditions were twice more frequently available to nonmanual as to manual professions. At the other extreme, the same data evidence that 7.3 percent of uneducated manual workers (or 6.2 percent of the total worker population) lived in overcrowded conditions (more than 3.1 persons per room) compared with only 1.0 percent of the nonmanual workers (Jarosinska and Kulpinska 1977, 143). In the rural areas the percentage of population inhabiting residencies with a low density (equal or below one person per room) was 26 percent for private farmers and 14 percent for those employed in the state-owned sector (rural cooperative and state enterprises) (Turski 1977, 85).

Similar differentiations continued in 1980, when the workers' families, although usually larger than the nonmanual workers' families, occupied by and large less housing space. Of all of the manual workers' households, 30 percent lived in one- and two-room apartments (a two-room apartment would be a dwelling unit consisting of a room and a kitchen; the latter is, in Polish statistics, counted as a room as well). This compares with 25 percent of nonmanual workers living in such small units. Average floor space was, respectively, 47.7 and 49.9 square meters; the average number of rooms per dwelling was 2.9 and 3.2; average space per inhabitant was 13.0 and 15.8 square meters; and the average number of persons per room, 1.2 and 1.0, respectively (Jarosz 1984, 110). There is a cultural and political meaning to this gap between living standards of manual and nonmanual workers. In Poland there are governmentally (centrally) imposed ceilings on the eligibility of floor space. Building regulations successfully encouraged substandard housing construction (small apartments). Although these regulations were supposed to affect all stratas equally, it is clear, as evidenced by the above data, that the nonmanual workers were able to bypass the regulations more successfully and that exceeding the regulated normative size of an apartment was easier for them than for manual workers.

Research done for the city of Warsaw indicates that according to the 1978 census the average size of a Warsaw apartment was even smaller, equaling 44.6 square meters. Therefore, the living conditions of the working class in big cities must have been worse than the national average. In Warsaw, for example, more than half of all apartments fall into the small-size category (30–49 square meters), and only approximately 5 percent fall into the large-size category (more than 80 square meters). Research on living conditions of the proletariat in other large and industrial towns indicate similar trends, with half of the unskilled workers inhabiting residences where the occupancy rate exceeded three people per room (Kobus-Wojciechowska 1974, 201; these data are for the city of Lodz).

Further differentiation is best seen when amenities in apartments are taken into account. In methodologically unique research carried out in 1972–1973 (Weglenski 1983) two main variables were considered as indicative of housing conditions: average number of people per room and the technical standard of the apartment. The latter index was calculated according to the availability of running water, sewerage, central heating, and a bathroom. Significant statistical correlations were found between housing conditions, income, education and the socioeconomic status of parents. For cities of various sizes the average density rate (number of persons per room in an apartment) was estimated and then compared against the survey data. In this way the undistorted influence of the place of residence on housing conditions in a city could be seen. Overall, the bigger the city, the lower the occupancy rate, varying from 1.77 (estimated 1.68) for towns with populations up to 5,000 to 1.58 (estimated 1.56) for cities with more than 200,000 people. In general, as the town's size increases, the average density rate decreases, or the housing conditions improve and the correlation between socioeconomic variables and housing quality becomes clearer. This means that in larger cities socioeconomic status, education, financial position and so on translate more directly into one's abilities to secure adequate housing, whereas in the smaller cities, no matter what the position or money earned, housing conditions are still determined by the availability of housing stock.

One can also hypothesize that the two processes (differentiation of access to housing according to the sociostructural position and differentiation of housing quality according to regional and spatial factors) operate simultaneously. This would mean that manual workers living in small- and middle-sized towns are doubly affected in their housing conditions: not only do they have to deal with the barriers created by social structure but they also have to cope with the overall regional disadvantage. In the big cities, on the other hand, "only" the socio-structural processes would operate.

Interestingly, the average density rate indicated by this research for the entire urban population was 1.61 and differed significantly from the official statistics published in 1974, which showed an average density rate of 1.23 persons per room (Weglenski 1983; Kulesza 1978, 166). However, even the less optimistic figure requires some statistical adjustment to take into consideration Polish cultural standards and statistical practices whereby a kitchen is used and counted as a separate room. It is not unusual that apart from being a place for preparation and consumption of meals, a kitchen also serves as a family room and a bedroom for some household members. This is particularly frequent in the multihousehold apartments where families are doubling up. Even when the kitchen does not function consistently also as a bedroom, it is statisically considered to be a "room in an apartment." A rough revised estimation, therefore, would make the Polish data more compatible with international statistics. If approximately 50 percent of the housing stock consisted of two-room apartments (which is an accurate estimate, since the absolute majority of the newly constructed apartments during the 1950–1970 period had one or two rooms; see Kulesza 1978, 165) and the other half were three- and four-room apartments, a realistic density rate would be 1.9–2.0 persons per room (1.61 + 0.29, where this last figure is calculated as a median of a 0.33 increase in the density rate for the smaller apartments and a 0.25 increase for the bigger ones). Therefore, if the kitchens were not used as bedrooms there would be approximately two persons per room in an average apartment in Poland.

Differentiation in the quality of housing in towns of various population sizes has been very strong. In the smallest category (up to 5,000 people) compared with the largest one (more than 200,000) the availability of amenities was as follows—for running water: 61.2 versus 92.0 percent; sewerage: 51.1 versus 87.6 percent; bathroom: 29.1 versus 74.9 percent; and central heating: 19.2 versus 68.9 percent.

Although there are few direct data about the proportion of substandard housing, it has to be made clear that determining what is substandard under the conditions of a shortage economy is relative. For example, the official statistics indicate that in the 1970s there was an increase in the absolute number of apartments not equipped with central heating. Central, water-forced heating is a must in the Polish climate where most apartments are heated from October to April. The fact that there is an increase in residences without this amenity (from 8.6 million in 1950 to 10.5 million in 1970) is not counted as an increase in substandard housing, although culturally the coal furnaces are already an anachronism.

Bureaucratically, substandard is defined as less than the minimum floor space per person (around 5 square meters or 7 square yards). In 1974, according to official data (Jarosinska and Kulpinska 1977, 144), the proportion of households (note that this does not reflect the number of persons) occupying substandard apartments so defined varied from 6 percent among manual workers to 1 percent among nonmanual workers.

Another assessment indicates that by 1980 there were approximately 650,000 apartments with floor space not exceeding 24 square meters. Those apartments were inhabited by 1.4 million people or 7 percent of population. The average space per person in those apartments was approximately 8 square meters. Bureaucratically, it would not be considered substandard, although culturally, it would certainly be so (Misztal and Misztal 1984, 325).

Since there are no available data about substandard housing, one can estimate its volume from the available information about housing conditions of those who are members of the housing cooperatives and who already obtained tentative promises of apartment allocation. Existing regulations require such members to give accurate proof of their current housing conditions. There is also information available about how many cooperative members are on waiting lists and on the volume of private construction. The latter is usually undertaken when a person does not foresee any chance of "breaking" into the waiting lists of housing cooperatives or into the communal housing-allowance scheme, and one can legitimately estimate that housing conditions of private investors are by and large not any better than those of coop members.

Currently, there are 731,000 coop members with tentative promises; 1.2 million so-called candidates, people who saved the necessary money for a down payment but have not been admitted to the coop as full members (since the cooperative is unable to determine when the housing would be available for them); and 1.1 million candidates who are in the process of saving money necessary for the original outlay. This means that the number of potential coop members was approximately 3 million by mid–1987 (Szyperska 1986, 8; *Solidarnosc* 1986, 15). These numbers are more or less fixed since the cooperatives do not accept new members in order not to increase the already conspicuously long waiting lists.

Of the waiting-list members, 51 percent are young couples without an independent apartment, and 80 percent live under extremely difficult conditions (high density, lack of amenities, moisture and so on). Extrapolation of these numbers for the 3 million potential members gives the following figures: 1.53 million people are couples without an apartment of their own; 2.4 million people live in substandard conditions. Accordingly, of the latter category, 65 percent or 1.56 million do not have independent housing (are doubling up), and 11 percent or 0.33 million live in apartments where the average space is below 5 square meters per person.

The above numbers reflect the differentiation of housing quality among those who have managed to register their interests with the state cooperative system before such registration closed in the late 1970s. Official statistics indicate that only 60.3 percent seeking to get an apartment are registered with the state system. Therefore, one can estimate that apart from the 3 million people making up the cooperative housing market there are an additional 2 million on the alternative market. Of these 2 million, an estimated 1.6 million live in extreme conditions; 1.04 million are deprived of individual housing units, and 0.176 million live in slums.

Total estimates, therefore, would indicate that of the 5 million people currently on the housing market, 3 million have housing conditions that are extremely difficult and either technically or culturally substandard; 2.6 million people live in forced doubling up, and 0.56 million live in slums.

Finance

Regulations regarding the financing of housing are unclear, redundant, and unequal for various types of housing and customers. The borderline is drawn by the character of construction. If there is individual investment (i.e., private construction of a one- or two-family house) a bank would lend money to an individual who holds the title of ownership to a particular lot, has demonstrated that this lot is situated on terrain suitable for private construction, has a council-approved project, and already has an outlay amounting to at least 33 percent of the estimated costs. No finance is normally available to cover the cost of lot purchase or preparatory construction. Estimated costs are based on the state-regulated price system of construction materials and workmanship. Market prices are double or triple the official ones. Therefore, one can assume that finance for individual construction is available only to the ceiling of approximately 5 to 15 percent of realistic investment costs and only after construction has already begun.

Alternatively, for collective construction (cooperatives or groups of investors or legally represented associations of home builders) finance is available only to investors and to construction enterprises that have applied for a construction permit at the city council. Construction is, therefore, centrally financed by the state bank (National Bank of Poland). The product, the apartments, is offered as a commodity to eligible customers. This is a peculiar socioeconomic arrangement. First, eligibility to become a market customer is determined by the co-operative or city council. Membership in a cooperative, the recommendation of the city council, or, in some cases, the recommendation of the employer is sufficient for one to be granted eligibility. Second, investors determine either centrally (i.e., cooperatives through the state-controlled union of cooperatives) or individually (i.e., the association of construction companies that build for their own employees) the financial conditions for eligible customers. Usually, the required down payment is not lower than 33 percent of the estimated construction costs, with the remaining sum payable to the builder in installments. In any case the bank lends to the builder who later collects individual repayments from the customers, invests the funds, or repays the bank. There are no general housing loans available to individuals, since one can become a purchaser only after having been determined as eligible. Under the conditions of an economy of shortage the state is the gatekeeper, determining people's access to the market and wielding ultimate control over the production and distribution of housing.

Several paradoxes and inequalities result from such regulations. For example, if somebody who already has an apartment has applied to obtain another (better, more adequate) apartment after having paid off the entire or part of the mortgage, this original unit has to be turned over to the "disponent" (i.e., to the cooperative or the state administration). No further loan is available to purchase this unit from the disponent since, by the bank's standards, the unit has been paid for. Therefore, such a unit can only be resold by the disponent for a lump sum that equals the amount of paid-up costs. The disadvantage is that such a reclaimed apartment cannot be refinanced; the advantage is that, in an era of skyrocketing prices of state-constructed housing, the reclaimed unit is sold for a fraction of its market value. Each disponent has a certain pool of such reclaimed stock that is not offered openly and is available only to those whose financial position guarantees that they can afford the monetary costs and whose social position is powerful enough to safeguard their clandestine bypassing of the waiting line. However, in some less affluent regions cooperatives are unable to find the prospective buyers that can or would like to lay out the equivalent of ten yearly incomes (Markiewicz 1987, 8).

Even in the event of "eligible" access to housing, the costs of it are soaring. For the less expensive option of the tenant cooperative (where the title of ownership remains with the disponent and cannot be acquired by a tenant) such costs were the following (numbers in parentheses reflect the amount of the down payment required per 1 square meter of the floor space): 1975, 4,050 zlo per 1 square meter (560 zlo per 1 square meter); 1980, 6,370 zlo per 1 square meter (900 zlo per 1 square meter); 1985, 26,000 zlo per 1 square meter (2,600 zlo per 1 square meter); 1987, 42,000 zlo per 1 square meter (4,200 zlo per 1 square meter). The increase in costs for the more expensive option of the owners' cooperative (tenant has the property title) has been even more symptomatic: 1975, 4,620 zlo per 1 square meter (1,020 zlo per 1 square meter); 1980, 6,650 zlo per 1 square meter (1,800 zlo per 1 square meter); 1987, 63,000 zlo per 1 square meter (12,600 zlo per 1 square meter) (Council of Ministers 1982).

The price of an apartment has, therefore, risen more than ten times during the past decade for the tenant cooperatives and approximately fifteen times for the owners' cooperatives.

The increase in construction costs can be best seen when those costs are compared to average income. In 1980 an average monthly salary was 6,040 zlo, so the cost of 1 square meter of housing in a tenant cooperative was equal to 105 percent of monthly income. The same cost in 1985 was equal to more than 200 percent since then the average monthly salary was 20,005 zlo (*Rocznik Statystyczny* 1986, 165, 166).

The 60 percent inflation rate in 1988 has affected the costs of housing. Simultaneous reform of the financial system of the state and the governmental declaration that housing should be removed from the domain of social welfare and turned into a commodity have further influenced those costs. Data for the city of Warsaw indicate that in the first half of 1988 1 square meter of housing space was traded for 200–250 thousand zlotys; at the end of the year comparable costs were in the vicinity of 900 thousand zlotys per square meter. One square meter of housing space cost 16.3 average monthly salaries (Fandrejewska 1989, 4). At the same time, monthly rent of privately leased apartments in Warsaw was the equivalent of three monthly salaries. In March 1989, following earlier governmental plans, the rents in state and municipal housing were increased by 60 percent.[2] This drastic increase notwithstanding, authorities have declared that even at these levels rents are still heavily subsidized. It is estimated that those costs will increase by 50 percent so as to narrow the gap between rents paid by tenants in public housing and those who rent on the open market. The costs of energy (gas, electricity, central heat) are also expected to increase by 50 percent.

STATE POLICIES AND THE ORGANIZATION OF THE HOUSING SYSTEM

State social policies in Poland have never reflected the serious nature of social problems resulting from unsatisfied housing needs of the population, nor have they adequately responded to the economic, political, or simply human aspects of such unsatisfied needs. As most of the data indicate, the housing situation in Poland has always been dramatic and has constituted a potential source of injustice, deprivation, and unrest. Investment strategies, as we have seen, have largely determined the immediate status of housing, and so have strategies of social development, which have stressed numerical growth of industrial workers without an accompanying development of the urban infrastructure.

In the early period (1944–1950) the state, through its central control system, monitored the availability of new apartments and the occupancy rate in those that were already inhabitable. Forced ''in-settlement'' of families to already inhabited apartments was a common practice meant to diffuse the pressure on the housing system. At this early stage the state allowed some pluralism of housing policies, and private investment was seen as a legitimate means of acquiring an apartment. Such policies were correlated with the period of economic reconstruction and could be seen as temporary measures only.

Forced Industrialization and Recommodification

Along with the introduction of forced industrialization the state took much firmer control over the housing system, especially since it was strategically significant to suppress any consumeristic appetites of the population in order to secure high rates of industrial growth and high levels of savings. Therefore, housing needs were considered to be of low strategic significance and the production output of high significance. Housing was centrally financed from the fund of collective consumption. In 1951 the entire housing stock became the property of the state, and the market was practically eliminated. Decommodification of housing was carried out through administrataive measures, and the state established a specialized housing authority within the already centralized city administration. The policies of construction and allocation of apartments were dominated by the priorities of employment, and the state made an effort to make sure that the most essential categories of employees of the crucial industrial branches got housing first. The recommendation of the employer was established as a criterion in the allocation of an apartment, and such recommendations included suggestions regarding the size and location of an apartment. Final decisions were made by the housing authority. During this period priority was given to members of the Communist party administrative apparatus, law enforcement institutions (militia and security services), army, and all sorts of employees of the state propagandistic and ideological machinery (including leading intelligentsia). Therefore, the state not only wiped out market forces from operation in the domain of housing but also, to a considerable degree, redefined criteria of social justice. The acute housing conditions, high density of tenants, and so on alone were not a sufficient criterion for allocation of an apartment, but the ''political importance'' certainly was. The new estates of state-constructed apartments were allocated to frequently homogeneous categories of dwellers, and until now there have been housing pockets in big cities where the families of those early settlers lived: the militiamen, the (former) party activists, and so on.

In general, those who were brought into the cities to reinforce the central bureaucratic apparatus or to revitalize the industry have experienced rapid and considerable improvement of living standards (housing included). Under the state-controlled policies of decommodification of housing the fact of being an approved and recommended migrant to the city was in itself sufficiently legitimate for allocation of an apartment. On the other hand, those who were not new city dwellers but who already resided in the cities were treated with lower priority and were confined to overcrowded housing in the old stock. During the decade of 1950–1960 there was only a slight decrease in the proportion of the urban population living in overcrowded conditions (29.9 percent and 27.3 percent, respectively), which suggests a continuous disadvantage for more than one-fourth of the urban population. At the same time, as Adam Andrzejewski suggested (1979, 268) there was a considerable improvement in the housing situation of those who already lived in noncrowded conditions, since approximately 20 percent of them moved to apartments with density rates lower or equal to one person per room. The state clearly used its control over housing as a tool to secure loyalty and to obtain legitimation in the eyes of strategically crucial categories of citizens. To obtain that result the state had to remove the market forces from operation and to introduce its own criteria that had little to do with social justice.

Transformation of the Role of the State

The end of the 1950s saw a shift in the entire package of welfare policies of the state, housing included. Following the October 1956 workers' uprising the proportion of social expenditures on the social infrastructure grew to an unprecedented 35.4 percent. Spending on housing construction reached 21.8 percent of the GNP, a record high never to be matched again. Those spectacular figures, however, came in a period of increased international tension and the concomitant demand for investments in heavy industry and in the military infrastructure. The result of those conflicting demands was that the state looked for possibilities of continuing its control over housing policies while changing the model of the entire social policies package. Original premises of state socialism were that while the work force would remain grossly underpaid, the state would provide for basic social needs from its centrally controlled fund of collective consumption. However, the pressures from below and the growth of the state bureaucratic apparatus resulted in some diversification of social structure. Despite initial monetary control, family budgets started to increase, mostly through extensive growth of employment (more members of households became employed). In the late 1950s the proportion of private investment in housing reached approximately 40 percent. Without transformation of the housing system the state would soon have been confronted with the emergence of a privatized sector, while the economic conditions for the operation of market forces were absent and more or less politically unthinkable. Under those circumstances the state adopted somehow more flexible economic policies that led to skimming of the excess money from the family budgets. Housing cooperatives were allowed to emerge. Originally, only tenant status was approved and the state maintained the upper hand over newly created institutions by including posts of chairmen in the party-controlled system of nomenclature. Confronted with social, political, and economic pressure, the state allowed some minimal pluralization of the housing system in order to be able to retain its overall control over housing.

At this very moment the welfare character of housing policies was no longer necessary, and the state moved quickly to introduce relatively high rents, security deposits, and council rates into the state or municipal housing system. Simultaneously, it allowed for a radical increase in the output of the housing industry while also allowing a considerable lowering of construction standards. New apartments were small, the buildings frequently lacked amenities such as elevators or even individual toilets, and so on. The housing cooperatives became economic and political intermediaries, authorities that could not be immediately identified with the state itself but that were capable of effectively diverting the welfare claims of the population from the state to bureaucratic and formally self-governing bodies. It was also convenient that institutions other than the state authority were able to carry out the operations of lowering technical standards, handling long waiting lines, and smoke screening the nonegalitarian distribution of apartments.

Interestingly, the proportion of housing investment in the state's general spending fell almost immediately after this transformation took place: from 21.0 percent in 1958 to 16.1 percent in 1961–1965 and 14.0 percent in 1966–1970. The state, thereby, managed gradually to withdraw from providing housing as a component of welfare while retaining its overall control over housing. Despite the 25 percent increase in the total output of new apartments during the 1960–1970 decade, housing remained a scarce good. The winding up of the state welfare policies did not shorten waiting lists.

The decade of 1970–1980 was marked by continuous and ever deepening stratification of Polish society. New, politically significant and economically potent sectors of the population (highly skilled workers, technocrats administering new branches of industry, party managers) received higher incomes, education, and increased entrepreneuriality, which were immediately translated into increased pressure on the housing system. At the same time, state expenditures on housing further decreased, reaching 13.0 percent in 1971–1975 and increasing only slightly after the 1976 wave of workers' unrest to reach 15.3 percent in 1976–1980.

Diversified and continuous demand for housing along with the fiscal crisis of the state, which bore the burden of ineffective and aborted modernization, led to a further amendment of housing policies. The previous model of tenant cooperatives was split into a dual one with the owners' cooperatives emerging fast. Soon the ownership option became available also within formerly "tenants only" cooperatives and within state-controlled municipal housing. Therefore, to cope with the pressure of its own upper-middle classes the state allowed an unprecedented move to partially reprivatize and recommodify housing. What used to be the domain of welfare policies now became the domain of market forces. However, although housing stock again became an economic commodity, the system of financing remained under strict political control of the state.

PROSPECTS: THE RECOMMODIFICATION OF HOUSING

In the late 1980s housing remains one of the most important and still unresolved social problems in Poland. This is true in many respects. First, there is the already mentioned dual gap between the available resources and the articulated needs of the population. This gap can be measured by, for example, the length of the waiting period. To "get" an apartment one either has to be accepted by a fairly complicated and tightly state-controlled system of housing provision (mostly cooperative, but still bound by endless restrictions and conditions) or one has to be able to buy an apartment on the open market. The first road is very long: it now takes twenty-five years from original membership in the cooperative to the time of receiving one's own apartment. The second road is very costly: in 1985 an average annual salary was only able to buy 7 square meters of housing space on the open market (the average "market price" was approximately 120,000 zlo per square meter [*Rocznik Statystyczny* 1986, 165, 166]), and the inflation of 1988 has increased the cost even more. The housing gap is also measured by the excess of the number of households over the number of apartments, meaning that two or more families have to live in the same apartment. Estimates for 1987–1988, made by unofficial Solidarity analysts and also by official governmental analysts indicate that 2.8 million to 3 million households did not have individual apartments (*Solidarnosc* 1986, 15; Szyperska 1986, 8). According to the Communist party's most recent housing program, approximately 4 million new apartments would need to be constructed by the year 2000 if by this date every family was to be provided with an independent apartment. Demographic trends (a large number of newlyweds and an increasing number of single households) further aggravate the situation, with the excess of demand over supply (measured by the ratio of households over apartments) reaching 2.08 in 1986 (2.04 in 1982). Figure 8.1 shows the population in collective households.

Second, the housing problem is unresolved because of the incapacitation of the state-owned building industry. In 1986 alone the state-controlled sector of housing construction was able to produce only 127,500 apartments (5,500 units fewer than in 1985), whereas the realistically formulated plan had estimated the output to reach 135,000 units. Therefore, 7,500 units (or 5.5 percent of the plan) were not built. Other data indicate substantial organizational deficiencies in the housing industry: most of the housing stock is being delivered in the last quarter of each year; in several regions plans were not realized at all due to mismanagement of materials or lack of a qualified labor force (Baczynski 1987, 5). At the same time only 62 percent of the productive capacities of the housing factories (that were supposed to supply enough prefabricated units to make the plans come true) were used. The deliveries of cement shrunk by 20 percent mostly due to a shortage of electric energy, and the shortage of various technical materials (usually piping for the central heating system, radiators, and so on) delayed a considerable part of the housing construction. For political reasons (the fear of decentralization of the allocation of housing) and economic reasons (shortage of construction materials, which are either in short supply, mismanaged, or otherwise wasted in bureaucratic allocation) the system does not allow private construction to grow, and the average citizen is entirely dependent on the state-controlled supply of housing. In 1987 the supply of housing was 112,600 apartments (5,500 fewer units than in the preceding year). To meet the demand for housing the output should reach approximately 300,000 units per year over the next two decades. However, under the current state of disorganization of the building industry, and also in view of the 20 percent cut in the production of construction materials (planned for 1989), the waiting lists are unlikely to become any shorter.

In January 1989 the Council of Ministers approved a new package of economic decisions that includes radical deregulation of housing policies. Confronted with high inflation of almost 66 percent per year the banks (which were deregulated as well) will pay adjustable interest rates on certified deposits and on deposits on housing loans. The prime rate was established at 66 percent, but some banks now offer even higher interest rates. Simultaneously, some of the new housing loans will be charged those new interest rates. As usual in the history of economic decisions in Poland, inconsistency and disorder make it impossible to estimate precisely the real costs of housing. It appears that certain loans awarded in late 1988 had a clause with the adjustable interest rate; hence their recipients would have to repay a ballooning mortgage loan. Almost at the same time, other loans did not contain the above-mentioned clause, and their recipients were given a guaranteed low interest rate. Presumably, further deregulation procedures expected later in 1989 will bring more free market mechanisms. Although credit is available to individuals and commercial customers alike, in practice it remains restricted to investors of large sums of capital.

The same decree has also changed some other aspects of financing housing construction. All recipients of loans are now considered equal, and in 1989 the banks began to provide loans that are governed by the same conditions for private, cooperative, patronage (built by large industrial plants), and municipal housing. It has also been acknowledged that approximately 1 million apartments in the state-owned stock require immediate renovation. The authorities have agreed that the title of ownership for such apartments will be granted to individuals, collectives, or private enterprises that will invest in their rehabilitation. It is expected that a considerable part of such older housing stock will be acquired (through investment in remodelling) and then leased on the private market.

Although the decisions toward "marketization" of housing are conspicuous, to date their scope is limited to the existing stock. The control over land still remains in the hands of the local units of state administration, and until land resources are truly freed, investment and profit will occur only in the already existing housing stock. The idea of the transformation currently taking place in Poland is that housing be completely removed from the agenda of social policies of the state, so that the obligation of providing housing will be entirely vested in the private sector and not in the socialist state. This shift occurred after the substantial restructuring of the Polish society in the 1970s, which allowed more affluent or more politically powerful segments of the population to take advantage of partial deregulation. Current processes determine the borderline between poverty and wealth, with those whose financial position depends on salaried labor remaining absolutely powerless and unable to improve their housing situation.

At the same time, for the segment of the population whose financial position depends upon financial speculation and engagement in profit-making market activities, housing becomes a true commodity that can be purchased, sold, or leased at high profit.

The period of 1980–1989 has been marked by three fiscal processes: the currency was devalued (inflation), the dollar was revalued, and the prices of housing were increasing. The increase in housing cost was much faster than the revaluation of the U.S. dollar. For those whose financial resources were not related to speculation in foreign currency or housing, an apartment became even less accessible than it used to be over the past forty years (compare figure 8.2).

Also, for the first time in the forty-year history of the Polish People's Republic the problem of the homeless has surfaced in the mass media. There are no general data regarding homelessness. The absence of such data results from the complete absence of any policies or legal regulations regarding the problem. It has recently been reported that the number of homeless in the city of Warsaw might be approaching 800. However, there is no single institution that is able to deal with this category of people. The city administration is incompetent, the police states that it has other things to do, and the department of social services admits that it has no funds to build a shelter. It is almost impossible to estimate the current number of homeless people nationwide, but one can expect that with further impoverishment of the population and with deregulation of housing policies and a declining role of the state in social housing provision the problem of homelessness will become more acute.

The unsatisfied needs of the population; the unresolved problems of housing production, delivery, and distribution; and also the absence of finance politics consistent with the transformation of social structures result in persisting political and social problems in contemporary Poland. Social inequality, differential access to housing, deprivation of cultural needs, socially unjustified differences in costs of housing, forced multigenerational family life, and protracted dependence of young couples on their parents are just a few of such problems. Interestingly, the third large wave of workers' unrest in this decade, which took place in August 1988, ended with Solidarity leader Lech Walesa's remarkable conclusion that Poland needs "an agreement that will yield pluralism, solidarity and housing" (*New York Times*, September 2, 1988, 6). This statement alone indicates the high priority of housing on the current, predominantly political agenda of Poland. Ivan Szelenyi is correct in his hypothesis about housing being the key problem for understanding state socialism (1987, 7). However, his ideas about the progressive impact of the market on state socialism have remained merely an idea. As the Polish example indicates, the recommodification did not contribute to a more equal distribution of housing, nor did it solve the housing problem. While freedoms offered by the market forces affected the average citizen with skyrocketing inflation, state control remained intact, and housing, even though recommodified, remained one of the scarcest goods, distributed unequally, dif-

Figure 8.1
Population in Collective Households, Poland, 1970–1985 (In Thousands)

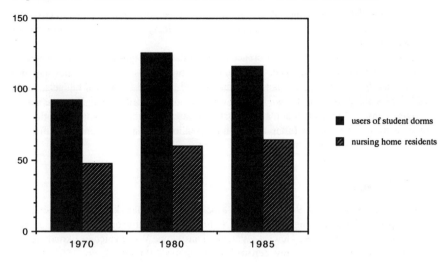

Source: GUS, 1980, 1985.

Figure 8.2
Cost of Housing and Average Income, Poland, 1975–1989

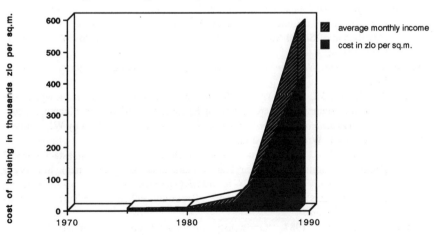

Source: Statistical data compiled by Krzysztof Frysztacki.

ferentiating people's life-styles and living conditions beyond socially legitimate limits.

NOTES

1. Accumulation spendings are expenditures from the government budget to cover the costs of investment in heavy industry, purchase of machinery, equipment, and construction of the new plants.

2. In legal terms there is no difference between these two types of housing. There is, however, a historical difference, since until the mid–1970s all "state" housing was constructed by the municipalities (city councils) and financed from local budgets. In the 1970s the state introduced its own housing construction financed directly from the central budget. Tenure of municipal and state housing is based on similar principles. Both types of housing can be bought (after a household is allocated an apartment) and they are bought from the state treasury.

REFERENCES

Andrzejewski, Adam. 1979. "Spoleczne aspekty polityki mieszkaniowej" (Social Aspects of the Housing Policies). In *Polityka Spoleczna* (Social Policies), 3d ed., edited by Antoni Rajkiewicz. Warsaw: Panstwowe Wydawnictwo Ekonomiczne.

Baczynski, Jerzy. 1987. "Stany Zerowe" (Zero States). *Polityka* 4, no. 1551 (January 24): 5.

Council of Ministers. 1982. Decrees no. 50 and 286. December 30.

The Economist. 1988. January 6–12. Editorial information.

Fandrejewska, Aleksandra. 1989. "Wynajme za milion" (For Lease for One Million Zlotys). *Polityka* 1, no. 1653 (January 7): 4.

Jarosinska, Maria, and Jolanta Kulpinska. 1977. "Czynniki polozenia klasy robotniczej" (Determinants of Social Status of the Workers). In *Ksztalt Struktury Spolecznej* (The Shape of Social Structure), edited by Wlodzimierz Wesolowski. Wroclaw: Ossolineum.

Jarosz, Maria. 1984. *Nierownosci spoleczne* (Social Inequalities). Warsaw: Ksiazka i Wiedza.

Kobus-Wojciechowska, Anita. 1974. "Zroznicowanie warunkow mieszkaniowych i sytuacji materialnej" (Differentiation of Housing Conditions and Financial Situation). In *Zroznicowanie Spoleczne* (Social Differentiation), edited by Wlodzimierz Wesolowski. Wroclaw: Ossolineum.

Kulesza, Hanna. 1978. "Warunki mieszkaniowe i ich przeksztalcenia w miastach Polski" (Housing Conditions and Their Transformations in the Polish Cities). In *Procesy urbanizacji kraju w okresie XXX- lecia PRL* (The Processes of Urbanization During the Thirty Years of the Polish People's Republic), edited by Jan Turowski. Warsaw: Ossolineum.

Markiewicz, Wojciech. 1987. "Gra w listy." *Polityka* 3, no. 1550 (January 17): 8.

Misztal, Barbara A., and Bronislaw Misztal. 1984. "Urban Social Problems in Poland. The Macrosocial Determinants." *Urban Affairs Quarterly* 19, no. 3 (March): 315–29.

New York Times. 1988. September 2, p. 6.

Rocznik Statystyczny (Statistical Yearbook). 1980, 1981, 1982, 1983, 1984, 1985, 1986. Warsaw: Glowny Urzad Statystyczny (Central Statistical Office).

Solidarnosc. Biuletyn Informacyjny (Solidarity. Information Bulletin). 1986. Vol. 148 (September 17): 15. Editorial.

Szelenyi, I. 1987. "Housing Inequalities and Occupational Segregation in Socialist Cities." *International Journal of Urban and Regional Research* 11, no. 1 (March): 1–8.

Szyperska, Urszula. 1986. "Chlopiec do Bicia" (The Scapegoat). *Polityka* 3, no. 1550 (January 17): 8.

Turski, Ryszard. 1977. "Przemiany klasy chlopskiej" (Transformations of the Peasant Class). In *Ksztalt struktury spolecznej* (The Shape of Social Structure), edited by Wlodzimierz Wesolowski. Wroclaw: Ossolineum.

Weglenski, Jan. 1983. *Urbanizacja* (The Urbanization). Warsaw: Ossolineum.

FURTHER READING

Ball, M., and M. Harloe. *Housing in a Socialist Country; the Case of Poland*. London: Centre for Environmental Studies, 1974.

Ciechocinska, Maria. "Government Interventions to Balance Housing Supply and Urban Population Growth: The Case of Warsaw," *International Journal of Urban and Regional Research* 11, no. 1 (1987): 9–26.

———. "Space and Living Conditions in Poland." *Social Indicators Research* 20 (1988): 59–77.

Dangschat, Jens. "Sociospatial Disparities in a 'Socialist' City. The Case of Warsaw at the End of the 1970s." *International Journal of Urban and Regional Research* 11, no. 1 (1987): 37–60.

Kuklinski, Antoni. "Investment Policies and Pathologies of Urbanization." In *Pathologies of Urban Processes*, edited by Kingsley A. Haines. Helsinki: Finnpublishers Oy; Wroclaw: Ossolineum,

———. "Industrialization Processes and Space Economy: The Experiences of Poland." In *Comparative Studies of Regional Development in Japan and Poland*. Japan: Tsuru University Press. 1987.

Misztal, Bronislaw, and Barbara A. Misztal. "Scarce State Resources and the Unrestrained Social Processes under Socialism." In *Housing and Social Policies under the Conditions of Fiscal Austerity*, edited by Willem van Vliet—. Westport, Conn.: Greenwood Press, 1987.

Misztal, Bronislaw, and Barbara A. Misztal. "Uncontrolled Processes in the Socialist City." *Politics and Society* 1: (1987): 145–57.

Regulski, Jerzy. *Rozwoj miast w Polsce* (Development of Towns in Poland). Warsaw: Panstwowe Wydawnictwo Naukowe, 1980.

Rodzina (The Family). Warsaw: Glowny Urzad Statystyczny (Central Statistical Office), 1981.

Spis Ludnosci i Mieszkan Metoda Reprezentacyjna z dnia 6.XII. 1984 (Population and Apartment Census with the Use of Representative Sample. 6 December 1984). Warsaw: Glowny Urzad Statystyczny (Central Statistical Office), 1986.

Spis Ludnosci Polski (Population Census). Warsaw: Glowny Urzad Statystyczny (Central Statistical Office), 1976.

III

NORTH AMERICA

9

Canada

J. DAVID HULCHANSKI

Political leaders and government housing officials continually remind Canadians that they ''are among the best housed people in the world'' and that Canada's housing system has provided ''an adequate supply of suitable accommodation at prices most people can afford'' (Canada Mortgage and Housing Corporation 1985a, 10). The key word in such claims is "most." Undoubtedly, most Canadians do enjoy a very high standard of housing relative to many other countries, and Canadian housing policy has played a significant role during the past forty to fifty years. But many Canadians still have great difficulty affording adequate housing appropriate to their needs.

TRENDS IN CANADIAN HOUSING CONDITIONS

As a result of both the Depression in the 1930s and the Second World War, Canada entered the postwar period with a large stock of old and substandard housing located in communities that often lacked adequate municipal services. Many households lived in overcrowded conditions or paid shelter costs that consumed a large percentage of their income. Since the mid–1940s these conditions have changed dramatically. Canada's housing institutions have evolved to meet the great surge in population growth and household formation.

Between 1941 and 1986 the population more than doubled, and the number of households and the number of dwelling units required more than tripled. In 1986 Canada's population was 25.3 million compared with 11.5 million in 1941; the number of households in 1986 was 9.3 million compared with 2.6 million in 1941. One of the more significant social and cultural trends is the decrease in average household size from 4.5 persons per household in 1941 to 2.7 in 1986. Along with overall population growth, this decrease in household size has played a particularly important role in housing demand throughout the postwar period. Overall population growth (natural increase and immigration) accounted for about two-thirds of the 6.7 million new households established between 1941 and 1986, and decreasing household size accounted for approximately one-third of new household formation. Thus a major restructuring in the living arrangements of Canadians has taken place in recent decades: there are many more one- and two-person households and more families with fewer children.

A dramatic shift in the urban and rural distribution of the Canadian population has also occurred. In 1941 only 54 percent of the population was urban, and only 30 percent of this urban population lived in cities with a population over 100,000 (see table 9.1). By 1981, 76 percent of the population was urban, and 52 percent lived in cities with more than 100,000 people. The single largest locational shift in population between 1941 and 1981 has been a decrease in the percentage of people living on farms—from 27 to 6 percent. The degree of urbanization is surprising to people who think of Canada as the world's second largest country (10 million square kilometers), close to half the size of the Soviet Union. Yet 7.7 million people, almost one-third of the total population, live in the three largest metropolitan areas of Toronto, Montreal, and Vancouver. Even in 1941, 22 percent (2.5 million people) lived in these three largest cities. (Table 9.2 provides recent population figures for Canada's fifteen largest metropolitan areas.)

Table 9.1
Urban Transformation, Canada, 1941–1981

	1941		1981		% Change
	000s	**% of Total**	**000s**	**% of Total**	**1941-1981**
Rural - Total	5,254	45.7	5,907	24.3	+ 12
Farm	3,117	27.1	1,436	5.9	- 117
Non-Farm	2,137	18.6	4,472	18.4	+ 109
Urban - Total	6,252	54.3	18,436	75.7	+ 195
under 10,000	1,259	10.9	2,285	9.4	+ 82
10-100,000	1,506	13.1	3,558	14.6	+ 136
over 100,000	3,487	30.3	12,593	51.7	+ 261
CANADA	11,506	100	24,343	100	+ 112

Source: Statistics Canada, *Census of Canada*, 1941, 1981.

Table 9.2
Population of the Fifteen Largest Metropolitan Areas, Canada, 1981 and 1986

Census Metropolitan Area	Rank 1986	Population ('000)		Percent Change 1981-1986
		1981	**1986**	
Toronto	1	3,130	3,427	9.5%
Montreal	2	2,862	2,921	2.1
Vancouver	3	1,268	1,381	8.9
Ottawa-Hull	4	744	819	10.1
Edmonton	5	741	786	6.0
Calgary	6	626	671	7.2
Winnipeg	7	592	625	5.6
Quebec City	8	584	603	3.3
Hamilton	8	542	557	2.8
St. Catharines	10	343	343	0.2
London	11	327	342	4.7
Kitchener	12	288	311	8.1
Halifax	13	278	295	6.6
Victoria	14	242	256	5.8
Windsor	15	251	254	1.2

Average Change 5.5%

Source: Statistics Canada, *Census of Canada*, 1981, 1986.

Table 9.3
Characteristics of Housing and Households, Canada, 1968–1986

	1968	1972	1976	1980	1986
Total Households(millions)	5.4	6.2	7.1	8.0	9.3
Persons per household	3.6	3.3	3.0	2.9	2.7
Rooms per household	5.3	5.3	5.3	5.6	5.7
Persons per room	0.68	0.63	0.57	0.53	0.48
Household Size					
1 Person	14%	15%	18%	18%	21%
2 Person	40	26	29	29	31
3 Person	18	16	18	18	
4-5 Person	30	29	29	29	27
6 or more Persons	16	13	8	6	3
Tenure					
Owners	63%	61%	62%	64%	63%
Renters	37	39	38	36	37
Owners without Mortgage	--	--	--	44%	50%
Year Dwelling Built					
Before 1940	41%	35%	28%	23%	20%
1940 to 1959	36	31	25	23	23
Since 1960	23	34	47	54	57
Type of Dwelling					
Single Detached	63%	60%	56%	58%	56%
Single Attached (Duplex)	37	40	44	8	9
Other (Apartment)				34	35

Source: Statistics Canada, *Household Facilities by Income and Other Characteristics*, catalogues
13–218 and 13–567. Ottawa, various years.

Canada has always been a nation of predominantly single detached homes, and although Canadians now live in smaller households in urban areas, the size of the average dwelling unit has increased slightly from 5.3 rooms in the 1940s to 5.7 rooms in the 1980s. In 1941 just over 70 percent of the housing stock consisted of single detached houses. Much of the housing built after World War II was in suburban districts around the larger cities, and many of these units were detached houses on large lots. By the mid–1980s about 56 percent of the housing stock consisted of single detached houses, a slight decline from about 63 percent in the mid–1960s. The continuing predominance of single detached houses accounts for the relative spaciousness of the average Canadian dwelling. (Table 9.3 provides a summary of the characteristics of Canada's households and housing stock for the years between 1968 and 1986.)

The quality of Canada's housing stock has improved dramatically since the 1940s. Housing in need of major repair fell from 27 percent in 1941 to 7 percent in 1981, and only 1.6 percent of dwellings lack basic facilities. The housing stock is in relatively good condition because most of it is fairly new. Only 20 percent of the current stock was built before 1941, and more than 55 percent has been built since 1960. Even renters have relatively high-quality housing. In 1980 only 2 percent of renter households were found to be overcrowded (dwellings with more than one person per room) and only 1 percent of rental units were found to be inadequate (lacking basic facilities).

One major characteristic of Canadian housing that has not changed significantly is housing tenure. Just over 60 percent of Canadian households own their own homes (table 9.4). The Depression of the 1930s reduced the home-ownership level from a high of 66 percent in the early 1920s to a low of 57 percent by the early 1940s. After World War II the home-ownership rate returned to the 66 percent level by the early 1960s and has since remained in the 60 to 63 percent range. Housing is also relatively affordable for most households, especially for the 50 percent of homeowners who have paid off their mortgage. Canadians spend, on average, less than one-fifth of their gross income on housing.

An aspect of housing tenure that has changed, however, is the composition of each tenure. In the twenty years between 1967 and 1986 the percentage of households in the lowest-income quintile who are homeowners has fallen from 62 to 38. For households in the highest-income quintile, the percentage of homeowners has increased from 73 to 86 (Statistics Canada 1987). There is a growing polarization of Canadian households based on income and tenure. A decreasing percentage of higher-income households are in the private rental sector, and an increasing percentage of lower-income households are renters rather than homeowners.

These national averages, however, tend to hide more than they reveal. It is only natural that averages and aggregate data for a country as wealthy as Canada would produce a rosy picture. A closer look reveals a much more troubled situation than the national averages, aggregate data, and percentages so often cited by government would indicate. The 75,000 people who live in the Yukon and the Northwest Territories, for example, are only now beginning to receive adequate housing appropriate to northern conditions. The thousands of urban poor and the deinstitutionalized individuals who are homeless or live in temporary shelters are still being ignored by policymakers (Oberlander and Fallick 1987; Hulchanski 1987). The most severe problems are found in the high-cost housing markets of Toronto, Montreal, and Vancouver; in rural areas; and on native reserves. For example, the housing conditions of Canada's native population are much worse than nonnative households. About 18 percent of native households live in overcrowded conditions compared with 2 percent of nonnatives; 13 percent of native households have no bathroom compared with 1 percent of nonnatives; and 16 percent of native households live in dwellings in need of major repairs, compared with about 7 percent for nonnatives.

The use of percentages in measuring housing progress can also be deceptive. In 1941, for example, when 27 percent of the housing stock required major repairs, the absolute number of such units was 700,000. In the 1980s the number

Table 9.4
Home-Ownership Rates, by Region, Canada, 1921–1986

	1921	1931	1941	1951	1961	1971	1981	1986
Atlantic Provinces	74.0	69.9	69.4	77.0	76.5	72.7	74.3	75.1
Quebec	55.8	47.9	44.6	48.6	49.0	47.4	53.3	54.8
Ontario	67.7	61.4	56.5	69.5	70.5	62.9	63.3	63.7
Prairie Provinces	73.7	69.0	64.4	72.4	73.4	70.0	66.0	66.6
British Columbia	56.8	58.5	59.0	69.6	71.0	63.3	64.4	62.9
CANADA	65.8	60.5	56.7	65.6	66.0	60.3	62.1	62.4

Source: Statistics Canada, *Census of Canada,* 1921–1986.

of units in need of major repair is surprisingly close to the 1941 number, about 600,000 units, even though these units represent only 7 percent of the now much larger stock of housing. Although it is true that "most" Canadians can afford good-quality housing, the Statistics Canada survey of households and incomes found that 970,000 renter households (27 percent of all renters) paid more than 30 percent of household income on rent in 1986. Furthermore, this is an increase compared to ten years earlier, when 23 percent of renter households paid more than 30 percent of income on rent (Statistics Canada, 1987,9). It is primarily the renters in the lowest income groups who are paying more than 30 percent of their income on housing (figure 9.1).

The rosy picture of Canadian housing conditions painted by government officials can primarily be found in selected urban and suburban districts where high incomes and ownership of detached houses are common. Lower-income households, many renters, and several demographic groups (single parents, young adults, single women, the elderly, natives, and the disabled) have great difficulty obtaining or affording appropriate and adequate housing. A much more detailed examination of housing data and trends is required for a more valid picture of housing conditions in a country as large and diverse as Canada.

CANADA'S HOUSING INSTITUTIONS

The dominant characteristic of Canada's housing system is the overwhelming degree to which housing is a market commodity. Slightly more than 95 percent of the housing stock is privately owned. There are only 425,000 nonmarket housing units in the country (about 4 percent of the stock). These are units subsidized by government and owned and managed either by government housing authorities, private nonprofit housing societies, or not-for-profit housing cooperatives. Although residential construction plays a major role in the economy, government has, for the most part, intervened indirectly, leaving the construction and ownership of most of the stock in the private sector.

Housing policy and programs are a shared responsibility between the federal and provincial governments, although it is the federal government that has generally played the major role. The Canada Mortgage and Housing Corporation (CMHC) is the federal government's housing agency with the responsibility for administering the National Housing Act (NHA). The CMHC is a crown corporation established in 1946 with a board of directors reporting to a federal minister responsible for housing. Under the mandate of the NHA, the CMHC functions partially as a financial institution that, since 1954, insures mortgages and partially as a government department responsible for housing-supply programs, housing-rehabilitation programs, research and demonstration projects, and the dissemination of housing information. The ten provincial governments also have housing corporations or housing departments that perform similar functions as those of the CMHC at the provincial level. Most of the social

Figure 9.1
Renters Paying 30 Percent or More on Rent, by Income Group, Canada, 1986

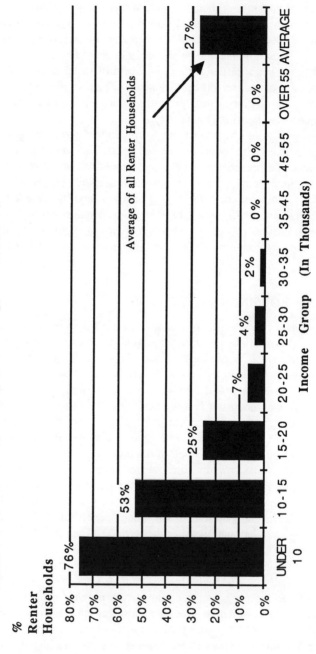

Source: Statistics Canada, 1987.

housing-supply programs have been jointly funded by the federal and provincial governments.

Residential construction has accounted for 5 to 6 percent of gross domestic product since the 1950s, and for most of the postwar period the construction of single detached houses has been the largest segment of new starts. During the 1950s construction of single detached houses represented 65 to 75 percent of all starts; during the mid–1960s to the late 1970s boom in rental and condominium apartment construction detached housing starts fell to the 40 to 50 percent range; and during the 1980s, with the fall in apartment starts, single detached starts have returned to the 60 percent level. Semidetached houses and row houses have generally averaged between 10 percent and 15 percent of all starts during the past few decades.

Because of the size of the country, the significance of single-detached-housing starts and the variable local building conditions and municipal regulations, new housing in Canada tends to be constructed by numerous private firms. The typical firm is small, building fewer than 10 units per year. The larger firms, which may build up to 2,000 units per year, are still relatively small compared to firms in other sectors of the economy. Few house-building firms operate in more than one market area, and no national firms building single detached houses are active in all major markets (Canada Mortgage and Housing Corporation 1987a, 20–21).

Developers of apartment buildings played a significant role in the housing industry from the mid–1960s to the mid–1970s, when apartment construction constituted a high proportion (40 percent to 50 percent) of all new residential construction. Many of these firms had originally been small builders of single detached houses, but as residential demand shifted toward apartment units, a number of house building firms became large successful real estate developers (Lorimer 1978). The shift in demand was due to several key factors: the baby-boom generation entering the housing market, the tend toward smaller house-holds, the increased demand for central city locations, and the general prosperity of the times, in particular the rising real wages and the increase in the number of two-income households.

Another important factor in the emergence of large-scale development firms was the introduction, during the late 1960s and early 1970s, of condominium tenure. The rapid growth in the construction of rental apartments quickly gave way by the mid–1970s to the more profitable development and marketing of condominiums. By the late 1970s virtually all large development firms left the rental sector, and most even sold their rental projects because a much greater and often quicker return on investment could be obtained outside the rental sector. As a result, the large development corporations diversified into office complexes, shopping centers, and industrial parks. Only a few remained in the residential sector, usually in the condominium market. As rental starts began to fall in the early 1970s a series of new subsidy programs and tax incentives were introduced that had the effect of stimulating additional rental starts but only during the life of the subsidy programs. Many of the subsidized units were also registered as condominiums to permit easy conversion to ownership status when market conditions were right.

Not only is construction carried out by the private sector, but residential finance in Canada is also largely private. Individuals and investors shop for mortgage funds from banks, trust companies, and other financial institutions. Although government mortgage loans through the National Housing Act did play a role in the past, no special institution or system for residential mortgage lending exists apart from the general money market. Even most social housing projects must obtain their mortgage financing in the private sector. Following the introduction of the National Housing Act in the mid–1930s, the government share of outstanding mortgage loans remained around 20 percent until the 1980s when its share fell to about 10 percent. Historically, life insurance companies were the most active lenders, and until mortgage insurance was introduced by the federal government in 1954, the country's major financial institutions, the chartered banks, were not allowed to make residential mortgage loans. Today, a variety of lending institutions compete for a share of the mortgage market, and shifts in market share occur from time to time (table 9.5).

FEDERAL HOUSING POLICY

After a decade-long depression and another half-decade devoted to the war effort, there was virtually no house-building industry. The existing stock was old, overcrowded, and in poor condition. A great deal of "catching up" was necessary. In 1946 the federal minister responsible for postwar economic recovery told the House of Commons that "adequate housing for the Canadian people is one of the major tasks before us" (House of Commons 1946, 3753).

Although the role of government in Canada's housing sector has grown significantly during the past fifty years, the approach established by the housing programs initiated in the 1930s and the 1940s have remained virtually unchanged. Canadian housing policy has focused almost exclusively on the *supply* of housing units in the *private* sector. Rather than a housing policy as such, there has been a series of housing programs designed to stimulate private residential construction as an instrument of macro-economic policy. There has been little concern over distribution issues.

The federal minister who developed Canada's postwar housing policy, C. D. Howe, told the House of Commons in 1946 that "it is the policy to ensure that as large a portion as possible of housing be built by private initiative" (House of Commons 1946, 3753). In 1955 the CMHC stated that "it has been a guiding principle of national participation in housing that, while the government may act to stimulate and supplement the house building market, it should not assume direct responsibilities . . . which could effectively be borne by private enterprise" (Central Mortgage and Housing Corporation 1956, 7). The federal government's 1985 *Consultation Paper on Housing* explained that "government has used

Table 9.5
Mortgage Loans Outstanding, by Type of Lending Institution, Canada, 1935–1985 (In Millions of Dollars)

Year	Life Insurance Companies		Chartered Banks		Loan Companies		Trust Companies		Credit Unions		Government & Gov. Agencies		Other		TOTAL
1935	405	43%			183	20%	97	10%			155	17%	95	10%	935
1940	412	44%			169	18%	86	9%			193	21%	73	8%	933
1945	339	45%			137	18%	66	9%			151	20%	53	7%	746
1950	901	50%			265	15%	113	6%			459	26%	62	3%	1,800
1955	2,016	48%	294	7%	444	11%	228	5%	211	5%	868	21%	109	3%	4,170
1960	3,412	36%	971	10%	698	7%	472	5%	390	4%	1,995	21%	1,454	15%	9,392
1965	5,662	30%	810	4%	1,839	10%	1,975	11%	695	4%	3,222	17%	4,415	24%	18,618
1970	7,723	25%	1,481	5%	2,868	9%	3,829	12%	1,353	4%	7,221	24%	6,170	20%	30,645
1975	10,364	17%	8,039	13%	6,560	11%	10,542	17%	5,205	8%	11,100	18%	10,561	17%	62,371
1980	16,319	13%	19,105	15%	12,956	10%	26,816	21%	15,619	12%	13,738	11%	21,351	17%	125,904
1985	21,666	13%	11,040	6%	42,553	25%	37,229	22%	21,659	13%	16,346	10%	20,968	12%	171,461

Source: Canada Mortgage and Housing Corporation, 1986b, table 78.

housing measures as an instrument of macro-economic policy" (Canada Mortgage and Housing Corporation 1985a, 23). In 1986 the CMHC stated that its objectives were "to assist in developing a climate of stability for the private market so that it can function effectively" and "to assist households in need who cannot obtain affordable, suitable, and adequate shelter in the private market" (Canada Mortgage and Housing Corporation 1986a, 12, 14).

This focus on starts and the near total reliance on the private market has been the subject of continuing criticism, but little has changed. In 1964 a major housing-policy review stated that "housing performance under the National Housing Act has been production oriented rather than distribution oriented, a quantitative operation qualitatively devoid of broad social objectives and economically inaccessible to many Canadians" (Ontario Association of Housing Authorities 1964, 49). The 1968 Federal Task Force on Housing and Urban Development found "ample evidence of imperfection within the existing market mechanism" and noted that housing "is a universal need, yet the private market on which Canadians have relied is anything but universal in its present scope and application" (Canada, Federal Task Force on Housing and Urban Development 1969, 14). A 1972 study of low-income housing policy noted that "production goals are adopted on the assumption that all Canadians will be decently housed if a sufficient number of units are produced so that there is one adequate dwelling for every Canadian family" (Dennis and Fish 1972, 29). The size, type, location, price, and tenure were left largely to the market and local regulations, with low-income households dependent on the filtering process. The 1972 study concluded that filtering had not worked. In his review of postwar housing policy Humphrey Carver, a senior CMHC researcher for twenty years, reported as follows:

The only interested party in the housing scene which didn't seem to get much attention at the staff meetings of CMHC was the Canadian family which couldn't afford home ownership. . . . The criterion of success was the number of new housing units provided under the National Housing Act. . . . To give some humanity to these statistics the expression used was "the number of new front doors," suggesting the grateful smiling faces of the families who would respond to the postman's knock. A subject that did not appear on the agenda was the question of what was behind the front door and what it looked upon. The environmental quality of the product was not considered important. (Carver 1975, 108)

The problem of producing enough new housing after the war was solved by the late 1960s when the house-building and house-financing capacity of the nation was no longer a problem. Canadian housing policy helped shape the mortgage-lending system, helped develop the house-building industry, and played a significant role in the municipal land-servicing process. House-production objectives were achieved, although distributional and equity considerations were ignored. The aim of Canadian housing policy has been to make ownership of a detached house and, more recently, a condominium apartment or townhouse, a feasible option for those able to qualify for a mortgage.

Public Housing, Nonprofit Housing, and Cooperatives

Reliance on the private sector and political and ideological resistance to an extensive government role in subsidizing nonmarket housing for low-income people was so great that a national public housing program was not implemented until 1949 (Bacher 1988). The city of Toronto used its own funds to build the nation's first public housing project in 1948 (Rose 1958). The 1938 National Housing Act contained provisions for assisted rental housing, but only subsidies for home ownership were ever implemented. Even the 1949 legislation that introduced a public housing program did not result in a great deal of activity.

During the fourteen years between 1949 and 1953, only 11,624 public housing units were built, amounting to 0.7 percent of the new residential construction (an annual average of 830 units). The federal minister responsible for housing in 1956 stated that "we would be justified in using public funds for housing only where private enterprise fails to meet the need" (Dennis and Fish 1972, 173). A member of the Board of Directors of CMHC explained in 1957 that "we are not competing with private enterprise who we assume will be building a more attractive product intended for those who can afford it." Public housing, he said, "should be based on economic and urban development considerations primarily and . . . the needs of individual tenants should be secondary" (Dennis and Fish 1972, 174).

The continued failure of the private sector to meet the need for low-rent housing and an unrealistic faith in filtering led to a decision to expand the public housing program in 1964. The new commitment to public housing resulted in 164,000 additional public housing units between 1964 and 1978 (an annual average of 11,680 units). By the late 1980s about 206,000 public housing units in about 4,700 projects had been built. These units comprise 2 percent of Canada's housing stock, and almost one-half of them are in Ontario. Most of the units (165,000) are provincially owned, with subsidy costs shared equally by the federal and provincial governments. The remainder are owned jointly by the federal and provincial governments with costs shared on a 75/25 percent basis. Rents are based on a federal or provincial rent-geared-to-income scale and generally equal 25 percent or less of the household's income. Sixty-three percent of the units are in high-rise buildings, and 86 percent of all public housing units are in good condition (Canada, Task Force on Program Review 1986, 56–61).

In the late 1970s the public housing program was phased out in most parts of the country and replaced by a much greater use of the public, private, and coop housing programs. This shift from public housing to the more socially mixed public, private, and cooperative nonprofit housing programs resulted from dissatisfaction with large-scale public housing projects for only the very poor. Since the early 1970s, nonprofit and cooperative housing have become the main vehicle for providing social housing assistance. By the mid–1980s the nonprofit and cooperative programs have accounted for 80 percent of new social housing units.

In addition to public housing construction, the federal and provincial governments lease about 36,000 rental units for low-income households. About half of the rent supplement units are in Ontario and the remainder are distributed across the country (Canada, Task Force on Program Review 1986, 51–54). This Rent Supplement program is used as an alternative to public housing.

Public, private, and cooperative nonprofit housing comprises the remainder of Canada's social housing stock—110,000 units developed and managed by public nonprofit housing corporations (provincial or municipal) and by private nonprofit housing corporations (church groups, unions, community organizations), as well as an additional 50,000 cooperative housing units. The 1964 NHA amendments provided funding for the first private nonprofit housing, but only 18,000 units were built until the 1973 NHA amendments expanded the nonprofit program and added funding arrangements for nonprofit continuing cooperatives.

Although housing cooperatives exist in many countries, they are usually similar to condominiums in that individuals make an equity investment and have the right to sell their share in the coop at market values and profit from any capital gain that may accrue. This type of market coop is virtually the same as owning a condominium. In Canada, condominiums and "nonmarket" continuing housing cooperatives are very different. Unlike condominiums, nonprofit housing cooperatives involve no equity investment by the residents. The federal coop housing program provides mortgage insurance and subsidies enabling lower- and moderate-income households to afford the monthly housing charges. An operating agreement covering the thirty-five year term of the mortgage guarantees ownership of the project by the residents on a nonprofit cooperative basis. It is the nonprofit and nonequity form of ownership combined with democratic self-management that distinguishes cooperative from condominium ownership. Cooperative housing in Canada represents a distinctly different tenure option for the ownership and management of housing. It is neither individually owned housing nor is it government owned and managed housing. Co-ops are within the public domain, like public housing; yet in practical and legal terms, they are owned by the people who live in them (Selby and Wilson 1988; Hulchanski 1987; and Laidlaw 1977).

In 1986 the Conservative government changed the orientation of the nonprofit and coop housing programs. It eliminated income mixing from public and private nonprofit housing that, in effect, reintroduced the public housing program. Cooperative housing continues as an alternative to home ownership for moderate-income households. The new orientation targets the public and private nonprofit projects to the extremely poor and recognizes the broader social objective of housing cooperatives—as an alternative to home ownership. Thirty percent of the units in the new co-op housing program receive rent supplement subsidies for lower-income households, thereby maintaining a social mix (Canada Mortgage and Housing Corporation 1985b).

Nonmarket housing has never received much attention from federal and provincial housing policymakers. Together, the public housing, rent supplement, nonprofit and co-op housing units comprise 4 percent of Canada's housing stock. In contrast to Canada's acceptance of strong public sector involvement in health and education, neither the state nor a majority of citizens have viewed the meeting of housing needs for all people as a public responsibility. The attention of policymakers and private citizens has focused primarily on problems of home ownership: development of private mortgage-lending institutions and provision of federal and provincial subsidies for home ownership. This focus has also neglected the private rental sector, which, as in many other Western countries, is in decline (Clay 1987; Hamnett 1984; Harloe 1985; Paris 1984). A declining private rental sector and a small social housing sector mean fewer options for the growing number of Canadians who cannot purchase a house.

Residential Mortgage Lending

With the exception of the small public and nonprofit housing programs, much of the history of Canadian housing policy is a history of a constant struggle aimed at improving the functioning of the private mortgage market to enhance opportunities for home ownership and, in doing so, to keep to a minimum the direct government role in the mortgage market.

Until the 1970s the major impediment to home ownership was the willingness of investors to lend sufficient funds in the residential mortgage market. Each time a crisis in mortgage availability arose, the federal government intervened with new incentives for private lenders. The first national housing legislation, the 1935 Dominion Housing Act, introduced joint mortgage lending between the government and the private sector (Hulchanski 1986, 27). The federal government extended the amortization period, absorbed most of the risk, subsidized the interest rate on its portion of the loan, and allowed private lenders to charge a higher than usual rate of interest on their portion of the loan.

The main elements of the joint loans introduced in 1935 remained intact until the creation of federal mortgage loan insurance in 1954. The intent was to end the joint-lending activity by creating a virtually risk-free investment for lenders. In exchange, the government retained the right to determine the lending terms, especially interest rates, to retain considerable influence over the mortgage market. However, the mortgage insurance scheme did not eliminate the need for direct federal mortgage lending. The scheme worked as long as rates of return on mortgage loans were equal to or better than other kinds of similar investments. When a crisis arose due to a lack of adequate mortgage funds in mid–1957, the CMHC was forced to intervene with massive direct mortgage lending to satisfy the "suburban house-builders of Canada" who were "hungry for funds to keep going" (Canada Mortgage and Housing Corporation, 1970, 21). In 1955 and 1956 the government financed only 700 homeowners each year, whereas in 1957 the CMHC financed 17,000 homeowners. In 1958 and 1959 government financing increased to 27,000 each year, and by the late 1960s more than 223,000 homeowners received mortgage funds directly from the government compared with fewer than 200,000 private sector mortgages financed under the NHA (Canada Mortgage and Housing Corporation 1970, 21). Mortgage lenders did not like the government-established NHA interest rate. In 1966 only 4,000 private sector NHA loans were made compared with nearly 28,000 CMHC loans.

Since the federal government gave no serious consideration to establishing a fully public residential mortgage lending system, its only option for decreased public involvement consisted of making mortgage terms much more attractive to investors. In 1967 the government introduced a new formula for setting the NHA mortgage interest rate, and in June 1969 it set the NHA interest rate free of any government regulation. The rate had been restricted by statute to a maximum of 2.25 percent above the long-term government bond rate. After June 1969 the only remaining difference between NHA and conventional lending was the risk-free nature of the NHA-insured mortgages. In addition, the government reduced the minimum term of the NHA mortgages from twenty-five years to five years, thereby eliminating long-term mortgage-rate security for homeowners (Smith 1974). Lending institutions began to enter the residential mortgage market in greater numbers, reducing the dominant role of life insurance companies (see table 9.4). While the pure market approach to mortgage lending pleased lenders, the higher interest rates increased costs for homeowners, and the shorter-term mortgages eliminated mortgage interest-rate stability. This introduced the use of a new term in the discussion of Canadian housing problems: *affordability*.

The term *housing affordability problem* first started to be widely used in the early 1970s. The 1970s was a decade in which a great deal of change took place in the macroeconomic conditions and housing-market conditions affecting virtually all aspects of the existing housing stock and the supply of new housing. Low-income households always had and continued to have a housing affordability problem. As a result of the difficult economic times during the 1970s, the problem of affording adequate and appropriate housing left the domain of households who were poor and began invading a significant proportion of the middle class, both tenants and homeowners. Macroeconomic and housing-market conditions made access to and maintenance of an expected standard of housing much more difficult.

One of the more obvious factors affecting "housing affordability," especially the ability of a family to purchase its first house, is interest rates. If interest rates remained relatively stable, house buyers had little to worry about. As interest rates rose in the 1970s and then became unstable in the early 1980s, access to home ownership and the risk of foreclosure among recent home buyers developed into a serious problem (see figure 9.2). From the early 1950s to the late 1960s the conventional mortgage interest rate was highly stable, ranging between 6 and 7 percent. From 1959 to 1965, for example, it stood firm at 7 percent. After the NHA mortgage rate was freed from any restrictions, it became unstable, jumping to 9 percent in 1969 and then fluctuating between 9 and 12 percent

Figure 9.2
Mortgage Interest Rate, Canada, 1951–1986

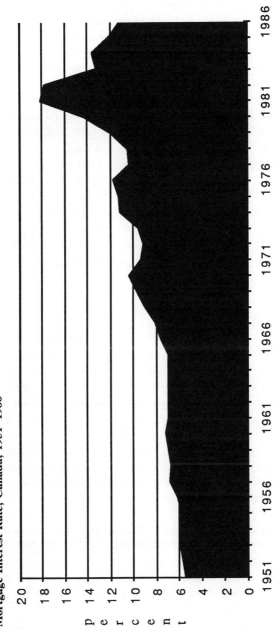

Source: Statistics Canada, *Canadian Economic Observer*, January 1988.

during much of the 1970s. The rate climbed to 18 percent in 1981 and 1982, reaching 21 percent in August 1981, and fell to 13 percent for two years and then to the 10 to 12 percent range.

The response to the problem of inadequate funds in the mortgage market was to make mortgages one of the safest and most lucrative investments. Still, this response generated new problems: access to home ownership and the threat of foreclosure. Many households, including those with two incomes, found it increasingly difficult to afford the purchase of a house in the major urban centers. In the early 1950s less then a third of all family households had more than one wage earner. By the 1980s more than two-thirds had two wage earners, and it took both incomes, rather than one, to qualify for a mortgage on an average suburban house. The home-ownership rate in Canada began to decrease in the 1960s from a historic peak of 66 percent in 1961 to 60 percent in 1971, and after many costly home-ownership-subsidy programs, the percentage of owners increased only slightly to 63 percent in 1986. By the early 1980s the federal government had classified more than 460,000 homeowners as being in "core housing need," that is, having severe problems affording their house (Canada, Task Force on Program Review 1986, 23). The political fallout of these conditions made short-term home-ownership-subsidy programs an inevitable part of the political process.

Home-Ownership-Subsidy Programs

During the early and mid–1970s the CMHC initiated several major home-ownership-subsidy programs. The early 1970s was a period of unprecedented house-price inflation. Between 1972 and 1974, for example, the cost of both the average resale house and the average new house rose by 53 percent whereas the average Canadian salary increased by only 22 percent (Schaffner 1975, 7). Home ownership became much more expensive relative to other cost-of-living factors, and incomes failed to keep pace. A greater proportion of households could not afford to buy a house. The CMHC's measure of the percentage of renters of prime home-buying age (twenty-five to forty-four years old) able to afford the average-priced house fell from 50 percent in 1971 to 17 percent in 1975 and 7 percent in 1981 (Canada Mortgage and Housing Corporation 1985a, appendix I, p. 15).

Political pressure on government from would-be home buyers and from the residential construction industry forced the creation of a string of expensive short-term subsidy programs through the 1970s and during the early 1980s. (Figure 9.3 provides a summary of federal home-ownership programs.) The government invented six new forms of primarily short-term subsidies in the 1970s and four in the early 1980s.

The first major benefit provided to homeowners after the 1969 changes in the NHA mortgage system was the exemption of the family house from capital gains taxes. In 1972 new tax rules introduced a 50 percent tax on capital gains with the exception of housing, thereby permitting homeowners to continue to benefit fully from appreciation. The exemption has become a permanent and popular housing subsidy. The capital-gains tax break allows homeowners to build up and shelter equity in their house, trade up to better houses, and eventually "cash in" their equity at retirement (or at any time). Unlike some countries, however, Canada does not allow homeowners to deduct mortgage interest and property-tax payments from taxable income. One result of the debate over the housing affordability "crisis" in the mid–1970s was the 1978 promise by the federal Conservative party to implement mortgage-interest and property-tax deductibility if elected. The Conservatives were elected but only as a minority government that lasted nine months, so the plan was never implemented, and it is now rarely mentioned (Shaffner 1979).

As the inflationary 1970s took its toll on the ability of households to afford the average house, a scheme to encourage renters to save for a down payment was introduced. The Registered Home Ownership Savings Plan (RHOSP) allowed up to $10,000 to be accumulated toward a down payment (from 1974 to 1985). Money placed in the RHOSP and the accumulated interest was exempt from income tax. In addition, to help moderate income households afford a mortgage, a five-year mortgage subsidy plan was introduced in 1973 (the Assisted Home Ownership Program, AHOP), and another 1974 program provided cash grants to help with the down payment (First-Time Home-Buyers Grant Program). About 95,000 households received AHOP-subsidized mortgages during the five-year life of the program. In addition, subsidy programs offering grants and loans to existing homeowners for renovations and insulation were introduced: the Residential Rehabilitation Assistance Program (RRAP) in 1974 and the Canadian Home Insulation Program (CHIP) in 1977.

In the early 1980s an economic slump and extremely high interest rates led to further programs to help out potential and existing homeowners. A short-term program, the Canada Mortgage Renewal Plan (CMRP), offered interest-rate subsidies for owners hit the hardest by the jump in interest rates, and in 1984 a permanent insurance scheme was introduced to protect owners from an increase of more than 2 percent in mortgage interest rates (the Mortgage Rate Protection Program). In 1982, when a sharp fall in starts was feared, the Canada Home Ownership Stimulation Plan (CHOSP) provided $3,000 cash grants as incentives for purchasing a house. To stimulate even more investment in residential construction in 1982, the Canada Home Renovation Plan (CHRP) furnished cash grants to a maximum of $3,000 per unit.

These home-ownership-subsidy programs, though very popular, were expensive and assisted few if any lower-income households. The three major programs in the early 1980s cost more than $1 billion: the CMRP cost $48 million, CHOSP $800 million, and CHRP $230 million (Canada Mortgage and Housing Corporation 1986a, 68–73). The foregone revenue from the nontaxation of capital gains on houses is estimated to be a $1.5 billion annual subsidy to homeowners. The RHOSP costs about $100 million per year (Dowler 1983, 56–75). (Figure

Figure 9.3
Evolution of Federal Home-Ownership Programs, Canada, 1945–1988

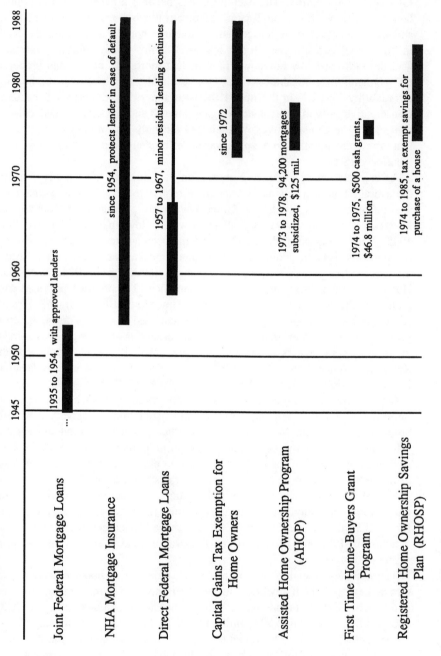

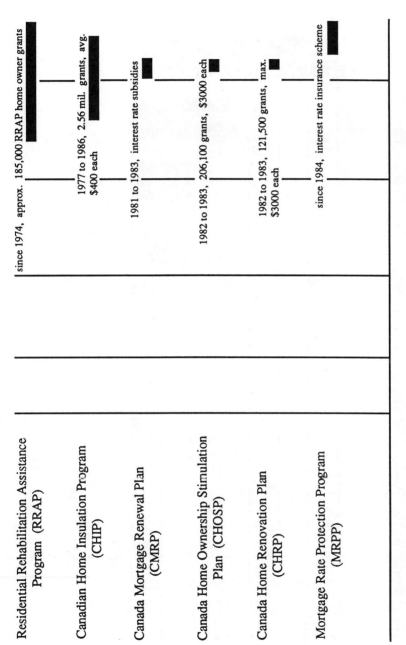

Residential Rehabilitation Assistance Program (RRAP)

since 1974, approx. 185,000 RRAP home owner grants

Canadian Home Insulation Program (CHIP)

1977 to 1986, 2.56 mil. grants, avg. $400 each

Canada Mortgage Renewal Plan (CMRP)

1981 to 1983, interest rate subsidies

Canada Home Ownership Stimulation Plan (CHOSP)

1982 to 1983, 206,100 grants, $3000 each

Canada Home Renovation Plan (CHRP)

1982 to 1983, 121,500 grants, max. $3000 each

Mortgage Rate Protection Program (MRPP)

since 1984, interest rate insurance scheme

Source: Compiled by J. D. Hulchanski, School of Community and Regional Planning, The University of British Colombia, April 1988.

Figure 9.4
Average Benefit from Federal Housing-Related Tax Expenditures, by Income Group, Canada, 1979

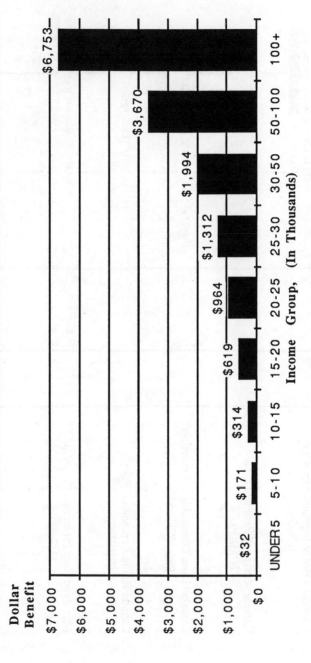

Source: Canada, Department of Finance, *Analysis of Federal Tax Expenditures for Individuals*, Ottawa, 1981, p. 12.

Table 9.6
Poverty, by Tenure, Canada, 1986

	Families		Unattached Individuals		Total	
	Poverty Rate	Number of Poor Families	Poverty Rate	Number of Individuals	Poverty Rate	Households in Poverty
Owners	7.3%	361,700	24.4%	187,000	9.4%	548,700
Renters	25.6%	489,300	38.0%	794,400	36.8%	1,283,700

Source: Canada, National Council of Welfare, 1988.

9.4 provides a Department of Finance summary of how unequally the housing-related tax expenditures are distributed.) Higher-income individuals receive most of the benefits of the housing subsidies provided through the income tax system. In comparison, the annual subsidy cost for all direct expenditures on the social housing units ever built in Canada for low- and moderate-income households— the public, nonprofit, and cooperative housing projects—was $600 million in 1982 and $773 million in 1983 (Canada Mortgage and Housing Corporation, 1986a, 68–73). As of 1986, only 1 percent of the federal budget had been spent on social housing.

Private Rental Housing Subsidy Programs

There has been little fluctuation in the percentage of Canadian households who rent their accommodations. In the late 1930s and early 1940s the percentage of renter households peaked around 45 percent and has since ranged between 35 and 40 percent. The poor performance of the private rental market and the severity and persistence of rental housing problems throughout this century has required the government to intervene continually. The early health and building codes were in large part directed at poor-quality rental stock. Residential rehabilitation programs, which began with the 1937 Home Improvement Act and the postwar urban-renewal and slum-clearance programs, have eliminated much of the poorest-quality rental stock. Since the market responds to effective market demand rather than social need, the reliance of Canadian housing policy on market forces has led to the huge disparity between the quality and the quantity of housing consumed by the poor and the rich. The poor simply cannot generate effective market demand in the rental sector. In 1986 about 500,000 families and 800,000 single-person households in the rental sector lived below the official poverty line (see table 9.6). About 37 percent of all renter households live in poverty compared with 9 percent of homeowners.

In her study of the federal response to rental housing problems during the past eighty-five years, Joan Selby concluded that ''despite the political and economic imperatives for government action which stemmed from early and continued

Figure 9.5
Evolution of Federal Rental Housing Programs, Canada, 1945–1988

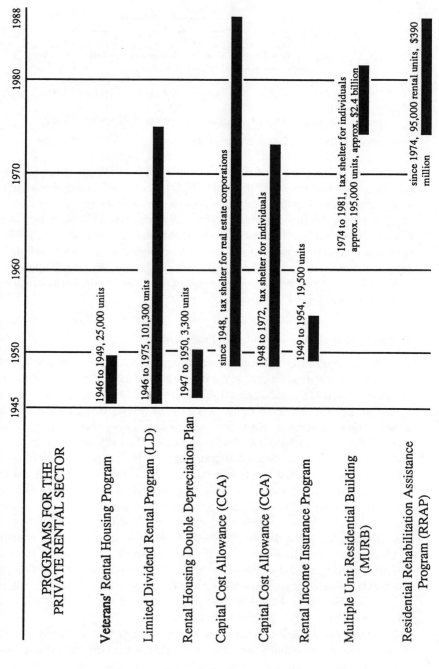

PROGRAMS FOR THE
PRIVATE RENTAL SECTOR

| | 1945 | 1950 | 1960 | 1970 | 1980 | 1988 |

Veterans' Rental Housing Program — 1946 to 1949, 25,000 units

Limited Dividend Rental Program (LD) — 1946 to 1975, 101,300 units

Rental Housing Double Depreciation Plan — 1947 to 1950, 3,300 units

Capital Cost Allowance (CCA) — since 1948, tax shelter for real estate corporations

Capital Cost Allowance (CCA) — 1948 to 1972, tax shelter for individuals

Rental Income Insurance Program — 1949 to 1954, 19,500 units

Multiple Unit Residential Building (MURB) — 1974 to 1981, tax shelter for individuals approx. 195,000 units, approx. $2.4 billion

Residential Rehabilitation Assistance Program (RRAP) — since 1974, 95,000 rental units, $390 million

Assisted Rental Program (ARP)

1975 to 1978,
122,650 units, $300 million

Canada Rental Supply Program (CRSP)

1981 to 1984, 21,700 units,
cost to 1986, $61 million

SOCIAL HOUSING SUPPLY
PROGRAMS

Public Housing Program

1949 to 1978, 206,000 units, minor activity continues

Public and Private Non-Profit Housing

since 1964, expanded in 1973, 110,000 units

Rent Supplement Program

since 1969, 36,000 units

Non-Profit Co-operative Housing

since 1973, 50,000 units

Rural and Native Housing Program

since 1974, 15,000 units

Urban Native and On-Reserve Housing

since 1978, 8,000 units

Source: Compiled by J. D. Hulchanski, School of Community and Regional Planning, The University of British Columbia, April 1988.

documentation of rental housing problems and prolonged advocacy for government intervention,'' the response has "been minimal, piecemeal and reactive, largely market supportive, and designed to challenge neither the principle of housing as a commodity nor the myth of market efficiency" (Selby 1985, 210). The resistance to developing a rental housing policy that effectively addresses the needs of lower-income households is due to four factors: (a) the reliance on the private sector for housing supply and housing-program delivery; (b) the focus on home ownership as the desirable tenure option; (c) the belief that severe housing problems are temporary aberrations rather than manifestations of fundamental, long-term problems; and (d) the view that housing is largely a local matter, with problems best left to municipalities and provinces to sort out (Selby 1985, 212).

The growth of the private rental stock has not been uniform during the postwar period. Only during the late 1950s and throughout the 1960s did market forces produce significant numbers of new rental units. After the war, to address the severe shortage, the federal government introduced two programs that directly subsidized rental starts, two providing tax benefits for rental investors, and one insurance scheme that guaranteed a certain profit level to investors (see figure 9.5). From 1945 to 1963, when 11,600 public housing units were built, the government subsidized a total of 83,500 private rental starts. Even the short boom in private rental starts during the 1960s was inadequate. To help meet the need for affordable rental housing, the government expanded the public housing program and increased the number of private rental units subsidized by the Limited Dividend Program.

When rental starts began to fall in the early 1970s two new subsidy programs resulted in 300,000 private rental units that were not targeted to the poor. They were short-term programs aimed at keeping the production of new units from falling more than they already had. The CMHC initiated the programs because some analysts claimed that the lack of rental investment was temporary, due to the unstable economic climate. Since the mid–1970s, however, almost all rental starts have been subsidized. As the *Consultation Paper on Housing* noted, "the federal government has devoted considerable resources to supporting rental production" spending "an estimated $4 billion to $5 billion in support of rental production" (Canada Mortgage and Housing Corporation, 1985a, 22). The gap between the economic rent of new units and the rent levels tenants can afford to pay has become increasingly large. There is no sign that the problem is temporary. Real incomes of average Canadian households declined during the early 1980s. The only private rental units built in the 1980s have been under government subsidy programs, and almost all multiple dwelling starts during the 1980s have been condominiums. Vacancy rates in the 1950s were about 5 percent. During the 1970s and 1980s they averaged closer to 2 percent, and many of the larger cities have rates persistently below 1 percent (see figure 9.6 for average vacancy rates between 1977 and 1986). It is in the context of market failure in the rental sector that most provinces maintain permanent rent regulations. Supply

Figure 9.6

Average Annual Vacancy Rates in Canada, 1977–1986 (In Private Rental Apartment Buildings with Six or More Units)

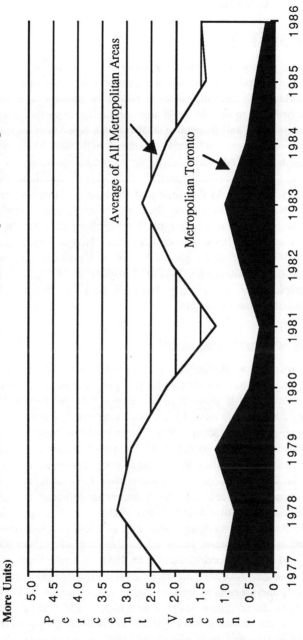

Source: Canada Mortgage and Housing Corporation, *Canadian Housing Statistics*, 1982, 1986b.

is not responding to demand; much of the demand is actually social need rather than effective market demand; and rental stock is being lost through condominium conversion and demolition.

MAJOR PROBLEMS

Canada has managed to construct a *partial* housing system during the postwar period. It is an exclusive system—it excludes those who cannot access the market. The nonmarket social housing sector is one of the smallest and least developed among major Western nations. The near total reliance on the private sector for supply, distribution, and maintenance of national housing resources means that people who cannot generate market demand will most likely not have their housing needs met. The market responds to market demand, not social need. The poor, in the past, were relegated to slum housing and their needs were, for the most part, ignored. As the quality of the housing stock improved after the 1940s there was less slum housing for the poor to disappear into. The gentrification that began happening during the 1970s further eliminated the lower-priced poor-quality inner-city housing stock (Ley 1985; Howell 1986). Canadian housing in the 1990s must deal with the legacy of a postwar housing policy that failed to address the housing needs of *all* Canadians and the impact of the adverse income, employment, and poverty trends of the 1980s that are affecting even more households than in the past.

A Policy of Crisis Management

A comparison of annual housing starts and the timing of new ownership and private rental-program initiatives supports the observation that Canadian housing policy consists of little more than a concern with production, that is, with maintaining a reasonable annual level of private sector starts (see figure 9.7 for annual housing starts, 1926 to 1986). The federal government adopted the first national housing legislation, the 1935 Dominion Housing Act and the 1938 National Housing Act, during the severe housing construction and employment slump of the Great Depression. Until that time there were no federal housing policy or programs, except for one home-ownership loan program for about 6,000 veterans after World War I (Jones 1978).

The introduction of mortgage insurance in 1954 followed the first serious postwar fall in housing starts. Housing starts leveled off at about 90,000 in 1948 and 1949 and then dropped to 68,000 in 1951. When it became obvious that mortgage insurance was not enough of an incentive for the private sector, the federal government began to lend mortgage funds directly in 1957. This intervention followed a decline in starts from a high of 138,000 in 1955 to 122,000 in 1957. A strong economy and continual direct lending by government helped maintain an increasing rate of starts until 1966. In response to a fear of another serious slump, the 1967 and 1969 freeing of the NHA interest rate and strong

Figure 9.7
Housing Starts in Canada, 1926–1986

Number of Units

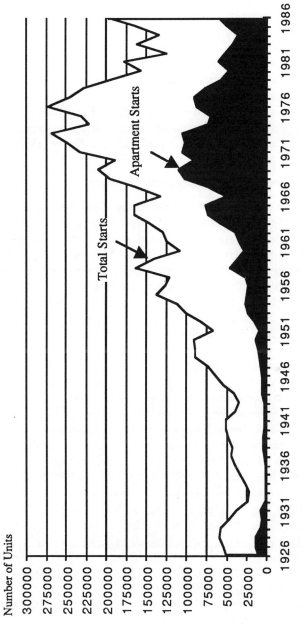

Source: Canada Mortgage and Housing Corporation, *Canadian Housing Statistics*, various years.

economic growth contributed to very high annual production levels until 1973. The sharp fall in 1974 and 1975 gave rise to a range of home-ownership- and rental-subsidy programs that temporarily boosted housing starts.

After housing starts reached an historic high of 273,000 in 1976, almost all of which were at least partially subsidized, annual starts continued to decrease. The high interest rates of the early 1980s led to another "outbreak" of short-term ownership- and private rental-subsidy programs. These programs did not reverse the downward trend very much but kept it from becoming worse. In the late 1980s starts began to recover due to stable interest rates, although most (60 percent) are single detached ownership units. The rental sector continues to be in a serious slump, and government fiscal restraint measures have reduced the level of social housing activity (Hulchanski and Drover 1987).

A Growing Housing-Affordability Problem

A number of economic trends during the 1980s indicate that many Canadians will have even greater difficulty affording housing in the 1990s.

The Decline in Real Family Incomes. Average real incomes of Canadian families fell by 6 percent between 1980 and 1984. Young families have been hardest hit, with a decline of 14 percent. This is a dramatic departure from trends between 1965 and 1976 when real incomes increased by 4.2 percent per year (Lindsay 1986, 15–16). A result of these trends is that by 1986 an estimated 3.7 million Canadians, 1 in 6, lived in poverty, a substantial increase of 215,000 since 1980. More than a million children under sixteen, 1 in every 6, are in low-income families (Canada, National Council of Welfare 1988, 2). By 1986, 1.9 million Canadians (7.5 percent of the population) were living on social-assistance payments, an increase from 1.4 million (5.7 percent of the population) in 1981 (Canada, National Council of Welfare, 1987, 8).

More Low-Income Single-Parent Families. During the period 1966–1986 the number of single-parent families increased 130 percent, whereas husband-wife parents increased only 42 percent. By 1986, 13 percent of all families were single parent compared with 8 percent in 1966. About 1.2 million children, or more than 14 percent of all children in Canada, lived in single-parent families. In 1986, 82 percent were headed by women, and women made up 94 percent of all young single parents (aged fifteen to twenty-four). About 60 percent of women single parents have incomes below the poverty line. The average income of female-headed single-parent families ($20,000 in 1985) was less than half that of husband-wife families with children ($44,000 in 1985). In 1986, 30 percent of female-headed single-parent families lived in single detached houses compared with 66 percent for other families with children. Also, 72 percent of female-headed single-parent families were renters, compared with 27 percent of other families (Moore 1987, 31–36).

The Aging of the Population. The population aged sixty-five and over is the fastest growing age group, and almost half (47 percent) of unattached elderly

Table 9.7
Share of Income, by Quintiles, Canada, 1951–1981

	1951	1961	1971	1981
Lowest Quintile	4 %	4 %	4 %	4 %
Second Quintile	12	12	10	11
Middle Quintile	18	18	18	18
Fourth Quintile	23	25	25	25
Highest Quintile	43	41	43	42

Source: Statistics Canada, 1984.

Canadians live in poverty. The number of elderly increased by 15 percent, from 2.4 million to 2.7 million, between 1981 and 1986, a growth rate more than three times that of the population as a whole (4 percent). The number of people over seventy-five increased by 19 percent (Devereaux 1987, 37).

These and similar income and poverty trends are occurring in the context of an already existing large gap between rich and poor in Canada and a very rigid income distribution. There has been little change in the distribution of income during the past thirty years (table 9.7). During the 1980s, however, there has been a measurable increase in economic inequality. Between 1980 and 1986 the bottom 60 percent of Canadian families saw their share of total national income fall from 37.6 percent to 36.5 percent, which is the equivalent of a $3 billion transfer. The top 20 percent of families (who have incomes exceeding $57,000 per year) accounted for all of the gain (Ross 1988, 20).

A Growing Urban Housing Crisis

The inability of an increasing number of households to afford adequate housing is already evident in the larger cities. In Toronto, for example, a 1987 report issued by the mayor notes that the shortage of affordable housing in the heart of Canada's largest metropolitan region "has evolved into a crisis." The vacancy rate in the rental market is 0.3 percent and the waiting lists for all forms of social housing are large and growing. The number of homeless people, especially women, youth, and families, is growing. From 1976 to 1985 more than 11,000 of Toronto's rental units were lost by conversion, redevelopment, and demolition. Gentrification displaced 54,000 people from rooms, flats, and apartments in converted family homes (owner-tenant properties) between 1976 and 1985. Rapidly rising land prices have outstripped gains in household incomes, making home ownership significantly less affordable and adding further to the pressure on the rental market. In 1972, for instance, the average Toronto house cost $28,000 and required about 32 percent of the median family income; by 1987 the median house price was $213,278 requiring 50 percent of the median income (City of Toronto 1987, 1–3).

PROSPECTIVE DEVELOPMENTS

Although a great deal of progress has been made during the past four decades in improving the standard of housing for most Canadians, many problems remain. Prospects for significant change in the near future are not good. Because of the generally high quality of the housing stock for most Canadians and the high cost and complexity of addressing remaining housing problems, it is too easy and convenient for the government and the housing industry to assert that housing markets are generally working well. To do otherwise invites more government intervention, which the housing industry opposes, and the spending of more money on housing, which is contrary to the fiscal restraint policies of the government.

Remaining housing needs will not be addressed until the ad hoc crisis-management orientation of housing policy is changed. The crises being managed, moreover, relate almost exclusively to issues of housing supply rather than distribution. Most Canadians will continue to be well housed while severe problems among a substantial minority—about 20 to 30 percent of all households, depending on the definition used—will likely worsen. The housing problem has tended to be framed in terms of conventional market analysis, which in turn limits the research and policy effort to a very narrow focus on marketplace transactions (the *processes* of the market). The *outcomes* of the market processes tend to be ignored. Rather than a housing affordability problem, it is conceptually more helpful to define the remaining housing problem as a resource-allocation problem: who gets what quality and quantity of housing at what percentage of their income and how this is decided. The housing debate is confused because problems and potential solutions are focused narrowly on subsidy programs and whether the country can afford them, rather than placing an emphasis on the allocative mechanisms of the economy—a fairer distribution of wealth, a less unequal wage system, and a less unequal allocation of housing resources. When we ask why, in the late 1980s, after more than fifty years of housing programs, so many Canadians have serious problems obtaining the housing they need, the only possible answer must point to the way housing resources are allocated. Canada is wealthy enough to guarantee every citizen adequate, appropriate housing at a reasonable cost. The accounts of housing-affordability problems that fill the media and much of the housing literature are, at their root, referring to a serious resource-allocation problem.

Forty years ago, in one of the first postwar studies of housing policy, Humphrey Carver noted that "the crucial and ultimate test of the effectiveness of housing policy is the condition of the worst-housed families in our communities" (Carver 1948, 123). The remaining unaddressed needs require making housing a priority and ensuring that resources are allocated appropriately. As Carver noted some forty years ago, "ultimately the solution to this central problem of housing lies in the formation of a philosophy concerning the rights and equities within our society" (Carver 1948, 128). Canadians have not yet made such a commitment, and narrow self-interest in housing and land markets continues to exclude a substantial proportion of Canadians from obtaining adequate and appropriate housing at a reasonable proportion of their income.

REFERENCES

Bacher, John C. 1988. "W. C. Clark and the Politics of Canadian Housing." *Urban History Review* 17, no. 1:5–15.

Canada. Federal Task Force on Housing and Urban Development. 1969. *Report of the Federal Task Force on Housing and Urban Development.* Ottawa: Information Canada.

Canada. National Council of Welfare. 1987. *Welfare in Canada: The Tangled Safety Net.* Ottawa.

———. 1988. *Poverty Profile, 1988.* Ottawa.

Canada. Task Force on Program Review. 1986. *Housing Programs in Search of Balance: A Study Team Report to the Task Force on Program Review.* Ottawa: Supply and Services Canada.

Canada Mortgage and Housing Corporation. 1970. *Housing in Canada, 1946–1970: A Supplement to the 25th Annual Report of Canada Mortgage and Housing Corporation.* Ottawa.

———. 1985a. *Consultation Paper on Housing.* Ottawa.

———. 1985b. *A National Direction for Housing Solutions.* Ottawa.

———. 1986a. *Annual Report, 1986.* Ottawa.

———. 1986b. *Canada Housing Statistics, 1986.* Ottawa.

Carver, Humphrey. 1948. *Houses for Canadians: A Study of Housing Problems in the Toronto Area.* Toronto: University of Toronto Press.

———. 1975. *Compassionate Landscape.* Toronto: University of Toronto Press.

Central Mortgage and Housing Corporation. 1956. *Housing and Urban Growth in Canada: A Brief from CMHC to the Royal Commission on Canada's Economic Prospects.* Ottawa.

City of Toronto. Office of the Mayor. 1987. *Proposals for a Housing Action Plan.* Toronto.

Clay, Phillip L. 1987. *At Risk of Loss: The Endangered Future of Low-Income Rental Housing Resources.* Washington, D.C.: Neighborhood Reinvestment Corporation.

Cullingworth, John Barry. 1987. *Urban and Regional Planning in Canada.* New Brunswick, N.J.: Transaction Books.

Dennis, Michael, and Susan Fish. 1972. *Programs in Search of a Policy: Low Income Housing In Canada.* Toronto: Hakkert.

Devereaux, Mary Sue. 1987. "Aging of the Canadian Population." *Canadian Social Trends,* Winter, 37–38.

Dowler, Robert G. 1983. *Housing Related Tax Expenditures: An Overview and Evaluation.* Major Report No. 22. Toronto: Centre for Urban and Community Studies, University of Toronto.

Hamnett, Chris. 1984. "Housing the Two Nations: Social-Tenurial Polarization in England and Wales, 1961–1981." *Urban Studies* 43:389–405.

Harloe, Michael. 1985. *Private Rented Housing in the United States and Europe*. London:
Croom Helm.

House of Commons. 1946. *Debates*. Ottawa.

Howell, Leigh. 1986. "The Affordable Housing Crisis in Toronto." *City Magazine* 9,
no. 1:25–29.

Hulchanski, J. David. 1986. "The 1935 Dominion Housing Act: Setting the Stage for a
Permanent Federal Presence in Canada's Housing Sector." *Urban History Review*
15, no. 1:19–40.

———. 1987. *Co-operative Housing in Canada*. CPL Bibliography 191. Chicago: Council of Planning Librarians.

Hulchanski, J. David, and Glen Drover. 1987. "Housing Subsidies in a Period of Restraint: The Canadian Experience." In *Housing Markets and Policies under Fiscal
Austerity*, edited by W. van Vliet—, 51–70. Westport, Conn.: Greenwood Press.

Jones, Andrew Eric. 1978. *The Beginning of Canadian Government Housing Policy,
1918–1924*. Occasional Paper #1/78. Ottawa: Centre for Social Welfare Studies,
Carleton University.

Laidlaw, Alexander F. 1977. *Housing You Can Afford*. Toronto: Green Tree Publishing
Ltd.

Ley, David. 1985. *Gentrification in Canadian Inner Cities: Patterns, Analysis, Impacts,
and Policy*. Ottawa: Canada Mortgage and Housing Corporation.

Lindsay, Colin. 1986. "The Decline of Real Family Income, 1980 to 1984." *Canadian
Social Trends*, Winter:15–17.

Lorimer, James. 1978. *The Developers*. Toronto: James Lorimer & Company.

Moore, Maureen. 1987. "Women Parenting Alone." *Canadian Social Trends*, Winter,
31–36.

Oberlander, H. Peter, and Arthur L. Fallick. 1987. *Shelter or Homes? A Contribution
to the Search for Solutions to Homelessness in Canada*. Vancouver: Centre for
Human Settlements, University of British Columbia.

Ontario Association of Housing Authorities. 1964. *Good Housing for Canadians: A Study
by the Ontario Association of Housing Authorities*. Toronto.

Paris, Chris. 1984. "Private Rental Housing in Australia." *Environment and Planning
A* 16:1079–97.

Rose, Albert. 1958. *Regent Park: A Study in Slum Clearence*. Toronto: University of
Toronto Press.

Ross, David. 1988. "Income Security: Not a Vintage Decade for Low-Income Canadians." *Perceptions* 12, no. 2:20–22.

Selby, Joan. 1985. "Urban Rental Housing in Canada, 1900–1985: A Critical Review
of Problems and the Response of Government." M.A. thesis, University of British
Columbia, School of Community and Regional Planning, Vancouver.

Selby, Joan, and Alexandra Wilson. 1988. *Canada's Housing Co-operatives: An Alternative Approach to Resolving Community Problems*. CHF Research Paper #3.
Ottawa: Co-operative Housing Foundation of Canada.

Shaffner, Richard. 1975. *Housing Policy in Canada: Learning from Recent Problems*.
HRI Observations No. 9. Montreal: C. D. Howe Research Institute.

———. 1979. *Housing Needs and Economic Policy: The Mortgage Interest and Property*

Tax Deduction Proposal. HRI Observations No. 19. Montreal: C. D. Howe Research Institute.

Smith, Lawrence B. 1974. *The Postwar Canadian Housing and Residential Mortgage Markets and the Role of Government.* Toronto: University of Toronto.

Statistics Canada. 1984. *Charting Canadian Incomes, 1951–1981.* Catalogue 13–581E. Ottawa: Supply and Services, Canada.

————. 1987. *Household Facilities by Income and Other Characteristics, 1986.* Catalogue 13–218. Ottawa: Supply and Services, Canada.

FURTHER READING

Arthur Anderson & Co. *Federal and Provincial Government Expenditures to Assist and Promote Rental Housing in Canada, 1976–1982.* Report prepared for the Canadian Home Builders' Association. Toronto: Arthur Anderson & Co., 1984.

Bacher, John C. "Canadian Housing 'Policy' in Perspective." *Urban History Review* 15, no. 1 (1986):3–18.

Bacher, John C., and J. David Hulchanski. "Keeping Warm and Dry: The Policy Response to the Struggle for Shelter among Canada's Homeless, 1900–1960." *Urban History Review* 16, no. 2 (1987):147–63.

Belec, John. "Origins of State Housing Policy in Canada: The Case of the Central Mortgage Bank." *Canadian Geographer* 29, no. 4 (1984):377–82.

Bourne, Larry S. "Recent Housing Policy Issues in Canada." *Housing Studies* 1 (1986):122–26.

Bourne, Larry S., and John Hitchcock, eds. *Urban Housing Markets: Recent Directions in Research and Policy.* Toronto: University of Toronto Press, 1978.

Bunting, Trudi E. "Changing Patterns in Inner-City Housing: A Canadian Example." Chap. 5 in *Housing and Neighborhoods: Theoretical and Empirical Contributions,* edited by Willem van Vliet—, Harvey Choldin, William Michelson, and David Popenoe. Westport, CT: Greenwood Press, 1987.

Canada Mortgage and Housing Corporation. *Housing in Canada, 1945 to 1986: An Overview and Lessons Learned.* Ottawa, 1987.

————. *Human Settlements in Canada: Trends and Policies, 1981–1986.* Ottawa, 1987.

Canadian Council on Social Development. *A Review of Canadian Social Housing Policy.* Ottawa, 1977.

Choko, Marc. "Montreal: Logement et Pouvoirs 1940–1960." *Les Annales De La Recherche Urbaine* 33 (March-April 1987):69–77.

Clayton Research Associates Ltd. *Rental Housing in Canada under Rent Control and Decontrol Scenarios, 1985–1991.* Toronto: Canadian Home Builders' Association, 1984.

————. *The Outlook for Residential Construction in Canada.* Ottawa: The Institute for Research in Construction, National Research Council of Canada, 1986.

Dansereau, Francine, Gerard Divay, and Jacques Godbout. "State Intervention and Alternative Tenure Patterns in Montreal." Chap. 8 in *Housing Needs and Policy Approaches: Trends in Thirteen Countries,* edited by by Willem van Vliet—, Elizabeth Huttman, and Sylvia F. Fava. Durham, NC: Duke University Press, 1985.

Goldberg, Michael A. *The Housing Problem: A Real Crisis? A Primer on Housing*

Markets, Policies and Problems. Vancouver: University of British Columbia Press, 1983.

Goldberg, Michael A., and Jonathan H. Mark. "The Roles of Government in Housing Policy: A Canadian Perspective and Overview." *Journal of the American Planning Association* 51, no. 1 (1983): 34–42.

Harris, Richard. "Boom and Bust: The Effects of House Price Inflation on Homeownership Patterns in Montreal, Toronto, and Vancouver." *The Canadian Geographer* 30, no. 4 (1986):302–15.

———. "Home Ownership and Class in Modern Canada." *International Journal of Urban and Regional Research* 10, no. 1 (1986):67–86.

Hertzog, Stephen, and Robert D. Lewis. "A City of Tenants: Homeowners and Social Class in Montreal, 1847–1881." *Canadian Geographer* 30, no. 4 (1986):316–24.

Hulchanski, J. David. *Shelter Allowances and Canadian Housing Policy: A Review and Evaluation*. Research Paper No. 147. Toronto: Centre for Urban and Community Studies, University of Toronto, 1983.

———. "Tax Costs of Housing." *Policy Options* 6, no. 5 (June 1985): 4–7.

Hulchanski, J. David. "The Evolution of Property Rights and Housing Tenure in Postwar Canada: Implications for Housing Policy." *Urban Law and Policy* 9, no. 2 (1988):135–56.

Hulchanski, J. David, and Beverly Grieve. *Housing Issues and Canadian Federal Budgets, 1968 to 1984*. Canadian Planning Issues No. 12. Vancouver: University of British Columbia, 1984.

Le Bourdais, Celine, and Michel Beaudry. "The Changing Residential Structure of Montreal 1971–81." *The Canadian Geographer* 32, no. 2 (1988): 98–113.

Lehrman, Jonas. "Innovative Compaction in Canadian Housing." *Habitat Intl.* 11, no. 3 (1987): 141–46.

Levine, G. J. "To Tax or Not to Tax?" *International Journal of Urban Regional Research* 11, no. 4 (1987): 543–66.

Ley, David. "Social Upgrading in Six Canadian Inner Cities." *The Canadian Geographer* 32, no. 1, (1988): 31–45.

Miron, John R. *Housing in Postwar Canada: Demographic Change, Household Formation & Housing Demand*. Montreal: McGill-Queens University Press, 1987.

———. *Housing in Postwar Canada: Demographic Change, Household Formation, and Housing Demand*. Montreal: McGill-Queens University Press, 1988.

Miron, John R., and John Barry Cullingworth. *Rent Control: Impacts on Income Distribution, Affordability, and Security of Tenure*. Toronto: Centre for Urban and Community Studies, University of Toronto, 1983.

Pratt, Geraldine. "Housing-Consumption Sectors and Political Response in Urban Canada." *Environment and Planning D: Society and Space* 4 (1986): 165–82.

———. "Housing Tenure and Social Cleavages in Urban Canada." *Annals of the Association of American Geographers*. 76, no. 3 (1986):366–80.

———. "Class, Home, and Politics." *Rev. Canada. Soc. & Anth/Canad. Rev. Soc. & Anth.* 24, no. 1 (1987):41–57.

Rose, Albert. *Canadian Housing Policies, 1935–1980*. Toronto: Butterworths, 1980.

Saywell, J. T. *Housing Canadians: Essays of the History of Residential Construction in Canada*. Discussion Paper No. 24. Ottawa: Economic Council of Canada, 1975.

Simon, Joan C., and Gerda R. Wekerle. "Planning with Scarce Resources: The Miniaturization of an Urban Neighborhood.'' Chap. 11 in *Housing and Neighborhoods: Theoretical and Empirical Contributions*, edited by Willem van Vliet—, Harvey Choldin, William Michelson, and David Popenoe. Westport, CT: Greenwood Press, 1987.

Skaburskis, Andrejs. ''Speculation and Housing Prices: A Study of Vancouver's Boom-Bust Cycle.'' *Urban Affairs Quarterly* 23, no. 4 (1988): 566–80.

Smith, Lawrence B. *Anatomy of a Crisis: Canadian Housing Policy in the Seventies*. Vancouver: The Fraser Institute, 1977.

Social Planning Council of Metropolitan Toronto. *A New Housing Agenda for Metropolitan Toronto*. Toronto, 1984.

Wade, Jill. ''Wartime Housing Limited, 1941–1947: Canadian Housing Policy at the Crossroads.'' *Urban History Review* 15, no. 1 (1986):41–60.

10

United States of America

PETER MARCUSE

THE CONDITION OF THE HOUSING SUPPLY

"Americans are the best housed people in history," reported President Reagan's Commission on Housing in 1982. Five years later, estimates of the number of homeless persons living on the streets or in emergency shelters ranged from a low of 300,000 to a high of 3 million (see below, "Security of Occupancy," *Homelessness*). All agree that the figure is higher than at any time since the Great Depression. The coexistence of the commission's conclusion with so many homeless can only be explained by a detailed examination of the system of housing provision in the United States.

Table 10.1
Persons per Household, United States, 1940–1988

Year	Persons Per Household	Year	Persons Per Household
1940	3.67	1978	2.81
1950	3.37	1979	2.78
1960	3.33	1980	2.76
1965	3.29	1981	2.73
1970	3.14	1982	2.72
1971	3.11	1983	2.73
1972	3.06	1984	2.71
1973	3.01	1985	2.69
1974	2.97	1986	2.67
1975	2.94	1987	2.66
1976	2.89	1988	2.64
1977	2.86		

Source: U.S. Bureau of the Census, 1988.

Quantity

The supply of housing in the United States has increased rapidly in the years since World War II. The rate of new construction has consistently surpassed the rate of population growth; between 1970 and 1988 population increased 16.7 percent, and year-round housing units increased by 35.4 percent. Household size has decreased in parallel from an average of 3.37 persons per household in 1950 to 2.64 in 1988 (table 10.1). In the past fifteen years alone, the number of one- and two-person households has increased from 46 to 55 percent of all households (Sternlieb and Hughes 1987, 39). But the number of vacant units has more than doubled, from 3,560,000 in 1960 to 8,324,000 in 1985 (U.S. Bureau of the Census: *Census of Housing* 1960, 1980; U.S. Bureau of the Census: *American Housing Survey*, various years).

These figures may be misleading, for the benefits of the rapid expansion in the housing supply have not been uniform for all population groups. Although average household size per unit has been declining, the U.S. Census defines a household as all of those occupying a housing unit; thus no figures are available for how many households (in the more conventional sense of a family group related by blood or marriage) are living doubled up or with relatives with whom they would prefer not to live. Nor do U.S. figures provide a measure of space per person, as most countries do, in square meters (or square feet) per person. The closest to a measure of crowding that U.S. statistics provide are the figures set forth in table 10.2, dealing with persons per room and "nonrelatives present." They show substantial improvement since 1950, but a significant remaining

Table 10.2
Measures of Crowding, United States, 1940–1987

Year	More Than One Person Per Room	Households With Unrelated Subfamily (x 1,000)
1940	20.2%	NA
1950	15.7	NA
1960	11.7	207
1970	7.4	130
1973	5.6	109
1974	5.3	137
1975	4.9	149
1976	4.6	189
1977	4.4	238
1978	4.2	257
1979	4.0	306
1980	4.5	360
1982	NA	372
1983	3.5	440
1984	NA	504
1985	2.8	526
1986	NA	505
1987	NA	566

Source: U.S. Bureau of the Census, 1988.

problem: about 2,496,000 households living at more than 1.0 person per room and 531,000 at more than 1.5 persons per room (U.S. Bureau of the Census: *American Housing Survey* 1988). When that problem is disaggregated, its dimensions become clearer. National figures obscure major local variations; the proportion of crowded units (with more than 1.0 person per room) ranges, among the thirty largest cities, from 2.7 percent in Columbus, Ohio, to a high of 15.5 percent in Honolulu, with New York at 8.2 percent, Chicago at 8.1 percent, and Los Angeles at 13.0 percent, all well above the national percentage (U.S. Bureau of the Census: *Census of Housing* 1980, vol. 1, ch. A 8).[1]

The adequacy of supply also varies dramatically by income. Overcrowding is most common among lower-income renters and is getting worse today. For renter households with incomes under $3,000 a year, nearly 10 percent were overcrowded in 1983, up from 5 percent just three years earlier (Dolbeare 1988). Among renter households with incomes of $3,000–6,999 a year, nearly 8 percent were overcrowded in 1983. The New York City Housing Authority reported in 1988 that as many as 43,000 families in the city's public housing projects were illegally doubling up, a problem that, according to the Housing Authority chair, is "growing geometrically."[2] The 1968 Housing Act estimated a housing shortfall of 26 million units over the following ten years, 6 million of which needed to be subsidized for lower-income households. Performance fell far short of achieving that goal; only 21.5 million units were built, 2.7 million of which were subsidized. National housing-production goals are no longer even being officially set by the government (President's Commission on Housing 1982, xxxv). The most recent estimate is that there will be a shortfall of 7.8 million units for low-income households by 2003, and that figure is conservative; it assumes low-rent units are occupied only by low-income households (Clay 1987).[3] Without this assumption, the shortfall might amount to more than 12 million units. The experiences of many potential housing voucher recipients who, though certificated for the program, are not able to use their federal subsidies because they cannot find standard housing to which to move confirm these nationwide statistics. In major cities such as Boston and New York, often as many as half of the vouchers are returned to the local housing authorities because adequate, affordable rental units cannot be found.

Quality

Housing quality has improved dramatically during the past fifty years for most but not all U.S. residents. The measurement of housing quality, never an exact science, has taken its twists and turns in the Census Bureau's enumerations. The relevant categories were "needing major repairs" in 1940, "dilapidated" in 1950, and "dilapidated" and "deteriorating" in 1960; the effort was abandoned entirely in 1970, when the Census of Housing was conducted for the first time by mail. The earlier category "dilapidated" survives only in the Annual Housing Survey, a sample survey undertaken in years between the Decennial Census.[4] The term *substandard* has frequently been used to cover both units considered physically in poor condition and those lacking piped hot and cold water, flush toilet, and bathtub or shower all for the exclusive use of the occupants of the unit.[5] Currently, the most widely used measurement of quality considers deficiencies in maintenance and equipment involving items such as breakdowns or inadequacies of heating systems, cracks in ceilings or walls, holes in floor, presence of rodents, and broken plaster or peeling paint.[6]

By such measurement, there has been rapid improvement since 1945. The figures for dilapidated units, for units with inadequate plumbing, and for units with deficiencies (table 10.3) all show a long-term reduction in poor-quality units. At the other end of the scale are the increases in quality and level of amenity in new single-family home construction (table 10.4); the indications are that the long-term trend to improvement has tapered off and may be over.

On the other hand, as those figures show, millions of Americans, most of whom are poor, are currently living in housing unacceptable by the prevailing standards of U.S. society; in 1985, on a scale of 1–10, 20.6 percent of renters and 7.6 percent of owners rated their dwellings less than 5 (U.S. Bureau of the Census: *American Housing Survey* 1983).

Attention to housing quality has broadened in recent years to consider neighborhood as well as individual unit characteristics. Neighborhood conditions may today be the most serious problem of housing quality in the United States. In

Table 10.3
Quality of Housing, United States, 1940–1983

Year	Dilapidated or needing major repairs	Lacking plumbing
1940	17.8%	NA
1950	9.8	NA
1960	6.9	7,899
1970	4.6	4,398
1980	NA	2,334
1983	NA	2,233

Sources: U.S. Bureau of the Census, *Census of Housing* and *American Housing Survey*, various years.

Table 10.4
Characteristics of New Housing Units, United States, 1939–1987

Year	Median Square Feet, New One-Family Houses	Median Square Feet, Existing One-Family Houses	Percent of All Units With Air Conditioning
1939	NA	1,591	NA
1949	NA	1,303	NA
1959	NA	1,500	NA
1960	NA	NA	12.4
1964	NA	1,512	NA
1969	NA	1,275	NA
1970	1,385	NA	36.7
1974	NA	1,295	49.3
1975	1,535	NA	4.6
1978	NA	1,500	NA
1980	1,595	1,488	55.0
1981	1,550	1,437	55.0
1982	1,520	1,525	57.1
1983	1,565	NA	59.1
1984	1,605	1,583	NA
1985	1,605	NA	60.6
1986	1,660	NA	NA
1987	1,155	NA	NA

Source: U.S. Bureau of the Census, 1988.

1985, 40 percent of renters and 37 percent of homeowners regarded their neighborhoods as deficient in one or more respects (e.g., too much litter, noise, or crime; streets needing lighting or repairs). Forty-five percent of renters and 50 percent of homeowners were dissatisfied with schools, police protection, public transportation, or other services (U.S. Bureau of the Census: *Annual Housing Survey*, 1982, tables A–2, A–3). In New York City, a quarter of all housing units were on streets on which there were also abandoned buildings, a key indicator of a problem neighborhood (Marcuse 1985b).

Table 10.5
Affordability Index, Existing One-Family Homes, United States, 1970–1986

Year	Affordability Index
1970	2.63
1971	2.75
1972	2.75
1973	2.75
1974	2.86
1975	2.99
1976	3.00
1977	3.16
1978	3.23
1979	3.38
1980	3.51
1981	3.48
1982	3.36
1983	3.37
1984	3.23
1985	3.20
1986	3.23
1987	3.29

Sources: U.S. Bureau of the Census, 1988; National Association of Realtors, *Existing House Sales*, 1987.
Note: The index is the number of years of income needed to purchase a median priced existing house with a median household income.

Price

Ownership. Home ownership is becoming increasingly expensive, particularly for newly formed households; in 1979, 44 percent of all households with residents between twenty-five and twenty-nine owned their own homes; by 1987 the figure had fallen to 36 percent (*Newsweek*, April 11, 1988, p. 65). In 1983, for the first time in more than twenty years, the nation's home-ownership rate fell. Although it was a small drop, from 65.6 percent to 64.6 percent, it is an important signal that what has long been considered "the American dream" is becoming less attainable (U.S. Bureau of the Census: *American Housing Survey* 1983). Mortgage interest rates over 10 percent seem to be a fixture now, whereas in 1970 they were 8.52 percent; in 1975 they averaged 9.10 percent, peaking at 16.52 percent in 1981, and now are about 12 percent (U.S. Bureau of the Census, 1986, 506).[7] (Table 10.5 sets forth the pattern.) The *affordability index* is the number of years' income the median household would have to spend to purchase the median-priced existing single-family home. When combined with rapidly escalating house prices, monthly mortgage payments rise geometrically, far faster than incomes.

In 1975 the average price of a new single-family house was $44,600, and the contract interest rate for a conventional first mortgage averaged 8.75 percent. With an 80 percent mortgage and housing costs at 25 percent of income, a family in 1975 would have needed a down payment of $8,920—65 percent of median family income that year—and, on a thirty-year level-payment mortgage, would have had a monthly mortgage payment of $280.69, which in turn required a minimum annual income of $13,473—2 percent below the nation's median family income that year.

In 1981 the average-price, new single-family house cost $94,100, and the contract interest rate for a conventional first mortgage averaged 14.1 percent. With an 80 percent mortgage and housing costs at 25 percent of income, a family in 1981 would have needed a down payment of $18,820—84 percent of median family income that year—and, on a thirty-year level-payment mortgage, would have had a monthly mortgage payment of $897.93, which in turn required a minimum annual income of $43,101—nearly double the nation's median family income that year (U.S. Bureau of the Census 1981). Although 1981 was the peak year for mortgage interest, the increase in the cost of home ownership is a long-term trend; real annual after-tax costs of a standard house increased from $5,375 in 1967 to $7,449 in 1987 and went from 22.2 percent of first-time buyer income in 1967 to 32.4 percent in 1987 (Apgar and Brown 1988, 20).

Since the high inflation rates of the late 1970s-early 1980s, adjustable (variable) interest-rate mortgages, in which interest rates change annually as general interest rates change, have come increasingly into use. Under them, the risk of inflation is shifted from lender to borrower, decreasing security of tenure and making savings for upward housing mobility more difficult with inflation.

Utility costs are an increasing component of homeowners' housing costs. The consumer price index (CPI) for fuel oil, coal, and bottled gas rose from 110.1 in 1970 to 685.8 in mid–1981; in that same eleven-year period, electricity prices increased by 175.5 points, compared with a 152.7-point rise in the CPI for all items (Bratt et al. 1986, xv). Continuing high oil and electricity prices, deregulation of natural gas, and aggressive rate-increase campaigns by utility companies all suggest that these costs will continue to be substantial.

Local property taxes have increased as local and state governments experienced fiscal crises and the federal government cut back traditional aid programs. Since the property tax—in effect, a sales tax on housing services—is highly regressive, low-income households are hit hardest. The median real estate tax bill for the 6.9 million homeowners with incomes under $5,000 in 1987 was $620, or almost 10 percent of their total income (U.S. Bureau of the Census 1987). Renters are equally burdened by such taxes, although they do not show up as direct payments but are folded into the rent payment to the landlord.

Of all owner-occupants, 57.8 percent had mortgages on their homes in 1985. The figure is up sharply from 44 percent in 1950 (U.S. Bureau of the Census 1988). The median amount in 1985 was $28,471. This is ten times the median nonhousing consumer debt and probably the biggest single item of expense for most home-owning families. The lower the income, the higher the proportion of it going to pay off a mortgage; two-thirds of all households earning under $5,000 paid more than 20 percent of their incomes for mortgage debt alone, compared with 6 percent of those earning over $50,000 (U.S. Bureau of the

Census 1988).[8] For higher income families, even that figure overstates the case, since often taking out or increasing a mortgage is simply a tax-advantaged (because mortgage interest is deductible from income for income tax purposes) way of borrowing money for other personal or business needs. For consumers, somewhat less than two-thirds of all debt is on mortgages, a figure that has remained remarkably stable during the past fifteen years, since rising gradually from about 52 percent in 1945 (U.S. Bureau of the Census 1975, 978).[9]

Rental. Housing costs for renters have become an increasing problem recently and may be the most critical aspect of the housing problem in the U.S. today. The figure of 30 percent of income for rent, already higher than the standard accepted by most developed countries and unrealistically high for lower-income households in the United States, is being exceeded for a larger and larger number of households (Stone 1988). For renters, between 1970 and 1983 median gross rent as a percentage of income rose from 20 to 27 percent (U.S. Bureau of the Census: *American Housing Survey* 1985). More than 10 million renter households paid 35 percent or more of their income for rent in 1985; 6.3 million paid 50 percent or more; and 4.7 million paid 60 percent or more. While less severe, the problem exists among homeowners too: 3.7 million homeowner households paid 50 percent or more of their income in housing costs in 1985. The affordability problem hits lower-income people the hardest: the median rent-income ratio for renter households earning less than $3,000 was over 60 percent (the *American Housing Survey* does not provide more specific figures at this level); for renter household in the $3,000–$6,999 income class it was 55 percent and for renter households in the $7,000–$9,999 class, 39 percent (U.S. Bureau of the Census: *American Housing Survey* 1983, table A–1).

The situation is likely to worsen in the foreseeable future. Landlord abandonment, arson, conversion of rental units to condominiums and cooperatives, gentrification, and other changes of land use are causing the existing rental housing stock to shrink as ongoing investment in older rental properties for in-place tenants becomes increasingly unprofitable. Indeed, a government report of a few years ago described rental housing as an "endangered species" (U.S. Comptroller General 1979; see also Downs 1983).

Tenure

The proportion both of owner occupancy and of single-family homes is among the highest of any country in the world, but its level has fluctuated significantly in the past. It is often assumed that owner occupancy and single-family housing are much the same thing, but this is not so: some single-family units are renter occupied, and the proportion of units in multi-family buildings that are owner occupied (as condominiums or cooperatives)[10] is increasing throughout the country. The assumption that owner occupancy means single-family housing may explain some of the frequently expressed popular preference for owner occupancy over renting as a form of tenure.

Table 10.6
Home Ownership, by Race, United States, 1920–1983

Year	Total		Suburban[1]	
	White	Black	White	Black
1920	48.2	23.9		
1930	50.2	25.2		
1940	45.7	23.6		
1950	57.0	34.9		
1960	64.4	38.4	73.4	51.6
1970	65.4	41.6	71.1	54.1
1980	67.8	44.2		
1983	67.7	45.0	71.4	51.9
1985	66.8	43.5	76.8	50.8

Sources: U.S Bureau of the Census, *Census of Housing*, 1960, 1970, 1980; *American Housing Survey*, 1983.
[1]Within SMSA, not in central city.

Home-ownership rates remained fairly stable until after World War I. In the 1920s they increased sharply (table 10.6) and then dropped back to their earlier levels under the impact of the Great Depression and its attendant mortgage foreclosures and unemployment. But in the immediate post–World War II period they increased sharply. Home-ownership rates also vary substantially by race (table 10.6); nonwhite households have about the same percentage of home-owners now as whites had before 1920 and are still 20 percentage points behind whites.[11]

Four interrelated factors explain the U.S prediliction for home ownership. The first has to do with both the early history and geography of the country. The immigration of European settlers that led to the founding of the American colonies and then the independence of the United States took place in a vast, sparsely settled country in a period of revolt against feudalism and political-economic systems dominated by strong centralized state authority. Individual enterprise and individual action without state "interference" were thus leitmotifs that played themselves out in housing as well as elsewhere. Since the geography of the country also made individual (actually, communal, but in contrast to governmental) effort the simplest method of settling new territory, and since the single-family house and individual ownership of houses individually built both meshed well with such a historical development in a region where land was abundant, individual single-family home ownership became the primary pattern in the new settlements. Even though the pattern did not prevail in the urban centers and was probably exaggerated in the common perception from the Civil War on, it became identified with good housing itself for most people. Even today, when the historical conditions that rendered it functional no longer exist and land costs have greatly increased, single-family home ownership remains the ideological, social, and psychological image of good housing for most Americans.

This historical logic has permitted the second factor promoting home ownership to become prominent. Ideologically, political as well as business leaders have long seen home ownership as buttressing stability, allegiance, thrift, hard work, and patriotism. Initially—at the time of independence—home ownership and land ownership were equated, and land ownership equaled ownership of an essential element for agricultural production; thus John Adams argued: "The only possible way . . . of preserving the balance of power on the side of equal liberty and public virtue is to make the acquisition of land easy to every member of society; to make a division of the land into small quantities, so that the multitude may be possessed of land and estates" (Letter to James Sullivan, May 26, 1776). By 1826, with Thomas Benton, who later coauthored the Homestead Act of 1860, the emphasis on the political element became clearer, and the relationship to production attenuated: "Tenancy is unfavorable to freedom. . . . It should be the policy of republics to multiply their freeholders, as it is the policy of nomarchies to multiply tenants" (U.S. Senate 1826, 727–38).

Conservative housing reformers, at the turn of the century, adopted the same posture: "Under no other method than small houses with open lots can we expect American institutions to be maintained," wrote Lawrence Veiller, and other reformers argued that "all observers agree that measured by the old standards, the apartment dweller shows a loosening of moral fiber. . . . [Home ownership] has great utility as automatically interesting the owner in government" (quoted in de Neufville and Barton 1987, 9).

The political-ideological content is as clear with Herbert Hoover, who called "the American Home . . . the foundation of American life" (Hoover Commission 1929, vol. 1), as it is with Franklin D. Roosevelt, who defended the establishment of the Homeowners Loan Corporation, one of the first major U.S. governmental measures intended to affect housing, which prevented widespread private mortgage foreclosures, by stating: "The broad interests of the nation require that special safeguards should be thrown around homeownership as a guarantee of social and economic stability" (quoted in Fisher 1931–1932).

Thus a strong political-ideological component undergirds public policies supporting home ownership. Those public policies themselves are the third factor in explaining the prevalence of home ownership in the United States. Governmental support for home ownership is reflected in federal mortgage-guarantee programs (FHA and VA; see below), which cover 29.2 percent of all single-family owner-occupied mortgaged units (61.0 percent of all such units are mortgaged).[12] But such support is even more important in the form of the tax advantages accruing to home ownership as opposed to rental (table 10.7). Figure 10.1 shows the evolution of the deduction and compares it with expenditures for assisted housing targeted to moderate- and low-income households. Although the distribution of tax benefits is clearly regressive—netting out benefits against

Table 10.7
Tax Expenditures Benefiting Homeowners, United States, 1984

Deductability of mortgage interest	$23,480,000,000
Deductability of real property taxes	8,775,000,000
Deferral of gain on sale if reinvested	4,895,000,000
Exclusion of $125,000 of gain on sale by elderly	1,630,000,000
Energy conservation credit	630,000,000
TOTAL	$39,410,000,000

Source: Figures are from table 15.1 and figure 15.1, in Dolbeare, 1986.

Notes: The figures shown, which are for 1984, do not include the benefits accruing from the failure to tax the imputed rental value of owner-occupied homes, but adequate information to estimate this benefit is not available. See U.S. Congress, Congressional Budget Office, 1981; and Simonson, 1981.

payments, Cushing Dolbeare estimated, net, that the average household earning under $10,000 received $125, and the average household earning over $50,000 received $1,860 (Bratt, Hartman, and Meyerson 1986)—such benefits are a powerful incentive encouraging home ownership generally.

Finally, the combination of inflation and prosperity will lead to investment in owner-occupied housing both for moderate-income households, whose other inflation-resistant investment opportunities may be limited, as well as for higher-income households. Some commentators have summarized this development under the catchy title of a "Post-Shelter Society" (see Sternlieb and Hughes 1980). Although the phrase is inappropriate for the overwhelming majority of residents, it accurately captures an important aspect of home ownership for a more affluent minority.

Security of Occupancy

Legal Protections. Mobility is very high in the United States, much higher than in most industrialized countries. It is estimated that one out of five households moves each year. To what extent such moves are voluntary is difficult to estimate; no doubt the overwhelming majority are. But security of occupancy is not guaranteed to most residents.

Security of occupancy is governed by the varying laws of the fifty states. For tenants, the historic imbalance that gave landlords the power to evict without requiring any reason, and with very limited notice, has been slowly adjusted since World War I to provide a set of limited protections for tenants in many states. Although only in the few jurisdictions having rent regulation is there any requirement that a landlord provide a justification for an eviction, in most states with or without rent regulations, tenants are entitled to notice of between one and six months, often depending on the grounds for eviction—eviction for non-payment of rent generally requiring the least notice. Courts have also frequently

Figure 10.1
Homeowner Deductions and Assisted Housing Payments, United States, 1977–1986

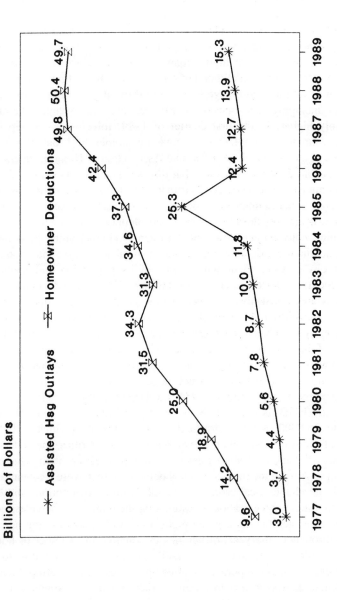

Billions of Dollars

✳ **Assisted Hsg Outlays**   ◁ **Homeowner Deductions**

Note: 1985 outlays reflected change to
capital financing of some already funded
public housing, not additional units.

Source: Courtesy of Cushing N. Dolbeare, Consultant on Housing and Public Policy, based on federal budget data compiled by
her for the Low Income Housing Information Service, Washington, D.C.

considered the situation of the tenants and their opportunities to find alternate accommodations in deciding the length of time to require before an actual eviction would be ordered. The general political climate often plays a role in such decisions.[13]

Although homeowners are relatively more secure in occupancy than tenants, they are potentially vulnerable to eviction if there is a mortgage foreclosure. Mortgage delinquencies are higher than at any time since the 1930s with a consequent increase in the likelihood of foreclosure.[14] In the first quarter of 1989, 4.6 percent of all home mortgage loans were thirty days or more past due, and in the high-unemployment states of the Midwest and Mid-Atlantic, the rate was considerably higher. In the first quarter of 1989, foreclosure—a step lenders generally resort to most reluctantly—took the homes of 1 out of every 345 mortgagees in the United States (National Association of Home Builders 1989).

Displacement. Best estimates are that displacement affects some 2.5 million Americans annually (LeGates and Hartman 1981). The reasons run the gamut: gentrification, undermaintenance, formal eviction, arson, unaffordable rent increases, mortgage foreclosures, property-tax delinquency, speculation in land and buildings, conversion of low-rent apartments to luxury units, condominiums or nonresidential uses, demolition, "planned shrinkage" (i.e., intentional withdrawal of city services to decant an area of its population and ready it for redevelopment), historic preservation (Hartman, Keating, and LeGates 1982). The victims are almost always lower-income persons, with a disproportionate number of nonwhites and elderly (LeGates and Hartman 1981). Legislation has been frequently introduced in Congress to protect displacees, but apart from the provisions of the Uniform Relocation Act, which requires that replacement housing be found for those directly displaced on-site from certain federally aided activities only, such legislation has not passed.

Homelessness. In the spring of 1984, the Department of Housing and Urban Development (HUD) issued a study estimating the number of homeless at from 250,000 to 350,000, a figure drastically below previous estimates (U.S. Department of Housing and Urban Development 1984). Critics charged political motivations—the administration's desire to minimize the problem—and shoddy methodology. Among the methodological defects charged were frequent reliance on patently unreliable local estimates, use of doubtful assumptions and extrapolation techniques, concentration on estimating the number of homeless seeking or using shelter facilities on a given night instead of estimating the number of homeless throughout the year, difficulties in counting the number of homeless who do not seek out formal shelter facilities, inadequate attention to "prehomelessness" such as temporary doubling up, and use of a "metropolitan area" definition that skewed results to minimize the final figure (Appelbaum 1984). The House subcommittee on Housing and Community Development held hearings on the HUD report on May 24, 1984.

All agree that those showing up at overnight emergency shelters today represent a full range of household types, ages, and races; no longer are only derelicts and alcoholics among the homeless. Causes include a variety of interacting factors, including poverty, unemployment, the deinstitutionalization of mentally disturbed persons, reduction of government benefit programs, and the loss of low-rent housing (Marcuse 1989).

Equality: Race and Gender

Housing issues today include more than inadequate, insecure, or unaffordable housing conditions. "Housing . . . is much more than shelter: it provides social status, access to jobs, education and other services, a framework for the conduct of household work, and a way of structuring economic, social and political relationships" (Achtenberg and Marcuse 1983, 207). Housing difficulties thus can have repercussions that go beyond the absence of decent shelter. This is particularly true of women, members of minority groups, and certain other particularly vulnerable groups. Minorities are held back educationally and in terms of employment opportunities as well as countless other ways by inadequate and segregated housing. Women tend to be confined to the traditional division of labor within the family and to limited labor-force participation, in part as a result of housing design and location (Hayden 1981). Housing patterns tend to keep classes, races, and subcultures separate and often antagonistic. "In this way, the housing crisis today expresses and perpetuates the economic and social divisions that exist within the society as a whole" (Achtenberg and Marcuse 1983).

Minorities face significantly more severe housing problems than the rest of the population. On all standard measures of housing conditions (affordability, physical inadequacy, overcrowding, and rates of home ownership), blacks and other minorities are consistently found to be worse off than whites. For certain minority groups, such as Native Americans and Hispanics, housing conditions are among the worst in the nation. Nearly one-fourth of all Hispanic and Native American households live in substandard housing; more than half of Native American families living in reservation areas inhabit substandard housing (Treuer 1982). Despite passage of the 1968 Civil Rights Act, discrimination based on race or ethnicity is still widely practiced and severely limits housing opportunities for minorities (Goering 1986).

Female-headed households also tend to suffer greater housing problems than the average household. For instance, 10 percent live in housing officially rated as inadequate, as opposed to 7.5 percent of all households (President's Commission on Housing 1982, 9). Even among higher-income households, suburban single-family homes are constraining for many women, limiting their economic and social opportunities and leaving them vulnerable to sexist patterns throughout their daily lives. For poor and single women with children, the problems are the most severe; housing standards in the United States today do not consider day care, nurseries, or even playgrounds essential elements of any housing development, although the campaign for them is vigorous and ongoing. Best estimates are that 25 percent of all rental units will not even admit households with children as tenants, as a matter of standard rental procedures (Van Vliet— 1988).

THE PRIVATE HOUSING INDUSTRY

Private is hardly an accurate term to describe the system of housing provision in the United States, even though more than 97 percent of all housing is privately owned and an even higher percentage privately built.[15] A private housing industry indeed exists and is the dominant force in the housing supply system, but it operates within, and is dependent on, governmental action at every step of the housing-provision process. The laying out and paving of streets; the supply of water; sewage disposal; utility provision (sometimes directly public, more often publicly regulated); building codes; zoning restrictions; health, fire, and safety codes; standards for materials; regulation of labor as to wages, hours, conditions of work, and safety standards; mortgage insurance; the financing and regulation of financial institutions; direct research and development; the setting of industrial and materials standards; the control of imports; the provision of those public services and facilities without which most persons would not be able to remain in occupancy of housing (schools, fire protection, sanitation pick-ups, and so on); the regulation of tenancy, including eviction controls, requirements, or prohibitions as to relations between landlord and tenant; mortgage foreclosure laws—all of these things are public activities.

''Private market'' and ''public intervention'' are thus inappropriate ways of dividing a discussion of the functioning of the U.S. housing system. The primary division is between the private profit-motivated (we consider nonprofits separately below) housing industry, on the one hand, and users or consumers of housing, on the other hand. Private producers and owners and private users interact with each other both in the private market and in the public arena, and governmental policies, like market changes, are largely a result of those interactions (see below, ''The Role of Government: History''). The major actors, their institutional forms, and their respective roles are described below.

The Construction Industry

The construction industry as a whole accounts for a significant part of the national income of the United States: 4.85 percent in 1987, down from a high of 5.6 percent in 1972 (U.S. Bureau of the Census 1986, 437). Residential construction accounts for between one-third and one-half of the value of all new construction put in place.[16] The overwhelming bulk of that residential construction is in single-family houses: between 70 and 85 percent in value, year in and year out (U.S. Bureau of the Census 1986, 722).

Although the aggregate size of the housing construction industry is substantial, its rate of growth has lagged behind that of the economy as a whole in the period since 1970 and certainly behind the growth sectors of the economy. Construction grew at three-quarters the rate of growth of the economy as a whole, about the same rate as manufacturing, two-thirds the rate of the service sector as a whole, and one-half the rate of health or legal services (U.S. Bureau of the Census 1986, 437). Employment in construction dropped from 5.4 percent of all employment in 1960 to 4.8 percent in 1985 (p. 410).

The industry has often been considered backward not only in its rate of growth but also in its organization and its use of technology.[17] As to rationalization, it has frequently been considered a fragmented industry, dominated by individual proprietors who stand to an efficient construction firm as mom and pop grocery stores stand to a supermarket chain. The facts suggest the picture is oversimplified. It is not, in fact, all small independents, although its degree of concentration is less than that of manufacturing as a whole. Of active corporations in construction in 1982, the largest firms (those with receipts of $10,000,000 or more) comprised 1.3 percent of the total but accounted for 39 percent of all receipts.[18] For all manufacturing, firms of similar size constituted 5 percent of all firms and accounted for 89 percent of all receipts. The modus operandi of the construction business makes number of employees a weak measure of volume of business, since subcontractors are so often used. Contractors who built twenty-five or fewer homes a year built only 13 percent of all single-family houses, many of the firms building more than that number and doing it largely through subcontractors rather than with their own work force (Sumichrast, Ahluwalia, and Sheehan 1979). Thus the degree of concentration is significant.

The technological development of housing construction, similarly, is low compared to many industries but hardly insignificant. The "capital-labor" ratio in construction is 4.3; in electrical machinery it is 12.0, in finance and insurance 19.5, in petroleum 103.0, in public utilities 170.8; only in apparel, with 4.0, is it lower, of all the major industry classifications (U.S. Bureau of the Census 1986, 528). But those figures relate primarily to the actual work of the "construction" component of the house-building industry, that is, the on-site activities. That component is a relatively small part of the final cost of housing; land acquisition, development, materials, financing, and professional services account for far more. (See table 10.8.)

Thus industrialization of on-site construction, for example, by greater use of factory-built modules, would, if it reduced the cost of on-site labor by 25 percent (considered a high figure by most commentators), only reduce the cost to the ultimate user by 2.5 percent. Even that reduction assumes an inflexible interest figure, included above under "debt retirement"; a 1 percent reduction in the interest rate is likely to produce a greater net savings to the end user than a 25 percent reduction in on-site labor costs.

As one commentator summarized the situation, "the existing construction industry is currently far more industrialized than one might think. . . . It would be unwise to expect to lower housing costs through the industrialization of the housebuilding process" (Stegman 1973).[19]

Mobile homes, once seen as the cure-all for increasing the supply of low-cost

Table 10.8
Costs of Housing Construction, United States (In Percentages)

	Percent
On-site wages	10
Materials and equipment	19
Profit and overhead	7
Improved land	13
Miscellaneous	3
	53
Debt retirement (inc. interest)	53
Real Property taxes	26
Utilities	16
Maintenance	5
	100%

Source: Figures are based on studies by McGraw-Hill, 1968, for the Kaiser Commission and reworked for this table.

housing, have found a steady niche for themselves in the U.S. housing system but at a much lower level than anticipated. At the highpoint of optimism about factory-built housing, with the U.S. Department of Housing and Urban Development putting major resources into its Operation Breakthrough to stimulate research and development and market aggregation for more efficient and economical housing production, mobile-home manufacturers succeeded in producing 576,000 homes in one year and accounting for one-third of all new single-family home sales; since that time their market share has varied, falling to less than 20 percent of that amount, although by 1981 it was back up to 35 percent (President's Commission on Urban Housing 1982, 85). (Table 10.9 shows the trends.) Both the price and the quality of these units ranks them near the bottom of what is being produced today; their sales are heavily concentrated in the southern states, where climatic conditions are less harsh than farther north. Their lesser durability reduces their cost advantages; financing for mobile homes is more often based on a ten-year depreciation schedule, thus increasing monthly costs compared to payments based on the more than thirty years anticipated for a conventionally built home. Although manufactured housing may bring new units within affordable prices for some households, and improvements in construction techniques, zoning practices, and tenure arrangement could improve quality and security, many see an emphasis on factory-built housing to meet low-income housing needs today as an attempt to lower standards for housing construction rather than increase its efficiency.

Table 10.9
Mobile Home Units Shipped, United States, 1956–1987

Year	Mobile Homes Shipped	Year	Mobile Homes Shipped
1956	125,000	1972	576,000
1957	119,000	1973	567,000
1958	102,000	1974	329,000
1959	121,000	1975	213,000
1960	104,000	1976	246,000
1961	90,000	1977	277,000
1962	118,000	1978	276,000
1963	151,000	1979	279,900
1964	191,000	1980	233,700
1965	216,000	1981	229,200
1966	217,000	1982	234,100
1967	240,000	1983	278,100
1968	317,950	1984	287,900
1969	412,690	1985	283,400
1970	401,000	1986	256,100
1971	497,000	1987	239,200

Source: U.S. Bureau of the Census, *Construction Reports*, Series C–20.
Notes: Units shipped, to 1978; units placed, from 1979. The difference in figures is not significant.

Finance

The financing of real estate transactions through mortgages is a major claim on credit markets in the United States. Total debt outstanding on residential mortgages sky-rocketed from $29.1 billion in 1946 to $2,162 billion in 1987.[20] Some commentators, pointing out that mortgage debt in this period has gone from 13.5 percent of the gross national product to 41.4 percent in 1980 (it dropped to 37.7 percent in 1984 [U.S. Bureau of the Census 1986, 432, 501]), have seen the pattern as leading to financial crisis and the brink of collapse for the financial system (Stone 1986, 41–67, 53–54). On the other hand, "other private credit" went up in parallel orders of magnitude, and consumer credit went up one and a half times as fast, going from 30 percent of mortgage debt in 1946 to 44 percent in 1985 (Stone 1986, 51; U.S. Bureau of the Census, 1986, 501–2). If the escalating use of credit by consumers (or government) is indeed leading to a crisis, it is not clear that expenditures for housing are a significant cause of that danger. Since the Tax Reform Act of 1986 has made other forms of interest nondeductible, we may see a shift to mortgage borrowing, with its interest remaining deductible, to finance expenditures or investments in fact having nothing to do with housing at all.

For many years, public policy had accorded a preferred position to mortgage lending. Under the complex system of government regulation and insurance established early in the New Deal in partial response to the widespread foreclosures following the Great Depression, thrift institutions—savings and loan associations, primarily—were permitted to pay a slightly higher interest rate on savings and given credit and deposit insurance protection, in return for a limitation of their lending activities to mortgage loans.[21] Through 1984 thrift institutions lent in general as much money for home mortgages as all other private financial institutions combined (U.S. Bureau of the Census 1988).

Mortgage insurance, administered by the Federal Housing Administration and the Veterans Administration, simply provides that if the purchaser of a housing unit is not able to repay a mortgage loan from a private bank or other lending institution, the FHA or the VA will make the repayment. One-half of 1 percent is charged a borrower as a fee for this insurance, and the proceeds of these fees are placed in a special insurance account. To date, the account is solvent, and no net governmental subsidies have been involved. It exercises a major impact on housing, however, by increasing the safety and thus the availability of loans in the housing sector; because loans up to 95 percent of the value of a unit (for the VA; less for the FHA) can be insured, it has permitted many to purchase homes who otherwise might never have done so or at the least might have to wait until their own savings had accumulated much longer.

To provide an order of magnitude of the above two impacts, consider the following: Some 57.3 percent of all owner-occupied units—32,195,000 units— were mortgaged in 1985 (U.S. Bureau of the Census 1986, 737). Of these units, about 24 percent had mortgages insured by either the FHA or the VA in 1985. The contribution of federal insurance is much less in the rental area: here only 20 percent of all units have insured mortgages. The extent to which government insurance is used depends directly on what the problems are in getting conventional—noninsured—mortgages: when money was scarce, as in the immediate postwar years, federally insured mortgages covered more than half of all new single-family houses sold; in more normal years, they have run between 20 and 40 percent; in 1985, they were 32 percent (1985, 728).

Land

The use of land is less regulated in the United States than in almost any of the other private market systems with developed economies (see "Planning, Zoning, and Land-Use Controls"). In much of the country, no governmental regulation controls the use of land at all, and only the private law of nuisance restrains the forms of exploitation. Whereas 10 million acres of land are currently in urban use (of 1,933,628,800 in the coterminous United States (1985, 6; estimates calculated differently show 2,265,000,000, p. 192) another 10 million acres or so are withdrawn from other uses, "ripening for active urban use" (Ackerman et al. 1962, 9), and that 20 million figure is expected to double by 2000. Between 1959 and 1974 land in urban areas increased by 46 percent and almost doubled between 1960 and 1980 (1985, 195).

Speculation in land is thus a major industry. In suburban areas, a doubling of prices in five years is not uncommon, and even land in the arid deserts of the

Southwest is bought and sold like shares of stock, sometimes with misrepresentations amounting to fraud, always with the hope of mammoth profits (Downie 1974; Feagin 1986). Although speculation is a consequence, rather than a cause, of the long-term rise in land prices, the minimally regulated use of land makes it one of the largest, and the most rapidly rising, components of housing cost in the United States.[22] The Kaiser Commission, in 1968, found that the site cost for a new FHA-insured home increased by 264 percent, rising from 12 to 20 percent of total house price between 1950 and 1967. At the same time, the size of the average lot decreased. Between 1967 and 1972, the price went up another 58 percent.[23] The Kaiser Commission found land the "fastest-rising element" of all major housing costs in 1968 (President's Committee 1968, 140); the President's Commission on Housing confirmed that finding fifteen years later (1982, 181).

Users

Consumers of housing have never organized effectively at the national level.[24] However, owner–occupants are a very potent political force in local and state politics in three major areas: first, decisions affecting local taxation, which, because such taxes are largely levied on real property, affect them directly; thus homeowners are behind many of the recent movements to put constitutional limitations on the ability of local or state government to levy taxes. Second, homeowners in many communities have fought to maintain the homogeneous, and thus often the exclusive, character of their communities. Such actions have often resulted in direct opposition to the movement of blacks and other minorities into suburban communities and account for restrictive economic zoning—for instance, by requiring four-acre lots for each private house—that is frequently found in wealthier suburban communities.[25] Homeowners, through community clubs and neighborhood associations, have been active in opposing developments that they believe will adversely affect their environment and property values in their neighborhoods. The projects opposed range from toxic waste dumps to shelters for the homeless.

Tenants have been a much more volatile force on the housing scene in the United States. No national organization of tenants has ever achieved stability or long-term effectiveness, although in the late 1960s the National Tenant Organization (see Marcuse 1971b) played a significant role in improving conditions for public housing tenants, and the National Tenants Union today organizes around certain national issues with some success. It helped defeat efforts to pass federal legislation restricting local rights to implement rent-control laws, for instance.

At the local level, there have been a few periods of high tenant militancy: after World War I, for instance, or during the ghetto rebellions in the mid- and late 1960s (Lawson and Naison 1986; Heskin 1983). But by and large tenants have not been a major political factor on the housing scene.[26]

THE ROLE OF GOVERNMENT: HISTORY

Government is not an independent force "intervening" in the housing market; its activities are integral to that market. Even in the days of the pioneers building log cabins with their own hands and the help of their neighbors, government was involved in the assignment, and then the protection, of title to the land on which those cabins were built. Courts created by government protect rights established by government; government agencies build roads and sewers, provide water, franchise electricity and gas, regulate construction, limit occupancy and uses, and tax and subsidize the values created; indeed, public activity itself creates much of the value of what is privately owned.[27]

A brief history of governmental action affecting housing in the United States shows how wrong the view is that government acts autonomously, that there is a central core of benevolence dictating governmental actions subject to the pressures of plural interest groups yet seeking the resolution of social problems as best it can. That history is a history of conflicts; in the postwar period, those conflicts might be summarized as follows:

1. In the economic sphere, over efforts to increase the profits of business activity in general, by ensuring the housing and the social discipline necessary for the essential work force, over controlling the cost of housing so as to avoid an undesirable upward pressure on wages, and over the allocation of resources and credit (and thus profits) among the various sectors of the economy, as opposed to efforts to improve the real standard of living of workers

2. In the political sphere, over efforts to use housing to support the political status quo and avoid political unrest growing out of dissatisfaction with housing, as opposed to demands for adequate housing as a political or civil right

3. Within the housing industry, over the magnitude and the division of profits among various groups directly involved in the production of housing, reflected in the prices of housing and its components, as opposed to the search for increased benefits from the use of housing

4. Over the uses and the amenities of housing, involving, among other issues, conflicts over location, standards, social patterns, and the provision of collective facilities and services, among the users of housing

These conflicts have influenced both private and public actions in the housing sector. Whether the resolution of any given conflict finds its expression in a private market arrangement or in a governmental action depends very much on which strategy best serves the interests of which party. The history of U.S. housing policies illustrates these points.

The Initial Postwar Years

The initial post–World War II years represent a fascinating study in "policy making," for they are a period in which the explicit debate on housing policies was more vigorous, deeper, more varied, more openly engaged in, than at any other period in the nation's history (with the possible exception of the early New Deal or the period of conflict in the mid–1960s)—yet what actually happened was only marginally affected by the debate and much more determined by the evolution of nonhousing-oriented political strategy and macrolevel economic forces.

The debate was so vigorous because the war had opened the door to new demands and new opportunities. The political stance of the returning veterans, the influence of the wartime alliance with socialist countries, the political ferment in Europe and throughout the world, the movement of blacks to urban areas and into the essential industrial labor force, the availability of resources at a level not approached since the Great Depression to deal with issues not tackled for fifteen years—all of these things created a tremendous and vocal ferment, including debates on housing policy both inside and outside the halls of Congress.

The debate concerned a number of issues that would appear central to housing policy: the nature and extent of public housing; the attitude to redevelopment, slum clearance, and rehabilitation; the mechanisms of housing financing; policies toward racial segregation; and generally the nature and extent of the government's role. The Housing Act of 1949 seemed to be the resolution of these debates. It reestablished and refunded public housing; it started (and created the legal mechanisms for) redevelopment of central city areas and slum clearance; it built a vast Veterans Administration and Federal Housing Administration mortgage insurance program aimed primarily at single-family owner-occupied housing. So it seemed to set major policy directions for some time to come as a result of extensive and democratic deliberations.

Yet the fact is that the major direction of policy (and the actual results of the 1949 act) were set by different factors. The two major ones were, first, on the economic front, the need for a major expansion of the internal market to use the productive capacity, and to absorb the buying power, built up during the war.[28] The private housing industry, from builders to financiers, from land developers to craft unions, were well served by the trend; only central city interests did not enjoy a piece of the action. Their efforts to get into the game dominated much of the conflict around housing policies for the next two decades, at the end interacting with even more powerful forces—economic changes in the nature of business activity and political changes in central city constituencies—to produce the conflicts of the mid–1960s.

The second major force determining the events of the post–1949 period was the political strategy chosen by the national political leadership to deal with the aspirations and alternatives evoked by the war. Winston Churchill's Fulton, Missouri, speech sounding the keynotes for the Cold War as international policy and Joseph McCarthy's unleashing of political repression at home represented the decision to put down, rather than conciliate, potential opposition. The pie seemed big enough and growing rapidly enough to buy off the veterans and many blacks. The level of funding of public housing, more generally the resources committed to pursue the goal of "a decent home in a suitable living environment for every American family" so ringingly proclaimed in the 1949 act, did not have to be very high if this was the approach. The carrots were VA mortgages, rising incomes to support suburbanization, and some improvement in absolute living conditions for minority groups; the sticks were political repression of the Left and fear-sustained integration of the moderates. The combination worked, and large state-assembled resources did not have to be redistributed progressively to achieve the goals. The tensions that lead to the welfare states of many European countries were only feebly reflected in the United States.

Central city interests did not initially come out well in this process. The redevelopment provisions of the 1949 act were limited in scope, clumsy in execution, and sparsely funded. The tie-in to the new housing provision was unwelcome; what downtown interests wanted was the means to clear land of unprofitable uses and assemble it for more profitable use. They wanted to take advantage of pent-up demand and to be able to adapt to changes in the nature of that demand because of shifts in modes of production and its spatial needs.

The 1954 Housing Act, with its much more flexible provisions for urban renewal and its much greater funding, provided the answer. In general, as one of the act's chief architects later described it, "the legislation was enacted with the purpose of placing greater reliance on private rather than governmental action." For central cities, it "was designed to place the major responsibility for development upon the private sector" (Cole 1979, 285).[29] It gave statutory support to the idea that urban renewal should contribute to improved housing by requiring, among other things, a workable program from each city wanting funds showing how such improvements would be brought about. But the "predominantly residential" requirement was but one of a number of loopholes permitting the result to vary substantially from the legislative declaration: areas being cleared were required only to be "predominantly" residential, and even this link to the goal of improving housing was interpreted flexibly to favor commercial redevelopment. Finally, a specific exception of 10 percent was provided from the residential requirement, and the figure was gradually increased until it reached 35 percent in 1965. It was expanded even farther by administrative manipulation (astute drawing of boundaries, counting questionable residential units, and so on). Pressures from the industry steadily weakened the housing link of urban renewal until it became transparently a central business district development game. Only strong countervailing pressures from two directions changed the situation.

Suburbanization (c. 1950–1964)

Suburbanization was the dominant trend in housing development and the dominant beneficiary of federal activities during the two decades following World War II. The encouragement of suburbanization was not the result of a "housing policy" but rather of a whole set of policies that came together to produce such a result. They included the massive construction subsidized out of the Highway Trust Fund, which facilitated suburban residents' access both to central city jobs and to jobs on the metropolitan fringe, the tax policies favoring home ownership, FHA and VA mortgage insurance programs, and propagation of the concept that the single-family suburban home was the ideal form of housing for the American family. The housing industry was a major driving force behind this policy; at the local level "pro-growth coalitions" saw to it that loose zoning and building regulations permitted the private market to build virtually wherever it wished (Mollenkopf 1975, 1983; Molotch 1976). The result was an unprecedented spate of new, single-family, owner-occupied housing construction that brought the percentage of U.S. owner occupancy from 43.6 percent in 1940 to 61.9 percent in 1960 (see table 10.6). The suburban proportion of the population in metropolitan areas similarly rose from 41.5 percent in 1950 to 48.6 percent in 1960 to 54.2 percent in 1970 (calculated from U.S. Bureau of the Census 1975, 40) and to 57.8 percent in 1980 (see U.S. Bureau of the Census 1986, 19).

Conflict and Revolt (c. 1964–1968)

The events that led up to the widespread unrest of the mid–1960s have been well recounted elsewhere (see Cloward and Piven 1972). The underlying changes in the forms of production, the types of jobs available, the educational system required to maintain incentives and productivity, the inequities in the distribution of the benefits of progress, all produced more or less violent and deep-seated confrontations in countries around the globe. The particularly urban and racial characteristics of the events in the United States distinguished them to some extent from those in most other countries. The changing composition and political stance of central city residents were critical to the events in the United States in the mid–1960s. Direct community resistance to the displacement caused by urban renewal was a significant part of the unrest. The civil rights movement and the ghetto revolts, from Watts in Los Angeles in 1965 to Detroit in 1968, shook up the establishment; the more ideological aspects of the new Left played a less decisive role here than elsewhere. The massive unrest produced the Civil Rights Act of 1964, the Demonstration Cities (later, for obvious reasons, renamed Model Cities) Act of 1966, and the comprehensive Housing Act of 1968, with its expanded funding for assisted housing construction and rehabilitation, development of new programs to meet groups and situations not touched earlier, changes in financing mechanisms, guarantees, and subsidies to reach lower-income households. The establishment of the cabinet-level Department of Housing and Urban Development in 1965, to replace the lower-level Housing and Home Finance Agency, was a symptom of the change in leadership attention to housing problems.

But the unrest of the 1960s never took solid political form. Although it dealt directly with governmental decision-making processes and challenged the distribution of political power, it was negative; no alternative organized force was generated that tried to substitute itself for the holders of formal power. The ghetto revolts lacked organization or ideology of their own; their spontaneous character was both their strength and their weakness. The working class did not enter the fray directly, even though parts of it—the public sector employees and their unions especially—benefited from it mightily. The 1960s found themselves increasingly in the anti-Vietnam War campaigns of the early 1970s and, because of weak organization, never returned to their earlier concerns. So the unrest of the mid–1960s did not produce a powerful continuing force for change in the direction in which it seemed to be heading.

Transition (c. 1969–1973)

The first Nixon administration (1969–1972), in the transitional period from unrest to response, witnessed an uncertainty as to the real balance of forces. The inclinations of the conservative national leadership, as represented by the Republican party, were clearly toward a return to the forcible putting down of the riots and a cessation of governmental programs in housing, particularly those with a redistributive component. Yet the momentum generated by the earlier period was not that easy to stop, and the certainty of stability at first not that clear. Thus in the early Nixon years, despite an explicit conservative orientation, public housing production was at its post–1950 peak (see table 10.10). Economic developments—the recession of 1969, the ending of the Vietnam War and confrontation with the shortages it had created, a weakened international economic position, all creating strong incentives for heightened government investment in stability-promoting domestic programs—perhaps contributed even more to the continuing federal presence in housing than did political considerations.

Response (c. 1972–1978)

Nixon's safe reelection in 1972 signaled the solidification of a basic shift in strategy by the political and economic leadership. The moratorium on all federal housing programs decreed by Nixon on January 1, 1973, was a statement that political unrest was no longer to be feared. If it appeared, it would be put down by force if necessary. To the extent that state housing programs constituted a buying off of a potential political opposition in the ghettoes, they were no longer considered necessary, nor are they today. The housing industry's role in policy formation thus became dominant, although limited by the influence of other and often competing business interests.

The 1974 Housing and Community Development Act represents a set of housing policies in which the influence of housing industry interests are more clearly reflected than at any time since 1954. The dominant note is privatization—not that that note was new; state subsidies had always been a tiny portion of

Table 10.10
Public Housing Units Started, United States, 1949–1983

Year	Public Housing Starts	Year	Public Housing Starts
1937	5,520	1964	23,396
1938	2,665	1965	35,652
1939	35,188	1966	29,370
1940	47,386	1967	36,002
1941	44,754	1968	59,207
1942	21,155	1969	59,571
1943	3,840	1970	77,039
1944	3,643	1971	70,925
1945	1,561	1972	50,713
1946	146	1973	28,457
1947	1,190	1974	31,041
1948	488	1975	24,532
1949	1,025	1976	20,887
1950	16,157	1977	12,080
1951	82,054	1978	11,330
1952	56,386	1979	21,868
1953	38,881	1980	40,528
1954	17,786	1981	45,607
1955	8,993	1982	25,100
1956	1,914	1983	27,060
1957	14,492	1984	22,443
1958	25,443	1985	11,133
1959	15,979	1986	6,385
1960	26,613	1987	5,861
1961	28,459		
1962	26,858		
1963	24,408		

Source: Unpublished data, U.S. Department of Housing and Urban Development, Office of the Assistant Secretary for Public and Indian Housing.
Notes: Year = fiscal year. Includes Indian housing and acquisitions without rehabilitation. Does not include leased housing.

expenditures on housing, and the funneling of those subsidies had always been through the private sector, as far as possible. Even redistributive programs could be accepted if there was enough private profit in them. The greater "popularity" of public housing after the introduction of turnkey development in 1966, by which private developers rather than public housing authorities initiated and executed the production of public housing, is an example; the acceptance of Section 236 when its tax advantages for limited-dividend private developers became apparent is another. The 1974 act placed the private sector formally on the throne, even if it was not until the Reagan administration that it received its full purple robes, crown, and scepter.

The Community Development Block Grant (CDBG) program and the Section 8 housing program were the two major contributions of the 1974 act. The CDBGs, which gave lump-sum grants to municipalities to spend according to their own priorities within certain very general federal guidelines, represented a limited political concession to the more urban-based leadership and constituencies that were to benefit from them. Funds were distributed according to a formula that reflected population, poverty, and age of housing stock (thus presumably reflecting need); the more urban consitituencies, and among them the older and "poorer" cities in particular, came out ahead. But the distribution *within* areas, study after study has shown, was much more regressive;[30] within the cities receiving funds, producer interests and the better-off among the eligible areas received benefits disproportionate to their needs. The survival and probable ascendance of the Urban Development Action Grant (UDAG) type of funding, by which only those projects are subsidized that can also attract private capital, is symptomatic of the same trend toward a siphoning of benefits away from the most needy. Working-class, minority, youth, and elderly pressures have always been more effective at the federal level in the United States than at the state or local level in all but a few communities; the shift to decentralization represented by the CDBG program, supported by the Nixon administration and those of Carter and Reagan thereafter, reinforced a regressive shift of benefits.

The Section 8 housing program is the closest the United States has come to a housing-allowance program. Its existing housing component, under which a subsidy is extended for the rental of existing private units, is almost a pure demand-side subsidy. Even its arrangement for the financing of new construction and rehabilitation gives maximum scope to the private sector: ownership of the subsidized housing, management, tax benefits, choice of location, size, occupancy, are all subject only to limited government supervision, left in private hands. The explicit housing-allowance program, tentatively supported as an experiment by the Nixon administration and the housing program of all housing programs able to function with the least public controls on the private market, perhaps lost support only because of the problem of limiting its coverage. Funding for supply-side programs can be easily limited; projects are considered administratively, and when funding runs out, no new projects are built. But a housing-allowance program is logically an entitlement program, like welfare. Keeping it restricted, as the Section 8 program does, is difficult to justify. How could one give some of those eligible help and not others? One could hardly go by priority of application without having a riot on the lines waiting at the door to file. Even with Section 8 certificates this has been a problem.

It may well be that the 1974–1975 recession prevented the next logical step toward reprivatization from being taken at that time: the absolute termination of progressive federal subsidies in housing. But even under the presumptively more liberal Carter administration (1977–1980), levels of funding were reduced. The Reagan administration, in office since 1980, simply has gone further and faster down a road that had been entered at least eight years earlier. The political pressures for progressive housing policies have been written off as not worth bothering with. The housing industry as a whole is not of that much consequence to the Republican party, which has closer links to the military-industrial complex. Much of the housing industry—property owners, flexible lending institutions, speculators, realtors—benefited from inflation and was doing quite well without further federal assistance in any event. Builders looked to lower taxes, controlled interest rates, and diminished government regulation as the ways to increase profits. The cost of a federal program to build for low-income households, given both the high interest rates and the political complexion of the administration, seem so high as to make it not worth fighting for.

Gentrification (c. 1980–1988)

The major change accompanying the election of Ronald Reagan as president was thus not in the adoption of a newly conservative housing policy. What was new under Reagan was the triumph of unmitigated privatization as an ideology: the conception that government should, on principle, play the least possible role in the provision of housing, with the transfer of governmental roles to the private sector wherever possible. The ideological change does not represent the triumph of one idea over another or even the political victory of a particular person or party over another. Rather, it mirrors a change in the balance of political and economic forces. Those groups that protested massively in the 1960s, awakening concern and fear among both private and governmental leaders, were now seen as defeated, no longer to be feared. The type of individualized resistance represented by street crime, drugs, and vandalism could be seen, and dealt with, as "social problems," rather than as societal problems—or, more callously, simply allowed to run rampant but confined to inner cities, areas of no interest to a business leadership whose basis for power lay elsewhere.

Gentrification is an apt symbol, if hardly a complete description, of the most current phase of urban change (see Marcuse 1985a for a detailed definition and discussion of the process of gentrification itself). Much of the restructuring of cities, earlier attempted through urban renewal and met with strong protest, is today accomplished through private gentrification, with only minor risk of embarrassment. Redistributive programs, which twenty years ago evoked conservative protest and taxpayer resistance, can now be abandoned; funding for new public housing, for instance, is completely terminated. Private entrepreneurs, restless under the governmental regulation required to keep the public peace in the 1950s and 1960s, can now, in the view of the national administration, be let go about their business unrestrained, without concern for social consequences. The opposition of the administration to the legislative proposals presented by Representative Barney Frank, calling for tight guarantees of relocation for households displaced through federally supported urban projects, is a sharp example.

The two terms of the Reagan presidency reveal (1) a sharp decline in federal expenditures (table 10.8) for housing the poor in any form, (2) a conversion of existing programs of governmental supply to programs supporting private supply by subsidizing demand, and (3) the endorsement of unbridled gentrification, with its accompanying displacement of the poor.

There is always a significant lag between expenditures and construction; in terms of new commitments, both are at a post–1949 low. The cutback is not accounted for by a decline in need; to the contrary, if homelessness is taken as an indicator, the need for federal action is greater now than it has been at any time since the Great Depression (see above, "Security of Occupancy," *Homelessness*).

The privatization of those programs that survive was already called for in the Report of the President's Commission on Housing. That commission called for the conversion of all existing programs for the support of lower-income housing to a single "Housing Payments" program (1982, chapter 2)—a term interchangeable with "housing vouchers" or "housing allowances" in the current U.S. debate. The program is described below; its net result is to permit landlords to collect somewhat higher rents from some tenants and to remove any restraints on such rents that either the earlier Section 8 program, with its "fair market rents," or the housing-subsidy programs, with their direct setting of rents, might have had.

Gentrification, however, is the symbolic center of the new phase of federal policy. It is often the other side of abandonment: the decline of "effective demand" for one set of units at the "decaying" edges of the central city and the increase in the market for luxury units near the city center or in areas of particular environmental amenity feed each other (Marcuse 1985a, 1986). Both sides of the process are supported by current federal policies providing Urban Development Action Grants for "revitalization" but not providing subsidy funds directly for low-income housing provision or rehabilitation. Local government, obeying the same underlying pressures that determine federal actions, implements a policy of triage (see Starr 1976; Marcuse 1982), cutting off funds, services, and facilities in poor areas, and providing tax abatements, infrastructure, loans and guarantees, and direct financing in gentrifying ones.

THE ROLE OF GOVERNMENT: PROGRAMS

Federal Taxation

Federal "tax expenditures" for housing—reductions in taxes that would otherwise be paid—are the single largest subsidy of the federal government in the housing field. In 1985 the staff of the Congressional Joint Committee on Taxation estimated that permitting homeowners to deduct from their individual income taxes the interest they paid on mortgages on their homes involved a cost to the federal government of $25,460,000. Permitting the deduction of real property taxes resulted in a fluctuating cost of $9,640,000. Not taxing certain gains on

Table 10.11
Households and Housing Subsidies (Tax and Direct), by Household Income,
United States, 1984

Income Household	Distribution		Monthly Average
	Households	Subsidies	
Under $10,000	25.7%	17.8%	$48
$10,000-20,000	25.8%	8.2	33
$20,000-30,000	18.9%	12.3	15
$30,000-50,000	20.0%	31.8	77
Over $50,000	9.6%	29.9	152

Source: Dolbeare, 1988.

sales of home (for the elderly, or where a subsequent purchase took place) involved a loss to the government of another $5,625,000,000.[31]

To provide a perspective on these figures, the total amount proposed by President Reagan to be spent in fiscal 1986 on all HUD Assisted Housing (social housing) was $1.5 billion, and the amount proposed for all Community Development activities at the federal level was $3.2 billion (Senate Subcommittee 1985, 1). The net distributional consequences of these tax and subsidy policies are shown in Table 10.11.

The Tax Reform Act of 1986 included a Low Income Housing Credit, hard fought for by low-income housing advocates as the only realistic policy to obtain financial assistance for low-income housing out of a very conservative administration. It permits an offset against income taxes (a tax credit) for eligible taxpayers of 9 percent of construction or rehabilitation costs for each of ten years for housing allocated to persons with incomes below 50 percent of the median, or 4 percent each year if allocated to persons with incomes below 60 percent of the median. Total credits are limited to $1.25 per capita. Its full results will not be known for some time; its quantitative impact is not likely to be large. New York City, for example, hopes to rehabilitate perhaps 2,000 units over several years with the credits (*New York Times*, 1988, 8/1); the estimated need in the city is for 678,000 units (Felstein and Stegman 1987, 7).

Public Housing

The public housing program, dating back legislatively to the United States Housing Act of 1937, provided for local housing authorities to be established by municipalities or counties (under state-enabling legislation), which were then authorized to borrow money by issuing tax-free bonds for the construction of housing to be owned and operated by the authority. The federal government then enters into an Annual Contributions Contract with the local Housing Authority under which it agrees to pay the part of the interest and principal on these bonds that the local authority cannot pay out of the rents it collects. Strict income

Table 10.12
Public Housing Units Construction Reservations (Units), United States, 1979–1985

1979	55,000
1980	37,000
1981	36,000
1982	12,000
1983	3,000
1984	8,000
1985	7,000

Source: Senate Subcommittee on Housing and Urban Affairs, 1985

limits are placed on eligibility for admission to public housing—80 percent of the median income for the area—and rents are fixed at a percentage of that income, earlier 25 percent but increased to 30 percent by the Reagan administration. At its inception, rents had been fixed first, at a level low enough not to compete with private enterprise, and income limitations were based on those rents. Conceived as a program in which the capital costs of a project would be subsidized but operating costs borne by the tenants (on the model of many European programs, the Gemeindebauten of Vienna, for instance), declining real incomes and rising costs of utilities, maintenance, and repairs created deficits for many authorities in the late 1960s, and in 1969 Congress, in the Brooke Amendments, undertook also to cover local operating deficits.

Public housing has never been popular with the middle class and has always been under attack from the Right as "creeping socialism." Standards were thus always kept very low, in design, amenities, and services, and residence in public housing is by and large considered undesirable. Those occupying it are stigmatized and looked down upon in many quarters. About 1.3 million units of public housing are now occupied in the United States, about 1.5 percent of a total housing stock of about 92 million units (U.S. Bureau of the Census 1988).

The Reagan administration has effectively halted all new construction under the program. The number of units for which construction funds were reserved in the past few years is shown in Table 10.12.

Other Social Housing Provision

Social housing managed by nonprofits has been a significant feature of the American housing scene only since 1968. Although several earlier programs had also permitted nonprofit or limited dividend sponsors to build and manage subsidized housing for lower-income groups, in 1968 the Section 236 program (rental) provided for a much greater role for nongovernmental organizations. (The Section 235 program, adopted at the same time, applied the same type of subsidy of interest rates to housing sold to lower-income households for owner occupancy.) In return for limiting profits, they were made eligible for federal guarantees on loans up to 100 percent of cost (for nonprofits) or 95 percent of cost (for limited dividend firms) with a commitment to subsidize the interest rate down to 1 percent to the extent necessary to enable households of lower income to afford the resulting rents within a stated percentage of their income. Eligibility for occupancy was limited to low- and moderate-income households: those with incomes low enough so that they needed the interest subsidies to afford the unit but high enough so that they could pay the resulting costs. Between the Section 236 program and its predecessors (Section 221 [d] [3] and the Rent Supplement program) some 688,238 rental units were actually built and occupied, 192,214 by nonprofits and 496,024, by profit-motivated limited dividends (Achtenberg 1989, exhibit 1.) Four hundred eighty-eight thousand, eight hundred and fifty-three units were built and sold under the Section 235 program (Low-Income Housing Information Service (LIMIS) 1989, table 3; U.S. Department of Housing and Urban Development (HUD) 1979, table A–36). Thus for a time, more housing was built under these programs than under public housing proper. (For urban renewal and rehabilitation programs, see below, "Local Government Actions.")

Housing Allowances and Demand-Side Subsidies

All of the above social housing programs were largely replaced by the Section 8 program in 1974. In part, this was because of various criticisms associated with each of these programs. Public housing, deliberately held to minimal standards and first de jure, then de facto, segregated, had never had a strong constituency behind it. The Section 235 program faced problems of quality and of nonpayment by purchasers who very likely should never had been in the ownership market to begin with but were convinced to enter it by aggressive real estate developers and builders who profited from each sale and had no further responsibilities for the housing they sold. Section 236 projects faced problems of amateur management, arrearages, and marketing, because of the tight range of incomes from which they could draw tenants. President Nixon commissioned a report to survey these and other difficulties at the beginning of his second term in office (U.S. Department of Housing and Urban Development 1974), but most observers believe he had already made up his mind to terminate them before the commission started its work, simply because they represented a social welfare approach to housing out of synchronization with his own conservative philosophy. Indeed, all of the criticisms set forth of the various existing programs could have been remedied by improvements in funding, administration, or guidelines, but the approach taken was rather to terminate and begin a different approach.

Under the new Section 8 program, the financing mechanism was different from any of these earlier programs. It hearkens back to the program for the leasing of existing privately owned units for public housing under Section 23 of the public housing legislation. Rather than paying the construction and some of the operating costs of publicly owned housing (as in the public housing program) or writing down the interest on private mortgages on units required to be rented or sold to lower-income households (as under sections 235 and 236), the Section 8 program authorized direct payments by the federal government to landlords who provided housing to low-income tenants, covering the difference between the "fair market rent" for that unit and rent paid by the tenants equivalent to 30 percent of their income. Maximum "fair market rents" were established for each municipality, tenants were certified eligible (having an income below 80 percent of the area's median) for the program by a local public agency (often a Housing Authority), and if an eligible tenant found a qualified unit, that is, in standard condition and of suitable size, within the permissible rent, the subsidy would come into effect and be payable to the landlord as long as the tenant occupied that unit and remained eligible. Originally intended to apply to existing units, it was expanded to cover substantially rehabilitated and newly constructed units also, with commitments running for up to fifteen years to the landlord as long as he or she found eligible tenants as occupants. Since its inception about 665,000 units have been newly built or substantially rehabilitated under the program, and another 1.1 million households participate in the existing housing part of the program. Thus those assisted by the program exceed by a small number those housed under the public housing program today, although public housing units are permanently part of the available low-income housing stock, whereas the commitment under Section 8 was originally at most for fifteen years, and that figure has now been lowered to five years.

The Reagan administration has undertaken to halt all new use of the Section 8 program and has proposed instead a system of "housing vouchers." Although Congress has refused to go along this year with a complete cessation of Section 8, funding has only been requested by the president for 12,100 net additional units (actually under the "voucher" program), and the future of the program is in substantial doubt.

State Government Actions

State government roles on housing are to be found in three areas: first, basic legislation-setting standards and, in a few cases, providing administrative mechanisms for the regulation of building and housing, generally applied at the local level. Examples include state building codes, eviction provisions, environmental standards, or labor regulations. Second, states have in the past twenty years in particular provided some assistance to low-, and even more to moderate-, income housing development, largely by way of assistance in financing through below-market-rate loans or loan guarantees. They have been effectuated through state-level Housing Finance Agencies, which have the power to issue bonds for housing purposes. New federal tax laws restrict the extent to which such bonds may be issued as tax-free instruments, but they remain a significant feature of the housing scene in the period of declining federal subsidies. In many states, such activities benefit primarily prospective homeowners, who are enabled to buy where without such assistance they would have rented. Finally, states have often pioneered in developing programs of support for housing that have then been adopted at the federal level. Although such experimental programs have never amounted to much quantitatively, they have provided a laboratory for innovation.

Local Government Actions

Local actions have in many ways more impact on the shape of housing in the United States than do federal ones. Legally, power to regulate land use lies with the states in the federal system and has been delegated by the states to the municipalities, with only limited state-level activities: to control supramunicipal environmental impacts, for instance, and to provide guidelines for what may be done in zoning or planning by localities. Localities, on the other hand, have and exercise very substantial powers to influence housing and land use. Much of the conflict around housing issues, therefore, is played out on the local rather than the state or national level.

Taxation. Real property taxes may constitute between 15 and 30 percent of the total cost of housing for a resident, running typically between 2 and 3 percent annually of the market value of a housing unit. (Their relationship to other housing costs is discussed above in "Price" and "The Initial Postwar Years.") The real property tax is the major source of revenue for most local (municipal, county, and special district) governments in the United States today; for city governments, it accounted for 52.1 percent of all revenues in 1983 (U.S. Department of Commerce 1986, 288) and has increased steadily from year to year, although as a percentage it has been moderately declining. It constituted, in 1983, fully 22.5 percent of all nonfederal sources of revenue and just over 10 percent of all taxes levied by all levels of government (U.S. Department of Commerce 1986, 264). Although economists disagree on the precise impact of such taxes, it seems clear that they are progressive through the middle range of incomes and thereafter become increasingly regressive.

In recent years, as the federal government's contribution to meeting lower-income households' housing needs has declined, local governments have been pressed to find programs and sources of revenue to make up the shortfall. General increases in property taxes have met voter resistance, but taxes contributing to public objectives have gained in popularity. Although the equity of abatements to stimulate housing production generally, or to assist commercial or industrial development, has been questioned, their use to stimulate construction or rehabilitation of properties to house lower-income families has come into widespread use.[32]

Other innovative approaches attempted by local governments range from rehabilitation and management of city-owned tax-foreclosed (abandoned) housing to below-market-rate loans to technical assistance and coordination of private housing activities, and assistance to self-help groups.[33] Public-private partnership is the public relations term often used to designate the various devices used to combine limited public funds with private profit-motivated activities in the hope of lowering the total costs of some housing below those that the private sector, without public action, would alone produce.

Rent Controls. Rent controls are authorized in only a few states—most prominently New York, New Jersey, California, Massachusetts, and the District of Columbia—and are in each case put into effect by local vote, pursuant to state-enabling legislation. Only New York City has consistently had some form of rent regulation since World War II. Both in it and in other cities, the actual impact of current controls is moderate. In most cities some form of vacancy decontrol or adjustment, in which a unit's rent can be set at an unregulated level when the current occupant moves out, exists. Part of the recent increase in condominium conversion may be accounted for by the desire of the owners of multifamily units, formerly built as rentals, to avoid the restrictions of rent control (for figures see Sternlieb and Hughes 1987, 126), although the desire to profit from the capitalization by the seller of tax advantages available to the occupant on the sale of a unit rather than its rental also plays a significant role.

The evidence on the actual impact of rent controls is fairly clear. They hold rentals down somewhat in areas in which scarcity would otherwise drive them up sharply. They do not hold rents down to levels that poorer tenants can afford. Rent-income ratios rise even in areas with strong controls. Landlords complain about a dampening effect on new construction from the existence of controls. Most new construction is at the upper end of the market and in any event exempt from control in every jurisdiction today. Other factors—interest rates, environmental controls, zoning—seem to have a much greater influence on the level of construction than do rent controls. Expenditures on maintenance might be expected to be constrained by limits on rental income; on the other hand, those expenditures are dictated by calculations addressed to maximizing long-term returns and may be independent of immediate income. Most studies find little relationship between rent regulation and maintenance and less between rent regulation and abandonment (Marcuse 1982). Landlords' returns are clearly higher without rent regulation than with it, or so landlords believe; otherwise they would not oppose regulation so hard; but most landlords probably continue to make a substantial return on equity regardless of regulation (see Marcuse 1986). Controversies about rent control generate much more heat than their demonstrable effects warrant, probably because they seem to challenge the ideological underpinnings on which trust in the private market rests (Marcuse 1986).

Landlord-Tenant Regulation. Landlord-tenant law in the United States originally relied on the two separate sets of common law rules: those governing interests in real property and those governing contracts. Under traditional real property law, tenants acquire an interest in property when they execute a lease. The transfer of that interest completes the landlord's obligations. Maintenance and upkeep, on the other hand, are a matter of contract; in the absence of a specific written provision, a landlord has no obligation to the tenant other than not interfering with the interest in the property granted the tenant at the time the lease is executed. Lack of maintenance, therefore, traditionally did not justify a symmetrical withholding of rent.

This unsatisfactory state of affairs has been largely modified by explicitly legislative provision in most states today. The market remains the most effective determinant of landlord and tenant behavior; in a loose market where supply exceeds demand, tenants' abilities to move out give tenants good bargaining power; in a tight market, the situation is reversed. For most lower-income tenants, the reality is a tight market. Under pressure from such tenants and those representing them, many states have now passed various measures setting forth minimum reciprocal obligations of tenant and landlord. These measures take various forms. Legislation providing for a landlord's warranty of habitability holds landlords to have warranted rented premises as suitable for occupation. Summary process and eviction laws provide accelerated means for a landlord to dispossess a tenant (accelerated in comparison to some earlier real property actions) but limit the grounds on which accelerated action is available and in some cases (where coupled with rent regulation) limit the grounds for any eviction. Other laws prohibit retaliatory evictions, in which an eviction is used to punish a tenant for complaining, for example, about building code violations. Rent withholding laws sometimes permit tenants to withhold rent if maintenance or repairs are not provided; in some states a receiver may be appointed by the courts to manage such property until it is repaired. The Uniform Residential Landlord and Tenants Act, drafted by the National Conference on Uniform State Laws, is an effort to bring states into a uniform scheme for regulating landlord-tenant relations but has not as yet achieved its goal.

Rehabilitation and Urban Renewal. Governmental efforts to aid directly in either the modernization or rehabilitation of existing housing units or in slum clearance and the assembly of land for new construction only date to after the end of World War II, even though site clearance for public housing and for highways had been used as a crude form of slum clearance already before the war. Their history has been described above. Under the initial redevelopment program established in 1949, local governments set up quasi-autonomous agencies, whose members were appointed by the local government but acted thereafter as independent bodies, with powers granted under state laws to condemn land and resell it to private developers or public agencies for reuse. The federal government underwrote two-thirds of the difference between the acquisition costs of the land and its resale proceeds (the "land write-down cost") for approved projects; local government financed the difference. In some cases, through the use of special tax districts, local governments allocated the increases in real property taxes paid by the new development to repay the bonds used to finance the local contribution to the land write-down costs. Such provisions were attractive to local leaders who saw that they made urban renewal virtually cost-free to local government; they were criticized by those who believed the benefits of urban renewal, including the higher taxes it produced, should be shared throughout the community.

The original redevelopment program, as adopted in 1949, envisioned clearance rather than rehabilitation as the main activity to be subsidized, focused on slum areas as its target, and contained no provision for replacement housing for that destroyed. As the result of experience and substantial protest, all three of these characteristics were modified over time. Rehabilitation rather than clearance was increasingly permitted; the proportion of the included areas required to consist of substandard housing was steadily reduced; and relocation of those displaced through public action was required, including new construction if no other suitable housing was available. An expanded public housing program was funded to meet the latter requirement. Despite these provisions, both conservative and liberal critics of urban renewal found in case after case that a net loss of low-income housing had taken place (see Weiss 1987), whether because the programs did not call for adequate relocation housing or because the administration was ineffective or, on occasion, corrupt (see Caro 1974 in regard to Robert Moses in New York).

Beginning in 1974, the formal Federal Urban Renewal program was officially discontinued, and comparable activities were permitted to go forward with federal help through the use of Community Development Block Grant funds or, for specific types of economic-development activities, Urban Development Action Grant funds. Lower funding levels and conflicting claims on available funds have reduced the impact of these programs in the housing field substantially.

Government support for the rehabilitation or modernization of deficient housing has never been substantial; the public role has been more to regulate then to subsidize. The two major programs involved at the federal level were Section 115 of the Housing Act of 1965, which provided direct grants to rehabilitate housing to be occupied by households within specified income limits, and Section 312 of the Housing Act of 1964, which provided for below-market-rate loans for a broader range of rehabilitation activities. Both were much used in conjunction with urban renewal in its heyday; the first is now officially dead; the second survives only at a trivial level of funding. Limited tax advantages for rehabilitation expenditures—permitting them to be amortized over five years, rather than their useful life, if they were designated for lower-income households—were phased out in the 1986 Tax Reform Act. Section 8 at the federal level (see above), local government tax-abatement programs, and a variety of loan programs using tax-exempt government bonds to provide below-market-rate loans are now the primary means by which the rehabilitation of older housing is supported by government.

Planning, Zoning, and Land-Use Controls. The location of housing within urban areas is subject to public control primarily through the instrument of zoning (in many rural areas and in one well-known urban area, Houston, Texas, there is no zoning, and locational decisions are determined by private market forces and agreements among private parties [covenants], with governmental regulation limited to areas affecting building standards and transportation and infrastructure relationships). Zoning is adopted by municipalities pursuant to state-enabling legislation, since under the U.S. federal system cities are creatures of the states. Most state-enabling legislation requires zoning to be adopted according to a comprehensive plan (see Kent 1964; Haar 1955). But such requirements have either resulted in paper plans, having no force in themselves and rarely even consulted, or have been interpreted to require only a rational basis for the zoning.[34]

The heart of most U.S. zoning ordinances is the separation of land uses. Housing is generally excluded from nonhousing zones and nonhousing from housing zones. Most zoning ordinances, even within housing zones, are hierarchical, excluding lower (higher-density) uses from higher-use zones. In addition, setback requirements, side- and rear-yard provisions, parking requirements, and height restrictions are found in most ordinances. Some use Floor Area Ratio (FAR) limits to control height and density by relating total floor area to lot areas. More modern ordinances may permit cluster development (in which houses may be grouped on a larger parcel with smaller individual lots but shared open space), may include performance standards, and may both limit the number of unrelated individuals that may live in a unit and prescribe a minimum floor space for the houses to be built.

Zoning is often used to exclude low-income households from moving into an area through large lot requirements or simply by limiting the areas set aside for multifamily (read: low-rent) housing or by requiring other expensive forms of development that raise the costs of housing within that area beyond what a low-income household can afford. A few states—New Jersey and, more recently, New York by court decision and Massachusetts by legislation—restrict the rights of municipalities to exclude people on this basis. The effort is being made in some cases to force municipalities to provide for lower-income housing; whether that will be successful remains to be seen, and it is thus far even being attempted in only a few places.[35]

The impact of local policies on gentrification, abandonment, and displacement is extensive.[36] Through policies of triage (see above, "Gentrification [c. 1980–1988]") or by the strategic use of tax abatements, urban renewal, public improvements, closing or opening facilities, upgrading or downgrading services, and revitalization may be encouraged; the benefits may or may not accrue to current residents. Actions to limit displacement, reverse abandonment, and ensure that the benefits of gentrification are equitably distributed may also be undertaken at the local level, through direct antidisplacement requirements, equitable allocation of budget expenditures, linkage plans requiring developments adversely affecting housing to contribute given amounts toward increasing low-income housing opportunities, and so on. Such provisions, however, exist in only a handful of municipalities to date.[37]

THE FUTURE

The future of housing in the United States will have its general direction set by basic demographic and economic changes; its actual shape within these broad limits will be dictated by public policies, about whose detailed future some predictions are also possible.

Demand: Limited Growth and Polarization

Demographic Factors. The baby boom of the period 1945–1965 and the baby bust of the period following are the dominant demographic characteristics that will affect housing demand in the next twenty years. Population projections are 60,875,000 households in 1990, 65,290,000 in 1995, and 69,313,000 in the year 2000. They are the middle-range projections of the U.S. Bureau of the Census. They suggest a continuing growth in the demand for housing but at a declining rate. Detailed analysis further suggests a continuing shift toward smaller households, although the recent sharp increases in the proportion of elderly will abate in the 1990s as the smaller generation born during the years of the Great Depression enters retirement age. Thus the overall projection is largely for a continuation of present trends in demand but with a shifting composition and at a slower rate (Sternlieb and Hughes 1987).

Income Distribution. Purely demographic analysis would lead to the conclusion that the above trends will result in increasing affluence and sharply rising effective demand at middle-income levels over the next twenty years. During this period, the baby-boom generation will have arrived at their peak earning years, thirty-five–fifty-four; their high proportion in the population should boost aggregate demand. But changes in the structure of the economy suggest that the picture may not be so simple. The reduction in manufacturing jobs and the demand for unskilled labor caused by the substitution of advanced machinery for labor, the low-wage competition from other countries, and the weakness of the labor movement all suggest an increasing number of permanently unemployed and very low-paid employed. At the other extreme, the demand for professional and technical personnel and the growth of the finance, real estate, insurance, and high-level service industries suggest a continuing growth of highly paid jobs. The magnitude of growth in the three segments of the market cannot be predicted accurately. What does seem clear is that the segmentation itself will increase, and the differentiation with effective demand and the growth of "ineffective" demand (i.e., those unable to afford housing in the private market) will both increase.

Public Policies

Public policies affecting housing in the United States historically have been determined by the balance of conflicting forces more than by governmental estimates of need or welfare. The present balance of power has led to a reduction of the federal role absolutely and the restriction of what remains to support for the private housing industry. Are there any indications that that balance will change in the foreseeable future? More specifically, is there any indication of heightened pressure from those needing or benefiting from more redistributive policies in housing?

Pressure for a change of policies exists and is slowly increasing. It has not escalated to the extent that might have been expected, perhaps for four reasons. First is a simple but often overlooked fact: it takes some time before changes of government policy are reflected on the ground at the local level, particularly in the area of housing. Thus in New York City for instance, public housing was still being built in 1988, although the last funds for new construction were allocated in 1981.

Second is that there has never been a long-term well-organized movement for progressive action politically in the United States; the absence of a labor party or a strong Left distinguishes the United States from many European countries.

The third reason for the as-yet-limited pressure for change may be the sharp edge that the administration has thus far succeeded in inserting between the "middle class," including a large segment of the working class, on the one hand, and the poor, the unemployed, minority group members, many women and elderly, and young people, on the other hand. Racism, sexism, and ethnocentrism play major roles in accentuating these divisions. Where the interests of moderate- and higher-income people are affected by the same problems that affect poor people, only then are poor people's problems also addressed (see Piven and Cloward 1977; Marcuse 1981). That situation has, for the time being, not risen to the level of widespread awareness among taxpayers, urban residents, and poor and working people of the United States.

The fourth reason for the lack of pressure for change is more speculative. State housing benefits for poor people may in fact never have been that significant anyway. At no time in U.S. history did more than 5 percent of the country's population benefit from the progressive aspects of governmental housing programs. Even that 5 percent received niggardly benefits, at the cost of social stigma, segregation, bureaucratic dehumanization, loss of control, and surrender of self-respect. It is no utopia that is being shattered; there is simply a little less meat in an already thin soup-kitchen stew. Anyone with any choice is already eating elsewhere. The state has never functioned, in the housing field in the United States, for the benefit of the needy. Many of the needy now hardly notice its withdrawal.

Only a substantial worsening of the conditions of the poor is likely to bring about any substantial upsurge of protest or pressure for change. If that worsening is confined to the poor, history suggests, as it was in the 1960s, the consequences for housing policy are likely to be shortlived. If it is accompanied by a worsening of conditions across a broad spectrum of income and racial or ethnic groups, the consequences may be longer lasting, as the experience of the Great Depression shows. Whether, when, and what kind of worsening will occur is a prediction that should hardly be ventured here.

Unbalanced Supply

In a housing supply system heavily dominated by the private market, supply will be a direct function of effective demand, at least in the absence of the type of major change in public policies alluded to just above. In general, a slower but steady growth in supply during the next twenty years can therefore be expected, increasingly upscale, with little provision for lower-income households. Indeed, the process of gentrification and the ending of federal subsidies to much existing housing both suggest a decline in available housing for the poor (see above, "Quantity"). Whether this expected pattern holds will depend on two factors. One is the level of economic prosperity; the business cycle, and long-term changes, may overwhelm all narrower housing-based influences and may negate the factors otherwise leading to moderate growth. The other uncertain factor is public policy: tax-law changes adverse to private housing production, subsidies for low-income households, and a shift in the politics of succeeding administrations may all be critical factors. At this time, however, a prediction of a radical change from existing patterns would be foolhardy.

Several lessons can be learned from the U.S. experience:

1. The profit motive is a powerful engine for increasing the supply and quality of housing for those economically able to pay its market price.

2. The attempt to regulate the private profit-motivated housing sector to provide housing for those not economically able to pay its market price is unlikely to succeed.

3. The attempt to subsidize the private profit-motivated housing sector to provide housing for those not economically able to pay its market price is likely to be plagued with one problem after another, as the conflicting motivations of the public and private actions collide with each other.

4. The extent and quality of public efforts to provide housing for those not economically able to pay its market price is more likely to be determined by the realities of political power and the threat posed by the ill-housed than on the extent of their need.

Finally—and this may be the cardinal lesson of the most recent past—the long-term hope that the filtering process in the private rental market will ultimately solve the housing problem, that "a rising tide will lift all ships," may finally have proved to be an illusion, as the experience of continuing new and more expensive housing construction for upper-income groups is more and more compatible with a consistent cost: income pressure on the middle class, a declining standard of living for the poor, and, most egregiously, an absolute lack of shelter for the homeless.

NOTES

1. The low figures for cities on this list are suspect; they include cities with rapid population loss and loss of units, and the delay in reporting lost units results in vacant units not practically available for occupancy being included in the vacancy rate.

2. Joseph Shuldiner, General Manager, New York City Housing Authority; Interview, February 11, 1989.

3. The conservatism of the assumptions is shown by the fact that Phillip Clay's figures

suggest a surplus of 1 million low-rent units in 1983, an unrealistic assessment, as he acknowledged (p. 24); Cushing Dolbeare, using less conservative assumptions, estimated that the shortfall in 1980 was already 1.2 million units. Dolbeare 1983.

4. Now "American" Housing Survey; a change of name that preserves the initials AHS but cloaks a change from annual to triennial for major components of the survey.

5. For a brief general discussion of the concepts and their history, see Marcuse 1979, 145–16 2. For a more general discussion of issues of measurement of quality, see Marcuse 1971a.

6. For an evaluation of the usefulness of indicators generally, see Goedert and Goodman 1977.

7. For conventional mortgages on new homes, see U.S. Bureau of the Census 1986, 506.

8. Ibid., p. 502.

9. U.S. Bureau of the Census 1975, 978. The figures from the two series are not fully comparable.

10. In cooperatives, title is technically in a corporation in which residents own stock and from which they rent their units, but operationally residents behave more as owners than as tenants.

11. The category is actually "black" and "other"; the categories and their definitions, unfortunately, vary significantly from census to census.

12. Of all residential mortgages, 9.5 percent are owned by federally secured pools of mortgages; that figure, however, largely overlaps with the figure for directly guaranteed mortgages. For both figures, see 1980 U.S. Bureau of the Census: *Census of Housing*, vol. 5, Residential Finance; and U.S. Bureau of the Census 1986, 738.

13. See, for instance the role of the New York State courts in dealing with the spate of threatened evictions in the immediate post–World War I period, recounted in Lawson and Naison 1986.

14. The Mortgage Bankers Association of America began keeping such records in 1953, but it is doubtful that the rate was higher in the postwar or war periods.

15. Many units that end in public ownership were built privately and then sold or otherwise transferred to government, for example, under the public housing turnkey program.

16. The recent range is from 37 percent in 1970 to 48 percent in 1986. U.S. Department of Commerce 1987.

17. For a good discussion of the issues of concentration and rationalization in the housing construction industry, see Schlesinger and Erlich 1986, 139–64. I am indebted to it for several of the references that follow.

18. Figures are for the industry as a whole; its residential component is at the least-concentrated end of the industry spectrum, but comparable separate figures are not available for residential construction. U.S. Bureau of the Census 1986, 518.

19. The major studies were undertaken by the President's Committee on Urban Housing (Kaiser Commission) 1968; and the National Commission on Urban Problems (Douglas Commission) 1968. Both were undertaken in the heyday of optimism as to the potential of industrialization of home building; their negative findings have only been reinforced since then.

20. Board of Governors of the Federal Reserve System, *Federal Reserve Bulletin*, monthly. The 1945 amount was virtually unchanged from 1925; see U.S. Bureau of the Census 1975, 648–49.

21. Building and Loan Associations, or Savings and Loan Associations, as they are more frequently called today, have a long history in the United States, dating from 1831, and still carry the ideological halo of self-help and mutual support. That characteristic, important in the early days of rapid growth and settlement, has long since given way to a thorough institutionalization. See Hanger 1904.

22. That result may appear contrary to economic theory: a large supply, and few restrictions on use, should increase the availability of the commodity and decrease the monopolistic aspect of particular locations. The intensity of use permitted at certain locations, however, leads to a higher demand at those locations than a regulatory-planning scheme that spreads development more evenly. One might thus expect that "nondevelopment" land would, symmetrically, be cheaper in the United States than in more regulated developed market economies. The data by which to judge that comparison are, however, lacking.

23. President's Commission, 1982, p. 211; see appendix D for caution regarding the representative character of figures; they do not track a single set of sites, among other things, but they are the best available on a national basis.

24. Where their interests are directly affected, however, their potential power is too strong to be ignored, even if that power is "unorganized." Thus the deductability of taxes and interest by homeowners on their homes was one of the major loopholes in the tax laws that, from the outset, the administration pledged itself not to tamper with in its wholesale reform of the federal income tax in 1986.

25. The Supreme Court, beginning with *Buchanan vs. Warley*, 245 U.S. 60, in 1917, has consistently held explicitly racial discrimination by the government unconstitutional in the area of land-use controls; in the recent *Mt. Laurel II* decision, the state of New Jersey has imposed an affirmative obligation on municipalities to provide for nondiscriminatory housing patterns. The support for segregation in housing provided by the Federal Housing Administration in its early years, however, is well documented (Rubinowitz and Trosman 1979).

26. In New Jersey, a statewide tenants organization has had some real political effect, and some tenant leaders believe a major untapped potential for political action remains to be tested. See Atlas and Dreier 1986.

27. For a sharp discussion in legal terms, see *Pennsylvania Central Transportation Co. vs. City of New York*, 1977.

28. Truman was quite explicit about the role of of housing: in his message to Congress of September 1945 he said, "The largest single opportunity for the rapid post-war expansion of private investment and employment lies in the field of housing both urban and rural . . . Such a program would provide capital to invest from six to seven billion dollars annually. Private enterprise in this field could provide employment for several million workers each year . . . A housing program . . . would in turn stimulate a vast amount of business and employment in industries which make house furnishings and equipment of every kind, and in the industries which supply the materials for them" (Barton and Matusow 1966, 92).

29. Albert Cole was, at the time of passage of the 1954 act, administrator of the Housing and Home Finance Agency, the predecessor of the Department of Housing and Urban Development.

30. See the work of the Center for Community Change's Community Development Block Grant Monitoring Project (including Marcuse with Medoff and Pereira 1982) and of the Brookings Institution and even HUD's own annual reports on the program.

31. Estimates of Federal Tax Expenditures for Fiscal Years 1984–89, Prepared for the Committee on Wage and Means and the Committee on Finance by the staff of the Joint Committee on Taxation, November 9, 1984, table 1.

32. New York City is a leader in the area. For a discussion of the pros and cons, and some alternate suggestions, see *City Limits*, Special Issue, December 1983.

33. Current information on such programs is maintained by the Citizens Information Exchange, reported on in the Journal of Housing, the magazine of the National Association of Housing and Redevelopment Officials in Washington.

34. See *Berenson vs. Town of New Castle*, 1975, (38 NY 2d 102, 341 NE 2d 136, 373 NV52d 672) and "Asian Americans for Equality," in *New York Law Journal*, August 14, 1985.

35. See *Mt. Laurel II, Southern Burlington County NAACP vs. Township of Mt. Laurel*, 92 N.J. 158, 456 A.2d 390, 1983, and *Asian Americans for Equality vs. Koch* in *New York Law Journal*, August 14, 1985, 11, decisions.

36. For a detailed discussion, see Marcuse, 1985a, 1984–1985.

37. The *Mt. Laurel* reasoning may ultimately require many more municipalities to act along these lines.

REFERENCES

Achtenberg, Emily. 1989. "Subsidized Housing at Risk." In *Housing Issues in the 1990s*, edited by Sara Rosenberry and Chester Hartman. New York: Praeger.

Achtenberg, Emily and Peter Marcuse. 1983. "Toward the Decommodification of Housing: A Political Analysis and a Progressive Program." In *America's Housing Crisis: What Is to Be Done?* Edited by Chester Hartman. Boston: Routledge & Kegan Paul.

Ackerman, J., M. Clawson, and M. Harris, eds. 1962. *Land Economics Research.* Baltimore: John Hopkins University Press.

Apgar, William C., and H. James Brown. 1988. *The State of the Nation's Housing, 1988.* Cambridge, Mass.: Joint Center for Housing Studies of Harvard University.

Appelbaum, Richard. 1984. Testimony before the Subcommittee on Housing and Community Development, Committee on Banking, Finance, and Urban Affairs, Subcommittee on Manpower and Housing, and Committee on Government Operations, May 24, 1984. Reprinted in *Housing the Homeless*, edited by Jon Erickson and Charles Wilhelm. New Brunswick, N.J.: Center for Urban Policy Research, 1986.

Atlas, John, and Peter Dreier. 1986. "The Tenants' Movement and American Politics." In *Critical Perspectives in Housing*, edited by R. Bratt, C. Hartman, and A. Meyerson. Philadelphia: Temple University Press.

Barton, J. Bernstein, and Allen J. Matusow, eds. 1966. *The Truman Administration: A Documentary History.* New York: Harper & Row.

Bratt, Rachel G., Chester Hartman, and Ann Meyerson. 1986. *Critical Perspectives on Housing.* Philadelphia: Temple University Press.

Caro, Robert A. 1974. *The Power Broker: Robert Moses and the Fall of New York.* New York: Knopf.

City Limits. 1983. Special issue, December.

Clay, Phillip L. 1987. *At Risk of Loss: The Endangered Future of Low-Income Rental Housing Resources.* Washington, D.C.: Neighborhood Reinvestment Corporation, May.

Cloward, Richard, and Frances Fox Piven. 1972. *The Politics of Turmoil*. New York: Vintage.

Cole, Albert N. 1979. "Federal Housing Programs: 1950–1960." In *The Story of Housing*, edited by Gertrude Fish. New York: McMillan.

de Neufville, Judith I., and Stephen E. Barton. 1987. "Myths and the Definition of Policy Problems: An Exploration of Home Ownership and Public-Private Partnerships." *Policy Sciences*, 20, no. 3: 181 ff.

Dolbeare, Cushing N. 1983. "The Low-Income Housing Crisis." In *America's Housing Crisis: What's To Be Done?*, edited by Chester Hartman. Boston: Routledge and Kegan Paul.

———. 1988. "The Low-Income Housing Crisis and Its Impact on Homelessness." Washington, D.C.: Advisory Commission on Intergovernmental Relations, March, typescript.

Downs, Anthony. 1983. *Rental Housing in the 1980s*. Washington, D.C.: Brookings Institute.

Feagin, Joe R. 1986. "Urban Real Estate Speculation in the United States." In *Critical Perspectives on Housing*, edited by Rachel Bratt et al. Philadelphia: Temple University Press.

Felstein, Carol, and Michael A. Stegman. 1987. "Toward the Twenty First Century— Housing in New York City." Paper prepared for the Commission on the Year 2000, New York, May. Mimeograph.

Fisher, Ernest M. 1931–1932. "Housing Legislation and Housing Policy in the United States." *Michigan Law Review* 31:320–45.

Goedert, Jeanne E., and John L. Goodman, Jr. 1977. *Indicators of the Quality of U.S. Housing*. Washington, D.C.: The Urban Institute.

Goering, John M., ed. 1986. *Housing Desegregation and Federal Policy*. Durham: University of North Carolina Press.

Haar, Charles. 1955. "In Accordance with a Comprehensive Plan." *Harvard Law Review* 68:1154

Hanger, G.W.W. 1904. "Building and Loan Associations in the United States." *Bulletin of the Bureau of Labour* 9, no. 55:1491–1572.

Hartman, Chester, Dennis Keating, and Richard LeGates. 1982. *Displacement: How to Fight It*. Berkeley, Calif.: National Housing Law Project.

Hayden, Dolores. 1981. *The Grand Domestic Revolution: A History of Feminist Designs for American Homes, Neighborhoods, and Cities*. Cambridge, Mass.: MIT Press.

Heskin, Allan David. 1983. *Tenants and the American Dream: Ideology and the Tenant Movement*. New York: Praeger.

Hoover Commission. 1929. *Report*. Washington, D.C.

Kent, T. J. 1964. *The Urban General Plan*. San Francisco: Chandler.

Lawson, Ron, and Mark Naison. 1986. *The Tenant Movement in New York City, 1904–1985*. New Brunswick, N.J.: Rutgers University Press.

LeGates, Richard T., and Chester Hartman. 1981. "Displacement." *Clearinghouse Review* (Chicago: National Clearinghouse for Legal Services) 15, no. 3 (July): 207–49.

Low-Income Housing Information Service (LIMIS). 1989. Special Memorandum, March.

Marcuse, Peter. 1971a. "Housing Policy and Social Indicators." *Urban Affairs Quarterly*, December.

———. 1971b. "The Rise of Tenant Organizations." *The Nation*, July; reprinted in *Housing in America*, edited by Daniel Mandelker and Roger Montgomery, 492–

99. Indianapolis: Bobbs-Merrill, 1973, 1979; also reprinted in *Housing Urban America*, edited by John Pynoos, Robert Schafer, and Chester M. Hartman, 49–54. Chicago: Aldine, 1973, 1981.

———. 1979. Rental Housing in New York City, 1975–1978. New York: Department of Housing Preservation and Development, Office of Rent Control.

———. 1981. "The Strategic Potential of Rent Control." In *Rent Control: A Source Book*, edited by John I. Gilderbloom. Santa Barbara, Calif.: Foundation for National Progress.

———. 1982. *Housing Abandonment: Does Rent Control Make a Difference?* Washington, D.C.: Conference on Alternative State and Local Policies.

———. 1984–1985. "To Control Gentrification: Anti-Displacement Zoning and Planning for Stable Residential Districts." *New York University Review of Law and Social Change* 13, no. 4: 931–52; reprinted in *Yearbook of Construction Articles*. Washington, D.C.: Federal Publications, 1985.

———. 1985a. "Gentrification, Abandonment, and Displacement: Connections, Causes, and Policy Responses in New York City." *Journal of Urban and Contemporary Law* 28: 195–240.

———. 1985b. "The State of the City's Housing." *City Limits* 10, no. 7 (September): 75–98.

———. 1986. *The Uses and Limits of Rent Control: A Report with Recommendations*. New York: State of New York, Division of Housing and Community Renewal, December.

———. 1989. "Housing as a Cause of Homelessness." In *People Without Homes: The Homeless in America*, edited by Carole Caton. New York: Oxford University Press.

Marcuse, Peter, with Peter Medoff and Andrea Pereira. "Triage as Urban Policy." *Social Policy*, Winter 1982, 33ff.

Mollenkopf, John. 1975. "The Post-War Politics of Urban Development." *Politics and Society* (Winter) 5: 2.

———. 1983. *The Contested City*. Princeton, N.J.: Princeton University Press.

National Association of Home Builders. 1989. *National Delinquency Survey* (Mortgage Bankers Association). Washington, D.C.

National Commission on Urban Problems (Douglas Commission). 1968. *Building the American City*. Washington, D.C.: U.S. Government Printing Office.

"Tax Credits Produce Housing for Poor." *New York Times*, January 17, 1988. Section 8, p. 1.

Pennyslvania Central Transportation Co. vs. City of New York, 1977. 42 N.Y. 2nd 324, N.Y.S. 2nd 914, 366 N.E. 2nd 1271.

Piven, Frances Fox, and Richard A. Cloward. 1977. *Poor People's Movements: Why They Succeed, How They Fail*. New York: Pantheon Books.

President's Commission on Housing, 1982. *Report*. Washington, D.C.: U.S. Government Printing Office.

President's Committee on Urban Housing (Kaiser Committee). 1968. *A Decent Home: Report of the President's Committee on Urban Housing*. Washington, D.C.: U.S. Government Printing Office.

Rubinowitz, Leonard S., and Elizabeth Trosman. 1979. "Affirmative Action and American Dream: Implementing Fair Housing Policies in Federal Homeownership Programs." *Northwestern University Law Review* 74 (November): 496–621.

Schlesinger, Tom, and Mark Erlich. 1986. "Housing: The Industry Capitalism Didn't Forget." In Bratt et al., eds, *Critical Perspectives on Housing*. Philadelphia: Temple University Press.

Simonson, J. C., 1981. *Existing Tax Expenditures for Homeowners*. Washington, D.C.: Department of Housing and Urban Development.

Starr, Roger. 1976. "The Changing Life of Cities." In U.S. Congress, House of Representatives, Subcommittee on the City, Committee on Banking, Finance, and Urban Affairs, 95th Cong., 1st sess. *How Cities Can Grow Old Gracefully*.

Starr, Roger. 1976. "The Changing Life of Cities." In U.S. Congress, House of Representatives, Subcommittee on the City, Committee on Banking, Finance, an Urban Affairs, 95th Cong., 1st sess. *How Cities Can Grow Old Gracefully*.

Stegman, Michael. 1973. "Reducing the Cost of New Construction." In *Housing in Urban America*, edited by Jon Pynoos, Robert Schafer, and Charles Hartman, 372–75. Chicago: Aldine.

Sternlieb, George, and James W. Hughes. 1980. "The Post-Shelter Society." In *America's Housing: Prospects and Problems*. New Brunswick, N.J.: Rutgers, Center for Urban Policy Research.

———. 1987. *The Dynamics of America's Housing*. New Brunswick, N.J.: Rutgers, Center for Urban Policy Research.

Stone, Michael. 1986. "Housing and the Dynamics of U.S. Capitalism." In *Critical Perspectives on Housing*, edited by R. Bratt, C. Hartman, and A. Meyerson, 41–67. Philadelphia: Temple University Press.

———. 1989. "Shelter Poverty." In *Housing Issues in the 1990s*, edited by S. Rosenberry and C. Hartman. New York: Praeger.

Sumichrast, Michael, G. Ahluwalia, and R. J. Sheehan. 1979. *Profile of the Builder*. Washington, D.C.: National Association of Home Builders.

Treuer, M. 1982. *Indian Housing, Worst in the Nation*. Boulder, Colo: Native American Rights Fund.

U.S. Bureau of the Census. 1981. *Current Population Reports*. Washington, D.C.: Government Printing Office.

———. 1960, 1970, 1980. *Census of Housing*. Washington, D.C.: Government Printing Office.

———. 1975. *Historical Statistics of the United States*. Washington, D.C.: U.S. Government Printing Office.

———. 1986, 1987, 1988. *Statistical Abstract of the United States*. Washington, D.C.: U.S. Government Printing Office.

———. Various years. *American Housing Survey* (*Annual Housing Survey* prior to 1983). Washington, D.C.: Government Printing Office.

U.S. Comptroller General, General Accounting Office, 1979. *Rental Housing, a National Problem That Needs Immediate Attention*. Report to the U.S. Congress. Washington, D.C.: Government Printing Office.

U.S. Congress, Congressional Budget Office. 1989. *The Tax Treatment of Homeownership: Issues and Options*. Washington, D.C.: U.S. Government Printing Office.

U.S. Department of Housing and Urban Development (HUD). 1984. *Housing in the Seventies: A Report of the National Housing Policy Review*. Washington, D.C.: U.S. Government Printing Office.

———. 1979. *Tenth Annual Report on National Housing Goals*. Washington, D.C.: U.S. Government Printing Office.

U.S. Senate. 1826. *Record.* 19 Congress, First Session. Washington, D.C.

U.S. Senate, Subcommittee on Housing and Urban Affairs, Minority Staff. 1985. *The Reagan Proposals in Congress: Fiscal 1986 Budget.* The Congress, April 16.

Van Vliet—, Willem. 1988. "The Housing and Living Arrangements of Young People in the United States." In *Handbook of Housing and the Built Environment in the U.S.*, edited by E. Huttman and W. van Vliet—, 313–345. Westport, Conn.: Greenwood Press.

Weiss, Marc. 1987. *The Rise of the Community Builders: The American Real Estate Industry and Urban Land Planning.* New York, Columbia University Press.

FURTHER READING

Adams, John S. *Housing America in the 1980s.* New York: Russell Sage Foundation, 1987.

Agpar, William C., Jr. *The Housing Outlook: 1980–1990.* New York: Praeger, 1985.

Appelbaum, Richard, and John I. Gilderbloom. *Rethinking Rental Housing.* Philadelphia: Temple University Press, 1988.

Burns, Leland S., and Leo Grebler. *The Future of Housing Markets: A New Appraisal.* New York: Plenum, 1986.

Clark, M.A.V. "Residential Segregation in American Cities—A Review and Interpretation." *Population Research and Policy Review* 5, no. 2 (1986):95–128.

———. "Understanding Residential Segregation in American Cities: Interpreting the Evidence (A Reply to Galster)." *Population Research and Policy Review* 7, no. 2 (1988):113–22.

Dolbeare, Cushing. "How the Income Tax System Subsidizes Housing for the Affluent." In *Critical Perspectives on Housing*, edited by R. Bratt, C. Hartman, and A. Meyerson, 264–271. Philadelphia: Temple University Press, 1986.

Downie, Leonard, Jr. 1974. *Mortgage on America.* New York: Praeger.

Galster, G. "Residential Segregation in American Cities: A Contrary Review." *Population Research and Policy Review* 7, no. 2 (1988):93–112.

Gilderbloom, John I., and Richard P. Appelbaum. *Rethinking Rental Housing.* Philadelphia: Temple University Press, 1987.

Hartman, Chester, ed. *America's Housing Crisis: What Is To Be Done?* New York: Routledge Chapman & Hall, 1983.

Hayden, Dolores. *Redesigning the American Dream: The Future of Housing, Work and Family Life.* New York: Norton, 1986.

Hays, R. A. *The Federal Government and Urban Housing: Ideology and Change in Public Policy.* Albany: State University of New York Press, 1985.

Hughes, James W., and George Sternlieb. *Dynamics of America's Housing.* New Brunswick, N.J.: Rutgers University, Center for Urban Policy Research, 1987.

Huttman, Elizabeth, and Willem Van Vliet—, eds. *Handbook of Housing and the Built Environment in the United States.* Westport, CT: Greenwood Press, 1988.

Listokin, David. *Housing Rehabilitation: Economic, Social and Policy Perspectives.* New Brunswick, N.J.: Rutgers University, Center for Urban Policy Research, 1983.

Marshall, Dale, and Roger Montgomery, eds. *Housing Policy for the Eighties.* Croton-on-Hudson, NY: Policy Studies Association, 1979.

Mitchell, J. Paul, ed. *Federal Housing Policies and Programs: Past and Present.* New Brunswick, N.J.: Rutgers University, Center for Urban Policy Research, 1986.

Molotch, Harvey. "The City as a Growth Machine." *American Journal of Sociology* 82 (1976): 2.

Phillips, David R., and Allan M. Williams. *Rural Housing and the Public Sector*. Brookfield, VT: Gower, 1982.

Pynoos, Jon. *Breaking the Rules: Bureaucracy and Reform in Public Housing*. New York: Plenum, 1986.

Rosenberry, Sara, and Chester Hartman, eds. *Housing Issues of the 1990s*. New York: Praeger, 1989.

Salins, Peter D. *The Ecology of Housing Destruction: Economic Effects of Public Intervention in the Housing Market*. New York: New York University Press, 1980.

Schwartz, David, R. Ferlauto, and Daniel Hoffman. *A New Housing Policy for America: Recapturing the American Dream*. Philadelphia: Temple University Press, 1988.

Shucksmith, Mark, et al. *Rural Housing: Recent Research and Policy Issues*. Elmsford, NY: Pergamon Books, 1987.

Stegman, Michael. *Housing Finance and Public Policy: Case Studies and Readings*. New York: Van Nostrand Reinhold, 1986.

Sternlieb, George, and James W. Hughes, eds. *America's Housing Prospects and Problems*. New Brunswick, N.J.: Rutgers University, Center for Urban Policy Research, 1980.

Tremblay, Kenneth R., Jr., and Don A. Dillman. *Beyond the American Housing Dream: Accommodation to the 1980s*. Lanham, Md.: University Press of America, 1983.

Turner, Margery A., and Raymond J. Struyk. *Urban Housing in the Nineteen Eighties: Markets and Policies*. Washington, D.C.: Urban Institute Press, 1984.

U. S. Department of Housing and Urban Development. *Report to the Secretary on the Homeless and Emergency Shelters*. Washington, D.C.: U.S. Government Printing Office, May 1984.

Weicher, John, et al. *Rental Housing: Is There a Crisis?* Washington, D.C.: Urban Institute Press, 1981.

Welfeld, Irving. *Where We Live: The American Home and the Social, Political, and Economic Landscape, from Slums to Suburbs*. New York: Simon and Schuster, 1988.

Wright, Gwendolyn. *Building the Dream: A Social History of Housing in America*. Cambridge, Mass.: MIT Press, 1983.

IV

CARIBBEAN AND MIDDLE AMERICA

11

Cuba

JILL HAMBERG

The mid–1980s marked a significant turning point in Cuban housing policy. New housing construction, as well as rehabilitation and maintenance, received increased attention and resources. Simultaneously, housing was called upon to play a central role in Cuba's most recent wave of economic reform. Two decades of piecemeal regulations and a growing recognition of the importance of maintenance and self-building culminated in the landmark 1984 General Housing Law. Years of the single-minded pursuit of state-built industrialized new construction gave way to a mixture of prefabrication and traditional technologies, state building along with individual self-building and collective self-help, and new construction together with rehabilitation.

STAGES IN HOUSING POLICY

Before discussing current trends in housing conditions, construction, markets, and institutions, it would be useful to trace briefly the highlights of housing policy since the 1959 Cuban revolution.[1] Further details are provided in later sections.

1959–1963

Housing-related legislation in the first years after the revolution halted evictions and rolled back most rents by up to 50 percent. The government did not nationalize urban land as such but did curtail land speculation by requiring private owners to sell sites at low uniform prices to anyone willing to start construction within six months. Most urban land coming into government hands was taken from speculators under a different law permitting confiscation of property of those leaving the country. The landmark October 1960 Urban Reform Law converted more than half of the urban tenants into homeowners. Most former owners were fully compensated, and many even received lifetime pensions. The rest of the tenants—those living in slum tenement buildings—were eventually given long-term rent-free leases, but their former landlords received no compensation. Households were permitted to own no more than one primary residence and one vacation home. Almost all private renting and subletting were prohibited. All units built or distributed by the government after 1961 were assigned with long-term leases (under the legal concept of "usufruct") at no more than 10 percent of household income.

The government experimented with an array of programs for new housing construction in the early 1960s, until the U.S.-inspired economic embargo and other construction priorities took their toll on housing. The lottery was transformed into a mechanism to finance housing. The largest and worst shantytowns were demolished; their residents built replacement housing through the Self-Help and Mutual Aid program. An extensive program of new construction in rural areas was initiated. Loans and technical assistance were made available for private construction by owner–occupants. Latrines and cement floors were provided to more than 100,000 rural dwellings, and electricity and other urban infrastructure were extended to thousands of houses in low-income urban neighborhoods.

1964–1970

During the rest of the 1960s, central government policy concentrated almost exclusively on new state housing construction, mostly in rural areas, although little was actually built. Instead, resources were concentrated on developing agriculture as well as the economic and social infrastructure.

1971–1975

After a major campaign, the 1970 sugar harvest set a record, but the effort severely disrupted the economy and also failed to attain its target of 10 million tons. It had the positive effect of provoking a profound reassessment of almost all aspects of Cuban life, including housing. The 1970 census indicated that central government agencies had built only a quarter of the houses and apartments constructed since 1959 (see table 11.1). The rest were self-built, often with some degree of informal local government support.[2] Although most of these units were of poor quality, it demonstrated tremendous pent-up demand and people's willingness to take action to provide their own shelter. A labor shortage in construction and other industries, coupled with disguised unemployment, led to the creation of a novel form of self-help: the "microbrigades." In this system, a group of employees from a given workplace formed brigades to build housing while the rest of the workers agreed to maintain production. The units were then distributed to employees from that workplace. During this period, state housing construction nearly tripled and partially shifted back to cities.

1976–1985

Many of the changes initiated in the early 1970s came to fruition in the second half of the decade. The 1976 Constitution established a system of elections (secret ballot, competitive) of officials to governing bodies on the municipal,

Table 11.1
Total Public and Self-Built Construction of Houses and Apartments, Cuba, 1959–1988

Period	Total Public and Private		Government Housing		Estimated Self-Built Housing	
	Total Units	Percent	Total Units	Percent	Total Units	Percent
1959–1970	416,400 (a)	100	99,600 (b)	24	316,800 (d)	76
1971–1975	212,000 (a)	100	81,000 (c)	38	131,000 (d)	62
1976–1980	246,000 (a)	100	82,000 (c)	33	164,000 (d)	67
1981–1985	342,000 (e)	100	135,000 (e)	39	207,000 (e)	61
1986–1988	302,000 (e)	100	85,000 (e)	42	118,000 (e)	58
Total	1,419,400	100	482,600	34	936,800	66

Sources: (a) Comité Estatal, 1984a, based on houses and apartments occupied in 1981 by year of construction; (b) Fernández Núñez, 1976, (c) Comité Estatal, 1980, note that only 6,000 units were built in 1971, but annual construction averaged 18,000 from 1972 to 1975; (d) Total minus government construction, (e) Comité Estatal, 1986; Instituto Nacional de la Vivienda, 1988; government construction includes permanent units built in agricultural cooperatives and by the military. See note 4 to the text for exclusions to self-built units for 1981–1988.

Note: Bohíos, units in tenements (i.e., rooms without exclusive use of sanitary services) and improvised housing are not included.

provincial, and national levels. Moreover, the country's geographic and administrative structures were reorganized and decentralized. The new Economic Management and Planning System, approved in 1975 and gradually implemented starting several years later, introduced self-financing in most workplaces, decentralized some economic decision making, instituted one- and five-year plans, and legalized a small self-employed sector.

In the housing field, major trends included growing attention to the maintenance and repair of existing housing, increasing the quantity and quality of informal self-building, and the decline of the microbrigades.

After nearly a quarter century of dispersed and uncoordinated housing laws, policies, and institutions and widespread public discontent about housing, Cuba's national legislature undertook the country's first comprehensive study of housing policy, culminating in the landmark 1984 housing law. It recognized the importance of self-building and attempted to resolve tenure, maintenance, inheritance, mobility, and payment issues. It converted leaseholders living in government-owned housing into homeowners, permitted limited short-term private rentals, fostered self-built housing construction, and updated existing legislation regulating housing management, maintenance and repair, evictions, and the buying and selling of land and housing.

1986–Present

By the mid–1980s Cuba had experienced a labor situation partially reminiscent of the early 1970s: a construction labor shortage coupled with unemployment, both disguised (overstaffed workplaces) and open (teens and young adults born during the 1960s baby boom). This situation coincided with economic difficulties precipitated by a sharp decline in hard currency to purchase imports and by distortions in the wake of the previous decade's economic reforms. At the same time, housing construction and repair enterprises, despite having greater resources, were proving woefully inadequate to meet the growing demand and expectations unleashed by the 1984 housing law.

The microbrigades, weakened but hardly moribund, were called upon to help address most of these problems. They were reorganized, revived, and given new tasks to such an extent that they became a central pillar of the reform process known as "rectification." In 1988 a new housing law was approved, retaining most of the basic policies of the 1984 law, but incorporating refinements contained in subsequent regulations and reflecting the new role of the microbrigades.

TRENDS IN HOUSING CONDITIONS AND CONSTRUCTION

By the mid–1980s Cuba's 10 million people lived in some 2.6 million housing units.[3] As of 1981, the date of the most recent census, two-thirds of this total were single-family houses; 15 percent were apartments (21 percent in urban areas); nearly 5 percent (mostly in Havana) were tenement units known as *cuarterías*, *casas de vecindad*, *ciudadelas*, and *solares* (inner-city slum housing where households live in one or two small rooms and share sanitary facilities); and 13 percent were *bohíos* (thatched-roof dwellings with walls of palm leaves or boards), representing two-fifths of all units in rural areas. More than half of the apartments and single-family houses were built since 1959, and two-thirds of them were self-built (see table 11.1).[4]

Housing construction has outpaced population growth, with average household size dropping from 4.6 in 1953 (year of the last prerevolutionary census) to 4.2 in 1981. The decline was sharpest in rural areas (5.4 in 1953 to 4.4 in 1981) but almost imperceptible in urban areas. Average household size actually increased in some localities, especially Havana, the nation's capital. In 1981 the average number of persons per room was 1.03 (excluding bathrooms, but including eat-in kitchens), and per sleeping room, 2.07, although on both measures the averages were somewhat higher for urban tenements and rural *bohíos*.

The quality of housing as a whole has improved since 1959 but not at the same rate in all regions or for all measures. In 1981 virtually all urban housing had electricity (as opposed to 84 percent in 1953). Rural electrification dramatically jumped from 9 percent in 1953 to 46 percent in 1981 but was still deficient in remote mountain areas. In the 1980s substantial progress was made in closing this gap by constructing small hydroelectric systems where feasible. In many other areas, small local generators provide current for a few hours a day until these remote settlements can be incorporated into the national electric system.

Water and sanitation have also improved but not quite as dramatically. In 1953 only one-third of all households had exclusive use of indoor piped water coming from a water main. By 1981 the proportion had increased to one-half (two-thirds in urban areas). A quarter obtained their water from wells (three-fifths in rural areas) and the remainder from rivers and streams. The proportion of urban units with exclusive use of indoor toilets increased from 45 percent in 1953 to 61 percent in 1981. In 1953 only 45 percent of rural houses had access to any kind of sanitary facilities, but this had risen by 1981 to 80 percent, mostly in the form of outdoor latrines.

Despite the fact that Cuba is still deficient in providing complete indoor plumbing, it enjoys a remarkably low infant mortality rate, 11.9 per thousand live births in 1988, perhaps the lowest among developing nations and lower than a number of European countries. Mortality and morbidity rates from diseases associated with poor sanitary conditions are also among the lowest in the Third World.

Cuba's remaining shantytowns and inner-city slums are small compared to those in other developing countries, but they nevertheless represent a starkly visible reminder of the legacy of underdevelopment and the lack of adequate maintenance and repair. In 1985, Cuba had 117,000 tenement units housing 322,800 people; 416 shantytowns (61 of which were in Havana) where 300,000 people lived; 355,000 *bohíos*; 93,000 units shored up, of which 50,000 can be rehabilitated; and 11,445 households containing 45,300 individuals—almost all in Havana—assigned to units declared dangerously uninhabitable. Frequent building collapses, with their related deaths and injuries, have led Havana officials to expand their existing shelter capacity of 3,800 beds in fifty shelters, to accommodate another 2,500 people.

HOUSING MARKETS, INSTITUTIONS, AND POLICY ORIENTATIONS

The National Housing Institute, established by the 1984 housing law, develops and coordinates housing policy on a national level and monitors the work of provincial and municial housing departments. The Ministry of Construction, several other ministries, the microbrigades, and local government agencies are responsible for building state-sponsored housing. The People's Savings Bank provides loans for private self-building and repairs. Local government agencies sell materials, run housing repair companies, and establish and enforce building and zoning regulations.

Tenure and Management

When the 1984 housing law was passed, slightly more than half of Cuba's 2.5 million households were owner–occupants, and another one-fifth lived in government-owned units for which they paid no more than 10 percent of their income in rent. The rest fell into a number of different categories. Many of these households held rent-free leases, including some 45,200 households living in rural new towns, 104,000 residing in urban tenements, and 23,000 very low-income families. Those who had built on land purchased in illegal or semilegal ways, or who simply squatted, were usually in a more ambiguous tenure situation.

One of the goals of the 1984 housing law was to establish a dominant and uniform tenure status by converting leaseholders into homeowners and legalizing most ambiguous or illegal situations.[5] By the end of 1988, 450,000 former leaseholders had become owners, and their "rents" were amortizing the purchase price of their dwellings. Another 330,000 had been granted title at no cost. A minority of households did not immediately become homeowners, including families receiving public assistance and those continuing to live in tenements and grossly substandard shantytowns, all of whom still retain rent-free leases. In addition, the tenure status of residents of the 145,000 units owned by or "tied" to workplaces received special treatment in the law.

Another purpose of the new law was to clarify responsibility for ordinary maintenance and major repairs. Residents of single-family dwellings (no matter what their tenure status) had always been responsible for all maintenance and repairs and continue to be so. Multifamily buildings, which are owned as condominiums, have been divided into two categories: some 33,000 low-rise structures, which are "self-managed" by residents' councils, and 650 high-rise elevator buildings, which are municipally managed in consultation with their residents' councils. All residents belong to the councils and are required to contribute a low monthly maintenance fee, which is set by the council in self-managed buildings within limits set by law. Local government pays an additional subsidy to help maintain the more expensive elevator high-rise structures.

These residents' councils have followed a long tradition of neighborhood activism since the revolution. Local block clubs, called Committees for the Defense of the Revolution (CDR), are active in local cleanup and beautification campaigns, as well as citizen anticrime patrols, blood drives, and other kinds of voluntarism. Most apartment buildings had residents' councils for many years—some more active than others—but their tasks were not always clearly defined.

New Construction

State-sponsored housing. The term *state-sponsored* covers a number of different programs and institutions:

1. *State brigades*: Since the early 1960s, more than one-half of all government built units have been erected by "state" brigades, which consist of regular employees of the Ministry of Construction (MICONS). These brigades concentrate on building housing in labor-scarce agricultural or industrial new towns and more complex high-rise dwellings in large cities.

2. *Microbrigades*: In their restructured form, the microbrigades are teams of thirty-three employees from one or more workplaces who labor under the supervision of skilled workers and technicians to build housing, 60 percent of which is then distributed to their workplace labor force, and the other 40 percent is reserved for employees of workplaces without microbrigades and for households living in dangerous situations and in buildings slated for demolition. Allocation of units within each workplace is decided in workers' meetings. Priority is given to those with outstanding job performance who need housing, but brigade members are not necessarily selected. Those remaining at the workplace agree to maintain production levels, and many also spend time on the construction project in the evening or weekends. Nearly half of the microbrigade members are assigned to build community facilities, while the rest erect housing.

In addition to workplace-based microbrigades, neighborhood-level "social microbrigades" also have been organized. Variations include residents of shantytowns building new housing and unemployed youth, housewives, and retired construction workers providing maintenance and repair services for deteriorated units in their own neighborhoods.

3. *Other workplace-related or institutional housing*: Aside from the Ministry of Construction, a limited number of other ministries directly build and manage housing—primarily the armed forces and the sugar and agriculture ministries—to ensure a labor force in labor-scarce or remote areas. In addition, some self-building is workplace related. Examples include agricultural cooperatives where members form informal building brigades and when enterprises, such as sugar

mills, occasionally provide land, materials, and building plans to their best workers. Twenty percent of agricultural land is still privately owned, 65 percent of which is incorporated into agricultural cooperatives.

4. *Local government*: Since the 1976 decentralization of many functions to local government—and to some extent before that step—local authorities have played an increasingly active role in different phases of housing construction, including establishing local materials industries, assigning land, and building urban infrastructure. Local governments also directly build housing with their own resources, but their more common role in the 1980s has been to move toward enforcing building codes and land-use regulations and offering technical assistance, land, materials, and equipment for self-building. In addition, administrative responsibility for the microbrigades has been transferred from MICONS to local government in some provinces, and some other MICONS functions may soon be decentralized as well.

Self-Built Housing. Under the 1984 law, low-interest bank loans are available to cover a wide range of building costs: materials for construction or repairs, land, architectural and other technical assistance, equipment rental, and contracted labor. To foster higher densities, especially in the largest cities, households may join together to build multifamily housing. Land or the right to build on roofs may be purchased from private individuals, as can permanent surface rights to state-owned land.

Financing and Payment

All state-built housing is financed out of the budget, in most cases the national budget, through MICONS but also through the ministries that directly build housing and through local budgets. Personal loans (not mortgages) are provided to purchase new units and for self-building and repairs by the People's Savings Bank, Cuba's only institutional source of consumer loans. However, credit is not available to buy existing units, privately owned land, or finance housing exchanges.

Since the revolution there has been an evolution in thinking about what, if anything, residents should pay for housing. The 1960 Urban Reform Law established several types of payment. Some existing homeowners with mortgage debt had their principal reduced by up to a third and interest on the debt was eliminated. The more than 200,000 tenant households who were converted into owners amortized the value of their units by continuing to pay their rents (most already rolled back in 1959) for between five and twenty years, depending on the age of the building. Hence by the 1980s virtually all of these households owned their units free and clear. Indeed, by 1972 only 10 percent of all households were still making some kind of amortization payment (Banco Nacional de Cuba 1975).

Leaseholders in most housing built or distributed by the government paid no more than 10 percent of income, although in practice the range was between 3 and 7 percent since rents were rarely adjusted upward when incomes increased or additional household members took a job. Residents of microbrigade housing built before the 1984 housing law paid a maximum of 6 percent of income to reflect the "surplus work" contributed either as microbrigade members or by working more on their regular jobs. Although the goal of eventually making housing free, proclaimed in the Urban Reform Law, was never fully attained, rent-free leases were granted to tenement dwellers and those living in rural new towns. Starting in the early 1970s very low income households were also exempted from paying rent.

The costs and form of payment for self-built housing varied widely, depending on a number of things: Was land obtained legally or illegally; at no cost, at the low legal cost, or at high free-market prices? Were materials obtained from nature, purchased from public agencies, received free, stolen, or bought on the black market? Was the unit a substandard shack or an oversized, high-quality residence? As a stopgap measure, in 1971 people who had already built on land they did not own were granted rent-free leases to their sites, but in all such future situations households were expected to pay 10 percent of their incomes for land rent in addition to any expenses of building their own dwellings.

By the late 1970s the whole tenure and rent-setting system began to appear unfair. Only homeowners acquired equity and could sell and bequeath their property. Whether households became owners or leaseholders was often a quirk of fate: for instance, whether one's workplace had a microbrigade or whether sufficient materials or land were available locally for self-building. Furthermore, income-based rents, at first glance apparently equitable, began to be perceived as unjust. Many families paid relatively high rents for small or poorly located housing, and others spent little for large, centrally located units.

In response to these objections, the 1984 law established a totally different payment system principally based on the "value" of the unit, including its size, construction quality, location, and depreciation. Under the new system, housing built or distributed by the government is amortized over a fifteen-year period (twenty years for high-rise buildings). Households unable to afford these payments could automatically have the term of the loan extended and their monthly payments reduced to 20–25 percent of income, and in some cases further reductions were possible. The 1988 law lowered the proportion of income paid by low-income families to 20 percent (for owners) and 10 percent (for renters). Loan payments averaged 16 percent of income in 1987. The relatively short repayment periods—and hence higher monthly payments—were deliberately set to absorb excess spending power in the economy.

In keeping with the economic reforms of the mid–1970s, differential interest rates and pricing policies were instituted. In the mid–1980s, purchasers of new state-built housing paid about 85 percent of production costs at 3 percent interest. Residents of microbrigade housing received a further 10 percent discount on the purchase price, and interest reduced to 2 percent. Agricultural cooperatives receive building materials at wholesale prices and pay 2 percent interest. Until

1989, households purchasing materials for repairs or construction were charged relatively high materials prices, are required to make a 15–25 percent down payment, and are charged 3 percent (new construction) to 4 percent (repairs) interest. But lower prices and more favorable loan terms are expected to be instituted shortly to make self-building more affordable.

Property and personal income taxes were abolished in the early 1960s. Therefore, disposable income is the same as actual income (except for the self-employed who pay a monthly business tax), unlike many industrialized countries where income taxes often represent 20–50 percent of personal income. Ongoing operating costs are relatively low, with no real estate taxes, heating bills, or liability insurance (although optional fire and disaster insurance is now available). Except for seriously deteriorated tenements, residents pay for all repairs, even those done by municipal enterprises and "social microbrigades," with discounts for contributed labor by residents.

Housing Distribution and Redistribution

New state-built housing has been allocated largely through workplaces, either based on job performance and need (microbrigades) or to attract or stabilize the labor force (agricultural new towns and industrial developments). Most existing units coming into government hands and some microbrigade housing is assigned to households living in unsafe situations. In the case of self-built housing, deliberate allocation occurs when state-owned land and the right to buy materials are assigned. Materials for repairs are sold, but decisions on who may buy scarce items are usually made by elected neighborhood committees. The National Association of Small Farmers allocates materials among agricultural cooperatives, and the members of each cooperative determine who will receive the completed units.

The "secondary" housing market is as important as the "primary" one. Before the 1984 law, private sales of land and housing were legal but only under limited circumstances. Government permission was required, and the state had first option to buy, having only to pay the "legal" price as determined under the Urban Reform law. The selling price between private parties was also limited to the "legal" price. Because of these restrictions, unauthorized sales at free-market prices were common, leaving many households without proper title to their dwellings or land. Even when carried out with government permission, under-the-table payments were frequent.

The 1984 law attempted to legalize and control what was occurring anyway. Provisions were made to legalize most previously illegal situations, and free-market prices were permitted for sales of land and houses. The state retained its right of first refusal, but apparently mostly as a form of land banking for future public projects and preventing housing from being erected in unsuitable areas. Within a year and a half after the law went into effect, overt speculation was so rampant that the government clamped down and began requiring that most sales be directly to the state, except in the case of property transfers to close relatives. This measure was later incorporated into the 1988 law. Speculators included private farmers who sold produce at high prices on the short-lived farmers markets, self-employed individuals, and black marketeers. Government agencies and state-owned companies also got into the bidding war, further pushing up prices.

Because of all of these problems with buying and selling, the most common way that Cuban families move is by exchanging their units. Before the 1984 law, the parties to the exchange retained the tenure status—leaseholders or homeowners—they previously held in their former residences. Hence it was not unusual to find "state-owned" housing developments partially occupied by people "owning" their own units. Since the new law converted the vast majority of households into owners, this is no longer a problem.

Since under the 1984 law home loans are personal loans, not mortgages, when families trade dwellings, they normally take their debt obligations with them. However, the 1984 law permits the parties to exchange their debt or one party to assume the debt on both dwellings. In some cases additional payments reflecting free-market prices are made, which remains perfectly legal despite the crackdown on private sales. People exchanging their units do not need prior government approval, but the 1988 law allows any of the parties involved or the government to challenge any specific trade.

Houses for exchange are announced in classified advertisements, a system replacing the cumbersome Housing Exchange Offices in the late 1970s. People also put up signs on their houses, at bus stops, and in grocery stores. Some individuals have taken on an informal broker function, often organizing exchange "chains," a sequence of interrelated transfers among three or more households.

Another form of "redistribution" is inheritance. Privately owned homes may be inherited, but a distinction is made between the right to occupy the dwelling and to receive its value. The current occupants, if they had lived with the now-deceased occupant for at least two years, if close relatives, and five years if not, cannot be thrown out whether or not they are heirs. These occupants amortize the value of the dwelling over a period of time to the government, which, in turn, reimburses the heirs.

MAJOR ISSUES AND PROSPECTIVE DEVELOPMENTS

Housing is widely acknowledged by Cuban leaders to be one of the country's most pressing problems. The 1984 and 1988 housing laws, the 1980s upsurge in housing construction, and the revival of microbrigades in all of their forms attest to their commitment to correct past mistakes and devote more attention and resources to this issue. But the importance of Cuba's housing problem reflects not only past neglect, errors, and the legacy of underdevelopment; it is, ironically, also the product of success in other areas, as other major problems have receded into the background in comparison to housing. Unlike the vast majority of

Table 11.2
Average Annual Public and Self-Built Construction of Houses and Apartments,
Cuba, 1959–1988

Period	Total Public and and Private		Government Housing		Estimated Self-Built Housing	
	Total	Per 1000 Pop.*	Total	Per 1000 Pop.*	Total	Per 1000 Pop.*
1959-1970	34,700 (a)	4.5	8,300 (b)	1.1	26,400 (d)	3.4
1971-1975	42,400 (a)	4.7	16,200 (c)	1.8	26,200 (d)	2.9
1976-1980	49,200 (a)	5.1	16,400 (c)	1.7	32,800 (d)	3.4
1981-1985	68,500 (e)	6.9	27,000 (e)	2.7	41,500 (e)	4.2
1986-1988	67,600 (e)	6.8	28,300 (e)	2.8	39,500 (e)	3.9

Sources: See Table 11.1, Sources.
Note: *Bohíos*, units in tenements (i.e., rooms without exclusive use of sanitary services), and improvised housing are not included.
* Population at midpoint of period (Comité Estatal 1988).

developing nations, Cuba is no longer plagued by mass unemployment, low wages, malnutrition, poor health care, illiteracy, and low educational levels, in part because resources were primarily devoted, during the revolution's first two decades, to stimulating economic development and providing educational and health facilities rather than housing. Moreover, housing is now accorded greater attention because of wider recognition of its role in promoting economic development, regional balance, orderly urban growth, and labor force and family stability.

Major housing issues confronting Cuban policymakers include:

Shortage

Cuban planners have estimated that it would be necessary to build 130,000 units a year (or 12 per 1,000 population) between 1980 and the year 2000 to replace lost housing, upgrade living conditions, eliminate overcrowding and doubling up, accommodate internal migration, and provide for demographic growth. This rate of housing construction would be 75 percent higher than the 1980–1985 average (see table 11.2) and approximates the highest annual rates in Europe during the postwar period (Donnison and Ungerson 1982).

Shortage reflects the interaction of two factors: supply and demand. Issues related to supply are discussed below in the context of building technology and productivity. Demographic and geographic factors are the most significant measures of demand since ability to pay has never been a criterion for access to state-distributed housing, although it influences the quality of self-built units. Cuba's rate of population growth has declined significantly since the mid–1960s and is among the lowest in the developing world. But by the early 1980s, the nation began to experience a veritable explosion in housing demand when the 1960s baby-boom generation started forming households. Continued rural to urban migration and the trend toward smaller families and a greater variety of household composition due to an aging population and low birth and high divorce rates have also increased overall demand. These trends are already influencing design features such as the number of rooms per unit, floor area per person, and building scale.

Building Technology, Productivity, and Design

The quantitative and qualitative aspects of the supply side of the shortage equation are intimately related to choices about construction technology and building standards and design.[6] During the wave of housing construction in the early 1960s, units were built to generous space and design standards using conventional construction methods. In rural areas single-family detached dwellings were erected on relatively large lots. Most urban units were in single-family detached residences or four-story walk-up apartment buildings. The exception was Habana del Este, an ambitious 2,300-unit development organized around the neighborhood-unit concept and the superblock, which combined high-rise and walk-up residential buildings with community facilities and commercial areas.

But by 1963 events soon forced a reevaluation of this approach. Construction materials for house building—most of which had been imported—became scarce due to the 1961 U.S.-imposed trade embargo, and what materials were available were soon diverted to more pressing needs.

For a variety of practical, and to some degree ideological, reasons, officials soon believed that they had no choice but to industrialize construction and to do so through the development of prefabrication. Conventional methods were hindered by the scarcity of imported wood to build forms for pouring concrete. A construction-worker shortage emerged, and it was especially difficult to find skilled craftsmen outside Havana. In the early 1960s Cuban officials estimated that 100,000 units a year would be necessary to relieve the housing shortage, and thus, it was believed, the solution had to be massive and speedy. They perceived industrialized construction as being rapid, requiring less labor, humanizing arduous tasks, and using far less wood than in conventional methods. Industrialization was also seen as congruent with the "scientific-technical revolution" and socialist planning.

Before the revolution, Cuba already had some experience with a domestically developed lightweight prefabrication system, later known as the Sandino system. In the early 1960s Cuba began developing its own and importing more advanced large-panel systems from Western and Eastern Europe. By the late 1970s Cuba was using some ten systems. In international conferences, Cuban delegates waxed evangelical about what they saw as the advantages of industrialized construction—as opposed to "appropriate" and "intermediate" technology—for both the developed *and* the developing world. They predicted that in Cuba even lightweight and semiprefabricated systems would soon be phased out in favor of the "more productive" large-panel systems.

But in reality Cuba has experienced a highly mixed system all along, and throughout the revolutionary period there have also been active proponents of using traditional systems and materials and devoting more attention to maintenance and repair of the existing stock. Self-built houses were and still are being built with traditional methods employed for generations, with occasional use of the Sandino system. The state-built sector was increasingly dominated by the use of large-panel prefabricated systems, but expected productivity gains materialized only sporadically. Cuban officials have repeatedly denounced construction delays due to materials bottlenecks caused by poor coordination and a perpetual tendency to start more projects than available resources can support. Cranes and other scarce heavy equipment and vehicles are vulnerable to breakdown, and both equipment and labor are often diverted to higher priority projects. The installation of water and sewer lines is often delayed, and finishing materials are in short supply, leaving otherwise completed units vacant for months or even years. Even when new units are occupied, basic infrastructure and community facilities and services often lag far behind or are completely ignored. End-of-the-year round-the-clock building "marathons" produce poor-quality structures, causing innumerable maintenance problems later.

Numerous past attempts have been made to remedy these long-recognized problems, but the shakeup in the construction industry provoked by the microbrigade revival may bear some fruits. The new policy is to finish projects before starting others, and more emphasis will be placed on completions than value produced. Services and infrastructures are to be built at the same time as housing. The demand for construction resources is pump priming the building materials industry, which is increasing productivity, adding extra shifts, and launching major investments to produce additional equipment and substitute imports (which represent 14 percent of building materials). Some transportation-induced losses and delays may be avoided, and quality enhanced, by the projected use of more on-site prefabrication.

Aside from construction-related problems, apartment-building and housing-development designs have also come under fire for their monotony and generally poor site planning. Although planners agree on the need to achieve high densities, they debate the best ways to achieve this goal. Officials have noted with irony the apparent contradiction of policies that stress building four- and five-story structures in rural new towns (to preserve agricultural land), while both planned and uncontrolled growth in cities has perpetuated urban sprawl. High-rise buildings have been put forth as the appropriate solution but have been criticized in recent years because of their higher per-unit cost (extra reinforcement for high winds and earthquakes), greater use of imported materials (elevators, structural elements), increased energy drain, and greater maintenance cost. Even many of those who support a judicious use of high-rise structures in large cities, and then only in downtown areas, on principal streets, and at major intersections, resist the policy—often sought by local officials—of building high rises in smaller cities and towns.

Critics have argued that sufficient densities can better be achieved by constructing high-density low-rise buildings, "in-fill" housing, and second stories on existing structures. New approaches to building design, construction, and site planning have emerged from lessons learned from historic preservation and urban-renewal projects, and a new appreciation of positive features of prerevolutionary housing (coinciding with similar trends in other countries). The decentralization of certain design responsibilities to the municipal level has fostered closer ties between architects, builders and users. For instance, in Havana, "bulky" walk-up buildings for small lots are being designed to blend into the surrounding area, including varying facades to avoid monotony. Building in rural areas is shifting back to one- and two-story units, usually with backyards.

Architects are striving to apply similar concepts in newly developing areas, including aspects such as mixed-use buildings, compact site plans, varied building heights, and maintaining the street as the focal point (unlike the "tower-in-the-park" superblock). Such designs seek not only to overcome the monotony in current housing design and site planning but also to respond to findings of Cuban studies indicating that undifferentiated open space tends not to be well used or maintained. Generous space standards between buildings, borrowed from cold European climates, are not well adapted to tropical conditions, where shade is of the utmost importance.

Most Cuban policymakers are still committed to the long-term development of industrialized construction, although they believe that the shift from traditional methods will take much longer than originally envisioned, and debate still continues on the shape and speed of the transition. Attempts are underway to adapt the installed prefabrication capacity to more varied design solutions. The need to mass produce materials for traditional self-built construction has led to greater emphasis on industrializing the manufacture of items such as bricks, cement blocks, and roof tiles, a form of industrialization relatively ignored in the past.[7]

Housing and Urban Growth

Cuba has been almost uniquely successful among developing nations in channeling most internal migration away from the capital and toward provincial capitals and other cities and towns, a feat accomplished *without* direct administrative measures to control internal migration. Before the revolution, Havana absorbed 52 percent of internal migration, in contrast to only 12 percent between 1970 and 1981. In that same period, towns between 2,000 and 20,000 population grew at an annual rate of 3.4 percent and cities from 20,000 to 500,000 inhabitants at 2.3 percent, in contrast to Havana (0.7 percent) and the country as a whole (1.1 percent).

Industrial location policy and improved living standards throughout the country have been the main factors responsible for this shift.[8] For instance, in 1959 Havana—with roughly a fifth of the nation's population—had 70 percent of all nonsugar industry and 63 percent of the doctors, but by 1984 these proportions had fallen to 30 percent in both cases.

Despite this relative achievement, Cuba has not yet been able to reach fully balanced regional development (Perdomo and Montes 1980). For instance, labor shortages are common in the countryside, especially in remote mountainous areas. As a result, a special plan has been developed to provide the necessary infrastructure to retain rural population in such areas. One key aspect of this strategy—pursued since the early 1960s—is to urbanize rural areas throughout the island by creating communities large enough to support social and consumer services. Four types of rural settlements, most of which have fewer than 2,000 inhabitants, have sprung up: (1) agricultural new towns (more than 350) for workers employed in the associated state farms (in many cases peasants were assigned these units after selling their land to the government) (Agüero 1980); (2) housing developments for sugar workers, in or near to existing sugar-mill towns; (3) new communities associated with agricultural cooperatives; and (4) spontaneously formed or enlarged hamlets.

Although the first three of these types of settlement have been "planned," they have not always been planned in relation to each other or to the broader urban system. Hence the size of many communities may have been appropriate for their related farms, but they are not large enough to sustain an adequate level of urban services. Moreover, over time household members find jobs elsewhere, retire, marry, divorce, and so on, often leaving few of the community's residents working in the associated agricultural or industrial enterprise. Some planners have argued for larger settlements housing people employed in a range of local activities, rather than the more dispersed and segmented approach common up to now.

Even successes have not been without their problems. Neglecting Havana in favor of other areas may have suppressed its growth, but it now is paying the cost in a severely deteriorated housing stock. Other cities grew more rapidly but often in problematic ways. Since 1959 the populations of Cuba's largest cities have doubled but their land areas have tripled, a result both of uncontrolled growth and of planned developments occupying more land than necessary.

The 1984 housing law declared a crackdown on uncontrolled construction. Until then, building and land-use regulations were either nonexistent or half-heartedly enforced. Starting in the mid–1980s, local authorities have more actively policed and even demolished some illegal dwellings in their early stages of construction. Moreover, loans are conditioned on obtaining a building permit. The decline in officially reported self-built completions from 45,000 in 1986 to

32,600 in 1988 in part reflects more effective enforcement of building and land use regulations (see also table 11.2).

Issues in Housing Distribution

Cuban policymakers have been striving to balance different objectives in distributing housing: economic development, equity, and improving conditions for those in the worst situations. They have also sought to combat corruption, or the appearance of it, by fostering collective, public forms of allocation. But balancing all of these objectives has been no easy task.

In the early years, "need"—defined in terms of living conditions rather than income—was the main determinant in urban areas for allocating units confiscated from people leaving Cuba. But when 150,000 applications were received for 7,000 vacant units, unduly raising expectations and making a fair choice impossible, the government handed the units over to trade unions to distribute among their members based on need. By the mid–1960s the number of Havana residents living in buildings on the verge of collapse had mushroomed. Therefore, the selection process was transferred back to local administrators using a municipal list of those in dangerous situations, thus opening the way for apparent corruption.

The establishment of the microbrigade system in the early 1970s coincided with a broader movement to increase productivity and deal with the apparent labor shortage through a variety of measures, including a law combating absenteeism and "loafing." Microbrigade housing, as well as other scarce consumer durable goods, were distributed in a public and collective fashion in workplace assemblies. But the criteria were based not only on need but also on "merit," which translated into good job performance and generally positive social behavior. Between 1971 and 1985, 40 percent of all state-built housing has been distributed in this way.

The rest of the government-built housing has been constructed primarily in labor-scarce areas and largely distributed in relation to workplaces. In agricultural new towns units have gone to former peasants and salaried rural workers. Only in new industrial areas, and existing cities and towns in underdeveloped regions, has an explicit bias existed toward managers, skilled workers, technicians, and professionals. Although seen as necessary to ensure balanced regional development in the absence of restrictions on internal migration and significant wage differentials, this policy has been criticized, and greater occupational balance in allocation is increasingly common in such areas.

Unlike state-distributed housing, the range in housing quality and user costs in self-built units has reflected ability to pay to a much greater degree. New regulations attempt to enforce minimum construction standards and prevent overbuilding. But in the countryside, the political and economic consequences of differences in housing quality are already apparent. The new homes of agricultural cooperative members tend to be of higher quality than the salaried cane cutters' new "low-cost housing." Small farmers, who have earned huge sums selling their produce in the short-lived legal farmers' markets or on the black market, have built even more elaborate abodes. This, in turn, discouraged them from joining cooperatives.

There are undoubted resentment and political costs to be paid if high-level or well-connected people are perceived to be receiving housing to which they are not otherwise entitled. But this problem, while always a danger (and despite some well-publicized cases), seems to be kept relatively under control by the dominance of public and collective distribution systems. It is on the other end of the spectrum—those who are deliberately denied better housing—that other problems may also arise. In the revolution's first years the worst shantytowns were cleared and their residents relocated to new housing, as a matter of simple justice and on the assumption that job opportunities and new housing would eliminate perceived antisocial behavior of some of their residents. The early Self Help and Mutual Aid program (run by the Welfare Ministry rather than the one dealing with construction) relocated former shantytown dwellers together in communities each averaging 100 families scattered throughout the largest cities. But this strategy was soon abandoned in favor of dispersing former residents of these settlements and other urban slum areas throughout new and existing housing to more fully integrate them into society and avoid stigmatizing them as former slum dwellers.[9]

After 1970 this approach changed markedly. Rewarding slackers with coveted housing was seen as being just as demoralizing to industrious workers as to pay loafers the same wages whether or not they came to work. A process of "creaming" the most active and hard-working families from the worst slums appears to have occurred, leaving behind those believed to have social problems. Indeed, each successive wave of concern about preventing juvenile delinquency and crime—still low by international standards—has been accompanied by studies of specific neighborhoods where antisocial behavior is thought to be concentrated. The new emphasis on rehabilitating slums, replacing shantytowns with new housing, and distributing a portion of microbrigade units to those in the worst housing is beginning to reverse this situation.

Tenure Security and Housing-Market Flexibility

The Urban Reform Law abolished private renting and subletting, with the exception of hotels, vacation homes, and "guest houses." But there was no forced "rationing" of living space, as occurred in the wake of wartime destruction in parts of socialist Europe. Small families in large houses were not forced to move to smaller units or share their homes with others. This situation has made it extremely difficult to accommodate the changes in household composition and internal migration. Families generously take in visiting friends and relatives but often find it impossible to get them to leave. Many divorced couples continue living together or with their former in-laws, sometimes along with their new spouses. People accepting jobs in distant provinces often live in hotels or worker hostels for extended periods, making it difficult to bring their families with them.

To deal with this situation, the 1984 housing law permits residents to rent out rooms on a short-term basis at free-market prices to no more than two households. It is seen as a transitional measure to provide more dwelling options for recently divorced people, married couples living apart, people doubling up with friends and relatives, and employees temporarily transferred to other parts of the country. Setting maximum rents was considered in the course of drafting the 1984 law but was rejected as an administrative nightmare to enforce. Cuban officials have stated they expect complaints about exorbitant rent levels and some redistribution of income toward "landlords" but that in the long run the only way to overcome this situation is to build more housing. The fact that renters usually share the same dwellings with their landlords tempers some of the worst potential abuses.

A potential landlord's greatest fear is that he or she will not be able to evict lease violators. Tenure security has constituted such an absolute right—nonpayment is dealt with by attachment of wages and unneighborly behavior usually through social workers or the criminal justice system—that the police are loath to carry out the few evictions that are ordered.

A more serious and controversial issue is the conflict between two rights: the right of owners to determine who lives in their homes, and the right of tenure security. The 1984 law and previous regulations had prohibited homeowners from evicting immediate family members. To discourage other unwanted household members from staying, owners could get a court order to withhold up to 50 percent of their income for six months. If they still refused to leave, an eviction could be ordered but was unlikely to be executed. Based on this experience, the 1988 law retained the government's role in arbitrating between household members and instituting wage withholding measures, but ended public responsibility for physically removing unwanted inhabitants. At the same time, additional household members were protected from eviction—regardless of their relationship to the owner—such as mothers with children, the elderly, those who contributed to acquiring or renovating the house, and others.

Achieving housing-market flexibility may conflict with other goals as well. Cuban policymakers seek to prevent housing from becoming a source of unearned enrichment. Hence they restrict home sales and take a dim view of house-exchange brokers. At the same time, they would like to encourage people to move to homes more appropriate for their family size and health needs and nearby their current workplaces or to underpopulated areas. But intra-, not to mention inter-, provincial swaps are difficult to arrange without intermediaries. Moreover, when the government cracked down on private free-market sales, it found people unwilling to sell because "legal" prices were so low, not only compared with free-market prices but also with those of new government units. Steep depreciation formulas left homes built more than twenty-five years ago worth only 30–40 percent of comparable new housing. The government responded by adopting a dual pricing structure: it buys dwellings at higher prices but sells at lower ones.

Popular Participation

Massive public participation in a vast array of civic and economic activities has consistently been a hallmark of the Cuban revolution. Yet at the same time, there has been a pervasive notion that in a socialist society the state can and should ensure that all citizens have the basic necessities of life. The evolution in policy regarding the microbrigades, self-built housing, and other forms of voluntary construction labor reflects both of these tendencies.

Self-Building. In the absence of clear national policy regarding self-built housing before the 1984 law, local governments, publicly owned enterprises, and assorted private individuals stepped in to fill the void. A 1985 study revealed that, aside from items foraged from the natural environment such as wood and thatch, self-builders obtained most of their construction materials from local agencies and workplaces and to a small extent from small-scale illegal private manufacturers. Indeed, even dwellings of wood and thatch had at least cement floors (Comité Estatal 1984a), and quality has steadily improved ever since materials (and limited credit to buy them) became increasingly available after the late 1970s.

Some land was obtained through legal private sales, but more frequently self-builders bought sites illegally or squatted on public or private land (sometimes with local government complicity or acquiescence). Some peasants owning land on the outskirts of cities and towns sold illegally subdivided lots. Infrastructure provision was minimal or absent. For instance, there were 300,000 illegal electrical hookups as of 1979 (one-sixth of all dwellings receiving electricity), which had been reduced by 1987 to 85,000 (half of them in the eastern provinces).

A special census of self-built housing conducted in 1983 (Comité Estatal 1983; Zschäbitz and Lesta 1988) revealed that 180,000 units had been completed between January 1981 and September 1983, and another 90,000 were under construction (including *bohíos* and other poor-quality units not included in other official statistics). Two-thirds of them were new units, and the rest were replacement housing. Of the 45,000 better quality units a year officially reported in 1986, one-fifth were replacement housing, one-quarter were additions to existing dwellings (usually on the second floor), and the rest constituted completely new houses (see also Zschäbitz 1988).

National recognition has stimulated more self-building and also has produced a new set of problems. By 1989, 135,000 units were under construction, creating a nearly insatiable demand for materials. Similarly, demand for state-owned sites greatly exceeded supply. Studies showed that the expense and difficulties of self-building tended to favor the more affluent, and self-building was associated with several well-publicized cases of black marketeering, speculation, and cronyism.

All of these factors led to measures designed to give priority to completing units rather than new starts and to allocate materials, land, and other building assistance to workers based on need, job performance, and social behavior. At the same time, municipal agencies, with the assistance of the block-level CDRs, are attempting to catch up with badly needed infrastructure.

Microbrigades. The reasons the microbrigades were created in the early 1970s, and revived in the mid–1980s, were essentially similar: pent-up housing demand in urban areas (especially Havana), labor shortage in construction, plummeting workplace productivity, and greater emphasis on collective allocation policies. Why then were they on the verge of elimination, and what explains their resurrection (see Mathéy 1988 for information on microbrigades in general)?

The microbrigades grew rapidly until 1975 and then leveled off when materials shortages prevented further expansion. In 1978 government officials proposed phasing out the program for a number of reasons. First, microbrigade housing was perceived to be of lower quality and higher cost than equivalent buildings erected by state brigades. Microbrigade workers, who continued to receive their regular salaries from their workplaces, earned on average higher wages than unskilled construction workers. Productivity was assumed to be lower since microbrigade members worked mostly on labor-intensive traditional and semi-prefabricated buildings, and it was believed they lacked the skills to be employed on some of the new large-panel and high-rise technologies.

Second, employees in workplaces without microbrigades and those living in unsafe and overcrowded dwellings were excluded, since almost all urban housing was distributed through the microbrigades. Third, the microbrigade system appeared to conflict with enterprise self-financing established by the new Economic Management and Planning System. Fourth, by the late 1970s overall productivity in the economy was increasing at a healthy rate, making it more difficult to remove workers without affecting production.

Despite trade union opposition, the slow phaseout began. In this "twilight" period, the microbrigades were paid through the Ministry of Construction, rather than their workplaces; some 20 percent of the units were allocated for relocation housing for those in dangerous situations or whose homes were cleared for public works; and working in a microbrigade increasingly became seen as an activity just for people needing housing.

Meanwhile, the expected benefits of state-brigade construction failed to materialize. The rate of new housing construction dropped; both quality and productivity declined; and infrastructure and related community and commercial facilities were largely ignored. Equipment, materials, and labor were often shifted to higher-priority projects. High turnover produced a less skilled and motivated building work force. Despite some degree of youth unemployment, construction remained unattractive. Labor shortages proved so acute that Havana started temporarily "borrowing" construction workers from the eastern provinces.

The factors leading to the 1986 revival of the microbrigades involved not only the construction ministry's evident failure to improve production of housing and other projects but also the array of events provoking or coinciding with Cuba's "rectification" process. They include wage inflation and overstaffing in many workplaces, the accumulation of vast sums of money—licitly or illicitly—by some self-employed and other individuals (and related corruption and speculation scandals), a decline in voluntary work, concern with juvenile delinquency and other social problems and the apparent association of some of these problems with slum housing, and severe contraction in imports purchased with hard currency, provoking temporary layoffs.

The microbrigades, in their revived forms, seemed to offer something for everyone. Prior objections evaporated: microbrigades were now seen as reducing costs and promoting higher quality, productivity, and efficiency. Employees in overstaffed workplaces maintain their ties and seniority while temporarily transferring to the microbrigade—a politically more palatable solution than massive layoffs—and their salaries are reimbursed to the workplace by the central government. "Social microbrigades" have provided neighborhood-based jobs for unemployed youth and involved local residents in repairing and rehabilitating their own buildings.

Costs are reduced by producing more with no increase in total salaries (except for those members of "social microbrigades" not previously employed). Higher productivity and quality in construction are achieved by a more motivated labor force, which can also call upon its own workplace to help resolve equipment and transportation bottlenecks. By developing their own productive infrastructure, microbrigades' resources are less vulnerable to being shifted to other projects. Moreover, microbrigades have been assigned to work on high-rise and other prefabricated buildings.

Unlike the 1970s microbrigades, which primarily concentrated on a few large-scale housing developments on the outskirts of major cities, the 1980s microbrigades are decentralized to each municipality. Hence the microbrigades have been in the forefront of seeking new designs for "in-fill" and contextual building. There is even talk of establishing "neighborhood architects," the design equivalent of the newly instituted local "family doctor."

Several of the themes of rectification appear in connection with the microbrigades. One is an emphasis on combining self-interest with unselfish assistance to others. This is manifested in the microbrigades by allocating 40 percent of units to others (50 percent in 1987 and 1988), by devoting nearly half of their efforts to building community facilities, and by ensuring that all employees in need in the workplace are equally eligible to receive housing, whether or not they participated in construction. In addition, voluntary work is an integral part of the microbrigade concept: brigade members themselves work longer hours than normal; others from the workplace help out evenings and weekends; other citizens contribute labor through their CDRs or their workplaces. Some microbrigades function only after regular working hours (usually residents of slums and shantytowns who have not been able to get paid leave from work or from workplaces that cannot spare workers). A few microbrigades building community facilities by day have formed nighttime microbrigades to erect housing.

Initial results have been impressive, but transitional and ongoing difficulties remain. Within eighteen months, Havana alone had more people incorporated in microbrigades than existed in the entire country in 1975. Inevitably, such rapid growth has created a variety of problems: organizational difficulties; shortages of tools, machinery, and safety gear; and the need to train a large number of people all at once. Materials shortages, especially for finishing work, has meant that once again new projects are started before others are completed. Although productivity gains through better management have been remarkable in a number of workplaces, in others, attempting to maintain production has meant putting in overtime. Workplaces, schools, and neighborhood organizations compete for voluntary workers, and it remains to be seen how long people can continue working so many hours without affecting their health, family lives, studies, and other commitments as well as the quality of construction.

CONCLUSIONS

Cuban policymakers now consider housing and community facilities to be an integral part of economic development after decades of viewing them as less important "nonproductive" investments. This makes it more likely that Cuba will attain its current goal of producing 9.5 units per 1,000 population by the year 2000.

The main challenge will be to use its resources effectively and efficiently to achieve that objective. Cuba has demonstrated considerable creativity and flexibility in correcting past mistakes and revising policy in response to changing situations. Self-building will probably represent at least half of new construction, and the main concern will be to improve quality, channel growth, and prevent illicit activities. Cuban officials generally prefer microbrigades over self-building for ideological and practical reasons: higher productivity through the use of higher technology and mass production, construction of community facilities and units for others in need, democratic allocation of units, contribution to controlling inflation and increasing productivity in the economy as a whole, and avoiding urban sprawl by promoting higher residential densities. Nevertheless, state brigades are favored in areas with greater labor reserves and to erect housing where needed to ensure a labor force for economic development; and self-building is encouraged for constructing additions and some "in-fill" housing, as well as in small towns and cities and the outskirts of larger urban areas.

As in other countries, Cuba's recent policies have involved privatization, deregulation, and decentralization, but with some notable differences. The main reasons for privatization were to foster a uniform tenure status (in a country where more than half of the residents were already homeowners), legalize ambiguous situations, and foster greater resident responsibility for maintenance and repair. There is some increase in payments (for maintenance fees and new owners), but tenure security is ensured, and low- and moderate-income families are protected.

Deregulation of renting and housing exchanges has provided greater flexibility to the housing market but at the cost of free-market prices. The about-face on deregulation of buying and selling, and the subsequent system of dual pricing, illustrates the difficulties even socialist economies have in suppressing unearned income from housing without draconian administrative measures, many of which have proved unworkable.

Cuba's greater decentralization of housing management and construction has been made possible by its earlier decentralization of government and economic functions, as well as Cuba's long-standing tradition of neighborhood activism.

Despite housing continuing to be a major problem in Cuba, its record stands in sharp contrast to the rest of Latin America and the Third World, where one-third to one-half of the urban population subsists in miserable slums and shantytowns and the rural population is even more poorly housed. Can Cuba's experience be applied elsewhere? Many of Cuba's housing policies, such as the microbrigades, would be virtually impossible to implement in capitalist countries, given private control of workplaces and unemployment. Cuba's experience, however, may be of greater relevance to socialist developed countries, many of which experience low productivity coupled with labor shortages, as well as to socialist developing countries, if their level of development is taken into account.[10]

NOTES

1. For more information on the history of Cuban housing since the revolution, and its landmark housing laws, see Acosta and Harody 1971; Agüero 1980; Castex 1986; Eckstein 1977; Fernández Núñez 1976; Fields 1985; Hamberg 1986; Mace 1979; Ortega Morales et al. 1987; Roca 1979; Segre 1980; and Vega Vega 1962, 1986. Some information in this article is based on materials that are not readily available, such as articles in newspapers, magazines, and professional journals; reports of speeches; conference papers and presentations; and personal correspondence and interviews. Please contact the author through the publisher to obtain any further citations. Note that most sources cited above do not discuss self-built housing; official statistics did not begin to reflect such construction more accurately until the mid–1980s.

2. The term *self-built* refers to informal actions initiated and largely organized by individual households to distinguish such activities from more formal self-help schemes. In practice, however, this kind of housing is rarely completely ''self-built''; the household usually receives assistance from family, friends and contracted labor.

3. Sources for this section include the Comité Estatal 1980, 1983, 1984a, 1984b, 1985; and Dirección Central 1976. See also Banco Popular de Ahorro 1988; and Luzón 1988.

4. *Bohíos*, which are impermanent structures (usually rebuilt every eight to ten years), and tenements (almost all of which were constructed before the revolution) are not included

in this figure. The 1980–1985 figures also exclude two other categories: (1) units with walls of wood and roofs of tarpaper or thatch (25,000 built during the 1981–1983 period); and (2) units with walls of adobe, mud, or palm leaf or board; and roofs of tile, metal, fibrocement, thatch, or tarpaper (38,000 in the same period) (Comité Estatal 1983).

5. For more information on the 1984 housing law and its regulations, discussed in this and other sections, see "Ley No. 48: Ley General de la Vivienda," 1984; Vega Vega 1986; and the entire July-September 1987 issue of the *Revista Cubana de Derecho*, which contains relevant articles as well as regulations regarding multiple dwellings, tied housing, tenements, pricing, sales, and others. For the 1988 housing law, see "Ley No. 65: Ley General de Vivienda," 1989.

6. For more information on construction technology, urban renewal, historic preservation, and other housing design matters, see the Cuban professional journals *Arquitectura Cuba* and *Arquitectura y Urbanismo*; and Coyula, 1985.

7. In her generally favorable discussion of Cuba's experience in industrializing construction, Jill Wells (1986) noted that the essence of industrialization is standardization and repetition, not necessarily full-scale prefabrication.

8. For generally sympathetic views on Cuban urban and regional planning see Acosta and Hardoy 1971; Barkin 1978; Gugler 1980; Landstreet 1981; and Susman 1987. For a more critical view, see Slater 1982. See also Diáz-Briquets 1988.

9. See Butterworth 1980; and Lewis, Lewis, and Rigdon 1977, 1978, for 1970 studies of relocated slum dwellers.

10. See Mathéy 1988 for a discussion of the possibilities of transferring the microbrigade concept to other contexts; the Summer 1985 issue of *Trialog* (Darmstadt, West Germany) devoted to shelter policies in socialist Third World nations; and Wells's (1986) description of the problems of transferring Cuban construction methods to other developing nations.

REFERENCES

Acosta, Maruja, and Jorge E. Hardoy. 1971. *Reforma Urbana en Cuba Revolucionaria*. Caracas: Síntesis Dosmil. English Translation: *Urban Reform in Revolutionary Cuba*. Occasional Papers 1. New Haven: Antilles Research Program, Yale University, 1973.

Agüero, Nisia. 1980. "La vivienda: experiencia de la revolución cubana." *Revista Interamericana de Planificación* 14 (June): 160–73.

Banco Nacional de Cuba. 1975. *Desarrollo y perspectivas de la economía cubana*. Havana: Banco Nacional de Cuba.

Banco Popular de Ahorro. 1988. "Población y fondo de viviendas. 1971–1985." *Economía y Desarrollo* 88, no. 2: 118–23.

Barkin, David. 1978. "Confronting the Separation of Town and Country in Cuba." In *Marxism and the Metropolis*, edited by W. K. Tabb and L. Sawers, 317–37. New York: Oxford University Press. Similar versions published in *Antipode* 12, no. 3 (1980): 31–40 (in English); and in *Boletín de Estudios Latinoamericanos y del Caribe* (Amsterdam), no. 27 (December 1979): 77–95 (in Spanish).

Butterworth, Douglas. 1980. *The People of Buena Ventura: Relocation of Slum Dwellers in Postrevolutionary Cuba*. Urbana: University of Illinois Press.

Castex, Patrick. 1986. *La politique de production-distribution du logement à Cuba*. Paris: Groupe de Recherche et d'Échanges Technologiques.

Comité Estatal de Estadísticas. 1980. *Anuario Estadístico de Cuba: 1980*. Havana.
————. 1983. *Censo de Viviendas Construídas por la Población, 1981–1983*. Havana.
————. 1984a. *Censo de Población y Viviendas: 1981. República de Cuba*. Vol. 16. Havana.
————. 1984b. *La población cubana en 1953 y 1981*. Havana.
————. 1986. *Anuario Estadístico de Cuba: 1985*. Havana.
Coyula, Mario. 1985. "Vivienda, renovación urbana y poder popular: Algunas consideraciones sobre La Habana." *Arquitectura y Urbanismo* 2:12–17. English versions: "Housing, Urban Renewal, and Popular Power: Some Reflections on Havana." *Berkeley Planning Journal* 2 (Spring-Fall 1985): 41–52; "Housing, Urban Renovation, and Popular Power." *Trialog* (Darmstadt, West Germany) 6 (1985): 35–40.
Díaz-Briquets, Sergio. 1988. "Regional Differences in Development and Living Standards in Revolutionary Cuba." *Cuban Studies* 18: 45-63.
Dirección Central de Estadística. 1976. *La situación de la vivienda en Cuba y su evolución perspectiva*. Havana: Editorial Orbe.
Donnison, David, and Clare Ungerson. 1982. *Housing Policy*. Middlesex, Eng.: Penguin.
Eckstein, Susan. 1977. "The Debourgeoisement of Cuban Cities." In *Cuban Communism* (3rd Edition), edited by I. L. Horowitz, 443-74. New Brunswick, N.J.: Transaction Books. Spanish translation: "Las ciudades en Cuba socialista." *Revista Mexicana de Sociología* 40, no. 1, (1978).
Fernández Núñez, José Manuel. 1976. *La vivienda en Cuba*. Havana: Editorial Arte y Literatura.
Fields, Gary. 1985. "Economic Development and Housing Policy in Cuba." *Berkeley Planning Journal* 2, nos. 1–2: 53–80.
Gugler, Josef. 1980. " 'A Minimum of Urbanism and a Maximum of Ruralism': The Cuban Experience." *International Journal of Urban and Regional Research* 4, no. 4: 516–34. Also published in *Comparative Studies in International Development* 15 (Summer 1980) and *Revista Mexicana de Sociología* 43 (October-December 1981): 1465–86 (in Spanish).
Hamberg, Jill. 1986. "The Dynamics of Cuban Housing Policy." In *Critical Perspectives on Housing*, edited by R. Bratt, C. Hartman, and A. Meyerson, 586–624. Philadelphia: Temple University Press. Reprinted as *Under Construction: Housing Policy in Revolutionary Cuba*. New York: Center for Cuban Studies, 1986.
Instituto Nacional de la Vivienda. 1988. *Resumen Anual*. Havana: Instituto Nacional de la Vivienda, Dirección de la Economía.
Luzón, José. 1988. "Housing in Socialist Cuba: An Analysis Using Cuban Censuses of Population and Housing." *Cuban Studies* 18: 65-83.
Landstreet, Barent. 1981. "Urbanization and Ruralism and Cuba." In *Dependent Agricultural Development and Agrarian Reform in Latin America*, edited by L. R. Alschuler, 147–68. Ottawa: University of Ottawa Press.
Lewis, Oscar, Ruth M. Lewis, and Susan M. Rigdon. 1977, 1978. *Living the Revolution*. Vol. 1: *Four Men*; Vol. 2: *Four Women*; Vol. 3: *Neighbors*. Urbana: University of Illinois Press.
"Ley No. 48. Ley General de la Vivienda." 1984. *Gaceta Oficial de la República de Cuba* 22:101–22.
"Ley No. 65. Ley General de la Vivienda." 1989. *Gaceta Oficial de la República de Cuba* 3: 5–32.

Mace, Rodney. 1979. "Housing." In *Cuba: The Second Decade*, edited by J. Griffiths and P. Griffiths, 121–30. London: Writers and Readers Publishing Cooperative.

Mathéy, Kosta. 1988. "Microbrigades: A Cuban Interpretation of Self-Help Housing." *Trialog* (Darmstadt, W.G.) no. 18: 24–30. Other versions of this article in *Bulletin of Latin American Research* 8 (Spring 1989) and *Habitat International* 12 (April 1989).

Ortega Morales, Lourdes, Alfonso Alfonso González, Angela Rojas Avalos, Gilberto Hernández Garmendía, and Obdulio Coca Rodríguez. 1987. *Nuevas tendencias en la política habitacional y la producción de vivienda en Cuba. Panorama de su desarrollo*. Hamburg: Technical University Hamburg-Harburg, Forschungsschwerpunkt 6, vol. 27.

Perdomo, José, and Norma Montes, 1980. "Las proporciones económicas territoriales en la República de Cuba." *Cuestiones de la Economía Planificada* 3 (March-April): 103–21.

Roca, Sergio. 1979. *Housing in Socialist Cuba*. Miami: Florida International University, International Conference on Housing Problems, 1979; in *Housing, Planning, Financing, Construction*, edited by O. Ural, 62–74. New York: Pergamon Press, 1979.

Segre, Roberto. 1980. *La vivienda en Cuba en el Siglo XX: República y Revolución*. Mexico: Editorial Concepto. Also published as *La vivienda en Cuba: República y Revolución*. Havana: Universidad de La Habana, 1985.

Slater, David. 1982. "State and Territory in Postrevolutionary Cuba: Some Critical Reflections on the Development of Spatial Policy." *International Journal of Urban and Regional Research* 6 (March): 1–33.

Susman, Paul. 1987. "Spatial Equality in Cuba." *International Journal of Urban and Regional Research* 2 (June): 218–42. Similar version published as "Spatial Equality and Socialist Transformation in Cuba." In *The Socialist Third World: Urban Development and Territorial Planning*, edited by D. Forbes and N. Thrift, 250–81. Oxford: Basil Blackwell.

Vega Vega, Juan. [1962]. *La reforma urbana de Cuba y otras leyes en relación con la vivienda*. Havana: n.p.

———. 1986. *Comentarios a la Ley General de la Vivienda*. Havana: Editorial de Ciencias Sociales.

Wells, Jill. 1986. *The Construction Industry in Developing Countries: Alternative Strategies for Development*. London: Croom Helm.

Zschäbitz, Ulrike, and Francisco Lesta. 1988. *Construcción por esfuerzo propio en la Ciudad de La Habana hasta 1985: Algunos alcances para su estudio tipológico*. Hamburg: Technical University Hamburg-Harburg, Forschungsschwerpunkt 6, vol. 36.

12

Mexico

PETER M. WARD

HOUSING AND MEXICO'S POLITICAL ECONOMY

My aim in this chapter is to introduce the reader to the nature of the housing problem in Mexico and to explore the ways in which the public, private, and "popular" sectors have responded.[1] The focus will be oriented primarily toward the public sector response, not because it is the most important (I will show that it is not) but because much has already been written about the nature and role of "irregular" settlement and self-help in Mexico. Since the early 1970s successive Mexican governments, like those in many other countries, have undertaken a more positive view of irregular settlement, frequently intervening to encourage upgrading and dwelling consolidation through the provision of services and public utilities, the legalization of "clouded" land titles, the creation of building materials yards and technical advisory centers, and so on.[2] I hope that the data presented in this chapter will allow cross-cultural comparisons to be made with other contributions to this book.

The nature of housing demand and supply does not occur in a vacuum but is closely tied to the changing political economy of a nation and region. Thus the construction industry forms an important part of the overall economic development process. Decisions about housing production and its location are an outcome of competing claims between different socioeconomic interest groups. Thus it is imperative to understand the contextual background in which policy and production are cultivated.

Development and Social Change, 1940–1970

The economic and social upheaval caused by the Mexican Revolution during the second decade of this century has given rise to one of the most stable and arguably least oppressive societies in Latin America. Yet it is also one of the most unequal. Neither rapid economic growth between 1940 and 1970 nor the enormous expansion in oil production during the late 1970s has significantly changed the levels of income inequality (Navarette 1970; Hansen 1974; Makin 1984), although both processes have generated major changes in the nature of economic activity. The principal beneficiaries of the Mexican "miracle" were the middle- and upper-middle-income groups: there was little trickle down to poorer sectors.

This "miracle" roughly spans the period 1940 to 1970 when the Mexican economy grew at more than 6 percent annually (more than 3 percent per capita). In some sectors such as manufacturing growth rates were considerably higher as import-substituting industrialization complemented investment in activities that produced goods for export. State support for capital under this model of "stable development" was exercised in several ways. Political stability was institutionalized through a single government party, the PRI (see list of abbreviations at the end of this chapter for all acronyms used in the text). Several public financial institutions provided the vehicle for large-scale state support in underwriting the development of basic industries and infrastructure such as electric power, railways, and roads (Hansen 1974). The scenario in agriculture was less impressive. Although overall production rates had increased very fast at the outset, they had declined to an average of 4.3 percent between 1950 and 1960 and to 2 percent in the latter half of the 1970s (Cockcroft 1983; Heath 1985).

The combined effects of intensifying income inequality, growing landlessness among the peasantry, and lack of governmental response to attend to the needs of rapidly swelling urban populations culminated in severe social unrest during the late 1960s (Tello, 1978).

These processes generated fundamental changes in the national economic structure and location of residence of the work force. Between 1940 and 1979 the proportion of the economically active population engaged in agriculture declined from 65 to 29 percent (Cockcroft, 1983, 183). Industry, on the other hand, raised its share from 15 to 28 percent, as did services from 19 to 43 percent. Total population increased rapidly from just under 20 million in 1940 to an estimated 77.4 million in 1985. In terms of location of residence, the center of gravity shifted ever more toward the urban. Industrialization strategies required cheap labor, much of which in the initial stages of development was to be found in rural areas. Thus many people moved: whereas only 22 percent of the national population in 1940 lived in centers of 10,000 people or more, by the early 1980s the figure was around 55 percent (Scott 1982, 53). If one takes a smaller population threshold to define "urban," the proportion is even higher (table 12.1).

The Economic Model of "Shared Development" Since 1970

The need to head off the social unrest alluded to above and to stimulate economic growth led the incoming administration of President Echeverría (1970–1976) to adopt a different approach—that of "shared development." The state took a more assertive role in economic affairs and created or revitalized a large number of state enterprises in the fields of production, distribution, and welfare (Tello 1978; Goulet 1983). The public sector expenditure on social welfare increased, and many new social development agencies were created. The real value of wages rose, and tax reforms were implemented. These changes were not achieved without cost, and strong resistance was encountered from the private sector and oligarchic groups that deepened into a political crisis during the latter years of the Echeverría administration (1975–1976).

Nevertheless, the economy continued to grow at a satisfactory rate during the 1970s (at an average 5.9 percent of GDP, 1971–1980), but it was not a smooth passage. There were three "depressions": first in 1971; the second between late 1974 and 1976, which lasted until President López Portillo (1976–1982) threw off the shackles of IMF intervention and quietly reflated the economy in 1978; the third after the economy had overheated, bringing about further currency devaluations and IMF intervention in 1982–1983. Oil has played a major role in the rags-riches-rags scenario. The groundwork for production was laid by Echeverría, enjoyed but mismanaged by López Portillo, and suffered by his successor (De la Madrid 1982–1988), saddled as he was by a huge foreign debt (much of it run up to finance oil production or set against it as collateral), high inflation, and overdependence on oil for foreign exchange earnings (Cornelius 1986). The economic emergency plan initiated by De la Madrid in 1983, directly

Table 12.1
Population Growth, Urbanization, and Housing Conditions, Mexico, 1960–1980

	1960		1970		1980		1985	
TOTAL POPULATION	34,923,129	100%	48,225,238	100%	66,846,833	100%	77.4m	100%
urban[1]	15,540,793	44.5	24,178,684	50.1	40,207,561	66.1		66.1
rural	19,328,336	55.5	24,046,554	49.8	26,639,272	39.9		39.9
TOTAL DWELLINGS	6,409,096	100%	8,286,369	100%	12,074,609	100%	14.5m	100%
urban	2,710,177	42.3	4,166,161	50.3	nd			
rural	3,698,919	57.3	4,120,208	49.7	nd			
OWNER HOUSEHOLDS[2]		nd		66%				67%
						68%		
AVERAGE NUMBER OF PEOPLE PER DWELLINGS	5.45		5.82		5.50		5.35	
QUALITY OF DWELLING: CONSTRUCTION - WALLS								
mud brick (adobe)		50%		30%		21%		19%
brick (tabique)		24%		44%		56%		61%
wood/embarro/other		26%		26%		23%		19%
QUALITY OF DWELLING:								
no water supply	4,339,115	68%	3,230,202	39%	3,541,445	29%	3.5m	24%
no drainage	4,557,626	71%	4,845,903	59%	5,916,514	49%	6.3m	44%

Source: Mexico: Population Census. 1960, 1970, and 1980 (various tables); 1985 data are drawn from the *IV Informe del Gobierno, Apendice Estadistico*, p. 353.

[1]Urban = more than 5,000 people.
[2]Owner households include those who may not have full legal title.

shaped by IMF orthodoxy, sought to reduce the public deficit by sharp reductions in public spending, to improve external payments through flexible exchange-rate policies in order to ensure competitiveness abroad, and to reduce inflation by tight fiscal and monetary policies, wage restraints, and so on (Navarrete 1986). Although considerable success was observed in most of these fields between 1982 and 1985 and Mexico was allowed to reschedule principal repayments on its debts and contracted new loans to manage its interest servicing, this was undone by the crash in oil prices early in 1986. Now it appears that Mexico once again is expected to lead the way with a new experimental economic strategy approved by the IMF in which major new credits have been contracted as part of a growth-oriented adjustment package in which the level of assistance varies in accordance with oil prices (Navarrete 1986).

Government and Politics: Who Rules?

The party political structure in Mexico is dominated by the Government party (the PRI), which regularly secures a large majority of the vote—by fair means or foul. This facade of democracy was fast becoming tarnished by the early 1970s (Gónzalez Casanova 1970), and steps toward political revitalization were undertaken through reforms in 1973 and 1978. These reforms widened the opportunities for the existence of opposition parties and gave them a guaranteed 25 percent of the seats in Congress. However, the PRI's role remains firmly that of ensuring quiescence and obedience among the working classes through its various sectors and of mobilizing electoral support when required (Hansen 1974; Smith 1979). The problem is that the PRI is finding this task ever more difficult as it is faced with an increasingly technocratic government that is less willing to engage in blatant partisanship and to direct favors and resources toward its own party and is faced with a more voluble and viable opposition (Ward 1986). The 1988 elections for presidency and legislature resulted in a narrow victory for the PRI after it had failed to accommodate demands for internal reform from leading radicals within its ranks, some of whom subsequently contested the election as a ''democratic front'' in combination with left-wing opposition parties. If it is to capture the political ground lost during the 1988 elections, then their narrow victory will oblige the PRI and the Salinas government (1988–94) to undertake major internal party reform and to initiate measures in the fields of housing and social development in order to achieve a dramatic improvement in living conditions (Cornelius et al. 1989).

The federal government in Mexico is a relatively independent apparatus to that of the party. Elected for nonrenewable six-year terms, the president has enormous power. He aims to reconcile a wide range of interest groups in his cabinet as part of a delicate balancing act of appeasing the political and economic elite. However, each administration inevitably creates imbalances and this partially explains the shift back and forth between activist and consolidatory presidents (Purcell and Purcell 1980; Smith 1979). Policy directions are firmly set by the executive and followed closely by cabinet secretaries. The six-year cycle creates a dynamic of its own: two years to form teams, identify policies, and secure resources; three years' action; and a final year of rundown and hustling to get into the incoming administration (Grindle 1977). It also results in major discontinuities of policy between one administration and the next. In effect, long-term planning is anathema in Mexico.

Thus since 1970 the economic background is one of shifting economic fortunes, growing intervention of the state in social and economic affairs, and an increasingly technocratic structure of government. Elsewhere I have sought to develop the argument that there is an increasing strain between the political party and the governmental technocratic bureaucracy (Ward 1986). Here the reader need only note that tension and recognize that housing policy in the late 1980s and early 1990s under President Salinas is likely to be informed by severe financial budgetary constraints and an attraction for less expensive solutions, more technocratic modes of decision making (specifically, greater efficiency and better value for the money), and growing pressures from the governing party to intervene preferentially on its behalf in urban development matters in order to offset some of the heightened social costs associated with ongoing austerity and, as outlined above, to recover substantially the PRI share of the vote.

HOUSING NEEDS AND HOUSING "DEFICITS"

The demand for housing in any society is itself a function of that society. Demands are shaped by the prevailing norms and customs relating to age at marriage and residence thereafter; by the ideology of ownership; by the articulation of fractions of capital associated with construction, financing, and distribution; as well as by existing opportunities for housing acquisition. A serious analysis of demand needs to take account of all of these processes. However, such a task is beyond the space constraints of this chapter, and I have sought only to identify the numerical demand for housing generated by population increase and rates of urbanization. Assuming an average household size at the level that prevailed at the beginning of each decade (see table 12.1), one can obtain a rough estimate of the likely annual demand for new dwellings.[3] For example, during the twenty-year period since 1960 the number of dwelling units required per annum in each decade would have been about 245,000 and 320,000. Figures in brackets on the bottom line of table 12.2 indicate the average actual public housing production levels achieved during earlier periods. Measured against demand they were inconsequential. Between 1965 and 1970 annual production for low-income groups represented approximately 8 percent of the total increase in dwellings; during the 1970s it rose to around 17 percent.

I estimate that during the 1980s, to accommodate national population increases assuming an average 5.5 persons per dwelling, it will be necessary to build around 476,000 dwellings each year, or, if one takes low- and middle-income housing then the public sector alone needs to sponsor 300,000 units each year according to government sources. As I note below, in spite of the somewhat exaggerated claims for production in, for example, 1985, the total was below 200,000, and a more accurate figure would be around half of that amount (i.e., approximately 20 percent of total annual demand and one-third of the total demand from the poorer sectors).

However, this offers only a partial perspective on the increase of housing stock relative to households: there is also a backlog of inadequate or substandard housing that needs to be replaced. In addition, there are families "stacked up" within the housing system who are dissatisfied with their residential arrangement because they have been unable to secure a dwelling of their own. This includes families who rent but wish to own or who share facilities with parents or with kin (Gilbert 1987). Nor is all existing housing satisfactory in terms of structure, services, and amount of sleeping space. Informal housing production within the popular sector (e.g., self-build irregular settlement) invariably comprises dwelling units built, at least temporarily, from provisional materials and without adequate servicing. Thus housing "deficits" and housing policy need to take account of production to improve residential living conditions. Each of the following tiers of demand adds significantly to the definition of "need" at any one time: (1) population growth and the formation of new households; (2) those households whose aspirations are blocked and who share or rent; (3) those whose homes are substandard, requiring improvement; (4) dwellings requiring replacement as they come to the end of their useful life.

One study (Mexico 1982) estimated the accumulated deficit that existed in 1970. In addition to the 3.6 million new units that were required to house the 1.9 million families without a dwelling and the 1.7 million living in extremely deteriorated conditions, the study identified the number of "actions" required to cover deficits of residential water supply and drainage (5.1 and 4.9 million actions, respectively). In the field of rehabilitation, some 4.8 million actions were required (Gónzalez Rubí 1984, 394).

A set of indicators (table 12.1) seek to identify the relative and absolute scale of housing deficits in Mexico between 1960 and 1980 according to the national population census. Two features emerge from an analysis of table 12.1. First, the high absolute deficiencies in house construction standards demonstrated by the poor quality of building materials and the lack of basic water services such as a piped water supply and drainage facilities. To allow comparability between the three censuses, it is necessary sometimes to take a fairly generous appraisal of what constitutes a household water supply—public standpipes in the street might reasonably be regarded as a perverse definition of a domestic service. Although it is not shown in the table, urban areas are generally better provided for than rural ones (Ward 1986, 88). Deficiencies in 1985 included a total of 3.5 million dwellings without an interior or exterior water supply and a large number of dwellings in which the walls were made of "traditional" or insubstantial building materials (table 12.1).

The second feature that emerges from table 12.1 is the substantial relative

Table 12.2
Formal Housing Production for Low-Income Groups, Mexico, 1947–1979

HOUSING AGENCY	1947-64		1965-70		1971-79		TOTAL	
Welfare agencies:	**57,002**	47%	**1,300**	1%	**5,139**	1%	**73,041**	9.6%
Civil pensions/ISSSTE	(45,302)		(1,300)		(4,375)			
IMSS	(10,600)		(nd)		(–)			
Military pensions	(1,100)				(764)			
Social Membership Funds	–	–	–	–	**276,561**	54%	**276,561**	36.4%
INFONAVIT					(213,785)			
FOVISSSTE					(60,811)			
FOVIMI					(1,965)			
Public Housing Agencies	**34,698**	28.7%	**36,016**	30%	**88,201**	17.3%	**158,915**	20.9%
INV/INDECO	(10,600)		(3,800)		(62,695)			
BANOBRAS/FHP	(24,098)		(16,644)		(19,550)			
FOVI (direct construction)	(–)		(15,572)		(5,956)			
Others	**29,500**	24.3%	**6,000**	5%	**34,454**	6.7%	**69,954**	9.2%
DDF	(11,700)		(6,000)		(32,198)			
PEMEX	(13,100)		(nd)		(nd)			
Trusts	(–)		(–)		(2,256)			
Private Housing Financed through FOVI/FOLGA	–	–	**76,443**	63.8%	**106,689**	20.9%	**183,132**	24.0%
TOTAL (average per annum)	**121,200** (7,129)	100%	**119,759** (19,960)	100%	**511,044** (56,783)	100%	**761,603**	100%

Sources: Adapted from Garza and Schteingart, 1978; also from sources noted on table 12.3, below.

Notes: The following notes also apply to table 12.3.

1. INFONAVIT. Data are for "completed dwellings," but each year's total also includes those dwellings begun and carried over from previous years. Dwellings constructed in the year specified vary between one-quarter and one-eighth of the totals declared. INFONAVIT, *Informes annuales*, 1979–1985; *Informes del gobierno*, various years, Sector Desarrollo Urbano y Ecología. The 1986 data are estimated from *Programa de vivienda, 1987*.

2. FOVISSSTE. Data are for "completed dwellings" under the scheme for financing "social modules." Credits for refurbishment or rehabilitation are not included. The 1980 and 1985 are from *Anexo Estadístico, Fondo de la Vivienda (FOVISSSTE)*. The 1981–1984 data are from *Informes del Gobierno*. The 1986 data are from "Cuadro anexo" Dirección de Proyectos FOVISSSTE.

3. FOVIMI/ISSSFAM. Housing funds for military personnel, now the Social Security Institute for Mexican Armed Forces. Comisión intersectorial de planeación, programación y financiamiento de la vivienda, *Estadística básica de vivienda, 1973–80*, and supplements for 1981–1982. The 1985 material is from a report to the Labour Congress by the Ministry of Housing, May 1985.

4. BANOBRAS/FHP. Data are for Fondo de Habitaciones Populares and include both "completed dwellings" and "urbanized plots" (sites and services). Data are from *VI Informe of José López Portillo*, Asentamientos Humanos, 56–57.

5. FONHAPO. Data are for various programs ("completed dwellings"; "improvements to existing stock"; "dwellings begun" in each year and are, therefore, always lower except in 1985 when budget adjustments provoked an attempt to complete almost twice as many units as would be initiated in that year. Documento interno de evaluación.

6. INDECO. This agency was being closed down during 1980–1981, and no data are given since the programs frequently cited for this period were initiated much earlier. Inclusion of the 15,000 sites and services units claimed by the agency for each year would be misleading since few were constructed.

7. DDF. Includes dwellings built by CODEUR, 'Plan Tepito,' and the Director General de Vivienda. *Informes del Gobierno*. Regularization of plots is not included.

8. Trusts within the SAHOP/SEDUE sector include fideicomisos for Monterrey (FOMERREY), Acapulco (FIDACA), Lazaro Cárdenas (FIDELAC), Puerto Vallarta (FPVALLARTA). *Informes del Gobierno*; various years. Data include completed dwellings, core units, urbanized plots.

9. Trusts not within the SAHOP/SEDUE sector include housing built for workers in the national petroleum and federal electricity industries. Again, it is likely that these data include housing completed from previous years rather than the annual increment of new housing. Comisión intersectorial.

10. Housing constructed in response to the earthquake damage. Most of the program was concentrated within the Federal District and took place in 1985–1987. Figures do not include 6,710 rehabilitated units by RHP (Mexico 1987, 3–4); 1,200 *rehabilitaciones* by "Phase II" (Mexico 1987, Fase II; 4), and 9,218 apartments in the Nonoalco Tlatelolco Program (Mexico 1986, 77).

11. Housing constructed using credit supplied through FOVI/FOGA and the Housing Finance Program. The 1981–1983 data are from the Banco de Mexico, *Informes annuales*; 1980 is an estimate derived from the amount invested in real terms assuming a similar ratio of real cost/dwelling unit for 1981; the 1984–1985 data are from the same source and are credits authorized each year.

415

improvement in housing conditions recorded during the decade 1970–1980. Population densities per dwelling declined; building materials became more substantial and permanent (see the proportion built of *tabique*), and the relative proportion of dwellings without water and drainage declined significantly. Despite these achievements, it is worth noting that in absolute terms the scale of the deficit in provision of services was as great or greater in the 1980s as a decade previously. In terms of its ability to reduce the deficit through housing improvements Mexico has "run fast to stand still." In 1980 there was an estimated national deficit of 4.7 million dwellings. Of them, 1.2 million new dwellings were needed along with 3.5 million dwellings that required rehabilitation or improvement (*Congreso de Trabajo* in *Unomasuno* January 24, 1983).

HOUSING PRODUCTION: WHO GETS WHAT AND FROM WHOM?

Access to housing is determined in Mexico in two ways: by income, and/or through eligibility (by type of employment) to one of the social membership funds, welfare agencies, or employee's unions. Income is the key variable. In Mexico approximately 77 percent of the economically active population in 1980 earned less than 2.5 times the minimum salary. This is a minimum subsistence wage that must be paid to those in formal employment and that varies according to region and type of job. In 1986 the average weekly minimum wage was around 20 U.S. dollars. In effect this means that if they fail to acquire housing through the public sector, four-fifths of the economically active population must rely almost exclusively on the private rental or private "informal" sector. Their incomes are too low for them to afford loans at commercial or "social" interest rates offered through the private sector. Sometimes, too, their work is unregistered or too ephemeral for them to be considered an acceptable risk for a home loan.

On the other hand, approximately 8 percent who earned more than five times the minimum salary may be regarded as well off. Those earning ten times the minimum salary would usually have access to bank loans (Stolarski 1982, 61). The majority of this group satisfy their needs through the private market—condominiums, custom designed houses, small "estates" (*quintas* and *fraccionamientos*)—and through private rental accommodations. Although they represent a small minority, they often occupy a proportion of the residential space far beyond their numerical importance. In between these two groups is a middle stratum (comprising approximately 15 percent) eligible for loans from banks and sometimes from professional funds such as the one for state employees (FOV-ISSSTE). As is the case in many developed countries, access to housing for these groups is not always easy, particularly in the case of first-time buyers, young couples, and so on. In Mexico these groups rent or purchase small homes or condominiums often through one of the public sector agencies for which they may be eligible or through the privately built state-guaranteed Housing Funds (FOVI/FOGA; see Table 12.2).

Of the two determinants of access, income has provided the primary filter in the past if only because the supply through the public sector has been severely limited.

Housing Supply through the Public Sector

There are three principal branches of public sector housing supply that have acquired importance in Mexico over the years (table 12.2): first, social security or welfare agencies for selected groups such as the Mexican Social Security Institute (IMSS) and the Civil Pensions and Retirement Directorate (largely for state employees and subsequently subsumed into the more important ISSSTE); second, the "social membership" housing funds specifically designed to accelerate the supply of housing to blue-collar registered workers (INFONAVIT) or to state employees (FOVISSSTE); third, agencies that have specifically been established to attend to housing needs of lower-income groups; they include the National Housing Institute, the National Public Works Bank (BANOBRAS), and their more recent offspring (INDECO and FONHAPO).

The temporal development and relative importance of these three branches is clearly demonstrated in table 12.2 and in figure 12.1. In the postwar period until 1964 overall production was limited—around 7,000 dwelling units per annum—and spread fairly evenly between the social security agencies and public housing agencies (including here the special program in the Federal District of Mexico City and houses produced for the Petroleum workers [PEMEX]). In short, the most-favored groups appear to have been those workers and employees in the more strategic industries, or those closest to government. Thus some public housing provision was made for government employees (almost exclusively lower-middle income groups through civil pensions, ISSSTE [rental accommodation], and housing provided by the Public Works' Bank), as well as for a select few of the better-off blue-collar workers. There was no pretense at attempting widespread coverage or of attending to the very poor. Preference was given to insured populations throughout this period; yet only one-fifth of the nation was covered. Little wonder that most of the poor in the rapidly expanding cities were driven into the "popular" sector.

The National Housing Institute was created in 1954 and promoted housing construction and improvement, especially in the provinces, although this, too, was largely oriented toward lower-middle-income groups. The same applies to the National Public Works Bank, except in this case most beneficiaries were based in Mexico City, and more than 12,000 apartments were built in 1960 as part of the now famous Nonoalco Tlatelolco housing project. Until very recently, this was the only period when rental accommodations were formally developed and rentals were low and adjusted only rarely so that they quickly came to represent a subsidy for the securely employed lower-middle classes.

Figure 12.1
Average Annual Level of Housing Production, by Principal Housing Agencies, Mexico, 1925–1987

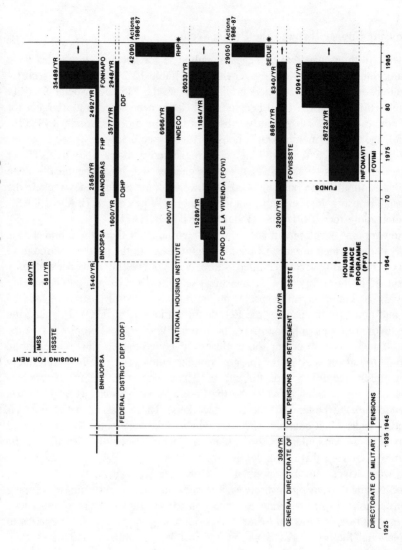

Sources: Adapted from Garza and Scheingart (1978); from data contained in tables 12.2 and 12.3 of this chapter.

*Postearthquake reconstruction.

The second period is marked by the beginnings of the Housing Finance Program (1964) established as part of the Alliance for Progress initiatives. This program channeled 30 percent of savings captured by private banks toward loans for the purchase and construction of "social interest" housing, with mortgages at 8 percent. It laid the basis for private development ostensibly for low-income groups, but as I note below, it in fact attended primarily to the middle-class needs.

Public sector production began to be significant in quantitative terms and genuinely low income in orientation only from 1970 onward. The explanation is discussed later, but both figure 12.1 and table 12.2 show the contribution made by the National Institute for Workers Housing Fund (INFONAVIT), which, between 1973 and 1976, generated more housing than the state sector had generated in the previous forty years. The INFONAVIT was modeled on Brazil's National Housing Bank (BNH) and was financed by a 5 percent tax paid on wages by workers, with matching levies paid by both employer and government. Between 1973 and 1976 the INFONAVIT engaged directly in house construction, which was allocated randomly by computer to blue-collar workers. Not surprisingly, however, such a rich source of patronage was eagerly fought over, and the all-powerful Mexican Workers' Confederation syndicate (CTM) won control from 1977/1978 onwards. The result was that the INFONAVIT came increasingly to finance approved schemes for approved worker groups rather than actually constructing the housing (Garcia and Perlo 1982). In effect, this meant those groups and organizations that towed the CTM line.

Also important between 1970 and 1979 were the Fund for State Employees (FOVISSSTE) and a "mopping-up" institution called INDECO, which adopted a troubleshooting brief incorporating a wide number of housing actions for the lower-income groups that fell outside the principal funds. The importance of INDECO is overstated by the data in table 12.2 and the actual units constructed under its aegis were much less than the 60,000 recorded. This figure may include some early sites-and-service experiments and the legalization of some plot titles for self-builders. The important point is that more than one-half of this hugely increased housing production during the 1970s came from the newly created funds (table 12.2). Yet between them, the INFONAVIT and FOVISSSTE were only able to meet 11.3 percent of the estimated total demand between 1973 and 1980 (González Rubí 1984).

Since 1980 the public sector housing production has expanded, although there are major difficulties in gaining an accurate picture of the number of new dwellings built in any one year. (As the notes to table 12.3 explain, the data displayed are inflated estimates of total new production in any single year.) In addition to the continued importance of the social membership funds a public housing agency now began for the first time to make a significant contribution. The FONHAPO was created in 1981 and strengthened from 1983 onward as a "popular" housing fund designed to support housing production for those people who earned up to or around 2.5 times the minimum salary and who were ineligible for support

Table 12.3
Formal Housing Production for Low-Income Groups, Mexico, 1980–1986

	1980	1981	1982	1983	1984	1985	1986
'Dwellings' completed: TOTAL (brackets = estimated production in each year [*])	67,479	91,564	107,312	115,906	170,118	194,606	247,254
		(46,080)	(53,015)	(88,329)			
Social Membership Funds							
- INFONAVIT[1] (est. in each year [*])	37,997	52,304	49,067	46,062	56,957	63,260	73,053
	(6,826)	(12,289)	(7,231)	(10,593)	(nd)		
- FOVISSSTE[2]	8,522	9,965	4,762	8,078	8,282	10,466[a1]	5,648
- ISSSFAM/FOVI[3]	485	500	426	nd	nd	nd	1,811
Public Housing Agencies							
- BANOBRAS/FHP[4]	1,201	3,782					
- FONHAPO[5] (est. in each year) [*]	–	–	17,933	26,061	62,668	35,272	45,082
			(504)	(7,467)	(27,243)	(67,410)	
- DDF[6]	300	1,970	1,594	1,570	2,547	6,757[a]	(4,090)
- Trusts within SAHOP/SEDUE[8]	725	533	638	2,570	2,454		
- Trusts outside SAHOP/SEDUE[9]	2,149	4,583	5,563	nd	nd		
- Renovación (Earthquake)[10]						9,269	42,090
- FONHAPO Fase II[10]							10,200
Private housing financed through FOVI/FOGA[11]	16,100	17,927	27,365	31,505	37,210	69,582[a]	79,802[a]

Note: nd = no data; (e) = estimate (preliminary figure only).

[a] The totals shown in brackets include only those dwellings that were completed in the year specified and do not include those that were carried over from the production totals of previous years. The figure in brackets, therefore, offers a more accurate estimate of annual production.

through the blue-collar workers' fund, INFONAVIT. This meant, in effect, low-earning self-employed workers and those in the "informal" sector. In practice, too, formal-sector blue-collar workers could benefit if they formed themselves into a local group and applied to the FONHAPO for support.

Obviously, if housing for this group was to be affordable it had to be inexpensive, and the FONHAPO's housing actions comprise sites and services, core units, support programs to assist self-builders improve their dwellings, upgrading programs that include credit for land regularization, acquisition of apartments by renters, and the construction of small completed homes (Mexico 1985). This input from the federal government has emerged as part of the National Housing Program, approved initially in 1979 and revised in 1984 through the Federal Housing Law and the creation of a National Housing Development Program. The first initiative of the program focused on "progressive" (self-help) housing and housing improvements for those earning between 0.75 and 2 to 3 times the minimum wage—thereby embracing the majority of the poor. Since 1984 subsequent initiatives have sought to reactivate the construction industry to supply completed dwellings for the salaried workers and also to extend support to unsalaried workers through agencies like the FONHAPO.

The level of public housing production for 1986–1987 has been greatly inflated by the earthquake reconstruction program. Severe damage and large-scale loss of life occurred in September 1985 as a result of the earthquake, much of which was concentrated in the downtown, working-class areas of Mexico City. Of the four programs coordinated by the Ministry of Urban Development and Ecology and the city government, two had a direct impact in the production of housing and the improvement of substandard and deteriorated dwellings. In a period of nineteen months the RHP built 42,090 new dwellings to replace those destroyed, renovated a further 6,220, and carried out repairs in 490 more (Mexico 1987, 3). Another program, "Phase II," was designed to carry out the reconstruction of 10,200 units and renovate 1,800 dwellings by the end of 1987. Together, these two programs cost a total budget of 444 million U.S. dollars, of which 46 percent came from a World Bank loan, the remainder coming from fiscal resources. Although both programs were highly subsidized, it has been estimated that cost recovery will amount to 50 percent of the building costs, which, compared to traditional public sector programs, will be 15–20 percent above the average level of cost recovery. Funds will be recycled through the FONHAPO to finance housing programs outside the metropolitan areas. Nevertheless, building upon their experience of what appears to have been an extremely successful reconstruction program, the Mexican authorities have undertaken to mobilize a major additional tranche of resources (of which it is hoped 235 million U.S. dollars will come from the World Bank) for fresh initiatives in national housing production.

Housing Supply through the Private Sector

If self-help ("popular") housing is included within the category of private supply, then it is this sector that has always dominated housing production in

Mexico. The rich look after themselves in the ways already described. The poor have acquired land illegally either through squatter invasions of vacant land or, more usually, through low-cost purchase from landlords, from unscrupulous real estate developers, or from peasants who hold use rights over land distributed to them as part of the postrevolutionary land reforms (Gilbert and Ward 1985). Whichever method is adopted, the land is unserviced, improperly titled, and fails to meet planning or local authority norms for residential developments. House construction is self-managed (if not self-built) by low-income "owners." Urban services and utilities, legalization of title (regularization), and home improvement takes place gradually in response to a wide range of factors that have been identified elsewhere in the literature.[4]

The emergence of low-income "irregular" settlements is largely a post–1945 phenomenon although *colonias populares* have existed in this form since the mid–1920s and probably much earlier (Perló 1979). Growth was especially rapid during the 1950s and 1960s when cities were expanding at rates of around 5 percent per annum due to a combination of high natural growth rates (around 3.5 percent per annum) and through cityward migration. For example, in Mexico City *colonias populares* housed 14 percent of the city's population in 1952 and extended over 23 percent of the built-up area, whereas in 1988 they had grown to include more than half the city's problem (of around 18 million) and covered a similar proportion of the urban area (Mexico 1958; Mexico 1977). Similar patterns of growth are to be observed in other Mexican cities, albeit a decade or so later (Legoretta 1984; Bazant 1985). Before the 1970s the areas were largely ignored by the authorities who turned a "blind eye" to the development of irregular settlements. However, the INDECO and other agencies established under President Echeverría during the early 1970s adopted more interventionist policies albeit that they were implemented in a highly ad hoc and partisan manner (Ward 1981, 1986). Policy-making toward these settlements has become increasingly oriented toward their physical improvement through servicing, through the regularization of "clouded" land titles, and through site-and-service schemes (Payne 1983; Linn 1983; Burgess 1985; Rodwin 1987). In the arena of regularization, national agencies such as the Commission for Land Tenure Regularization (CoRett) have been expecially influential, complemented by statewide agencies and programs. On the other hand, the FONHAPO has been at the forefront of promotion of sites and services, while city authorities have undertaken major extensions to their servicing networks, thereby stimulating "upgrading" and the physical improvement of irregular settlements.

Rental accommodation is also important in Mexico. In 1980 an estimated 44 percent were nonowners according to the National Census—many of whom rent. Yet until very recently there has been no formal government-led production of rental housing (with a single minor exception noted earlier [figure 12.1]). Rental accommodations for the poor have been left to the private sector. In Mexico City rent-control legislation during the 1940s effectively froze rents below a certain level and acted as a disincentive to property owners to develop rental accommodations. Much of the low-cost rental opportunities that developed sub-sequently comprised inner-city shackyards on land sites awaiting redevelopment (the "lost cities") or were tenements constructed in the *colonias populares*, particularly the older and well-established districts nearer to the city center. Unfortunately, there has been a lack of research into nonownership, but recent evidence suggests that access to land for ownership is becoming more difficult (Gilbert and Ward 1985). Plot densities are rising in irregular settlements; the average size of house plot is declining; and the average age at which renters move from nonownership to ownership has increased—indicating a tightening land market in Mexico (Gilbert 1987). Although the wages earned by renters and owners are broadly similar, owner households are larger, the heads are older, and they are more likely to have other members of the family in paid employment, thereby raising the total household income significantly above that of renter households (Gilbert 1987). The demand for cheap rental accommodations and the large scale of this demand has only recently been recognized by the government with some minor supports given to the production of rental housing. In addition, programs have recently been established to enable renters to acquire their homes and become owner–occupiers (*Comercio Exterior*, November 1987, p. 906).

Formal private production of housing for low-income groups only began with the Housing Finance Program in 1964. Two housing trusts were created within the Central Bank of Mexico: one to develop housing (FOVI), the other to provide financial guarantees and credit supports (FOGA) to private sector housing initiatives for lower-stratum income groups. Both trust funds have provided a strong stimulus to private intervention in so-called social interest housing, but they have consistently failed to reach the lowest paid. Beneficiaries need to enjoy reasonably high salary levels and income security. Nonetheless, private production has been important. Between 1965 and 1970 it provided 64 percent of formal housing production (table 12.2), and since the rise of the social membership funds and later more direct intervention by public housing agencies, the FOVI/FOGA has financed around one-quarter of total formal production (tables 12.2 and 12.3). The 1984 National Housing Program established four types of private housing production eligible for support from FOVI/FOGA, each with different interest rates. The least expensive, designed for those earning between 2.0 and 2.8 times the minimum wage, carries a repayment rate of 15 percent. This compares with the more expensive housing designed for those earning between 6.3 and a maximum of 7.5 times the minimum wage for whom the interest rate is 30 percent. When inflation was between 60 and 100 percent per annum, such interest rates represented heavy subsidies.

This review of formal housing production in Mexico since 1947 has shown that production was oriented initially to those worker and employee groups that enjoyed strong union support. Although there has been a gradual broadening of coverage during the latter part of the period, in effect the beneficiaries have been lower-middle income groups or the better-off working classes thereby accentuating patterns of social inequality. Only since the creation of the INFONAVIT, and later still the FONHAPO, has the state made a significant intervention in housing production that is genuinely directed to the poorest social groups. Even so, total production has been inadequate to keep pace with demand so that throughout the whole period analyzed here, the majority of Mexico's poor have had to take responsiblity for shelter into their own hands and have sought access through irregular settlement processes. It is difficult to see how the Mexican authorities will ever generate sufficient housing to reduce the housing deficit significantly. However, the FONHAPO-type programs combined with heavy investment in servicing and legalization programs for the irregular settlements have achieved a substantial relative improvement in housing conditions throughout most of the country.

THE RATIONALE FOR CHANGING STATE INTERVENTION IN HOUSING PROVISION

As I have argued, housing production in any society does not evolve in a vacuum. It is partially a response to changing ideology of urbanism and home ownership. It is also a response to the process of capital accumulation: the expression by different fractions of capital to intensify their profit taking in various arenas of housing development—land, construction materials, finance and circulation, and so on. It is also a response to demand making from the grass roots. The extent to which different social groups mobilize around demands for housing or around inequalities in its supply will shape the level and form of state intervention. Elsewhere I have argued that housing and servicing in Mexico become part of cannon fodder for political mediation and "statecraft" (Ward 1986; see also Malloy 1985). These arguments guide my explanation of the changing nature of housing production since 1947.

Between 1947 and 1964 one has to explain not so much the nature of public housing production but its absence. This was a period of sustained economic growth, successful industrialization, and rapid urbanization. The development philosophy at that time was one of "modernization" and the gradual trickle down of the benefits of growth throughout the social pyramid. Depending upon the ideology of the government of the day at a national or local level the rise of illegal settlements was a temporary problem that would be overcome as populations changed their value systems from rural and traditional to urban and modern. References to slums as rural aberrations in the city are legion during these decades. The inability to afford orthodox methods of housing acquisition was viewed as a temporary time-lag problem between growth and the trickle down of wealth generated. Conveniently, too, this "world view" reinforced the elite's self-perception of its moral responsibility to exercise power and to act paternalistically on behalf of the poorer social groups (Perlman 1976).

Thus housing production between 1947 and 1970 was characterized by the following features. First, a blind eye was cast at the dramatic expansion of illegal settlements. Only where they threatened to encroach upon specific interest groups, occupied valuable land sites, or detracted from the modern image of certain parts of the city were they likely to be removed. Bulldozing and evictions were justified by an ideology that emphasized poverty and poor housing as an outcome of inappropriate "traditional" or rural values (Perlman 1976). For example, one large area of low-income, dilapidated housing was removed for the huge scale (12,000 apartments) lower-middle-income housing project of Nonoalco Tlatelolco and developed by the BANOBRAS just north of the city center. Between 1953 and 1966 the DDF imposed a ban on new low-income land subdivisions that it saw as "Zones of shacks or huts made from scrap and throwaway materials such as boards, sheets of bitumen-covered cardboard in which people live without any services and without sanitation" (*Diario Oficial*, October 3, 1962). Although it proved impossible for the DDF to prevent the spread and densification of irregular settlements, it was able to withhold systematic introduction of services to such areas.

Second, positive discrimination was exercised on behalf of those labor groups that were most powerful. Hence housing developments were undertaken on behalf of subgroups within the military, the railway workers, and among the state-owned oil-company workers. These groups either had powerful unions and the ear of the power elite within Mexico or had forged welfare agencies that undertook certain housing actions on their behalf. Of more general benefit to blue- and white-collar workers, respectively, were the IMSS and ISSSTE, which developed some limited housing for rent and which, because of its low cost, became a virtual supplement to wages. Only occasionally were housing actions undertaken that were not specific to identifiable labor groups such as rent controls in 1943 and 1947 and some housing in the Federal District. Invariably, these actions were in response to mini-crises in state management. For example, during the 1940s rent controls were instigated to minimize and offset demands for wage increases in the Federal District (Mexico 1977, 30). Also, worker housing was initiated by the Department of the Federal District as part of the aforementioned hard-line repressive policy toward illegal settlements within the city boundary (Aguilar Martínez 1986). The important point to recognize is that the amount of public housing production was very limited and that it was used to coopt and to pacify certain powerful labor groups in strategic sectors or industries.

The pattern of housing production began to change from the mid-sixties onward in response to a variety of pressures and initiatives. Especially significant in 1964 was the creation of the Housing Finance Program (PFV). As figure 12.1 shows, most agencies active in the housing field received a major fillip to their programs dating from that time. Others emerged entirely as a result of the existence of the PFV—most notably the FOVI. The PFV was created using seed capital derived from the Alliance for Progress, which was a continent-wide set of reforms designed to weaken the likely success of any further Cuba-style socialist experiments. That it was adopted in Mexico can be explained in part by the growing middle and lower-middle classes whose low earning power often left them bereft of access to housing through the private sector. The FOVI offered new financing and financial guarantees for the so-called social interest housing that emerged and that was "raided" (acquired) by lower-middle-income and better-off worker groups. There is also evidence from the early 1960s onward that pressures were growing from within the construction industry for some pump-priming government initiative that would enhance an expansionary building program nationwide (Mexico 1977, 82).

A dramatic change in housing production occurred in the late sixties. The FOVISSSTE, INDECO, DGHP, and, in 1973, INFONAVIT all date from this time. Not only did total housing production rise sharply from this point onward, but the range of governmental action widened to cover support for irregular settlements through regularization programs, servicing, supports for self-help, and so on. Why at this time? Most important was the intense social unrest that had begun to threaten political stability. By the late sixties it was becoming clear that conditions were deteriorating. The hoped-for trickle down of wealth had not occurred: economic development had not led to improved income distribution—quite the opposite (Navarette 1970; Makin 1984). Nor had lower middle-class groups been kept prosperous by a trickle down that had fallen into their laps. The problem was that it was largely the upper-income groups that had benefited most. Many intellectuals wanted an expansion of job opportunities especially in the professions; others wanted political reforms. In the countryside, too, the opportunities for land distribution through agrarian reform had dried up, production of staples was declining, and the livelihood of *campesinos* was threatened (Varley 1985; Heath 1985). The extremely bad living conditions in the (by now) huge areas of irregular settlement that existed in many cities were thrown into sharp relief in the public domain once the 1970 census results began to be published. In addition, communities were beginning to hammer on the doors of city authorities either to demand action to improve services or to mobilize and remonstrate politically (Ward 1981). Public demonstrations were the order of the day between 1968 and 1971.

Government policy shifted markedly as a result. As we observed early in this chapter, the whole ideology shifted to one of "shared development." One can debate the sincerity of this policy shift, but the important point is that housing became a key element in the political calculus of achieving social peace. Governmental response toward irregular settlements shifted away from a "laissez faire" approach that had favored capital accumulation for illegal land developers and industrial employers at the expense of low wages and acute deprivation in people's residential living conditions. Instead, a more "interventionist" stance was adopted. Actions designed to offer legal security to illegal settlements, the introduction of basic services, and supports for self-building were initiated.

Between 1971 and 1976 a large number of agencies were established often with inadequate budgets and ill-defined, overlapping responsibilities. In part this was deliberate: "lightweight" actions of troubleshooting agencies such as IN-DECO gave the impression that the government was concerned and that action was being undertaken, yet without laying out the large-scale resources required to deal with the problem. The opportunities for involvement of different housing agencies with overlapping responsibilities heightened this impression and also created opportunities for manipulation, for splitting constituencies, and for the expansion of a "divide-and-rule" control over troublesome social groups (Ward 1986). Moreover, there were other reasons for the policy changes that do not relate to social unrest. International opinion has shifted away from orthodox housing solutions toward support for self-build (Ward 1982; Rodwin 1987). To the extent that external financial sources were important for housing, then, this policy change was likely to be significant.

Since 1977 governmental policy toward private sector "popular" housing production has entered a new phase that might best be described as "technical management." The aims are the same—to achieve social peace and to offset unrest, particularly during economic austerity after 1982. But instead of achieving this through bureaucratic manipulation, cooption, and patron clientelism, the government has begun to emphasize greater efficiency and the delivery of services. Land regularization is being systematically pursued; illegal land developers are no longer condoned; services are introduced with community participation and the recovery of costs directly and through local property-based taxation. These policies also reflect growing conventional wisdom that housing production in developing countries will be enhanced by government intervention to make the market operate more effectively—removing supply bottlenecks and monopolies, minimizing subsidies, emphasizing cost recovery, providing security of tenure, and so on (Linn 1983; Rodwin and Sanyal 1987).

Another major response from 1970 onward has been far greater housing production. In addition to the social unrest already cited, this increase was also an outcome of labor pressure from the Workers' Confederation (CTM), which had been pressing for implementation of Article 123, which made employers responsible for providing housing for workers (García and Perló 1982). Although this aspect of the Constitution had never been seriously confronted, coming at this particular conjuncture, it did direct attention toward possible joint state-private employer activity in the housing market. The INFONAVIT was the offspring of that liaison. More recently still, the FONHAPO has added significantly to housing production for the most economically disadvantaged groups effectively excluded from all other forms of formal housing supply. Both agencies are making significant contributions to contemporary housing production (figure 12.1). Many dwellings built in 1986–1987, though, were a one-time response to damage sustained by the earthquake.

CONTEMPORARY POLICY: HOUSING UNDER AUSTERITY

If 1970 marked an important break point in the scale of state intervention in the housing sector, 1978–1979 saw an equally important shift in the nature of policy. The U.N. HABITAT conference held in Vancouver in 1976 proved to be a watershed that stimulated a shift internationally away from orthodox housing schemes toward initiatives that "sponsored" self-help and the production of lower-cost dwelling units. In Mexico a housing directorate in the Human Settlements and Public Works Ministry formulated a National Housing Program that was approved in 1979. This program was directed at those earning less than 4.0 times the minimum wage and offered completed dwellings for formal salaried workers, as well as other housing that embodied self-help principles and renovation ("progressive" and "improved") and designed mostly for unsalaried workers earning 0.75 to 2 and 3 times the minimum wage.

However, this was a period of rapid economic reflation and expansion based upon expected oil revenues and foreign loans. During the last four years of the López Portillo administration (i.e., 1978–1982) 2.7 million housing actions were to be undertaken, 1.1 million of which would be in the arena of "progressive" (self-help) housing, 658,000 "completed" dwelling units, and 964,000 actions to improve existing stock. Even a casual glance at the reported production levels on table 12.3 indicates that these targets were never met, although housing production was raised significantly (figure 12.1).

Within the housing bureaucracy two important changes occurred. First, the FONHAPO emerged in 1983 from being a low-key department in the BAN-OBRAS. Not unnaturally, given its appearance during the lame duck phase of the presidency, its fortunes remained uncertain until the following administration had considered the agency's future. Second, a potential cash-flow crisis within the INFONAVIT was averted by changing a law that would have required repayment of worker contributions to those who had not benefited from the agency during its first ten years of operation. It was also determined that the INFONAVIT should direct greater attention to housing production for its lesser-paid affiliates.

The economic crash in 1982 and the period of austerity that followed offer an important insight into housing management at a time of intense social hardship. Faced with a sharp rise in unemployment and underemployment, a decline in real wages, and reductions or removal of subsidies on subsistence items, social welfare policy (of which housing forms a part) became a critical ingredient in a country's ability to burrow through the recession and to offset social unrest. Within four months the old Human Settlements Ministry had been recast and the new Ecology and Urban Development Ministry (SEDUE) unveiled a Program of Immediate Housing Action (PVAI) designed as a realistic response to the housing problem. In general, it aimed at controlling land speculation, the development of federal land reserves, promoting community participation in urban service installation as well as in self-help and sites-and-services, and regrouping the financial systems to cover the least protected social groups.

In 1984 the government passed a Federal Housing Law that consolidated and developed many of the policies identified under the so-called Immediate Housing Action Program a year earlier. The new law established a National Housing System under the SEDUE and a National Housing Program for Housing Development (PRONADEV). Seen as the most ambitious piece of housing legislation ever, the PRONADEV sought to mobilize resources equivalent to almost 1 percent of the GDP, which in 1984 alone would have had the effect of generating some 400,000 jobs and 270,000 housing actions benefiting a total 1.5 million people. Specifically, 44 percent of these actions (28 percent of resources) were to be in the field of "progressive" (self-build) housing; 40 percent (some 60 percent of resources) "completed" housing (i.e., fully completed and serviced); 9 percent on housing improvement (2 percent of overall budget), and 7 percent on "other" initiatives. Once again, even the inflated figures in table 12.3 suggest a substantial underperformance on these targets. Notable, however, is the significant contribution to housing production achieved by the FONHAPO particularly from 1984 onward. In 1988 the government for the first time formally undertook a rural housing program when it created the Rural Housing Fund as a separate sub-fund within FONHAPO, designed to attend, primarily, to the needs of farmworkers—especially those in important areas of production (cotton, *cacao*, tobacco, and so forth) and those closely tied to the National Farmworkers' Federation (CNC), itself an important pillar of the government party.

A new system of financing was adopted that obliged the recently nationalized banking system to underwrite the production of "social interest" housing at interest rates affordable to purchasers. Different housing modules were proposed for different economic groups. Type 1 housing was designed for those earning 2.0–2.8 times the minimum salary (xMS), paying 15 percent interest; Type 2 aimed at those earning 3.2–4.2 xMS at 19 percent interest; Type 3 for 4.3–6.2 xMS at 25 percent; and Type 4 for 6.3–7.5 xMS at 30 percent. When annual inflation was running between 60 and 100 percent, this represented a substantial subsidy to house buyers. Interest repayments on loans contracted through the FONHAPO, INFONAVIT, and FOVISSSTE were even lower.

In short, post–1982 crisis management has led to a further increase in public sector involvement in housing production. However, despite inflated targets and exaggerated reported levels of production, supply remains well below the demand. The different housing-delivery systems have consolidated into three broad areas: social membership funds in which the INFONAVIT dominates, public housing agencies in which the FONHAPO has emerged as the most significant, and private sector construction over which the state increasingly exercises guidance to ensure affordability by the lower-middle and better-off working classes. Set alongside the initiatives designed to respond to the needs of those living in irregular settlement, it is apparent that the overall institutional structure has, in fact, deepened the long-standing tendency in Mexico to create a variety of differentially served constituencies. The major difference today with that of the past is that these constituencies are much larger and, usually, more adequately financed. Nonetheless, the splitting up of different social groups has important ideological and political consequences. Ideologically, it strengthens the belief that each social group is being "looked after" by an agency specifically charged with acting on that group's behalf. This weakens any move toward collective cross-class mobilization and demand making, and the creation of multiple constituencies enhances the facility with which the state can employ methods of "divide and rule."

CONCLUSION: THE DETERMINANTS OF HOUSING PRODUCTION

I have tried to account for the evolution of housing production and allocation in Mexico. In reviewing the overall economic process there is some evidence of a systematic relationship between housing policy and specific interest lobbies. Thus since the 1940s specific labor groups were able to win concessions for themselves and develop housing for their affiliates. It seems probable that pressure from the Construction Industry Chamber was significant in raising the tempo of public sector involvement in "social interest" housing projects during the early sixties, although it is debatable whether this would have happened in the absence of offers of funding from abroad. I have observed, also, how the powerful CTM syndicate has been kept passive and supportive by allowing it to shape the INFONAVIT housing policy in a way that maximizes its control over patronage from that institution.

Although internal lobbies are important, they do not offer a complete explanation. Important, too, are external events. It is impossible to explain the emergence of public housing policy in Mexico without reference to external pressures. The Alliance for Progress initiative was critical in the creation of a Housing Finance Program and allowed the state to respond to pressure within the construction industry. The barrage of self-help orthodoxy that has been delivered from international agencies such as the World Bank, tied as it often is to external credits, has undoubtedly promoted the marked shift in housing policies. The collapse in oil prices was another external shock that, combined with poor internal housekeeping between 1978 and 1982, obliged a period of economic austerity after 1982. This forced the Mexican government to rethink how it could respond most effectively to the housing needs of its lower-paid workers.

Also, the September 1985 earthquake disaster is likely to be perceived in future years as having had a dramatic effect in the evolution of housing production. It demonstrated that given political commitment, huge fiscal resources could be generated for a housing program (matched, in this case, by external credits). It showed, also, that good-quality housing could be built quickly using small-scale construction firms. This management experience—together with criticism that the huge diversion of resources to the capital city was inappropriate coming precisely when the government was seeking to decentralize investment in public utilities away from Mexico City—is likely to be carried over into a more adequately financed national housing program.[5] Given the success of the program to produce high-quality completed dwellings richly painted in deep blues, pinks and greens, the popular perception of appropriate assistance from government appears to have switched from one of aided help to that of demand for completed apartments painted in strong colors.

I have also argued throughout this chapter that public sector housing response cannot be divorced from the political process. Increasingly, housing production, policy, and bureaucratic delivery systems have been designed to intensify state control over the low-income populace and to induce their passivity. This has probably always been the case, but the difference in recent years has been the widening of coverage to embrace an even larger proportion of the population. This has been achieved through the elaboration of different "tiers" of policy from the relatively expensive condominium projects for state employees to the financial assistance for home improvements given by the FONHAPO to, say, a group of garbage-dump pickers. Although there is some attempt to ensure that interest rates are progressive (i.e., lower for the lowest paid), the high levels of subsidy on all housing loans means that those who receive the largest home loans inevitably benefit the most, and this favors the FOVISSSTE, INFONAVIT, RHP, and, to a lesser extent, FOVI/FOGA. The stratification of delivery systems reinforces and replicates the stratification of social groups, and this is not a historical accident. It is part and parcel of the wider process of political mediation. As the current government responds to the narrowness of its 1988 electoral victory, the relationship between the delivery of housing, social control and preferential treatment for party-linked groups is likely to intensify.

ABBREVIATIONS

AURIS	Acción Urbana y de Integración Social
BANOBRAS	Banco Nacional de Obras
BNH	Banco Nacional de Habitacão (Brazil)
BNHUOPSA	Banco Nacional Hipotecaria Urbano de Obras Públicas
CODEUR	Comisión de Desarrollo Urbano
CoRett	Comisión para la Regularización de la tenencia de la tierra
COPEVI	Centro Operacional de Poblamiento y de Vivienda
CTM	Confederación de Trabajadores Mexicanos
DDF	Departamento del Distrito Federal
DF	Distrito Federal
DGCP	Dirección General de Centros de Población (SAHOP)
DGHP	Dirección General de Habitación Popular (DDF)
FHP	Fondo de Habitaciones Populares
FIDACA	Fideicomiso Acapulco
FIDELAC	Fideicomiso Lazaro Cárdenas
FIDEURBE	Fideicomiso de Interés Social para el Desarrollo Urbano de la Ciudad de México

FOGA	Fondo de Garantía de Vivienda
FOMERREY	Fideicomiso Monterrey
FONHAPO	Fideicomiso Fondo de Habitaciones Populares
FOVI	Fondo de Vivienda
FOVIMI	Fondo de Vivienda Militar
FOVISSSITE	Fondo de vivienda del Instituto de Seguridad y Servicios Sociales de los Trabajadores al Servicio del Estado
FPVALLARTA	Fideicomiso Puerta Vallarta
IMF	International Monetary Fund
IMSS	Instituto Mexicano de Seguro Social
INDECO	Instituto Nacional de Desarrollo de la Comunidad
INFONAVIT	Instituto Nacional del Fondo de Vivienda para los Trabajadores
INV	Instituto Nacional de Vivienda
ISSSTE	Instituto de Seguridad y Servicios Sociales de los Trabajadores al Servicio del Estado
PCP	Procuraduría de Colonias Populares
PEMEX	Petróleos Mexicanos
PFV	Programa Financiero de Vivienda
PRI	Partido Revolucionario Institucional
PRONADEV	Programa Nacional de Desarrollo de Vivienda
PVAI	Programa de Vivienda de Acción Inmediata
RHP	Renovación Habitacional Popular
SAHOP	Secretaría de Asentamientos Humanos y Obras Públicas
SEDUE	Secretaría de Desarrollo Urbano y Ecología
SPP	Secretaría de Programación y Presupuesto

NOTES

1. I am indebted to Noemí Stolarski, Advisor to the director of planning and budgeting of Renovación Habitacional Popular. Her great assistance in the collection of much of the housing data and the innumerable discussions that we held are deeply appreciated. Responsibilities for the argument and for any errors that have crept into the statistical analysis are mine alone. The 1986 field research for this chapter was made possible by a grant from the Small Grants in the Humanities of the British Academy, which is also gratefully acknowledged. A second research grant, this time from the Nuffield Foundation, made it possible to conduct fieldwork in 1988 and to amend and add material relating to 1988.

2. See, for example, De la Rosa (1974); Turner (1976); Centro Operacional de Poblamiento y de Vivienda (1977); Ward (1982); Durand (1984); Legoretta (1984); Bazant (1985); Gilbert and Ward (1985); Varley (1985); and Ward (1986).

3. I recognize that this is an extremely crude way of estimating demand. Average

family size per dwelling is not normative but is, itself, a reflection of the available supply. Thus these are likely to be conservative estimates of demand.

4. See, for example, Ward (1978); Burns and Shroup (1981); Angel (1983); Strassman (1984); and Varley (1987).

5. "Report of a Group of Foreign Experts on Selected Aspects of the Reconstruction of the Inner City Area of Mexico City" (Delivered to the Minister of Ecology and Urban Development, October 1986). The author was a member of the group. Arising from the success of the housing reconstruction program, the SEDUE hoped to win further loans from the World Bank for its 1987–1988 housing program.

REFERENCES

Aguilar Martinez, Guillermo. 1986. "Contemporary Urban Planning in Mexico City: Its Emergence, Role and Significance." Ph.D. thesis, University of London.

Angel, S. 1983. "Upgrading Slum Infrastructure: Divergent Objectives in Search of a Consensus." *Third World Planning Review* 5:5–22.

Bazant, Jan. 1985. *Autoconstrucción de vivienda popular*. Distrito Federal: Trillas.

Burgess, Rod. 1985. "The Limits of Self-Help Housing Programmes." *Development and Change* 16:271–312.

Burns, L., and D. Shroup. 1981. "The Effect of Resident Control and Ownership in Self-Help Housing." *Land Economics* 57:106–14.

Centro Operacional de Poblamiento y de Vivienda. 1977. *La producción de vivienda en la zona metropolitana de la ciudad de México*. Distrito Federal: AC.

Cockcroft, J. D. 1983. *Mexico. Class Formation, Capital Accumulation, and the State*. New York: Monthly Review Press.

Cornelius, Wayne. 1986. "The Political Economy of Mexico under De la Madrid: The Crisis Deepens, 1985–1986." Center for U.S.-Mexican Studies Research Report Series, no. 43. La Jolla, Calif.: University of California, San Diego.

Cornelius, W., J. Gentleman, and P. Smith, (eds). 1989. *Mexico's Alternative Political Futures*. Center for U.S.-Mexican Studies, Monograph Series, no. 30. La Jolla, Calif.: University of California, San Diego.

De la Rosa. 1974. *Netzahualcóyoltl: un fenomeno*. Distrito Federal: Testimonios del Fondo.

Durand, J. 1984. *La ciudad invade el ejido*. Distrito Federal: Casa Chata.

García, Beatriz, and Manuel Perló. 1982. "Estado, sindicalismo oficial y políticas habitacionales: analisis de una década del INFONAVIT." Distrito Federal. Mimeograph.

Garza, Gustavo, and Martha Schteingart. 1978. *La acción habitacional del estado mexicano*. Distrito Federal: El Colegio de México.

Gilbert, Alan. 1987. "Latin America's Urban Poor: Shanty Dwellers or Renters of Rooms." *Cities*, February, 43–51.

Gilbert, Alan, and Peter Ward. 1985. *Housing, the State, and the Poor: Policy and Practice in Three Latin American Cities*. Cambridge: Cambridge University Press.

Gónzalez Casanova, Pablo. 1970. *Democracy in Mexico*. New York: Oxford University Press.

Gónzalez Rubí, Rafael. 1984. "La vivienda, un desafio atroz." *Comércio Exterior* 34 (May, July, and August):390–96, 592–98, 728–34.

Goulet, Dennis. 1983. *Mexico: Development Strategies for the Future.* Notre Dame, Ind.: University of Notre Dame Press.

Grindle, Merilee. 1977. *Bureaucrats, Politicians, and Peasants in Mexico: A Case Study in Public Policy.* Berkeley: University of California Press.

Hansen, Roger. 1974. *The Politics of Mexican Development.* 2d ed. Baltimore: Johns Hopkins University Press.

Heath, John. 1985. "Contradictions in Mexico's Food Policy." In *Politics in Mexico*, edited by George Philip. London: Croom Helm.

Legoretta, Jorge. 1984. *La autoconstrucción de vivienda en México: el caso de las ciudades petroleras.* Distrito Federal: Centro de Ecodesarrollo.

Linn, Johannes. 1983. *Cities in the Developing World: Policies for Their Equitable and Efficient Growth.* Oxford: Oxford University Press.

Makin, John. 1984. "Self-Help Housing in Mexico City and the Role of the State." Ph.D. thesis, Heriot Watt University.

Malloy, James. 1985. "Statecraft and Social Security Policy and Crisis: A Comparison of Latin America and the United States." In *The Crisis of Social Security and Health Care*, edited by Carmelo Mesa Lago, 19–50. Pittsburgh: University of Pittsburgh.

Mexico. Instituto Nacional de Vivienda. 1958. *Las colonias populares de la Ciudad de Mexico: problemas y soluciones.* Distrito Federal.

———. Centro Operacional de Poblamiento y de Vivienda. 1977. *La producción de vivienda en la zona metropolitana de la ciudad de México.* Distrito Federal.

———. 1982. *Necesidades esenciales en Mexico: Vivienda. Situación actual y perspectivas en el año 2000.* Distrito Federal: Siglo XXI.

———. Fideicomiso Fondo de Habitaciones Populares. 1985. "Una visión sobre el Fondo Nacional de Habitaciones Populares." Mimeograph.

———. Secretaría de la Presidencia. 1986. *El gobierno Mexicano* 46 (September).

———. Renovación Habitacional Popular. 1987. *Síntesis de la memoria del programa, 1986–7.* Distrito Federal.

Navarrete, Ifegenia. 1970. "La distribución del ingreso en Mexico: tendencias y perspectivas." In *El perfil de México en 1980*, edited by David Ibarra, et al. 15–71. Distrito Federal: Siglo XXI.

Navarrette, Jorge. 1986. "Mexico's Economic Policies and External Debt Management: An Overview of Recent Issues and Experiences." Paper delivered to the Centre of Latin American Studies, Cambridge, November 27, 1986. Mimeograph.

Perlman, Janice. 1976. *The Myth of Marginality: Urban Poverty and Politics in Rio de Janeiro.* Berkeley: University of California Press.

Perló, Manuel. 1979. "Politica y vivienda en México, 1910–52." *Revista Mexicana de Sociología* 3:769–835.

Purcell, S., and J. Purcell. 1980. "State and Society in Mexico." *World Politics* 32:194–227.

Rodwin, Lloyd, ed. 1987. *Shelter, Settlement, and Development.* Boston: Allen & Unwin.

Rodwin, Lloyd, and Bishwapriya Sanyal. 1987. "Shelter, Settlement, and Development: An Overview." In *Shelter, Settlement, and Development*, edited by Lloyd Rodwin, 3–31. Boston: Allen & Unwin.

Scott, I. 1982. *Urban and Spatial Development in Mexico.* Baltimore: Johns Hopkins University Press.

Smith, Peter. 1979. *Labyrinths of Power: Political Recruitment in Twentieth-Century Mexico*. Princeton, N.J.: Princeton University Press.

Stolarski, Noemí. 1982. *La vivienda en el Distrito Federal: situación y perspectivas*. Distrito Federal: Dir. Gral. de Planificación.

Strassman, W. P. 1984. "The Timing of Urban Infrastructure and Housing Improvements by Owner Occupants." *World Development*:743–53.

Tello, Carlos. 1978. *La política económica en México, 1970–1976*. Distrito Federal: Siglo XXI.

Turner, J. 1976. *Housing by People*. London: Marion Boyars.

Varley, Ann. 1985. "Urbanization and Agrarian Law." *Bulletin of Latin American Research* 4:1–16.

———. 1985. " 'Ya somos dueños'. Ejido land regularization and development in Mexico City." Ph.D. thesis, University of London.

———. 1987. "The Relationship Between Tenure, Legalization and Housing Improvements: Evidence from Mexico City." *Development and Change* 18:463–81.

Ward, Peter. 1978. "Self-Help Housing in Mexico City: Social and Economic Determinants of Success." *Town Planning Review* 49:38–50.

———. 1981. "Political Pressure for Urban Services: The Response of Two Mexico City Administrations." *Development and Change* 12:379–407.

———. 1982. *Self-Help Housing: A Critique*. London: Mansell.

———. 1986. *Welfare Politics in Mexico: Papering Over the Cracks*. London: Allen & Unwin.

FURTHER READING

Aguilar, Adrian Guillermo. "Urban Planning in the 1980s in Mexico City." *Habitat Intl.* 11, no. 3 (1987):23–38.

Ball, Michael, and Priscilla Connolly. "Capital Accumulation and the Mexican Construction Industry, 1930–1982." *International Journal of Urban and Regional Research* 11, no. 2 (1987):153–71.

Cummings, S., L. F. Paradis, C. N. Alatriste, and J. Cornelis. "Community Development in a Mexican Squatter Settlement: A Program Evaluation." *Population Research and Policy Review* 7, no. 2 (1988):159–188.

De la Cueva, Antonio Azuela. "Low-Income Settlements and the Law in Mexico City." *International Journal of Urban and Regional Research* 11, no. 4 (1987):522–542.

Gilbert, A. *Housing and Land in Urban Mexico*. San Diego: University of California, Center for U.S.-Mexican Studies. Monograph no. 31, 1989.

Gilbert, Alan, and Peter Ward. "The State and Low-Income Housing." In *Urbanization in Contemporary Latin America*, edited by A. Gilbert. et al., 79–128. Chichester: Wiley, 1982.

Mexico. Banco Nacional Hipotecario. *El problema de la habitación en la Ciudad de México*. Report. Distrito Federal, 1952.

———. Centro Operacional de Poblamiento y de Vivienda. *Investigación sobre vivienda: las políticas habitacionales del estado mexicano*. Distrito Federal, 1977.

Pezzoli, Keith. "The Urban Land Problem and Popular Sector Housing Development in Mexico City." *Environment and Behavior* 19, no. 3 (1987):371–397.

Poulantzas, Nicos. *Political Power and Social Classes*. New York: New Left Books, 1973.
Stephens-Rioja, Kathryn. "Land and Shelter Important Issues for a Growing Metropolis." *Built Environment* 8, no. 2 (1982):1–9.
Stepick, Alex, and Arthur D. Murphy. "Brief Communications: Comparing Squatter Settlements and Government Self-Help Projects as Housing Solutions in Oaxaca, Mexico." *Human Organization* 39, no. 4 (1980):339–343.

V

SOUTH AMERICA

13

Brazil

SUZANA PASTERNAK TASCHNER WITH CÉLINE SACHS

References

Further Reading

TRENDS IN HOUSING CONDITIONS (1940–1984)

Background

Brazil is a country characterized by strong regional and social differences. The population's income is distributed in an extraordinarily differentiated way. In 1983 the poorest 50 percent got only 13.6 percent of the total national income, while the wealthiest 10 percent received 46.2 percent of this income (Jaguaribe et al. 1986, 18). According to Pesquisa Nacional por Amostragem de Domicilios—National Survey by Housing Sampling (PNAD) data (1984), 66 percent of the economically active population earned up to twice the minimum wage (this means Cr $97,176.00 or U.S. $66.30 in 1984 and Cz $6,240.00 or U.S. $60.80 in 1988). This ratio varies according to regions: it is 77.6 percent in the Northeast, the poorest region, and 53 percent in the Southeast, the richest. About 34 percent of the Brazilian households are above the poverty line, earning up to twice the minimum wage per month in 1984 (PNAD).

Regional disparity is translated into the concentration, in 1984, of 44 percent of the 131 million Brazilians in 11 percent of the Brazilian area: the Southeast Region, the location with the strongest economic strength in the country and where the metropolitan areas of São Paulo (12.5 million inhabitants in 1980) and Rio de Janeiro (9 million inhabitants in 1980) are located. These two metropolitan regions had, in 1975, approximately 49 percent of the Brazilian industrial production capacity (Geiger 1985, 15).

The growth rate of the number of housing units was, until the seventies, lower than demographic growth, increasing the scarcity of houses, especially in cities, for a rapidly urbanizing population (the urban population increased from 45 percent in 1960 to 67.6 percent in 1980, and it is estimated to have reached 72.7 percent in 1984 (PNAD 1984). Starting in the seventies, the populational-growth rate decreased and the growth of housing units was above the demographic growth, especially in urban areas, reflecting a strong investment in house building during these years (1970–1984—see table 13.1), resulting from the establishment of the National Housing Bank (BNH). This bank was founded in 1964 as a support for the military regime, which started in 1964. The bank was closed in 1986, eighteen months after the (indirect) election of the first civilian President after the military coup d'état.

Negative demographic growth rates for the rural population appeared for the first time in the seventies. This explains the lower attention generally given to studies of the rural environment. Although precarious and with little infrastructure benefits, the scarcity and very poor quality of rural housing are insignificant

Table 13.1
Annual Growth Rates for Population and Housing Stock, Brazil, 1940–1984 (In Percentages)

| Year | Annual Growth Rate | | | | | |
| | Demographic | | | Housing | | |
	Urban	Rural	Total	Urban	Rural	Total
1940-50	3.8	1.6	2.4	4.0	1.6	2.4
1950-60	5.5	1.6	3.0	5.5	1.2	3.0
1960-70	5.2	0.7	2.9	4.9	0.2	2.7
1970-80	4.4	-0.6	2.5	5.6	0.1	3.6
1980-84	4.3	-1.8	2.4	6.6	-0.1	4.7

Sources: Instituto Brasileiro de Geografia e Estatistica (Brazilian Institute of Geography and Statistics) (IBGE), Demographic and Building Census, 1940, 1950, 1960, 1970, and 1980; Pesquisa Nacional para Amostragem por Domicilios (PNAD), National Survey for Sampling per Domicile, 1984.

Table 13.2
Private Home Ownership, by Region, Brazil, 1940–1984 (In Percentages)

Year	Brazil	Southeast	Northeast
1940	43.7	34.2	47.6
1950	52.1	40.6	58.7
1960	57.1	46.7	64.0
1970	60.3	54.4	66.5
1980	61.8	55.3	66.7
1984	63.4	58.3	70.2

Sources: IBGE, Building Census, 1940, 1950, 1960, 1970, and 1980; PNAD, 1984.

when compared to the problems of urban housing, especially in the periphery of large cities.

Tenure. Basically, tenure alternatives in Brazil are either private rental or private ownership. Government builds houses but sells them as any private agency does. (Table 13.2 shows the growing rate of home ownership for Brazil as a whole as well as for the wealthiest [Southeast] and for the poorest [Northeast] regions, where the percentage of home ownership was above 70 in 1984.)

Many specialists are used to associating home ownership with higher-income levels. In Brazil, however, where the trilogy of periphery/irregular settlements/ self-help housing accounts for a large part of the housing stock, home ownership and social classes are often inversely related. In this country, the price of land and of construction is high, and a large part of the population cannot afford a house in the free market. Therefore, the purchase of a plot of land in the periphery and the use of their own labor are the resources that provide them with access to housing.

For instance, in São Paulo, the proportion of rental houses was lower in the periphery ring—the poorest area (35.2 percent in 1980)—than in the central and intermediate rings (56.6 and 40.3 percent) (Pasternak Taschner 1987). The percentage of rental houses in urban Brazil has decreased from 49 in 1940 to 28.5 in 1984, representing almost 42 percent fewer rented units in these forty-four years. The transition to home ownership occurred between 1920 and 1950 although the trend varied according to cities and regions (Villaça 1986, 51).

The 1940s show the obsolescence of the "rental-house" model. The growth differential between the population and the housing stock, shown in table 13.1, and the strong rural-urban migration contributed to an increase in rents that had already reached very high levels when the first Tenancy Law was promulgated on February 20, 1942, freezing rents and making it difficult for owners to repossess their property.

This kind of state intervention discouraged the construction of rental buildings especially in urban areas. For example, in São Paulo, the percentage of rental housing decreased from 78.6 in 1930 to 59.3 in 1950 and to 38.2 in 1970 (Bonduki in Valladares 1983, 146). In 1980 this proportion increased again (40.0 percent), showing the beginning of the crisis of BNH, as explained later.

On the other hand, the ideology that only home ownership could provide economic and social security, representing an insurance against an uncertain future in a country where inflation was usually high and unemployment cycles frequent (unemployment insurance was established only in 1985) was spread. Brazilian housing policy was entirely oriented toward increasing private ownership. Diffusion of home ownership, especially among less-favored classes, was one of the main explicit objectives for the creation of the National Housing Bank (BNH) in 1964.

Nowadays the importance of home ownership is far from being only ideological. Home ownership provides status and opens doors for loans and for mortgage credit. It is not only a safe investment but also an efficient defense against inflation and arbitrary state intervention in the real estate market, which has been misguiding both landlords and tenants during the 1980s.

Quality. 1. *Material quality*: The census rates the housing units as durable or inadequate; *durable housing units* are those built mainly with permanent materials for the floor, walls, and roof (table 13.3). A strong trend of improvement in housing quality can be noticed, even in the poor northeastern area. However, the indicators are deficient. Mud houses, covered with straw and with dirt floors,

Table 13.3
Proportion of Durable Houses, Brazil, 1940–1984

Year	Brazil	Southeast	Northeast
1940	32.9	60.4	19.9
1970	73.8	85.1	59.3
1980	88.3	96.2	69.8
1984	91.9	-	-

Sources: IBGE, Building Census, 1940, 1970, 1980; PNAD, 1984.
Note: These data are not available for 1950 and 1960.

are certainly inadequate. Neither the house's maintenance status nor the quality of materials or installation nor the age or any other element except for the type of construction material are taken into account (Vetter 1981, 290). Additionally, quality does not include security in relation to tenure. During recent years, the old shacks in squatter settlements of the wealthier cities have started to be replaced by masonry units. However, this does not mean that these houses are suitable, considering the insecurity of permanence in invaded sites.

There are no reliable statistics on squatters. Even in the major cities, the figures are very often conflicting. According to the city planning secretary of Rio de Janeiro there are 1,740,818 *cariocas* living in squatter settlements, 32 percent of the city's population. "It seems that the tendency to exaggeration is still unshakeable; however, nothing authorizes us to believe that IBGE data, which showed only 628,170 squatters in Rio in 1980, are more reliable" (Ferreira dos Santos 1984, 29).

In São Paulo, the squatter population was around 7.0 percent or 630,000 people in 1985 (Pasternak Taschner 1986b). But the official planning agency in 1984 counted 558,000 people or 5.7 percent of the total population (São Paulo 1985). São Paulo, an industrial metropolis, is slightly different from the other Brazilian capitals, where rural immigration and subemployment, in addition to the strong concentration of private land ownership, have caused an abundance of squatting during the "Brazilian economic miracle" (1973–1979). During this period, the income concentration was mirrored spatially in the increase of the annual rate of squatter population from 27.6 percent per year (1973–1975) to 34.6 percent per year (1975–1979) while the population grew by 4.4 and 3.2 percent per year. Between 1979 and 1985 the squatter population grew by 12.4 percent per year, compared with 3.1 percent for the city as a whole. The economic crisis of 1987 has caused a new increase of squatters. Decidedly, Brazilian cities are becoming huge squatter settlements.

2. *Housing density*: The number of people per house in Brazil (table 13.4) has been declining: for Brazil as a whole between 1940 and 1984 there was a drop of 17.0 percent; urban-housing density declined by 18.9 percent, and rural-

Table 13.4
People per House in Urban and Rural Regions, Brazil, 1940–1984

Year	Urban	Rural	Total
1940	5.2	5.3	5.2
1950	4.9	5.3	5.1
1960	4.8	5.4	5.1
1970	4.9	5.4	5.3
1980	4.5	5.1	4.7
1984	4.2	4.9	4.3

Sources: IBGE, Demographic and Building Census, 1940, 1950, 1960, 1970, 1980; PNAD, 1984.

housing density declined by 7.6 percent. The index rise in 1970 is a result of trends during the 1960s, when increases in housing stock were clearly lower than demographic growth (table 13.1). There are also regional differences. In 1940 housing density was lower in the Northeast (4.95) than in the Southeast (5.23). In 1984, the situation was reversed: in the Southeast it was 4.34 (a reduction by 2.42 percent in forty-four years); in the northern region, including the Amazon, whose population has increased in the past thirty years, it was 5.12. This rate is similar to that of 1940, but it is a considerable decrease compared with the figure of 6.0 in 1960.

Brazil's North and Midwest regions have experienced high demographic growth rates (5.02 and 4.05 percent, per year, in the 1970–1980 decade), resulting from a national policy that promoted human settlements in those areas. However, the population increase in the North region in the 1970s although resulting in this huge growth rate, is only a little more than 2.2 million inhabitants, lower than the growth recorded in São Paulo. In any event, the migration to the North was translated into a higher housing density than for the rest of Brazil.

Since a dwelling's square floor area is not included in the census, the average number of persons per room has been used as an indicator, and more than one person per room is defined as unacceptable (table 13.5). The number of persons per room considered acceptable varies greatly according to social groups, cultures, and countries (United Nations 1967, 47–48).

However, the way this indicator is collected in Brazil shows a serious underestimation: First, the U.N. recommendation that the minimum size of a room should be sufficient to contain an adult's bed (at least 4 square meters) is not followed (United Nations 1964, 65). Also, the United Nations advised the exclusion of the bathroom from the total number of rooms. Data from the census and PNAD do not allow for this exclusion, because there is no information on the use of rooms (except for the bedroom), and even the bathroom and the kitchen are classified as bedrooms when they are used as places to sleep.

Table 13.5
Persons per Room and per Bedroom, Brazil, 1940–1984

	Persons per room			Persons per bedroom		
Year	Brazil	Southeast	North	Brazil	Southeast	North
1940	1.2	1.1	1.4	-	-	-
1950	1.1	1.0	1.4	2.5	2.3	3.1
1960	1.1	1.0	1.6	2.5	2.4	3.3
1970	1.1	1.0	1.7	2.5	2.4	3.4
1980	0.9	0.9	1.4	2.3	2.3	3.0
1984	0.8	-	-	2.1	-	-

Sources: IBGE, Demographic and Building Census, 1940, 1950, 1960, 1970, 1980; PNAD, 1984.

Bearing these limitations in mind, one sees in table 13.5 a decrease in average room density, which is strongest in the Southeast, the wealthier region. In the border regions, with a more recent colonization, the indicator is higher than the national average, and it increases until 1970, reflecting a densification of the already precarious housing situation that resulted from the differential between the growth of the housing stock and the population in the area.

Data for 1984 show, for Brazil, 27.0 percent of the housing units with an average of more than one person per room. Overcrowding is more critical in the rural areas, where 36.0 percent of the houses show an average of more than one person per room and 6.5 percent more than two persons: however, also in the urban areas the situation is serious, with respective figures of 24.3 and 4.3 percent.

The situation is even more serious with respect to the average number of persons per bedroom, especially considering what qualifies as a bedroom. In spite of this deficient definition, the number of persons per bedroom, even in the wealthier region, is more than two. The long-term trend shows a slow but steady decrease. However, it is alarming that in 1984, 39.2 percent of all Brazilian housing units contained more than two persons per bedroom and 13.2 percent more than three persons per bedroom. Overcrowding was still worse in rural areas, where 46.4 percent of the units had more than two persons per bedroom and 16 percent more than three. In urban areas the proportion of units with more than two and more than three persons per bedroom was, respectively, 36.8 and 12.4 percent.

3. *Public services*: Housing sanitary conditions are among the most important indicators of the quality of the urban utility services. (Table 13.6 shows the improvement, both for the country as a whole and for its two more heterogeneous regions, of water-supply conditions.) There was an increase of almost 300 percent

Table 13.6
Public Service Indicators: Water Supply, Suitable Destination for Dejecta, and Electrical Connections by Region, Brazil, 1950–1984

	Percentage of Houses Connected to								
	Public Water System			Sewers and/or sceptic tank			Electrical Energy		
Year	Br.	SE.	NE.	Br.	SE.	NE.	Br.	SE.	NE.
1950	-	-	-	13.1	23.5	3.6	24.6	40.4	8.4
1960	21.1	36.0	5.3	23.8	40.4	6.1	38.5	58.2	49.8
1970	33.3	51.6	12.4	26.6	43.8	8.0	47.6	68.8	23.3
1980	54.9	72.6	31.6	39.6	58.0	17.0	68.3	85.2	43.5
1984	62.2	81.7	42.6	47.9	68.7	16.0	79.4	91.5	56.8

Sources: IBGE, Building Census, 1950, 1960, 1970, 1980; PNAD, 1984.
Notes: Br. = Brazil; SE = Southeast; NE = Northeast. Data are not available for 1940.

in the number of domiciles connected to public water services between 1960 and 1984, partially as a result of the PLANASA program, launched by the BNH in 1971 (Jorge 1987). This is equivalent to stating that there was an annual increase of 4.6 percent, which was lower in the Southeast (3.5 percent per year) than in the Northeast (9.1 percent per year). In spite of this effort, the regional differential increased.

Sanitary improvement also appeared in relation to the destination of dejecta, since almost 50 percent of Brazilian domiciles in 1984 had a correct destination for domestic waste—public sewers system or septic tank (in this case it should be considered adequate only when it is regularly maintained and cleaned and when its location and surrounding soil conditions are suitable). The annual increase of domiciles with a correct destination for dejecta between 1950 and 1984 was 3.9 percent per year for the country as a whole. Similarly, table 13.6 shows not only the alarming sanitary situation in the Northeast but also the increasing differential between this region and the Southeast. This is translated into a child mortality rate of 71.6 per thousand of children born alive in the Southeast and 124.5 per thousand of children born alive in the Northeast (data from 1982).

In 1984 almost 60 percent of the houses enjoyed public garbage-collection services; 29 percent disposed of the garbage either in unused lots or threw it into rivers, especially in the rural regions. Electrical connections are the public utility service most frequently available.

Conclusion. The indicators, somehow, permit the measurement of housing quality. However, to use them to estimate the proportion of unsuitable housing is dangerous. The concept of adequacy is relative, and the concrete characteristics of a "standard house" vary from country to country, from region to region, among social groups and, above all, with time (Pradilla 1976; Havel 1968; Pasternak Taschner 1983).

Following the minimum requirements established by the United Nations (1962), we will see that the 8.2 percent of housing units built with rough materials (nonfinished wood boards, mud, straw) are unsuitable, as well as 13.23 percent of houses with more than three persons per bedroom and 37.8 percent houses without piped water (approximately 11 million units in 1984). However, the housing indicators are supplied separately by the Brazilian census, exactly the way they were prepared and recorded for this work. Without special tabulations there is no way to know whether the mud house is supplied with water and/or sanitary facilities or whether the house provided with suitable material and sanitary conditions is overcrowded.

Some estimates state that around 3 percent of the houses in the country are "substandard." A special tabulation for the metropolitan area of Rio de Janeiro in 1974 has shown that more than 480,000 units had unsuitable water and sewer conditions, representing 31.6 percent of the total of houses (Vetter and Simoes 1980).

ROLE OF HOUSING INSTITUTIONS AND ORGANIZATIONS

General Overview

At least five historical landmarks can be seen in the Brazilian popular housing policy. The housing solution during the slavery period (until 1888) was the *senzala* (slave quarters); during the first industrialization stage (1890–1929) the slums and "workers' villages" appeared. Then, in the 1930s, simultaneously with a spontaneous urban-expansion process and, consequently, a decline in the housing situation due to the increase of migration flows to urban areas, state intervention started through the social security system. After the military coup in 1964, the federal government proposed the construction of mass housing by the National Housing Bank. Finally, after the bankruptcy of the BNH, Brazilian housing policy has lacked direction. The Housing Finance System (SFH) has been paralyzed since November 1986.

During the slavery period, the owner designated part of the construction to slave quarters, close to the manor house, where the slave manpower was sheltered and secluded. The slaves represented a fundamental asset for the owner, who protected it from loss due to escape or death. The slave housing, that is, the housing of workmen during the slavery period, was the insurance of the slavery itself.

The abolishment of slavery by the end of the nineteenth century happened parallel with the expansion of cities dedicated to agricultural trade. Coffee exports created an urban infrastructure for the founding of industries. A work market was established and expanded in the cities, and immigration, both internal and foreign, affected the urban-housing conditions.

Adjacent to the increasing slums, "workers' villages" arose. Industrial entrepreneurs built blocks of houses for the workers near their plants (Blay 1978, 1985). Housing was an attraction factor for the few existing skilled workers needed by the industry. When these workers entered into this system, they created roots and agreed to receive lower salaries since the loss of their jobs also meant the loss of their homes. From the companies' viewpoint, housing was a point of leverage over the workers. This system became useless when the constant migration brought an increasingly large labor pool that was increasingly skilled.

Therefore, in the 1940s and 1950s, the trilogy of periphery/self-help housing/ irregular settlements was dominant for the poor people particularly in São Paulo. One of the possible alternatives for the poor population was the purchase of a lot in the developing periphery and building a house by self-help. In Rio de Janeiro, the particular topography contributed to the proliferation of houses in invaded sites on the mountains—the *favelas* (squatter settlements).

The difference between the two housing solutions also was due to income and employment levels: in São Paulo the concentration of industrial investments guaranteed labor and wages while in Rio unemployment and subemployment rates were always higher. Consequently, for the poor people in Rio the sole alternative was living in huts in invaded land.

Until 1930 both production and distribution of the housing units were left to the discretion of private initiative (Bonduki 1982; Ribeiro and Pechman 1983; Farah 1985). The thirties saw a change in this pattern. Through the Retirement and Pension Institutes (IAPs), created in the decade and organized in accordance with occupational categories (industry workers, railroad workers, bank workers, and so on), the state started to interfere directly in the supply of houses by constructing isolated housing estates for selected categories of workers, for example, housing estates for bank workers, railroad workers, and so on. The very first steps of state intervention in housing date from 1920: a presidential decree ruling the construction of rental houses for "workers and proletarians" (Financiadora de Estudos e Projectos—Grupo de Arquitetura e Planejamento 1985; Azevedo and Gama de Andrade 1982). In 1923 the first Retirement Savings Bank was created for railroad employees.

Between 1937, when the Retirement and Pension Institutes' assisted housing programs were started, and 1964, when these activities connected to social security ended, 279 housing estates were built in the country, totaling 47,789 dwellings. In the same period, 76,236 houses were financed, built, or acquired by social security members (Farah 1985, 74).

Change of the state intervention pattern can only be understood in the broader framework of the changes in Brazilian society at large since 1930. This year the Getulio Vargas dictatorship started. He was a populist leader, who represented the victory of industrial sectors over the landed gentry. Industrialization caused the rapid growth of urban population, increasing the housing problem. Additionally, looking for popular support, Vargas intervened in the real estate market, issuing the draconian "Tenancy Law," which froze rents and made it difficult for the landlords to repossess the property. This measure disorganized the rental housing market, discouraging investors.

Workers demanded housing from the state to be provided through the Social Security Institutes, identified by the lower classes as an institutional channel responsible for meeting consumption needs. As a result, state intervention increased, and in 1946 another agency for housing finance and construction was created, no longer tied to any professional category as were the IAPs: The Popular Housing Foundation. Its ambitious plan was to build houses for sale and for rent, to support the industry of construction materials, to implement basic sanitation projects, and to define construction standards and policies. Until December 1960 it built 143 housing estates, containing approximately 17,000 units, with a floor area ranging from 60 to 70 square meters.

The Target Plan of the 1956–1960 government did not specify anything in relation to housing construction. However, it stimulated the civil construction industry and the construction materials industry by the founding of Brasilia, the new capital of the republic of Brazil. Housing became of great concern to the next government (1961–1962) not only because of the critical housing situation but also because of the importance given to housing by the Alliance for Progress, the reform program launched by President Kennedy, with the help of the World Bank and the Interamerican Bank, as a protection against the influence of the Cuban Revolution. At that time the Interamerican Bank proposed the financing of a Housing Assistance Plan and the replacement of the Popular Housing Foundation by the Brazilian Housing Institute. Emphasis would be given to private home ownership as a policy to limit worker rebellions and to support individual social mobility. The plan's objective was that the Brazilian Housing Institute would build 100,000 compact units in eighteen months, with services supplied by the municipalities and with mortgage payments of 20 percent of the minimum wage. This project presaged the National Housing Bank, created immediately after the coup of 1964.

In 1964 the Brazilian economy was in serious crisis. Inflation was 100 percent per year. The GNP growth rate was 10.3 percent in 1960 and 5.3 percent in 1962 and dropped 1.5 percent in 1963 and 2.4 percent in 1964. By stimulating the construction industry through a public-financed housing-construction program, it was expected that the economy would improve since the construction industry absorbed mostly unskilled labor, especially rural migrants. It also had important multiplier effects, stimulating indirect employment and the construction materials industry. The growth of jobs in civil construction during the 1960s was 8.2 percent per year and during the 1970s, 6.2 percent per year, compared with 5.2 percent and 7.7 percent per year for the industrial sector as a whole (table 13.7). The 1981–1983 crisis was more strongly felt in the construction area, with a decline in jobs in 1980–1984 of − 1.8 percent per year, while the

Table 13.7
The Economically Active Population in the Civil Construction Sector and in the Industrial Sector, Brazil, 1950–1984

Year	Industrial Sector (Total)		Construction Industry	
	N	%	N	%
1950	2,427,364	14.2	584,644	3.4
1960	2,940,242	12.9	781,247	3.4
1970	5,295,417	17.9	1,719,714	5.8
1980	10,674,977	24.4	3,151,094	7.2
1984	10,923,994	21.8	2,926,441	5.9

Sources: Faria, 1983, p. 146; PNAD, 1984.

other industrial sectors were able to maintain a 1.5 percent growth of the employed population.

The sector of the civil construction industry was responsible for 13.8 percent of the new jobs from 1960 to 1970 and for 10.1 percent from 1970 to 1980. In addition, in Brazil, the construction industry does not depend on imports, making it a privileged instrument in conjunctural economic policy.

The creation of the National Housing Bank in 1964, only five months after the military takeover, was possible only because of the existence of the studies and projects for the planned Brazilian Housing Institute, with a different economic approach, but with a similar ideology. The fact is a good example of continuity in policy orientation and of reuse of technical solutions in different political contexts. Within the income concentration model chosen by the 1964 government, it made sense to help to buy a house instead of raising salaries.

Therefore, the establishment of the Housing Financing System (SFH) followed a strategy of the authoritarian state, striving to find in housing an instrument to legitimate itself using "the dream of home ownership" spread through the entire Brazilian society. Above all, it was a way to supply employment to nonskilled manpower, making civil construction attractive to domestic capital and acting as a buffer to the economic recession (Bolaffi 1977, 1983; Azevedo and Gama de Andrade 1982; Valladares 1978, 1983; Pasternak Taschner 1975; Veras and Bonduki 1986; Maricato 1987).

The BNH was created with the authority to "guide, discipline, and control" the Housing Financing System and to promote the construction and acquisition of houses, especially by lower-income groups. Its history is the course of its institutional performance, its implementation, its search for higher financial rationality, changing its mechanisms in accordance with the needs arisen in each sociopolitical conjuncture.

The SFH and BNH have been discussed in numerous places. The Housing

Table 13.8
SFH (Housing Financing System) Funds' Share, Brazil, 1967–1984

Year	Savings		
	Compulsory	Voluntary	Induced
1967	93.4	3.8	2.8
1973	41.6	49.6	8.8
1980	36.3	56.4	7.3
1984	30.9	62.1	7.0

Sources: Sachs, 1987; Pasternak Taschner, 1975.

Financial System, which financed 4.4 million housing units between 1964 and 1985, is often cited as an example of an ingenious institution for channeling an important part of national savings toward the execution of construction programs. Its funds came from three sources:

1. *Compulsory savings*, represented by the payment of the service Time Guarantee Fund (FGTS) managed by the BNH. The FGTS represents the deposit by an employer of 8 percent of the payroll in an account in the name of an employee, managed by the BNH, yielding quarterly interest and inflationary correction. These savings can be collected by the employee in case of dismissal from the job, purchase of one's own business, marriage, and purchase of property from the SFH.[1]

2. *Voluntary savings*, the Brazilian Savings and Loans System (SBPE). Collection of resources voluntarily deposited in a savings account. These deposits yield 6 percent interest per year and get monthly inflationary correction.

3. *Induced savings*, government savings funds given to financial agents or to borrowers.

There is an increasing share of voluntary private savings in the SFH resources (table 13.8). This important change in the composition of SFH resources had the effect of making housing finance inaccessible to the low-income population, since there is a significant difference between the use of the money from the two main sources. The FGTS money remains available a long time for BNH since the employee can only collect it upon dismissal, purchase of one's own business, marriage, or purchase of property from the SFH. Besides, this FGTS loan is paid at a low interest rate (3 percent per year) with inflationary correction. The savings accounts loans are paid at 6 percent interest per year with inflationary correction and should be available whenever their owners need them. The impossibility of having a higher amount of cheaper money from the FGTS reduced the bank's investments in subsidized housing for low-income classes (COS: Carteira de Operações de Natureza Social—Social Operations Agency).

The housing market became segmented by the division of the work among the various public and private agents under the control of the BNH, each one of them serving one of these segments. For example, the "popular market" (for families earning up to three times the minimum wage and later up to five times) would be served by the COHABs (Housing Companies at the local or state level). The "economic market" (for families with an income ranging from three to six times the minimum wage, increased later) was served by housing cooperatives, nonprofit associations for occupational categories acting as intermediates between the borrowers and the BNH. The "medium market" was designed to serve families with an income above six times the minimum wage. Here, the most active operator was the SBPE (Brazilian Savings and Loans System), serving the so-called middle class and the sector of deluxe construction for the upper class.

The complex relationship between the state and the private industry can be summarized as follows: the SFH agents worked with private building contractors while the BNH controlled the market through building standards, terms for payment, and interest rates. The BNH also acted as the guarantor of funds for construction in a very peculiar way, as shown in the following example: a private construction contractor sold a house to someone and received the entire amount in cash from the BNH. The debt was transferred to the bank. The buyer did not pay directly to the contractor but to the bank. Thus the builder ran no risk. The bank guaranteed the money in cash. This way, the SFH intended to stimulate the private building industry.

Over the years, the BNH's policy has undergone changes. M.P.B. Veras and N. Bonduki (1986) distinguished five stages:

1964–1967: The BNH's major function was to institute a monetary correction in the loan contracts to compensate for inflation.

1967–1971: During this time the BNH expanded its resources as it became the FGTS manager and the country's second bank. Its functions were also expanded to include urban development and sanitation.

1971–1979: The BNH was reorganized. It still operated as a bank, dealing directly with the public, but it was connected to the Interior Ministry and transferred resources only to its agents (private banks, housing cooperatives, state housing companies). The Popular Housing Plan was established (1974) and subsidies were implemented. Another significant change was the attempt to minimize the effects of monetary correction, since salary readjustments were below inflation and many borrowers were not able to keep up with mortgage payments. The financing system was improved by means of the Salary Equivalence Plan (PES) whereby the debtor balance was readjusted quarterly but the monthly mortgage payments were readjusted according to increases in the minimum wage or to an occupational category collective-bargaining agreement. In the PES plan the Compensation Fund for the Salary Variation (FCVS) was responsible for the debt: If there was any debt after the payment of the last installment at the end of the term established, the FCVS would underscribe the debt. If the opposite occurred (that is, if the debt had been repaid before the last installment), the remaining balance would be credited to the fund. This was theoretically possible depending on the inflation rate and on the time of purchase of property. Calculations showed that for expected inflation rate and salary readjustments the FCVS could remain balanced. During this period there was an attempt to gain popular legitimization for the bank's methods of readjusting mortgage payments according to salaries. Before this period, discrepancies had occurred several times. Many buyers could not afford to pay the mortgage installments. Before the PES implementation, banks estimated that around 30 percent of the buyers had discontinued or were overdue in their payments.

1979–1983: This was an ambiguous phase, strongly affected by the economic crisis of 1981–1983 and characterized by the beginning of more flexible financing models, oriented toward popularization. However, in 1983 the growing difference between the large upward correction of mortgage installments and the smaller salary increases overburdened the Salary Variation Compensations Fund and increased the number of defaults. Starting in 1982, salaries were readjusted annually at indexes of 100 percent and BNH installments at a rate of 130 percent. Inflation in 1983 was 157 percent, reaching 215 percent in 1984. Additionally, the readjustment of the SFH assets and liabilities was not synchronized, and they were made at different times. Besides, they were expressed in different values, over which different correction indexes were applied. While debt balances were adjusted quarterly according to the UPC (Basic Capital Unit), the mortgage installments were adjusted either annually or biannually according to specific indexes, and salaries were expressed in *cruzados* and adjusted either annually or biannually.[2] The gap between the adjustment of the debt and of the mortgage installments generated a huge residue, burdening the FCVS. The SFH financial problems had started.

1983–1986: This period is characterized by the bank's crisis and bankruptcy. The construction of finished units was too expensive and the bank had no funds. As the housing crisis continued, programs such as site-and-services, with or without core units, assisted self-help housing, and the like were launched on a larger scale.

Low-Cost Housing: Plans and Reality

The BNH was originally conceived as the main spearhead of the social policies of the military regime and created as a bank to promote private home ownership among low-income classes, but it has subverted the intended objectives. Monies meant to finance low-cost public housing and, in part, obtained through compulsory savings from the working class have been diverted to feed real estate speculation and construction of middle-class and luxury housing. Indeed, out of the 4.4 million units financed through the SFH between 1964 and 1985, only one-third of the loans benefited low-income families (that is, those earning up to five times the minimum wage) representing two-thirds of Brazilian families in 1984, equivalent to only 12.9 percent of the total allocated resources (Sachs 1987, 136).

The BNH's Annual Report (Banco Nacional de Habitação 1982) estimated demand for the 1980–1985 period, including the construction of new units and the improvement of existing houses, at 6.65 million units and recognized that 82.8 percent of this demand accounted for households in the COHABs range (up to five times the minimum wage), 10.8 percent for households between five and ten times the minimum wage, and only 6.4 percent for households with higher income.

From 1964 to 1985, 13 percent of SFH resources were used to meet the needs of 83 percent of the population, whereas 87 percent of the resources were used for the needs of the remaining 17 percent of the population, that is, the middle and upper classes (Cavalcanti de Albuquerque 1985).

From January 1, 1980, to June 30, 1985, 615,690 COHAB loans were granted, corresponding to 11 percent of the population's needs during this period. This is far from enough, even though in the past five years the SFH has built almost as many COHAB units as in the preceding fifteen years.

The BNH's performance shows that its policy was successful as an instrument for ideological domination (home-ownership model), as a job generator in civil construction (especially up to 1980), and as a promoter of the housing industry—between 1964 and 1986 the Brazilian housing stock increased by 18.25 million units, of which 4.4 million used SFH resources, that is, 24 percent of the new housing benefited from BNH resources.

Owing to its free-market model the SFH has handled housing as a problem of investment-return, and when it has used subsidies, it has done so in the wrong way. The Salary Variation Compensation Fund ended up operating as a large subsidy, in an indiscriminate manner, when it amortized the debt balance, both for medium- and high-income families and for poor families. Few of the workers that contributed with their FGTS benefited with houses.

In addition, large sums of the BNH's money were directed to urban development (urban renewal, highway system, underground train) and to sanitation (32.3 percent of its 1985 budget). This money was very seldom returned to the BNH by the municipalities that loaned it, thereby contributing decisively to the bankruptcy and extinction of the institution by the end of 1986. The BNH, perverted by its own contradictions, illustrates the limits of a social housing policy not embedded in an economic and social policy.

The basic problem is not the Housing Financing System but poverty. Until a few years ago it was perfectly possible to make houses of 50 square meters affordable for individuals in the range from one to three times the minimum wage. After this, Brazil went to "core houses," with 23 square meters. Today, this has been reduced to units with 7 square meters, containing only a kitchen and sanitary facilities, and even this has become unaffordable (Lerner 1980, in von Zastrow 1987).

HOUSING MARKETS AND POLICY GUIDELINES

The Rural Housing Market

The rural housing market is unknown. Brazilian rural population is extremely poor: 28.5 percent of the households earn less than the minimum wage; 32.7 percent earn between one and two times the minimum wage per month. The housing model in force until the 1970s was the house granted by the landowner, usually the farmer. The implementation of Rural Social Security caused the rural landowners to enforce a mass dismissal of workers, due to the fear of workers' demands who, therefore, lost their houses. In the 1980s a large part of the population working in the agricultural sector has lived in rented houses in the periphery of urban centers. They are the *bóia-fria* (cold-food), mobile rural workers that are given this name because they eat in the fields, without time to heat the food they bring from home. They are paid daily, and they have no formal work contract and therefore do not enjoy any of the rights of urban workers (the FGTS, eight-hour work day, thirty-day remunerated vacations, ninety-day maternity leave, unemployment insurance, social security, and so forth).

The Urban Housing Market

The urban housing market in Brazil can roughly be divided into three large segments:

1. *The illegal market*: It groups the various submarkets covering invaded land (either gradually or by collective actions—squatter settlements, a new phenomenon in Brazil, contrary to other Latin American countries) and invaded housing units. At least 2 million urban households earning less than a minimum wage (9.1 percent of all urban households) are part of this market. Very probably also, the almost 4 million households with monthly incomes between one and two times the minimum wage (16.5 percent of the urban households in 1984) cannot afford a house outside this market, which, therefore, covers about 25 percent of all urban households.

2. *The private commercial market*: It consists of private rental housing and private home-ownership units controlled by private landlords and private industry, either with their own capital or BNH-transferred capital. The 8.8 million urban households with more than five times the minimum wage (38.4 percent of the Brazilian urban households) can surely buy or rent any type of housing within this market, either units produced on order from the houseowner, from a speculative builder or from a state developer. Readers must bear in mind that most of the SFH financing was targeted for the medium-income households (above six times the minimum wage). This market is operated mainly by private agents making up the Brazilian Savings and Loan System (Property Credit Societies, Savings and Loan Associations).

The private commercial market also serves poorer strata (two to five times the minimum wage) since public housing is not sufficient. In São Paulo, for example, COHAB's production from 1964 to 1985 amounted to only 2.5 percent of the city housing stock in 1985 (Sachs 1987, 94). Dwellings in this market segment are located in the "periphery" of urban centers, built by house owners (self-help) or by a small builder. The labor force that builds the house is not always strictly family. The incidence of paid labor is in fact far from negligible:

more than a half of the households living in self-built houses used it during the construction.[3] When home ownership is out of reach, these people become part of the slum population or live in backyard rooms (the so-called periphery slums). People in these income brackets would certainly be qualified for units built by public housing if there were enough of them. They are part of the 7.9 million urban households with incomes between two and five times the minimum wage (34.5 percent of the total of urban families in 1984) who could not afford to buy a public house.

3. *The public market*: It consists of the units built by public promotion (CO-HAB). Generally, construction is done by private contractors. Approximately 1.5 million units, averaging 40 square meters, were targeted for families with two to five times the minimum wage.

The illegal market is far from homogeneous. Although there are no data for Brazil as a whole, in São Paulo, field surveys conducted in 1980 have shown an increasing trade of shanty houses. The commodification trend is seen in the higher amount for a hut in 1987—14 times the minimum wage—compared with the price of a similar shanty house in 1982—around ten times the minimum wage. Even land is now commercialized: the right to use a site in a well-structured squatter settlement in São Paulo must be bought by the user from the first invader, and the price is rising (Pasternak Taschner 1983).

One of the most generalized beliefs is that squatter settlements are built exclusively by the dwellers, with extremely low-cost waste materials. The reality in São Paulo and Rio has shown that specialized builders as well as "shanty-house manufacturers" thrive in the settlements. Cavalcanti (1984) in a study performed in *favelas* in Rio de Janeiro found a builder in the Santa Maria *favela* who had already built 100 houses in the *favela* with the help of relatives. The "manufacturers" sell wood panels in modules, supplied with door and window. They are a response of a popular technology to the demand for more units with less construction time. The supply price for a 20-square-meter shanty house built this way was seven times the minimum wage in 1980, a good example of popular ingenuity applied to meet a demand ignored by the "formal market."

From Eradication of Favelas to Their Upgrading

The first basic form of state intervention in housing, following the international trend, was the removal and relocation of the *favelas*. This policy, in force during the 1960s, saw squatter settlements as a focus of disease, crime, social disorders, and marginality. This pathology would be extinguished with the extirpation of the settlement from the urban fabric and the relocation of the squatters to suitable units. In Rio de Janeiro, between 1962 and 1974, 26,193 shanty houses and 139,218 people were removed (Valladares 1978). In São Paulo, removal never reached either the violence or the size reached in Rio.

However, since the seventies, it has become clear that relocating the squatters to traditional housing estates has failed. This failure was evidenced by the abandonment and sale of the apartments and the return of squatter settlements (Valladares 1978; Rush 1974; Perlman 1976, 1977; Blanck 1980). Nowadays the removal is used only in emergency situations.

Therefore, instead of putting squatters in a final housing unit, there was an attempt to locate them in so-called Temporary Housing Villages (VHP) in São Paulo and in the Proletarian Parks in Rio de Janeiro. The theories that mediated this form of intervention held that the squatter settlements were the first housing alternative for the migrants, a "springboard" to the city, a required first stage for integration into the city. At the VHP the basic concern was to shorten the "compulsory time" spent by the immigrants in the squatter settlements. Therefore, the local state supplied certain basic infrastructure elements such as piped water and sewers systems, collective bathrooms, and laundries. Government social assistance also helped people to get jobs and provided occupational training. It was expected that after one year families would be able to find housing from the private commercial market or from the public market. Criticisms of this project were many. In addition to the implicit assumption of social integration, empirical data soon showed that many squatters were not at all recent migrants and the squatter settlements were not always their first living locations. In São Paulo, for instance, in 1980, approximately 41 percent of the family heads had lived in other places in the city, before living in the squatter settlements, and there they had paid rent or had even been owners (Pasternak Taschner 1978). The growth of squatter settlements is due to pauperization rather than to migration. Many migrants living in squatter settlements did not come first to the shanty house where they were interviewed.[4] They had moved in the urban space, following a logical path in the process of increasing prices of urban land and of pauperization of the working class, from central areas to the periphery, from masonry houses to shanty houses (Pasternak Taschner 1983).

By the end of the 1970s, it had become clear that the squatter settlements would remain and that the repressive bulldozer policies had failed. It had also become clear that the squatter settlements did not represent a malfunction of the economic and social system but were the physical expression of its contradictions. The large increase in the squatter population and the growing political pressures demanded new solutions. Paradoxically, public authorities started looking for legal norms and suitable standards for illegal settlements.

By the end of 1979 the PROAGUA Program was started in São Paulo. It proposed the extension of the water network to the squatter settlements, first to those located in sites belonging to the municipality. In the same year, the PRO-LUZ (supply of electrical power to *favelas*) was created, and in 1987 electrical power had been installed in practically all the shanty houses of São Paulo. Additionally, more ambitious projects of upgrading squatter settlements have been started although at small scale. From March 1983 to December 1985, more than 151,000 families benefited from the upgrading program, almost 12 percent of the total of squatter families in São Paulo.

Another project, PROMORAR, implemented in June 1979, proposed the eradication of squatter settlements, replacing the shanty houses with masonry houses in the same location and legalizing the site ownership. In São Paulo, until 1986, eleven PROMORAR housing estates were built, with 3,142 units delivered and 2,380 units under construction. The PROMORAR offered to each family a core unit (room and bathroom) with the possibility of extension by the dweller. The sites, services, and community equipment (e.g., nurseries, schools, outpatient clinics) were supplied by the local government.

The midseventies also showed a change in the public upgrading policy at the federal level. The BNH practices, which were previously exclusively concerned with the construction of housing estates and turnkey housing units changed to include sites-and-services programs—intended for families with less than three times the minimum wage—squatter upgrading programs, as well as an assisted self-help program launched in 1984 in an attempt to reach the poorer strata. However, these alternative housing schemes did not go much beyond the pilot-project stage, using only 1.6 percent of the SFH's resources, benefiting 250,000 out of 4.4 million families.

In summary, from 1964 to 1979, when directed toward the low-income strata, the BNH built large housing estates. At that time, it was the national and foreign experts' consensus that mass production, supported by industrial methods, would solve the housing issue. The change and evolution of these ideas and practices in the 1970s because of scholars like J.F.L. Turner (1976) was intensified under the stimulus provided by the United Nations conferences on the Environment (Stockholm 1972) and on Habitat (Vancouver 1976). The "reform" solutions, in opposition to mass production of housing estates, included upgrading, institutional self-help housing, and sites-and-services programs (World Bank 1986).

The starting point of the reform solutions was twofold: first, the excessive financial cost of the classical solutions of public housing; second, the unacceptable political cost of the destruction of spontaneous settlements. The search for alternative solutions has been the focus of many discussions. A. Gilbert (1982) stated that the adoption of programs to consolidate the squatter settlement areas arises from the fact that they do not directly threaten private property. For example, in Chile in the 1970s and in São Paulo in 1987, it was more advantageous for owners of real estate in the periphery to collect the government's indemnity after having their sites invaded than to invest in sites-and-services. H. Harms (1982, 23–24) stated that the "new" housing programs are the dominant class strategies, and they were implemented because they would serve as instruments to help in conjunctural crises and to contain social uprisings. (In São Paulo they appeared with the most conservative city government in the past twenty years).

As elsewhere, in Brazil there is a debate on pros and cons of self-help housing. In a simplistic manner, we can summarize the debate as a "rightist" and a "leftist" polemic (Valladares 1985). The rightists hold that the poor are best able to solve their housing problems by themselves, and the state is responsible for helping them by means of assisted self-help housing and sites-and-services programs. Among the main reasons in favor of "self-help" are flexibility, dweller control, low cost, and participation.

Critics (the leftists) claim that besides exploiting the working class, self-help represents a transfer to the poor of the state's responsibility for housing provision. The numerous criticisms of the alternative housing programs result from two factors. The first is primarily ideological, related to the principle of using self-help housing and stressing its equivalence to exploitation of the work force (Pradilla 1976; Harms 1982; Burgess 1982). Second, there is a certain skepticism generated by assessments already conducted by experts contracted by the World Bank (Rodell 1983; Crooke 1983). These assessments show the deviation from the initial goals, considering the contracting of manpower and high turnover of residents in the areas where projects occur (Ward 1982; Burgess 1985). In addition, it was noticed that the implementation of services raised the land's price, starting a gentrification process.

A "new left" consisting mainly of young architects and sociologists that work side by side in urban social movements have been defending the idea that self-managed, self-help housing, free from the state or linked to the state only to get resources, is the way to educate the poor for collective solutions (Bonduki 1986).[5]

The experience is still too brief to allow for a valid evaluation of the incipient reforms. In any case, many experts argue that since approximately 40 percent of all urban houses are self-help constructed, it is better to assist and finance this type of housing, thus ensuring a better technical quality and saving human resources. In response to the leftists' argument that this practice camouflages worker exploitation, they reply that self-help builders themselves appropriate the increased house value. Additionally, one must take into consideration that the "parallel" job market created by self-help activity is far from insignificant.

In 1948 approximately 28 percent of the manpower employed in civil construction declared itself "independent" (PNAD 1984). They include both self-help and the periphery's small builders and masons who find room to work at the fringe of capitalist production, without being directly included in a capital wage relation, in a way very similar to that of the independent producer. Working on repairs, for sale or rent, the small builder is characterized by taking direct part in construction work. His activity at the fringe of capitalist production puts him in the unique position of producer and distributor of housing to a population having a similar income level (Mautner 1986).

MAJOR PROBLEMS

The basic housing problems in Brazil can be divided into four groups: (1) poverty, (2) sociospatial segregation, (3) contradictions and bankruptcy of the Housing Financing System, and (4) excessively centralized decision making.

Table 13.9
Distribution of Monthly Household Income, by Region, Brazil, 1984

Salary * (MW)	Urban		Rural		Total	
	N (x 1,000)	%	N (x 1,000)	%	N (x 1,000)	%
up to 1	2,092	9.1	2,105	28.5	4,197	13.9
+1 to 2	3,779	16.5	2,339	31.7	6,118	20.2
+2 to 5	7,910	34.5	2,032	27.5	9,942	32.8
5+	8,823	38.5	843	11.4	9,666	31.9
no income	133	0.6	32	0.4	165	0.5
no declar.	174	0.8	38	0.5	212	0.7
TOTAL	22911	100.0	7389	100.00	30300	100.00

Source: PNAD, 1984.
*Minimum wage (MW) in 1988 is approximately U.S. $60 per month.

Poverty

Poverty and an uneven income distribution are the roots of the housing crisis. In 1983 the wealthiest 5 percent of the population got more than one-third of the national income. Of all Brazilian households, 34.1 percent are under the poverty line (i.e., with incomes less than two times the minimum wage, or about U.S. $720 per year) in a country where the per capita income is around U.S. $2,000 per year (table 13.9). This situation is both directly and indirectly the result of an unfair distribution of opportunities and wealth that, within a different framework, could stop existing at this same level of GNP.

Given this income distribution, the task of providing each citizen with decent housing is very difficult and impossible without subsidies. Considering that families need at least to pay for food and transportation to work and school, they have no money left to purchase a house. According to a survey on family expenditures, families earning from two to five times the minimum wage can spend from 10 to 16 percent on housing.

For the very poor, rent-supplement programs could be considered (public rental housing, which is unusual in Brazil; Bolaffi 1986). Also existing reform alternatives such as sites-and-services and assisted self-help housing could be increased. In government-assisted self-help housing, cost reduction amounts to around 60 percent. In a recent 40 square meters pilot project (Cavalcanti de Albuquerque 1985) a house cost around 600 UPC (U.S. $4,800), not including the remuneration of the self-help builder. A 20 square meters COHAB core unit cost 400 UPC (U.S. $3,200). The self-help form of housing production, although despoiling and cruel to the worker, minimizes the need for financial savings, which low-income strata do not have, and it is supported by surplus work (i.e., a number of hours worked in the building process, in addition to normal worked hours in other activities), a resource usually available in low-income families.

Sociospatial Segregation

The Brazilian conjuncture of accelerated urbanization and salary erosion have triggered a powerful mechanism of social exclusion and urban segregation, two fundamental traits in the Brazilian urban development. From this also arises the poor quality of the units, which are currently inhabited by the poor. On the one hand are the workers, with little or no qualification, who form the "city of producers" but are excluded from the "city of consumers" (the part of the city with an urban infrastructure, such as the sewage system, telephone, pavement, public transportation, and urban services like shops, medical services, schools, and so on). On the other hand is a minority that is able to enjoy the urban benefits. Between the two ends are middle class and skilled workers who try to reach the consumption style of the wealthy stratum, very often through huge sacrifices.

Social polarization is inscribed in space. The urban centers and the wealthy neighborhoods contain the majority of the infrastructure and benefit from a real estate boom. Medium-size and large cities show high-rise buildings. On the other hand, the poorer majority is restricted to an increasingly distant periphery. This causes an enormous expansion of the urban area, with an exaggerated horizontal growth at extremely low densities. In São Paulo, for instance, the gross demographic density dropped from 110 inhabitants per hectare in 1914 to 72 inhabitants per hectare in 1986. Poor peripheral sections of São Paulo—the wealthiest Brazilian metropolis—contain 52.2 percent of all residences supplied with piped water and 32.7 percent with sewer services, while in wealthier neighborhoods located downtown, 99.6 percent of the houses have a piped water supply and 98.8 percent have sewers (Pasternak Taschner 1986a). In downtown São Paulo, more than 50 percent of the families earn more than ten times the minimum wage; in the periphery, 70 percent earn less than five times the minimum wage, and they spend an average of three hours and fifteen minutes commuting each day. Land prices in São Paulo vary from 0.3 OTN (U.S. $2.4) per square meter to 23 OTN (U.S. $184) per square meter.[6] These figures exclude the more expansive central sites.

Brazilian cities are characterized by an irrational use of land and infrastructure. M. A. Campanario's (1984) study of the real estate market and social exclusion in São Paulo estimates 12.8 percent empty urban space in the downtown area, 22.6 percent in the so-called intermediate ring, and 57.9 percent in the poorly served periphery, creating a vast horizontal, impoverished urban landscape, where the costs of establishing new sites and infrastructure are enormous.

Contradictions and Bankruptcy of the Housing Finance System

The complexity of the SFH financial support arises from the need to make the long-term investment (up to twenty-five years) compatible with savings accounts on a short-term basis within an economic environment characterized by high inflation (more than 100 percent per year since 1983; in 1987 the inflation rate was around 325 percent).

In addition, the synchronization of the SHF's assets and liabilities was undermined by the effects of the high inflation. The difference between the readjustments of the debt balances (quarterly) and the readjustment of the mortgage installments (annual or biannual) generated a deficit that grew bigger as the difference between them increased and led to the system's bankruptcy in 1986.

If the salary readjustments had been higher than the inflation rate of less than 100 percent per year, it would have been possible, at least theoretically, not to have deficits left after the mortgage-expiration term. Unfortunately, this is not what happened. The increases in minimum wages during 1982–1984 were lower than the inflation rate and the index of upward adjustment of the mortgage installments. The population's pauperization increased the deficit, burdening the Salary Variation Compensation Fund (FCVS) and eventually leading to the system's financial crash in 1986. For example, in 1983 the index of upward adjustment of the minimum wage was 109.4 percent, the inflation rate was 156.6 percent, and the mortgage-installment adjustment was 130.4 percent. In 1984 these figures were 179.4, 215.3, and 191.0 percent.

This financial crash had far-reaching consequences for the Brazilian economy. The SFH was responsible for the management of funds valued at six times the nation's funds for payment, 50 percent of the current foreign debt, and more than twice the federal government's revenue (Cavalcanti de Albuquerque 1985, 75).

In fact, the Housing Financial System was based on the assumption of continuous and fast economic growth. It was not able to bear the 1981–1984 crisis accompanied by high unemployment and pauperization. With the economic crisis, SHF's support base—the savings accounts—were weakened by the withdrawal of money to supplement domestic household budgets. The FGTS funds were also depleted by the increase in unemployment. According to A. Barros de Castro and F. E. Pires de Souza (1985) industrial employment decreased by 20 percent between 1981 and 1983, and the number of unemployed and subemployed individuals was estimated in 1983 at 13 million, a quarter of the economically active population (Jaguaribe et al. 1986).

Ironically, the Cruzado Plan of monetary reform and economic stabilization was the finishing blow for the SFH. The artificial freezing of prices, decreed in February 1986, was followed by a consumption boom with the withdrawal of approximately 28 million cruzados, about 20 percent of all savings (300,000 OTN or U.S. $2.4 million, in February 1986) from the savings accounts.

Except for the Itaquera housing estate in São Paulo, the SFH did little to improve the quality and to reduce the cost of construction by investing in technological innovation. It favored the principle that an intensive labor technology contributed to job generation. G. Bolaffi (1983) was one of the few to state that capital-intensive technology could reduce construction cost and simultaneously not reduce the number of jobs. With lower cost, the same amount of money could be used to build more. Then it would be possible to guarantee an equivalent number of jobs in the sector, probably more qualified and better paid jobs.

In Itaquera, technologically advanced models and scale economies from the construction of more than 40,000 apartments permitted COHAB in São Paulo to sell its units at U.S. $69 per square meter when the average price per square meter in São Paulo was U.S. $170. Self-help housing and sites-and-services options are more in line with the resources available for housing, but it would be unrealistic to think that the housing problems of a city such as São Paulo, with more than 10 million inhabitants, could be solved with the division of land into small lots and technical help for self-help construction. High-rise solutions are also necessary.

Excessive Centralization

During the twenty-two years of military government from 1964 to 1985, decisions and resources were strongly centralized. The extreme centralization of public finance is evidenced by the following data: in 1984, out of 100 cruzeiros of taxes collected in São Paulo, 63.7 went to the federal government, 30 to state government, and only 6.3 to the municipality (Wilheim 1985). Part of the federal funds were returned to the municipalities but subject to strong national political influences. The recovery of the BNH or any other bank that will take its place (in 1988 in the hands of the Federal Savings Bank [CEF]) will have to go through the decentralization of investment decisions. Contrary to what has been happening in the past twenty years, the decisions cannot be made in Rio de Janeiro or in Brasilia and then applied in uniform programs across a country as heterogeneous as Brazil as if the conditions and needs were all the same.

The first program adopted was the construction of housing estates and new houses for sale. In large cities, cost problems resulted in peripheral locations and in the reduction of both the floor area and the quality of housing. The second program adopted since the eighties replaced the policy of granting house building only to large companies. Instead, resources were allocated to self-help housing and upgrading. However, the cost of the land and of the services still weighs decisively in social housing. Brazil lacks consistent policies to control real-estate speculation, especially in large cities. Additionally, almost no resources are allocated to the improvement and recovery of deteriorated properties, an absurdity in any developing country. Very often enormous built-up areas are destroyed and reconstructed, wasting resources and eliminating historic elements.

PROSPECTS

A quantitative evaluation of the SFH's performance shows that it helped build 4.4 million units, that is, 24 percent of the total housing increases between 1964 and 1986. Out of these 4.4 million, a little more than 1.2 were for low-income households (up to five times the minimum wage) and about 250,000 units were financed for programs such as sites-and-services, squatter upgrading, and assisted self-help housing schemes.

Today, what are Brazil's most important housing challenges? A brief estimate of the investments required to solve the problem is discouraging:

1. To meet a 2.4 percent per year demographic growth (3.15 million new inhabitants annually) and considering an average of 4.34 persons per dwelling (table 13.4), 725,000 new units need to be built each year.

2. The housing stock consists of 30.3 million units. Assuming an average life span of fifty years, 606,000 new houses need to be built per year just to replace deteriorated units.

3. If approximately 34 percent of the existing stock needs improvements and assuming that the remodeling of each house is, on average, equivalent to one-half of a new house, this amounts to the construction of about 5,151,000 units. Doing this in ten years means building 515,000 new houses each year.

In summary, the annually required construction including demographic deficit, replacement, and quality improvement adds up to 1,846,000 units during each of the next ten years.

Based on the average of 40 square meters per unit for popular housing, that is, housing for low-income people, 73.84 million square meters per year will need to be built. At an estimated unit cost of 15 UPC per square meter (U.S. $110 per square meter) (not taking into consideration the total wages of the self-help builder), the required annual investment in the housing sector would be 1,110 million UPC, or U.S. $8.1 million dollars.

Considering that the total GNP amounts to U.S. $260 billion, the required housing investment represents 3.1 percent of the GNP. Including also investments related to public services such as water, sewers, lighting, and streets layout and paving, the figure reaches 6.2 percent of the GNP, without taking into account the land's price (by way of comparison, the foreign debt service takes approximately 4 percent of the GNP).

Brazilian savings capacity reaches, at most, 20 percent of the GNP; the modal percentage is between 16 and 18 percent. To invest one-third to solve housing problems is beyond the country's investment capacity, especially when it urgently needs improvements in the agricultural sector to maintain growth in the food supply for a rapidly urbanizing population, expansion of health care, social security and education services, and savings to update and expand its manufacturing industry. H. Jaguaribe and associates (1986), in an optimistic estimate, said that Brazil has the capability to invest the equivalent of 12.5 percent of its GNP in social issues. In 1984 social expenditures were about 10.5 percent of the GNP. The improvement of life standards is urgent in Brazil, especially in the most backward regions. The literacy rate for those over fifteen years of age is 78.7 percent, ranging from 60.0 percent in the Northeast to 86.3 percent in the Southeast (PNAD, 1984). In 1975 the proportion of the population with a suitable diet was only 32.8 percent; 17.3 percent had a deficit of more than 400 calories per day (Knight et al. 1979). The result is a generation of undernourished illiterates.[7]

Thus a first challenge is the allocation of approximately 6 percent of the GNP to housing excluding labor costs. This figure could be streamlined by cutting the investment on improvements and establishing goals less ambitious than the construction of all required units in one decade.

The second challenge is related to another question: what part of the population can afford a 40 square meter unit, the COHAB standard, even without paid labor? Such a house will cost 600 UPC or U.S. $4,800. We can assume a monthly loan repayment over twenty years, free from interest, that would demand from the families a mortgage of 2.5 UPC or U.S. $18.30 per month. Budget studies of low-income families recommend a maximum commitment of 10 percent of their income for housing, so as not to cut back excessively on daily living expenditures, basically food, transportation, and health. Thus for payment of the 40 square meter unit, minimum family income would have to be approximately 25 UPC or U.S. $200 monthly. However, 34 percent of the population has a monthly income less than twice the minimum wage, and approximately 16 percent earn between two and four and a half times the minimum wage. Therefore, at least 50 percent of the population cannot pay even for the minimum unit.[8]

What modifications should be made in the urban and housing policies and practices to respond to the housing needs? First, assuming that the use of nonpaid labor will continue, it is necessary to streamline and make the construction process less expensive by means of appropriate technologies and light, prefabricated, tax-free manufactured elements for self-help housing programs. Doing this would combine technological innovations and higher productivity with intensive labor. Also needed is research on highly productive work processes, on new techniques for work-site management, on assembling construction elements, and on less expensive materials—wood, concrete, or masonry panels; pressed earth; and cardboard. Second, it is necessary to find a consistent urban policy that can control land prices and land speculation. For a large part of the population the sole feasible solution today is to have plots of land leased from the government. Finally, it is necessary to develop partnerships between the national government, the society, and the private market in which the role of each would be clarified, leaving to the central government the task to foster and support local initiatives, both public and private.

The demand for housing cannot be addressed in isolation. Without tackling the income structure and the sharing of the benefits produced by society, the housing policy proposals are bound to remain more or less unsuccessful palliatives in the face of growing poverty, continuously reproduced by the dominant model of economic accumulation. The paths discussed herein can, undoubtedly, improve life and housing conditions. But one cannot expect housing to be more equitable than the conditions that generate it.

ABBREVIATIONS

BNH	Banco Nacional da Habitação (National Housing Bank)
CEF	Caixa Econômica Federal (Savings and Loans Federal Bank)
COHABS	Companhias de Habitação (Housing Companies [State or Local])
COS	Carteira de Operações de Natureza Social (Social Operations Agency)
FCVS	Fundo de Compensação de Variação Salarial (Salary Variation Fund)
IAPs	Institutos de Aposentadorias e Pensões (Retirement and Pension Institutes)
IBGE	Instituto Brasileiro de Geografia e Estatística (Brazilian Geography and Statistics Institute)
OTN	Obrigação do Tesouro Nacional (National Treasure Bonds)
PES	Plano de Equivalencia Salarial (Salary Equivalence Plan)
PLANASA	Programa Nacional de Saneamento (National Program of Water Supply and Sewage Systems)
PNAD	Pesquisa Nacional para Amostragem por Domicílios (National Housing Survey)
PROAGUA	Programa de Abastecimento de Agua para Habitações Sub-Normais (Water Supply Program to Squatter Settlements)
PROLUZ	Programa de Eletrificação das Favelas (Electrical Power Supply Program to Squatter Settlements)
PROMORAR	Programa de Erradicação da Sub-Habitação (Eradication Program of Sub-Standard Dwelling)
SBPE	Sistema Brasileiro de Poupança e Empréstimo (Brazilian Savings and Loans System)
SFH	Sistema Financeiro de Habitação (Housing Financing System)
UPC	Unidade Padrão de Capital (BNH Readjustable Units or Basic Capital Unit. It was adjusted quarterly according to Brazilian inflation)
V.H.P.	Vila de Habitação Provisória (Temporary Housing Settlements)

NOTES

1. FGTS (Fundo de Garantia por Tempo de Servico)—Guarantee Fund for Time of Work—is used only for employees. It represents a deposit of 8 percent of the company's

payroll in the name of the employees. This amount is not deducted from their wages. Self-employed and public officers are not granted the benefit of the FGTS.

2. UPC (Unidade Padrao de Capital) means Basic Capital Unit and is adjusted quarterly according to Brazilian inflation. In March 1988 it was equal to U.S. $8.

3. According to preliminary results of the author's current research.

4. Average length of residence in São Paulo squatter settlements has increased: in 1973, 40.8 percent of family heads living in squatter settlements had been living there for less than one year; in 1980 this was only 15.3 percent.

5. This self-managed, self-help housing was tried in São Paulo in 1986. It was designed for the inhabitants of a squatter settlement in the south periphery of the city. The squatters, with only the help of professors and students of an architectural college, built their masonry houses.

6. OTN (Obrigacoes do Tesouro Nacional)—National Treasure Bonds—differ from the UPC because they are adjusted monthly.

7. Historically, the growth rate for the Brazilian GNP has been above 7 percent per year; in 1973 it reached 13.6 percent, its peak. From then on, it has been progressively dropping, although figures were high until 1980, when it was slightly above 7 percent. In 1981 a strong economic recession started and was reversed in 1984. It started again in 1987 (Dupas 1987).

8. These calculations do not include subsidies. On the other hand, they also do not include the land cost, interest, and management of construction programs.

REFERENCES

Azevedo, S. and L. A. Gama de Andrade. *Habitacão e Poder. Da Fundação da Casa Popular ao Banco Nacional de Habitação*. Rio de Janeiro: Zahar.

Banco Nacional da Habitação. 1981, 1982, 1983, 1984. *Relatórios Anuais*. Rio de Janeiro.

Barros de Castro, A., and F. E. Pires de Souza. 1985. *A Economia Brasileira em Marcha Forçada*. Rio de Janeiro: Paz e Terra.

Blanck, G. 1980. "Bras de Pina: Experiência de Urbanização de Favela." In *Habitação em Questão*, edited by L. Vallandares, 93–124. Rio de Janeiro: Zahar.

Blay, E. 1978. "Habitação: a politica e o habitante." In *A luta pelo espaço*, edited by E. Blay, 75–86. Petrópolis: Vozes.

———. 1985. *Eu não tenho onde morar: vilas operárias na Cidade de São Paulo*. São Paulo: Nobel.

Bolaffi, G. 1977. A Casa das ilusões perdidas: Aspectos socio-economicos do Plano Nacional da Habitação. In *Cadernos Cebrap* 27, Saõ Paulo: Brasiliense.

Bolaffi, G. 1983. "A questão urbana: produção de habitações, construção civil e mercado de trabalho." *Novos Estudos Cebrap* 2, no. 1 (April): 61–68.

———. 1986. "Os mitos sobre o problema da habitação." *Espaço e Debates* 17:24–32.

Bonduki, N. 1982. "Origens do problema da habitação popular in Saõ Paulo." *Espaço e Debates*, no. 5 (March-June): 1–11.

———. 1986. "Produção da Habitação através de ajuda mútua e auto-ajuda." Paper presented at the annual meeting of Anpocs, Campos de Jordão, October 22–24. Mimeograph.

Burgess, R. 1982. "Self-Help Housing Advocacy: A Curious Form of Radicalism. A Critique of the Work of John Turner." In *Self-Help Housing: A Critique*, edited by P. Ward, 56–27. London: Mansell.

————. 1985. "The Limits of State Self-Help Housing Programmes." *Development and Change* 16, no. 2:271–312.

Campanário, M. A. 1984. "O Mercado de Terras e a Exclusão Social na Cidade de S.Paulo." In *Terra de Habitação versus Terra de Espoliação*, edited by P. J. Krischke, 11–30. São Paulo: Cortez.

Cavalcanti de Albuquerque, M. C. 1985. *Habitação Popular: Avaliação e Propostas de reformulação do S.F.H.* São Paulo: Escola de Administração de Empresas de S.Paulo, 92 pp. Mimeograph.

Cavalcanti, L., and Guimaraens, D. 1984. *Morar: A casa brasiliera.* Rio de Janeiro: Avenir.

Crooke, P. 1983. "Popular Housing Supports and the Urban Housing Market." In *People, Poverty and Shelter*, edited by R. Skinner and M. J. Rodell, 173–91. New York: Methuen.

Dupas, G. 1987. *Crise econômica e transição democrática.* São Paulo: Klaxon.

Farah, M.F.S. 1985. "Estado e habitação no Brasil: o caso dos Institutos de Previdência." *Espaço e Debates* 16:73–82.

Faria, V. E. 1983. "Desenvolvimento, Urbanização e Mudanças na Estrutura do Emprego: A Experiência Brasileira nos Últimos Trinta Anos." In *Sociedade e Política no Brasil Pós-64*, edited by B. Sorj and M.H.T. de Almeida, 118–63. São Paulo: Brasiliense.

Ferreira dos Santos, L. N. 1984. "Em trinta anos passou muita água sob as pontes urbanas . . ." *Espaço e Debates* 11:28–40.

Financiadora de Estudos e Projetos-Grupo de Arquitetura e Planejamento. 1985. *Habitação Popular.* Inventário da Ação Governamental. São Paulo.

Geiger, P. P. 1985. *Expansão da classe média e do setor público e urbanização no Brasil.* Paper presented at the symposium "A Metrópole e a Crise," Instituto de Geografia da U.S.P.

Gilbert, A. 1982. "The Housing of the Urban Poor." In *Cities, Poverty, and Development*, edited by A. Gilbert and J. Gugler, 81–115. Oxford: Oxford University Press.

Harms, H. 1982. "Historical Perspectives on the Practice and Purpose of Self-Help Housing." In *Self-Help Housing: A Critique*, edited by P. Ward, 17–53. London: Mansell.

Havel, J. E. 1968. *Habitat et logement.* Paris: Presses Universitaires de France.

Jaguaribe, H. et al. 1986. *Brasil 2000: para um novo pacto social.* Rio de Janeiro: Paz e Terra.

Jorge, W. E. 1987. "A politica nacional de saneamento pós 64." Doctoral thesis, Faculdade de Arquitetura e Urbanismo da Universidade de São Paulo.

Knight, P. T. et al. 1979. *Brazil: Human Resources Special Report.* Washington, D.C.: The World Bank.

Mautner, Y. 1986. "The Building Industry Which Works at the Fringes of Capitalism: The Cases of São Paulo." Paper presented at the Annual Meeting of Bartlett International Summer School (BISS). Dessau, July.

Pasternak Taschner, S. 1975. "Espaço e População." Master's thesis, Universidade de São Paulo.

————. 1983. "Moradia da Pobreza: habitação sem saúde." Doctoral thesis, Universidade de São Paulo, 684 pp.

————. 1986a. "A cidade dos "Sem Terra." *Sinopses* 9:268–304.

————. 1986b. "Squatter Settlements: The Facts and the Policies." Paper presented at the International Conference on Housing Policy, Gävle, Sweden, June, 71 pp.

————. 1987. "Habitação e Adensamento Urbano." Paper presented at the I Simpósio Nacional de Planejamento e Engenharia Urbana, Escola Politécnica da Universidade de São Paulo, November 11–12.

Perlman, J. 1976. *The Myth of Marginality: Urban Poverty and Politics in Rio de Janeiro*. Berkeley: University of California Press.

Pradilla Cobos, E. 1976. La ideologia burguesa y el problema de la vivienda: critica a dos 'teorias' ideológicas." *Ideologia y Sociedad*, no. 19 (October): 17–35.

Ribeiro, Luis L. de Queirós, and Roberto Pechman. 1983. *O que é a questão da moradia*. São Paulo: Brasiliense.

Rodell, M. J. 1983. "Sites and Services and Low-Income Housing." In *People, Poverty, and Shelter*, edited by R. J. Skinner and M. J. Rodell, 21–52. New York: Methuen.

Rush, B. S. 1974. "From favela to conjunto: the experience of squatters removed to low cost housing in Rio de Janeiro, Brasil." Cambridge, Mass., March. Mimeograph.

Sachs, C. 1987. "Evolution et limites de la promotion publique de logements populaire a S. Paulo." Doctoral thesis, Institut d' Urbanisme, University de Paris XII-Val de Marne.

São Paulo (Municipio). Secretaria Municipal do Planejamento. 1985. *Conheça sua região*. Série Informes. São Paulo.

Turner, J.F.L. 1976. *Le Logement est votre affaire*. Paris: Ed du Seuil.

United Nations. Department of Economic and Social Affairs. 1962. *Statistical Indicators of Housing Conditions*. Statistical Papers, Series M, no. 37. New York.

————. 1964. *Handbook of Household Surveys*. Statistical Papers, Series F, no. 10. New York.

————. 1967. *Methods of Estimating Housing Needs*. Statistical Papers, Series F, no. 12. New York.

Valladares, L. do P. 1978. *Passa-se uma casa. Análise do Programa de Remoção de Favelas do Rio de Janeiro*. Rio de Janeiro: Zahas.

————. ed. 1983. *Repensando a habitação no Brasil*. Rio de Janeiro: Zahar.

————. 1985. "Politicas alternativas de habitação popular: um voo sobre literatura internacional." *Espaço e Debates* 16:33–52.

————. 1987. "La recherche urbaine au Brésil: bref aperçu de son évolution." Paris: *Cahiers du Brazil Contemporain*.

Veras, M.P.B., and N. Bonduki. 1986. "Politica Habitacional e a luta pelo direito á habitação." In *A cidadania que não temos*, edited by M.L.M. Covre, 39–72. São Paulo: Brasiliense.

Vetter, D. M. 1981. "Problemas conceituais e operacionais na avaliação da "adequação" das condições através de indicadores elaborados com dados dos Censos e das PNAD's." *Revista Brasileira de Estatistica* 42, no. 168 (October-December): 283–314.

Vetter, D. M., and L. L. Simões. 1980. "Acesso a infra-estrutura de saneamento básico e mortalidade." *Boletim Demográfico* 10, no. 4 (April-June).

Villaça, F. 1986. *O que todo cidadão precisa saber sobre habitação*. São Paulo: Global.

Ward, P. M., ed. 1982. *Self-Help Housing. A Critique*. London: Mansell Publishing Limited and Alexandrine Press.

Wilhem, J. 1985. "As Cidades da Nova República." *Senhor 205*, (February 20): 54–62.
World Bank. 1986. "Urban Development Countries: Issues and Priorities." Paper presented at the DAC-OECD Meeting on Urban Development, Paris, October 7–8, 24 pp. Mimeograph.
Zastrow, J. L. von. 1987. "O sistema Financeiro da Habitação agride a classe média." *Gazeta Mercantil*, July 13, 4.

FURTHER READING

Batley, R. "Who Makes Housing Policy in India and Brazil." *Local Government Studies* 13, no. 3 (1987):19–25.
———. "National Housing Banks in India and Brazil." *Third World Planning Review* 10, no. 2(1988):203–208.
Maricato, E. *Politica habitacional no Regime Militar*. Petrópolis: Vozes, 1987.
Pasternak Taschner. "Favelas do Minicipio de São Paulo: resultados de pesquisa." In *A Luta pelo espaço*, edited by E. Blay, 127–47. Petrópolis: Vozes, 1978.
———. "Las Favelas del Municipio de San Pablo." *Revista Interamericana de Planificacion* 14, no. 54 (1980): 50–67.
Pasternak Taschner, S., and Y. Mautner. *Habitação da Pobreza. Alternativas de moradia popular em São Paulo*. FAU USP-FUPAM, Cadernos de Estudo e Pesquisas PRODEUR, 1982. 238 pp.
Pradilla Cobos, E. "Notas sobre el problema de la vivienda." *Ideologia y Sociedad* 16 (January–March 1976).
Sachs, C. "The Growth of Squatter Settlements in São Paulo: A Study of the Perverse Effects of the State Housing Policies." *Social Science Information* 22, nos. 4, 5 (1983): 749–75.
Valladares, L. do P. "Working the System: Squatter Response to Resettlement in Rio de Janeiro." *International Journal of Urban and Regional Research* 2 (1978):12–25.
———. "Housing in Brazil: An Introduction to Recent Literature." *Bulletin of Latin American Research* 2 (1983):69–91.
Valladares, L. "Popular Housing in Brazil: A Review." In *Housing Needs and Policy Approaches: Trends in Thirteen Countries*, edited by W. van Vliet—, E. Huttman, and S. Fava. Durham, N.C.: Duke University Press, 1985.
World Bank. 1986. *Urban Development Research at the World Bank*. Washington, D.C., 22 pp.

14

Colombia

JOSÉ OSPINA

Colombia covers approximately 1.5 million square kilometers in the northeastern corner of the South American continent, about five times the area of France (Cardona 1986). The majority of the population is very young. In 1986, 65 percent of all Colombians were under the age of twenty-four. Population is

Table 14.1
Population Growth, by Region, Colombia, 1938–1986

Year	Total Population	Urban	Rural
1938	8.7 million	31%	69%
1951	11.6 million	39	61
1964	17.5 million	53	47
1973	21.1 million	64	36
1986	28.0 million	67	33

Source: Cardona, 1986.

concentrated in the fertile Andean region and in the coastal areas to the north and west of the country. Recent population growth has been concentrated in the urban areas (see table 14.1).

Migration from the countryside has been the primary cause of the rapid urban growth. Evidence for this comes from a 1973 survey of the population of the four major cities showing that, for example, in Bogota 50 percent of the population consisted of recent migrants (Cardona 1987). This pattern almost certainly occurred because these large cities also were recipients of 65 percent of all national financial investments (Santana 1981).

The same survey also showed the following job distribution: industry (25.5 percent), service and domestic (30.6 percent); underemployed (31.9 percent); and unemployed (15.5 percent). "Underemployment" refers to irregular income-earning activities that rarely guarantee a "legal minimum" income (Cardona 1987). The irregularity or absence of employment for nearly half of the country's population, added to the lack of any effective social security system, makes it impossible for a large proportion of the population to secure adequate housing and services.

The *salario minimo* ("minimum legal" salary level) is calculated by the government as the sum needed for the basic necessities for a family. In 1982 this minimum salary was estimated at Col $9,500 (about U.S. $115) per month, and it was suggested that, nationally, 30 percent of all families had incomes below this level (Ramirez Soto 1981). In urban areas this proportion was even higher. In Bogota, 37 percent of the families were said to be below the minimum (Molina 1981).

In Colombia, as in other Third World countries, only the wealthier part of the population has access to decent housing at prices they can afford. For the rest, the private commercial sector has not been able to provide a solution. Neither have state initiatives that so far have been limited to subsidizing private developers and a small proportion of owner–occupiers. The main source of housing for the poor population has been and continues to be "illegal" settlement, now constituting the country's major source of new dwellings. However, the housing thus produced is far from adequate. Only an accelerated, state-supported development of the nongovernmental sector, the growing network of community housing organizations, can provide a more satisfactory alternative.

TRENDS IN HOUSING CONDITIONS AND CONSTRUCTION

Housing Deficit

The total number of existing dwellings increased from 1.9 million in 1950 to 4 million in 1982 (Unidad de Programacion Global and Unidad de Desarrollo Regional y Urbano 1981). In 1982 the national housing deficit was estimated at 800,000 dwellings (Ramirez Soto 1981), although other researchers have placed it closer to a million. It was estimated that this deficit was growing at a rate of 60,000 dwellings per annum (Santana 1981). The deficit is concentrated in the four major cities—Bogota, Medellin, Cali, and Barranquilla—accounting for about 73 percent of the total deficit. Bogota alone accounted for about 47 percent of the deficit, with an estimated shortage of 375,000 dwellings (Santana and Casasbuenas 1981).

Some 71 percent of those affected by this housing shortage earned less than Col $18,000 per month, and a further 21 percent of those affected had earnings between Col $18,000 and Col $36,000 per month. Only 8 percent of those affected by the deficit were in higher income brackets (Ramirez Soto 1981). It is clear then that the main reason for lack of access to adequate housing is the low income of a large proportion of the population.

Tenure Patterns

The predominant form of tenure in Colombia is owner occupation. In 1973, 55 percent of the population was estimated to occupy their own homes. Surprisingly, this proportion has been declining. Many of these dwellings are in "illegal" settlements but are often gradually improved by their owners. Roughly half of them provided rented accommodations for lodgers.

Many of these homes are loan funded, from private or public sources, and it was estimated that on average 40 percent of income was spent on repayment of loans (Brille 1981). Those on lower incomes, however, pay up to 80 percent of income on repayments (Negocios 1985).

A large percentage of the population, about 32 percent in 1973, was dependent on rented housing, almost entirely from the private sector (Unidad de Programacion Global and Unidad de Desarrollo Regional y Urbano 1981). This proportion has been increasing, and by 1982 it was about 39 percent (Santana and Casasbuenas 1981). Tenants pay an average of 32 percent of their income on rent, but in urban centers it can be as high as 43 percent (Unidad de Programacion Global and Unidad de Desarrollo Regional y Urbano 1981).

Rented housing accounts for some of the worst housing conditions in Colombia. Some have argued that the financial disincentives to private rental (rent freezes legislated since 1943) have discouraged landlords from providing a good level of management and maintenance, particularly for low-income rentals. There is some truth in this, but it is also likely that rent increases would deprive lower-income families of their major source of accommodations.

Another 13 percent of the population occupied housing as licensees or squatters, with no tenancy rights. In addition to owner occupation, rental, and licenses, hybrid forms of tenure such as leasehold arrangements have been tried by some cooperative organizations (e.g., Cooperativa Medica del Valle, Cali) to give tenants the benefit of eventual owner occupation. However, these arrangements have not become widespread.

Housing Conditions

In 1973 a national survey of existing dwellings revealed that 90 percent were family houses, 8 percent were flats, and 2 percent were boarding houses (*inquilinatos*) or other forms of accommodations. Most rented accommodations were provided in family houses, and overcrowding was common in single-family rooms (Santana and Casasbuenas 1981). Since the first waves of rural migration into the urban centers in the 1930s and the growth of "illegal settlements," substandard housing conditions have been a chronic aspect of Colombia's pattern of urban development. In 1970 the illegal settlements contained about half of the country's urban population (Janssen 1984). These settlements were substandard by the very nature of their production. They often lacked adequate roads and walkways. They were rarely provided with sewers and other essential services. The dwellings were often (at least initially) makeshift and poorly constructed. They were rarely served by adequate community facilities such as health, education, and recreation.

Researchers have suggested that about 10 percent of Bogota's housing is substandard, that is, lacking in at least one essential service or inadequately built. In Medellin, the proportion of substandard dwellings is 20 percent, in Baranquilla 50 percent, and in Cali 30 percent (Foro 1985). Results of a survey of illegal settlements in sixty-nine urban centers, carried out between 1972 and 1975 by the Instituto de Credito Territorial (ICT), indicated 617,000 substandard dwellings, housing approximately 4.5 million people (Soto Sierra 1981).

Illegal settlements do not have a monopoly of bad housing conditions. The *inquilinatos* are also notorious. They are boarding houses created by the subdivision of formerly middle-income houses in the older parts of the cities. The problems there are usually overcrowding, lack of repair and maintenance, and overuse of sanitary facilities. In Bogota, in 1981, for example, 183,736 families were said to live in such single rooms, with an average occupancy of six persons per room (Santana and Casasbuenas 1981). It is not only the *inquilinatos* that are overcrowded, however, since most low-income rented accommodations are also provided in family houses in "illegal" settlements.

Standards of Construction

More than half of the dwellings built in the urban centers have been built illegally, so standards of construction are often wanting. Nonetheless, it is evident that conditions in these areas vary, and they often improve through the years. Many settlements have been successful in acquiring services, and occupants have replaced makeshift wood and cardboard structures by reinforced concrete and traditional oven-baked brick. In a few others, improvement programs have been undertaken to provide community facilities and to improve the layout.

Often, new dwellings will be makeshift structures, built out of temporary materials like cardboard, asphaltic felt, tin, and wood. In time, the occupants will substitute permanent materials, like bricks or concrete blocks and asbestos cement or tin roofing sheets. It is usual at this stage that occupants employ semiskilled labor. An indication of this process is that the national percentage of dwellings with some "permanent" building materials increased from 72.7 percent in 1964 to 86.2 percent in 1973 (Unidad de Programacion Global and Unidad de Desarrollo Regional y Urbano 1981).

The "legal" private sector, the state sector, and the nongovernmental housing sector have, to date, relied primarily on conventional building technologies, usually reinforced concrete structures filled in with kiln-baked bricks or concrete blocks. Recently, light prefabrication and modular building systems have been introduced primarily by large developers but also by state housing organizations and nongovernmental organizations.

Some low-income projects promoted by state organizations and nongovernmental agencies have recently attempted to develop appropriate and intermediate building technologies and materials, which make better use of local resources and are more suited to self-build techniques. Examples of this are the use of bamboo by the ICT in Manizales, stabilized pressed earth blocks in ICT housing in Tunja, and fiber-cement roofing sheets in a self-build scheme by Fundacion para el Desarrollo Integral de Manizales y Caldas (FUNDEMOS), a community housing organization in Manizales. Research centers like the Escuela Nacional de Autoconstruccion in Manizales have been set up to develop and teach these technologies.

Services and Infrastructure

All housing provisions in Colombia are dependent on the supply of infrastructure and services by the different statutory authorities. These institutions are often centralized and bureaucratic, have a tendency to overlap and duplicate, and can present serious difficulties for the development of housing projects, even for those operated by the state (Foro 1985).

The Ministry of Public Works is responsible for public roads and highways, whereas the Fondo Financiero del Desarrollo Urbano (FFDU) provides funding for other urban facilities. Municipal Water and Electricity Boards provide the respective supplies and connections. Schools and health centers are also the responsibility of statutory bodies.

The service bodies (like water and electricity) are often capitalized with foreign loans. Within the current framework of currency devaluation, this has meant that their charges are "index linked," making the acquisition of these services an added economic burden for low-income families.

The combination of bureaucratic inertia and high costs has made the acquisition of services a major housing problem. Their absence is common in "illegal" settlements, and their acquisition is perhaps the major required improvement. Of the 5 million inhabitants of the country's northern coast, it is estimated that only 16.2 percent have access to sewerage and only 45 percent to running water (Santana 1981). In the rural areas, absence of services is the norm; 67 percent of dwellings in towns of less than 20,000 inhabitants have no water or electricity (Unidad de Programacion Global and Unidad de Desarrollo Regional y Urbano 1981).

Finance

Before 1970 loan funding for house building had been made available primarily by two organizations. One was the Instituto de Credito Territorial, which loaned at subsidized interest rates; the other was the Banco Central Hipotecario (BCH), which loaned at fixed-interest market rates. The ICT has traditionally been funded from compulsory investment from private financial institutions plus an additional contribution from the national budget. The BCH was funded primarily from deposits but also contributions from public sources. Thus the ICT has been the primary recipient of subsidies, and it has targeted those of lower-income sectors, whereas the BCH has operated at commercial rates of interest and primarily targeted middle-income sectors. Several smaller state and municipal institutions also loan for house building and purchase, like the Fondo Nacional del Ahorro, which caters to civil servants; the Caja Agraria, which funds rural housing; and various other specialist funds.

From 1960 to 1970 an average of 60 percent of the loans for house construction were provided by the BCH. The ICT's contribution was more modest, although in the years 1962–1964, due to an influx of Alliance for Progress credit, it financed the building of a large number of dwellings. During these two years, 43 percent of dwellings built in Bogota were funded by the ICT, compared with only 14 percent in the previous two years (Jaramillo 1980).

Before 1970 both subsidized ICT loans and nonsubsidized BCH loans were made at fixed rates of interest. The ICT and BCH loans had a sliding scale of interest according to the type of project receiving the loan: thus a loan for a self-built dwelling in 1962 would have an interest rate of 8 percent per annum (plus 1 percent for insurance). This rate would be increased yearly. A BCH loan for low-income house building in the same year would have an interest rate of 14 percent per annum, which also would be increased annually.

In 1970 the liberal administration of Pastrana Borrero sought to strengthen the financial sector of the economy by encouraging private investment in building. The mechanism for achieving this was index linking of loan funds. The UPAC (unit of acquisitive power) was created, whereby a yearly index figure was worked out on the basis of current interest rates plus the current rate of inflation.

To pursue this financial formula, the setting up of new private sector financial institutions was authorized: the Corporaciones de Ahorro y Vivienda (CAVs), building societies that operated the UPAC system. The BCH was also transferred to the UPAC system. This was coupled with a slashing of the budgets of the existing state housing institutions. The immediate result was a virtual take over of the funding of house building by the new corporations. Growing availability of private loan funds justified a reduction in the budgets of subsidized state housing institutions, and public funding of house building reached an all time low (Jaramillo 1981).

The risks and the costs of the new funding mechanisms made them practically inaccessible to those with low incomes. Although the CAVs eventually supplied 70 percent of the capital for building, it has been estimated that 70 percent of the loans have been made to private developers, 30 percent to high- and middle-income buyers, and none at all to those with lower incomes (Ramirez Soto 1981).

The ICT, on the other hand, continued to operate on the fixed-rate principles but used differential rates for different types of property. Thus a "minimal" dwelling (35 square meters) would have a rate of 19 percent per annum, whereas an "intermediate" dwelling (72 square meters) would have a rate of 24 percent per annum. Both would be increased yearly by 15 percent. The ICT loans were not index linked, but annual percentage interest rate increases rose dramatically since 1970 (ranging from 15 to 18 percent every year).

The combination of the targeting of investment to higher-income housing (implicit in the UPAC system) and the curtailing of subsidies for low-income housing caused an apparent growth of "illegal" private sector housing (Ruiz Gutierrez 1987), as well as an inflation of land and building prices, primarily in the urban centers (Santana 1981).

In 1982 the government of Belisario Betancur attempted to redress this imbalance by two principal measures: (1) trebling the budgets available to state housing bodies to allow them to build an additional 60,000 homes per year and (2) obliging CAVs to invest in low-income housing to produce an additional 50,000 homes per year (Giraldo Isaza 1981).

About half of the dwellings produced with subsidized funding were to be aimed at those earning less than a "legal minimum" income; 100 percent loans would be available to allow people to purchase the homes thus built. Loans were given to nonprofit and community-housing organizations to develop their own projects, but the majority of dwellings were built through traditional partnership arrangements with private developers.

With these elements, the ICT was able to achieve its ambitious target, and 122,505 dwellings were financed from 1982 to 1984. The BCH financed an additional 44,000 dwellings during this time, mainly through nonprofit housing organizations (Foro 1985).

The coexistence of two loan structures (fixed interest and index linked) created significant inconsistencies in the targeting of subsidy, as a comparison of the two systems shows (Jaramillo and Equipo de Investigaciones Urbanas 1985):

Interest Rates in 1984

	ICT	UPAC
Sites-and-services project	19.8% per annum	32.2% per annum
Self-build project	19.8%	30.4%
Basic dwelling	23.0%	30.4%

Nonetheless, these measures were relatively successful. House building during the Betancur administration surpassed all previous levels.

However, there have been fundamental criticisms of the ICT program and its long-term effects. One is the apparent inability of many of those who have purchased homes to make the required loan repayments. By the end of 1983, loan arrears stood at Col $20 billion, and many developers with which the ICT had contracted to build these dwellings could not be paid. Another problem was the low planning and building standards of the dwellings produced by private developers under "cofinancing" schemes and the lack of adequate services and infrastructure for these projects. The ICT has been accused in some quarters of building "official shantytowns" (Negocios 1985).

With the change of government in 1985, a new liberal administration pledged to keep housing on the agenda. However, given the political pressures against the public subsidy of housing and the country's deteriorating political and financial situation, maintaining earlier levels of public investment seems unlikely. At the same time, private investment in the UPAC system has been rapidly declining, with capital tending to go abroad. All of this has had negative repercussions on the country's housing situation.

HOUSING MARKETS, INSTITUTIONS, AND POLICY ORIENTATIONS

Urban development and housing policy have traditionally been determined by the region's economically dependent role. During the Conquest, native towns became administrative and military centers for the Spanish Crown. Fishing villages became ports for the export of raw materials and the import of manufactured goods. The population of these urban centers remained relatively small. By 1700, for example, the population of Bogota (Colombia's capital) represented only 2.8 percent of the nation's total.

This dependent role did not change with independence. Lacking capital investment and markets to enable the development of a significant industrial sector, the country's role after 1800 continued being that of supplier of raw materials and importer of manufactured goods. Hence the country's population remained predominantly rural. By 1928, for example, the population of Bogota was still only 3 percent of the country's total.

The first significant wave of urban growth came in the early 1930s. The Great Depression had weakened the economies of the developed countries, causing raw material exports to lose their value and making it difficult to secure imported goods. National capital was obliged to turn to local production of consumer goods and light industrial products such as textiles, beer, and cement.

This shift in financial priorities brought with it a political shift. The "landed" Conservative party was ousted from power (after forty years rule) by a radical Liberal party that pursued reforms that promoted urban development. The electoral basis for this shift was primarily the new industrial workers, so many of these reforms were aimed at improving workplace conditions, consolidating trade union rights, and subsidizing urban low-income housing. All of this greatly accelerated the growth of the urban centers: the population of Bogota, for example, doubled from 1938 to 1951 (Torres 1971).

This period brought with it a struggle between the rich and the poor for control of the central areas of cities. In 1924, for instance, the municipal authorities of Bogota attempted to clear a central slum area known as Paseo Bolivar to make way for "residential" development. Resistance was fierce, and although the clearance was eventually carried out, it appears to have discouraged further clearances. Eventually, wealthier families abandoned the center and South of the city to the poor, moving to the distant North. Low-income settlements expanded toward the South and East where a majority of industries were based.

By the late 1940s Colombia's short-lived "industrial revolution" had ground to a halt. The economies of the developed nations had recovered from the Depression and actually extended their influence as a result of World War II. Foreign investment (mainly North American) gradually gained control of local manufacture, and financial institutions gained a dominant role in the economy and in national policy. The ownership of land was concentrated in fewer hands, and agriculture became increasingly mechanized (Jaramillo 1980).

A movement for extensive political reform was cut short in 1948 with the assassination of Jorge Eliecer Gaitan, a radical presidential candidate. This led to a bloody civil war and four years of military rule. This civil war was fought primarily in the countryside, in turn accelerating the migratory process. Urban population thus increased dramatically during this time, from 39 percent of the total in 1951 to 64 percent by 1973. Most of this growth was contained in the illegal settlements of the main urban centers (Cardona 1987).

The Provision of Housing

Colombia's present housing conditions and policies are rooted in its historical development. At the time of its conquest by Spain, its native inhabitants had developed indigeneous building technologies and methods, using locally available material, implemented through various forms of mutual aid, which enabled them to house themselves. As colonization progressed, these technologies and methods were complemented by the feudal practices of the conquering nations.

As urban centers developed, most housing was secured privately. However, the inadequacies of this sector in providing for middle- and low-income sectors led to the development of a large "illegal" private sector, as well as state intervention and the development of a "nonprofit" sector.

Legal Private Sector Provision. When urban growth began to speed up after the 1930s, those who could afford it could still secure good housing. Native architects were available from newly formed architectural schools to design European- or American-style houses. Building materials were either produced locally or imported. The fact that labor was inexpensive and most materials plentiful meant that impressive homes could be built for those with available capital. Occasionally, foreign architects were commissioned to design and supervise more prestigious buildings (Jaramillo 1980).

Those with higher incomes would usually commission the building of their own homes. This was the norm until about 1950, when "legal" housing production passed almost entirely into the hands of private developers. They usually had access to capital and large areas of land in the periphery of major cities and could provide "off-the-shelf" houses for sale or rent. They were often linked to financial institutions and employed their own architects and builders. Their scale of operation allowed them to invest in high-technology "building systems," although import restrictions and the relative cheapness of labor made conventional building technologies cost effective (Clavijo 1981).

In 1970 a Liberal administration further aided the fortunes of private developers with the introduction of index linking. This was presented as a way of regenerating industry and promoting house production. New private sector financial institutions were created (Corporaciones de Ahorro y Vivienda—CAVs) to trade in index-linked loan funds. Eventually, 70 percent of all investment in housing was index linked, and public investment in housing was reduced. Most of this funding, however, was going to luxury housing and commercial development and little to the production of low-income housing (Ramirez Soto 1981).

In 1982 President Betancur enacted legislation obliging CAVs to invest half of their takings in low-income housing, a measure that forced many developers into this type of provision, although many nonprofit housing organizations also became the recipients of this investment.

The legal private sector also provided housing for rent for high- and middle-income families. This primarily took the form of single-family houses, but several developers also built apartments for rent.

In addition, there were a few private sector low-income housing initiatives around this time, particularly associated with major industrial developments. One example was a project to provide housing for workers at El Peñol, a major hydroelectric dam, and at Cerrejon, a major new coal source on the northern coast of the country. However, such projects were the exception.

"Illegal" Private Sector Provision. The primary source of both rented and owner-occupied housing for those on lower incomes has been the "illegal" private sector. It is a relatively consistent characteristic of housing for the poorer population that it contravenes existing legislation in terms of transfer of ownership, planning requirements, construction standards, infrastructure, and service requirements or simply standards of repair, hygiene, and overcrowding. This "illegality" is primarily a product of the low income of its users within a fundamentally "free" housing market.

This sector is primarily made up of the many "illegal" settlements that have sprung up in and around the urban centers since the 1930s. Initially, rural migrants set up these settlements on land they did not own or on land they did own but where building was restricted, using their own labor and traditional materials and techniques (bamboo, mud, thatch, and so on). Later, rural technologies and local materials were abandoned in favor of conventional building and industrial materials, and many settlers also became landlords to other low-income families.

A "borderline" case of this "illegal" private sector is the *inquilinatos*, or boarding houses set up in large, older properties, abandoned by the wealthy in their exodus to the suburbs. They have been subdivided by private landlords and rented out, often to whole families in one room. Apart from overcrowding and inadequate sanitary facilities, many of these buildings have deteriorated rapidly through lack of investment in maintenance and repair.

"Illegal settlements" rapidly became the country's main form of low-income housing. From 1938 to 1950, 54 percent of all new units in Bogota were "illegal," compared with 29 percent during the 1928–1938 period (Jaramillo 1980). From the 1950s onward, a growing number of settlements became evident, displaying even worse conditions than the earlier ones. Much of this housing was not "owner occupied" but rented out to other low-income families.

Around the 1970s several government bodies began to take an interest in the activities of the "illegal" settlers. This was partially due to a growing concern with the activities of the *urbanizadores piratas*, or black-market developers, who exploited the settlements. These individuals would select land that was of little agricultural value on the periphery of the cities and where building or services were restricted, persuade the owner to sell, or simply squat the land. They would then subdivide it without official approval and sell individual plots to low-income families. Sale prices would be considerably lower than that of "legal" plots but still much higher than the price originally paid. Families would also be offered short-term loans at high interest rates for purchase. Once sold, the land would be occupied collectively by the families, who would erect makeshift shacks to prevent eviction.

The government's aim in intervening in this sector was not to ban self-building. It was not even to dispense with the *urbanizador pirata* since it was recognized that low-income housing provision depended on this institution. It was merely an attempt to control the most extreme abuses in this sector. By all accounts even this has been done half-heartedly, and some authorities have even suggested giving *urbanizadores piratas* a freer hand (Arango 1986).

A series of flexible planning norms (*Normas Minimas*) was introduced in major cities that allowed for the gradual self-build development of housing, and basic regulations governing transactions between self-builders, owners, and self-build developers and organizations were enacted. The Superintendencia Bancaria, a supervisory body for banks, was (inappropriately) charged with surveillance of this sector.

Self-builders and "pirate" developers who failed to comply with regulations could be "intervened" by the Superintendencia, which would take over the housing and hand it over to an agency of the ICT (the Agencia de Urbanizaciones Intervenidas) that was charged with "normalizing" the settlements. In practice, the agency was rarely able to do much good. Inhabitants would find it difficult to obtain services and infrastructure, since they were deemed "illegal" and would have no guarantee of the security of their housing. In contrast, settlements with effective community organizations, left to their own devices, were often able to sort out their own problems (Foro 1985).

Some of these settlements achieved an impressive level of popular organization. In Bogota, a residents' organization called the Comite Pro-Defensa de los Barrios Orientales successfully defended communities from a municipal development project for many years. The Central Nacional Provivienda and the Movimiento Civico Nacional have also organized the inhabitants of some of these settlements and provided technical services for improving their conditions (Janssen 1984). By 1982, Departamento Administrativo Nacional de Estadistica (DANE) estimated that 65 to 70 percent of the dwellings in Bogota had been built "illegally"—a total of about 600,000 dwellings (Foro 1985)—and similar proportions were true of other urban centers.

State Housing Provision. The first major attempt by the national government to promote low-income housing was contained in legislation enacted in 1928 that required municipal authorities to invest 2 percent of their yearly budget in "workers' housing." To implement this objective, the Caja de Vivienda Popular, a municipal housing body, was set up in Bogota. However, municipal bodies like this were rarely effective.

In 1939 municipal housing was superceded by a national housing authority, the Instituto de Credito Territorial (ICT). It had access to subsidized capital and contracted work from private builders. These dwellings were then sold to individual families by means of low-interest mortgages from the institute. The number of houses built initially was very small, geared toward public employees and "key" workers. From 1928 to 1950 public housing (including municipal housing bodies) accounted for the production of only 3,500 dwellings, compared with 57,000 built by the private sector.

A further state contribution to housing provision at this time was the setting up in 1932 of the Banco Central Hipotecario (BCH), the national mortgage bank, that collected savings and investments and loans for building and house purchase at commercial interest rates. However, the services of this body were confined to middle- and higher-income groups (Jaramillo 1981). The political crisis of 1948 was followed by civil war and four years of military rule. In 1957 the military government was replaced by civilians, pledged to defusing some of the country's most explosive conditions. This was particularly pressing after the success of the Cuban Revolution. They were helped in this task by the Alliance for Progress that (through USAID) provided dollar loans for a variety of "community-development" programs. Exceptional low-income housing projects were initiated, such as Ciudad Kennedy, a "new town" of more than 80,000 people, covering 450 hectares of land outside Bogota. Half of the dwellings were built through self-help aid and many more through a combination of self-help and private contract. Apart from housing provision, a program of community development was undertaken with considerable success (Rocha Sanchez 1970). Government housing performance during this time reached an all-time peak. The ICT alone built 84,829 dwellings from 1960 to 1964, more than half through self-help aid schemes (Mondragon 1979).

Experiments were also carried out in the field of low-cost building technology. The CINVA (Centro de Investigacion Nacional de Vivienda) institute, attached to the Universidad Nacional, a state university, researched the use of local building materials and self-building techniques. One of its products was the CINVA-RAM, a block-making machine that is used in self-building throughout the world today.

By 1965 the climate of reform had ended. That year only 2,399 dwellings were produced by the ICT. Although yearly production levels rose to about 10,000 in subsequent years, they remained well below earlier levels. The reason given for this change in policy was the escalating cost of repaying inflationary foreign loans undertaken to finance the earlier programs, but there was also an implicit political decision to rely more on the private building sector.

Instead of self-help aid and direct development of projects, the ICT turned to "cofinancing" with private developers. In this arrangement, the ICT would provide funds for construction, and a developer would provide technical services, labor, and sometimes land. On completion of the scheme the ICT would pay the builder for its contribution and allocate individual dwellings for sale to families by means of subsidized mortgages. This arrangement was essentially a subsidy to private enterprise and private ownership. It did not guarantee that the housing built would remain in the low-income sector. Nor did it benefit the families with the lowest incomes. However, the contribution of state housing organizations has not been negligible. Between 1970 and 1982 approximately 1,120,000 were funded or built by state housing organizations (Santana and Casasbuenas 1981).

In 1982 a coalition of several political currents, from traditional Conservatives to Christian Democrats, came together behind a "maverick" Conservative (Betancur) and successfully ousted the Liberal party from power. They offered, among other things, a program of major reforms, aimed at increasing public and private investment in housing, particularly low-cost housing, and its infrastructure in order to improve conditions and regenerate the economy. In housing terms, they aimed at stopping the growth of the deficit and reducing it by 20 percent per annum.

Toward this end, the budgets of state housing organizations were trebled, and CAVs were compelled to invest 50 percent of their receipts in low-income housing (Giraldo Isaza 1981). This funding was made available both to private developers and to the growing network of nongovernmental housing organizations that relied strongly on self-building and community self-help. With these elements the government was able to achieve an all-time record for house building (Foro 1985).

Betancur's failings in other spheres, however, particularly his failure to generate industrial growth and to curb violent factions to the Left and the Right, paved the way for the return of the Liberal party to power. The new government nominally adopted Betancur's radical housing policies and promised new measures to support the effort of nongovernmental social housing organizations. However, given the declining political situation now faced by the country it is unlikely that such policies will be a priority.

Nongovernmental Bodies. Cooperative housing in Colombia also made a start around the 1930s, providing homes for clerical workers and professionals at less than market prices. The Cooperative de Habitaciones de Medellin, for instance, on the basis of members' savings and by employing its own development and architectural staff, became one of the city's major housing developers. At that time, cooperative initiatives were rarely evident in lower-income sectors.

The next great impetus for the nongovernmental sector came from the state itself. In 1958 "Accion Communal" legislation created a simple legal framework for neighborhood organizations, the Juntas de Accion Communal (JACs). They were small, locally managed neighborhood councils set up to undertake a variety of community-development projects. They were coordinated and often funded by the Ministry of Government, which employed a professional staff to give them legal and technical advice. Although not originally intended to act as self-build organizations, in years to come many JACs took on this role (Velez 1984).

Throughout the sixties and seventies, church-linked and philanthropic organizations attempted to create model neighborhoods, often based on self-building and mutual aid. Examples of this are the Casitas de la Providencia in Medellin and the Minuto de Dios development in Bogota.

However, the most significant development of nongovernmental community housing organizations has taken place since the late 1970s, stimulated by increased need for housing and minimal government provision of low-income housing. A 1986 survey showed an extensive network of organizations throughout the country, developing housing and other facilities for their members on the basis of self-help. The survey identified a total of 522 organizations: 133 JACs, 19 foundations, 152 associations, 83 cooperatives, 98 organizations with "other" legal forms, and 32 organizations with no legal form at all. Collectively, they were carrying out projects for more than 89,000 dwellings (Molina and Henao 1986). Other researchers have suggested that this survey was incomplete and that there are now more than 1,000 such organizations (Foro 1985).

Most of these organizations were found to provide low-income housing. Most relied on self-building by future occupiers to reduce the cost of the dwellings. Most used an element of self-funding by future occupiers from savings, pensions, or loans. Most undertook loans, either subsidized or UPAC, to build. Some had developed "appropriate" building technologies that allowed them to self-build more effectively, and many produced their own building materials. Some had not stopped at housing but sought to provide their members with a range of social services, including employment, health, and education (Ospina 1987).

Given the size and potential of this movement, various attempts have been made to coordinate their fragmented activities and to create a national coordinating body to represent them. In October 1982 several independent housing organizations came together to form the National Federation of Popular Housing Organizations (FEDEVIVIENDA). Apart from this, a number of heterogeneous regional and national bodies have sprung up, attempting to coordinate and represent the different groupings. Whereas the FEDEVIVIENDA had twenty-two affiliated bodies in 1983 (mainly large associations), Camara Colombiana de la Autogestion (CONSTRUYAMOS), a government-sponsored federation, had sixty-six (mainly JACs), a cooperative committee in Cali had twenty-five affiliated coops, a federation in Cundinamarca had two dozen more, and so on. This organizational fragmentation has undoubtedly been an obstacle to the development of a strong, independent movement.

The Conservative government of Belisario Betancur declared 1984 the "Year of the Self-Builder" and sponsored a number of joint activities (such as a National Exhibition of Projects) that were instrumental in focusing official and public attention on the movement. However, this did not prevent the same government from enacting legal measures that make life harder for the community housing organizations. One such measure was the Superintendecia Bancaria's "Regulation 052." This regulation was supposedly aimed at protecting individual members of self-build organizations. It required such organizations to repay individual members who decided to withdraw both their financial contribution to date (including interest) and the cash equivalent of the labor they had contributed to the scheme so far. In practice, the regulation could have bankrupted many small self-help projects that barely had enough working capital to cover day-to-day costs. The FEDEVIVIENDA launched a campaign against these measures that gained the support of other federations and succeeded in getting the legislation suspended.

In August 1985 the FEDEVIVIENDA joined with other housing bodies in the country's first "Unified Housing Congress." Participants included CONSTRUY-AMOS del Valle, a breakaway group from the government-sponsored federation, the Movimiento Civico Popular, Provivienda, and a national tenant's association. Representatives from 350 organizations attended, representing about 100,000 families (Ospina 1987).

PROSPECTIVE DEVELOPMENTS

From the 1930s to today, most functions of housing production and development, ownership, and management have been left up to individual and private enterprise. The state has limited its intervention to regulating these activities and using rent controls and subsidies to ensure that at least a limited number of lower-income families benefit from this activity. On the whole, this intervention has been ineffective, and the majority of low-income families depend for housing on an inadequate "illegal" private sector.

It would be unrealistic to expect the state to provide an alternative to the private sector, since it does not have the organizational infrastructure, the funding, or the political consistency to undertake such a role. This has been demonstrated by the brief periods when this has been attempted (e.g., 1962–1964).

A more realistic proposal would be for the state to move in a more determined manner in the direction it is already going. This approach is oriented toward "enabling" community-housing organizations to build and possibly manage housing with the active participation of the communities that they serve.

In 1984 the Conservatives lost power, mainly through their inability to control growing social unrest. A new Liberal government was elected whose housing policy was basically similar to its predecessor, emphasizing the need for state intervention and public investment in low-cost housing.

One of its primary proposals has been the strengthening of the self-help housing movement, so it can become the major provider of social housing. A number of measures were suggested by a Liberal party working group on housing to make this possible:

1. Streamlining the legal and technical framework, so that organizations can develop their programs without bureaucratic obstacles (such as obtaining permits to accumulate savings, building permits, and so on).

2. Making subsidized funds available through the Instituto de Credito Teritorial and the Banco Central Hipotecario, so that these organizations can successfully complete their programs.

3. Making technical assistance available through the SENA (the government's national training organization), so that these projects have the benefit of professional assistance.

Municipal authorities will also be encouraged (by giving them additional resources from central government) to make land and services available for these projects in order to complete about 90,000 dwellings by 1988 (Liberal Party 1985).

These policies show a growing awareness in all political currents of the need for the state to concentrate on supporting the growing "community-housing" movement, if an alternative to the "illegal" private sector is to be found. However, recent information indicates that these measures have not had the desired effect. ICT is facing bankruptcy and has cut back its activities drastically. Proposed urban reforms have not led to the expected release of land for social housing but to a shortage of suitable land. Also, the organizers of these projects have had to face violence or even assassination for their efforts.

To be genuinely effective, the community housing alternative would require a coherent program to strengthen these organizations, to provide them with an integrated legal and financial framework in which to function and with essential resources like land, finance, and technical skills. Also, subsidy of low-cost rentals or the promotion of alternative tenures (like co-ownership or leasehold) would help close the gap between the benefits derived by those that rent and those that own. Above all, it is necessary that the government respond, enter into a dialogue with the representatives of the community-housing organizations.

In the present climate of political and financial instability it would be unrealistic to expect determined measures like these. However, in the long term there is unlikely to be any other way forward. In any case there is no doubt that the community-housing organizations will continue their activities, contributing their experience to an eventual solution.

REFERENCES

Arango, A., Carlos. 1986. *La Lucha por la Vivienda en Colombia*. Bogota: Ecoe Ediciones.

Brille, Ines Useche de. 1981. "El Banco Central Hipotecario y la Vivienda Popular." In *La Vivienda Popular Hoy en Colombia*, edited by Pedro Santana, 27–35. Bogota: Centro de Investigacion y Educacion Popular.

Cardona, Lucy de. 1987. "The Relationship between Working-Class Women and Their Housing." Paper presented to the IYSH International Women in Housing Conference, Sheffield, U.K.

Clavijo, Hernando. 1981. "La Produccion Privada y Estatal de Vivienda en la Decada

de los Setenta.'' In *La Problematica Urbana Hoy en Colombia*, 189–215. Serie
Teoria y Sociedad. Bogota: Centro de Investigacion y Educacion Popular.

Foro Nacional por Colombia. 1985. ''Documentos del Foro.'' Paper presented to the
Primer Congreso Unitario de Vivienda Popular, Bogota, August 17–19.

Giraldo Isaza, Fabio. 1981. ''El Sector de la Construccion de Vivienda y la Vivienda
Popular.'' In *La Vivienda Popular Hoy en Colombia*, edited by Pedro Santana,
57–149. Bogota: Centro de Investigacion y Educacion Popular.

Janssen, Roel. 1984. *Vivienda y Luchas populares en Bogota*. Bogota: Ediciones Tercer
Mundo.

Jaramillo, Samuel. 1980. *Produccion de Vivienda y Capitalismo Dependiente: el Caso
de Bogota*. Bogota: Editorial Dintel.

————. 1981. ''La Politica de Vivienda de Betancur: sus Raices y sus Alcances.'' In
La Vivienda Popular Hoy en Colombia, edited by Pedro Santana, 167–91. Bogota:
Centro de Investigación y Educacion Popular.

Jaramillo, Samuel, and Equipo de Investigaciones Urbanas. 1985. *Entre el UPAC y la
Autoconstruccion: Comentarios y Sugerencias a la Politica de Vivienda*. Con-
troversia 123–24. Bogota: Centro de Investigacion y Educacion Popular.

Liberal Party (Colombia). 1985. ''Programa de Vivienda Popular.'' Unpublished discussion, Bogota. Mimeograph.

Molina, Humberto. 1981. ''Reactivacion Economica by Redistribucion del Ingreso en la
Politica de Vivienda.'' In *La Vivienda Popular Hoy en Colombia*, edited by Pedro
Santana, 149–67. Bogota: Centro de Investigacion y Educacion Popular.

Molina, Humberto, and Carlos Henao. 1986. *Directorio Nacional de Autoconstruccion*.
Bogota: Fondo Nacional de Formacion Professional de la Industria de la Construccion (FIC).

Mondragon, Luz Angela. 1979. ''Politica de Vivienda del Estado Colombian.'' In *Colombia: Vivienda y Subdesarrollo Urbano*, edited by Humberto Molina, 445–527.
Bogota.

Negocios (Editorial). 1985. ''Vivienda: Una Bomba a Punto de Estallar.'' In *Revista
Negocios*, 26–34. Bogota.

Ospina, Jose. 1987. *Housing Ourselves*. London: Hilary Shipman Ltd.

Ramirez Soto, Javier. 1981. ''El Programa Gubernamental de Vivienda.'' In *La Vivienda
Popular Hoy en Colombia*, edited by Pedro Santana, 3–9. Bogota: Centro de
Investigacion y Educacion Popular.

Rocha Sanchez, Lola. 1970. ''Ciudad Kennedy: A New Town in Bogota.'' In *The Role
of Housing in Promoting Social Integration*, 120–96. New York: United Nations
Department of Science and Education.

Ruiz Gutierrez, Fernando. 1987. ''The Problems of Spontaneous Settlement in Bogota.''
Paper presented to the International Symposium on Housing, Yokohoma, Japan.

Santana, Pedro. 1981. ''Movimientos Populares y Revindicaciones Urbanas.'' In *La
Problematica Urbana Hoy en Colombia*, 215–39. Serie Teoria y Sociedad. Bogota:
Centro de Investigacion y Educacion Popular.

Santana, Pedro, and Constantino Casasbuenas. 1981. ''Hacia una Politica de Vivienda
Popular en Colombia.'' In *La Vivienda Popular Hoy en Colombia*, edited by Pedro
Santana, 191–283. Bogota: Centro de Investigacion y Educacion Popular.

Soto Sierra, Javier Pedro. 1981. ''Un Nuevo Enfoque en las Soluciones Habitacionales
para Sectores de Muy Bajos Ingresos.'' In *La Vivienda Popular Hoy en Colombia*,

edited by Pedro Santana, 45–57. Bogota: Centro de Investigacion y Educacion Popular.

Torres, Camilo. 1971. "Bogota, Pre-industrial City." In *Revolutionary Priest: The Complete Writings and Message of Camilo Torres*, edited by John Gerassi, 63–64. London: Jonathan Cape.

Unidad de programacion Global and Unidad de Desarrollo Regional y Urbano. 1981. "La Edificacion de Vivienda en Colombia." *Revista de Planeacion y Desarrollo* (Bogota) 13, no. 3:11–91.

Velez Vanegas, C. A. 1984. "Accion Communal, Esfuerzo de Todos." *Revista de Auto-Construccion y Vivienda Popular* no. 4 (May): 11.

FURTHER READING

Gilbert, A. "Pirates and Invaders: Land Acquisition in Urban Colombia and Venezuela. *World Development* 9 (1981):657–78.

Hammer, Andrew M. *Bogota's Unregulated Subdivisions: The Myths and Realities of Incremental Housing Construction.* World Bank, 1985.

Ospina, Jose. "Self-Help Housing and Social Change in Colombia." *Habitat International* 9, nos. 3–4 (1985): 235–49.

―――. "The Self-Help Housing Movement in Colombia." *Cities*, 1985, pp. 314–18.

VI

MIDDLE EAST

15

Egypt

LATA CHATTERJEE

Although Egypt is a relatively large country in Africa, with an area of 1.05 million square kilometers, its population of 48 million is concentrated on approximately 4 percent of the land mass that constitutes the Nile valley and delta. Egypt would be an extension of the Sahara desert without the Nile; consequently, the rural and urban population has always been concentrated within the geographic area irrigated by the Nile. This uneven spatial distribution has caused Egypt's nondesert population density of 1,250 persons per square kilometer in 1982 and an estimated 1,380 square kilometer in 1985 to be one of the highest densities in the world (Economist Intelligence Unit 1985). This geographical characteristic of the concentration of population in the narrow confines of the Nile valley and delta provides a context for many of the housing problems in Egypt. This particular characteristic also provides the fundamental parameters within which housing policies to address these problems need to be defined, since loss of the scarce agricultural land through housing sprawl is a major problem facing the country.

The uneven distribution of population has been further exacerbated by rapid urban growth in the past few decades. Due to rural urban migration, the annual growth rate in urban areas in the 1976–1985 period was approximately 4.0 percent, even though the annual rate of natural increase was around 2.8 percent. By 1980, 44.3 percent of the total population lived in urban areas, and the urbanization rate was expected to continue to increase (United Nations 1986a). Moreover, the total urban population of 19.25 million is also unevenly distributed and approximately 60 percent of the total urban population is concentrated in the two metropolitan areas of Cairo and Alexandria. It is in these metropoles and the three canal cities of Suez, Port Said, and Ismalia, that housing problems are most acute. Rapid population growth and its spatial redistribution through rural-urban migration increases the need for housing, and the housing sector is particularly important to Egypt.

The Egyptian government, contrary to that of the majority of developing countries, recognized the need to support housing for low-income groups early in its phase of development planning. Under Nasserism, a form of socialism, the government intervened in the housing sector and played an active role in improving the housing availability and standards of low-income households. In spite of the promulgation of tough regulations and the channeling of large investments, the public sector was able to address the problem only partially. Undoubtedly, more low-income Egyptians are better housed than they would otherwise have been without these programs. Nevertheless, the scale of the problem has combined with the inadequacy of public resources to focus attention on the necessity for combining the relative strengths of both the private and the public sectors to minimize, if not overcome, the problem. Currently, there is much analysis of the housing problems, the strengths and weaknesses of past policies, and the means for rationalization of the housing sector that would involve the relative strengths of both the public and private sectors.

Many of the housing problems in Egypt are common to those of other developing countries, and since they have received extensive coverage in the housing literature, no attempt is made to provide a comprehensive description of these problems. Rather, this chapter highlights the roots of the housing problem in Egypt, describes the past policies of the government, summarizes the findings of studies that have evaluated these policies, and discusses the alternatives that can address the problems within the socioeconomic context of modern Egypt. In the light of the limited space and the scale of the problems, this chapter can, at best, be viewed as a brief introduction to the subject.

TRENDS IN HOUSING CONDITIONS AND CONSTRUCTION: 1950–1985

There is only fragmentary and inadequate information on housing in the national economy. This can be partially explained by the difficulty of collecting information in a developing country wherein most of the value added is in the unorganized sector. In the unorganized sector housing construction is done by local artisans, often on an irregular and piecemeal basis. In this form of production no centralized information is kept on costs and value added. In addition, much of this construction is illegal in that agricultural land is urbanized and the housing units are often constructed in contravention of planning laws. Consequently, the only official information that is available on housing construction pertains to legally authorized housing in urban areas. These numbers underestimate the volume of construction since through sample survey data it has been estimated that the unauthorized, illegal sector in urban areas can account for as much as 75–90 percent of the new construction (Abt Associates 1982).

Although statistical data to assess accurately the volume of housing construction in the economy as a whole are lacking, we can piece together a picture of the role of housing in the national economy from several studies that have focused on specific cities or specific target groups. Egypt, relative to other countries in Africa, has had several housing studies, and a scholar of Egyptian housing is relatively fortunate with respect to housing literature. However, these studies have focused on limited aspects of housing problems and have used survey data to provide an assessment of the housing-consumption patterns and behaviors of specific target groups in a few geographical areas, particularly in Cairo and Alexandria. Inasmuch as the most severe housing problems are in the larger cities, this information, even though it provides only partial coverage of the country, is very valuable. This chapter draws on these studies to augment the 1976 Census, which provides the only reliable data that are available on a countrywide basis.

According to the 1976 Census, Egypt's total housing stock was 7.3 million units of which approximately 3.5 million were in urban areas (Central Agency for Public Mobilisation and Statistics [CAPMAS] 1976). At the aggregate level the census data indicated that there was no deficit since there was no homelessness in rural areas and there was a vacancy rate of 3.4 percent in urban areas. The National Urban Policy Study (NUPS) (PADCO 1980), which did a very comprehensive analysis of this data, stated that for the country as a whole the construction of housing had kept pace with the growth in population in the 1960–1976 period. The Abt Associates (1982) study of Cairo found that the number of dwelling units constructed in the 1976–1981 period had grown at an annual average rate of 5.9 percent, with the annual growth of apartments at an approximate 6.5 percent rate. Thus in 1981 there was a vacancy rate of 5.5 percent. In urban areas with 5,000 or more persons there were 1.03 dwelling units per household (PADCO 1981).

However, this aggregate data has to be interpreted with caution. Severe housing shortages exist in specific housing markets where the natural increase in population has been aggravated by rural-urban population movement. In cities such as Cairo and Alexandria there are acute housing deficits for specific income groups. A. Rageh (1984) estimated that the housing shortage in Cairo was around 299,000 units. However, at that time 500,000 people lived in the cemeteries, and almost 1 million lived in one-room units. Thus his estimates of the true housing deficit appear to be conservative.

Aggregate figures obscure the real nature of the quantitative aspects of housing since the need for housing is locality and income specific. In countries, such as Egypt, undergoing large-scale rural-urban and interurban migration, it is possible to have the simultaneous existence of a surplus of dwelling units, as the 1.03 dwelling units per household signify, and severe housing shortages. The Abt study addressed the issue of the apparent anomaly between an increasing housing shortage and large vacancy rates. They noted that in Cairo high vacancy levels existed in the luxury range in which dwelling units carried price tags far beyond the range of the ability to pay of even affluent households. Moreover, vacant units were held by speculator investors in expectation of higher returns due to the rapid inflation in the price of dwelling units, and owners often carried vacant apartments for their own or their dependents' future use due to the strict rent-control and tenant-eviction laws. The national picture also reflects the surplus of dwelling units in rural areas and small towns where the housing problem is qualitative rather than quantitative. In these areas housing problems relate to the unavailability of potable water and sewerage facilities rather than to the availability of dwelling units.

Rapid urbanization in the 1960–1975 period caused an urban housing scarcity that reached crisis proportions by the end of the seventies. The housing shortage in Egypt may have reached 1.5 million units by 1979 if city specific housing shortages are added up (Cooper 1982, 270). In the period new urban households formed at an annual rate of 90,000, whereas new housing units increased at an annual rate of 28,000. This method of accounting provides a contrary picture to that which emerges from a perusal of aggregate statistics that ignores locality and income class. Due to this increasing shortage, urban housing has been conceived of as an investment priority sector in the eighties. According to government estimates 103,558 new units were constructed in 1980, which was at least twice the average rate of the 1970s (Economist Intelligence Unit 1985). Table 15.1 provides information on authorized housing construction in urban areas during the 1970–1980 period. Only the 1980 construction matched the estimated growth of households.

The census of 1976 did not provide information on the age or condition of the stock so only general assessments could be made in the NUPS study. However, related indicators suggest that modest improvements have been made in the quality of the housing stock. There was a reduction in the percentage of single-room dwelling units from 36.3 percent in 1964 to 20.5 percent in 1976.

Table 15.1
Dwelling Units Completed in Urban Areas, Egypt, 1970–1985

	1970	1975	1979	1980	1985
Total Population[1] (in millions)	32.3	36.9	40.8	43.8	48.5
Urban Population[1] (% of total population)	42.3	43.5	43.8	43.8	44.6
Authorized dwelling[2] units completed in urban areas (x 1,000)	32.0	50.0	90.9	103.6	NA

Sources: [1]United Nations, 1986b, table 6; [2]United Nations, 1986c, table 15.7.
Note: The 1979, 1980, and 1985 population figures are estimates.

With respect to infrastructure improvements, buildings with access to sewerage increased from 21 percent to 29 percent and those with electricity from 37 to 62 percent in the 1960–1976 period. With respect to water connections, the national average of 48 percent consisted of a range from Port Said with an 85 percent connection rate to Qena with a 26 percent rate. The percentage of households connected to water and power were higher in the metropolitan areas. CAPMAS statistics indicated that 74 and 90 percent of the households were connected to water supplies in Greater Cairo and Alexandria, respectively, and both had power connection rates in excess of 80 percent. William Wheaton (1981), using CAPMAS data, noted that the room-occupancy rate had declined from 2.3 in 1960 to 1.9 persons in 1976. However, there is no consensus about these improvements. Mark Cooper (1982, 270) noted a deteriorating trend in housing quality and mentioned that the proportion of households without proper housing grew from 21.7 percent in 1970 to 31.9 percent in 1977. Since population is growing at a faster rate than the growth in the housing stock of the larger cities, we can expect regional variations in housing quality and access to services.

Some information on the size of the urban housing stock and new construction, for the 1960–1976 period for selected governorates, is shown in table 15.2. Although dated, it does provide the latest available data on the spatial distribution of the stock. The highest growth rates are registered in Giza and Qalyubia, which are in metropolitan Cairo.

The best source of information on the macroeconomic aspects of the role of housing in the economy is the National Income Statistics. Data on the contribution of the housing sector to the national product is available by industry of origin, at 1981–1982 constant prices, for 1977 and 1981. Two indicators of trends in the housing-construction sector are (1) housing as a component of gross domestic product (GDP) and (2) the amount of employment provided through that sector (table 15.3). The overall contribution of housing construction to the GDP has

Table 15.2
The Urban Housing Stock, Egypt, 1960–1976

Governorate	Dwelling Units (N)		Average Rate of Growth of Housing Stock (in %)
	1960	1976	
Cairo	782,254	1,140,216	3.8
Alexandria	323,722	477,262	4.0
Giza	173,086	337,882	6.9
Gharbia	105,831	168,142	4.7
Qalyubia	72,710	149,719	7.5
Dakhalia	89,543	145,719	5.0
Other (18)	873,543	1,152,956	3.3
Total Urban Stock	2,391,424	3,478,738	3.8

Source: PADCO, 1981.

remained constant, around 3.6 percent, in both periods. However, its share of the construction sector declined between 1977 and 1982 from more than three-quarters to slightly less than two-thirds. This is partially a result of the increase in the share of the construction sector with respect to the GDP and partially the difference in the growth rates of the GDP and the housing sector. Although the GDP grew by 45 percent between the two periods, housing grew by 40 percent. The declining share of housing is further corroborated by employment figures. Employment in housing grew by only 18 percent compared with the growth of 45 percent in the construction sector; consequently, housing employment as a percentage of construction employment declined between these two periods.

However, we should interpret these figures with caution since this information provides only an incomplete picture of the level of activity in the housing sector inasmuch as housing construction includes a substantial amount of "own account" work that is not accounted for. Given the size of the unorganized sector, we should expect a downward bias in the estimates provided on residential building, relative to the construction sector. Since the construction sector includes items such as bridges, factories, and dams where the activity is much more organized and larger in scale, a more accurate assessment of nonresidential construction activity is feasible. With respect to capital formation, the contribution of residential buildings to gross fixed capital formation has hovered around 43 percent during the 1973–1979 period (United Nations 1987).

Table 15.3
Selected Indicators of the Role of Housing in the National Economy, Egypt, 1977 and 1981–1982

STRUCTURE OF GDP (# fixed factor cost constant 81-82 prices - in millions of U.S. $)	1977[1]	1981-82[2]
Total GDP	9,360	13,565
Total Construction	455	737
Housing	346	483
Construction as % of GDP	4.9	5.4
Housing as % of GDP	3.7	3.6
Housing as % of Construction	76.1	65.5
EMPLOYMENT		
Construction (x1,000)	457.1	664.0
Housing (x1,000)	144.8	171.3
Construction Employment as % of total employment	4.6	5.7
Housing Employment as % of construction employment	31.7	25.8

Source: Computed from *Quarterly Economic Review*, 1985, Supplement, Economist Intelligence Unit. London: Economist.

[1]In 1977, 0.391 Egyptian pound was the equivalent of 1 U.S. dollar.

[2]In 1981–1982, 0.70 Egyptian pound was the equivalent of 1 U.S. dollar.

THE ROLE OF HOUSING INSTITUTIONS AND ORGANIZATIONS

In Egypt a distinction is commonly made between two systems of housing provision—the formal and the informal. The formal system, which consists of legal and authorized construction, can be further subdivided into three sectors: public, private, and cooperative. Informal housing, which consists of dwelling units built on illegally subdivided land in contravention of planning permission and standards, can be subdivided into two sectors: housing built by legal owners of the building sites but without building permits and housing built by squatters on occupied public land. The informal sector is very significant with respect to the total number of units constructed, and remarkable gains have been made in the provision of housing by the informal sector in the past two decades (Abt Associates 1982). In the informal sector community organizations are effective agents for improving access to and quality of housing services. The institutional and organizational makeup of the housing sector can best be discussed in the context of the public, private, and cooperative institutions.

The public sector has had a direct impact on housing delivery since the 1952 revolution, and until 1974 it was a major provider of low-income housing in the metropolitan areas. In the initial stages of public sector housing intervention, following the 1952 revolution, the government clearly defined the role of the actors in the supply sector and distinguished between private institutions, co-operatives, and the public sector. Private sector companies were allowed to construct luxury housing, whereas the public sector was involved in residential land development and the construction of subsidized housing. Cooperatives developed land and built housing for their members who were drawn predominantly from middle-income groups. However, since *Infitah*, the open-door policy of Sadat, the role of the government both as a provider and regulator of housing has diminished, and the private sector has had a more direct impact on the availability and distribution of housing for both lower- and upper-income groups. The relative importance of the two sectors—public and private—and their constituent institutions thus varies between the two periods associated with the political philosophies of Nasser and Sadat.

Several public sector institutions are involved in the housing sector. Currently, national ministries, departments of housing and planning in the governorates, public construction companies such as the Arab Contractors, and special-purpose agencies such as the General Authority for Housing and Building Cooperatives (GAHBC) are involved in the provision of housing and related utilities. Although the Ministry of Housing and the Ministry of Reconstruction and New Communities are the two primary agencies, the Ministries of Defence, Awkaf (Religious Affairs), Agriculture, and Industry in addition to Housing departments of the governorates develop housing. The activities of these various public providers are not coordinated by any agency, and there are severe problems that arise from overlap and/or fragmentation (Dames and Moore 1981).

There are also various legislative bodies such as the Housing Committee of the People's Assembly, the courts, and religious councils such as the Shura Council that have important impacts on the housing sector through the laws that are passed. There are research organizations such as the General Organization of Housing, Building and Planning Research (GOHBR), which conducts housing research for the government, often in collaboration with foreign consulting companies. For example, the GOHBR jointly with Abt Associates and Dames and Moore conducted a study on informal housing. With the Ministry of Housing and Ministry of Reconstruction and New Settlements it is conducting a study that is focusing on standards, costs, and criteria for developing housing for low-income groups. There are also several infrastructure agencies such as the General

Organization for Greater Cairo Water Supply that have impacts on housing and residential land development.

The institutional structure of the housing sector is much too complex to deal with in a chapter of this size, and the reader is referred to the Dames and Moore study (1981). Since many of the government institutions and activities are common with other countries, only two relatively unique aspects of public sector involvement are discussed. They are (1) residential land development in new communities and (2) the role of public sector construction firms.

New Communities: Residential Land Development and Housing

As noted earlier, a distinguishing attribute of Egypt is the limited area with easy water availability for agriculture. To protect the arable land and decrease the pressure for urbanization on it by private formal and informal builders, a primary objective of the government has been the development of desert areas for housing. The government emphasizes land development in desert areas, and national investment has been channeled into new communities such as the Tenth of Ramadan, Fifteenth of May, 6th October, and satellite towns of Al Abour and Al Amal (Ambar 1984).

The Ministry of Reconstruction and New Settlements is responsible for the development of three types of new communities on desert land—self-contained new towns, satellite towns around the major metropolises, and new settlements. New towns, such as the Tenth of Ramadan, plan to channel both housing and employment away from existing cities. Deep subsidies have been provided by the government to meet this national objective of land and housing development in the desert. Fully urbanized plots were sold for nominal prices to attract middle-income households; however, most of this land has been held for speculative purposes, and little private sector housing has been built in the new towns. Rapid construction of affordable housing for low-income workers was attempted through government assistance. However, the cost of housing construction was 35 percent higher than expected, making the housing too expensive for workers. A 1982 revised plan, in recognition of these problems, has downsized plot sizes from the original 600 square meters to 120 square meters and has embarked on building worker housing with reduced standards.

Satellite towns such as Al Abour or Fifteenth of May are conceived of as partially independent centers, diverting housing requirements away from congested central areas of Cairo. The projected sizes of satellite towns around the major metropolises vary from 250,000 to 500,000 inhabitants. The primary target group is the low- to middle-income households, the group currently involved in arable land destruction through the informal housing sector. For example, in Al-Abour the first stage of the plan calls for 11,800 serviced sites and 5,050 dwelling units with plots ranging from 72 square meters to 252 square meters, with 82 percent of the plots 135 square meters or less. The gross density of the residential area will average 480 persons per hectare. The reader is referred to the PADCO (1981) report, which presents a detailed and comparative assessment of the space and infrastructure standards of the new communities.

Public Sector Construction Firms

Before the sixties large-scale land development had been in the hands of private companies such as the Heliopolis and the Al Maady Companies. However, in 1952 they were nationalized and made into public companies. In addition, new companies such as Nasr City were established on a similar model. The Development and Popular Housing Company was established in 1954 to build low-cost public housing units even though the units were fully financed through government loans. In more contemporary times the Arab Contractors is a very large public enterprise that is involved in the construction of housing and infrastructure in the new towns and satellite communities.

Public sector construction firms are the most important formal sector agents involved in the development of land and dwelling units. Although there are numerous small, private firms, the majority of formal construction is done by the public nonprofit companies. The national and state governments promote housing through the provision of low-cost capital and construction subsidies; however, the public construction companies actually develop the land and construct the housing units. After *Infitah* in 1974, the construction industry became even more powerful and the large public construction firms became important agents in the building and reconstruction boom. The predominant interest of these construction firms lies in large-scale residential land development in the satellite cities and new communities in the arid areas or in large-scale slum-clearance schemes in central cities that seek to replace low-income housing by luxury housing and hotel and office complexes. Hinnebusch (1985) mentioned the case of the demolition of lower-income neighborhoods in central Cairo that the construction and real estate interests had lobbied for and pushed through the Housing Committee of the People's Assembly, in spite of strong community opposition. This tradition of public land development and construction of new housing has been retained in spite of the move to a less-controlled economy.

Some of the public sector construction companies, such as the Cairo Company and the Arab Contractors, have developed financing schemes for marketing their housing units. The Cairo Company sells preconstruction equities in its buildings and selects the eventual housing-unit purchasers from among the bondholders using a priority ordering based on the number of bonds owned and the chronological order of bond purchases (USAID 1977a). Eventually, the bonds are applied to the purchase price. This scheme allows the company to overcome the problem of construction financing and helps purchasers by permitting them to phase their investments incrementally. A below-market interest rate is paid to the bondholders, and the principal and interest are guaranteed. Given the high rates of inflation in house values, this scheme is very attractive to potential homeowners, and the bonds have been fully subscribed. Arab Contractors has gone into joint ventures with foreign investors for housing projects that are exempt from rent control in perpetuity and free of taxes for the first five years after completion. The housing units are sold to foreign investors and nonresident Egyptians who can purchase units in foreign currencies, reserving the right of reconversion to the currency of purchase. This scheme has a dual purpose; it allows the company to pay for its imports of building materials from foreign currencies and also ensures a superior quality of finish. However, such innovative financing schemes are suitable only for the upper end of the housing market.

Middle-income households depend on subsidized loans channeled through the GAHBC. The GAHBC was established in 1954 to encourage and facilitate the formation of housing cooperatives, and it has become the most effective institution for the provision of moderate and middle-income housing. The GABHC acquires land, develops sites, and supervises the design and construction work at the site. The cooperatives are also permitted to plan and design the buildings; however, GAHBC sets standards and supervises construction in such cases. It favors intermediate-sized subdivisions and condominium ownership.

Cooperatives are formed among groups having a common profession, for example, teachers, police officers, engineers, and the like. Subsidized financing, in the form of below-market interest rates, is provided to groups for the development of cooperatives and to individual members of cooperatives for the purchase of their units. Cooperatives pay 5 percent interest on the loan with an amortization period of fifteen years. Individual members pay a 6 percent rate of interest. The GAHBC does not have its own capital, and its operating expenditures are received from the national budget. The GAHBC is authorized to borrow from the commercial banks at market interest rates and to relend to the members at subsidized interest rates with the government underwriting the difference. By 1983–1984 total government financing of cooperatives had reached U.S. $214.3 million. (Note: Exchange rate, national currency per U.S. dollar—1968–1972:0.435; 1973–1978:0.391; 1979–1984:0.700.)

The housing finance system in Egypt is still in a rudimentary form, even though there are various institutions involved in finance. There are formal and informal sector institutions. In the formal sector there is a National Housing Bank and several mortgage banks (Wildeman 1984). Of them, the Real Estate and Credit Bank (Crédit Foncier Egyptien) and the Arab Land Bank are dedicated to real estate and housing finance. In addition, commercial banks contribute to housing finance through loans to cooperatives and construction companies. However, such loans are a small proportion of the portfolio of commercial banks. The combined efforts of all of these institutions—public and private—is not commensurate with the need for housing finance.

Low-income households do not benefit from formal institutions, and the informal sector housing study found that less than 10 percent of the purchasers in Cairo had either borrowed from or had savings in the banks in 1981. Most units constructed in the informal sector depend on informal finance mechanisms.

Various mechanisms are used in the informal sector that are common to developing countries, for example, rotating credit societies known as the *gamiya* in Egypt, installment purchase of land, building material loans, and incremental retirement of contractor and builder fees. The interest rate in the informal financing can vary from zero percent to usurious rates. There is no information that allows a quantitative assessment of the flow of funds and terms of credit in this sector. If the scale of construction is used as an indicator, the informal financing system must be very effective.

Low-income households depend on community efforts such as the *gamiya*. The gamiya is an institutional mechanism that permits households with limited means to pool their savings. These savings are often channeled to capital expenditures and in the housing sector are used by owners for down payments on land and building materials and by renters for key money (Abt Associates 1982; Wikkan 1985). Since land and building materials can be bought on an installment system, the *gamiya* can be used as a source of housing finance. Since no interest is charged, this form of short-term credit is popular among low-income households.

The *gamiya* involves the formation of a savings club by a voluntary group of individuals in which a fixed amount of savings per period—weekly, biweekly, or monthly—is specified. One member of the group receives the pooled savings in each period, and the savings club is dissolved after each member has received an installment. A household can be a member of more than one *gamiya* at any time. The amount of periodic savings and the length of the savings cycle vary, and there can be *gamiya* suited to the savings capacity of an individual household.

Another source of informal finance is key money. Key money is the practice of collecting an up-front payment for the right to rent (i.e., get the key) from the property owner. Since rents are controlled and eviction of tenants is almost impossible, key money permits the contract rent to approximate the true market rent. Of the Cairo households, 20 percent reported paying key money, but among movers in the 1980–1982 period the rate was 53 percent of the households (Abt Associates 1982, 173). Key money is a particularly valuable form of finance since land and building materials can be bought on an installment basis. Debts for land, labor, or building materials are often retired from the key money received by the building owner. The land subdivider or building materials supplier provides a form of informal finance to creditworthy buyers. There is an initial down payment, and the remainder is retired, usually in twelve monthly installments (USAID 1977b). Interest is charged informally—either in the form of an extra installment or as priced into the land costs. Because of Islamic principles these extra payments are rarely viewed as interest payments by either party— they are predominantly viewed as fees or compensations. These informal, short-term financing practices, fairly common in developing countries, are used extensively among low-income households in rapidly expanding informal settlements.

A major source of funds for land purchases in the informal sector is the repatriation of funds by labor migrants to Arab countries. Since housing is a highly prized investment due to the rapid inflation in land and house prices, it provides a reliable form of investment for the Egyptian worker who temporarily migrates for this purpose. The scale of the importance of repatriation can be gauged from the fact that $35,714,000 was sent from abroad in 1981 compared with $10,800,000 in 1971. A sizeable proportion of these funds has been channeled into the housing sector, at least as confirmed by specific studies (Culpin, Clifford and Partners 1982; Davidson 1984).

HOUSING MARKETS AND POLICY ORIENTATIONS

Four major groups are involved in the production of housing: the government through the Ministries of Housing at the national and the governorate levels; public sector construction companies that are required to devote 15 percent of their profits toward the production of worker housing; the formal private sector, which consists of small construction firms and engineers' constructing units that have building permits; and the informal sector.

The Public Sector

Historically, housing policies in Egypt have been primarily geared toward increasing equity, and most programs were designed in favor of low-income groups. This involved the active participation of the public sector in new construction of public housing as well as in the stringent regulation of rents in private sector housing. Public sector activities can be broadly divided into three categories—construction and management of public housing that carries rental subsidies; public development of subsidized land in new communities for housing built for resale to consumers; and the provision of credit subsidies to cooperatives for housing construction and ownership. Since development of new communities and public support of cooperatives have been discussed earlier, in this subsection the characteristics of the public housing program are highlighted.

Under President Nasser low-income housing was built, for the first time in Egyptian history, on a massive scale. The state emphasized the construction of public housing to meet its social equity goals. The Development and Popular Housing Company was established in 1954 to build low-income housing units in Cairo. In the 1957–1962 period the government allocated $200 million for the construction of 300,000 new public housing units. The annual production in the 1960–1970 period fluctuated between 10,000 and 20,000 units with the construction of 11,000 units on an average; a record that has not been equaled in the later decades (El-Messiri 1985). One-, two-, and three-bedroom dwelling units were constructed in large, five-story walk-up housing complexes. The average size of 12 square meters per person compares favorably with the public housing space standards of other Third World countries. The low-income units ranged in size from 25 to 65 square meters with 52 square meters as the average (Rageh 1984).

These housing projects were predominantly constructed in urban areas. The 1976 Census showed that approximately 70 percent of all public housing units were built in the five major cities: Cairo, Alexandria, Port Said, Ismalia, and Suez. These buildings were often built on newly developed land on the outskirts of rapidly growing cities and metropolitan areas, such as in Imbaba to the west and Helwan to the south of Cairo. The peripheral location posed initial hardships for the dwellers since the housing units were distant from the jobs and social networking areas of the households. Since there was often a lag in transportation and other infrastructure construction, this led to considerable dissatisfaction on the part of consumers and critical evaluations from analysts of public housing policies. As urban development engulfed these projects over time, the attitude toward these projects changed. Public housing is currently considered to be very desirable by low-income households, and 60 percent of the renters and 51 percent of the owners of informal housing expressed a preference for public housing (Abt Associates 1982, 149). Ninety-two percent of the occupants of public housing expressed satisfaction with the program.

To make public housing affordable to low-income households, rents were set at nominal levels. Units were rented at highly subsidized rates of $4.00 to $7.00 per month for two- and three-bedroom units, respectively, in 1976. Then rents were virtually unchanged until 1982. In Cairo median rents were $7.85 per month for a room in private housing compared with $2.50 in public housing. The incidence of key money was remarkably different—$22.9 versus $285.7. Moreover, the real cost was often reduced by the household through a subletting process in which a household would rent one of the rooms illegally. Although such subsidized shelter costs made public housing immensely popular with low-income households, the program placed enormous fiscal burdens on national and local governments since these rates do not reflect construction or the operating costs. Such deep subsidies restricted the ability of the public sector to meet housing requirements.

However, the financial commitment to public housing declined in the seventies due to the high cost of the program and the deep subsidies attached to each unit. The public sector did not have enough resources to meet the increasing housing needs. Moreover, there was a shift in resource allocation in favor of new towns so as to contain the explosive growth of the major cities and increase colonization of the desert. The Sadat regime was unprepared to emphasize public housing, and its modest program did not target the poor. After 1973, 60 percent of the units were reserved for the army and public employees, irrespective of income (Hopwood 1985). Due to the combined effect of these factors there are acute housing shortages in the major urban areas. In the eighties the emphasis was placed on the construction of new satellite communities to relieve some of the existing pressure in major metropolitan areas.

Although public housing units exist in most governorates, the majority of the units were built in Greater Cairo and Alexandria. The spatial distribution of units, as reported in the NUPS study, is shown in table 15.2. Although 22.2 and 13.8 percent of the public housing buildings were constructed in the Cairo and Alexandria governorates, the number of dwelling units in the metropolitan area is higher than these figures suggest. For example, the Cairo metropolitan area includes portions of the Giza and Qalubiya governorates. The units constructed in these governorates, such as the large complex in Shubra, are not included in the Cairo figures but indeed belong to the metropolitan area.

Public housing programs for the middle-income groups were also popular. The average dwelling units ranged from 90 square meters for three-room apartments to 120 square meters for four-room apartments. Buildings costs were $10 per square meter compared with $7 for the low-income housing. These programs were discontinued due to the lack of resources.

In light of the housing-needs gap the public sector recognized the importance of rapid construction. So policies favored industrialized building since theoretically both time and money could be saved through manufacturing of prefabricated systems. Since a large volume of construction would benefit from scale economies, a strong argument was made in favor of developing national capability in prefabricated systems. However, this policy has been unsuccessful and most factories are underused. Lack of infrastructure and cement are major impediments to the development and use of the prefabricated building blocks.

Although public policies have increased the welfare of many households, the scale of activity has not been commensurate with the total needs of housing. Even though public housing benefited thousands of households, the scale of construction could not keep pace with the rapid increase in urban households. There have been, and continue to exist, severe shortages of housing for low- and moderate-income households in urban areas.

Private Sector Housing

Remarkable improvements have been made in urban housing conditions in the seventies and eighties largely due to the activities of the private sector (PADCO 1980). The inability of the public sector to meet the increasing housing needs brought about by rapid urbanization and rising incomes caused the private sector to address the slack. Indeed, the private sector has always been active in Egypt, except in the two decades following the 1952 revolution. With the open-door policy and the lifting of government restrictions in the seventies the private sector has once again become very active. Three categories of housing are produced by the private sector in Egypt. Luxurious apartments, often costing more than $500 per square meter, are produced for sale. There is an ample supply of luxury housing. Rental apartments are produced for the middle-income groups. There is an insufficient construction of such units. Low-income units are built by traditional craft methods in formal, informal, and squatter settlements. This is the most rapidly growing component of private sector housing construction.

Private sector development of land and the construction of luxury housing had been an active component of the supply sector in Egypt in the forties and fifties. The Heliopolis and Al Maadi companies, noted earlier, constructed for this sector. However, in 1962 a law was promulgated that controlled rents and set the permissible rate of annual return at 5 percent of the value of the land and 8 percent of the value of the buildings. Subsequently, rental returns were set back even further due to the imposition of security and defense taxes on rental incomes. These various forms of rent adjustments dampened the vigor of the private construction and rental sectors. In 1977 the rent-control formula was modified, and high-quality housing was exempted from such controls. The law also allowed an increase in rents where upgrading and restoration had taken place (Ambar 1984). This encouraged the channeling of private sector resources to upper-income housing, and there is currently an oversupply of luxury units.

Since the public sector was unable to meet the housing needs of low- and moderate- income groups, a dynamic informal sector developed. Most of the housing constructed in Egypt is informal (Abt Associates et al. 1982). Informal housing, while built on legally owned land, is illegal in that the buildings are constructed on nonurban land and in contravention of existing planning and building regulations. Almost 84 percent of the dwelling units constructed in Cairo and 91 percent of the units constructed in Beni Suef, a small town, in the 1970–1981 period were in the informal sector. The estimates of the General Organization for Housing, Building, and Planning Research (GOHBPR 1981) are presented in table 15.3. In recently constructed housing the structural quality of the building is comparable to, if not superior to, formal housing (Abt Associates 1982). However, infrastructure is significantly less well supplied than in formal sector housing since most informal households build the dwelling unit before installation of utilities. Political considerations affect the timing of the extension of the infrastructure, so differences between formal and informal persist over time. Although not all informal housing has desirable structural or infrastructure standards, this sector has rapidly added to the stock.

Housing Cooperatives

Rent reductions in the sixties severely affected the supply of new rental housing for middle-income groups as the private rental sector virtually stopped new construction after the enforcement of the rent-control laws. Since the public sector lacked the resources to meet the housing needs of all income groups, the government instituted a cooperative housing program for those households that could afford their shelter in condominium-type units. Middle-income household savings were channeled into cooperative housing. The government provided subsidies for land development and reduced interest rates to aid this owner-occupancy sector as has been discussed earlier. The 1981 Housing Law continues to support cooperative activity through provision of loans and preferred allocation of building materials. In the 1983–1984 fiscal year, financing was provided at a 5 percent interest rate to cooperatives (and 6 percent to individuals) for a fifteen-year maturity period. Total government financing had reached U.S. $214.3 million by 1984 (Rageh 1984).

Cooperative housing exists primarily in urban areas of most of the governorates. Condominiums were built on large subdivisions, for example, in Madinat Al-Awqaf and Al-Mohandissin in Cairo. In smaller towns the cooperative program favored intermediate-sized subdivisions. Cooperative membership was largely drawn from the professional classes. While originally the program was restricted to owner occupancy, currently furnished rental units are available in cooperative housing since furnished apartments are not subject to rent control laws.

MAJOR PROBLEMS

Egypt's housing problems result from factors that are common in Third World countries—rapid population increase, internal migration from rural to urban areas, a large low-income population, inadequate investment in the physical infrastructure, rapid escalation in land and building materials costs, and the deterioration of the existing housing stock. We can broadly classify Egypt's housing problem into five subclasses: an increasing housing deficit that is not keeping pace with the rapid population growth in urban areas; the resulting high density of occupancy and poor environmental amenities, particularly for low-income groups; the high cost of developing land for housing in arid areas; the rapid proliferation of informal, illegal housing on scarce agricultural land; and an affordability crisis caused by an increasing gap between the cost of and a household's ability to pay for housing. Since many of these issues have already been discussed in this chapter, in this section three additional issues—land development, housing affordability, and housing finance are discussed.

The population of Egypt is concentrated in an area that occupies 4 percent of the country. The remaining 96 percent of the country of approximately 1 million square kilometers is composed of sandy and rocky deserts. Consequently, there is a competition between urban and rural activities for use of the scarce nondesert land where water is easily available for human use. A fundamental problem, then, is the rational and optimal allocation of scarce land between the built environment and agricultural uses. Since housing accounts for 60 percent of the built environment, housing development is inextricably tied to the overall land development policy issue. It has been noted earlier that the government has emphasized land development in the desert and has channeled impressive amounts to that end. However, only a small majority of households have been attracted to the new towns, and the pressure on existing urban areas continues to mount. Inflation in land prices is a very serious problem.

Residential land prices increased from $4.70 to $9.20 per square meter in the late sixties, \$15.30 to \$25.60 per square meter in the seventies, to \$42.90 to \$371.40 per square meter in the early eighties in the Cairo metropolitan areas (Dames and Moore 1981). It was common to find land prices that have increased at compound annual rates of 25–40 percent in Cairo in the 1970–1980 period. Land at Nasser City that sold in 1973 for \$12.80 per square meter increased to \$142.90 per square meter in the early eighties. Such rapid rates of inflation in fringe areas have fueled land speculation and the conversion of agricultural land to urban uses. To dampen these rates the government instituted a vacant land tax of 2 percent of appraised value. However, this tax has not been very effective due to the creation of intermediary "contractors" who buy up agricultural land and subdivide them into small building lots in anticipation of future urban development. A substantial amount of erstwhile productive agricultural land is lying fallow and cannot be reconverted to agricultural use due to this fragmentation.

A 1973 law forbade conversion of agricultural land, and it was strengthened in 1979. These laws, which made agricultural land conversion a criminal offense subject to a jail sentence, have failed to stop the process. For example, LANDSAT satellite imagery showed that between 1972 and 1978 urban land use increased in the rural governorate of Qalyubiya by 25 percent and agricultural land decreased by 10 percent (Dames and Moore 1981).

Costs of building materials and labor have increased at annual rates of 15–20 percent, at rates higher than the general price index. The resulting increase in total housing costs has significantly contributed to an affordability problem in Egypt. Although there is considerable wealth in Egypt, the average annual family income in 1982 was \$1,343.00. Even if 25 percent of the income could be devoted to housing, the average family would be able to afford 17 square meters of space, which is about 3.7 square meters per capita. This is a low space-consumption standard by U.N. requirements. Given the distribution of household incomes, a housing unit of 40 square meters could not be afforded by 60 percent of Cairo households (Rageh 1984). Much of the housing problem stems from this affordability crisis that results from a combination of low incomes and rapid inflation in land and housing costs. A very dramatic expression of this affordability problem is the colonizing by low-income households of the necropolis in Cairo. Anywhere from 200,000 to 500,000 live in the area of old graves in what is often colloquially termed the City of the Dead.

The affordability problem causes poor environmental conditions as well. Parsons, Brinckerhoff, and Sabbour (1981, 52) noted that the expansion areas lack sewerage facilities and that a majority of households in such sections use holding tanks. Holding tanks are drained occasionally, and it is common to find excess sewage spillage on the streets. The animal-drawn draining carts often empty the raw sewage into canals and open ditches with serious negative health implications. Similar problems exist in the solid-waste-collection sector. Private sector garbage collectors—the zabalin—prefer to service higher-income dwelling units due to the higher value of waste materials generated by the upper-income households. Although the recycling of such waste provides some income to the *zabalin*, low-income household waste has little or no recyclable value. Poor areas are not serviced, leading to garbage pileups on streets and vacant lots.

Various efforts have been made to facilitate the production of affordable housing for low-income groups. Most well known among them is the Ismalia Demonstration Project at Hai el Salam and Abu Atwa, started in 1977 (Davidson 1981; Culpin, Clifford, and Partners 1982; Blunt 1982). These projects made a concerted effort to provide unsubsidized, yet affordable housing to a range of low- and moderate-income groups, including the very poor. They sought to do this by offering a wide range of plot sizes and utility-service levels, combined with user control over plot development. F. Davidson (1984) and G. Payne (1985) documented the discrepancy between plan and reality. Approximately 75 percent of all low-income plots were not available to the poor and captured by middle-income groups. In evaluating the several reasons that explained this behavior they noted the influence of politicians, planners, and aid agencies. The reader is referred to the several insightful analyses that highlight the problems of delivering affordable housing to the poor. Jan Rowland's (1985) documentation of the Kabutti upgrading project in Port Said provides additional information about the constraints surrounding the provision of affordable housing to the poor that result from value positions, attitudes, and rigidities of central government planners and ministry officials.

The housing sector would be more capable of meeting the unsatisfied demand for units if households could have access to long-term financing. However, the housing finance system is still in a rudimentary form relative to need. Although there are various institutions, as discussed earlier, there is a poor mobilization of funds from households. The financing institutions depend on governmental allocations and thus there is limited availability of funds. There is also the problem of a lack of a strong secondary market to provide liquidity. Clearly, the liquidity constraints have limited the ability of institutions to provide funds to the housing sector. The reader is referred to several USAID funded studies that have dealt exhaustively with the complex issues surrounding the strengthening of the currently weak housing finance sector and the mobilization of savings from households (USAID 1977b, USAID 1981; Richard Pratt Associates 1979).

PROSPECTIVE DEVELOPMENTS

Egypt's population is expected to grow from 41 million in 1980 to 70 million by the year 2000 (PADCO 1982). Of this, 37 million are expected to be urban— 16 million in Cairo alone. Without innovative measures such population pressures can only lead to acute housing problems that have not only economic but also severe political ramifications. In recognition of this the government has focused once again on housing. A first step is the estimation of housing needs, with a specification of targets against which performance can be evaluated. The Ministry of Housing estimates an additional need for 3.6 million housing units in the

Table 15.4
National Housing Plan, Egypt, 1981–1985

Year	Number of Units (x 1,000)	Average Cost Per Unit	Total Cost (in millions)
1981	110	4,956	636
1982	125	5,123	723
1983	135	5,264	780
1984	145	5,362	828
1985	160	5,446	924

Source: Ettouney, 1984, table 2.
Note: Cost converted to U.S. dollars.

Table 15.5
Housing Plan: Distribution of Units, Egypt, 1981

Housing Class	Number of Units (000)	Percent of Stock	Average Area (sq. m.)	Average Unit Cost
Economic	60.5	45	45-50	2,827
Middle	40.7	37	70-80	5,574
Upper Middle	8.8	8	100-120	9,600
Total	110.0			4,956

Source: Ettouney, 1984, table 3.
Note: Cost in U.S. dollars.

1984–1999 period. However, estimates of need vary greatly since they depend on different accounting formulas and projections of growth. The Shura Council puts its fifteen-year estimate of needs at 4.4 million units (Economist Intelligence Unit 1985).

The National Housing Plan specified a one-year urgent plan (1979–1980), a five-year plan (1981–1985), to be followed by additional five-year plans to meet the 3.6 million dwelling units estimated to be required by the year 2000. The target for the increase of urban housing in the 1982/1983–1986/1987 plan is 800,000 new units with an escalating rate of construction during the plan years. It calls for the construction of 185,000 units in the final year of the plan. (Selected information on plan targets for each of the plan years is shown in table 15.4. In table 15.5 the planned distribution of the dwelling units between the various socioeconomic groups for 1981 is shown.) Although an emphasis has been placed on low income groups, the estimated cost of the dwelling units suggests that the units are unlikely to be accessed by low-income groups. Perhaps moderate- and middle-income groups will benefit as in the case of the Ismalia Demonstration Project. These two tables also provide some information on expected costs. Total expenditures on housing and related utilities (including infrastructure) are expected to be an average of U.S. $2.1 billion a year, and total building and construction activity is expected to yield a gross output of U.S. $23.2 billion over the total plan period. These statistics, as noted earlier, do not take into account the much larger, unauthorized informal sector housing construction.

A second step lies in the development of an integrated set of policies that can help in the meeting of the targets. These policies have to be designed for various components of housing, since housing is a complex good that is produced and allocated through the interaction of several markets—land, building materials, credit, and labor. Inefficiencies and bottlenecks in any of these markets can lead to a glaring gap between the rhetoric of planning and the implementation of targets. Policy issues pertaining to the credit, land, and building materials market have already been alluded to, and no attempt is made to repeat them in this section. However, labor-market policies also have to be addressed. For example, a primary cause of inflation in housing prices has been the outmigration of skilled construction workers to the Gulf countries. This has had several negative effects. Higher-skill workers have been lost; the wages of all domestic construction workers have inflated rapidly, thereby increasing the cost of housing; the repatriation of funds has inflated land costs and encouraged agricultural land conversion to urban uses; and the growth of the concomitant informal sector has imposed severe burdens on planning and service-delivery agencies.

Fresh attempts have to be made to deal with these complex and interrelated issues. It has been noted in this chapter that in recent years both private and public sector investment in housing and the rate of housing production has increased rapidly. Although efficiency gains have been made, the situation for low-income groups has worsened with the move toward a less-controlled housing system. The government is trying to address this problem, and a 1981 Housing Law specifies that two-thirds of the 15 percent of the profits of public sector companies should be channeled for the construction of worker and low-income housing.

The need to develop land for housing is an acute necessity from a social welfare perspective. Since 1973 land prices have increased by 500 percent in the country as a whole, and this has put an enormous pressure on agricultural land since the easiest land to develop for informal housing is the agricultural land. There is no evidence that the prohibitive laws are working. In Egypt, as a whole, there is an annual loss of 60,000 *feddans* or 1 percent of the national agricultural land (Dames and Moore 1981). Direct losses to housing and the infrastructure are augmented by indirect losses to speculative transfers of ownership and laying fallow productive land. Steps have to be taken to protect existing agricultural land. Negative instruments such as defensive laws, regulations, fines (that is, the use of the police powers of the state) are not likely to stem the destruction of agricultural land. Although there is a political commitment toward the preservation of agricultural land, the only feasible management approach is to channel the energies of the informal sector toward nonagricultural, urbanized land.

Clearly, the enormous expenditures made in creating new towns in the desert such as the Tenth of Ramadan failed to meet the objectives of drawing population away from the metropolises. The government's satellite town program such as in Al Abour is a policy change that has much greater potentials. The past experience of Heliopolis, Maadi, and Nasser City provide some evidence of the success of land and housing development in proximity to the major urban centers. There is some hope in this change in tactic to meet the dual needs of agricultural land preservation and increase of urban housing supply.

An aggressive public housing program is required for the very poor; however, there is currently less political support for this. Experience with the Ismalia demonstration project clearly shows that community upgrading and the development of projects such as Abu Atwa are likely to be more appropriate for the moderate-income groups. Yet these self-help solutions are popular with the government, given the current emphasis on the mobilization of the private sector initiatives for housing supply. Although the upgrading and sites-and-services strategy will not address the needs of the very poor, who lack even minimal resources to help themselves, it can help a sizeable majority of moderate income households who can and do generate savings and are operating in the incremental housing-construction sector.

There is much that needs to be done to improve the efficiency and equity aspects of housing in Egypt. As a relatively low-income country, with depressed oil prices, there are real resource and feasibility constraints. However, planners have choices—the limited resources of the housing sector can be channeled to expensive, large projects that benefit the wealthy, or they can be used to ensure the delivery of adequate housing and the meeting of basic needs of the poor. The future depends on the political will to tackle the problems of housing outlined in this chapter.

REFERENCES

Abt Associates. 1982. *Informal Housing in Egypt*. Cairo: United States Agency for International Development.

Ambar, A. 1984. "Cairo: 1800–2000." In *The Expanding Metropolis*, 91–120. Proceedings of seminar held in Cairo. Singapore: Concept Media.

Blunt, A. 1982. "Ismalia Sites and Services and Upgrading Projects: A Preliminary Evaluation." *Habitat International* 6, nos. 5–6: 587–97.

Central Agency for Public Mobilisation and Statistics. 1976. *Census of Buildings and Dwelling Units in Urban Towns*. Cairo: A.R.E. Government Printing Office.

Cooper, Mark. 1982. *The Transformation of Egypt*. Baltimore: Johns Hopkins University Press.

Culpin, Clifford, and Partners. 1982. *Ismalia Demonstration Project*. Final Report. Vol. 1. London.

Dames and Moore. 1981. *Cairo Metropolitan Area Land-Use and Infrastructure Development Study*. Cairo: USAID.

Davidson, F. 1981. "Ismalia: From Master Plan to Implementation." *Third World Planning Review* 3, no. 2: 161–78.

———. 1984. "Ismalia: Combined Upgrading and Sites and Services Project in Egypt." In *Low-Income Housing in the Developing World*, edited by G. K. Payne. London: Wiley.

Hinnebusch, R. 1985. "Political Participation and the Authoritarian Modernizing State in the Middle East—Activists in Syria and Egypt." *Journal of Arab Affairs* 3, no. 2: 131–55.

Economist Intelligence Unit. 1985. *Quarterly Economic Report, Supplement*. London.

El-Messiri, S. 1985. "The Squatters' Perspective of Housing: An Egyptian View." In *Housing Needs and Policy Approaches: Trends in Thirteen Countries*, edited by Willem Van Vliet—, Elizabeth Huttman, and Sylvia F. Fava, 376. Durham, N.C.: Duke University Press.

Ettouney, S. F. M. 1984. "Low-Income Families Housing: Note on Egypt's Experience." In *Low-Cost Housing for Developing Countries*, edited by Central Research Institute at Roorkee, vol. 2, 853–60. New Delhi: Sarita Prakashan.

General Organization for Housing, Building, and Planning Research. 1981. *Construction Industry Study*. Cairo: A.R.E. Government Printing Office. Appendix 8, The Informal Sector.

Hopwood, D. 1985. *Egypt: Politics and Society: 1945–84*. Boston: Allen & Unwin.

PADCO Inc. 1980. *The National Urban Policy Study: Working Paper on Urban Development Standards and Costs*. Cairo: A.R.E. Government Printing Office.

———. 1981. *National Urban Policy Study (NUPS): Cairo Concept Plan*. Cairo: Ministry of Development, A.R.E. Government Printing Office.

Parsons, Brinckerhoff, and Sabbour. 1981. *Basic Infrastructure for Provincial Cities*. Cairo: USAID.

Payne, G. 1985. "Ismalia Revisited: A Personal Assessment of the Hai El Salam and Abu Atwa Projects." *Open House International* 10, no. 3: 22–24.

Rageh. A. 1984. "The Changing Pattern of Housing in Cairo." In *The Expanding Metropolis*, 133–40. Aga Khan Seminar held in Cairo. Singapore: Concept Media.

Richard Pratt Associates. 1979. *Housing Finance in Egypt: Prospects for Development*. Cairo: USAID.

Rowland, Jon. 1985. "Kabbutti Upgrading Project, Port Said." *Open House International* 10, no. 3.15–21.

United Nations. 1986a. *Construction Statistics Yearbook, 1984*. New York.

———. 1986b. *Demographic Yearbook, 1983–84*. New York.

———. 1986c. *Statistical Yearbook, 1983–84*. New York.

———. 1987. *National Accounts Statistics, 1984*. New York.

USAID. 1977a. *Housing and Community Upgrading for Low-Income Egyptians*. Cairo: Joint Housing and Community Upgrading Team, Ministry of Housing and Reconstruction, A. R. E. and USAID.

———. 1977b. *Housing Finance in Egypt*. Report of the Joint Housing Team for Finance. Cairo: Ministry of Housing and Reconstruction, Ministry of Planning Arab Republic of Egypt with the Office of Housing.

———. 1981. *Housing Finance: An Analysis of Prospects for Increased Activity*. Cairo.

Wheaton, William C. 1981. "Housing Policies and Urban 'Markets' in Developing Countries: The Egyptian Experience." *Journal of Urban Economics* 9:242–56.

Wikkan, Unni. 1985. "Living Conditions among Cairo's Poor: A View from Below." *The Middle East Journal* 39, no. 1:7–26.

Wildeman, R. C. 1984. "Housing Finance in Urban Development." In *The Expanding Metropolis*, 195–99. Proceedings of seminar held in Cairo. Singapore: Concept Media.

FURTHER READING

Aga Khan Award for Architecture. In *The Expanding Metropolis: Coping with the Urban Growth of Cairo*, 238. Proceedings of seminar held in Cairo. Singapore: Concept Media, 1984.

Bayad, Mohsen A. "Housing and Urban Development in Egypt." Ph.D. dissertation, Stockholm, Royal Danish School of Architecture, 1979.

Central Agency for Public Mobilisation and Statistics. 1976. *The General Population and Housing Census*. Cairo: Arab Republic of Egypt Government Printing Office.

Chiri, Tayssir. "Housing in Egypt." *Open House International* 10, no. 3 (1985): 6–9.

Economic Commission of Africa. *Socio-Economic Indicators, 1984*. Addis Ababa, Ethiopia, 1986.

Hardoy, Jorge E., and David Satterthwaite. *Shelter: Need and Response. Housing, Land, and Settlement Policies in Seventeen Third World Nations*, sec. 1, 9–54. London: Wiley, 1981.

Ilbert, R. "Heliopolis: Colonial Enterprise and Town Planning Success?" In *The Expanding Metropolis*, 61–42. Proceedings of Aga Khan Award for Architecture held in Cairo. Singapore: Concept Media, 1984.

Ministry of Development. *New Towns for the Greater Cairo Urban Region*. Cairo: A.R.E. Government Printing Office, 1980.

Ministry of Housing. *Implementation Plan for the Upgrading Program, 1980–83*. Cairo: A.R.E. Government Printing Office, 1982.

———. *National Housing Policy*. Cairo: A. R. E. Government Printing Office, 1979.

Ministry of Planning. *Proposed Five Year Plan (1978–82): The Housing Sector*. Cairo: A.R.E. Government Printing Office, 1977.

Mohavenzadeh, F., L. Supria, and N. Chowchiri. *The Housing Construction Industry in Egypt*. Technology Adaptation Program Report 80–13. Cambridge, Mass.: MIT Press, 1980.

Neamatalla, Mounir. "Urban Service Delivery." In *The Expanding Metropolis*. Aga Khan seminar held in Cairo. Singapore: Concept Media, 1984.

Skinner, R. J., and M. J. Rodell, eds. *People, Poverty, and Shelter*. New York: Methuen, 1983.

Soliman, A. "Housing the Urban Poor in Egypt: A Critique of Present Policies." *International Journal of Urban and Regional Research* 12, no. 1 (1988):65–86.

Stewart, Roy. "The Development of the City of Suez." *Third World Planning Review* 3, no. 2 (1981):179–200.

Waterbury, John. *Cairo: Third World Metropolis—in Housing and Shelter*. American University Field Staff Report, part 2. Hanover, N.H., 1976.

Wikkan, Unni. *Life among the Poor in Cairo*. London: Tavistock, 1980.

Yinon, Oded. "The Significance of Egypt's Population Problem." *Middle Eastern Studies* 18 (1984): 378–86.

Ziegler, F., and H. Knikkink. "New Ameriyah City: Planning for Limited Public Control." *Open House International* 5, no. 3 (1980): 2–9.

16

Israel

NAOMI CARMON AND DANIEL CZAMANSKI

Israel is known in the world as the country of the *kibbutz*—a unique cooperative small settlement—and as a source of advanced agricultural technology. Actually, it is an urban society, with an interesting experience in urban planning of old and new cities. Ninety percent of its citizens live in urban areas, and only 7 percent live in cooperative villages. By the middle 1980s, most Israelis possessed decent homes. In rural areas the common types are one- and two-story buildings with one to four dwelling units. In urban places most residents live in multi-unit two- to four-story buildings. Considering that housing conditions were very poor when the state was established in 1948 and that the population has increased more than fivefold in the past forty years, the achievements of Israel's housing policy are noteworthy.

The purpose of this chapter is to describe and analyze the evolution of Israel's housing policy in a context of a continuing transformation from a centrally planned to an increasingly market-oriented economy. Based on this analysis, a few lessons are drawn from the Israeli experience that may be relevant to both developing and developed countries.

(Note: Wherever quantitative data are reported in this chapter without their sources, they are based on data of Israel's Central Bureau of Statistics, usually on its annual *Statistical Abstract*; see Central Bureau of Statistics, Various years.)

THE EVOLUTION OF HOUSING POLICIES

Housing policy in Israel has been aimed at two national-interest goals—immigrant absorption and population dispersal—and one private-interest goal—the provision of satisfactory housing to every household. Three periods can be distinguished in the evolution of Israel's housing policy, and different goals were emphasized in the various periods. In the early one the first two goals were dominant; the government and its institutions played a central role, and the production of new housing was very high. In the past decade the third goal has come to the forefront; the focus has turned from quantity to quality, and the government is retreating gradually from its deep involvement in the housing market.

1948–1964: Housing in the Service of National Goals

The state of Israel was born in 1948 with very serious housing problems. The population was composed of two major groups, a Jewish majority and an Arab minority. No statistical data are available about the housing conditions of Arabs in that early period, but the presumption is that conditions were very poor. A survey of Jewish households in 1946 found that the average density in city dwelling units exceeded three people per room (Carmon 1979).

The years 1948–1951 were a period of massive Jewish immigration to Israel; about 700,000 people arrived in these three years, and the Jewish population of

Israel doubled. Most immigrants, both those who survived the Nazi regime in Europe and those who were forced out from Middle Eastern and North African countries, were penniless refugees. The young state, while still fighting its Independence War, took upon itself the heavy task of providing a roof over their heads.

The first 100,000 immigrants were housed in abandoned British military barracks. When they were filled, the *Ma'abarot*—special transit camps—were erected. The construction material was light and of inferior quality: tents, cloth on wooden frames, tin sheets, and little shacks, all used to provide minimum shelter. In the collective memory of Israelis, the term *Ma'abarot* has had a negative association: very poor housing conditions that were planned to be used for a maximum of two to three years, but its remnants were part of the landscape for about twenty years. Looking back as planners, we can appreciate the endeavor; the *Ma'abarot* were part of an ambitious development plan. They were located in consideration of employment opportunities and needed services. There were three major types: those that were located near large cities, where some employment was available; those in agricultural districts, which later became *Moshavim*—cooperative small settlements; and those at points earmarked for new development towns. Moreover, from the outset, health, educational, and other social and public services were provided to the residents of the eighty-one *Ma'abarot*, scattered throughout the country toward the end of 1951.

When the 20.4 percent annual rate of population growth of the first three years dropped to the still high rate of 3.0–5.5 percent in 1952–1964, Israel stopped building transition camps and turned to its major enterprise of constructing ''hard'' housing. More than 500,000 units were built in this period, 70.0 percent by the central government and its institutions. Just one-quarter of this massive public building activity was aimed at improving the poor housing conditions of veteran citizens in the cities of Israel, while three-quarters were directed toward achieving the two major national goals: first, immigrant absorption, by providing a dwelling unit to each family of immigrants as soon as they arrived and by liquidation of the transit camps; second, population dispersal, by constructing new towns and new villages in the periphery of Israel. Sometimes considerations of immigrants' rapid integration into Israeli society were in conflict with the goal of population dispersal. When this happened, the government usually gave priority to the latter national-defense-related goal over the more individually oriented notions of socioeconomic integration (Cohen 1969; Van Vliet—1985).

Toward the end of the period only 4,000 households remained in transition camps, and one could count about 400 new small agricultural settlements (most of them cooperatives) and some 30 new development towns with modern housing, infrastructure, and services, most of them in the less-populated areas of the Galilee and the Negev. Almost all of them were planned and constructed first by the Department of Housing in the Ministry of Labour and since 1961 by the new Ministry of Housing.

1965–1976: Housing Policy in Transition

A few changes took place in the beginning of this period:

- A drop in immigration: during the early 1960s some 50,000 newcomers arrived each year. In 1965 the net migration balance was 23,000, followed by 8,300 in 1966 and reaching a low of 4,300 in 1967 (it increased thereafter).
- Economic slowdown: in the middle 1960s the economy of Israel experienced a recession with considerable unemployment, especially among construction workers.
- Public awareness of social gaps: for quite a few years Israeli society had succeeded in ignoring the correlation between socioeconomic status and ethnic origin in the Jewish population, but local demonstrations and writings by journalists as well as academics awakened public awareness.

The Ministry of Housing was traditionally a strong institution, and it fought against reduction of its resources, in spite of a reduction of needs. It continued with the construction of big quantities, even when a surplus of empty dwelling units was gradually growing, especially in the development towns. But in addition, the ministry searched for new missions. In response to the new circumstances, it established at first a few governmental-municipal companies for slum rehabilitation in the large cities and then a governmental Urban Renewal Authority (Alexander 1981). Allocating more resources to the veteran population and to older buildings was an important innovation of the 1960s.

In the early seventies, the governmental housing policy was criticized from various directions. It was accused of imposing an excessively heavy burden on the state budget, of causing a very rapid increase in the price of dwelling units (Borukhov and Pines 1976), and of creating discrepancies between demand and supply (Lerman 1976). The pressures caused the Ministry of Housing to change some of its policies. It still tried to build many units by itself, but part of its budget (a small part for the time being) was transferred from supporting the supply side to assisting the demand side. There was a partial transformation from subsidizing dwellings to subsidizing mortgages for eligible persons, initially for newly married couples only. A second important change was the new opportunity to receive a subsidy not only for purchasing a new publicly built apartment, but also for purchasing a privately built apartment, either new or old. The size of the subsidy was coordinated with the level of household need (by income and family size), but it was bigger and with less rigid eligibility criteria in the remote development areas compared to centrally located settlements.

A clear sign of the struggles regarding housing policy in this transitional period is found in the opinion statements that were commissioned by the Ministry of Housing from housing experts (Baruch 1969; Ben-Shachar 1974) and in the proceedings of the committees that were established to investigate the governmental housing policy (Avi Zohar 1976). Their conclusions supported and encouraged processes that were on the way anyhow: the reduction of direct involvement in the housing supply and an improvement in the assistance terms on the demand side, especially to low-income families.

1977–1989: From Government Control to Market Control

In the middle seventies, the real crisis in housing was over. Nearly every household had a dwelling unit for itself, and tenure was secure for most of them, by ownership (70 percent) and public tenancy (15 percent). The number of families in housing distress (dilapidated or overcrowded units) rapidly decreased and was estimated at 64,000 at the end of 1974 (Slijper 1977). At the same time social norms were changing, and the public widely expressed a preference for a higher standard of living and for less public involvement in various spheres of economic life. These changes became clear toward the end of the first long period (thirty years) of the regime of the Labor party but obtained full legitimacy and more rapid implementation when the right-wing parties of the Likud took over in 1977.

The share of newly built public housing dropped from about half to less than a quarter of the number of residential units built in the middle eighties. Although in the past, public housing meant units that were initiated, planned, and constructed directly by governmental bodies, the term is currently used when the initiative is public, while most of the planning and almost all of the actual construction is carried out by private companies with some financial support from the ministry. The Ministry of Construction and Housing still allocates a considerable part of its resources to supporting housing and services in areas to which the government gives higher priority, such as Jewish settlements in the West Bank that were fostered by the Likud government. But a higher percentage of housing investment is directed not to collective goals but rather to promoting individual welfare in the form of improved housing.

Some two-thirds of the public housing solutions (the ministry's term for the yearly number of dwelling units the construction or the renovation of which was supported by the Ministry of Construction and Housing) have been directed in recent years toward families in need. Most of them were either newly married couples or residents of distressed areas. Allocating considerable resources to poor veteran residents and to their children in their old homes and neighborhoods, instead of constructing new buildings for newcomers and for new development areas, is a new current trend in Israel's housing policy.

TRENDS IN HOUSING CONSTRUCTION AND CONDITIONS: 1948–1987

Housing-construction activity and housing conditions need to be viewed in the perspective of the unique rates of population and economic growth that Israel has experienced since its independence. As shown in table 16.1, there was a tremendous growth of population in the first few years of statehood, with high

Table 16.1
Growth of Population and Residential Construction, Israel, 1948–1987

| | Population | | Residential Construction | | | |
| | | | Dwelling Units | | Square Meters | |
Year	End of Period (x 1,000)	Yearly % of increase	Completed (x 1,000)	% Public	Completed (x 1,000)	% Public
1948	872					
1950-54	1,717	13.8	196	78	7,812	61
1955-59	2,089	4.3	130	82	9,247	54
1960-64	2,526	4.1	135	73	12,842	44
1965-69	2,930	3.2	152	46	13,044	34
1970-74	3,422	3.6	219	41	21,335	33
1975-79	3,836	2.3	220	45	21,835	34
1980-84	4,200	1.9	155	36	18,160	25
1985-87	4,331	1.6	68	22	8,960	15
Total			1,275*	45%	113,235	35%

Source: Central Bureau of Statistics, various years.
*Including about 50,000 temporary dwellings.

rates between 1955 and 1974 and low rates since 1975. The number of completed dwelling units was very high at the beginning, reflecting the urgent need to accommodate the biggest wave of immigrants. After fifteen years of lower numbers of added new units, record numbers were reached in the 1970s reflecting increased rates of immigration in the early 1970s and the improvement of economic conditions in a country that managed to triple its GNP in the first twenty years of its existence.

The area of completed new housing (the column of square meters in table 16.1) tells a somewhat different story. There were great fluctuations in the early seven years (not shown in the table), when very large quantities of small public housing units were constructed, followed by a steady growth of the housing industry, especially private building, with a peak in the middle 1970s (1972–1977) and back to a steady high number of square meters and a lower number of completed units in the early 1980s.

The picture for 1980–1984 requires special explanation. The Israeli inflation of the early 1980s was among the highest in the world; the GNP growth rate arrived at a complete stop, and population growth was very low. Nevertheless, investment in housing as expressed in additional square meters was much higher

Table 16.2

Growth in Gross National Product and Selected Housing Conditions, Israel, 1950–1985

| Year | GNP per Capita | | Average Square Meters of Completed New Dwelling | | | % Population Living | |
	1980 NIS[1] (x 1,000)	Average Annual Change	Total	Public	Private	3+ persons per room[2]	up to 1 person per room[2]
1950	7.70		32	28	50	n.a.	n.a.
1955	10.14	6.3%	56	45	75	n.a.	n.a.
1960	12.79	5.2	63	57	81	24	30[3]
1965	16.74	6.1	76	61	92	18	40[3]
1970	20.85	4.9	93	74	104	11	47
1975	25.48	4.4	92	73	110	8	53
1980	26.51	.08	108	80	120	4.4	59
1985	26.47	0	115	86	126	3.5	58[4]

Source: Central Bureau of Statistics, various years.

[1]U.S. $1.00 = 7.5 1980 NIS.

[2]Kitchen and bathroom are not counted as rooms.

[3]Estimate.

[4]The calculation was changed; had it been the former, the figure would have been about 6 percent higher.

compared to the 1960s, when both population and GNP were growing rapidly. This seems to reflect the economic fact of increased household affluence and the social norm that accords the dwelling unit high importance as the family nest and as a highly appreciated status symbol. It seems that the government's reduction of inflation from 400 to 20 percent a year in the mid–1980s has considerably suppressed the housing market, but it is too early to assess the new trends.

The share of public housing was about 80 percent of completed dwellings in the early years and dropped to about 20 percent in the late 1980s (table 16.1). If one looks at area rather than the number of dwellings, the share of private construction was not so small even in the 1950s. This means that even when government building captured most of the market, private companies dominated the market of larger apartments. In addition to the big differences in size, there has been a difference in the geographical dispersal of private and public construction. Throughout the years, some 65 percent of the private units were built in the districts of Tel Aviv and central Israel, another 20–25 percent in the cities of Jerusalem and Haifa, and only 10–15 percent in the rest of the country. As for public construction, 60 percent was concentrated in the above-mentioned urban areas, and 40 percent was scattered in the northern and southern districts, in which there was almost no privately built housing.

Housing conditions in Israel have changed dramatically over the years. This is clearly illustrated (table 16.2) by the average size of a completed new dwelling which increased almost fourfold in thirty-five years. In these years the average household size in Israel decreased from 4.0 to 3.6, and the combination of smaller households and far bigger apartments is expressed in the density rates. At present, nearly 60 percent of the population live in spacious living conditions of as low as one person per room or less (kitchens and bathrooms are not counted as rooms), and only 3.5 percent live in what was defined as overcrowded conditions—three or more persons per room. Whereas in the mid–1950s, 10 percent had no running water in their dwellings and 20 percent had no electricity, today there is a universal service in these categories. Basic home appliances were missing in many homes of the 1950s: some 70 percent did not have a refrigerator and a similar percentage did not have a modern stove. In 1985 nearly every household was equipped with both a refrigerator and a stove; 90 percent had televisions, and 70 percent had telephones.

There are few data available about the differences in housing conditions between socioeconomic groups. The little that is known is that homelessness is negligible and that very close to every home is of hard construction with all of the basic amenities, but there are big differences in the construction quality and in living space between the various groups. Compared to other countries, Israel has a high percentage of low-income families who own the dwelling units they live in. According to data from the two recent general censuses of Israeli population, 45 percent of the households in the eighty-four distressed urban neighborhoods of Project Renewal owned their dwellings in 1972 and 54 percent in 1983. The average density (persons per room) dropped in these years from 1.7 to 1.2 in the distressed neighborhoods, compared with 1.4 to 1.0 in the general population (Hovav and Ben-Yitzhak 1986). Hence the high involvement of the government of Israel in the housing market not only has enabled every household to have a shelter but also has reduced the disparities in housing conditions between residents of better-off and distressed neighborhoods and has decreased the high correlation between level of income and home ownership that is common in other countries.

THE ROLE OF HOUSING INSTITUTIONS

Initiative, Design, and Construction

Veteran cities in Israel are either a few thousand years old (Jerusalem, Nazareth) or the products of private construction activity in the beginning of the current century by settlers of modern Israel (Tel Aviv, Petach Tikva). But there are hundreds of new settlements, most of them small agricultural villages and some thirty new towns, that were initiated, designed, developed, and constructed by public authorities, that is, central government institutions. Israel is a centrally managed country with relatively little authority in the hands of local bodies, including municipalities. Thus local authorities have very little control over new public housing in their areas. But they have more control over the initiative and construction activities of the private sector that has actually dominated residential design and building in the central parts of the country, in city centers, and in their prestigious suburbs.

The differences in architectural design between public and private projects are not as visible in Israel as in many other countries. Israeli architecture followed European styles and standards, with less-than-optimal consideration of local climate and the various housing traditions that immigrants brought from all parts of the world. Rectangular boxes of two- to four-story walk-ups are the most common type of upper-middle to lower-class urban housing in the coastal strip as well as in mountain and desert regions.

In recent years, however, more attention has been paid to creating housing design sensitive to people (Carmi 1980; Gerstel 1980) and to planning "climate-conscious" buildings (Hassid et al. 1982, 1983). It is interesting to note that the public and not the private sector was usually the leading force in innovative design. In a typical scheme of an Israeli dwelling unit, full advantage is taken of every corner, and it is clearly divided into a public area with the relatively large open space of a living room connected to the entrance area, the kitchen and the dining space, and a private area of small, closed bedrooms. This design started appearing in public projects of the sixties and was gradually developed by private builders. Throughout the years, the Ministry of Housing has initiated many experimental housing projects, from Shikun Ledugma in Be'er Sheva and Kiryat Gat during the sixties to new neighborhoods in Jerusalem, and new towns for Arab bedouins in the seventies and eighties (Ministry of Construction and Housing 1980).

In the middle eighties a statement of the functions of the Ministry of Housing included the following (Israel Government 1986): directing and regulating residential housing construction in the country, preparing development plans for high-priority areas, designing and constructing settlements and neighborhoods by government decisions, advancing construction methods, and developing housing codes and eligibility criteria for housing assistance. This means that the ministry takes the overall responsibility for directing housing activities and is still somewhat involved in actual construction. However, the role of developers and building contractors has significantly increased since the middle seventies. Indeed, frequently they depend on governmental allocation of national land, and/or subsidized development costs, and/or intermediate financing by the ministry, and/or the ministry's commitment to purchasing a certain percentage of unsold units in development areas. But the governmental department of urban planning and design has been considerably reduced in recent years, and the number of construction workers who are paid by the government is a fraction of what it used to be. Another important change in the public construction activity is that whereas in the past it was directed solely by national goals, recently, it has been influenced by market considerations. Even the governmental implementation arm of the Housing and Development Company Ltd. has recently been evaluated by its profits (Hacohen 1987).

Finance

Israel invested a high percentage of its gross domestic product in housing construction: 13.7 percent in 1950, about 10 percent in most of the years between 1953 and 1980, and 5 percent in 1985. In the first years, these investments were divided almost equally between public and private financing, but gradually government financing was reduced to less than a quarter of the total investment in residential construction.

The big change in governmental financing policy was the partial transition from supporting the supply side to subsidizing the demand side through mortgages to eligible target populations. By the middle eighties, 95 percent of all mortgages were provided through the special mortgage banks, most of which are public companies whose shares are kept by the government, commercial banks, and the general public. The system has been very centralized, with four big mortgage banks keeping 85 percent of the assets (Gabriel 1985). The government-managed mortgages are given for twenty-five years with 5 percent real interest. They cover 20–50 percent of an average apartment unit's price (some $50,000 in Tel Aviv area) (Tel Aviv Municipality 1986, 215) and are allocated according to eligibility criteria determined by the level of need (income and size of family). About one-fifth of the mortgages are private, fully indexed, usually very limited in size (up to $10,000), and given ordinarily for no more than ten years at 7.5 to 12.5 percent interest. Recently, there have been signs of change in the mortgage market. Private banks negotiate mortgages for longer periods with lower interest rates, and a secondary mortgage market is being developed.

The government-directed mortgages are highly subsidized, because they are not fully indexed (a very important benefit in high-inflation conditions) and because of their low interest rate. About two-thirds of them go to households that do not own a dwelling unit, most of whom are either newly married couples or new immigrants. The other third goes to households that may own an apartment but are eligible for public assistance because of poor housing conditions or because they want to purchase a unit in a development region. Assistance is given to buy a unit of up to 85 square meters to a family with up to four members. Bigger families and households who settle in designated areas (distressed neighborhoods and development settlements) may purchase bigger units and still be helped by a subsidized mortgage. In addition to offering assistance in purchasing, the Ministry of Housing provides a small number of highly eligible households temporary housing allowances to pay rents in the free market. More common are publicly rented apartments in which the disadvantaged groups live, pay symbolic rents, and have secure tenure. The public holding companies, the budget of which comes almost solely from the Ministry of Housing, are surveyed in the next section.

Management

Seventy percent of Israel's citizens own their dwelling units. Only a small percentage occupy a single-family house, and the majority live in what is defined by Israeli law as "common houses," buildings with two to many units, each of which is privately owned while the common areas (stairways, yards, and so on) are commonly owned. The law requires each "common house" to have an elected building committee, the role of which is to care for current maintenance and to collect money for this purpose from all of the inhabitants. The result is that most common houses in Israel have been moderately maintained throughout the years. The level of maintenance has improved recently in many places, where awareness of "quality of life" has increased and where the semivoluntary Association for Housing Quality has provided technical consulting and access to loans in convenient terms to interested building committees.

More than half of the 30 percent of dwelling units that are not owner occupied are owned and managed by the public through the public holding companies: Amidar (with most of the property), Amigoor, and the governmental-municipal companies in the big cities. The residents—immigrants and low-income families in the development areas and in low-status city neighborhoods—pay very low rents, and several thousand ("welfare cases") pay no rent at all. Yet tenure is secured throughout a tenant's life, and there is no obligation to leave when income improves. Residents are encouraged to purchase their units for lower-than-market price with very convenient loans. Many of them have taken the opportunity, and thus the current number of publicly owned and managed apartments is about one-third of the number that had been transferred to the management of the public holding companies.

The market of control-free rental dwelling units is small, about 10 percent of the housing market. Most apartments are reasonably maintained by their landlord, but common leases are for short periods, a year or two. The relatively high rental fees require at least middle-class income to afford them.

Finally, a common housing arrangement in the older parts of several cities is renting for "key money." This historical arrangement (not available for apartments that were built after the mid–1950s) provides secure tenure for very low rent in return for a relatively high down payment, often paid decades ago by the tenant. It contributes to the poor maintenance of old buildings in the center of cities, especially in Tel Aviv, which has about half of this stock. Pressures from various sides are likely to bring a change of laws that will enable landlords to receive higher rents and pay for better maintenance.

Renovation and Rehabilitation

Most of the housing stock in which Israelis are living has been built in the past forty years. In spite of that, there is a great need for renovation and rehabilitation. There are three major reasons for this: the low quality of construction work, especially in the fifties when hundreds of thousands units were hastily built for newcomers to the new state; the low level of maintenance, especially of publicly rented apartments; and a very rapid increase in the standard of housing in the country. The construction of large and well-designed apartments in recent years has caused units that were built in the fifties and sixties to be considered inadequate and substandard.

Project Renewal, a national program for social and physical rehabilitation of distressed neighborhoods throughout the country, was started in 1976 and has been intensively active since 1979 (Carmon and Hill 1988). Ninety neighborhoods were gradually included in the project, in which some 15 percent of Israeli citizens reside. In 1987 the project was in a phasing-out stage in twenty neighborhoods, a dozen residential areas were added to the project, and other neighborhoods are waiting to be included. The housing side of Project Renewal, in which some 50 percent of its budget has been invested (the rest was allocated to social programs), is managed by the Ministry of Housing without involvement of private companies. Local decision making and implementation are administered by an appointee of the ministry, a neighborhood project manager, who works with a local steering committee that is composed of officials and area residents in equal numbers. The main housing programs are: the renovation of building exteriors and yards (beneficiaries: 50 percent of the households in the designated areas), partially by the public holding companies and partially through do-it-yourself renovation activities; encouraging residents to purchase the housing units they occupy on favorable terms (10 percent have taken the opportunity); interior renovation (15 percent); and a uniquely successful program of loans for housing enlargements in buildings of up to four stories (10 percent) (Carmon and Oxman 1986; Carmon and Gavrieli 1987).

Within the framework of Project Renewal special attention is given to the growing group of elderly residents. In a few neighborhoods, experimental "sheltered housing" can be found, that is, elderly households live in their own units that are part of a defined area providing special services for its residents, especially maintenance, health, and community services. In other neighborhoods a special old-age renovation standard was executed in apartments of the elderly in need.

The housing enlargement program of Project Renewal has had an important unintended outcome. Its visible success encouraged local authorities in many cities and towns to change previous attitudes and old local regulations and to encourage housing enlargements in nonproject neighborhoods. Thus a slow process by which small dwelling units are changed and renovated to be in line with housing standards of the Israel of the eighties is gradually developing. Low-income families are eligible for subsidized loans for this purpose, whereas higher-income households use their own resources.

CURRENT ISSUES

Affordability for Moderate-Income Households

Years ago, when the phenomenon of two to three households crowded into one dwelling was common, the major housing problem was housing availability. But by the middle 1980s, there was no evidence of homelessness in Israel, and the rate of shared occupancy was close to negligible. The number of housing units is now higher than the number of households, and there are vacant dwelling units in every town and city, especially in the development towns.

As described above, low-income households, especially the very low income group, usually have secured tenure for very low rent, and a few thousand do not have to pay at all. But there is a serious affordability problem for the upper-low and moderate-income groups who do not want to live in the development areas. The number of publicly rented units for these groups is declining, because tenants tend to purchase their old units from the public holding companies and because most of the new public housing in the nondevelopment areas is for sale and not for rent. There is just a small market of privately rented apartments, and most of these units can be rented only for short periods for relatively high rent (20–40 percent of average income). Most people want to buy their places of living, but prices are high—four to five times the average annual gross income of an urban employee's household (Goldman 1981)—and mortgages are small. There is a common norm of parents assisting their newly married children with purchasing their first dwelling place, but not all Israeli parents can afford it. The special difficulties of the low-moderate income groups were expressed in a survey of households' expenses of 1980, where the lowest quintile of nonworking households were found to pay 14 percent of their net income for housing, compared with 20 percent of the lowest quintile of employed workers and 13 percent of the upper quintile of the employed population (Central Bureau of Statistics 1983).

Improvement of Old Buildings

Of the housing units in Israel, 75 percent are either very old or built under the constraints of public housing and, therefore, have up to three small rooms (including a living room), a small kitchen, and a tiny washroom. In contrast, present housing standards are high: 70 percent of new, privately constructed units of the middle 1980s have at least four and frequently more rooms; rooms are much bigger with various kinds of modern amenities in a wide variety of building types. Hence a major current issue is the ability to improve the housing stock and to make it compatible with the new needs and desires of its residents.

This problem is socially and politically sensitive since a majority of occupants of the less-desirable housing are Jewish people of Asian and African origin. They constitute somewhat less than 50 percent of the Jewish population in Israel but some 80 percent of the population of distressed neighborhoods.

Organized housing renovation and the first experiments with housing enlargements started in the 1960s. Most were the result of individual initiative. The numbers grew throughout the 1970s, but housing enlargements were still limited to one- and two-story buildings, that is, where the physical construction and the organizational dilemmas were relatively easy to handle (Carmon and Oxman 1986). It was not until the 1980s that Project Renewal (see above) provided hard evidence that renovation and large expansions are possible physically, organizationally, and economically not only in low-rise but also in the most common type of buildings in Israel, the three- and four-story walk-ups with multiple entrances (Weinberg 1986). In various places there are the beginnings of a "movement" of housing enlargements (Lamdoon 1988). Most enlargers belong to the modest to lower-middle income groups and live in what was constructed as public housing. A large part of the investments in these improvements is private, but there are places where public assistance is needed in the form of cutting red tape, community work, or subsidized loans. Providing such assistance increases the chances of avoiding physical and social deterioration of neighborhoods with inferior housing stock, but it is seldom provided outside Project Renewal areas.

Housing for Arab Citizens

The percentage of Arab citizens in Israel (1967 borders, that is, exclusive of the West Bank and Gaza Strip) has increased from 12 percent in 1950 to 18 percent in 1985. There are big differences between the housing conditions of Arabs in Israel, compared to the Jewish population. Whereas 60 percent of the Jews live in urban areas of more than 50,000 persons and another 20 percent in towns of 20,000–49,999 persons, the comparable rates for Arabs are 22 percent and 15 percent respectively. Whereas a majority of the first group live in multi-unit buildings and somewhat fewer than 70 percent own their dwellings, a majority of the second group live in single-family houses and some 80 percent own their places. From these points of view the Arabs have advantages over the Jewish population, but since their average family size is much higher—6.14 compared with 3.35 (1984)—they are disadvantaged from the point of view of housing density: 2.12 persons per room among Arabs compared with 1.09 average density among Jews (1984). Hence, high density is still an unsolved issue in the Arab sector. Other major housing hardships have almost disappeared; in the early 1960s only half of the Arab households had a toilet in their homes, but in the early 1980s more than 90 percent had at least one toilet, and 98 percent had not only running water but also hot water for bathing in their dwellings.

At present, the most aggravating housing problem in Arab villages and small towns in which most Israeli Arabs live is lack of adequate land on which to build a desirable, traditional type of house. One way of solving the problem would be to enlarge the area where housing construction is permitted in these settlements. An alternative solution would be to give up some of the traditional norms by selling family land to nonfamily members or to accept modern housing arrangements, that is, to accept three- and four-story buildings and agree to live with other families in the same building.

In the mixed Jewish-Arab cities there are many mixed neighborhoods, but on the whole, the two groups tend to live separately, each in its own residential area. Frequently, Arabs suffer from discrimination when they try to enter the Jewish housing market. Discrimination is felt also in lower standards of maintenance in Arab neighborhoods and in fewer governmental housing programs for them. In the mid–1980s some eligibility criteria for housing loans were changed to ease the way for Arabs, but government treatment still differs by religion.

Market Efficiency

The extent of housing-market efficiency is discernible through the speed with which demand and supply are matched. A common test of efficiency requires comparing actual rates of return on housing assets with rates that would be expected in an efficient market, whereas the nature of real estate market data causes researchers to accept the assumption that expected returns are constant over time (Guntermann and Smith 1987). However, available data and research findings in Israel do not enable any such efficiency evaluations.

Therefore, we use the rate of housing vacancies as an indicator of market efficiency. The average vacancy rate in Israel (1983) was 9 percent, with big differences among the various places. According to Aliza Haber-Fisch (1985), the smaller the settlement, the higher the vacancy rate, and the more active the government in the housing market in a certain settlement, the larger the rate of vacancies in it. In the cities of Jerusalem, Tel Aviv, and Haifa, there were no more than 6–8 percent vacant units, whereas in two remote development towns the rates were 43 and 47 percent, and there were ten small development towns with 20–33 percent vacancies. Hence the government seems to have made many "inefficient" housing decisions. But several government officials argue that building new and improved subsidized housing for citizens of these development towns is the only way to attract them and convince them to stay in these settlements rather than move to more central places. If this is so, it may be considered as a conflict between the goal of maximizing profit on investments and the national goal of population dispersal. The question still remains whether population dispersal could not be promoted through more efficient means.

The same question applies to the ways of promoting immigrant absorption through housing provision. Israel is proud of its achievements in supplying adequate housing to the big waves of immigrants that reached it, mainly by means of government construction. But there has been no systematic evaluation of the efficiency of this government activity (such as the one suggested by Raymond Struyk and John Tuccillo [1983]). The current retreat of the government from the housing market is related more to the ideological approach of reducing collective intervention in private decisions than to a rigorous analysis of costs and benefits.

Another aspect of the efficiency of Israel's housing market involves the technical aspects of the housing industry. This is still a traditional and labor-intensive industry that has barely adopted standard prefabricated production methods. One of the consequences is an average long building duration that has been about twenty months per dwelling in the recent decade. In addition, only limited efforts have been devoted to designing houses in accordance with local climate and energy-saving requirements. The only exception is solar waterheaters, which can be seen on the roof of almost every house in Israel.

Compatibility of Housing Policies

The above-mentioned conflict between efficiency of the housing market and the decision to build many dwelling units in the development towns is one example of the dilemma of compatibility of policies. Another very important conflict is between new construction of apartments and rehabilitation of old urban areas. As Katherine Bradbury, Anthony Downs, and Kenneth Small (1981, 1982) clearly showed for the urban United States, the construction of new, improved housing units in numbers that exceed the increase in households is a major cause of deterioration and abandonment of old neighborhoods. This is true for Israel as well. The pressure of the housing industry to continue high rates of residential construction in spite of very slow population growth contradicts the policy of revitalization of old neighborhoods (Carmon 1987).

For many years urban areas in Israel suffered from the inability of public and social services to keep pace with the rapid development of residential construction. In recent years, however, this incompatibility problem is in a process of being solved in the Jewish sector. In most new housing projects services are constructed simultaneously with the dwelling units, and in older areas Project Renewal has contributed to the completion of missing municipal and community services. In the Arab sector, which is rapidly growing, their problem has not yet been solved.

REVIEW AND CONCLUSION

Housing policy in Israel has been aimed at three goals: immigrant absorption, population dispersal, and the provision of adequate housing to every household. In the early years of the state, in the 1950s and 1960s, the government built most of the new dwelling units and directed most of its investments toward achievement of the first two goals. The management of housing policy, like the management of the country in general, had a strong socialistic character. The Ministry of Housing functioned in a manner more similar to its counterparts in Communist countries than to the ones in the free Western world. It was a tool for realizing national goals, with little concern for private needs and preferences.

The results were impressive not only physically but also socially. Social integration of Jewish people from more than a hundred countries was advanced through housing arrangements. People from different origins found themselves living together in a public housing project, going to the same supermarket and medical clinic, and sending their children to the same school. It was not an easy transition; lessons were slowly learned from experience (Carmon and Mannheim 1979), and Israel is still far from solving its social-integration problems. But research-based evaluations and predictions in the 1980s are more optimistic than those of ten to twenty years ago (Peres 1983), and some of the progress can be attributed to socially integrated housing.

After basic needs were met, after every immigrant had an apartment, and after thirty new towns and a few hundred villages were constructed, housing policy gradually acquired a market orientation. This happened in the last years of the socialistic government and was pushed ahead in the late 1970s and early 1980s under governments of the Right. In recent years, the government has supported residential construction in preferred regions, but most housing activity is now directed by profit considerations.

The exaggerated stimuli and responses that were part of Israel's forty-year history, especially the fivefold increase in the size of population, represent an interesting laboratory for examining the making of modern housing policy in developing and newly developed countries. The way we interpret the facts is that the success in solving the most acute problems and in achieving a dramatic improvement in the housing conditions of all citizens is attributable—to a large extent—to the extensive government involvement in the housing market during the early years. In those years, despite the wars and the economic difficulties, housing had high priority in the allocation of publicly managed finance and manpower. Later, the success enabled a continuous withdrawal of the government from the housing market. It seems that the fine tuning that is required now in the matching of demand and supply may be best achieved by the private sector. This sequence of housing policies may be relevant to many countries with severe housing problems.

Hence in the big debate regarding privatization of the housing sector in developing countries (Sanyal 1986), our experience supports a mixed approach. Governmental involvement seems to be critical in assisting the first stages of mass construction for low-income households, but this does not mean that public agencies should continue to control the units and the areas that were assisted by them. On the contrary, once the residents are there, every effort should be made to privatize the continuous housing process.

Another lesson that our analysis of Israel's housing policy may suggest is to take into consideration the high social and economic costs of a rapid improvement in housing standards. When considerable improvement becomes common in one group of a society, its very existence makes the housing of other groups inadequate and substandard. This will cause feelings of relative deprivation and social unrest, unless large investments are directed toward rebalancing the living conditions.

Is such rebalancing possible when we deal with heavy and naturally inflexible goods like housing? Our analysis shows a few directions for providing a positive answer. For the weaker strata of society, public intervention is required, and Israel's Project Renewal for social and physical rehabilitation of distressed neighborhoods is a good example of what can be done on time, that is, before deterioration reaches a point of no return. For many of the residents of the distressed residential areas, and certainly for people with more economic capability, the name of the game is private ownership and permissive building permits. Home is such an important asset and status symbol in modern societies that households will do a lot to improve it with their own resources, once they are given the chance. Hence encouraging self-help housing improvement by incumbent residents seems to be the best road to both preventing urban decline and increasing the stock of decent housing.

The era of high demand for new housing is almost over in most developed countries. The challenge for the future is making the currently big stock adaptable to the new emerging needs and changing preferences of its residents. One more lesson to be drawn from the Israeli experience is that not only can the interior of old residential buildings be adapted but also many of them can be externally changed and considerably expanded to compensate for low standards of the past.

REFERENCES

Alexander, Ernst. 1981. *Neighborhood Renewal in Israel: History and Context.* Working Paper. Haifa: Technion, S. Neaman Institute.

Avi Zohar, Meir. 1976. *The Report of the Committee for Determining Criteria for Housing Assistance* (in Hebrew). Jerusalem: The Ministry of Construction and Housing.

Baruch, Nisim. 1969. *Criteria for Supporting Public Housing* (in Hebrew). Jerusalem: Consulting and Research Company.

Ben-Shachar, Haim. 1974. *The Policy of Housing Subsidies in Israel* (in Hebrew). Ramat Gan: The Institute for Information.

Borukhov, Eliahu, and David Pines. 1976. *A Quantitative Evaluation of the Factors in Rising Dwelling Prices in Israel* (in Hebrew). Tel Aviv: Tel Aviv University, Department of Economics.

Bradbury, Katherine L., Anthony Downs, and Kenneth A. Small. 1981. *Futures for a Declining City: Simulations for the Cleveland Area.* New York: Academic Press.

———. 1982. *Urban Decline and the Future of American Cities.* Washington D.C.: The Brookings Institute.

Carmi, Ram. 1980. "Human Values in Urban Architecture." In *Israel Builds, 1977,* 3d ed., 31–44. Jerusalem: Ministry of Construction and Housing.

Carmon, Naomi. 1979. "Neighborhood Policy: The Israeli Experience." In *Neighborhood Rehabilitation in Israel*, edited by Naomi Carmon and Moshe Hill, 91–113. Research Report. Haifa: Technion, S. Neaman Institute.

———. 1987. "The Current Depression in Housing Construction: A Desirable State" (in Hebrew). *The Economic Quarterly* 38, no. 132:61–66.

Carmon, Naomi, and Tamar Gavrieli. 1987. "Improving Housing by Conventional versus Self-Help Methods: Evidence from Israel." *Urban Studies* 24, no. 4:324–34.

Carmon, Naomi, and Moshe Hill. 1988. "Neighborhood Rehabilitation without Relocation or Gentrification." *Journal of the American Planning Association* 54(4):470–81.

Carmon, Naomi, and Bilho Mannheim. 1979. "Housing Policy as a Tool of Social Policy." *Social Forces* 58, no. 1:336–51.

Carmon, Naomi, and Robert Oxman. 1986. "Responsive Public Housing: An Alternative for Low-Income Families." *Environment and Behavior* 18, no. 2:258–84.

Central Bureau of Statistics. Various years. *Statistical Abstract of Israel*. Jerusalem: Hamakor Press. Annual.

———. 1983. *Family Expenditure Survey, 1979–80*. Part B. Special Series No. 711. Jerusalem.

Cohen, Erik. 1969. "Population Dispersal and Social Integration as Conflicting Goals" (in Hebrew). In *Mizug Galuyot*. Proceedings of a conference at the Hebrew University, 143–57. Jerusalem: Magnes Press.

Gabriel, Stuart. 1985. "Housing Policy in Israel" (in Hebrew). In *Resource Allocation for Social Services*, edited by Yaakov Kop. Jerusalem: Center for Social Policy Studies in Israel.

Gerstel, L. 1980. "Planning for Man in Movement in an Urban System." In *Israel Builds, 1977*, 3d ed., 67–72. Jerusalem: Ministry of Construction and Housing.

Goldman, Morris, ed. 1981. *Society in Israel, 1980: Statistical Highlights*. Jerusalem: Central Bureau of Statistics.

Guntermann, Karl L., and Richard L. Smith. 1987. "Efficiency of the Market for Residential Real Estate." *Land Economics* 63, no. 1:34–43.

Haber-Fisch, Aliza. 1985. *Jewish Urban Settlements, 1972–1983* (in Hebrew). Jerusalem: Ministry of Construction and Housing.

Hacohen, Orly. 1987. *Housing Institutions in Israel*. Working Paper. Haifa: Technion, Faculty of Architecture and Town Planning.

Hassid Shmuel, Michael Poreh, Dan Even-Or, and Daniel Wegner. 1982, 1983. *Energy Conserving Buildings Project*. Research Reports. Haifa: Technion-Israel Institute of Technology, Building Research Station.

Hovav, Hagit, and Yehuda Ben-Yitzhak. 1986. *Changes in the Population of Project Renewal in Light of the General Census of 1972 and 1983* (in Hebrew). Jerusalem: Ministry of Construction and Housing, Team for Social Policy.

Israel Government. 1986. *Government Year Book*. Jerusalem.

Lamdoon, Alex. 1988. *Flexible Housing: Expansion of Dwelling Units in Multistorey Buildings*. Master's thesis. Haifa: Technion, Faculty of Architecture and Town Planning.

Lerman, Robert. 1976. *A Critical Overview of Israeli Housing Policy*. Jerusalem: Brookdale Institute.

Ministry of Construction and Housing. 1980. *Israel Builds, 1977*, 3d ed. Jerusalem.

Peres, Yochanan. 1983. "Why Is It Difficult to Cope with Inter-Ethnic Relationships in

Israel?'' In *On the Difficulty of Being an Israeli*, edited by Alouph Hareven. Jerusalem: Van Leer Foundation.

Sanyal, Bishwapriya. 1986. ''Learning before Doing: A Critical Evaluation of the Privatization Concept in Shelter Policies of International Institutions.'' *Open House International* 2, no. 4:13–21.

Slijper, Joseph. 1977. ''Housing Distress in Israel'' (in Hebrew). *Social Security* 12–13:163–73.

Struyk, Raymond J., and John A. Tuccillo. 1983. ''Defining the Federal Role in Housing: Back to Basics.'' *Journal of Urban Economics* 14:206–23.

Tel Aviv Municipality. 1986. *Statistical Yearbook*. Tel Aviv: Center for Economic and Social Research.

Van Vliet—, Willem. 1985. ''Housing Policy as a Planning Tool.'' *Urban Studies* 22, no. 2:105–17.

Weinberg, Ariela. 1986. *Housing Enlargement in Multi-Unit Residential Buildings with Project Renewal Assistance*. Master's thesis. Haifa: Technion, Faculty of Architecture and Town Planning.

FURTHER READING

Darin, Dan. ''The Evolution of the Urban Land Lease System in Israel.'' *Habitat Intl.* 11, no. 1 (1987):83–95.

Ginsberg, Y., and R. W. Marans. ''Social Mix in Housing: Does Ethnicity Make a Difference?'' *Journal of Ethnic Studies* 7, no. 3 (1979):101–12.

Lithwick, Irwin. *Macro and Micro Housing Programs in Israel*. Discussion paper D–47–80, Brookdale Institute/Joint Distribution Committee, Jerusalem, 1980.

Meyer-Brodnitz, Michael. ''Physical Change and Self-Help Housing in Arab Settlements in Israel.'' *Habitat Intl.* 9, no. 2 (1985):141–75.

Seelig, M., and J. Seelig. ''Architecture and Politics in Israel: 1920 to the Present.'' *Journal of Architectural and Planning Research* 5, no. 1 (1988):35–48.

Shaham, I. ''Public Housing in Israel.'' In *Public Housing in Europe and America*, edited by J. S. Fuerst, 52–66. New York: Wiley, 1974.

VII

AFRICA

17

Kenya

KINUTHIA MACHARIA

The post–World War II period has seen Kenya move from being a British colonial state to an African independent state and, in the process, inheriting development problems and continuing to be dependent on Britain and other Western nations. Like most other developing countries in Sub-Saharan Africa (e.g., Gambia, Tanzania, Ghana), urban development in Kenya was not a priority during the colonial administration. It became a priority only when the urban center served the colonialists' interests, for example, as a marketplace, a recreation center, or an administrative center and also as a transportation and communication link to Western European capitals. The town policies during the colonial period alienated the Africans; in Kenya it was not until after World War II that housing was considered for the Africans who worked in the factories and in the Europeans' homes. Even then, however, housing policy in Kenya could well be summarized by this quotation from a letter to the colonial state written by E. R. Cousins who was then a special commissioner and the acting commissioner for lands: "With the exception of a few detribalized Africans, petty traders, shop keepers, caterers or self-employed artisans, the African is not a town dweller. He has one foot in the reserve and comes to town merely to work. He does not need to acquire a permanent home there and what he wants is lodgings either free or for rent.'' (Vasey 1953).

The housing crisis notable in most African cities, like Nairobi, Lagos, or Dar es Salaam, has its origin in the biased colonial urban policy that did not plan early enough for the African majority. In the past twenty years, however, the crisis cannot be blamed solely on its origins. Also, the performance of the modern state—budgetary reforms toward housing, building bylaws, policies toward population and rural-urban migration, and establishing housing institutions—has to be examined to understand the current shortage and substandard quality of housing.

The housing conditions in both urban and rural Kenya are generally poor. In the rural areas, however, there is ample space and therefore a housing shortage or overcrowding, typical problems of the urban areas, are not significant. The quality of rural housing is poor, but with rising agricultural incomes from coffee and tea in some districts like Kericho, Kiambu, and Muranga, it is improving. Thus instead of thatch roofs, corrugated iron and brick roofs have become more fashionable and affordable for the small-scale farmers. Housing problems in Kenya are therefore more prevalent in urban areas. For this reason, this chapter emphasizes urban low-income housing.

TRENDS IN HOUSING CONDITIONS: 1945–1985

The major elements determining the condition of housing in Kenya are previous colonial housing policies, supply relative to need, ownership rates, spatial and social segregation, differential financing of public and private housing, and prices and rents. The interaction of these elements results in overcrowding, insufficient supply, polarized housing classes, and slum and squatter development, especially in larger cities like Nairobi and Mombasa. Anthony O'Connor (1983) has made similar observations in other major cities of tropical Africa.

Over the years, the following tenure forms have come into existence in the urban areas: rental, ownership, and pool houses. Rental is the most widespread. It is seen by most of the urban dwellers as a half-way solution toward solving the problem of house ownership in the towns. Contrary to some popularized arguments by World Bank and United States Agency for International Development (USAID) staff who think urban Kenyans are satisfied with rental units and are not as interested in owning houses in the urban areas, my discussions and observations with Nairobi residents show that they would like to own their own houses and are saving toward that goal. Unfortunately, they do not have enough money to buy their own houses or to construct on a plot allocated in the sites-and-services schemes. (Macharia 1985). They end up as renters due to their inadequate financial means. Thus they are renters by constraint and not by choice. Even in the case of those planning to retire in the rural areas, they aspire to have an urban house that they could rent to the new migrants from the rural areas. The fact that an owner in a housing project funded by USAID or the World Bank chooses to be a renter in another residential estate that is usually cheaper than rent on his own house should not be misunderstood as "a desire to be a renter." Instead, it should be interpreted as a need to raise more money to meet other needs like children's education, or family support while living in a cheaper unit than one's own house. This is one way that the urbanite in a Third World city has learned to survive economically in a situation of few economic opportunities.

It is not the case that migrant workers in cities necessarily return to rural places of origin during periods of illness, unemployment, or when reaching old age. The neat theoretical process by which capitalist firms draw labor from subsistence enclaves in periods of high demand and return them when no longer needed does not correspond to the actual experience in many peripheral communities. Kenya is one such example. The available empirical literature (Lomnitz 1977; Roberts 1978) indicates that although return migration frequently occurs, a large proportion of migrants stay in cities and manage in time to firm up their positions within the urban economy (Portes 1981).

There are different forms of rental houses. They include company-owned houses strictly rented to employees; government pool houses especially for senior civil servants; private rentals, that is, individually owned houses rented out to other people, especially the middle class and also the low-income groups like those in squatter settlements (Amis 1984); and local council, like the city of Nairobi, rental units. The last type used to form a majority of the rental houses, but the individually owned houses put up by the private sector are now more predominant mainly in large cities like Nairobi and Mombasa.

Ownership, especially owner-occupied, is another common tenure, especially among middle-income groups who have received loans using the security of their jobs as collateral. I refer to this as permanent ownership as opposed to temporary ownership, which is common among the low-income groups in squatter settlements or in the sites-and-services schemes.

One of the characteristics of urban housing, especially for the Africans since 1945, has been overcrowding. In the late 1940s, the colonial government put up rental rooms of 10 by 10 feet to accommodate working African male adults. Officially, these male adults were to leave their families in the rural areas, and they were not expected to host friends or relatives without permission. Obviously, this could not be enforced, and as the rural areas got more impoverished, rural-urban migration picked up, and this contributed to overcrowding. The formerly one-man room now was occupied by three to four persons. Some even accommodated families, sometimes two families, causing further overcrowding. In 1968 only 5.3 percent of the African population lived in urban areas, compared with 84.8 percent of the non-African population. Despite the small percentage of Africans in urban areas, they constituted the overwhelming proportion of those looking for houses in Kenya's towns. However, housing for them was proportionally the lowest in numbers and standards compared with that of the non-Africans.

Between 1948 and 1962 urban Africans increased by 174 percent (Bloomberg and Abrams 1965), while non-Africans increased by 85 percent. Early projections that Africans would urbanize in greater numbers during the 1960s and 1970s have now been realized. The African urban population has risen from 6.5 percent of the total (population) in the 1960s to at least 15.0 percent in the 1980s, nearing 20 percent by 1990.

Despite what may be considered a low percentage of urban population in Kenya, urbanization has been occurring at a very rapid rate. Efforts to house new urbanites by both private and public sectors have not matched the numbers of the newcomers, and overcrowding continues in the towns. In 1965 it was observed that overcrowding was an exceedingly serious situation among urban African households. This was particularly the case in Nairobi and Mombasa. In Nairobi, for example, it was estimated that 57 percent of single rooms were occupied by three or more persons. In Mombasa, for the same kind of room, the percentage of three or more occupants was 49 percent (Bloomberg and Abrams 1965, 151).

Bloomberg and Abrams also noted that even at the extremely high ratio of three or more persons per room (10 feet by 10 feet), 49 percent of all urban African households were overcrowded (52 percent in Nairobi). In 1979, for example, household size indicated an average of 4.25 persons per household in Nairobi and Mombasa, 4.43 in other urban areas, and 5.65 in the rural areas (Republic of Kenya 1979).

The low-income housing areas are an extension of what was in the 1950s and the 1960s designated as African housing areas. The conditions of the housing for these Africans were poor; they were situated mainly in the flatlands of most towns, while the non-Africans occupied the "hills" (referred to as "Milimani" locally). The house types were mainly dormitory-like with various rooms that were later and until now occupied by different families. The general environment was poor. For example, in 1965 water closets were accessible to occupants in only 49 percent of urban African households, and they were generally shared with other households. Pit latrines or bucket collection were common for many African households ranging from 65 percent in Mombasa to 24 percent in Nairobi, with other towns averaging 50 percent. Although bucket collection has been done away with in almost all Kenyan towns, the pit latrine now still accounts for 40 percent of the low-income housing units. In the rural areas pit latrines are predominant with no less than 98 percent.

Home ownership in the urban areas is almost a luxury. This has been the same in the 1960s, the 1970s, and even now in the 1980s. In the 1960s, for example, only 11 percent of the African households owned their houses, ranging from less than 3 percent in Nairobi to 30 percent in Mombasa, with 6 percent in the other towns (Bloomberg and Abrams 1965). The percentage in Mombasa was higher than in Nairobi because land is cheaper there and the local council

Table 17.1
Reported Completion of New Private and Public Residential Buildings in Main Towns, Kenya, 1981–1985

	Number		Estimated Cost Ksh* Million	
Year	Private	Public	Private	Public
1981	1,918	206	27.19	3.72
1982	2,083	443	32.71	5.00
1983	981	790	15.46	9.05
1984	646	552	10.00	16.73
1985	444	15	11.88	0.17

Source: Adapted from Republic of Kenya, 1986b, pp. 147–48.

allowed construction of the Swahili houses. These houses are inexpensive and use materials, like coconut leaves for roofing, that are readily available. The percentage of house ownership has risen with the years, but in proportion to the current urban population figures, it is still low. Based on City Council estimates, and my own observations, home ownership in Nairobi, for example, is about 15 percent, in Mombasa 40 percent and in other Kenya towns about 30–35 percent. Houses in the rural areas, on the other hand, are almost 100 percent individually owned. However, their quality is much lower than that in the urban areas.

Housing segregation in the urban areas is no longer by race or color in the 1970s and the 1980s but is mainly based on income. For example, African urban housing of the 1950s and 1960s is low-income housing in the 1970s and 1980s. The European housing, which is still intended for the Europeans, in the towns like Nairobi or Mombasa, is comparable to upper-income housing today. The former Asian housing could today be the middle-income housing. In Kenyan towns, however, the Asians have been very conservative and have tried to keep some residential areas strictly to themselves through covert ways—for example, raising the house value beyond the market price, not advertising house sales in the public media but rather using social networks based on religion, family, or friendship. Middle-class African groups, mainly business, academic elites, and especially university graduates, are successful in "creating" housing estates that may be well labeled "middle class." The low-income groups have often moved from bad to worse: from 100 square foot rooms during colonial rule to makeshift cardboard shacks during the 1970s and the 1980s. This is particularly the case in major towns like Nairobi where about one-third of the almost 1.5 million people today (1989) live in slum or squatter settlements.

Table 17.1 shows reported completions of private and public residential buildings. They are mainly houses for the upper- and middle-income groups usually unaffordable for more than 60 percent of the urban residents who are either in the low-income group or in the lower middle class (earning less than $1,500 per annum). The private sector, especially after the Kenyan coffee boom (1979–

1980), invested in residential buildings, especially in 1981–1982. The public sector (the state) was not spending as much in the same years by comparison.

Sources of finance for residential housing have been both private and public. Until the 1960s and 1970s, most of the towns' residential houses for the Africans (later for the low-income group) were built from public funds. The private sector has mainly invested in high-income and upper-middle-income residential housing. It is more profitable and worth speculating for. The state, in the current Development Plan (1984–1988), is encouraging the private sector to engage in construction of low-income housing. No major trends in the private sector's provision for low-income housing have been recorded yet, since that shift is just taking place gradually.

The 1986 paper *Economic Management for Renewed Growth* (Republic of Kenya 1986a) also stresses the major role the private sector is expected to play in the economy. This will include housing provision in urban areas, a role that the public sector has led in during the past twenty years. I argue that although the government is encouraging the private sector to provide housing for the population, this may benefit only the middle- and high-income groups. The private sector is profit oriented. It does not envision investing in low-income housing where it is needed the most by the low-income groups and also the lower-middle-income groups. The private sector has also realized a monopoly now that fewer public houses are being produced. This has led to skyrocketing house prices that prohibit many people, especially the low-income groups, from owning a house. Inevitably, many have become renters against their will.

Foreign financing from organizations such as the World Bank, which sponsored the Third Urban Housing; USAID; and the Commonwealth Development Bank (which sponsored construction of Buruburu residential estates with about 4,100 three- to four-bedroom houses mainly occupied by middle-class Africans) plays a major part in housing provision; this will continue in the years ahead as urban residential housing continues to lag behind urban population growth.

Median sales prices and rents in most of the towns and especially the major ones, Nairobi and Mombasa, vary. However, unlike the United Nations recommendation that a reasonable expenditure on housing should not exceed 25 percent of the family (or individual's) income, it takes up to 40 percent in rent and mortgage payments (for those in mortgage programs) in almost all of the towns. In the amount of monthly payment, there is an insignificant difference between owners and renters. The significant difference is that in the long run, the owner will actually own the house, while the renter will continue to be renting. It is not surprising, therefore, that slums and squatter areas are expanding, and overcrowding remains the characteristic of low-income urban dwellings.

THE ROLE OF HOUSING INSTITUTIONS AND ORGANIZATIONS

Until the late 1970s, housing institutions in Kenya had been established and run by the state. In the 1970s private financial institutions with provisions for loans to construct urban residential homes came into existence, and they continue to increase in numbers. The parent housing institution is the Department of Housing, which is part of the Ministry of Housing and Urban Development. This has been part of the central government establishment since 1948, under different names, charged with increasing housing output in urban areas and improving the quality of housing in both rural and urban areas.

The Ministry of Housing derives its powers from the Constitution and from such legislation as may be enacted from time to time. The minister in charge may confer enforcement powers on local councils in the regulation of sanitation, construction, and similar matters (Public Health Act of Kenya, Section 126).

The National Housing Corporation (NHC), as it came to be known in 1966, was founded in 1952 as the Central Housing Board. It is the central government's main institution to implement its policies and to coordinate housing design, construction, standards, and sanitation in all local councils. The NHC is also empowered to borrow money for its purposes to the extent and as such as may be approved by the minister. Loans are made from the Housing Loan Fund, which consists primarily of money borrowed from the Development Fund of the Government and Commonwealth Development Corporation. The World Bank and USAID also contribute to this loan fund.

The NHC is empowered by the Constitution to make loans to local authorities and supervise local housing projects. The corporation has also been involved in pilot housing schemes in towns such as Thika and Nakuru, where low-income houses built mainly with locally available materials have been constructed. The NHC is charged with formulating, reviewing, and modifying policy and policy- and program-implementation guidelines for shelter and urban-development projects. It is also expected to coordinate the activities of all implementing agencies and to handle the financial and physical programming of housing and urban development. This institution, headed by bureaucrats and political appointees, and with its headquarters in the capital city, Nairobi, has been responsible for project delays in many towns. Evidence of such delays were found in Thika, where a housing project that should have been completed in 1975 actually had not been started in 1981 (Macharia 1983). Conflicts based on the NHC's housing-design recommendations have arisen with local authorities. For example, in Mombasa, where a majority of the residents are Muslims, the NHC design guidelines for a housing project were not culturally acceptable to the residents. The NHC did not take into consideration the locals' objections and advice. This led to the failure of the project (Stren 1978).

However, the NHC continues to play a leading role in the implementation of housing policies and programs through sites-and-services schemes for low-income earners, rental-housing development, and mortgage housing and in assisting individuals to develop private houses in rural housing programs (Republic of Kenya 1986b). Although the 1986 paper on economic management (Republic of Kenya 1986a) intended to reduce the role of public organizations in spending government funds, the NHC is still carrying out its housing programs for the low-income groups as evidenced by two large projects it was undertaking in

1988 ("NHC Ready" 1988). If the government policies as outlined in the 1986 paper will be implemented, the role of the NHC in housing-policy implementation will be reduced. This may have adverse effects in the provision of low-income housing in most urban areas.

In 1985 1,009 housing units were completed compared with 2,398 units in 1984. This was due to the fact that provisional approved expenditures on housing decreased from $7,938 million in 1984–1985 to $5,625 million in 1985–1986, a decline of nearly 30 percent. (Table 17.2 shows the total number of housing units completed by the corporation during the past five years.) The sites-and-services scheme encouraged and strongly recommended by the central government, has been funded through the NHC, and almost every town has one. This is one of the major housing programs designed for low-income groups. It encourages people in this income group to invest in housing of "substantially reduced costs." The government provides sites, basic services, and infrastructure like roads, sanitation, water, and standard plans; the public then constructs the houses with permanent materials. In 1985, 882 such units were completed compared with 2,099 units in 1984. As previous critical studies of sites-and-services schemes have shown, the low-income group, which is usually the target group, has not benefited from this program (Stren 1978; Macharia 1985; Chana and DeKruijff 1981).

The Housing Research and Development Unit (HRDU), founded in 1971 and part of the College of Architecture and Engineering of the University of Nairobi, is another public institution. It is charged with initiating and undertaking research projects on low-cost housing, urban-improvement programs, building-materials-construction techniques, house-plan designs, training and community-development aspects of housing, and urban-development programs. Despite the formal guidelines, the HRDU's policy recommendations take a long time to be enacted in actual housing programs. Its impact on housing design and development in Kenya has yet to be felt.

Housing finance institutions could be divided into two categories: public and private. The public ones are charged with mobilizing financial resources for housing development and participating in the secondary mortgage market, particularly for middle-income housing. The Housing Finance Company of Kenya (HFCK) is the most prominent public financial institution with the ability to lend up to $46,875 to a family buying a house in the major towns of Nairobi, Mombasa, and Kisumu. The loan is payable at a 14 percent interest rate, which is lower than that of the commercial banks or the private financial houses, which charge 17–19 percent. The HFCK has benefited up to 60 percent of the present homeowners in the major towns. The beneficiaries are mainly the middle-income groups, which can afford a sizable down payment (at least 10 percent of the house value) and can also show evidence through collateral or family income or the ability to repay the loan.

The private financial institutions have also targeted the middle-income and upper-income groups who can afford to invest in them. They operate as savings

Table 17.2

Housing Units Completed or Supported by the National Housing Corporation, Kenya, 1981–1985

Units Completed	1981	1982	1983	1984	1985
Province					
Nairobi	1,072	2,311	–	284	–
Coast	–	13	50	13	50
North-Eastern	–	–	–	–	–
Eastern	–	70	98	2	–
Central	–	–	187	–	45
Rift Valley	1,577	354	302	199	745
Nyanza	106	180	–	1,900	169
Western	–	–	50	–	–
TOTAL NUMBER	2,755	2,928	687	2,398	1,009
Of which site and service[1]	2,719	2,550	598	2,099	882

Value of Units Completed (in Ksh x 1,000)	1981	1982	1983	1984	1985
Nairobi	963	2,031	–	4,106	–
Coast	–	155	116	166	302
North-Eastern	–	–	215	–	–
Eastern	–	263	330	4	–
Central	–	–	908	–	618
Rift Valley	1,821	1,333	–	550	1,737
Nyanza	185	432	–	1,500	210
Western	–	–	511	–	–
TOTAL VALUE	2,969	4,214	2,080	6,236	2,867

Source: Republic of Kenya, 1986b, p. 149.

[1]As noted elsewhere (Macharia, 1985), the sites-and-services schemes have failed to provide housing for the urban poor. Instead, middle income groups have benefited. The poor have been pushed from such schemes to slums and squatter settlements.

and loan banks. Like the HFCK, they also expect at least 10 percent down payment of the total house cost and evidence of the ability to pay back the loan. Their interest rates are usually higher by about 2–3 percent compared with those of the publicly supported HFCK. These private financial institutions have helped about 30 percent of those who own homes by providing loans that they might not have received from public financial institutions. In 1986, however, six of the leading private house-building societies (as most of them are called) had to close following government orders due to substantial debts they had incurred from the major commercial banks in Nairobi. Some of the leading ones that closed and had their directors arrested to answer charges included the Rural-Urban Credit Finance Company, and Continental Credit Finance Company. In 1987 the Pioneer Building Society also closed. The impact this had in the public eye was that many people lost faith in the private financial institutions. This was the case with the building societies, and those who had invested there divested their money and reinvested it in more established commercial banks. The ability for such private institutions to finance and help in construction of new houses was also put to doubt. The 1986 paper suggesting more private sector participation in housing provision may become another case in Kenya's development where policy statements have usually taken too long to be implemented.

Finally, there is the National Cooperative Housing Union (NACHU), founded in 1983. It was established to sponsor, implement, and manage cooperative housing programs. The government continues to provide technical and financial assistance to the NACHU until it becomes self-supporting. For the majority of low-income employees who are members of this cooperative society at their workplace, this might be one promising way to own a house in the urban area.

Besides the local institutions, international development agencies like the World Bank, USAID, Overseas Development Authority, and Commonwealth Development Bank have contributed to at least 40 percent of the completed houses in urban areas during the past fifteen years. The Commonwealth Development Bank provided funds for construction of Buruburu Estate estimated to have at least 4,000 residential units in Nairobi. USAID provided funds for the Umoja Housing Estates in Nairobi, with an estimated population of 30,000 living there. Since the early 1970s, a number of both bilateral and multilateral international development agencies have participated in the government's efforts to increase availability of housing, particularly for the low-income families.

The housing outputs expected from the World Bank through the Third Urban Project and USAID are examples of foreign institutional responses to the housing problem (table 17.3). Assistance has also come in the form of housing loans in secondary towns. In 1984–1985 USAID loans were estimated at $187,500; loans of the World Bank for the Third Urban Project were estimated at $468,750. In addition, foreign aid has included technical support to about a dozen major urban housing projects (Republic of Kenya 1987). Notable achievements resulting from these initiatives include the development of local authority and an institutional capacity to implement and administer housing-development programs and vastly

Table 17.3
Planned Physical Housing Output, Kenya, 1983/1984–1987/1988

	Serviced Plots	Rental	Upgrading	Mortgage/ Tenant Purchase or Owner Builder	Total
Nairobi	7,000	400	200	1,150	8,750
Mombasa	2,300	–	1,200	–	3,500
Kisumu	1,500	100	3,500	–	5,100
Other Municipalities	1,300	200	500	–	2,000
Other Towns	664	210	–	–	874
Rural Housing	–	–	–	4,200	4,200
Third Urban	3,700	–	6,300	500	10,500
USAID Project	1,500	400	1,500	–	3,400
Mortgage Housing Project (NRC)	–	–	–	100	100
Staff Mortgage (Govt.)	–	–	–	1,800	1,800
Urban Pool Housing (Govt.)	–	–	–	80	80
Institutional Housing	–	500	–	–	500
Local Authority Housing	–	4,000	–	–	4,000
Private Sector Development	–	4,000	–	–	4,000
	–	4,300	–	6,400	10,700
TOTAL	**17,964**	**14,110**	**13,200**	**14,230**	**59,504**

Sources: Republic of Kenya, 1984–1988, p. 168; 1987.

improved access to housing finance in suitable towns by middle-income families and to some extent low-income families. Short courses are available locally and abroad for the local authority staff responsible for housing-policy implementation; also residential technical officers have in some cases collaborated successfully with the housing officers and town planners where specific proposals are being implemented. This kind of education is necessary for those officers entrusted with implementing housing policies in the local councils.

HOUSING MARKETS AND POLICY ORIENTATIONS

The provision of housing is in both public and private hands. The public sector represented by the central government through local authorities has been at the forefront since the colonial days. Provision of housing for the civil servant in what has been referred to as "pool housing" continues. Government-owned houses provide homes to only about one-quarter (about 20,000) of the senior civil servants. The public sector has also encouraged and supervised the provision of sites-and-services schemes targeted for low-income groups in almost all towns.

The private sector, on the other hand, has concentrated on the provision of upper- and middle-income housing, mainly in the major towns. The expectation is that those developers will mobilize land, financial, and technical management resources for low-cost housing. They also should package suitable housing projects jointly with specific local authorities. The paper on economic management calls for local government to work with private developers in subdividing land, the acceleration of regularization of land tenure among existing subdivisions, and the charging of market prices for government-operated sale and rental housing. It is still too early to measure the impact of this collaboration and how much this will revolutionize the capacity of low-cost housing in Kenya. Given the profit drive of the private developers, however, we may not expect many low-cost housing units to emerge from these efforts. Moreover, it appears there is a market for low-cost housing sought by those who would otherwise have occupied middle-income housing. This means that those who should have been eligible for the low-cost housing will be pushed down the line to informal sector housing in slums and squatter settlements—substandard housing that the state would have claimed it is eliminating.

The informal sector housing in squatter settlements, such as Mathare in Nairobi, Kiandutu in Thika, and Pandipieri in Kisumu, has put up shelter for the majority (85 percent) of the urban poor. In Nairobi alone, about 400,000 people are estimated to be living in informal sector housing. This kind of housing also accounts for 200,000 people accommodated in other towns. The houses constructed in the informal sector use locally available materials like wattle and mud, carton boxes for walls and roofs, and grass or old corrugated iron sheets for roofs.

Informal sector housing, like the informal sector economy, has come about as a result of the formal sector's not providing enough housing for the thousands of urban dwellers who have migrated to the towns in the past twenty years. Informal sector housing can be found near the industrial areas of most of the major towns. About half of those living in such housing depend on the industries for jobs as casual workers; the rest are self-employed in the informal sector. For example, women are food sellers outside major industries. Other locations for informal housing include areas near or along river banks, particularly the Nairobi River in Nairobi and also Mathare. The land near the river banks is unsuitable for prime development. It is also easy to occupy it and put up temporary housing since it is public land; given its low value for development, the government or the city council does not take immediate action to evict those putting up structures. When many have settled there, it becomes cumbersome to evict them.

Until the mid–1970s the government's policy was to bulldoze such housing sites. But the numbers of those occupying them kept increasing, and the policy to bulldoze was revised in 1976. After this date eviction of such temporary housing occurs only when there is a clear alternative of where the evicted will be housed. It takes time for an eviction order to be served due to the many levels of bureaucratic decisions. Sometimes it is too late, and it takes time to be effective, especially when there may not be a ready reasonable alternative.

Despite the lower standards of the informal housing, it has given shelter to many who would otherwise have been homeless and sleeping in the streets (now only 1 percent of the urban dwellers). In most cases, the homeless are mentally or physically disabled. Instead of not recognizing this kind of housing, the government should put more efforts in upgrading informal housing, preferably in its present location. Although the government recognizes the informal sector as contributing to the national economy, in 1986 police harassment in various economic subsectors such as hawking and food selling was still going on. Negative attitudes and threats of demolition of informal housing in Mathare and Kibera continue, too, despite the official recognition of the informal economy. Movement of the people in such housing can be too expensive, both to the government and to the occupants. The people also get attached to a certain location, where they begin their informal economic activities, which they usually stand to lose if they move (Macharia 1983).

Housing policy and its implementation are very much linked with the country's general economic and political development. The government's minimum building standards, which require a house of at least two rooms made of permanent materials, pose an obstacle to housing production in urban areas that would match the ever-increasing urban population. It appears that the government's standards may be deliberate and intended to develop and improve employment in the construction industry. For example, despite plenty of wood in the country, timber houses in urban areas are discouraged with the excuse that they could be a fire hazard. Instead, stone houses, which are more expensive and require more time to construct, are stipulated by the building code. I argue that the objective of the government in this case may be to create more jobs among the low-income groups who will be employed in the quarry and on the building site to straighten and curve the stones as required by the masons. This creates jobs for the local artisans and graduates of village polytechnics who would otherwise be unemployed. However, this does not increase housing output.

Housing construction plays an important part in the nation's economy. A number of factories in major towns are planned. However, a major obstacle is lack of housing for the workers. Housing and industrial expansion are inextricably combined. Thus I suggest closer collaboration between the government and factory owners. The government, which owns most of the land, could make it available on reasonable terms to factories, especially those with at least 250 employees. These factories could devise an acceptable housing scheme either in the form of a cooperative or a rental scheme. This would ensure more production in the factories and workers housed in quarters with a clean environment and standard sanitation. A few factories like Kenya Canners in Thika and Kenya Breweries in Nairobi have housing for about half of their workers. This type of public-private partnership would be beneficial for all parties involved.

Housing also plays an important part in absorbing unemployment both in the building trades and in the materials industries, some of which have been suffering adversity due to the lag in construction activity. Increasing housing activity will increase employment and this would be very compatible with the government's general policy of increasing employment, particularly in the urban areas.

MAJOR PROBLEMS

Housing development in Kenya cannot be looked at in isolation from other government programs. Therefore, the general problems facing most developing countries—for example, large foreign debts, lack of enough capital for planned projects and especially foreign currency to pay for imported materials, corruption at top-level management, and high rates of inflation—have direct negative effects on housing production.

Kenya, however, in addition to having these general problems, has its own specific problems that have contributed to the housing crisis. Among them are the high population increase, especially among the youth, and poor housing in the rural and urban areas. Kenya's population is growing at a rate of 3.9–4.0 percent annually (Republic of Kenya 1983a), which is the highest growth rate in the world. The population will more than double in the next twenty years to about 38.6 million by the year 2003, compared with 18.7 million estimated for 1983 (Rourk and Roscoe 1984). In 1979 there were eighty-eight urban centers with at least 2,000 residents, and this number is expected to be higher in the near future. In 1985 the urbanization rate in Kenya was estimated to be 15 percent and it is expected to rise to 25 percent by 2003 (Struyk and Nankman 1986). More urban development is needed to solve the housing problems.

Rapid rural-urban migration continues due to pressing factors such as landlessness, unemployment, famine, and drought in the rural areas. The urban areas do not offer jobs immediately to the new migrants and have unemployment rates of 10–15 percent. The new migrants, however, perceive more opportunities in the towns, and at least 40 percent of them are engaged in the informal economy as street hawkers, metal and wood artisans, and garment makers (Macharia 1986). These informal economic workers make a better income than they would have made in the rural areas. On the other hand, their income, an average of about $625 a year, may not be enough to rent, buy, or build the minimum standard house in the urban area.

High building standards that require at least a two-room house with kitchen and bathroom, made of permanent materials, have been a major constraint on urban housing provision in the past twenty years. The existing housing standards are beyond the reach of the low-income and even the lower-middle-income groups and would require unsustainable levels of subsidy from the public sector were they to be enforced effectively. In 1985 such a minimum standard house would have cost $5,625. An estimate of median household income by Michael Lee (1983, 36) was $2,153 for urban areas and $3,171 for metropolitan Nairobi and Mombasa. Even with such conservative estimates, it is evident that the costs of the standard "simplest" house is too high to be afforded by more than half of the needy target groups in the towns. The subsidy in the sites-and-services scheme has been $875, which was estimated to cover the costs of the roof (and this subsidy not increasing). With rising costs in housing materials, it will be hard for the majority to afford formal housing.

Unequal distribution of property in Kenya's mixed economy has had effects on land prices in the urban areas. Although most of the land is still publicly owned, 40 percent of the urban land is now in private hands. This has brought about land-speculation practices that have hiked land prices and in turn the housing prices. For example, in 1980 the price of a house in middle-income or high-income residential areas was $31,250. The price had more than doubled in 1985, to about $75,000. This is particularly the case in Nairobi. Because of heavy foreign investment in Nairobi, with a number of international organizations having their headquarters there (e.g., United Nations Environmental Programme [UNEP], Habitat, many foreign embassies), prices of housing have gone up tremendously, and this affects almost every person planning to own a house in Nairobi. This, however, works to the benefit of the landlords who are usually senior government officers, directors of private and public companies, and other highly paid elites.

Delays in construction have also contributed to the housing problem. Cases of housing projects that could have been completed five to ten years earlier are not uncommon (Macharia 1985). Such delays have usually come about due to stringent and slow bureaucratic machinery, especially in the Department of Housing and the National Housing Corporation in Nairobi. The bureaucratic elites sitting in their Nairobi offices have on many occasions ignored suggestions and advice from the Municipal Councils which in most cases know what is best for their local community. Such conflicts have caused delays in release of funds, approval of house plans, and sometimes the failure of a proposed project to take off. The case of Mombasa (Stren 1971) and the ill-fated Kariobangi sites-and-services scheme, which was built too far from the workplaces of prospective occupants, are examples (Stren 1978). The 1986 paper on economic management advocates decentralization in development planning to what has come to be referred to as "district focus." The "district focus" planning will, one hopes, sensitize the local leaders to the local needs. Delays of project implementation may come to an end. It is too early to suggest what impact this will have on housing. My skepticism is based on the fact that the funds for projects like housing will still be controlled from the Treasury in Nairobi. The extent to which the decentralization policy will be translated into successful projects will be seen in the near future.

Corruption and disagreements among elected municipal council officials who want to extend favors to their electorate have also caused housing-project delays in many towns in Kenya. Funds approved by the government or a donor agency for housing projects have usually been returned unspent at the end of the approved fiscal year. This is despite the housing shortage and overcrowding in most towns. Thika town (Macharia 1983) and Nairobi ("Nairobi," 1985) are examples of conflicts that have led to the failure of housing projects that could have been the homes of many today.

Consultation on the needs of the local people could also ensure appropriate housing designs and locations that may be acceptable to the local communities. Local authorities should be free of nepotism, tribalism, and internal political conflicts, allowing them to be entrusted with grants available from donor agencies. Donors, like USAID or the World Bank, should stop laying out building plans and designs unacceptable to the local needs. If the Swahili Muslims, for example, do not favor a bathroom inside the house but prefer one outside based on cultural practices (like not going to the bathroom in the presence of one's in-laws), this should be accommodated in proposed housing designs.

PROSPECTIVE DEVELOPMENTS

The 1981–1985 housing output of the formal sector, including public and private, is far below that which will be needed to meet projected basic housing needs, while the standards are far in excess of those affordable by the low-income families. In the 1984–1988 *Development Plan* (Republic of Kenya 1983b), it is estimated that 250,000–280,000 new housing units would be required to meet fully the basic needs in urban areas alone. At current capacity (table 17.3), the government is unlikely to produce more than 45,000–55,000 urban housing units in the next five years. To meet this wide gap, informal sector housing output will have to be facilitated and upgraded and formal sector standards reduced.

D. W. Rourk and A. B. Roscoe (1985) estimated that there were 343,000 households in the metropolitan areas in 1983. About 16 percent of the dwelling stock in Nairobi is estimated to be substandard because of the absence of water and sanitary facilities, the quality of the structure, or excessive densities. Of this stock, two-thirds (59,000 units) is estimated to be upgradable, primarily through the provision of an infrastructure, and one-third (29,500 units) is not upgradable and must eventually be replaced. This observation by Rourk and Roscoe is for Nairobi only, showing the need of more new units. Projecting to the future, I agree with the observation made by J. Raymond Struyk and Piet Nankman (1986, p. 18) that "the emphasis in Kenya's housing strategy should be on the producing of a very high volume of new housing units. Upgrading the comparatively small number of deficient units should take second place to a very concerted effort to produce more housing."

A total of 23,800 new units per year are estimated to be required in the metropolitan areas between 1984–1988 if the needs of new households are to be met. In addition, a twenty-year upgrading program for the metropolitan areas would require the upgrading of 2,950 units per year, bringing the total construction requirement to almost 26,000 units per year during this period. These efforts may not fulfill all housing needs, especially given that urban population growth (natural and from rural-urban migration) will still be increasing. Although I support the government efforts to reduce population through family-planning methods, I suggest the encouragement of self-help building within the informal sector. As has been mentioned earlier, the 1986 official recognition of the informal sector has embraced only a few subsectors, such as metal artisans and taxis, which do not include slum and squatter housing. Local councils like the City Commission in Nairobi are still reluctant to recognize such housing. What this suggests is that the understanding of the policy of "official recognition" of the informal sector is unclear or has yet to be implemented practically. Upgrading in squatter settlements could be evidence of the acceptance of informal housing, but this was still not the case in 1988. The observation by Struyk and Nankman (1986) that up to 40 percent of urban housing is in unserviced areas is correct, and this has not changed even with the government's subsequent policy. The government response should be to develop land in the squatter-settlement areas and a more aggressive upgrading program than there is now. Such an approach aimed at increasing shelter through the informal sector would involve measures to increase the security of land tenure, lowering the minimum building standards (e.g., by allowing the use of temporary materials initially that may be replaced later as the family gets more income); redirecting financial savings toward low-cost housing; and finally, providing a greater degree of cooperation between the public and private sector in the provision of urban housing. More research on locally available raw materials and culturally acceptable house designs should be encouraged. The impact of donor agencies on urban housing should also be reevaluated with the idea of making them more accountable to local needs.

REFERENCES

Amis, P. 1984. "Squatters or Tenants: The Commercialization of Unauthorized Housing in Nairobi." *World Development* 12:87–96.

Bloomberg, L. N., and C. Abrams. 1965. *United Nations Mission to Kenya on Housing*. New York: United Nations.

Chana, T., and G. J. de Kruijff. *Case Studies of Site and Service Schemes in Kenya*. Nairobi: Housing and Research Development Unit, University of Nairobi, 1981.

Lee, Michael. 1983. *Kenya Housing Demand: An Interim Assessment*. Nairobi: United States Agency for International Development.

Lomnitz, Larissa. 1977. *Networks and Marginality: Life in a Mexican Shantytown*. New York: Academic Press.

Macharia, Kinuthia. 1983. "Housing in Kenya for Low-Income Groups: Site-and-Service Scheme in Thika." Unpublished paper. Nairobi: University of Nairobi, Department of Sociology.

————. 1985. "Low Income Housing in Kenya: The View from the Bottom." *International Journal of Urban and Regional Research* 9, no. 3:405–19.

————. 1986. "Urban Informal Sector in Nairobi." Paper presented to a conference held at Johns Hopkins University, Baltimore, October 14.

"Nairobi City Council Dissolved." 1985. *Weekly Review* (Nairobi), June 21.

"NHC Ready to Develop Two Major Housing Projects." 1988. *Daily Nation*, May 13.

O'Connor, Anthony. 1983. *The African City*. New York: Africana Publishing Co.

Portes, Alejandro, and John Walton. 1981. *Labour Class and the International System*. New York: Academic Press.

Republic of Kenya. 1979. *Population Census*. Nairobi: Government Printer.

————. 1983a. *Census Survey Report*. Nairobi: Government Printer.

————. 1983b. *Development Plan, 1984–1988*. Nairobi: Government Printer.

————. 1986a. *Economic Management for Renewed Growth*. Sessional Paper No. 1 of 1986. Nairobi: Government Printer.

————. 1986b. *Economic Survey, 1986*. Nairobi: Government Printer.

————. 1987. *Economic Survey, 1987*. Nairobi: Government Printer.

Roberts, Bryan R. 1978. *Cities of Peasants: The Political Economy of Urbanization in the Third World*. London: Edward Arnold.

Rourk, D. W., and A. B. Roscoe. 1984. *An Assessment of National Housing Needs and Affordability in Kenya*. Washington, D.C.: Office of Housing and Urban Programs, United States Agency for International Development.

Stren, R. 1971. "Policy, Local Politics, and Urban Development: A Study of Low-Cost Housing in Mombasa." Ph.D. dissertation, University of California, Berkeley.

————. 1978. *Housing the Urban Poor in Africa. Policy, Politics, and Bureaucracy in Mombasa*. Berkeley: Institute of International Studies, University of California.

Struyk J. Raymond, and Piet Nankman. 1986. *Developing a Housing Strategy for Kenya: Recent Housing Production, Market Development, and Future Housing Needs*. Washington, D.C.: The Urban Institute.

Vasey, Ernest Albert. 1953. *Report on African Housing in Township and Trading Centres*. Nairobi: Government Printer.

FURTHER READING

Chana, T. "Nairobi, Dandora and Other Projects." In *Low-Income Housing in the Developing World*, edited by G. K. Payne, 17–36. New York: Wiley, 1984.

Hake, A. *African Metropolis: Nairobi's Self-Help City*. London: Chatto and Windus, 1977.

Kitching, G. *Class and Economic Change in Kenya.* New Haven: Yale University Press, 1980.

Leesmith, D., and P. A. Memon. "Institution Development for Delivery of Low-Income Housing—An Evaluation of the Dandora Community Development Project in Nairobi." *Third World Planning Review* 10, no. 3 (1988):217–38.

Leys, Colin. *Underdevelopment in Kenya.* Berkeley: University of California Press, 1975.

Macoloo, G. C. "Housing the Urban Poor—A Case Study of Kisumu-Town, Kenya." *Third World Planning Review* 10, no. 2 (1988):159–74.

Muwonge, J. W. "Urban Policy and Patterns of Low-Income Settlement in Nairobi." *Population and Development Review* 6 (1980):595–613.

Yahya, S. *Review of Kenya's Building By-Laws.* Nairobi: Housing Research and Development Unit, 1983.

18

Ghana

SETH OPUNI ASIAMA

Ghana, a West African country, has an area of about 240,000 square kilometers and a population of about 12.5 million. Average monthly temperatures are above 20 degrees centigrade all year, and in the North temperatures can rise above 35 degrees centigrade during the day. The coastal people depend on fishing for mackerel, herring, and barracuda. In the North arable agriculture is the main occupation with the main crops being yams, guinea corn, maize, ground nuts, and rice. In the South, cassava, rice, cocoyams, and plantains are grown, with cocoa being the most important cash crop. Livestock is popular in the North although sheep, goats, and poultry are kept by people all over the country. The country is rich in minerals with gold, diamonds, manganese, and bauxite being of great export value. Timber is also exported in large quantities.

The country's economy is heavily dependent upon imported commodities. This is due to the poor industrial base and the overreliance on cocoa as an export crop. The poor economy led the government, in 1983, to embark on an Economic Recovery Program (ERP) with assistance from the World Bank and the International Monetary Fund. The currency, the Cedi, which sold for U.S. $1 = ¢2.75 in 1983 was devalued and exchanged at U.S. $1 = ¢176 at the close of 1987. Per capita gross domestic product (GDP) is U.S. $380.

The country gained independence from Britain in 1957 after a century of colonial domination. In 1960 the country became a republic under an executive president, Kwame Nkrumah. Since independence the country has seen three civilian governments and four military coups. Since 1981 the country has been ruled by a military cum civilian dictatorship under Jerry John Rawlings.

Population is concentrated in the South and in the middle belt of the country. The capital city, Accra, has a population of 859,640, and the other main towns are Kumasi (348,880), Sekondi-Takoradi (116,498), Tema (131,222), and Tamale (136,828).

Like many countries in the developing world, Ghana lacks adequate and reliable statistics on housing. Information relating to important issues such as the housing stock, density levels, tenurial arrangements, and the quality of housing are either nonexistent or unreliable. This has been largely due to the

Table 18.1
Growth Patterns of Some Major Towns, Ghana, 1960–1984

| Town | Absolute Figures | | | % Growth |
	1960	1970	1984	1970-1984
Accra	347,815	564,194	859,640	52
Kumasi	180,642	260,286	348,880	34
Sekondi-Takoradi	85,617	112,056	116,498	4
Cape Coast	41,230	51,653	57,700	12
Bolgatanga	5,613	81,719	31,500	68
Tamale	40,443	83,653	136,828	63
Koforidua	34,856	46,235	54,400	18
Sunyani	12,160	23,072	36,100	56
Ho	14,518	24,199	37,200	54
Tema	14,937	60,767	131,222	116

Sources: 1960, 1970, and 1984 census data.

low level of practical interest that successive governments have had in housing. Few studies have been commissioned on housing, and even they have had little impact on the data base relating to housing owing to their narrow and often specialized scopes. Housing has, in the past, been left largely in the hands of the private sector, represented by individual operators whose motives have generally been conditioned by their personal desires to own property rather than investment.

It is also significant that there has been an almost total focus of attention on the urban communities. The high rate of rural-urban migration has swelled the populations of the urban centers and has increased the pressure on urban amenities and services. Owing to the social and political implications of this state of affairs, governments have, in the past, devoted the scarce alleviating resources to the urban sector, giving little attention to the rural communities.

Ghana has experienced a high growth rate in its urban population. In 1960, 23 percent of the population was classified as urban; this increased to 29 percent in 1970 and to 31 percent in 1984. In 1970 the populations of the three largest cities, Accra, Kumasi, and Sekondi-Takoradi, represented about 11 percent of the country's total population; this had risen to 12 percent in 1984. (Table 18.1 shows the pattern of population growth in some major towns between 1960 and 1984.) Much of this growth has been due to migration. Between 1960 and 1970 the annual national growth rate was 2.4 percent whereas the growth rates for almost all urban centers was 3.0 percent or more. One result of this growth has been an acute housing shortage.

TRENDS IN HOUSING CONDITIONS AND CONSTRUCTION: 1945–1988

As expected, housing conditions in terms of the quality of housing, the character of housing, and amenities have been altered during the 1945–1988 period. So also have modes and materials of house construction. The greatest influences in these metamorphoses have been European acculturation manifested through Christianity and education, which accompanied the period of colonialism. As more and more of the natives converted to Christianity and became educated in the ways of the whites, they tended to adopt the tastes and preferences of whites in food, clothing, and housing. These influences are still being manifested in the housing preferences of a majority of the people and by the institutional framework of town planning that operates in the country.

Housing Quality

It is probably true that notions of overcrowding are recent and can be traced directly to European acculturation. In the rural areas density levels generally have been low. The pressure on housing in the urban centers has raised density levels significantly, but the desire to provide accommodations for one's kith and kin seems to override all other considerations. Nevertheless, there is little doubt that density levels are significantly high.

There is no definite rule defining the limits of overcrowding in the country. A reasonable assumption would be that more than 2.0 persons per room is indicative of crowded conditions, and more than 2.5 persons per room is indicative of severe overcrowding (Quarcoo et al. 1967, 76). Severe overcrowding has been identified in most of the regional capitals (e.g., Accra [2.8], Kumasi [3.9], Sunyani [3.8], and Koforidua [3.5]). These figures, however, conceal the spatial differences that exist in density levels within the towns.

In good residential areas—such as the airport residential area and Roman Ridge residential area in Accra, the Nhyiaeso and Danyame residential areas in Kumasi, and the Ridge residential area in Cape Coast—it is easy to see that in some cases rooms are underused since the number of rooms in such houses increases in relation to the other parts of town. In cases in which households occupy single rooms, density levels are high. For example, in a study of the Asawasi Housing Estate in Kumasi, it was found that when households occupied single rooms, in 61.7 percent of the cases density levels were between three and six persons to a room, and cases in which there were eleven, twelve, and fifteen people to a room were reported; out of a sample of 2,900 single-room households surveyed throughout the country, 28 percent were found to be sleeping six or more (Owusu et al. 1973, 34).

Tenure

Tenurial arrangements for housing span a wide spectrum. The private sector has traditionally been responsible for housing provisions in the country. Central government provision is recent, and the earliest evidence of public housing provision was after the earthquake in 1939 when housing estates were developed in Accra. The Action Plan (Ghana Government 1986) estimates that the private sector has provided about 80 percent of the country's housing stock. The tenure of house builders ranges from freeholds to licenses.

In many cases the house builder in the private sector, who is usually a private individual, builds on land that he acquires with his own resources. His title to the land may be a freehold, a leasehold, or merely possessory. When the house builder has a freehold, he holds his land and house in free and unfettered ownership.

A system of tenure for house builders that has become popular is the leasehold. Leaseholds are often given for ninety-nine years to house builders (fifty years to foreigners) by landlords who are often traditional overlords (i.e., chiefs or family heads). This period is regarded as being long enough to enable the house builder to recoup his investment and still enable the community to retain its interest in land. A third variant of land holding is that of the possessory title. In this case, the house builder has an interest in housing land not beyond the mere possession of such land with the desire to acquire either a freehold or a leasehold interest in the future. The house builder in this case is not to be identified as a squatter (i.e., one who has no legal estate in land on which he builds) because he has the land with the consent of the landowner (Asiama 1984).

The proportion of households in the rental sector is not well documented. In a survey of households in low-income areas in Kumasi, G. A. Tipple (1982, 34) found that more than 75 percent of his sample were renters. Owusu and Associates (1973) also found that about 95 percent of their nationwide sample rented their accommodations. These results could have been influenced by the nature of the samples chosen—low-income earners. This high proportion of tenants does not, however, reflect an investment motive in housing. In a survey of houseowners in Madina, a suburb of Accra, S. O. Asiama (1980, 229) reported:

Houses were constructed mainly as accommodation for the owner and his nuclear family. . . . Few of them had more than one reason for building their houses, though the desire for a place to live was paramount; 68% said they constructed their houses in order to have a place to live. This number was made up of 39% of respondents who said the desire for a place to live was their only reason and 29% who gave a secondary reason as either the desire to leave a heritage for their children (27%) or the desire to have an investment for their money (2%). The investment motive did not feature prominently as only 7% gave investment as the only reason they constructed their houses.

The Madina survey showed that 56 percent of landlords shared their houses with tenants.

Housing tenure in the public sector has been a combination of rental and outright ownership. The emphasis has been on rentals. Historically, houses built with public funds by the State Housing Corporation and the Tema Development Corporation have been let to their occupants, and only a small proportion has been sold. In 1971, however, this policy changed significantly when the government decided that public housing should be sold to the occupants, particularly houses owned by the Tema Development Corporation. It is significant to note that even when public houses have been sold, the land still remains in the ownership of the central government. Hence the owners remain tenants of the state although they pay only ground rents, which are generally very low. There is still a proportion of public estates in the rental sector, although it is shrinking. In 1976, for example, out of the total stock of 1,097 units in three State Housing Corporation estates in Kumasi, 22 percent were rented, and the remainder were on hire-purchase terms.

A number of employers and organizations also provide accommodations for their staff during the tenure of their employment. They may be either in the private sector or in the public sector. The major public organizations are the Civil Service, the Ghana Cocoa Board, and the universities. In lieu of rent, they usually forego a percentage (normally, 10 percent) of their salaries. The Social Security and National Insurance Trust (SSNIT) began a Workers' Housing Scheme in 1974 under which the trust intended to construct apartments in all regional capitals for workers. The trust would sell the apartments to public and private organizations that would let them to their staffs. By the end of March 1989 the nineteen blocks of apartments to provide accommodations for 963 workers in Dansoman (Accra) had reached advanced stages of construction, and 532 apartments had been occupied.

House Type

House types in the country differ in terms of class and location. Housing standards in the upper-middle class and high-income group areas (officially referred to as first-class residential areas) are high. This housing, such as that found in the airport residential area, Roman Ridge and East Legon in Accra, or Nhyiaeso and Danyame in Kumasi is characterized by buildings of high quality set in large compounds. Plot sizes are, on the average, 100 feet in width and 120 feet in length. Some houses have been provided with luxuries such as swimming pools and air conditioners. Piped water and electricity are standard. Services such as door-to-door refuse collection, first-class access roads, and high-class schools are provided in such communities. The housing is mainly owner occupied, one-family dwellings.

Housing standards in lower-middle-class areas (officially referred to as second-class residential areas) are of good-quality construction. They are usually higher than the ground floor with the two-story building being predominant. The houses are typically in multiple occupation with the landlord also living on the same premises although there are absentee landlords. Plot sizes are about 80 feet by 80 or 100 feet.

Third-class residential areas are the areas occupied by the low-income population and include slums and spontaneous settlements. Qualitatively, as expected, the housing in these areas is of lower standards than that in the other two areas. In terms of standards, two main variants may be identified within this category. First is the traditional housing. It makes up the center of towns— the original townships before urbanization and its concomitants caught up with them. Such housing is usually of poor quality in design and structure. Modern concepts of ventilation, sanitation, and drainage have had little or no impact in this sector. The houses are closely packed together with little or no space between them. It is not unusual to find the windows of one house opening into the compound of another house. The houses are usually of mud, and it is usual to find that they have been rendered with Portland cement and painted. Most of the houses are occupied by members of the extended family and are often termed family houses, although one might find that a few rooms have been let to tenants. They are often referred to as compound houses. Examples of such settlements are James Town in Accra and Ashanti New Town in Kumasi.

The second variant is the Zongo, a migrant settlement to be found on the outskirts of most towns. Slum conditions are characteristic of these settlements, and they constitute the country's stock of spontaneous housing.

Location

Urban sprawl in the country has not yet attained alarming dimensions even though cities like Accra and Tema are moving toward conurbations. This is mainly due to the land-ownership structure and the urban-planning regulations, which make it difficult to control urban growth.

Because land ownership is in private hands, house builders build wherever they are able to obtain land without having to contend with government regulations. The laws regulating urban development are not automatic. For example, the Town and Country Planning Ordinance of 1945, which regulates planning in the country, provides that development control by the central government is applicable only when the minister responsible for planning has declared an area to be a Planning Area. In many urban areas, the areas so defined do not include all of the city.

Building activities are now often taking place on the fringes of the urban centers since vacant land is available only in such places. This has, in part, been the result of a sudden surge of house construction in the period 1979–1986 when governments in Western Europe (particularly West Germany) tightened immigration and Ghanaians who were illegal immigrants were sent home. Some of the returnees invested in housing on the urban fringes such as Achimota, Taifa,

Dome, Ashalebotwe, and Agboba in Accra and Kwadaso Extension, Boadi, and Anwomaso in Kumasi.

Few building activities have taken place in small towns and rural communities owing, perhaps, to the lack of amenities such as piped water, electricity, and good roads in such areas. People, however, tend to build in their hometowns when they are nearing their retirement age and intend to resettle in their hometowns. Again, there is little assistance, such as mortgage finance, given to help housing development in the rural areas and small towns since it is generally assumed that owing to low population pressure, there is no housing problem there.

Special Population Groups

Housing provision in the country is rarely targeted for special population groups except in loosely defined terms such as "workers" or "low-income earners." Because such terms are loosely defined, the houses provided rarely reach the target groups strictly defined. For example, a Low-Cost Housing Committee was set up in 1972 by the central government to provide houses for people in the low-income groups. To satisfy this objective the committee planned to build houses at an average cost of less than ¢4,000 (U.S. $2,353). By 1975 the average cost of a house was about ¢9,000 (U.S. $5,294), and this effectively put the completed houses beyond the reach of the low-income earners as previously defined by the committee.

Housing has also been provided by agencies for particular groups in different employment categories such as the military or nurses. They are generally tied to the continued employment of the occupant in that particular organization.

Construction

The rate of house construction between 1945 and 1988 has been low in relation to the demand for housing, particularly in the urban areas. Reliable statistics on housing output is hard to come by owing to the poor statistical base of the housing industry. However, an indication of the rate of house construction by the private and public sector in the period immediately after independence is given by the situation existing in Accra, the capital city. In 1957 a United Nations Technical Assistance Housing Mission to the Gold Coast suggested that to ease the housing situation in Accra alone, 3,000 houses must be constructed annually. In the first decade after independence only 2,533 houses were constructed in the city.

In 1960 the Statistical Service recorded a total of 106,023 houses in the urban areas; this number had increased by 68 percent to 178,519 in 1970. This means that the average annual production of houses in the urban areas was 7,250. Relating this figure to the population growth rate, the annual growth rate was 2.9 new houses per 1,000 population.

The situation was probably better in the rural areas, which in 1960 had about 83.3 percent of the country's housing stock and about 77 percent of the total population. By 1970 this relationship had improved because the rural areas had 80.1 percent of the housing stock and 71 percent of the country's total population. It is obvious that in terms of household formation absolute figures of population growth have little significance since the influence of rural-urban migration greatly increases the rate of household formation in the urban areas. In 1986 it was reported that the average annual national output of housing was estimated at 12,000 compared with an estimated need of 70,000 units, giving an average annual performance rate of 17 percent (Ghana Government 1986).

House construction has traditionally been the job of skilled artisans. It is typical to find, in the rural areas, buildings that have been constructed to no particular specifications or building plans. This could be explained by the general informality surrounding house building owing to the near absence of any planning-enforcement agencies. To some extent, this problem also exists in the urban areas. In a survey of Madina, a suburb of Accra, it was found that 11 percent of the houses were constructed without any building plans (Asiama 1984, 179). This is probably due to the low level of appreciation on the part of the landlords for the merits of planning and the fact that the planning authorities often have not been efficient. In the case of Madina, the area had, at the time, not been declared a Planning Area and thus did not fall within the purview of the planning laws. Of those buildings for which building plans exist, a significant number show some fundamental deviations in construction from the prepared plans.

Also characteristic of the house-construction industry is the prevalence of incremental housing practices. This may be viewed on two levels. First, house builders, constrained by financial difficulties, may provide themselves with the barest minimum accommodations, generally a bedroom or two with or without a kitchen—cooking may be done in the open space in front of the house—and a small temporary enclosure behind the house for a bathroom. Such houses may not have toilets, and their occupants may use a public toilet in the neighborhood. With time, house builders, with the security gained by living in their own house, may complete their units. Second, house builders may span their building activities over a long period (sometimes about ten years), again owing to financial constraints or due to unavailability of building materials on the market; house building may thus proceed in stages such as the foundation, the walls, the roof, and finishing.

Materials

Materials employed in building differ between the rural and urban areas and among the various geographical regions of the country in view of the climatic differences. In the urban centers, construction materials are controlled by the local authorities. For example, the Accra Building Regulations, 1944, of the

Accra City Council provide in Regulation 36: "(1) All walls of buildings shall be composed of masonry, burnt brick, cement blocks, cement concrete, reinforced concrete or other approved materials. No sun-dried bricks, swish or other similar material shall be used. (2) Walls, external, or internal, of buildings shall not be constructed either wholly or in part of corrugated iron or timber without the written consent of the Municipal Engineer." These legislated materials are those that the planning and local authorities would allow in Accra and most of the urban centers. It is significant that mud, the traditional building material, was legislated out of use. This was no doubt the effect of European acculturation. The extent to which such dictates have affected the housing problem in the country may never be known, but in a country where cement is largely imported and thus expensive, there is no doubt that a nearly-total reliance on cement in construction will lead to poor housing output. In spite of the legislation, however, it is not unusual to find mud houses in almost all urban centers, generally built before planning and building regulations became effective.

The 1969 Post Enumeration Survey published by the Census Office in 1970 showed that as many as 54 percent of the buildings in the urban centers are of mud construction, and cement blocks accounted for 38 percent. A regional distribution showed that in the Greater Accra region 60 percent of the houses were built with cement blocks. The western and central regions had 39 percent, the Ashanti region 33 percent and the Volta region 32 percent of the buildings constructed with cement blocks. In the northern and upper regions mud houses accounted for 82 percent of the total housing stock, and the Brong Ahafo region had 80 percent, the eastern region 66 percent, and the western and central regions 58 percent. Recent data are not available yet from the 1984 census, but it was expected that in 1988 a greater proportion of houses would be cement-block construction.

In the rural areas, a significant proportion of houses are constructed of mud largely because planning and building regulations are almost nonexistent and house builders thus have the freedom to seek more practical solutions to their housing problems. Roofing materials are generally of metal (corrugated iron or aluminum sheets), corrugated asbestos sheets, or concrete. They are fairly durable materials and are also in general use in the urban areas.

In terms of geographical distribution, housing in the northern and the upper regions differs from that in the South of the country owing to the peculiar climate. Mud buildings roofed with thatch are more prevalent in the northern sector. This combination ensures that the rooms are cool during the day, when the weather can be hot, and warm during the night when it can be very cold. In fact, thatched roofs are provided for about 52 percent of the houses in the urban centers of the northern sector.

Finance

Finance for house building is generally private. It includes personal savings, gratuities, and social security benefits. Institutional finance has been used to some extent, but there is no doubt that its influence on house provision is minimal.

In the Madina Survey discussed earlier, only 5 percent of house builders were found to have financed their housing activities through institutional finance, and 2 percent received help from their extended families. The rest financed their building operations from their own resources.

The low reliance on institutional finance may be due to the conditions under which such finance may be obtained, discussed in the next section. However, one major reason appears to be the attitude of the people themselves. In Madina it was found that even if the conditions were reasonable, more than a third of the respondents would not accept mortgage financing. Predominant among the many reasons given was that they did not like taking loans because of the possibility of foreclosure in case of default (Asiama 1984, 180).

Among renters, the higher the income level, the lower the proportion of income spent on housing. Paradoxically, this relationship is inversely related to the provision of amenities in that the lower the proportion of income spent on housing, the higher the level of amenities provided in the house (Owusu et al. 1973, 66). Higher-income groups enjoy better accommodations.

D. J. Owusu and Associates (1973, 66) found that, on the average, people spend about 12.7 percent of their income on rents, although wide differences among the various income categories exist. For example, the very low paid spend about 25 percent of income on rents whereas the highest paid spend about 8 percent.

For many people in salaried employment, a rent allowance of 20 percent of one's gross salary is provided by one's employer. When an employee is given housing by his employer, he contributes 10 percent of his gross income toward rent payments. This, however, is far below the rental payment that may be not less than twice a person's income. For example, housing in Cantonments, North Labone, or North Kaneshie in Accra, adequate for a university lecturer whose gross basic monthly salary is about ¢13,700 (U.S. $76.00), might cost about ¢40,000 (U.S. $222) a month (i.e., almost thrice). The tenant however, contributes only 10 percent of his salary, and the employer pays the rest.

THE ROLE OF HOUSING INSTITUTIONS AND ORGANIZATIONS

Design

It is probably true to state that, except in a few cases, there are as many designs as there are houses in Ghana. This shows the versatility of the Ghanaian house builder. Designs for housing are generally prepared by skilled draftsmen, and it would appear that their output is adequate, particularly in the case of small houses for residential occupation. In the Madina Survey it was found that draftsmen rather than professional architects prepared 74 percent of the designs (Asiama 1984, 179). Their fees are competitive, and this helps to maintain their attraction to house builders. Most draftsmen work in offices in which their jobs do not normally include house designs, so they carry out their designing on the side.

In the public sector, the State Housing Corporation has standard designs (SH Types) for its housing programs on its estates. They are often borrowed by public bodies that provide housing for their staff. It is significant that a majority of such designs are altered by those who eventually purchase the houses. Two reasons may be adduced for this. First, it would appear that the designs are inadequate for the target population and, second, that as their income increases, purchasers find it necessary to enlarge their houses.

Finance

Finance for house building is generally generated from the house builder's own resources. This is true in spite of the existence of financial institutions capable of giving mortgages for housing. One of the reasons given is the attitude of the people themselves; the other is the conditions under which these institutions grant mortgages.

Theoretically, anyone can secure a loan from a commercial bank for housing or any other venture. However, in practice, these avenues are restricted. The commercial banks do not discriminate between investments in housing and other investments; for this reason, the interest rates charged are excessive if the loan is to be invested in housing owing to the general low turnover in housing and hence the long pay-back period. The Bank for Housing and Construction (established in 1972) and the First Ghana Building Society (the only building society in the country, established in 1956 by the central government) are the major financial institutions specializing in mortgage financing. According to the rules of the bank, the only qualification for a mortgage is for the applicant to be a depositor of at least six months' standing. The maximum pay-back period allowed for mortgages is twenty years, and the rate of interest charged is 26 percent. The society specifies that applicants for mortgages must be members of at least three years' standing; the maximum pay-back period is twenty-five years or the applicant's sixty-fifth birthday, whichever is earlier. (Table 18.2 shows the performance of the bank since its inception.) There is no doubt that in relation to housing demand, the bank has not performed creditably.

In addition to the bank and the society, other financial institutions provide mortgage housing finance to special groups. They include the State Insurance Corporation, which grants mortgages to its employees, the university senior staff, and senior officers of the Ghana Armed Forces. The maximum amount that can be granted is ¢500,000 (U.S. $2,841.00). Mortgages of up to ¢250,000 (U.S. $1,420) attract a compound interest of 10 percent, and those exceeding ¢250,000 (U.S. $1,420) attract 14 percent. These rates are considerably lower than the 26 percent currently being charged by the Bank for Housing and Construction, thus making the corporation's facility popular; however, between 1975

Table 18.2
Mortgage Loans Issued by the Bank for Housing and Construction, Ghana, 1974–1985

Year	Number of Houses Financed	Amount	
		¢ (000)	US $ (000)
1974	19	434.40	255.50
1975	109	2,342.40	1377.80
1976	74	2,492.50	1466.20
1977	43	1,645.00	967.60
1978	17	1,097.00	645.30
1979	8	583.30	216.00
1980*	2	38.80	14.40
1981	5	385.40	142.70
1982	2	740.00	274.00
1983	7	1,208.60	13.40
1984	7	1,439.60	16.00
1985	4	1,159.18	12.90
TOTAL	**297**	**13,566.18**	**5,401.80**

Source: Compiled from records of the Bank for Housing and Construction, Accra.
*Supplementary loans.

and 1985 the corporation granted only 639 mortgages, again a low performance rate.

A special mortgage-finance scheme, the Public Servants' Housing Loan Scheme, was established in 1975 to be applicable only to Ghanaian public servants whose salaries are paid by the controller and accountant-general. A maximum amount not exceeding five times the gross annual salary of the applicant is granted to public servants for the purpose of building their own houses. Interest on the loan is 2.5 percent on the reducing balance. Repayment is by monthly deductions from the applicant's salary by the controller and accountant-general, who pays such deductions to the Public Servants' Housing Loan Scheme Board, administrators of the scheme. Such monthly deductions must not exceed 20 percent of the applicant's basic monthly salary, and total repayment should not exceed thirty years. Thus, clearly, the scheme is targeted toward a specific income group.

The National Mortgage Financing and Guarantee Scheme was established in 1976 with four objectives:

1. To promote the financing of the construction of dwelling houses by private individuals for their personal occupation

2. To finance the construction of dwelling houses by organizations engaged in housing development

3. To provide for an indemnity by the Bank of Ghana (the country's central bank) in regard to losses incurred by financial institutions participating in the scheme arising out of defaults in payment of loans by them under the scheme

4. To provide for the establishment by the Bank of Ghana of a secondary mortgage market in Ghana

To qualify for a loan under the scheme one must be in employment approved by the Bank of Ghana and must keep an account with the financial institution from which the loan is sought for not less than three years. The rate of interest on loans under the scheme is 2 percent above the current savings deposit rate of interest on the reducing balance of the mortgage, and the amount of mortgage is not to exceed 95 percent of the cost of the proposed development. On August 31, 1989, the interest rate under the scheme stood at 20 percent.

Some schemes are restricted to rural communities. The peculiar characteristic of these schemes is that assistance is given in terms of materials rather than money. Under the Roof Loans Scheme, building materials are supplied to selected applicants of villages, which have approved Roof Loan Societies, to roof their housing units to prevailing standards. A corollary to this is the Wall Protection (Home Improvement and Repairs) Loans Scheme under which building materials are supplied to members of village cooperative housing societies to plaster and paint their walls and to provide doors and windows and proper drainage around the building. These loans are repayable at low interest rates. By the end of 1986, 13,900 persons had benefited from the Wall Protection Scheme.

Building and Development

There are few institutions that specialize in house provision, and many of them are in the public sector.

- The State Housing Corporation: The output of the corporation by the end of 1986 was estimated at 200 units per annum against a projected target of 2,000 units per annum.

- The Tema Development Corporation: The main objective of the corporation is to improve the housing situation in Tema and to redevelop the slum areas of Tema through the building of eighteen self-contained residential communities with a total of 28,500 housing units by 1985. However, the corporation did not add to its housing stock during the three years ending in 1987 and has a total housing deficit of about 10,000. Between 1974 and 1984 the corporation's annual output of housing was about 200 units.

- Redco: This is a subsidiary of the Bank for Housing and Construction specializing in housing development. It declared a projected annual output of 1,000 units at its inception in 1979, but as of the end of 1987 it had not completed a single house.

• The Prefab Concrete Products Company: This company is concerned with the production of large concrete-panel prefabricated housing units. Its installed capacity is 400 housing units per annum, but as of the end of 1987 it was producing only 100 units per annum.

In addition to these organizations, other state organizations have been involved in housing using their own generated funds (such as the Social Security and National Insurance Trust, the State Insurance Corporation, and the banking institutions) or central government budgetary allocations for housing (e.g., staff bungalows, nurses' quarters, army housing). Together, they have been projected to add about 1,000 units to the housing stock every year, but in reality they have never reached the 100-unit mark (Ghana Government 1986, 7).

In the rural areas, the Department of Rural Housing and Cottage Industries engages in a Rural Co-operative Housing Scheme under which the department assists twenty or more rural dwellers who form cooperative societies to build houses. Until the end of 1986, the department had undertaken the construction of 1,806 units out of which 972 units had been completed with the remainder at various stages of completion.

Public housing delivery agencies have performed very poorly, and the reasons for this are rooted in corruption, nepotism, lack of initiative, and unworkable bureaucracies. Funds allocated for house building have often been misapplied and dissipated.

Few institutions operate in house building in the private sector. One of the largest and the most successful is CFC Estates, which has built a large estate in Tesano and Dome in Accra. After the 1987 Budget Statement and Economic Policy was issued there was a proliferation of real estate development companies wanting to take advantage of the concessions offered in the housing sector. It is too early to assess the impact they will make on the housing industry, although current evidence suggests that financial constraints will make most of these companies unviable.

Most house building (about 80 percent) is done by private individuals. Reliable statistics do not exist, but much of this building is done through self-help in the rural areas. In the urban areas, small-scale builders (called masons) may be contracted to construct the house, usually under the supervision of the house-owner.

Management

Housing management in the country is private and individualistic except in the case of institution-provided housing in which case the institution may provide some estate-management functions. Such institutions usually run an estate-management department that undertakes such tasks. The State Housing Corporation, the Tema Development Corporation, the State Insurance Corporation, and the Social Security and National Insurance Trust all have their own estate-management departments.

In the private sector, there are a few professionally qualified estate managers offering management services. They rarely have been patronized by property owners because few property owners find such external managers necessary. It is also because the phenomenon of large residential estates is generally unknown outside the public sector.

Renewal

Urban-renewal programs have not been a characteristic of the housing scene in Ghana. This has not been for the lack of opportunities because there are many slums needing renewal. The reason has been that urban renewal is an expensive task that in a developing country can be successfully tackled only by the state machinery. The willingness on the part of the state to undertake such tasks has, until recently, been very poor.

Two renewal projects stand out for mention. The Koforidua urban-renewal project was undertaken in about 1974 and involved the elimination of substandard houses and the resettlement of the affected population. It entailed the complete redevelopment of the project area with recreational facilities and so on. According to the Technical Memorandum prepared for the project, three main objectives were to be achieved by the project:

1. The redesigning and improvement of the land-use plan of the area
2. The building of adequate parking lots in the area
3. The improvement of the road network so that it will offer the capacity to move people and goods within and outside the area easily and conveniently

Unfortunately, the project was beset by many difficulties, the least being the lack of finance, and by the end of 1989 the redevelopment had not been completed.

One major urban renewal project that is likely to serve as a prototype for other projects is the East Mamobi Upgrading Project in Accra. The project, which is funded by the World Bank, began in 1986 and is estimated to require three years for completion. The project involves the provision of basic roads, drainage, water supply, electricity, sanitation, and garbage disposal in a 30 hecter sector of Nima-Mamobi east of the Nima highway and north of the Nima stream inhabited by approximately 19,000 people. Initial estimates placed the total project cost at U.S. $3 million.

HOUSING MARKETS AND POLICY ORIENTATIONS

The country has lacked a coherent policy on housing. The state's attempt at rationalizing operations in the housing industry has been ad hoc and has lacked consistency. Government policy has been strewn among various development planning objectives (none of which has ever been fully implemented), speeches of politicians, various uncoordinated administrative instructions and suggestions, and directives in the government media. This has made assessments of housing achievements difficult since they rarely relate to any set objectives. This needs to be set against the background of frequent changes in government.

In 1986 the government, the Provisional National Defence Council (PNDC), introduced the first serious attempt at formulating a national housing policy in a document, The National Housing Policy and Action Plan. According to the document, "the ultimate goal of the country's housing policy is to provide adequate and affordable housing with infrastructure facilities to satisfy the needs of her people." This, according to the document, should be achieved through the realization of these objectives:

1. shifting of emphasis of the government from completed houses to the provision of infrastructural/serviced sites;
2. creation of a sound financial body for effective planning implementation and co-ordination; monitoring and evaluating all action plans and programmes emanating from this policy;
3. ensuring easy access to housing land, security of tenure and effective land-use management;
4. intensifying and encouraging the development and use of local building materials, through research and pilot prototype projects. And also ensuring a continuous flow of both building materials and needed skills;
5. an appraisal of all abandoned housing in the public sector and the completion of feasible rehabilitation. In the case of units in the private sector, concessionary reliefs will be given for the rehabilitation of those that can be readily converted into communal housing;
6. improving rural housing through its integration with the dominant economic activity in a particular area; and
7. the improvement of housing standards through the orderly growth of settlements based on effective planning and control.

These objectives are to be achieved by a National Housing Board to be established under the chairmanship of the secretary (minister) responsible for public works and housing. At the end of March 1989, however, the board had not been established.

In the 1988 Budget Statement and Economic Policy the government introduced several policy objectives relating to the housing sector. These and the aforementioned objectives are discussed and evaluated below in relation to specific topics.

The Provision of Housing

The 1986 Action Plan estimates an annual average output for the period (1987–1990) of 28,750 even though the annual housing requirement is estimated at

70,000 units. Thus it is expected that a total of 115,000 housing units will be constructed under the plan. They will be made up of 91, 7, and 2 percent low-, medium-, and high-income units distributed throughout the country. Although the plan envisages that the entire infrastructure base will be financed from the public sector with supplemental funds from the National Housing Fund, only 2 percent of the units will be directly provided by the public sector.

Agencies in the public sector that would have responsibility for this are the State Housing Corporation, the Tema Development Corporation, the Public Works Department, the State Insurance Corporation, the Social Security and National Insurance Trust, and Redco. In the rural sector, the Department of Rural Housing and Cottage Industries would have the responsibilities of providing housing and infrastructure.

In the private sector four organizations are identified for the mobilization of resources in house provision: the First Ghana Building Society, the Credit Union, the Ghana National Association of Teachers (GNAT), and the Cocoa, Coffee, and Sheanut Farmers Association. Although they, except for the first one, are not housing organizations, the plan envisages that they would be interested in diverting resources into housing provision. It is significant to note that in the plan no particular incentives are given to those organizations to induce them to do this.

The plan provides for some subsidy for housing developers through the granting of "tax holidays" (i.e., periods for which no taxes will be paid) to newly established large-scale building-materials factories in accordance with the country's code on investments and the reduction of interest rates on housing loans to house builders to less than 75 percent of the commercial interest rate. The 1988 Budget Statement and Economic Policy also grants tax relief to housing developers. Corporate Tax for Real Estate Companies has been reduced by 10 percent, and companies and persons who invest part of their profits in residential real estate development will be allowed to offset up to 50 percent of such investment against the ensuing year's tax liability. In addition, the Economic Policy Statement grants a five-year tax holiday to real estate developers and allows any losses incurred during the tax holiday period to be carried forward for another two years. Furthermore, purchasers of houses from real estate companies, the State Housing Corporation, and the Tema Development Corporation are to be exempted from payment of stamp duty. The sales tax on locally produced building materials was also reduced to 10 percent from 20 percent.

In terms of actual expenditures, the Economic Policy plans to spend ¢1.25 billion (U.S. $7.1 million) renovating all government bungalows and to complete ongoing public housing projects. This amount constitutes about 0.9 percent of the GNP for 1988. In addition, the government plans to spend ¢2.6 billion (U.S. $14.8 million) between 1988 and 1990 to provide infrastructural facilities for housing and to provide financial assistance to the state's housing-development institutions to complete various projects initiated by them.

The plan makes no detailed provision for the development of housing associations and housing cooperatives except in the rural sector where mention is made of the fact that housing cooperatives will be promoted. The National Housing Board also has, as one of its functions, to "encourage and develop housing cooperatives and provide incentives to private developers." The focus, apart from the few houses to be constructed by the public sector, is to be on real estate development companies. The plan provides that "in the utilization of the funds the Board will seek ways of encouraging the development of large housing programs to take advantage of economies of scale in construction. Single developers should be discouraged as much as possible."

Evaluation

The housing policy does not form part of a national development strategy. For example, it does not relate to important national concerns such as the alleviation of unemployment, the location of job opportunities outside the main urban centers, and the fight against inflation. This makes difficult the assessment of the achievements of the policy. It also means that housing is viewed as a physical rather than socioeconomic entity.

The relationship between the National Housing Board and the Ministry of Works and Housing has not been clearly defined. If the ministry is to continue in its present form and organization, the National Housing Board would be merely another bureaucracy. If the board is to be efficient, the housing wing of the ministry may have to be dismantled. This would eliminate unnecessary interference from the ministry.

The 1986 Action Plan's provisions ignore the role the individual has played in the housing sector through self-help housing by placing a high premium on the role of real estate development companies. Owing to the high cost of housing finance, these companies must provide for the capital rather than the rental market. This means that only the rich would benefit from these arrangements. If the goal of the housing policy to house as many people as possible is to be achieved, the focus of attention must be on the individual who builds a house through self-help. The policy must provide the conditions under which people, particularly the poor, can build their own houses.

It is expected that through the implementation of the housing policy and action plan some jobs will be created to help ease the problem of unemployment. Although this has not been quantified owing to the poor statistical base of the country, one of the functions of the National Housing Board is the "training of manpower resources to support the implementation of the stated objectives."

Although the plan fails to incorporate housing into the development strategies for the country, it does mention the need to meet the housing needs of special groups like the Ghana National Association of Teachers, the Ghana Private Road Transport Union, the civil servants, the police, the prison service, and the military. This will, it is expected, help to increase productivity in those sectors, if the houses benefit those most in need.

MAJOR PROBLEMS

Land

One of the most fundamental problems of housing in Ghana is the issue of affordable land for housing. The institutional framework of landholding impedes the development of housing particularly for the economically disadvantaged.

The land market in Ghana is characterized by a dual system of ownership—the traditional sector, which is predominant, and the state sector. In the traditional sector land is owned by tribes and families with authority to deal in land vested in the tribal heads (chiefs) and family heads. Land acquisition for housing (or any other purpose) is therefore controlled by them. They determine who is to receive land grants, how much is to be charged for land, and how much land is to be offered for sale. The choice of beneficiary of land grants is not always dependent on economic considerations but at times on one's social and political standing in society. Land prices in this sector are high, particularly in the urban areas, owing to the high demand.

Other features of the traditional market in land include the time it takes to acquire interests in land. Apart from the time it takes to investigate the title of the prospective vendor and to identify the real owners of the land, the procedures instituted by the government to monitor the land-acquisition process—such as the granting of Ministerial Concurrence, stamping, and registration—sometimes take more than a year. The sector is also characterized by insecurity of titles. Primarily, the problem is one of identifying the real owners of land and whether they have authority to deal in land. This problem is compounded because the high demand for urban land leads people to make hasty decisions to develop land before they have satisfied themselves about the title being passed on to them (Woodman 1969). The result is usually a long chain of litigation over titles, which is not only time consuming but expensive and reduces the development financial resources of the purchaser. Again, owing to the large number of traditional authorities, each with its own traditions and customs, land tenure is not uniform. In some urban centers (notably Sekondi-Takoradi, Cape Coast, and Accra) the traditional authorities are themselves not certain who constitutes the final authority with respect to land. In Sekondi, for example, the *Omanhene* (paramount chief) believes he has a right to confirm all grants of land made in the city, whereas the *Ahenkofi* chief (a subchief under the *Omanhene*) also claims to be the final authority over a large part of the city's land. A similar problem occurs in Cape Coast where the *Omanhene* and the head of the Ebiradze clan are in conflict over who constitutes the final authority. The effect of this uncertainty of titles among the owners is that people are not sure who is capable of giving a title secure enough to justify the expenditure of money on land.

In the public sector, land management is in the hands of the Lands Commission, a seven-member body appointed by the central government with a secretariat that has offices in all ten regional capitals. In late 1987 the government appointed subcommittees of the commission to oversee the activities of the commission in the regions.

Theoretically, publicly owned land is accessible to all Ghanaians on an equal basis of ''first come, first served'' (i.e., one who presents an application earlier will receive priority over all applicants who follow regardless of any other factors). In practice however, many qualifications exist in regard to this general principle.

Public lands are accessible only when the applicant's spouse has not benefited from a grant of land from the commission. The rule is that each nuclear family is entitled to only one plot of land in the public sector.

To qualify to own a plot of publicly owned land a person must have a favorable bankers' reference that shows that he holds, in his account, a sum of money that will enable him to carry out building operations on the land he seeks. The grantee must also promise the commission to commence building operations within twelve months of the grant of the land and to complete them within thirty-six months from the same date.

Even though there are no specific official rules making an applicant's occupation a factor determining eligibility to own a public plot, examination of the beneficiaries of allocations by the commission shows that senior civil servants, senior army personnel, senior public officers (e.g., staff of state corporations and other parastatal organizations), and the senior staff of the universities stand a better chance of securing grants from the commission than any other group of people.

Again, a grant by the commission costs nothing to the grantee. One is required to pay a development charge ranging between ¢1,000 (U.S. $5.68) and ¢5,000 (U.S. $28.41) depending on the location of the land one seeks, to cover the cost of providing services such as access roads, electricity, water, and drainage facilities. In the face of spiraling inflation in the Ghanaian economy, this figure is woefully inadequate. Nevertheless, the state provides these services and, in effect, subsidizes the already well off. In addition to paying the development charge, the grantee is expected to pay a ground rent annually, since all grants made by the commission for housing are leaseholds for ninety-nine years (fifty years in the case of expatriates).

The security of tenure for a grantee of publicly owned land is almost absolute. Since the state is the landlord, the grantee can expect no interference from any other person claiming to have a better title. Thus as long as the grantee observes the terms of the covenants in the leasehold document, he can be sure of title for as long as the lease lasts.

The period for acquisition of public land is on the average thirty-six months between the time the grantee submits an application and the time the application comes up for discussion by the commission. This is primarily due to the low supply of land in this sector in relation to the demand, but it is also due to the inefficient bureaucracy. Thus in either the private or public sectors, land for housing presents a formidable problem particularly to the economically disadvantaged.

Finance

There are numerous financial arrangements under which house builders can obtain financing. However, all of them are very problematic.

Of primary concern is the level of interest rates in the economy. Owing to the government's monetarist economic recovery program, interest rates have been significantly raised to stimulate savings and to discourage borrowing as a way of checking inflation. This is having deleterious effects on those sectors that are yet to be developed such as the housing and agricultural sectors. Mortgage finance has become too expensive, and when it is to be used for housing, it becomes prohibitive. This is because the long payback period in the housing sector makes high interest payments uneconomical. By the close of 1987 interest payments stood at 26 percent. Few people could afford this. One effect of this would be that housing developers would produce housing for sale rather than for rental. Second, those who operate in the capital market as purchasers must already have accumulated the purchase price since it would be uneconomical to borrow money to purchase their houses. Third, the poor who want to build their own houses cannot afford to take mortgages. The result is that only the rich can participate in the market for housing.

Even when one wants to take the risk and seek mortgage finance from the financial institutions, the conditions under which they lend means that few people can qualify for such assistance. The majority of people, particularly those with low income, have not acquired banking habits. Under a government directive in late 1986 all state employees were to open bank accounts into which their salaries would be paid. Although the primary objective was to check the fraudulent payment of salaries to nonexistent employees, the measure was also aimed at creating a savings habit among the populace. It is yet to be seen whether the primary objective of the policy has been achieved, but evidence so far suggests that salaries paid into banks are almost instantly withdrawn by their recipients. This may be due to the poor economic situation, which makes it difficult to live on less than one's full income. In the rural communities, a similar measure that required cash payment for agricultural produce (such as cocoa, coffee, sheanuts) to be made in checks has not produced a higher propensity to save since farmers often take out all of the money. Perhaps time and a better economic climate will inculcate the savings habit.

This state of affairs is even worse in the nonformal sector because few people save in the banks. The nature of transactions in this sector makes savings undesirable since people must always have their monies nearby to make purchases when required (Asiama 1985). Thus a requirement of a good savings account by the banks becomes onerous so that few people qualify for mortgages.

Building Materials

Building materials also provide considerable problems in the housing sector. Owing to the fact that a significant proportion of materials needed for housing is imported from abroad, building materials are often scarce. This scarcity has led to high prices of these commodities. When housing has to compete with the demand for such materials by other sectors in the construction industry, the cost of housing becomes prohibitive and few people can participate in house building, particularly when they cannot afford to take mortgages.

As an illustration, by the end of 1987, a 50 kilogram bag of cement cost approximately ¢1,700 (U.S. $9.70). This meant that house construction was curtailed considerably since few people could afford this. Of perhaps more significance was the fact that building maintenance was also curtailed owing to the scarcity and the high cost of the materials. Thus not only was house construction curtailed but also the existing stock was not being maintained. It is significant to note that the official price of cement (i.e., government-approved price) at this time was about ¢950 (U.S. $5.40). However, a majority of the population lacked the essential "credentials" to obtain the cement from the government agencies who sold at that price. The government responded and, in accordance with the economic recovery program, gave permission for individuals, who had the means, to import cement to be sold in the open market. This had the effect of temporarily reducing the price because many traders responded to this by increasing the supply. However, this was short lived since the import duties payable made cement importation uneconomical at the new price.

Also of some significance are the different prices of building materials (even at the official price) found in the country. As one moves farther away from the capital, Accra, prices escalate to take account of transport costs. This means that building materials become more expensive in the hinterland and the northern sectors of the country, areas, ironically, where more buildings are needed and incomes are lower.

Rent Control

Another area of discontent is rent control. This was introduced soon after World War II to ensure that the increase in demand for housing in Accra, owing to the large influx of returning servicemen who had decided to stay in Accra rather than return to their rural habitats, did not lead to high rents in the city. After independence, urbanization outstripped the provision of houses giving landlords advantages over tenants. The Rent Control Act, 1963 (Act 220), was enacted not only to check rent increases but also to regulate landlord and tenant relations (e.g., security of tenure, responsibility for repairs).

Rent control has assumed a more prominent place in the housing market since 1972 when the Rent (Amendment) Decree, 1972 (NRCD 153), was passed stipulating that rents of rooms not exceeding 12 feet by 12 feet be fixed at ¢5.00

(U.S. $4.50) per month. This was followed in 1979 by the Rent Amendment Decree (AFRCD 5), which again fixed rents arbitrarily. In 1982 the Rent Control Law was passed (PNDCL 5), and it pegged the rent for a single room at ¢20.00 (U.S. $7.00) per month from an open-market rent of about ¢70.00 (U.S. $25.00). The law also stipulated that when house rents exceeded ¢1,000 (U.S. $350.00) per month, a rent tax of 50 percent was to be exacted. In 1986, the Rent Control Law (PNDCL 138) was passed removing the authority to deal with most landlord and tenant disputes from the courts to Rent and Housing Committees established under the law.

The effect of these measures has been a certain wariness on the part of the landlords. Although statistical data are lacking, many tenants seem to collude with landlords to subvert the existing controls on rent. This suggests that the law is out of step with the realities of life in the country. Another effect seems to be that new house construction is moving away from housing for the low-income earners, the sector that is more susceptible to rent controls. This is because rents for middle-income properties are not controlled, and taxes on rent income have not been enforced. If this trend continues it is likely that housing will become a critical issue in the economic and political development of the country as the existing stock of low-income houses is not maintained or replaced. Many landlords in first-class residential areas in the large cities, particularly Accra and Kumasi, now demand the payment of rents in convertible currency, principally the U.S. dollar. This is a response to the poor economic situation of the country. What it means, however, is that a dual housing market is created in the country. Typical rents in the airport residential area in Accra hovered around U.S. $1,200 per month by the close of 1987. Exchanging this for the Ghanaian Cedi at the official rate of exchange of U.S. $1 = ¢176 gives a total of ¢211,200 per month. Similar properties let to Ghanaians were commanding rents of about ¢70,000 (U.S. $398) per month. With such a huge difference there is no doubt that more and more landlords will opt for the foreign-exchange market.

PROSPECTIVE DEVELOPMENTS

In the absence of reliable statistical data, forecasting future developments in housing becomes a hazardous task. The discussion that follows is thus based mainly on scattered evidence.

Housing Demand

Housing-demand patterns are likely to remain in their present forms for some time. Owing to the poor adjustment between rural development and urban growth, rural-urban migration is likely to continue. This means that urban single-person households are likely to continue to increase and the need for the type of ac-commodations desired will persist. In the past few years, the poor economic situation in the country has resulted in many of these single-person households migrating to other countries to earn a living. This has, to an appreciable degree, helped to ease the urban housing situation since their stay in urban areas has only been transitory. With the prospects of economic recovery at home, the unfortunate collapse of the once-buoyant Nigerian economy, the diminished attractiveness of Libya to Ghanaian migrant workers, and the tightening of immigration laws in Europe, it is likely that a significant proportion of these rural-urban migrants will stay, thus increasing the demand for urban housing.

In the rural areas, housing demand will be mainly in the quality of housing. Current trends suggest that better and more durable buildings will be constructed in the rural communities. This is largely due to the flow of capital from the overseas migrant workers and from an improved urban economy into rural areas. Most of such capital flow is being manifested in new construction of houses using modern materials and modern designs and improvement of the existing stock. There is some indication that this trend will continue. The growth of cooperative housing societies is also likely to alter the character of demand for rural housing (Thompson 1980). This is because the kind of housing being constructed appears to be underlying a perpetuation of nuclear-family individuation in the rural communities (Caldwell 1966). Whereas in the past most individuals have been content with a room or two in the ancestral or family house in the village, thus fostering and strengthening family ties, now with the development of cooperative housing societies, prosperous individual family members join a cooperative to build a single-family house, thus moving out of the family house. When this happens, there is little doubt that the individual will become less likely to contribute to the improvement of the family house. This will be unfortunate since the family house is a focal point for all of the extended family. It is usually the house in which rites of passage for family members are performed (Kilson 1974).

In urban communities, it appears that the compound house is going out of fashion. This is because more and more families now prefer the privacy afforded by single-family housing units. Largely due to low rents many compound houses are also poorly maintained, thus further reducing their attractiveness to prospective occupiers and the demand for them.

Housing Supply

Housing supply will, in the immediate future, lag behind demand because there is no evidence to suggest that the current constraints on housing provision will be eliminated. In the government's National Housing Policy and Action Plan, 1987–1990, it is estimated that the annual housing requirement is 70,000 new units. The government plans to produce an annual average of 28,750 units. Even if the plan is successfully implemented (by June 30, 1988, there were no signs of its implementation), there will be a planned average annual deficit of 41,250 units. Thus irrespective of current and projected efforts Ghana will have to bear with the housing problem for some time.

Current evidence suggests that the nature of the houses being supplied will be to satisfy the demand of middle- and high-income earners. This is partially due to the effect of rent-control legislation, which has, predictably, been focused consistently on low-income housing, thus making investments in that sector not profitable. It is also due partially to the economics of housing. Owing to high interest rates on mortgages, housing investors expect a short payback period and thus high returns in the short term. The low-income sector cannot play a part in this scenario.

Policy Directions

The direction of Ghana's housing policy for the immediate future has already been discussed in relation to the government's National Housing Policy and Action Plan. This shows a trend toward the government playing the role of a facilitator in housing to enable the private sector to be involved more actively in housing provision. It would appear, however, that a reliance on real estate development companies in this respect, as envisaged by the government, will not extend housing to the low-income earners and the rural communities owing to the poor economic situation. Although these companies may be efficient in a macro sense, they cannot address the real housing needs of the country since a majority of the populace cannot participate in the market. Although privatization of housing provisions is desirable and, perhaps, a much better alternative to public provision, it would be more beneficial to rely on individual efforts because this might prove more productive in terms of actual needs satisfied than attempting to reap economies of scale that might be associated with real estate development companies.

It appears that housing policy will focus on slum upgrading projects in the immediate future. In November 1987 the government published a document, *Programme of Actions to Mitigate the Social Cost of Adjustment* (PAMSCAD), which itemized some projected plans to mitigate the deleterious effects of the World Bank and International Development Agency (IDA)-sponsored economic recovery program of the country on urban centers. If this program is implemented, inner-city renewal projects might become a feature of housing programs in the future.

Another potentially significant policy direction is the development of indigenous building materials to reduce the import volume and, hence, the cost of housing, as called for in the Housing Policy and Action Plan.

Agenda for Research

Current research has focused on housing land to identify rational and workable land policies to provide cheap land with secure titles to urban settlers, particularly the low-income earners. Work is also being done on a compilation of housing statistics relating to housing development, occupancy rates, house types, and so on. The role of financial institutions in housing is also being investigated as are building materials. It is expected that in the immediate future these studies will continue.

The National Housing Policy and Action Plan identifies the following areas as "major" research areas to which immediate attention will be given:

1. Improvement of inexpensive on-site materials for increased utilization in housing construction
2. Erosion control in settlements
3. Identification and development of local sources of structural and masonry binders
4. Building costs
5. Improvements in building construction practices
6. Standardization of building components and their fabrication and the construction of timber structures

Additionally, the following areas might prove useful if studied:

1. Building regulations: Building regulations and codes relevant to the Ghana experience need to be examined within the context of the social and political circumstances of the country.
2. Planning regulations: They need to be investigated to provide a technical background to housing in the country. The existing planning law was passed in 1945, and there is no doubt that, functionally, it is outdated, owing to demographic and economic growth in the country since that date.
3. Urban services: Housing does not mean only buildings; it also includes those services and amenities, like access roads, refuse collection, and utilities, that make housing meaningful. The management, delivery, and economics of these services need to be researched.
4. Filtering: It needs to be examined whether houses filter down to people of lower economic status as their occupants move out into better housing. One needs to know whether filtering is along economic lines or along kinship lines.

Institutions involved in housing research are mainly the universities and the Building and Road Research Institute of the Department of Housing and Planning Research in the University of Science and Technology. There is little doubt, however, that owing to the poor institutional financing of housing research, much of the research will still be conducted by individual academic researchers.

REFERENCES

Asiama, S. O. 1984. "The Land Factor in Housing for Low-Income Urban Settlers: The Example of Madina, Ghana." *Third World Planning Review* 6:171–84.
———. 1985. "The Rich Slum Dweller: A Problem of Unequal Access." *International Labour Review* 124:353–62.

Caldwell, J. C. 1966. "The Erosion of the Family: A Study of the Fate of the Family in Ghana." *Population Studies* 20:5–26.

Ghana Government. 1986. *National Housing Policy and Action Plan. 1987–1992.* Accra: Ministry of Works and Housing.

Kilson, Marion D. 1974. *African Urban Kinsmen: The Ga of Central Accra.* London: C. Hurst.

Owusu, D. J., R. K. B. Bofa, and C. C. T. Blankson. 1973. *A Housing Survey in Ghana.* Accra: National Low Cost Housing Committee.

Quarcoo, A. K., N. O. Addo, and M. Peil. 1967. *Madina Survey.* Legon: Institute of African Studies, University of Ghana.

Thompson, P. A. 1980. "Co-operative Housing as a Solution to the General Housing Problem in Ghana." Paper presented at the National Housing Seminar, University of Science and Technology, Kumasi, March 17–22.

Tipple, G. A. 1982. *Housing in Kumasi.* Research Report No. 4. Kumasi: Department of Planning, University of Science and Technology.

United Nations. 1957. *Housing in Ghana.* Report of Technical Assistance Housing Mission to Ghana. New York.

Woodman, G. R. 1969. "Palliatives for Uncertainty of Title: The Land Development (Protection for Purchasers) Act 1960." *University of Ghana Law Journal* 6: 146–58.

FURTHER READING

Acquaye, E., and S. O. Asiama. "Land Policies for Housing Development for Low-Income Groups in Africa." *Land Development Studies* 3 (1986):127–43.

Afele, L. K. *National Housing Estimates.* Current Report No. 6. Kumasi: Building and Road Research Institute, 1978.

Albert, Frants. "Urban Land Use in Ghana." *Ekistics* 249 (1976):109–17.

Asiama, S. O. "Social Analysis, Urbanisation and Land Reform in Ghana." Ph.D. dissertation, University of Birmingham, 1980.

Bobo, B. F. "Population Density, Housing Demand and Land Values: The Case of Accra, Ghana." *Journal of African Studies* 4 (1977):140–60.

Brand, R. R. "The Spatial Organisation of Residential Areas in Accra, Ghana with Particular Reference to Aspects of Modernisation." *Economic Geography* 48 (1972):284–98.

Farrow, J. E. *Alternative Housing Policies for Ghanaian Cities.* Current Report No. 9. Kumasi: Building and Road Research Institute, 1975.

Ghana Government. *Report of Committee on National Housing Policy.* Accra: Ministry of Works and Housing, 1976.

———. *Programme of Actions to Mitigate the Social Costs of Adjustment.* Accra: Ministry of Finance and Economic Planning, 1987.

Tipple, A. Graham. "Housing Policy and Culture in Kumasi, Ghana: A Study of Constraints and Resources." *Environment and Behavior* 19, no. 3 (1987):331–52.

———. "Housing Policy and Culture in Kamasi." *African Urban Studies* 15 (Winter 1983):17–30.

———. *Housing Conditions and Household Characteristics in Kumasi: A Survey of Existing Data.* Research Report No. 3. Kumasi: Department of Planning, University of Science and Technology, 1980.

19

South Africa

TIMOTHY HART

HOUSING POLICY AND APARTHEID

The evolution of post–World War II housing policy in South Africa cannot be understood apart from the broader sociopolitical agenda of separate development (Soussan 1984) that has led, over time, to the complex web of racially discriminatory laws and practices that have come to be known as apartheid. But these laws and practices have not remained monolithic and immutable. Since the late 1970s the state has faced a deepening political and economic crisis, and a neoapartheid order has begun taking shape (Cobbett et al. 1986). South African housing policy is both an aspect and a result of "modernizing" (Adam 1971) apartheid, and it is in the housing arena that some of its sociospatial manipulations (Smith 1982) have been most consistently and powerfully felt. Furthermore, some of the most virulent opposition to aspects of apartheid has been expressed in and around the built environment (Sutcliffe 1986).

It is incorrect to associate racial legislation and apartheid entirely with the Afrikaner-dominated Nationalist party (Pirie 1984), which gained a majority in the white Parliament in 1948, and which has ruled without a serious threat to its majority for forty years. Apartheid and neoapartheid are associated in this chapter with the period extending from 1948 to the present, but the underlying imperatives, the labor requirements of a capitalist economy, and the protection of white privilege and supremacy (Smith 1982) predate the use of the term *apartheid* and the Nationalist government. The foundations of apartheid, and of racially based housing policy, had been laid long before 1948.

The major policy instruments of apartheid have been those effecting and entrenching racial segregation, such as the Group Areas Act and related legislation specifically applicable to blacks (Maasdorp 1980; Pirie 1984), and "influx-control" measures controlling and directing the movement of people (particularly blacks) between peripheral labor-rich reserves and urban areas (Horrell 1982; Morris 1981). Two levels of segregation have emerged as a result of the body of influx control and segregation laws: a division between "common" South Africa and the "homeland" black reserves and a patchwork of white, "colored" (mixed race), Asian, and black (or African) areas in nonhomeland South Africa (Smith 1982). Rigid territorial apartheid has proved difficult to sustain, however, and the scrapping of overt influx control in 1986 was symptomatic of wide-ranging reformist policy restructuring.

Against this background, South African housing policy has displayed a broad rationale and purpose but also vacillation and contradiction in the formulation and implementation of reforms. Nonwhite and in particular black housing policy bears the imprint of modernizing apartheid and also the legacy of persistent and frequent change and reorganization. This process can be described in the context of three broad phases.

Townships and Passes (1948 to 1961)

The term *township* is used throughout this chapter to describe segregated black residential areas adjacent to towns and cities in "common" South Africa.

During this first phase, policies and instruments of apartheid were elaborated and refined (Morris 1981). So-called pass laws served to entrench a stable black work force and residential population in white cities and towns, while directing surplus labor to migrancy and to agriculture (Hindson 1987b). The development of segregated mass public housing estates (townships) on the peripheries of the cities became the hallmark of this period. In rural and homeland areas housing was provided through a process of local "self-help" (Hendler 1986).

Homeland Development and Urbanization (1962 to 1977)

In the second phase, passes continued to differentiate between urban and migrant labor, but influx control came under pressure from a growing surplus population (Hindson 1987b). Influx measures were tightened, and homeland development emerged as the dominant dimension of apartheid policy. In pursuit of homeland development, decentralized industry was established in and around homelands, and steps were taken to promote homeland settlement (Hendler 1986; Hindson 1987b). These steps included the erosion of tenure rights in urban townships, the curtailment of township building programs, and the relocation of many nonhomeland urban and rural communities (Hindson 1987b; Morris 1981).

Resistance and Reform (1978 to 1986)

Township violence and industrial activism became more frequent and widespread during this period, and the division between homelands and the remainder of South Africa became blurred by a flood of cross-border commuters from peri-urban settlements close to the metropolitan centers (Hendler 1986; Hindson 1987b). The state came under extreme pressure to address political and economic crises and growing contradictions in apartheid policy. Reforms accepted the permanence of black settlement in nonhomeland cities and towns, and new institutions were introduced to accommodate regional labor markets (Hendler 1986; Hindson 1987b). Along the lines of monetarist economic policy elsewhere in the world, the state also moved to privatize low-cost housing by introducing measures to encourage the private sector and self-help and by seeking to sell public housing stock (Glover and Watson 1984).

These phases reflect core elements of national policy affecting settlement and housing, but they are by no means discrete. The thread that runs through this chapter is inevitably that of discrimination and relative disadvantage based on race. The degree of disadvantage is frequently different for various racially defined groups, so it is necessary to make use of terminology that reflects official racial classification. The emphasis throughout the chapter is on black housing, because it is in this context that apartheid has been most thoroughly applied, and it is here where its effects have been most acutely felt. The discussion thus has a particular tone and thrust, one that is possibly markedly different from that which might characterize an examination of white housing and housing policy.

TRENDS IN HOUSING CONDITIONS AND CONSTRUCTION

Modernizing apartheid and shifts in housing policy have had a profound physical effect on South African housing. The state has dominated as a financier and a supplier of formal housing for blacks, coloreds, and Asians and in this role has acted as a major determinant of quality, quantity, and conditions of tenure. But while the state has been an important source of housing it has also acted as an agent of dislocation between predominantly poor people and existing housing stock, through massive population relocations in support of urban and regional racial separation (Mare 1980; Platzky and Walker 1985).

During the most recent policy phase, the private sector has become more prominent in the formal black housing market, in response to unfavorable conditions in the white market and policy-driven moves to open the black townships to the formal construction industry (Hendler 1986). Informal settlement and squatting have remained important housing processes throughout the period under review, reflecting an ongoing popular struggle to gain access to a residential niche closer to the major employment centers.

Trends in Residential Type, Quality, and Quantity

Formal Housing. Statistical information about housing in South Africa is for the most part inadequate and unreliable, especially for blacks. Indeed, no South African census has ever counted the number of houses occupied by blacks (De Vos 1987c). Since 1948, an important feature of formal housing provision has been the central role of the state in black, colored, and Asian housing. The involvement of the state in this sector reflects both the implementation of apartheid and the income-based constraints that have limited the access of blacks, coloreds, and Asians to the private housing market (Boaden 1978; Dewar 1980; Sutcliffe 1986). By contrast, the formal private sector has been particularly active among whites, as is shown for selected periods during the second and third phases of apartheid housing policy (table 19.1).

Table 19.1
Dwelling Units Erected by the Private Sector and the Department of Community Development, South Africa, 1972–1976; Housing Financed by the Private Sector and the State, South Africa, 1980–1984

	White	Colored	Asian	Black (1)
Construction				
Priv. sector	161,178	15,894	7,251	5,015
Dept. C. D.	26,185	61,591	12,515	40,862
Finance				
Priv. (2)	132,903	15,091	8,552	6,756
State (3)	6,450	46,840	27,005	33,663

Sources: De Vos, 1987c, p. 7; Morris, 1981, p. 80.

Note: C.D. = Community Development.

(1) Black residential areas.

(2) Excluding the homelands.

(3) Excluding the independent homelands.

Changes in the balance between state and private sector sources of housing over time and across regions have been most pronounced in black areas, for reasons relating to shifts in settlement policy under modernizing apartheid and to fluctuations in the economic fortunes of the country (Sutcliffe 1986).

Following World War II, housing for working-class groups, of all races, was in critically short supply (South African Institute of Race Relations 1957). During the townships and passes phase, the state sought to entrench a settled black city population and to control the entry of outsiders through influx control (Hindson 1987b). In and around the "white" cities, sites-and-services self-help schemes were officially sanctioned (Davenport and Hunt 1974; Morris 1981), and a mass housing program for blacks was launched, through urban municipalities, giving rise to comprehensively planned segregated townships and standardized houses. A four-room 40 square meter prototype developed early in this phase became the backbone of township housing schemes, together with a slightly larger five-room variant (Morris 1981). In physical terms, the scale of the mass housing initiative was impressive, with the Johannesburg Housing Division erecting 40,682 houses in Soweto between 1948 and 1960 (Morris 1981), and 11,047 houses in one year between July 1957 and June 1958 (Lewis 1966). Between 1957 and 1960 the Durban Corporation erected 5,115 houses in Kwa Mashu, and by 1958 the Pretoria municipality had built 12,448 dwellings for black people (Morris 1981).

From the early 1960s onward, the thrust of settlement policy under apartheid was increasingly directed toward a framework of separation based on the homelands. The allocation of state funds for family housing in the homelands was progressively increased (Hendler 1986), and in a dramatic about-face, a battery

Table 19.2
Number of Houses Built for Blacks, South Africa, Phase 2, Selected Years

Year	"White" areas	Homelands
1967/8	14 369	4 233
1970/1	8 566	11 364
1973/4	7 573	7 963
1976/7	6 109	29 241(1)

Source: Smit and Booysen, 1981, p. 91.
(1) This figure is inflated by the incorporation of existing townships into homeland areas.

of restrictive measures was introduced over a decade to inhibit black housing processes in the townships (Morris 1981). These measures included tighter influx control, restrictions on the erection of family housing, no compensation for improvements to state houses, and the withdrawal of black-property ownership rights (Morris 1981; Smit and Booysen 1981).

In this new policy context, the mass township housing campaign abated, resulting in a decline in the provision of formal township housing (table 19.2). With the growth of homeland populations during this period, and despite the establishment of new homeland towns and commuter settlements, state housing increasingly lagged behind demand in all parts of the country, aggravating conditions of overcrowding and adding impetus to informal settlement, the erection of backyard shanties, and subletting (Morris 1981; Smit and Booysen 1981). In the townships living conditions progressively deteriorated, and even conservative official figures showed an average of thirteen people per household in 1985 (De Vos 1987c).

The early part of Phase 3 saw increased state investment in black housing, linked partially to a changed subsidy structure and subsidized home ownership for black employees of the state (Hendler 1986). A modest resurgence of public housing activity in black areas outside the homelands accompanied the reform initiatives, and the state financed an average of 7,728 houses per year between 1980 and the end of 1985 (De Vos 1987c). The vast housing backlog was barely touched, however, and dissatisfaction with housing often combined with other grievances to spark violent protests (Hendler 1986). A wave of such violence swept through the country in 1985 and 1986. The growing economic and political crisis in housing was accompanied, after 1975, by efforts to shift a part of the burden for the provision of low-cost housing to the private sector and to the low-income group itself and by associated strategies to depoliticize black housing through privatization (Glover and Watson 1984). In 1975 the state reintroduced township home ownership, based on a system of a thirty-year leasehold (see discussion of tenure status). The so-called "new dispensation" (Lea 1980) has now come to comprise several interlinked elements, including the introduction of a commercially bondable ninety-nine-year leasehold tenure in the townships (Boaden 1979; Morris 1981), the sale of land and the facilitation of private development in the black townships (Hendler, Mabin, and Parnell 1986), the sale of state-owned mass township housing to tenants (Hardie and Hart 1986; Mabin and Parnell 1983), and the promotion of controlled sites-and-services schemes in black residential areas (Bekker and Humphries 1985; Hart and Hardie 1987).

Against the background of the shortage of black housing, the crippling income disadvantage of most of the black population and continued state control over racial zoning and the supply of residential land, the new dispensation seems likely to have a modest impact on the physical dimension of the housing crisis, at least in the short term. Between 1980 and 1984 the formal private sector financed only 7,108 housing units for blacks in the "common" areas of South Africa and the nonindependent homelands (De Vos 1987c). There is accumulating evidence, however, of the growing involvement of private developers, contractors, and odd-jobbers in formal township housing, encompassing the erection of houses, renovations and additions, and specialized subcontracting in sites-and-services self-help schemes (Hart and Hardie 1987; Hendler 1986; Hendler, Mabin, and Parnell 1986). There is also a resurgence of state sanctioned self-help schemes, and it seems possible that they will replace the townships as the dominant "legal" residential environment for urban black people outside the homelands, especially if standards are not unrealistically enforced (Hart and Hardie 1987; Nell 1987).

Informal Housing. The importance of informal housing in the provision of shelter for colored, Asian, and black South Africans should not be underestimated. In fact, throughout the apartheid era, most privately supplied black housing has been in the illicit squatter settlements that have sprung up close to urban areas in "common" South Africa (Maasdorp 1982) and in the informal settlements that have mushroomed in the homelands and especially the peri-urban niches close to urban and industrial nodes (Graaff 1987; Smit and Booysen 1981). The distinction between squatting and homeland informal settlement is sometimes not clearly made in secondary information sources, making the task of integrating the already incomplete data on informal housing all the more difficult.

In the late forties, several squatter groups occupied land close to existing black residential areas in Johannesburg (Davenport and Hunt 1974; Stadler 1979), and early in 1947 the squatters were estimated to number some 60,000 (Hellman 1949). In 1946 Durban had an estimated 30,000 shack dwellers (Morris 1981), mirroring a postwar popular response to housing shortages, the high costs of tenancy, and poor living conditions countrywide (Morris 1981).

Squatter settlements in or close to "white" towns and cities were an early and predictable target of slum-clearance programs in the townships and passes phases of housing and settlement policy (Smith 1982). Large-scale demolition of shacks took place in Durban after 1958 (Maasdorp and Humphries 1975), but actions against squatters, supported by increasingly punitive amendments to the Squatters Act of 1951 (Horrell 1982), became a feature of the entire period 1948

Table 19.3
The Population of Selected Squatter and Homeland Informal Settlements, South Africa, Selected Years

Area	Size of settlement	Date	Type
Durban	30 000	1946	Squatter
Johannesburg	60 000	1947	Squatter
Durban (Cato Manor)	120 000	late 50s	Squatter
C. Town (region, coloured and black)	130 000	1977	Squatter
C. Town (Crossroads)	20 000	1978	Squatter
	60 000	early 80s	Squatter
Port Elizabeth	70 000	early 80s	Squatter
East London (Mdantsane)	100 000	late 70s	Homeland
Pretoria (Winterveld)	300 000	late 70s	Homeland
Durban (Malukazi, KwaMagaga, Adams Mission, Dassenhoek)	105 000+	1980	Homeland
Durban (Inanda)	500 000	early 80s	Homeland
Pietermaritzburg (Edendale)	250 000	early 80s	Homeland
Bloemfontein (Onverwacht)	200 000	early 80s	See note

Sources: Bekker and Humphries, 1985, p. 86; Hellman, 1949, p. 248; Maasdorp, 1982, p. 147; Maasdorp and Haarhoff, 1983, p. 39; Morris, 1981, p. 38; Smit and Booysen, 1981, pp. 90–93; Smith, 1982, p. 33–34; South African Institute of Race Relations, 1979, 1985; Sutcliffe, 1986, pp. 145–46.

Note: Onverwacht (or Bochabelo) has become a focus of settlement for relocated people in the Orange Free State. The population estimate is conservative, as are many of the estimates listed in this table.

to 1986 (Hindson 1987b; Smith 1982; Soussan 1984). Squatter clearance is but one facet of the broader program of population relocation that gained momentum through the 1950s, peaking during the homeland development drive of the 1960s and 1970s. It has been estimated that more than 3 million people were moved between 1960 and 1983 (Platzky and Walker 1985), sometimes to segregated residential areas in "white" towns and cities, but in the vast majority of cases to the homelands.

Although squatters have always been subject to removal, the huge informal settlements that mushroomed in the homelands in the 1970s were allowed to grow relatively unhindered (table 19.3). Declining agricultural production and the growth of a landless population in the homelands contributed to the rapid expansion of informal towns within commuting range of metropolitan areas, and these towns thus became integrated into regional metropolitan-centered labor markets straddling apartheid boundaries (Hindson 1987b). Winterveld in Bo-phutatswana is an example of such informal urbanization. Winterveld is close to Pretoria, and it surrounds formal border towns that were designed to house cross-border daily commuters to the industrial areas north of Pretoria (Smit and Booysen 1981). As in similar settlements elsewhere in South Africa, the residents have diverse places of origin, with many having been relocated from white farms, from "black spots" in "common" South Africa, and from deproclaimed black townships in towns adjacent to homeland territory ("Winterveld" 1980).

Informal towns are highly visible, but considerable "infill" settlement, in the form of backyard shelters, has taken place in the formal townships outside the homelands. Sporadic campaigns to eradicate backyard shacks have been mounted in many townships, but they remain an important form of housing for blacks in urban areas outside the homelands. In the early 1980s, an estimated one-fifth of the population of black townships in Port Elizabeth occupied illegal makeshift shelters (Bekker and Humphries 1985).

Trends in Tenure Status and Finance

Tenure Status. Throughout the four decades under review, whites, coloreds, Asians, and blacks have had differing levels of access to secure residential tenure, in large measure due to the implementation of legislative measures to restrict influx and to create residential areas for the exclusive occupation and ownership of racially defined communities. Among blacks outside the homelands, tenure has been withdrawn and granted at the whim of the state, in support of the prevailing thrust of settlement and housing policy. Thus secure tenure for a selected group of urban "insiders" in the cities and towns was supported during the townships and passes phase, only to be withdrawn when the focus of apartheid policy shifted to the homelands. Township property-ownership rights were re-introduced just before the start of the reform policy phase and have been twice revised in the ongoing drive to entice private developers and to consolidate a permanent and stable black home-owning class.

Freehold ownership (ownership in perpetuity) is probably the most common form of residential tenure in the white areas, and until recently, a steadily increasing proportion of whites occupying houses has been able to take ownership (table 19.4).

Apartments, however, became a more prominent component of overall white housing stock between 1951 and 1970 (table 19.5), a trend that almost certainly continued into the 1980s. Since most apartments were rented (84.5 percent in 1981), the increase in owner-occupied houses was probably counterbalanced by growth in the number of rented apartments (South Africa 1983). The sectional title, introduced in 1971, made it possible for apartment dwellers to become the registered owners of their units (Shandling 1983). It may well be the case, thus, that after 1971 the relative number of rented apartments decreased.

Coloreds and Asians have rights of property ownership in the prescribed group

Table 19.4
Proportion of Owner-Occupied and Rented Houses in Major Metropolitan Areas, Whites, South Afirica, 1965–1981

Year	Percent owner-occupied	Percent rented
1965	69.8	23.4
1969	75.6	15.5
1973	77.7	11.6
1977	79.3	12.7
1981	77.6	14.9

Sources: Adapted from South Africa, 1968, 1970, 1974, 1978, 1983.

Table 19.5
Ratio of Houses to Apartments in Major Metropolitan Areas, Whites, South Africa, 1951–1970

Year	Percent houses	Percent apartments
1951	85.4	14.6
1960	84.1	15.9
1970	79.3	20.7

Source: South Africa, 1983, pp. 1, 19.

areas, but throughout the various phases of apartheid and neoapartheid housing policy, a degree of residential insecurity has prevailed (Dewar 1980). The Group Areas Act is responsible for some of this insecurity, in that it has been instrumental in relocating large numbers of coloreds and Asians and placing many others under threat of relocation (Dewar 1980). Relocation, the escalation of property prices in well-located group areas (South African Institute of Race Relations 1968), and the fact that an estimated 50 percent of coloreds and 30 percent of Asians cannot afford to purchase even low-cost housing without assistance (De Vos 1987b) has led to a proliferation of short-term renting, tenancy in state-subsidized housing, and, in some areas, absentee landlordism (Dewar 1980). The relative demand for owned and rented housing among coloreds in Cape Town is illustrated by the 1983 waiting list in terms of which 10,915 families were seeking to buy and 20,380 to rent (South African Institute of Race Relations 1984).

Tenure for blacks in the cities has been most closely related to the various shifts in emphasis in settlement policy under apartheid. As an adjunct to the township sites-and-services schemes of the townships and passes phase, a thirty-year leasehold tenure was introduced, and between 1955 and 1968 some 112,848 leaseholders had been registered (Hendler 1986). During the fifties, however, preapartheid freehold rights were withdrawn, and blacks were moved from inner-city enclaves such as Sophiatown in Johannesburg (Morris 1981; South African Institute of Race Relations 1957) to outlying segregated townships.

In 1968, during the homeland-development phase, the granting of leasehold tenure in the townships was stopped, and various measures to strip township tenure of permanence were introduced (Morris 1981). Apart from existing lease-holders, who were prohibited from bequeathing owned houses to their heirs (Morris 1981), this move effectively barred township residents from access to home ownership unless they bought property in the homelands.

A thirty-year lease scheme was reintroduced in 1975, but only black people who qualified to live in the townships in terms of influx control were allowed to participate. In a widely applauded reform initiative, a ninety-nine-year lease-hold was introduced in 1978 (except in the Western Cape "colored labor pref-erence" area), allowing blacks access in principle to private sector housing finance. The state announced its intention to sell large portions of its township housing stock to tenants in 1983 (Hardie and Hart 1986; Mabin and Parnell 1983), underpinned by the ninety-nine-year leasehold scheme. The new tenure dispensation was also designed to pave the way for greater private sector in-volvement in the provision of black housing.

In general, township dwellers have been slow to take up home ownership. The mass housing sale was greeted with suspicion despite (or because of) gen-erous incentives (Hardie and Hart 1986), with some 12.7 percent of the 345,640 township houses available for purchase having been taken up between 1983 and the middle of 1985 (De Vos 1987a). Formal self-help schemes in the townships have tended to be modest in scale, and privately funded and built houses have only recently been erected in significant number (Hendler 1986; Hendler, Mabin, and Parnell 1986). The most important impediment to black home ownership in the new policy environment is undoubtedly income (Boaden 1979; Hendler 1986; Mabin and Parnell 1983), with 84 percent of black households in South Africa estimated to be unable to acquire a low-cost dwelling without assistance (De Vos 1987b).

Finance. Much of the housing for middle- and higher-income groups in South Africa has been financed by specialized savings and loan organizations called building societies and, since 1982, by commercial banks (De Vos 1987b; Jack 1977; Maasdorp 1980). Mortgage bonds from these sources have gone mainly to whites (Maasdorp 1980). Low incomes have limited access to private sector loans for coloreds and, to a lesser extent, Asians. Rocketing interest rates in the early and mid–1980s reduced the effective demand for mortgage finance in all sectors of the population. Between 1980 and 1985 the interest rate on a loan of R20,000 ($25,641 [U.S. $1.00 = R0.78 in 1980]) almost doubled from 10 to 19 percent (Hendler 1986).

Before the introduction of the ninety-nine-year leasehold at the start of the reform policy phase, access to building-society finance was largely denied blacks in urban townships, because the conditions of residential tenure provided insuf-ficient security (Morris 1981). In exceptional cases, however, township Admin-istration Boards were prepared to stand surety for business and home-improvement loans (Hendler 1986). Even with the ninety-nine-year leasehold

Table 19.6
Housing Expenditures and Dwelling Units Erected, Department of Community Development, South Africa, 1972–1976

	Percent total expenditure	Percent total houses erected
Whites	42.0	18.6
Coloureds	40.9	43.6
Asians	11.4	8.9
Blacks	5.7	28.9

Source: Adapted from Morris, 1981, pp. 80–81.

and the promised introduction of freehold in the townships, the building societies and banks made limited progress in the black housing market, largely due to low black incomes but also to conservative lending practices, high physical standards requirements, and, for some black borrowers, the distant and unsympathetic image of formal lending institutions (Hardie, Hart, and Strelitz 1987; Nell 1987).

Throughout the period 1948 to 1986, the state has directly and indirectly provided most of the formal low-income housing finance. It is difficult to find figures that detail the year-by-year apportionment of state housing finance among race groups, but there is evidence from the homeland development phase to suggest that although the majority of state-financed dwelling units were erected in colored and black residential areas, a significant proportion of the available funds was made available to whites (table 19.6). The implication, of course, is that the houses built for whites were of a higher standard than those provided for the other groups.

Before and during World War II state finance for black housing was negligible (Hendler 1986). After the war, during the townships and passes phase, state investment in black housing showed steady growth from a small initial base, increasing (in real terms) by a factor of 2.3 between 1949 and 1957. The government spent a total of R37.35 million ($51.88 million [U.S. $1.00 = R0.72 in 1953]) during this time, mainly on the construction of township housing around Johannesburg and the towns of the Witwatersrand (Hendler 1986).

State financing policy for black housing during the townships and passes and homeland-development phases was based on the notion that the townships should be self-sufficient. In terms of this view, highly subsidized "subeconomic" loans remained available for white, colored, and Asian housing, but they were phased out in favor of "economic" loans for black housing (see "The Role of Housing Institutions and Organizations" for a more detailed discussion of subsidies). In 1950–1951 nearly 75 percent of state funds for black housing were made available at subeconomic subsidized interest rates. By 1956–1957 less than 3 percent of the funding allocation was offered on subeconomic terms (South African Institute of Race Relations 1959). This placed tremendous financial pressure on township residents, who were forced to pay market-related economic rentals (Morris 1981).

Table 19.7

State Expenditures on Black Housing Outside the Homelands, South Africa, Selected Years

Years	Value (R million deflated to 1967 base)
1967–8	14.4 ($20.0 million)
1970–1	7.8 ($10.8 million)
1973–4	5.7 ($ 7.9 million)
1976–7	2.7 ($ 3.8 milliom)

Source: Adapted from Hendler, 1986, p. 82.
Note: U.S. $1.00 = R0.72 in 1967.

Table 19.8

Direct State Investment in Black Housing as a Proportion of Total Investment in Housing, South Africa, Selected Years

Year	Total investment (R million, 1975 base)	Percentage to black housing
1975	173.84 ($234.92 million)	6.3
1979	208.07 ($281.18 million)	14.4
1983	131.39 ($177.55 million)	25.5

Source: Adapted from Hendler, 1986, p. 89.
Note: U.S. $1.00 = R0.74 in 1975.

It also forced local authorities to pursue aggressive income-generating strategies, such as a monopoly over the sale or sorghum beer in the townships (Hendler 1986; Morris 1981).

During the homeland-development phase state housing finance was increasingly diverted from the townships to the homelands. Between 1971 and 1977 annual state investment in black housing outside the homelands was half of that invested between 1962 and 1971 (in real terms). By contrast, annual investment in homeland housing from 1971 to 1977 was between three and four times higher than during the period 1962–1971 (Hendler 1986). The steady decline in state housing expenditures outside the homelands in the latter portion of the homeland-development phase is illustrated in table 19.7.

State investment in black housing outside the homelands gre.7 significantly in the period following the township riots in 1976, as in fact did the black housing portion of the total state investment in housing (table 19.8). Black housing and residential circumstances figured predominantly in the reformist agenda, but even increased funding allocations remained disproportionate against the background of the accumulated black housing backlog.

It is unclear exactly how increased state funding for black housing during the reform and resistance phase (up to 1986) was spent. Various new forms of "color-blind" subsidization introduced from 1979 onward (Dewar 1985; Morris

1981; Hendler and Parnell 1987) must have absorbed a considerable proportion of the state housing budget (see "The Role of Housing Institutions and Organizations). In addition, expensive housing schemes were undertaken in designated decentralized growth nodes, extensive physical upgrading programs were initiated in some riot-torn black townships (Bekker and Humphries 1985), and land and infrastructure were provided for sites-and-services schemes (Hendler 1986) outside and within the homelands.

THE ROLE OF HOUSING INSTITUTIONS AND ORGANIZATIONS

State Organizations and Institutions

Before World War II the role of public organizations in housing was largely restricted to the administration of regulations pertaining to orderly housing practices (Cloete 1977). The Central Housing Board (CHB) was established in 1920, mainly to oversee state housing loans, at first predominantly for whites (Hellman 1949; Hendler 1986). The CHB was replaced by the National Planning and Housing Commission (NPHC) in 1944. Until 1957 the NPHC acted as the main conduit of state housing funds to local government (Hendler 1986). The Housing Act of 1957 put new structures in place (South African Institute of Race Relations 1958), and many of them played a central role in the formulation and implementation of apartheid housing policy. Major neoapartheid restructuring accompanied political and economic reform, and by 1986 many of the custodians of the orthodox apartheid order had been stripped of crucial functions or had been abolished completely.

The National Housing Fund. In terms of the 1957 Housing Act, the National Housing Fund (NHF) became the primary coordinating body for state housing finance (South African Institute of Race Relations 1958). It received an annual grant from Parliament and was obliged to repay only the interest. In turn, the NHF housing loans to local authorities were redeemed over a certain period, constituting a second source of income for the fund (Boaden 1979; Hendler 1986). Since its establishment, the NHF has passed from the jurisdiction of the Department of Health to the Department of Community Development and then to the Department of Public Works and Land Affairs (Hendler 1986). The most recent move followed the establishment of colored and Asian houses of Parliament in 1984 (South African Institute of Race Relations 1985) and placed the NHF under the control of the new white-dominated multiracial executive cabinet before eventual fragmentation between "own affairs" departments (white, colored, and Asian) and black housing organs (Hendler and Parnell 1987).

The Department of Community Development. The 1957 legislation that established the NHF also provided the foundation for the National Housing Commission (NHC) and the Bantu Housing Board (BHB) (South African Institute of Race Relations 1958). The NHC replaced the NPHC, and it assumed responsibility for state-funded white, colored, and Asian housing (Maasdorp 1980). Its brief was that of acquiring land for residential purposes and to evaluate and administer housing loans (Dewar 1980). Requests for housing loans from local authorities were thus to be channeled through the NHC, which would then obtain funds from the NHF. The BHB performed a similar task with regard to black housing in urban areas outside the homelands (Dewar 1980) until it was subsumed by a "deracialized" NHC in 1979 (Hendler 1986; South African Institute of Race Relations 1980).

In the 1960s the Department of Community Development (DCD) consolidated its role as the pivotal state agency (Cloete 1977) in the planning and execution of housing policy under apartheid, especially with regard to finance. The racially based NHF and BHB were attached to the department, and it was also charged with the development of group areas, the rehousing of households "disqualified" in terms of the Group Areas Act, the removal of slums, rent control, and urban renewal (Dewar 1980; Maasdorp 1980).

The NHC absorbed the BHB in 1979, and the DCD was reconstituted as the Department of Public Works and Land Affairs in terms of neoapartheid constitutional changes that were promulgated in 1983 (South African Institute of Race Relations 1986). The tricameral Parliament held its first session in the spring of 1984. Blacks were not included in the new Parliament, and despite the participation of coloreds and Asians, the final balance of power was designed to remain firmly in the hands of the established white government (South African Institute of Race Relations 1986). The renamed DCD relinquished many of its housing portfolios to "own-affairs" departments of local government and housing (South African Institute of Race Relations 1986), but while housing became an "own affair" for whites, coloreds, and Asians, the NHC remained in place pending its planned replacement by the respective racially defined administrations.

Administration Boards. During the townships and passes phase of apartheid housing policy and for much of the subsequent homeland-development phase, white local authorities were the implementers of low-income housing projects in the black townships. In 1971 Bantu Administration Boards (ABs) replaced white municipalities and acted as the local agents of the Department of Bantu Administration and Development, which was the central body responsible for the control and administration of the affairs of black people (Bekker and Humphries 1985). The ABs, now firmly under the wing of the state, were given sweeping powers. They included the provision of township housing, the administration of townships, and the enforcement of influx control. In this role, the ABs were at the front line of apartheid housing policy as it applied to blacks (Bekker and Humphries 1985), and they bore the brunt of escalating black resistance in the 1970s and 1980s.

The presence of the ABs in the townships was pervasive, but it was short lived as reformist restructuring manifested itself at local level. From the outset of the reform phase in 1978, especially against the background of the introduction of leasehold tenure, sites-and-services schemes, and the privatization of state-owned mass housing, the role of the ABs changed from one of almost exclusive control of black housing in the townships to that of sharing of this process with others (Bekker and Humphries 1985). In addition, the establishment of black local authorities after 1982 eroded the authority of the ABs in the area of local government administration (Bekker and Humphries 1985).

From the early 1980s onward the ABs were, for the most part, bankrupt (South African Institute of Race Relations 1984). They retained access to state funds after the demise of the BHB (Hendler 1986), but sources of supplementary income, like the sale of sorghum beer and other liquor, proved unreliable and increasingly unprofitable (Bekker and Humphries 1985; Stadler 1987). In addition, costs increased, and post–1976 repair and upgrading projects placed an extra burden on budgets that were already in deficit (Bekker and Humphries 1985). The economic malaise of the ABs thus accompanied the reformist political agenda, and their downfall was consummated when they were abolished in 1986.

Homeland Institutions. In the mid–1980s the provision of housing in the homelands was the responsibility of the respective homeland administrations (South African Institute of Race Relations 1986). During the 1960s, all homeland towns were administered and financed by the South African Bantu Trust (SABT)(Smit and Booysen 1981), under the jurisdiction of the Department of Bantu Administration and Development (renamed the Department of Plural Relations and Development and then the Department of Co-operation and Development)(Maasdorp 1980). The responsibility for the provision of housing was shared between the homelands, the SABT (later the SA Development Trust), and various homeland development corporations throughout the 1970s, using funds voted by the Treasury (Maasdorp 1980; Smit and Booysen 1981). The ABs also played a significant role in the development of homeland townships, through their technical services sections (Bekker and Humphries 1985).

Private Organizations and Institutions

In broad terms, the activities of private (and especially profit-oriented) housing organizations have tended to focus on the provision of housing for the middle- and upper-income strata of South African society (Jack 1977). It would be incorrect to conclude, however, that profits have not been made by the private sector in low-income housing. Even before reform-based policy shifts opened up new business opportunities, private lenders benefited when they assisted with the funding of township housing, private contractors built houses for the state, and the state used materials mostly from private sector suppliers (Hendler, Mabin, and Parnell 1986).

Building Societies and Banks. Building societies were estimated in the mid– 1970s to be the source of finance for 80 percent of all formal private sector housing (Jack 1977). Commercial banks entered the home-loan market in 1982 (De Vos 1987b). South African building societies are specialized savings banks that raise short-term savings deposits on the open market and that make mortgage bond finance available to qualified borrowers (De Vos 1987b). Increasing numbers of bonds have, in recent years, been made available to coloreds, Asians, and blacks, but for the most part they have served a predominantly white market (Maasdorp 1980). Even with ninety-nine-year leaseholds in the townships, the building societies have proved to be cautious in extending finance to blacks. They have tended to demand high building standards and have considered numerous small loans to be uneconomic (De Vos 1987a). It has been argued that blacks and coloreds have contributed to the income of building societies, with little commensurate service other than interest (Jack 1977).

Utility Companies. Nonprofit housing utility companies (established in terms of Section 21 of the Companies Act) have for decades provided serviced sites and housing for lower- and middle-income households throughout the country, particularly among coloreds and whites in Cape Town and lately among blacks, Asians, and coloreds in many of the major metropolitan areas (Jack 1977; South African Institute of Race Relations 1965).

The Urban Foundation. The Urban Foundation (UF) was established in the wake of the Soweto riots in 1976. It is funded by private sector donors (Lea 1980), and it has acted as a pressure group for big business, urging an improved quality of life, particularly among urban blacks (Bekker and Humphries 1985; Hendler 1986; Stadler 1987). The UF supported the massive Soweto electrification project (Stadler 1987), and it was prominent in the lobbies for a ninety-nine-year leasehold (Hendler 1986) and black home ownership (Smith 1982). More recently, it has been active in campaigns to end influx control and group areas.

Since its inception, housing has been a priority for the UF, and it has involved itself in demonstration self-help schemes and the establishment of low-cost financing structures. Several housing-utility companies are affiliated with the UF.

Private Contractors and Developers. Private contractors and developers have played an important role in the provision of housing and residential services in South Africa, even in the sphere of state housing where they have often acted as subcontractors to local authorities and ABs. Since the early 1980s, large township development and construction companies have become increasingly active in black townships, usually as an extension to established business in other markets (De Vos 1987b; Hendler 1986). Smaller firms have also proliferated in the black urban areas.

HOUSING MARKETS AND POLICY ORIENTATIONS

Housing Provision and Allocation Mechanisms

Public Sector. As has been demonstrated in previous sections, systems of housing provision in South Africa have evolved in two broad streams, each influenced to some degree by shifts in apartheid settlement and housing policy. On the one hand, there is housing developed by a nongovernment or private sector, for a predominantly white but increasingly nonwhite market, and on the other hand, there is housing provided by the state for a predominantly black, colored, and Asian market.

State housing falls into three broad categories: (1) subsidized housing for low-income whites, coloreds, and Asians; (2) single-sex dormitory accommodations for migrant workers and mass township housing in urban areas outside the homelands; and (3) homeland housing. During the period under review, housing provided by the state has been based on and controlled by overlapping and changing direct and indirect allocation measures relating first to spatial zoning, second to delivery systems, and third to subsidy structures.

1. Spatial zoning and segregation: Despite the modernization of apartheid, the central principle of racial residential segregation has remained as a thread linking the three phases. Under apartheid and neoapartheid policy, all housing has thus been subject to the allocation of segregated race space, and land and housing have been used in various ways to control and manipulate residential settlement, especially among blacks, coloreds, and Asians. Instruments for the segregation of urban blacks predate apartheid by several decades, but after 1948 comprehensive influx-control legislation restricted access to the urban townships to qualified urban insiders. In the early 1950s group-areas legislation provided for the consolidation of racially exclusive residential areas for whites, coloreds, and Asians (Hindson 1987b; Pirie 1984; Stadler 1987).

In all three policy phases, land for black township housing has been provided in limited quantity and in carefully selected locations (Nell 1987). During the townships and passes phase, new tracts of residential land were opened up on the fringes of the ''white'' cities but were separated from them by ''buffer strips'' of open or industrial land (Morris 1981). The establishment and extension of nonhomeland townships was virtually frozen during the homeland-development phase, and township land allocations remained severely curtailed in many areas right until the end of the period under review. However, the rationale underlying the distribution of new township land changed markedly during the reform phase. Deconcentrated growth areas within daily commuting distance of the major cities became an important focus of land allocation as housing policy sought to accommodate and reinforce the metropolitan-centered labor markets that emerged when homeland population concentrations mushroomed in niches close to the cities (Hindson 1987b).

Apartheid influx control sought both to perpetuate migrant labor and to underpin the established urban workforce housed in the townships (Hindson 1987b). The criteria for township access were clearly laid out in Section 10 of the 1952 Urban Areas Act (Lea 1980; Morris 1981), in terms of which qualifiers had to have been born in an area and lived there continuously, or they had to have worked for one employer for ten years or several employers for fifteen years (Morris 1981). Influx control was policed particularly strictly in the homeland-development policy phase, but during the 1970s large-scale urban squatting and commuting from border homeland settlements increasingly challenged the insider-outsider rationale of the influx laws (Hindson 1987b). In the face of the growing dysfunction of the legislation and in response to an increasingly vocal private sector lobby, Section 10 was finally scrapped in 1986.

Group-areas land allocations and the associated population relocations began in earnest during the 1950s and have continued into the 1980s. Planning and implementation have been directed by the white-controlled Group Areas Board (Pirie 1984), and it has been instrumental in securing for whites the best residential land, centrally located, and in "sectors with strategic significance and commanding topography" (Pirie 1984, 212; Western 1982). The result for coloreds and Asians has been that although subsidized housing has to some extent addressed problems of affordability, the costs of living are artificially elevated by the transport implications of residence on the urban fringe (Dewar 1985). The future of the Group Areas Act has recently become the source of heated political debate and a platform for colored and Asian groups that have elected to participate in the tricameral Parliament. The Nationalist government has proved intransigent on the issue, but it has chosen not to pursue group-areas contraventions in selected inner-city "grey" residential areas (Pirie 1986).

2. *Centralized delivery system*: Throughout most of the period reviewed in this chapter, state-funded low-cost housing has been almost exclusively financed via the National Housing Fund. During this time, the NHF loans have required adherence to the Housing Code (Dewar 1980; 1985), which over the years has tended to act as a powerful centralized source of control over the delivery and physical standards of state housing. As a result of its emphasis on physical quality and the quantity of units, the code has had considerable impact on NHF-supported housing, leading to the use of industrialized building methods and to mass-produced housing (Dewar 1985). With the fragmentation of the NHF in the wake of the tricameral dispensation, the implementation of the Housing Code is likely to become more flexible, as different housing departments interpret its provisions according to their own interests.

3. *Subsidy structure*: There are several forms of housing subsidization in South Africa, and some of them reflect clearly the shifting motives of apartheid housing policy. Particular subsidy schemes have had an impact in the more affluent private sector dominated housing markets, but in the public housing arena a system of centrally controlled, direct, low-income housing subsidization has underpinned state housing schemes, mediating supply, affordability, and the physical characteristics of the housing stock (Dewar 1985). This system was put in place in the early phases of apartheid housing policy and has been restructured during the recent reform phase.

State subsidization of housing for low-income households is differentiated according to income categories, and for a time it was also differentiated by race (Dewar 1980; 1985). In terms of income, subsidies have been divided into "economic" and "subeconomic" categories. The boundary between the two has changed over time, but using 1980 as an example, households were deemed to be subeconomic if their heads earned less than R150 ($192 [U.S. $1.00 =

R0.78 in 1980]) per month and economic if they earned between R150 and a ceiling determined by household size (R540 [$692] per month in the case of a household with five or more dependent children). The "economic" rate of interest in 1980 was 9.25 percent (the market rate of 11.25 percent less a 2.0 percent NHF subsidy). For an intermediate category earning between R150 and R250 ($192–$321), the interest rate was 3.5 percent. In both of the above categories the loan redemption period was thirty years. Economic subsidies have been made available for both rental and purchase, with rentals calculated by amortizing actual construction costs over the period of the loan. Due to the escalation of building costs, this has meant that old houses are relatively cheaper to rent than new (Dewar 1980).

As the system stood in 1980, subeconomic subsidized rates were restricted to rentals only, at interest rates of 1 percent or less and with a loan redemption period of forty years (Dewar 1980). Subeconomic subsidies for black housing were phased out in the mid–1950s and were reintroduced in 1979 when the BHB was abolished and the low-income subsidy system was deracialized (Dewar 1985; Hendler 1986; Morris 1981). Subsidy discrimination in the prereform housing-policy phases was based on the requirement that the segregated townships be financially self-sufficient. During the homeland-development phase the state adopted the position that it had no responsibility to subsidize the housing of blacks, who were seen to be in the "white" cities purely to work (Morris 1981).

Recent shifts in the emphasis of low-income housing subsidization reflect the determination of the state to divest itself of its former role as a major landlord (Hendler and Parnell 1987), particularly in black, colored, and Asian residential areas. The subsidy system introduced in the mid–1980s clearly favored ownership above tenure, with state funds directed predominantly to the provision of serviced sites and infrastructure. As categories of subsidization stood in 1986, state assistance in the provision of serviced residential sites was limited to the group earning R800 ($351 [U.S. $1.00 = R2.28 in 1986, after steep devaluation of the Rand in the 1980s]) or less per month. Subsidies for housing were restricted to certain welfare categories, including homes for the aged, housing for those earning R150 ($66) or less, state-sanctioned self-help schemes, and housing-utility companies (De Vos 1987b).

Profit and Nonprofit Private Sector. Private sector housing can be classified according to provision and allocation mechanisms as follows:

1. *Detached and high-density contractor-built housing*: This is typically housing designed for markets where there is sufficient effective demand, mostly in white urban areas and to a more limited extent in Asian, colored, and black areas. In recent years, a sharp drop in effective demand in the white housing market, coupled with policy-led efforts to encourage private sector construction activity in the townships, has led to increased "fortune hunting" in the black market (Hendler 1986). Racial segregation and land allocation potentially constrain the supply and quality of land for private residential development, as they

certainly have done for groups other than white (De Vos 1987c; Dewar 1985; Nell 1987).

Segregation aside, three major state interventions have modified markets for housing in this category. First, the subsidized loans available to members of the civil service (Dewar 1980; Hendler and Parnell 1987) have enabled many of this group to purchase a first house or to move up-market. Restricted originally to whites, civil service housing subsidies were opened to coloreds and Asians in 1975 (South African Institute of Race Relations 1980) and to blacks after the introduction of the ninety-nine-year leasehold in 1978. Second, the nonracial first-time homeowners' subsidy introduced in 1983 broadened access to ownership, with a marked impact on the number of privately built new houses in the black townships (Hendler and Parnell 1987). Third, rent control in privately owned buildings occupied before June 1966 has constrained rent increases. The first stage in a process of decontrol was initiated in 1978 (Dewar 1980). Rent control has benefited mainly whites, among whom the largest formal private rental market has operated (Dewar 1980).

2. *Employer-provided housing*: This ranges from detached housing to single-sex hostels for black migrant workers (Wilson 1972) and employer-provided rooms for black, colored, and Asian domestic servants (Cock 1980) in white households. The latter form of dormitory housing is typically in white backyards or atop apartment buildings. Throughout the apartheid and neoapartheid housing-policy phases, accommodations for domestic workers have stood out as a thorny contradiction between the labor requirements of a white residential elite and the principle of racial residential segregation. Since 1948, and especially during the first two phases of apartheid housing policy, there have been attempts by the state to restrict the size of the nonwhite population resident in white areas (South African Institute of Race Relations 1957; Horrell 1971).

3. *Owner-built housing*: This category includes all so-called self-help housing, whereby those seeking housing have exercised some control over the provision of residential infrastructure and dwellings. The major manifestation of self-help housing in South Africa, as shown in the first section, is that of informal housing in the homelands and its illicit "squatter" counterpart in and around the cities. The growth and distribution of legal and illegal informal settlement is the physical expression of popular initiative in the face of relocation and the destruction of existing housing, inadequate systems of housing supply, and locational disadvantage as a result of movement and settlement policy under apartheid. In a sense, therefore, squatting and informal settlement are as much the product of formal structures of housing allocation and control as they are of the informal private sector.

Policy Focus and Effects on Housing Markets

It is clear that whereas public housing has come to bear the stamp of housing policy and modernizing apartheid, nongovernment sources of housing supply have also been influenced by allocation mechanisms controlled by the state. Reforms undoubtedly have begun to reshape the roles of the state and private sectors in the nonwhite housing markets but still within the confines of spatial zoning and residential segregation. Throughout the period under review, the racial segregation of living places has remained the focus of housing policy, and despite the scrapping of influx laws and the variable policing of the Group Areas Act, many of the effects of racial residential zoning continue to be felt in black, colored, and Asian housing markets.

The Effects of Group Areas Legislation. The implementation of the Group Areas Act (GAA) had led, by 1981, to the relocation of 375,000 coloreds, 172,000 Asians, and 8,000 whites (Pirie 1984). Another estimate suggests that more than 840,000 people had been moved by the mid–1980s (Platzky and Walker 1985). In terms of housing markets, the GAA has promoted the destruction of existing dwellings by aggravating urban decay in areas threatened with removal and by demolition (Maasdorp 1980). It also has tended to allocate land on the urban fringes, imposing additional travel costs on communities that often have limited resources (Nell 1987). As a result, artificial shortages of land and housing have been created, especially in areas close to central workplaces and facilities, inflating values by as much as 70 percent in some colored and Asian group areas (De Vos 1987c; South African Institute of Race Relations 1968; Stadler 1987).

Tenure patterns also have been modified as a result of state involvement in the development of new group areas, and as implementation has progressed, increasing numbers of coloreds and Asians have become state tenants (Pirie 1984). Recent reform moves have sought to reverse this trend, for example, by selling public housing stock to registered tenants. The privatization of housing does not address the loss of urban centrality, however. Nor does it deal directly with social losses accompanying the translocation of whole residential enclaves. Among these losses are the disruption of education, worship, and recreation (Pirie 1984).

The Effects of Influx Control and Racial Zoning for Blacks. One of the most obvious outcomes of attempts to direct and control black urbanization and urban settlement has been the emergence of peri-urban homeland informal settlement on a large scale. Little has been written about housing markets and housing conditions in the homelands. For example, the housing implications of the relocation of around 3 million black people (Platzky and Walker 1985) in the name of separate development remain to be studied and documented fully, as indeed do other social and environmental consequences (De Wet 1987). In so-called relocation townships, some of the results of moving people from the cities to new homeland towns have included the allocation of residential sites without reference to kin and friends, increased commuting distances, more expensive accommodations, and higher priced consumer goods (De Wet 1987).

In the urban townships, influx control and segregation measures have powerfully shaped and manipulated housing markets, first by limiting legal access to housing to qualified "insiders" (Hindson 1987b), second by withdrawing and reintroducing ownership at the stroke of a pen, and third by limiting the overall supply of residential land (De Vos 1987a). One of the results of these interventions has been the emergence of squatter and lodger groups with no rights and few residential options, hence with a limited chance of winning a better deal in a market segment characterized by overcrowded lodgings, shack landlordism, and rental exploitation.

Significant Successes and Failures

One of the most significant housing events of the reform phase was the 1983 announcement by the Department of Community Development of its intention to sell around a half-million state-owned houses. The houses available for purchase were mostly in the black townships, but a number were also in white, colored, and Asian residential areas (Hardie and Hart 1986). The so-called Big Sale was promoted on the basis of ownership and secure tenure and became almost symbolic of the new policy dispensation for black people. The sale was welcomed as a significant turning point by a broad spectrum of the media and also by several associations concerned with the affairs of urban blacks (Mabin and Parnell 1983).

With generous pricing structures and aggressive promotion, the DCD was clearly eager to ensure the success of the sale. However, it was soon evident that the sale was moving slowly. By the end of 1984, 11.0 percent of the available township units had been sold, increasing to 12.7 percent by mid–1985 (South African Institute of Race Relations 1985). Some of the most serious problems were in the black areas, and official sources were quick to point to the lack of private loan finance (South African Institute of Race Relations 1985) and the action of political pressure groups as factors retarding the sale. Other commentators singled out low incomes (Mabin and Parnell 1983) and official tardiness in the surveying of sites for the ninety-nine-year leasehold (Hardie and Hart 1986).

Research among township dwellers themselves, however, revealed a multi-faceted apartheid legacy that the Big Sale planners had failed to anticipate. Thus the sale and the ninety-nine-year leasehold system were greeted with suspicion, potential purchasers discovered that loan repayments far exceeded rentals based on construction costs in the 1950s and 1960s, and serious questions were raised regarding the resale of township houses in a context of residential immobility due to the housing shortage (Hardie and Hart 1986).

MAJOR PROBLEMS

Discrimination

It will be obvious throughout this chapter that discriminatory policies and practices permeate almost every facet of housing in South Africa, influencing supply, quality, and options. Many of South Africa's major housing problems have roots in discrimination and in the imperatives that underpin apartheid as a whole. This is not to imply, however, that South Africa would have no housing problems without apartheid, but if gross economic indicators are any measure of the resources available to address the supply of housing, the problems here should be less acute than in most other African countries.

Shortage

A persistent crisis in the supply of housing, particularly for blacks, coloreds, and Asians, is a feature of the period reviewed in this chapter and indeed of many decades before (Hellman 1949). Immediately after World War II, acute housing shortages were evident for all sectors of the population. The breakdown of housing construction during the war was an aggravating factor, but particularly for blacks, this simply perpetuated decades of relative inactivity among the white local authorities that were, in 1923, charged with the responsibility of facilitating the provision of housing in segregated townships (Hellman 1949). In 1947 it was reported that the immediate requirement for black housing was around 154,000 units, with further accommodations required by 106,900 black migrant workers (Hellman 1949). A symptom of the postwar housing crisis was the erection of illicit shantytowns around the cities and a burgeoning population living in "flimsy and inadequate" temporary shelter (Hellman 1949, 246).

Despite unprecedented state activity in the provision of mass low-income housing during the 1950s and 1960s, the persistent housing-supply crisis became an issue of widespread discussion and debate following the township riots of 1976 (Lea 1980). There was considerable disagreement about numbers, but various estimates of the shortage of housing mirrored conditions immediately after the war. The Venter Commission report, published in 1984, estimated the 1980 urban housing shortfall to have been 6,130 units for whites, 51,870 units for coloreds, 39,610 units for Asians, and 160,540 units for blacks (South African Institute of Race Relations 1985). The calculated housing shortfall for blacks did not include the four "independent" homelands of Transkei, Ciskei, Bophutatswana, and Venda, and it was widely acknowledged to be an underestimate (South African Institute of Race Relations 1985) that failed to take account of the housing needed simply to redress the gross overcrowding of the black townships. More recent estimates suggest, according to a variety of scenarios, a black housing shortage (in urban areas outside the homelands) of between 238,000 and 832,000 units (De Vos 1987c).

In international perspective, statistics for the early eighties show that the average annual number of housing starts in the United States has equaled 0.65 percent of the total population and in Australia 1.0 percent. Equivalent figures for South Africa are 0.98 percent for whites and around 0.14 percent for blacks in urban areas outside the homelands (De Vos 1987a). The number of housing units (of whatever physical quality) destroyed in actions against squatters and as a result of various forms of relocation remains a matter for speculation, but even without accounting for these cases, it is clear that building activity in the early 1980s offered little hope of ending the accumulated backlog in black housing.

Quality

The quality of housing environments is related to elements of the physical environment such as houses and services; location relative to work, schools, shopping, community facilities, and other households; and conditions of occupancy (Boaden 1978). Problems relating to all of these facets of housing quality are not unique to a single population group, but they have been, and remain, most acute in Asian, colored, and black residential areas.

Sterile Physical Environments and Overcrowding. The housing environments created by mass construction of low-cost housing consist for the most part of monotonous rows of look-alike houses (Dewar 1985; Morris 1981). The houses are generally of a relatively high physical standard, but they are small, inflexible, and in some cases in disrepair. Pressure on township housing has led to the overcrowding of these units, with occupancy rates of sixteen or more per house reported in some areas (De Vos 1987c). Dissatisfaction with township houses has been identified as a further factor retarding the housing sale, as has the question of which members of extended families occupying such houses have the social and legal right to secure ownership (Hardie and Hart 1986).

Poor Services. In line with the early apartheid view of blacks as providers of labor in white towns and cities, physical infrastructure was either not provided in the townships, or it was of inferior quality (Nell 1987). In 1976 only 15 percent of black townships had water-borne sewerage. In the same year, only a small number of townships, mostly close to the major metropolitan areas, offered electricity or water reticulated to individual houses (Smit and Booysen 1981). In the homeland informal settlements and in squatter areas services are sometimes almost nonexistent (Morris 1981), and group areas removals have often separated colored and Asian communities from established and high-quality services in the white towns and cities. The upgrading of township services is one of the thrusts of reformist housing policy, but with inflation and the sheer scale of the task, the costs are high.

Lack of Choice. Under apartheid housing policy, several forces have acted to restrict access to land and housing, and the result is that coloreds, Asians, and especially blacks have been able to exercise limited choice as regards housing and tenure (De Vos 1987c; Morris 1987). Even when income should allow choice, constrained housing markets have limited mobility.

Insecurity. Even with new tenure dispensations in the recent reform phase, insecurity remains a part of township existence. A history of draconian intervention, coupled with apparent policy vacillation, has led many township dwellers to view new policies stressing the permanence of blacks in white areas with cynicism (Hardie and Hart 1986). Group areas legislation remains a source of insecurity among those remaining communities still threatened with removal (Pirie 1984).

Commuting Distances. Residential segregation, in its various forms, has created a subpopulation of predominantly low-income long-distance commuters. In the case of segregated areas on the outskirts of the cities, commuting distances may be around 20 kilometers in one direction (Sutcliffe 1986). Many blacks (close to 800,000 in 1982) commute daily from peri-urban homeland settlements to nonhomeland workplaces, incurring enormous transportation costs. Public transport on some of the major commuter routes is subsidized by the state (Smit and Booysen 1981; Sutcliffe 1986).

Unrepresentative and Ineffective Local Government. Despite the fact that some black town councils were given administrative control over most local government functions in 1982 (Bekker and Humphries 1985), this did little to improve living conditions. From the outset the black town councils suffered a lack of credibility, with 1983 election percentage polls ranging between 36.6 and 5.9 (South African Institute of Race Relations 1984), and they also inherited the financial difficulties of the Administration Boards (South African Institute of Race Relations 1984). These problems were compounded by the enormous costs of upgrading inadequate services and by a lack of local government experience (Nell 1987). In 1984 council buildings and councillors themselves became the target of township demonstrators, and many councillors resigned (South African Institute of Race Relations 1985). In the latter years of the reform policy phase, the system of black local government has remained in considerable disarray (Cobbett, et al. 1986).

Affordability

Affordability depends on several variables, including income, the cost of housing, and the proportion of household income available for housing. In 1985 the estimated average monthly income of white households was R2,050 ($919 [U.S. $1.00 = R2.23 in 1985]). For Asians, coloreds, and blacks the estimates were R1,071, R671, and R352, respectively ($480, $301, and $158) (De Vos 1987b).

Based on the distribution of incomes in each group, and estimated household subsistence levels (HSLs), it has been calculated that in 1985, 9 percent of the whites, 30 percent of the Asians, 50 percent of the coloreds, and more than 80 percent of the blacks required assistance to purchase low-cost housing. On the same basis, 2.4, 8.2, 31.2, and 56.4 percent of the whites, Asians, coloreds, and blacks were shown to have no disposable income for housing (De Vos 1987b). It is generally acknowledged that the HSL figures underestimate household expenditures (De Vos 1987b), especially for outlying areas where commuting costs are high and the cost of living is inflated by expensive consumer goods (Dewar 1985). Thus the estimates cited above are almost certainly con-

Table 19.9
Population, South Africa, 1985 and 2000 (x 1,000)

	1985		2000	
Blacks	21 197[1]	72.0%	34 770[2]	76.8%
Asians	802[1]	2.7%	1 108[3]	2.4%
Coloureds	2 854[1]	9.7%	3 607[3]	8.0%
Whites	4 591[1]	15.6%	5 817[3]	12.8%
Total	29 444	100.0%	45 302	100.0%

Sources: [1]South African Institute of Race Relations, 1986, p. 2; [2]Simkins, 1985, p. 46; [3]de Vos, 1988, p. 8

Note: Estimates marked (3) exclude the independent homelands. It is likely that the relative numbers of whites, coloreds and Asians in these areas will remain small.

servative. Indeed, it has been suggested that more than 70.0 percent of the colored heads of households living in rented accommodations in Cape Town fell below the breadline in 1981 (Dewar 1985).

PROSPECTIVE DEVELOPMENTS

Housing Demand and Demographic Trends

The major demographic shifts between 1985 and 2000 are expected to be the rapid growth of the black population relative to other groups (table 19.9) and an accelerated migration of black people to towns and cities outside the homelands as a result of the abolition of overt influx control.

Given the present housing stock, it has been calculated that an additional 218,000 housing units will be required for whites (excluding those in the independent homelands) by the year 2000. For coloreds and Asians in the same geographical area, 192,000 and 93,000 units will be required, respectively (De Vos 1987b). An estimated 2,695,000 houses will have to be provided to meet black housing requirements outside the homelands by the year 2000 (De Vos 1987b).

Most housing built for whites, coloreds, and Asians until the year 2000 will be in towns and cities, since it is projected that 91, 78, and 95 percent of these groups will be urban at the turn of the century (Simkins 1985). The picture is more complex for blacks, because of uncertainty regarding the scale and destination of postinflux-control migration and the diverse manifestations of black urban settlement under apartheid (De Wet 1987; Graaff 1987; Hindson 1987b; Simkins 1985). If it is assumed that homeland rural populations stabilize between 1990 and 2000 and that growth rates in metropolitan areas equal those in homeland urban and "fringe" (peri-urban) areas, more than 70 percent of black population growth until 2000 is likely to be in the metropolitan and homeland urban and peri-urban areas (35 percent in the former and 36 percent in the latter) (based on Simkins 1985). The implication of these figures is that the often-discussed challenge of providing black housing in the cities will be matched by a less-recognized task in the homelands.

Sociopolitical and Economic Trends

Resistance and Protest. Resistance and protest have accompanied the evolution and implementation of apartheid and neoapartheid housing policy, and conditions in the built environment have often provided the focus for mass demonstrations and civil unrest. Issues that have galvanized protest have included group areas removals (Pirie 1984), rent increases, evictions (South African Institute of Race Relations 1984, 1985, 1988), the carrying of influx "passes" (South African Institute of Race Relations 1960, 1961), service levy increases, and the lack of electricity (South African Institute of Race Relations 1984). During the reign of apartheid and neoapartheid, housing-policy protest action has spread, becoming more frequent and involving increasing numbers of people (Stadler 1987). Major urban riots occurred in 1976, 1980, 1984, and 1985 (Morris 1981; South African Institute of Race Relations 1977, 1981, 1985, 1986; Stadler 1987), and by 1987 rent and service boycotts had extended to more than fifty townships countrywide (South African Institute of Race Relations 1988). A wave of violence spread through townships in the Natal Midlands in 1987 and 1988, fuelled by conflict between rival black political organizations (South African Institute of Race Relations 1988). Partial and national "states of emergency" have been declared in response to upwellings of protest and resistance since 1960 (Webster 1987). Emergency powers have enabled the state to deploy a batter of repressive measures, including detentions without trial and army and police patrols in the townships. A partial state of emergency declared in 1985 was briefly lifted in March 1986, to be reintroduced nationally in June of the same year. By the end of 1988 the national emergency was still in place.

The Economic Crisis. Following a short-lived boom in 1983 (Von Holdt 1986), the South African economy entered a deep recession in 1984. The recession was characterized by increasing foreign debt, declining gross domestic product per capita (Sutcliffe 1986), tax increases, bankruptcies, inflation (around 16 percent in 1984), and burgeoning unemployment (Von Holdt 1986). Township unrest and the declaration of the 1985 state of emergency reversed mild positive trends in 1985, and another downswing ensued (South African Institute of Race Relations 1986). Although not necessarily the primary cause, the economic hardship faced by tenants probably added impetus and broader appeal to the wave of rent boycotts that swelled dramatically from 1984 onwards (Hendler 1986).

Policy Directions

The recent reform movement must be understood in the context of the growing political crisis in South Africa (Sutcliffe 1986; Todes and Watson 1986) and economic circumstances that have eroded the basis for grand social engineering in the style of early apartheid (Cobbett et al. 1986). In housing, reform initiatives have reflected attempts to reinforce and broaden a stratum of settled urban black people and to allow them some participation in local political structures. They have also signaled the determination of the state to shift some of the economic and political burden of black housing to the private sector. The reform program thus has had several facets including the promotion of secure urban tenure and home ownership for blacks, the facilitation of movement in regional labor markets, the installation of black local authorities in the townships, and the expansion of the roles of the business sector and self-help home builders in the provision of low-income housing and infrastructure.

Beyond individual reforms, the abolition of the pass laws confirmed a changing view of apartheid in state circles. By affording black labor greater mobility across the insider-outsider apartheid divide, government policy-makers signaled growing recognition of de facto regional urban agglomerations straddling homeland borders and also the recognition of a permanent black residential population in various settings within these metropolitan regions (Hindson 1987b).

A regional strategy that in some respects discards the rigid territoriality of orthodox apartheid now appears to underlie the long-term strategic thinking of the state (Cobbett et al. 1986; Hindson 1987b). This thinking was given substance in housing terms with the recent establishment of Regional Services Councils (RSCs). Moves toward the establishment of black local government in the townships began early in the reform drive but floundered as a result of popular rejection and the lack of a viable revenue base. The first RSCs began operation in 1987 amid some confusion and controversy (South African Institute of Race Relations, 1987). The RSCs offered the possibility of redistributing resources across regional racial boundaries (Cobbett et al. 1986) and, based on a system of business taxes and levies, they forced private sector involvement in the funding of urban services in the townships and elsewhere in designated regions. By the end of 1987 some of the sixteen established RSCs had embarked on ambitious upgrading projects in the townships under their jurisdiction (South African Institute of Race Relations 1988).

Although RSCs are a significant departure from the prereform apartheid vision of discrete self-supporting black townships, they still operate within a framework of residential segregation. The participating local authorities have jurisdiction only in racially defined areas. Furthermore, RSC representatives will be nominated by the participating local authorities, and the number of representatives will depend upon the consumption of RSC-provided services. In practice, this means that the RSCs will be dominated by the white municipalities (Cobbett et al. 1986).

Against the backdrop of the growing policy accommodation of regional labor markets and strategies to promote permanent and politically stable settlement within urban regions, racial zoning and the allocation of racially exclusive land remain in place as mechanisms for the manipulation of settlement. The ''orderly urbanization'' policy announced in 1985 makes provision for the new regional pattern of black urbanization, but it envisages the orchestration of metropolitan and "deconcentrated" urban growth through indirect market incentives and disincentives (presumably subsidies and taxes) and via direct squatter and slum-control measures vested in existing legislation and bylaws (Hindson 1987a; South Africa 1985). Clearly, the direct measures can be used in the manner of the defunct influx laws, especially if coupled with selective control of the supply and location of segregated residential land. Successive amendments to squatter legislation (culminating in 1988) have sought to apply this principle by progressively sharpening punitive removal clauses, while making provision for controlled settlement in areas designated by central and now regional authorities. The orderly urbanization policy stresses nondiscrimination and the recognition of market forces, but since it is predominantly the urbanizing black population that will be affected by efforts to channel urban migration and to plan the distribution of new urban residential areas, it is difficult to imagine how orderly urbanization will avoid further discrimination.

Beneath reformist regional strategy, the notion of racial residential segregation remains entrenched for the foreseeable future. The homelands are now cemented in a web of constitutional and administrative structures, and black townships are being incorporated into regional arrangements as racially defined units. Furthermore, controversial legislation has provided for racially mixed "free settlement" enclaves, partly in response to the ongoing "greying" of white inner city and suburban areas (South African Institute of Race Relations 1988), but racially defined spheres of influence remain central to the "own affairs" structures of the tricameral Parliament.

In reviewing South African housing policy and modernizing apartheid, it is essential to be aware of the complex underpinnings of the reform process, and also its likely limits. An important question in South African political debate is precisely how far the Nationalist government is prepared to proceed with the dismantling of orthodox apartheid.

It would be a mistake to dismiss changing housing policy and broad reform as cosmetic, however. They will undoubtedly bring about new interests and alignments within the fabric of the built environment (Cobbett et al. 1986; Mabin and Parnell 1983), altering the lived experience of that environment for many people.

Agenda for Research

The South African housing question, and the political economy in which it is embedded, has recently become the focus of growing scholarly attention. Many areas of the potential research terrain have hardly been touched, however, and there remains a great deal to be done.

In the first instance there is an urgent need for more empirical research (Hendler, Mabin, and Parnell 1986). Priorities that suggest themselves immediately are the monitoring of housing supply, distribution, and use and of the ongoing effects of segregation and relocation. At this level, the paucity of basic housing-oriented research in the homelands is striking. It is as if housing questions are seen to have less substance there.

There is also a need to understand the roles of, and outcomes for, the various interests involved in the new policy dispensations. Reformist housing policy will bring about new opportunities and threats for the residents of South African cities (Mabin and Parnell 1983; Cobbett et al. 1986). Among many others, the following particular groups appear to deserve further research attention: squatters, tenants in self-help schemes (Gilbert 1982), new homeowners committed to formal finance (Hardie, Hart, and Strelitz 1987); private builders and materials suppliers (Hendler 1986); the providers of formal and informal housing finance, and those households that have invested heavily in homeland urban areas.

Beyond research that reflects somewhat passively on housing processes, however, there is also a need for researchers to look at possibilities and prospects for broadening democracy in housing in the short and medium term (Cobbett et al. 1986) and also in a postapartheid future. There are doubtless lessons to be learned from postcolonial Africa and from countries occupying positions similar to that of South Africa in the world economy. But forward-looking research should not only address hypothetical futures; it should also work toward recognizing and assisting progressive and constructive forces at work right now.

ACKNOWLEDGMENT

A draft of this paper was read by Simon Bekker, Tobie De Vos, David Dewar, Graeme Hart, Paul Hendler, and Willem Van Vliet—. I have sought to address their many comments, but I accept responsibility for the final product.

REFERENCES

Adam, H. 1971. *Modernizing Racial Domination: The Dynamics of South African Politics*. Los Angeles: University of California Press.

Bekker, Simon, and Richard Humphries. 1985. *From Control to Confusion: The Changing Role of Administration Boards in South Africa, 1971–1983*. Pietermaritzburg: Shuter and Shooter.

Boaden, Bruce G. 1978. "The Urban Housing Market in an Apartheid Economy." *African Affairs* 77, no. 309:499–511.

———. 1979. *The Financial Aspects of Black Homeownership with Reference to the New 99-Year Leasehold Legislation*. Johannesburg: University of the Witwatersrand, Department of Business Economics.

Cloete, J. J. N. 1977. "Government Housing Institutions." In *Housing People*, edited by M. Lazenby. Johannesburg: A. D. Donker.

Cobbett, W., D. Glaser, D. Hindson, and M. Swilling. 1986. "South Africa's Regional Political Economy: A Critical Analysis of Reform Strategy in the 1980s." In *South African Review 3*, edited by South African Research Service, 137–68. Johannesburg: Ravan.

Cock, Jacklyn. 1980. *Maids and Madams*. Johannesburg: Ravan Press.

Davenport, T. R. H., and K. S. Hunt. 1974. *The Right to the Land*. Cape Town: David Phillip.

De Vos, T. J. 1987a. *The Black Urban Housing Market* (R/BOU 1419). Pretoria: National Building Research Institute, Council for Scientific and Industrial Research.

———. 1987b. *Financing Low-Cost Housing* (R/BOU 1426). Pretoria: National Building Research Institute, Council for Scientific and Industrial Research.

———. 1987c. *Housing under Group Areas and Influx Control Legislation*. Special Report No. BOU 88. Pretoria: National Building Research Institute, Council for Scientific and Industrial Research.

Dewar, David. 1980. "A Low-Income Urban Housing Policy Framework for South Africa." Ph.D. dissertation, University of Cape Town.

———. 1985. Housing Policy in South Africa: An Evaluatory Overview. *RSA 2000* 7, no. 1: 19–34.

De Wet, C. 1987. "The Impact of Environmental Change on Relocated Communities in South Africa." *Development Southern Africa* 4, no. 2:312–23.

Gilbert, A. 1982. "The Tenants of Self-Help Housing: Choice and Constraint in the Housing Markets of LDC's." *Development and Change* 14:449–77.

Glover, Christine, and Vanessa Watson. 1984. "The 'Affordability' of the New Housing Policy and Its Likely Impact on the 'Coloured' Housing Crisis in Cape Town." In *Second Cornegie Inquiry into Poverty and Development in Southern Africa*. Paper 161. Cape Town: South African Labour and Development Research Unit, University of Cape Town.

Graaff, J. F. de V. 1987. "The Present State of Urbanisation in the South African Homelands: Rethinking the Concepts and Predicting the Future." *Development Southern Africa* 4, no. 1: 46–66.

Hardie, Graeme J., and Timothy Hart. 1986. "Homeownership and the 'Big Sale' of State-Owned Housing: A View from the Townships." *The Property Economist, Opinion Survey* 5:1–12.

Hardie, Graeme J., Timothy Hart, and Jill Strelitz. 1987. "Housing Finance and Home-ownership: An Investigation of Practices, Perceptions, and Problems in the Context of Five Urban Townships." *Planning and Building Developments* 90:85–93.

Hart, Timothy, and Graeme J. Hardie. 1987. "State-Sanctioned Self-Help and Self-Help Homebuilders in South Africa." *Environment and Behaviour* 19, no. 3:353–70.

Hellman, E. 1949. *Handbook on Race Relations in South Africa*. London: Oxford University Press.

Hendler, Paul. 1986. "Capital Accumulation, the State and the Housing Question: The Private Allocation of Residences in African Townships on the Witwatersrand, 1980 to 1985." M.A. dissertation, University of the Witwatersrand, Johannesburg.

Hendler, Paul, Alan Mabin, and Susan Parnell. 1986. "Rethinking Housing Questions in South Africa." In *South African Review 3*, edited by South African Research Service, 195–207. Johannesburg: Ravan.

Hendler, Paul, and Susan Parnell. 1987. "Land and Finance under the New Housing Dispensation." In *South African Review 4*, edited by G. Moss and I. Obery, 423–32. Johannesburg: Ravan.

Hindson, Doug. 1987a. "Alternative Urbanisation Strategies in South Africa: A Critical Evaluation." *Third World Quarterly* 9, no. 2:583–600.

———. 1987b. *Pass Controls and the Urban African Proletariat*. Johannesburg: Ravan.

Horrell, Muriel. 1971. *Legislation and Race Relations*. Johannesburg: South African Institute of Race Relations.

———. 1982. *Race Relations as Regulated by Law in South Africa*. Johannesburg: South African Institute of Race Relations.

Jack, D. 1977. "Non-government Housing Agencies." In *Housing People*, edited by M. Lazenby, 127–31. Johannesburg: A. D. Donker.

Lea, J. P. 1980. "The New Urban Dispensation: Black Housing Policy in South Africa, Post Soweto, 1976." Paper presented at the conference of the African Studies Association of Australia and the Pacific, La Trobe University, Victoria, August 23–24.

Lewis, P. 1966. "A 'City' within a City: The Creation of Soweto." *South African Geographical Journal* 48:45–81.

Maasdorp, Gavin G. 1980. "An Effective Alternative Housing Policy for South Africa." In *South Africa: Dilemmas of Evolutionary Change*, edited by J. Opland and F. van Zyl Slabbert, 197–223. Grahamstown: Institute of Social and Economic Research.

———. 1982. "Informal Housing and Informal Employment: Case Studies in the Durban Metropolitan Region." In *Living under Apartheid*, edited by D. M. Smith, 143–163. London: Allen & Unwin.

Maasdorp, Gavin G., and Errol Haarhoff. 1983. *Housing Policy in Conditions of Rapid Urbanisation*. Durban: University of Natal, Economic Research Unit.

Maasdorp, Gavin G., and A. S. B. Humphreys, eds. 1975. *From Shantytown to Township*. Cape Town: Juta.

Mabin, Alan, and Susan Parnell. 1983. "Recommodification and Working-Class Home Ownership: New Directions for South African Cities." *South African Geographical Journal* 65:148–66.

Mare, E. 1980. *African Population Relocation in South Africa*. Johannesburg: South African Institute of Race Relations.

Morris, Pauline M. R. 1981. *A History of Black Housing in South Africa*. Johannesburg: South Africa Foundation.

Nell, Matthew A. E. 1987. "Housing South Africa's Black Population." *Juta's South African Journal of Property* 3, no. 5: 2–7.

Pirie, Gordon H. 1984. "Race Zoning in South Africa: Board, Court, Parliament, Public." *Political Geography Quarterly* 3, no. 3:207–21.

———. 1986. " 'More of a Blush Than a Rash': Changes in Urban Race Zoning." In *South African Review 3*, edited by South African Research Service, 186–94. Johannesburg: Ravan.

Platzky, Laurine, and Cherryl Walker. 1985. *The Surplus People: Forced Removals in South Africa*. Johannesburg: Ravan Press.

Shandling, A. 1983. *Your Property and the Law*. Cape Town: Blackshaws.

Simkins, Charles. 1985. "Projecting African Population, Distribution, and Migration to the Year 2000." *RSA 2000* 7, no. 1: 41–46.

Smit, P., and J. J. Booysen. 1981. *Swart Verstedeliking: Proses, Patroon en Strategie*. Cape Town: Tafelberg.

Smith, David M. 1982. "Urbanisation and Social Change under Apartheid: Some Recent Developments." In *Living under Apartheid*, edited by D. M. Smith, 24–46. London: Allen & Unwin.

Soussan, J. 1984. "Recent Trends in South African Housing Policy." *Area* 16, no. 3:201–7.

South Africa (Republic). 1968. *Statistics of Houses and Domestic Servants, 1938–1965.* Report 11–03–02. Pretoria: Government Printer.

———. 1970. *Statistics of Houses and Domestic Servants, October 1969.* Report 11–03–05. Pretoria: Government Printer.

———. 1974. *Statistics of Houses and Domestic Servants, October 1973 and of Flats, May 1973.* Report 11–03–09. Pretoria: Government Printer.

———. 1978. *Statistics of Houses and Domestic Servants, October 1977 and of Flats, May 1977.* Report 11–03–13. Pretoria: Government Printer.

———. 1983. *Statistics of Houses and Domestic Servants, October 1981 and of Flats, May 1981.* Report 11–03–17. Pretoria: Government Printer.

———. 1985. *Report of the Committee for Constitutional Affairs of the President's Council on an Urbanization Strategy for the Republic of South Africa.* Pretoria: Government Printer.

South Africa Institute of Race Relations. 1957. *A Survey of Race Relations in South Africa, 1955–1956.* Johannesburg.

———. 1958. *A Survey of Race Relations in South Africa, 1956–1957.* Johannesburg.

———. 1959. *A Survey of Race Relations in South Africa, 1957–1958.* Johannesburg.

———. 1960. *A Survey of Race Relations in South Africa, 1958–1959.* Johannesburg.

———. 1961. *A Survey of Race Relations in South Africa, 1959–1960.* Johannesburg.

———. 1965. *A Survey of Race Relations in South Africa, 1964.* Johannesburg.

———. 1968. *A Survey of Race Relations in South Africa, 1967.* Johannesburg.

———. 1977. *A Survey of Race Relations in South Africa, 1976.* Johannesburg.

———. 1979. *A Survey of Race Relations in South Africa, 1978.* Johannesburg.

———. 1980. *A Survey of Race Relations in South Africa, 1979.* Johannesburg.

———. 1981. *A Survey of Race Relations in South Africa, 1980.* Johannesburg.

———. 1984. *A Survey of Race Relations in South Africa, 1983.* Johannesburg.

———. 1985. *A Survey of Race Relations in South Africa, 1984.* Johannesburg.

———. 1986. *A Survey of Race Relations in South Africa, 1985.* Johannesburg.

Stadler, Alf. 1979. " 'Birds in the Cornfield': Squatter Movements in Johannesburg, 1944–1947." *Journal of Southern African Studies* 6, no. 1: 93–123.

———. 1987. *The Political Economy of Modern South Africa.* Beckenham: Croom-Helm.

———. 1988. *A Survey of Race Relations in South Africa, 1987/1988.* Johannesburg.

Sutcliffe, Michael O. 1986. "The Crisis in South Africa: Material Conditions and the Reformist Response." *Geoforum* 17, no. 2: 141–59.

Todes, Alison, and Vanessa Watson. 1986. "Local Government Reform, Urban Crisis and Development in South Africa." *Geoforum* 17, no. 2: 251–66.

Von Holdt, Karl. 1986. "The Economy: Achilles Heel of the New Deal." In *South African Review 3*, edited by South African Research Service, 303–19. Johannesburg: Ravan.

Webster, David. 1987. "Repression and the State of Emergency." In *South African Review 4*, edited by South African Research Service, 141–72. Johannesburg: Ravan.

Western, J. 1982. "The Geography of Urban Social Control: Group Areas and the 1976 and 1980 Civil Unrest in Cape Town." In *Living under Apartheid*, edited by David M. Smith, 217–29. London: Allen & Unwin.

Wilson, F. 1972. *Migrant labour in South Africa*. Johannesburg: Christian Institute of Southern Africa.

"Winterveld." 1980. *Work in Progress* 15:79–91.

FURTHER READING

De Vos, T. J. *Urbanisation and Housing Requirements in South Africa*. Paper presented at the International Conference on Population Development, Johannesburg *Sun*, October 13, 1988.

Hart, Deborah W. "Political Manipulation of Urban Space: The Razing of District Six, Cape Town." *Urban Geography* 9, no. 6 (1988):603–28.

Hendler, Paul. *Urban Policy and Housing*. Johannesburg: South African Institute of Race Relations, 1988.

Mashabela, Harry. *Townships of the PWV*. Johannesburg: South African Institute of Race Relations, 1988.

McCarthy, Jeff, and Dan Smit. *The South African City: Theory in Analysis and Planning*. Johannesburg: Juta, 1984.

Parnell, Susan. "Land Acquisition and the Changing Residential Face of Johannesburg 1930–1955." *Area* 20, no. 4 (1988):307–14.

———. "Public Housing as a Device for White Residential Segregation in Johannesburg, 1934–1953. *Urban Geography* 9, no. 6 (1988):584–602.

Pirie, G. H. "Housing Essential Service Workers in Johannesburg: Locational Constraint and Conflict." *Urban Geography* 9, no. 6 (1988):568–83.

Rycroft, A., ed. *Race and the Law in South Africa*. Cape Town: Juta, 1987.

Tomlinson, Richard. "South Africa's Urban Policy: A New Form of Influx Control." *Urban Affairs Quarterly* 23, no. 4 (1988):487–510.

Van Onselen, Charles. *Studies in the Social and Economic History of the Witwatersrand, 1886–1914*. 2 volumes. Johannesburg: Ravan, 1982.

VIII

ASIA

20

Singapore

J. JOHN PALEN

References
Further Reading

TRENDS IN HOUSING CONDITIONS AND CONSTRUCTION: 1945–1985

The Republic of Singapore occupies a unique niche, beginning with its particular geography and extending to the scope and comprehensiveness of its housing policies.* Singapore occupies an island comprising 620 square kilometers or 238 square miles. Fully half of the land area is comprised of built-up residential, commercial, or industrial areas. All of Singapore's 2.6 million ethnically multiracial population (77 percent Chinese, 15 percent Malay, 6 percent Indian, and 2 percent other) is classified as urban. A separate city government no longer exists; the island is governed by a seventy-nine-member, unicameral Parliament.

Singapore's population density of nearly 4,000 persons per square kilometer is one of the highest in the world—about ten times that of the Netherlands, the most densely populated European nation. Singapore is also unique in the degree to which the government is directly involved in building and managing the nation's housing stock. As of 1989 Singapore had 85 percent of its population residing in government-managed housing estates—a majority of the units in the estates being high-rise apartments. Of those residing in such public housing, four-fifths are purchasing rather than renting the unit the occupy. One authority goes so far as to state that "Singapore's effort in social housing is quite remarkable, and along with Norwegian housing, the most impressive in the world" (Pugh 1985, 287).

Singapore was founded in 1819 by Sir Stanford Raffles as a trading base for the British East India Company, and it remained a British colony until 1959. Singapore unexpectedly achieved full independence as an independent nation after a break with Malasia in 1965. At that time:

One-third of the total population lived in "temporary" wooden structures, with attap-thatch, zinc, or bitumen sheet roofing. Most of these people, perhaps over 500,000, were squatters—occupying land they had no legal right to occupy. . . . Most of the deteriorated or dilapidated structures had no piped water, bathing or toilet facilities, many had no electricity. Another 23% of the population lived in structurally non-sound shop houses (row houses) which were characteristically overcrowded. (Buchanan 1972, 192)

During the past quarter century, Singapore has moved from underdeveloped to newly developed status. Singapore's GNP is higher than that of the other Asian "Little Tigers" of Hong Kong, South Korea, and Taiwan and is the

*This research was aided by a grant from the Division of International Programs, National Science Foundation.

second highest in Asia ($7,940 in 1987), trailing only that of Japan. From independence in 1965 through 1983 Singapore's official annual growth rate of 7.4 percent was one of the highest in the world ("Economy Strong" 1983). Although poverty persists, Singapore's expanding professional class enjoys a comfortable and affluent life-style (Crossette 1984, 122). Going to the city's center from the ultramodern Changi Airport, one travels landscaped expressways bordered by mile after mile of government-built, high-rise housing. Downtown Singapore, especially along Orchard Road, boasts one of the most extensive luxury hotel and shopping areas anywhere on the globe, and the business district has an impressive skyline of high-rise office buildings. Most of this construction has occurred during the 1970s and 1980s.

Singapore is a health place to live with once-epidemic diseases such as malaria being eradicated. In 1988 the infant mortality rate of 7.4 per 1,000 was lower than that of the United States (9.9) and that of the United Kingdom 9.1 (Population Reference Bureau 1989). Population growth is moderate. The 1988 annual rate of natural increase was 1.2 percent, compared with 2.5 percent growth in 1965 (Population Reference Bureau 1989).

Since achieving internal self-governance in 1959, Singapore's only prime minister has been Lee Kuan Yew. Mr. Lee, a man of considerable ability and deeply influenced by the work ethic, has increasingly sought since the mid–1970s to instill in Singaporeans a belief in meritocracy and self-reliance. Throughout the years, his ruling Peoples Action Party (PAP) has largely reversed its initial strongly socialist orientation favoring social welfare and social equality and has replaced it with emphasis on hard work and meritocracy with the biggest rewards going to the biggest achievers.

Singapore, under his guidance, enjoys a largely corruption-free government, a controlled press, no independent judiciary (jury trials were abolished as inefficient), and a largely rubber-stamp Parliament. Its political system has been characterized as "top down" and "predemocratic" (Pugh 1985).

Colonial Period: 1945–1960

The British colony of Singapore emerged from World War II Japanese occupation with a severely deteriorated and overcrowded housing stock (Teh 1975, 4). Crowded shop houses and squatter shacks were the norm. A full third of the population was packed into roughly 1,000 acres in the center of the city where densities were, in some cases, more than 1,000 persons per acre (*Report of Singapore Housing Committee* 1948).

When Singapore gained full control over its own internal affairs in 1959, the city–state had reached a population of 1.6 million and annually was adding 40,000 to 70,000 persons, or 7,000 to 10,000 families (Liu 1982, 134). Even critics of Singapore's political policies acknowledge that the housing situation required drastic action (George 1973).

Housing Development Board

Surveys done in 1960 indicated that between 1961 and 1970 a minimum of 147,000 new housing units would be required—80,000 to relieve existing over-crowding, 20,000 to resettle families displaced by central city redevelopment, and 47,000 to account for the population increase (Liu 1982, 135). To deal with the crisis, the Singapore government established a statutory Housing and Development Board (HDB) in 1960 (Housing and Development Act, Chapter 271). The HDB is somewhat misnamed in that it is a statutory authority that manages all housing programs. It was given exceptionally wide-ranging powers, and empowered to erect, convert, or improve any building for sale, lease, rental, or other purpose. The HDB was also empowered to clear and redevelop slums and other urban areas and to develop rural areas for resettlement. It was also to manage these areas and make mortgage loans. Since 1974, the Urban Redevelopment Authority has been the statutory body responsible for nonhousing urban redevelopment.

The initial goal of the HDB was to construct the maximum number of units in the shortest time and at the lowest cost. These initial apartments could most charitably be described as spartan and functional. The HDB's European-influenced architects favored the then popular high-rise buildings. Thus what was constructed were Emergency Housing Estates comprised of high-rise buildings containing very small (23.5 square meters or 240 square feet) one-room apartments with a minuscule kitchen and bathroom.

The second five-year building program (1966–1970) saw the introduction of an improved range of one-room to three-room apartments. During the last quarter of a century, there have been several generations of apartment designs—from Emergency to Standard to Improved to New Generation and Model A. Each new prototype has increased the size of the unit and improved the interior amenities and quality of workmanship. By the 1980s some ninety blocks of the original one-room Emergency flats had been demolished as part of an upgrading of housing stock (Housing and Development Board 1983, 16).

Of the housing that the HDB had built from 1960 to 1985, the amount of construction has consistently increased over the various five-year building programs (table 20.1). As of 1989, 85 percent of Singapore's population resided in HDB housing, and the HDB estimates that it could cater to 98 percent of the population. The HDB manages more than 500,000 units of subsidized apartments—primarily in high-rise buildings. Thus, except for the wealthy in private housing and a decreasing minority in older traditional housing, the HDB has a de facto monopoly on housing in Singapore. For most of its population, the Singapore government has provided adequate housing.

Housing Queues

By the 1980s Singapore had largely relieved its postwar housing backlog. Demand for new units peaked at 115,000 in 1982. There is still a two-year

Table 20.1
Number of Housing Units Built under HDB Five-Year Housing Programs,
Singapore, 1960–1985

Years	HDB Housing Units Built
1960–65	55,000
1966–70	65,000
1971–75	110,000
1976–80	130,000
1981–85	155,000

Source: Housing and Develppment Board, *Annual Reports*, various years.

waiting list for the more popular public housing units due to new family formation and to the economic reality of HDB housing being substantially less expensive than private sector housing. The HDB housing is substantially removed from market forces. Sale prices of apartments remained constant from 1964 to 1974 and rental prices until 1979. These prices were adjusted up more than 40 percent in the early 1980s but are still well below private market costs. Private market housing costs often have run four to five times that of an equivalent-size HDB unit.

Thus queueing up for more desirable HDB units reflects not so much unmet housing needs as the inability of all but the most affluent to afford private sector housing. As long as such differences remain, there will be "housing shortages" and waiting lists for the larger and better located HDB apartments. The near monopoly of HDB housing also means that unlike some countries (e.g., United States), public housing includes all social classes except the affluent. There is no negative stigma attached to living in public housing.

The Singapore government no longer sets targets regarding the number of public housing units to be built. Rather, housing programs are triggered in part by waiting-list demands and in part by the government's willingness to provide HDB budget subsidies. The latter fluctuates with political conditions. For example, in the late 1970s the government became less willing to absorb rising costs of housing and sought to shift costs to occupants. However, the by-election of October 1981 saw a Workers Party candidate defeat the PAP candidate, thus becoming the first non-PAP member of Parliament in two decades. The prime minister attributed the setback to housing issues, and the amount of housing resources and government involvement in "grassroots" community development was increased. As the remaining traditional kampong-type housing and shop houses have continued to be razed, the only housing alternative to HDB estates is becoming private luxury bungalows or high-rise apartments. The cost of private market apartments and townhouses begins at roughly U.S. $200,000.

Amenities

The level of amenities in Singapore housing is the highest in Southeast Asia. Although in 1970 only 64 percent of the housing units in Singapore had flush toilets, today all HDB units have sanitary amenities. Least likely to have sanitary facilities are the decreasing number of zinc-roofed houses found in squatter settlements (the traditional attap-thatch houses are virtually extinct) and some remaining central city slum units, about 45,000 housing units in 1985. In 1985 unsewered but habitable units comprised approximately 13 percent of all housing stock, down from 33 percent in 1970. The majority of these units are scheduled for removal. Squatters and shop-house dwellers are being resettled at a rate of 20,000 persons per year. (*Squatter* is somewhat a misnomer in Singapore since the housing is generally of sound quality.)

Piped, potable water is available to virtually all households in Singapore, and electricity is found in more than 99 percent of all household units. Because of its location near the Equator, heating facilities are unnecessary. Air-conditioning is standard in all major stores, offices, and shopping centers. All taxis are air-conditioned as are almost all private autos. Approximately one out of four HDB families owns an auto. Bedroom air-conditioning is standard in middle-class households, and whole-house air-conditioning is increasingly normative in upper-middle-class homes.

New Towns

As of 1990 the HDB plans to have completed or under construction fifteen New Towns, or major housing estates. These New Towns radiate out along four corridors—one east to Changi Airport, one west to Jurong Industrial Estate, and two to the north. Transportation to and from some of the more outlying New Towns will be greatly aided by the new MRT subway system under construction. The largest New Towns of 150,000 to 200,000 persons are designed into neighborhoods of roughly 20,000 to 30,000 and then into smaller precincts of 3,000 to 4,000 persons. Finally, open balcony space is designated as a "courtyard in the sky," including groupings of six to eight families of immediate neighbors. Designating "courtyards" is in response to concern over lack of neighboring in the high-rise buildings (discussed in "Major Issues").

New Towns contain hawker (eating) stalls, commercial establishments, schools, and even light industry, but it would be inaccurate to think of them as independent communities. They are not removed from the city as in the British model (Schaeffer 1970). (Singapore is de facto 100 percent urban.) Most of the New Towns occupy locations that are clearly part of the city and, in some cases, part of the central city. The earlier New Towns come closer to what in North America would be labeled urban-renewal districts.

The initial 1960s estates such as Bukit and Ho Swee were composed of central city, very basic, emergency one-room and two-room apartments. City-located

New Towns, built later in the decade, such as Queenstown and Toa Payoh had bigger apartments and more amenities. These New Towns were organized on a neighborhood concept and included facilities such as markets, eating stalls, schools, and cinemas. The seventies again saw better-designed projects such as Clementi New Town, built farther out but still physically part of the city. The 1980s New Towns, even farther out, occupy land that was previously largely not developed. In this way, they differ from the first New Towns, which were built on large land parcels of previously occupied and then cleared land.

New Towns generally progress from first proposal to finished New Town in fewer than ten years. This is made possible by compulsory acquisition powers under the Land Acquisition Act of 1966. In Western Europe and North America, projects have often been slowed—or even stopped—by concerns over historic structures or by long legal battles waged by area residents. This has not occurred in Singapore. Compulsory acquisition powers are effectively beyond court challenge or citizen protest. Once the government decides to clear a site for a housing estate, the debate is over. The Land Acquisition Act permits the government to acquire any property deemed necessary for national development. Normally, such acquired land is compensated, but in practice it is essentially confiscated. Compensation to landowners is based on value as of 1973 or at the time of notification, whichever is lower. The rate was nominally adjusted upward in 1986. When determining value, no account is taken of the potential value of the land. The government justifies its policy on the grounds that in land-scarce Singapore, the government should not have to pay for land speculation (Wong and Yeh 1985, 41).

ROLE OF HOUSING INSTITUTIONS AND ORGANIZATIONS

Housing Development Board

In Singapore housing and the HDB are synonymous. Except for high-income private housing, virtually all housing units constructed since 1960 are operated and managed by the Housing Development Board. The HDB has been the nation's sole housing authority since 1982, when it took over the government Housing and Urban Development Company (HUDC). (The HUDC's mandate had been to build larger and higher-quality apartments for those middle-class Singaporeans whose earnings placed them beyond HDB eligibility qualifications but who could not afford the large step to private market luxury housing.) The HUDC in its eight-year existence built only 4,400 housing units. When it went out of business in 1982, the HUDC flats and maisonettes ranged in cost from approximately U.S. $80,000 to $130,000.

Also under the HDB since 1982 are the 24,000 housing units previously managed by the Jurong Town Corporation. (Jurong is the industrial and oil-refining town built on Singapore's West Coast during the 1970s.) The HDB also sees to the building of other facilities ranging from sports centers to mosques and buys, clears, develops, and sells industrial and commercial property. Since 1966, the HDB has also been involved in land reclamation projects from the ocean. As of 1985 some 16.5 square kilometers, or 3 percent of the island's 1960 size, was reclaimed land.

To operate all of the above, the HDB has an organization of almost 13,000 employees with extensive research and computer-services departments. In many respects, the HDB is designed to be a bureaucratic government within the government. The HDB, since 1975, has not publicly released any of its numerous in-house studies and controls all data released to researchers. Housing is considered a politicized issue; information provided supports PAP political positions.

Allocation

Since independence, housing and economic development have been the government's prime concerns and a de facto test of nationhood. To achieve social stability, the government has sought to provide affordable housing for all but the lowest-income citizens. Rental costs commonly take about one-fifth of a Singaporean's income. Income eligibility limits cover about 90 percent of the households—all but the most affluent and the poorest residents. As noted, 85 percent of the population already resides in HDB housing. Except for the wealthy, the government essentially has a housing monopoly.

Throughout the years, there has been a progressive relaxation of both the minimum number of required persons per household and the maximum income allowed for application for HDB housing.[1] Until 1967 the minimum household size for applying was five persons (three persons for one-room apartments). Today, the minimum household size for applying is two persons. For reasons of social policy, the government does not favor single-person households, so young singles mostly reside with their families unless they can afford private market housing.

HOUSING MARKETS AND POLICY ORIENTATIONS

Home-Ownership Program

The Singapore government is committed to home ownership. In 1964 the government initiated a Home Ownership for People Plan. The scheme was substantially modified in 1968 to allow purchasers of HDB apartments to use their compulsory Central Provident Fund (CPF; social security) contributions. Forced savings can be used both for a down payment and a monthly mortgage payment. It cannot be used for a rental payment. Singaporeans, as of the late 1980s, contributed 25 percent of their income, and employers contributed another 10 percent to the CPF (the percentages undergo periodic adjustments). Residents purchasing apartments are allowed to use these compulsory savings to purchase HDB apartments under favorable terms. A down payment of 20 percent can be deducted from the purchaser's CPF, as can monthly payments for as long as twenty years. The Home Ownership Scheme has been extremely popular since the purchase can be made without reducing monthly disposable income (Pugh 1985). As of 1988, four-fifths of all HDB apartments were being purchased rather than rented. More than three-quarters of HDB home buyers use their CPF to provide both their down payment and monthly installments. Nine basic models of up to five rooms (six counting kitchens) are available to home purchasers. (Purchase, however, does not provide income tax benefits such as those found in the United States.) After five years of ownership, a household can sell its apartment at market rates and keep any capital gains.

To encourage 100 percent home ownership, the government has made it increasingly difficult to obtain HDB rental housing. Since 1981, only one-room and two-room apartments (with kitchen) are available for rental, and currently, the head of household must be over age twenty-nine with the household income below S $800 (U.S. $364) a month. By squeezing out rental housing, the government can move toward its ideological goal of 100 percent home ownership. By taking the mortgage payment from the forced-saving CPF account, it ensures that low-income purchasers will not fall delinquent in their payments. Not yet fully addressed are the long-term consequences in taking funds from what was initiated as a compulsory payment fund for retirement.

Subsidies

The HDB income falls short of its revenue by about 12 percent a year (Housing and Development Board 1983, 8). The HDB supplements its financial position by the sale of land for commercial and industrial usage (Liu 1982). It also gets revenues from activities it manages such as parking lots. Government loans to the HDB account for one-third of the development budget each year, and HDB activity contributes 4 to 5 percent of the gross domestic product (Housing and Development Board 1983, 8). The HDB Housing Program also requires a government subsidy of about 2 percent of the government's annual budget (Wong and Yeh 1985).

More difficult to determine than the amount of overall subsidy is the amount of subsidy per housing unit. The HDB claims its subsidized prices are 25 to 40 percent below actual construction costs ("Housing Subsidies" 1981). However, there is controversy regarding the accuracy of these claims. Until 1987 land costs were not included in figuring the selling price. The consensus among local housing experts is that the HDB may not know its exact per-unit costs when land acquisition and organization overhead are included. Thus the 25–40 percent figures should be taken with caution.

High Rises

Undergirding Singapore's housing policies is the unquestioned belief that the nation's limited land area necessitates that public housing be high rise and high density. As the HDB expressed it, "High-rise is still land-starved Singapore's only option" (Housing and Development Board 1983, 6). This belief has been propagated by planners and government officials for two decades. Construction firms that profit from high-rise techniques also strongly support the belief that high-rise construction is the only option. Singapore adopted the overseas town-planning ideology of high-rise building in the early 1960s and has strongly resisted change since.[2]

Research by Cedric Pugh indicates that Singapore could have built a medium density mix of one-, two-, three-, and four-story buildings, and the HDB argument of severe land-supply constraints is based more on mythology than systematic analysis (Pugh 1985, 1987). Since Singaporeans generally prefer lower-rise housing, it would be politically difficult, at this point, to acknowledge the lack of necessity for building high-density, high-rise estates. Even among well-educated Singaporeans it is an accepted belief that the HDB had no alternative but to build high-rise buildings.

A second and related belief is that low-rise housing is more expensive to build than high-rise housing. Most Singaporeans believe this because, in Singapore, private low-rise housing costs more to purchase than HDB-built high-rise apartments. The mid–1980s movement of the HDB toward mixing four-story and even two-story buildings into new housing estates, thus, was not based on the rationale that these units were less expensive or more desirable but that they "offset the dwarfing effect of tall towers and blocks, offering more interesting spaces between blocks" (Housing and Development Board 1983, 6). After promoting high-rise housing for more than two decades, the HDB still passionately combats the view that low-rise housing is more practical, or more economical, or even possible.

Renovation

For a quarter of a century Singapore has razed its historical buildings and neighborhoods with only marginal consideration given to the alternatives of restoration or modernization. As of 1985, the government had completed only one housing-redevelopment project—the one-block preservation of Emerald Hill. Opposition to restoration lessened somewhat in the late 1980s, but there is still no Singaporean conservation or architectural preservation lobby and no important local organizations pushing revitalization. Revitalization is still perceived as primarily an interest of Western expatriates.

Singapore's Land Acquisition Act facilitates the clearance and rebuilding rather than the restoring of neighborhoods. As previously noted, once government officials decide to rebuild a district, the land is compulsively acquired, and neither litigation by owners nor pleas of residents can stop redevelopment. A notable example is Singapore's Chinatown outdoor market, with its crowded street stalls and lively shop houses. This dilapidated area, which served as Singapore's major Chinese market as well as one of the city's prime tourist attractions, was closed in 1983. By 1984 part of Chinatown had already been leveled for a modern shopping center, high-rise housing, and office buildings, and the street stalls had been moved into the massive concrete Kreta Ayer Hawker Complex. Ironically, pictures of the old Chinatown street market remained a major feature of Singapore's tourist promotion information. Stall holders in the Kreta Ayer Complex complained that their business was down as much as 65 percent (Letter to Editors 1984). Following widespread public complaints, some restoration of the not-yet-razed sections of Chinatown is being undertaken.

Likewise, historically and socially vibrant, but dilapidated, Buggis Street, Singapore's late-night food and street market noted for its well-dressed transvestites, was closed in 1985. The East Coast Road outdoor restaurants, famous for their chili crabs, were relocated to more modern and less colorful surroundings in 1986. More importantly, the Serangoon Road neighborhood, the commercial and communal soul of Singapore's Tamil Indian community, is still slated for redevelopment. (For a history and description of this area, see Siddique and Shortam 1982). Only an excess capacity of new shopping centers has temporarily saved most of this historic area from razing.

One sociological explanation for government officials' preference for razing and rebuilding is that many upper- and middle-class Singaporeans are but a single generation removed from the poverty of slums and squatter settlements. Although Americans generally consider it laudable to recall how one worked oneself up from poverty, in contemporary Singapore poverty is not something to be recalled; it is something to distance oneself from. The destruction of old neighborhoods helps in this goal. The embracing of a "new Singapore" philosophy can, thus, be viewed as a means of selectively eliminating the past. By design, contemporary Singapore is largely ahistorical.

MAJOR ISSUES

Ethnic-Racial Policies

Singapore's housing programs augment its ethnic-racial policies. The expressed national goal has been to create a multiracial, multiethnic society. The population is 77 percent Chinese, 15 Malay, 6 percent Indian, and 2 percent others. Malay, Chinese (Mandarin), Tamil, and English are all official languages, but English is the language of administration. Politically and economically, the Chinese are dominant, with the Malays as a group occupying the least-advantaged position.

Singapore, like Malaysia and Indonesia, underwent serious Chinese-Malay conflict during the 1960s. To reduce such intercommunal strife, Singapore's housing policy was designed to break up the traditional—and racially exclusive—kampongs and urban neighborhoods and to intermix ethnic-racial groups in new high-rise housing estates. During the 1960s early clearance of resisting ethnic squatter areas was helped, it has been charged, by "fires of convenience"

(George 1973, 102). As fears of intercommunal strife have abated, there have been modifications of the ethnic mixing policy. There even have been attempts in recent years to resettle jointly the members of fishing kampongs.

Destruction of specific neighborhoods also has served the PAP political purposes. "Neighborhoods with a history of opposing the government were often the first to 'benefit' from urban renewal, the old tenements torn down and their inhabitants scattered throughout the island" (Bellows 1983, 76). Such policies have all but destroyed the community-based ethnic Malay and Tamil political parties.

Finally, destroying the slum area helped break the political and economic power of the powerful criminal gangs or tongs that, during the colonial period, controlled slum neighborhoods. The razing of the slums and disbursing of their populations with other policy actions such as preventive detention without trial broke the power of the gangs. The razing and redevelopment of neighborhoods was designed not only to achieve better housing but also to reduce ethnic strife, destroy the power bases of political foes, and control criminal gangs.

Housing for the Elderly

A potential problem is providing housing for the elderly. Due to declining birth rates, the proportion of the population under age fifteen has declined from 43 percent in the census of 1957 to 38 percent in 1970 and 27.1 percent in 1980 (Singapore Council 1981, 6). By contrast, the proportion aged sixty and above increased dramatically from 3.8 percent in 1957 to 5.7 percent in 1970 and 7.2 percent according to the 1980 census. Demographic projections indicate further increases to 9.7 percent in the year 2000 and 18.5 percent in 2020 (Singapore Council 1981, 6). As of 1987 life expectancy was seventy-three years (Population Reference Bureau 1988).

Housing Development Board housing was not designed with an elderly population in mind. High-rise housing, particularly those units requiring entrance by walking up stairs, were constructed on the assumption of healthy and mobile tenants. There are no apartments especially designed for the disabled or those confined to wheelchairs. Public housing specifically built for the elderly such as that found in Europe and North America does not exist in the HDB estates.

Social Control

One of the more significant (and overlooked) aspects of Singapore's housing four-fifths of its population in HDB housing estates is the role of the HDB as a major agent of social control. Upon achieving most of its physical planning agenda, the HDB has increasingly become involved in social management. It sees itself as much a manager of people as a manager of buildings (Housing Development Board 1983, 10). The HDB consciously plays the self-described role of "social policeman" and "social engineer."

The HDB housing rules seek to promote acceptable social conformity. Policies dictate not only how one can physically modify the apartment one is purchasing and but how one can change social behavior. Single persons under middle age, as previously noted, cannot rent or buy HDB apartments since the Singapore government does not approve of unmarried, young adults having their own apartments. Unmarried, single-parent families have even greater difficulty getting housing since they are considered "one of the causes of crime and poverty" (*Sunday Times*, London, 1984, 18). Being an HDB homeowner does not mean one's right to an apartment is permanent or that the householder can use the apartment solely as he or she chooses. Families can be evicted, for example, if a member of the family is caught vandalizing HDB property or if the apartment is used to sell noncensored videotapes. Nor is there hesitation on the part of HDB officials to enforce government rulings. As volunteered by one HDB official, "We'll even go around and investigate at ten in the evening, if we think something is going on we don't allow" (*Sunday Times*, London, 1984, 18). This intervention is justified by Prime Minister Lee who, in a 1986 speech commemorating the nation's achievements, stated that "we wouldn't be here (nor) have made the economic progress, if we had not intervened in very personal matters—who your neighbor is, how you live, the noise you make, how you spit (or where you spit), or what language you use" ("Housing Subsidies" 1986, sec. 1, p. 8).

Since the HDB controls virtually all of the affordable standard-quality housing in Singapore, even the threat of eviction can be a powerful tool for social control. As expressed by a sociologist member of Parliament: "You may say that all this produces a conformist culture. But what we say is that we don't have to pay the price the British pay for non-conforming individualism—and that price is Britain's high crime rates" (*Sunday Times*, London, 1984, 18).

The HDB probably already is the principal social control agent on the island. Whether the board can resist the temptation to attempt to manage further the residents' behavior remains to be determined.

Neighboring

The replacement of the traditional kampongs, with their high degree of social interaction, has led to concern over decreasing patterns of neighborliness. Sociological research indicates that these concerns have a factual basis (Chen and Tai 1977; Hassan 1977; Walters 1978). Riaz Hassan's extensive study of 400 lower-income families living in public housing found that in the housing estates, the practice of "keeping oneself to oneself" was the norm—fewer than 10 percent of the children under ten years old were ever allowed to play outside the small families' apartments with children of other families (Hassan 1977). Peter Chen and Tai Ching Lim found that among HDB dwellers, 18 percent reported no contact of any type with their neighbors (Chen and Tai 1977, 91). Similarly, whereas while 59 percent of kampong dwellers discussed problems with neighbors, only 17 percent of the HDB dwellers did so (Chen and Tai 1977, 91).

Not all high-rise dwellers welcome greater involvement with neighbors. About half of the National University students J. John Palen interviewed in a nonrandom sample expressed no real interest in greater neighboring (Palen 1984). They preferred privacy. In this regard, they resembled the archtypical urbanite described in classical urban theory (Wirth 1938).

The government is attempting to encourage neighboring in HDB buildings through establishing HDB-organized resident groups. Independent self-help groups were established in the early 1980s, which led to the banning of independent resident organizations in HDB-managed housing estates. Singapore is a managed society where citizen independence is often perceived as a potential problem rather than a civic virtue.

PROSPECTIVE DEVELOPMENTS

One reason that educated upper-middle-class Singaporeans seek private rather than HDB housing is to avoid HDB involvement in, and regulation of, what they consider matters of personal taste and preference. However, most of the population lacks the private market option. On the other hand, younger Singaporeans entering apartment-purchase ages have grown up in an era of relative prosperity and may not be as amenable to HDB bureaucratic direction. What can be said is that Singapore's housing programs have, in terms of quality of housing for the average citizen, provided arguably the best housing in Asia. The HDB projects house 85 percent of the population and are generally efficiently and tightly managed.

Overall, Singapore has a remarkable record in providing decent reasonably priced housing for most of its population. For the past quarter century, its level of performance has surpassed other developing and newly developed nations. Singapore moves toward the new century in the enviable position of having most of its basic housing needs met, except for the poor. During the next decades, the emphasis will be on upgrading housing quality rather than on housing availability. Air-conditioning, for example, probably will be a standard feature in most HDB homes a decade from now.

In terms of providing standard-quality, reasonably priced housing for most of the population, Singapore's housing policies have to be given very high marks. The social consequences have been more mixed. Singapore's high-rise estates efficiently provide good-quality, if somewhat esthetically and socially sterile, housing. If the price for this efficiency has been the weakening of the close human relationships found in the kampongs and old neighborhoods and an increase in social control, it is a price most Singaporeans appear willing to pay.

NOTES

1. Specific income figures are not provided since they are constantly being readjusted by the government. Specific housing programs are often modified or changed with a

speed unknown in most other nations. Thus the pattern of Singaporean programs rather than specific details is of primary importance.

2. This commitment to defending government ideology often includes the National University of Singapore. See, for example, Chua 1988.

REFERENCES

Bellows, Thomas J. 1983. "Big Fish, Small Pond." *Wilson Quarterly*, Winter, pp. 66–85.

Buchanan, Iain. 1972. *Singapore in Southeast Asia*. London: G. Bell and Sons.

Chen, Peter, and Tai Ching Lim. 1977. *Social Ecology of Singapore*. Singapore: Federal Publications.

Chua, Beng-Huat. 1988. "Sociology of Public Housing: A Comparative Perspective." Paper presented to the American Sociological Association Meeting, August 28, Atlanta.

Crossette, Barbara. 1984. "The Opulence of Singapore." *New York Times Magazine*, December 16, pp. 122, 124, 142–148.

"Economy Strong." 1983. Singapore, *Straits Times*, November 21.

George, T. S. J. 1973. *Lee Kuan Yew's Singapore*. London: Andre Deutsch.

Hassan, Riaz. 1977. *Families in Flats*. Singapore: Singapore University Press.

Housing and Development Board. 1983. "New Vistas for the Eighties." HDB presentation at the High-Rise/High-Density Singapore Conference, Singapore, September 5–9, 1983.

"Housing Subsidies." 1981. Singapore, *Straits Times*, August 13.

Liu, Thai-Ker. 1982. "A Review of Public Housing in Singapore." In *Our Heritage and Beyond*, edited by J. Jayakumar, 133–53. Singapore: NUTC. Letter to Editors. 1984. Singapore, *Straits Times*, March 13.

Palen, J. John. 1984. Survey of National University of Singapore Students. Unpublished paper.

Population Reference Bureau. 1989. *1989 World Population Data Sheet*. Washington, D.C.

Pugh, Cedric. 1985. "Housing Developments in Singapore." *Contemporary South East Asia* 6:275–307.

———. 1987. "Housing in Singapore: The Effective Ways of the Unorthodox." *Environment and Behavior* 19 (May): 311–30.

Report of Singapore Housing Committee, 1977. Singapore: Singapore Government Printing Office.

Schaeffer, Frank. 1970. *The New Town Story*. London: MacGibbon and Kee.

Siddique, Sharon, and N. L. Shortam. 1982. *Singapore's Little India*. Singapore: Institute of Far East Asian Studies.

Singapore Council on Social Services. 1981. "Social Policy and the Elderly in Singapore." Report of Singapore Council on Social Services.

Sunday Times. 1984. London, February 26, p. 18.

Teh, Cheang Wan. 1975. "Public Housing in Singapore." In *Public Housing in Singapore*, edited by Stephen Yeh, 1–22. Singapore: Singapore University Press.

Walters, Michael. 1978. "The Territorial and the Social: Perspectives on the Lack of Community in High-Rise/High Density Living in Singapore." *Ekistics* 45, no. 270 (June): 236–41.

Wirth, Louis. 1938. "Urbanism as a Way of Life." *American Journal of Sociology* 44 (July): 1–24.

Wong, Aline, and Stephen Yeh, eds. 1985. *Housing a Nation: Twenty-Five Years of Public Housing in Singapore*. Singapore: Housing and Development Board.

FURTHER READING

Goh, Lee E. "Planning That Works: Housing Policy and Economic Development in Singapore." *Journal of Planning Education and Research* 7, no. 3 (1988):147–62.

Hassan, Riaz, ed. *Singapore: Society in Transition*. Kuala Lumpur: Oxford University Press, 1976.

Housing and Development Board. *HDB Annual Report 87/88*. Singapore, 1988.

Huff, W. G. "Patterns in the Economic Development of Singapore." *The Journal of Developing Areas* 21 (1987):305–26.

Lim, W. S. W. "Land for Housing the Urban Poor in Free Market Economy of Third World Countries—with Singapore as a Case Study." In *Land for Housing the Poor*, edited by Shlomo Angel et al. Singapore: Select Books, 1983.

———. "A Tale of the Unexpected: The Singapore Housing Experience." *Habitat International* 12, no. 2 (1988):27–34.

Smith, Russell A. "Recreation for High-Rise Living in Singapore." *Habitat Intl.* 11, no. 3 (1987):123–39.

Wang, L. H., and Anthony G. O. Yeh. "New Town Development as a Means to Urban Growth: The Singapore Case." *Asian Geographer* 4, no. 2 (1985):113–28.

Wong, A. K., and S. H. K. Yeh. "Housing a Nation—25 Years of Public Housing in Singapore." *Third World Planning Review* 9, no. 2 (1987):196–.

———, and Stephen Yeh, eds. *Housing a Nation: Twenty-Five Years of Public Housing in Singapore*. Singapore: Housing and Development Board, 1985.

Yeh, S. H. K., and E. F. Pang. "Housing Employment and National Development: The Singapore Experience." *Asia* 31 (1973):8–31.

Yeh, Stephen, ed. *Public Housing in Singapore*. Singapore: Singapore University Press, 1975.

Yeung, Y. M., and D. Drakakis-Smith. "Public Housing in the City States of Hong Kong and Singapore." In *Urban Planning Practice in Developing Countries*, edited by J. L. Taylor and D. G. Williams. Oxford: Pergamon, 1982.

21

China

DAVID K. Y. CHU AND R. YIN-WANG KWOK

Table 21.1
Population and Value of Social Product, China, Selected Years

YEAR	TOTAL[1] POPULATION MILLION	%	URBAN[2] POPULATION MILLION	%	RURAL[3] POPULATION MILLION	%	TOTAL PRODUCT[4] OF SOCIETY BILLION US$ (RMB)	PER CAPITA US$ (RMB)
1949	541.67	100	57.65	10.6	484.02	89.4	15.18 (55.7)	28.02 (102.83)
1958	659.94	100	107.21	16.2	552.73	83.8	64.20 (213.8)	96.99 (322.97)
1966	745.42	100	133.13	17.9	612.29	82.1	110.94 (306.2)	148.83 (410.77)
1976	937.17	100	163.41	17.4	773.76	82.6	275.79 (543.3)	294.27 (579.72)
1979	975.42	100	184.95	19.0	790.47	81.0	493.03 (764.2)	505.46 (783.46)
1985	1045.32	100	382.44	36.6	662.88	63.4	549.12 (1630.9)	525.32 (1560.19)

Since 1949, Chinese housing has been provided within a socialist system. The general assumptions are that under this system housing is primarily a social welfare and income subsidy; therefore, this sector is planned in relation to social needs, and housing is mainly supplied by the state. This chapter reviews housing conditions and construction in contemporary China in light of these assumptions.

In a socialist system of development, policy is determined by the state, and most of the implementation of development is through a combination of the public and private sectors, with much greater emphasis on the public sector. Development, therefore, relies heavily on the government. The governmental structure is divided into three levels. The state level—central government—provides the policy-decision and coordination as well as the resource-allocation organization. General housing policy and investment decisions are made at this level. The intermediate level—provincial and district government—provides the organization for policy transmission, coordination, and adjustment of local decisions. The local level—city, county, and subcounty government—provides the implementation body of the policy. In analyzing Chinese housing policy, like any other policy, the key governmental levels are the state and the local levels—the legislative and executive branches.

In contemporary Chinese development since 1949, when the present regime

Table 21.1 (continued)

INDUSTRIAL PRODUCTION VALUE		AGRICULTURAL PRODUCTION VALUE		OTHERS[5]	
BILLION US$ (RMB)	PER CAPITA US$ (RMB)	BILLION US$ (RMB)	PER CAPITA US$ (RMB)	BILLION US$ (RMB)	PER CAPITA US$ (RMB)
3.81	7.04	8.88	16.40	2.48	4.58
(14.0)	(25.85)	(32.6)	(60.18)	(9.1)	(16.80)
32.52	49.28	17.00	25.75	14.68	22.25
(108.3)	(164.11)	(56.6)	(85.76)	(48.9)	(74.10)
58.84	78.93	32.97	44.23	19.13	25.66
(162.4)	(217.86)	(91.0)	(122.08)	(52.80)	(70.83)
160.3	171.05	69.95	74.64	45.53	48.58
(315.8)	(336.97)	(137.8)	(147.04)	(89.7)	(95.71)
289.23	296.52	122.32	125.41	81.48	83.54
(448.3)	(459.6)	(189.6)	(194.38)	(126.3)	(129.48)
294.8	282.03	154.2	147.52	100.1	95.76
(875.6)	(837.64)	(458.0)	(438.14)	(297.3)	(284.41)

Source: State Statistical Bureau, 1986.

Note: The value of RMB was calculated from State Statistical Bureau, 1986, p. 481. That in 1985 was 2.97 RMB to U.S. $1 and its former value of 1950 as 3.67, 1958 as 3.33, 1966 as 2.76, 1976 as 1.97, and 1979 as 1.55.

[1] Referring to population of twenty-nine provinces, autonomous regions, and municipalities on the mainland.

[2] Referring to population living in areas under the administration of cities and towns.

[3] Referring to population of counties but excluding those living in towns of a county.

[4] Referring to the sum total of gross output in value terms, produced by the following five material production sectors: agriculture, industry, construction, transport, and commerce (catering and supply and marketing of materials included).

[5] Referring to the production value of construction, transport, and commerce sectors.

began, urbanization took place relatively slowly since the population movement was controlled successfully. In recent years, as restriction has been relaxed and definition of urban places has widened, urban population has increased more rapidly, but essentially the People's Republic of China (PRC) is still a rural country (see Table 21.1). The socialist government, despite its radical development-policy changes during four decades, has been effective in producing real economic growth. In both agricultural and industrial sectors, the absolute growth has been impressive (table 21.1).

Table 21.2
Ownership Structure of Housing Stock in Cities, China, 1978–1984 (Floor Space in Square Meters x 1,000)

Ownership	1978	1979	1980
Rental Units Built and Managed by Municipality's Housing Management Bureau	172,690 (33.4)	184,270 (31.6)	191,550 (29.8)
Rental Units Built and Managed by Various Ministries and State-owned/Collectively owned Enterprises	238,190 (46.1)	282,730 (48.5)	333,060 (51.9)
Privately owned in Urban Areas	105,900 (20.5)	116,050 (19.9)	117,580 (18.3)
TOTAL	516,780 (100)	583,050 (100)	642,190 (100)

Economic reform since 1978 has transformed the Chinese socialist economy from a closed-state planned economy into a more open mixed economy. Previously, all production units and enterprises were state owned (public ownership means that both capital and profits or losses accrue to the various levels of government) or collectively owned (shared ownership mainly organized under the auspices of the public bodies below the county or city district government); the private sector was suppressed almost to extinction. Economic-reform policies in 1978 and 1984 have opened the economy for foreign investment and market processes, reintroduced an individual (private ownership) economy, and encouraged a collective economy. Commodity production for market and profit is advocated. All of this indicates a radical change in development policy.

Chinese housing provision in the urban and rural sectors is treated entirely differently. For reasons of scale economy, residential density, industrial concentration, construction technology, and externalities, the state takes on a much greater responsibility in the urban sector. Before economic reform, new urban housing was primarily provided by the state, with a small and almost insignificant private sector. Only since 1978 has urban private sector housing been encouraged. The rural sector, where 63.4 percent of the population resided in 1985 (State Statistical Bureau 1986, 71), relies mainly on private efforts.

In the urban sector, private housing comprises owner-occupied units and rented units; however, the population of private housing is relatively small. The majority of urban housing is state owned either by the ministries or the municipal governments. Until the recent introduction of commodity housing, all state-owned

Table 21.2 (continued)

1981	1982	1983	1984
203,440	213,030	222,700	232,400
(28.7)	(27.2)	(25.4)	(24.1)
380,340	437,160	503,720	567,530
(53.6)	(55.8)	(57.6)	(58.8)
125,770	133,680	148,560	164,600
(17.7)	(17.0)	(17.0)	(17.1)
709,550	783,870	874,980	964,530
(100)	(100)	(100)	(100)

Source: Qi, 1985, pp. 59–62.
Note: Figures in parentheses are percentages.

units were for rent.[1] As early as 1956, private housing, particularly the rental units and absentee landlord housing, were confiscated under the joint-management movement, and more than half of the urban residential accommodations were transferred into the state sector (Howe 1968, 87). During the Cultural Revolution (1966–1976), private housing was systemically transferred into state ownership. After 1978, private units, particularly those owned by overseas Chinese, were gradually returned to their owners. Because of the political stigma of home ownership and the limited resources to maintain private units, many previous owners have been content to leave their units in government hands. The estimate of public and private ownership in the urban sector in 1984 was 82.9 and 17.1 percent (table 21.2). In the rural sector all housing is privately owned and owner occupied. The land-reform movement in the early 1950s distributed all of the rural housing units to the farmers. During the Cultural Revolution, there was some effort to provide housing collectively in the most advanced agricultural units. But subsequently, these units were transferred into private ownership.

TRENDS IN HOUSING CONDITIONS AND CONSTRUCTION: 1945–1985

Housing conditions vary tremendously in China. Sharp contrasts are found between cities and countryside. Even among the cities, differences in living conditions are noticeable. The worst housing conditions, in terms of space provision, are found in the largest cities in China (table 21.3). Other cities are not as crowded. Rural households enjoy much more living space than their urban counterparts.

Amenities

The urban households, although having much less space than their rural counterparts, enjoy much better amenities in terms of water provision, sewerage, and other modern conveniences. Plumbing and independent toilets, for example, although still not universal in urban houses, are almost nonexistent in the countryside. Central heating in the South and air-conditioning in general are still a luxury in China. Except in hotels and office buildings, coal-fire hearths are employed for both cooking and heating by the urban households, whereas the rural households supplement coal with firewood and grasses to reduce their energy bills.

Housing conditions were revealed in a 1985 survey on urban and rural household income and expenditures (table 21.4).[2] Compared to previous surveys, the situation in 1985 shows tremendous improvement (table 21.4). Urban housing conditions had been worsening since 1949 partially because of the rapid population increase and partially because of insufficient investment in the housing sector (for details, see the section on financing). The downward trend was not reversed until 1978. Since then, large amounts of money from various sources have triggered a construction boom resulting in a less tense supply and demand situation.

Urban Ownership

Ownership of land and housing stock differs significantly between urban and rural areas. During the late 1950s and early 1960s, there was a transformation to socialist home ownership. Units with a floor area over 150 square meters in large cities, over 100 square meters in medium cities, and over 50 square meters in small cities were put under state or collective ownership. The total floor area involved amounted to 100 million square meters (Qi 1985, 60). After socialist transformation, urban units under private ownership were few and mainly owner occupied. Their proportion further declined because of the rapid increase in housing stock added by the government ministries and the state-owned enterprises, mainly for their own staff and workers (table 21.2). Collectively owned urban units were few before 1978; their staff and workers thus relied heavily on the housing stock under the municipality's Housing Management Bureau.[3]

Rural Construction

In rural areas, all land is owned by local government bodies, but houses are mainly built by individuals with their own finance and sometimes their own labor, with construction materials available in the local market. The role of the

Table 21.3
Housing Conditions, by Community Size, China, 1985

HOUSING CONDITIONS	LARGEST CITIES	LARGE CITIES	MEDIUM CITIES	SMALL CITIES	RURAL AREAS
Average Number of Persons per Household	3.68	3.86	3.86	4.08	5.12
Average Living Space per Household	22.30	26.57	27.59	29.28	75.26
Average Number of Rooms per Household	1.81	2.09	2.15	2.26	5.11
Average Living Space per Capita (sq.m.)	6.00	6.91	7.19	7.28	14.70
Average Auxilliary Floor Space per Capita (sq.m.)	1.92	1.47	2.14	2.20	2.64

Sources: State Statistical Bureau, 1986, pp. 579, 582, and 595.

Table 21.4
Living Space per Capita, China, 1949–1985

Year	Living space Per Capita in Chinese Urban Households	Qi's Estimates of Living Space Per Capita in Chinese Cities (Sq.m.)	Floor Space Per Capita in Chinese Peasant Households	Living Space Per Capita in Chinese Peasant Households
1949-52		4.5		
1957			11.30	
1977	3.6			
1978	4.2	3.6	10.11	8.1
1979	4.4	3.7		8.4
1980	5.0	3.9	11.59	9.4
1981	5.3	4.1		10.2
1982	5.6	4.4		10.7
1983	5.9	4.6	14.25	11.6
1984	6.3	4.8	15.38	13.6
1985	6.7		17.34	14.7

Sources: State Statistical Bureau, 1986, pp. 582, 595; Qi 1985, pp. 59–62 (his statistics include cities but exclude towns).

collectives in rural housing provision is dwarfed by individual efforts (table 21.5). Before 1980, with low incomes and only traditional skills, peasants could afford to spend only a small percentage of their income on housing (table 21.6).

As in other agrarian societies, Chinese farmers have developed traditional housing construction skills based on locally available building materials and the inherited indigenous construction methods. Sun-baked bricks were easily made and were widely available in rural areas, but this type of construction was susceptible to damage by climatic conditions, especially rain and snow. Consequently, most of the houses were of adobe structure, and housing expenditures were largely for minor house repairs (Lin 1986). However, since 1981, peasants have spent an ever increasing amount of their disposable income on their houses (table 21.6) and their emphasis in expenditures has also shifted from minor house repairs to major repairs and reconstruction. According to Lin (1986), this included the enlarging of existing houses and the building of new ones and replacing adobes with kiln-baked brick and even cement prefabs. Because of the technical limits of the traditional building materials and construction methods, housing units are usually one or two stories high. Even with modern construction technology, the highest rural buildings are normally three stories. Although building materials have been vastly improved and fairly modern building technologies are available, the design of rural housing has not changed significantly. Finally, because of the policy of farm-land conservation and greater availability of modern technology, the general trend is from one-story to multistory structures.

Urban Construction

In urban areas, subsidized housing has long been regarded as part of the reward and fringe benefits that the Chinese state-owned and collectively owned units offered to their staff and workers. This also explains the relatively low percentage of their expenditures on housing (table 21.7). Indeed, with an average 3.85 persons per household in 1985 and a per capita rent of U.S. $2.67 (7.92 RMB), each household is paying an average of U.S. $10.27 (30.49 RMB) annually for a unit with an average size of 32.96 square meters of floor space of which 25.48 square meters is regarded as living space (State Statistical Bureau 1986, 577–95). In other words, in 1985 each square meter gave a gross return of U.S. $0.31 (0.93 RMB) to the supplier with a capital cost of U.S. $59.60 (177 RMB). The annual return was approximately 0.5 percent of the capital cost; it would take 200 years to recover the capital costs discounting maintenance and depreciation. The exceedingly low and slow return of capital practically limited the possibility of recovering capital investment. New construction therefore depended almost entirely on new investment. Consequently, the greatest constraint on urban housing is financing.

Housing design naturally aims at cost minimization. The early housing design attempted to reduce the most costly building elements, such as bathrooms and kitchens, which are provided on a shared basis. Self-contained units were later

Table 21.5

Investments in Residential Buildings, China, 1982–1985

	1982		1983		1984		1985	
	US$ M.	('00M RMB)	US$ M.	('00M RMB)	US$ M.	('00M RMB)	US$ M.	('00M RMB)
Stated-owned Units	9,184	(169.91)	8,480	(167.06)	7,539	(168.87)	8,367	(248.51)
of which for capital construction	7,624	(141.05)	6,349	(125.07)	6,004	(134.50)	n a	n a
for technical updating and transformation	1,560	(28.86)	2,131	(41.99)	1,534	(34.37)	n a	n a
Urban Collectives	n a	n a	560	(11.04)	546	(12.23)		(2)
Urban Individuals		(1)	794	(15.65)(3)	1,209	(27.09)		(1)
Rural Collectives	n a	n a	396	(7.81)	805	(18.04)		(2)
Rural Individuals		(1)	10,868	(214.10)	10,686	(239.38)		(1)
TOTAL			21,122	(416.10)	20,786	(465.61)	21,603	(641.63)

Sources: *Statistical Yearbook of China*, 1983 pp. 302, 303; 1984, p. 299; 1985, p. 413; 1986, p. 369. The value of RMB was calculated from State Statistical Bureau, 1986, p. 481; that in 1985 was 2.97 RMB to U.S. $1. Its former value was 2.24, 1.97, 1.85, 1.67, 1.49, 1.55, 1.72, 2.78, and 3.37 for 1984–1978, 1965, and 1957, respectively.

Note: M = million; na = not available.

(1) The sum of urban and rural individuals in 1982 was U.S. $9,783,000 (18,000,000 RMB); in 1985 it was U.S. $12,206,000 (36,254,000 RMB). According to *China Encyclopaedia Yearbook*, 1982, p. 665, rural individuals' contribution in that year amounted to U.S. $8,649,000 (16,000,000 RMB).

(2) The sum of urban and rural collectives in 1985 was U.S. $1,030,000 (3,058,000 RMB).

(3) According to Qi, 1985, the policy of housing construction by urban individuals with their own finance or help from their working units was officially endorsed in May 1983, but the activity began as early as 1979; see also table 21.8.

Table 21.6
The Significance of Housing in Household Income and Expenditures, China, 1957–1985

YEAR	AVERAGE PER CAPITA LIVING EXPENDITURE				OF WHICH ON HOUSING					
	RURAL		URBAN		RURAL		URBAN		%	
	US$	(RMB)	US$	(RMB)	US$	(RMB)	US$	(RMB)	RURAL	VRBAN
1957	21.03	(70.86)	65.88	(222.00)	0.44	(1.49)	1.53	(5.16)	2.1	2.32
1964	n a	n a	78.26	(220.68)	n a	n a	2.04	(5.76)	n a	2.61
1965	34.21	(95.11)	n a	n a	0.97	(2.69)	n a	n a	2.8	n a
1978	67.48	(116.06)	n a	n a	2.13	(3.67)	n a	n a	3.2	1.93
1981	n a	n a	273.56	(456.84)	n a	n a	3.81	(6.36)	n a	1.39
1982	n a	n a	254.59	(471.00)	n a	n a	3.82	(7.08)	n a	1.80
1983	126.04	(248.29)	256.81	(505.92)	13.98	(27.56)	3.89	(7.68)	11.1	1.82
1984	122.23	(273.80)	249.75	(559.44)	14.32	(32.12)	3.48	(7.80)	11.7	1.39
1985	106.87	(317.42)	246.54	(732.24)	13.29	(39.46)	2.67	(7.92)	12.4	1.08

Sources: Except for the 1978 percentage figure, which was given by Lin, 1986, p. 97, the rest is taken from State Statistical
Bureau, 1986, pp. 577, 583, and other issues of the *Statistical Yearbook of China*.
Note: na = not available.

Table 21.7
Unit Costs of Completed Residential Buildings (State-Owned Sector), China,
1957–1985

YEAR	COST	
	US $/SQ.M.	RMB/SQ.M.
1957	13.94	47
1962	18.41	56
1965	21.18	59
1978	51.71	89
1979	64.50	100
1980	75.80	113
1981	76.63	128
1982	72.80	135
1983	76.58	151
1984	71.33	160
1985	59.60	177

Source: State Statistical Bureau, 1986, p. 385.

provided for families when the economy improved. Most of the new housing is six-story walk-ups built to eliminate investment in elevators with a space standard of 4 square meters per person (Kwok 1973, 193). Low-rise housing construction uses a labor-intensive method with cross-wall construction and prefabricated floor and roof slabs (Kwok 1981).

For industrial workers, dormitories were built in the 1950s and 1960s as an experiment to provide low-cost housing. Several single workers shared a room, with bathrooms communally provided, thus reducing the space standard to 2.5 square meters per person. After the initial phase of the new enterprise, the ratio of single workers to workers with families began to change drastically (Kwok 1973, 228–29). Dormitory housing proved to be an inadequate long-term solution.

Modern high-rise housing with elevators has been built with modern construction technology—first in Beijing (Zhang 1979, 21–24) and subsequently in many metropolises and large cities. Many of these units were built for and allocated to white-collar workers and cadres who get political priority.[4] In exceptional conditions, blue-collar workers are given these modern units if their work units can afford the cost (such as in Special Economic Zones) and the local supply is abundant.[5]

Private initiatives have resumed an important position in urban housing construction (table 21.5). From 1978 to 1984 the growth rate of this sector has surpassed the state-owned and collectively owned sectors (Qi 1985). Since 1982 private ownership has contributed to more than one-tenth of the floor area completed each year in the towns and cities (table 21.8). In 1984 urban individuals contributed 13 percent of the total investment in residential buildings in urban areas (table 21.5). Consequently, the relative decline of housing stock owned by individuals was stabilized in 1982 and stayed around 17 percent. Part of the reason for the private housing-construction boom was that after 1978 many housing units were returned to private hands, particularly to Chinese overseas ("Cultural Revolution Victims Win Back Homes," October 20, 1984).

There were several reasons for returning housing to previous owners. Housing maintenance and management costs exceeded extremely low rents. It has been estimated that the Chinese government collected annually U.S. $0.32 per square meter (1.2 RMB per square meter) of rent for housing, but it paid U.S. $0.69 per square meter (2.6 RMB per square meter) for maintenance and repair (Zhong, March 21, 1987). Returning housing units to private owners would not only transfer those costs back to the owners, thereby reducing public expenditure, but also would allow the local government to collect property taxes, which are extremely low but are one of the basic revenue sources. Because of the relatively small proportion of private housing, private units are mainly owner-occupied. Shifting the large number of urban renters to owners requires that the state supply new and better-quality housing, provide attractive economic incentives for home ownership, and declare explicitly that home ownership is acceptable socially and ideologically. Without these measures, prospective owners will not convert their personal savings into private housing investment.

Since 1979, China has advocated commodity housing to stimulate private housing market demand and to provide an alternative to the existing highly subsidized housing. Whether this policy can increase the proportion of private ownership has yet to be seen; what can be confirmed at present is that commodity housing has undoubtedly channeled additional investment and resources toward enlarging the urban housing supply.

HOUSING ADMINISTRATION AND ORGANIZATION

Relatively little is known about the precise functions and responsibilities of the administrative housing organizations. Recent work on urban housing administration, largely the result of field interviews, still does not give a complete account (Badcock 1986, 152–55). This section attempts to provide a brief account, albeit incomplete, of the supply institutions in urban housing provision.

Two central commissions—the State Planning Commission (for long-term planning) and the State Economic Commission (for annual planning)—control

Table 21.8
Privately Built Houses in Cities and Towns, China, 1979–1984

YEAR	FLOOR AREA BUILT		TOTAL INVESTMENT		(I) & (II) AS % OF THE TOTAL URBAN FLOOR AREA*
	(I) IN TOWNS (Sq.m. x 1,000)	(II) IN CITIES (Sq.m. x 1,000)	US $ (million)	RMB* (million)	
1979	n a	951	n a	n a	n a
1980	1,326	2,403	154.28	230	3.9
1981	3,709	4,730	203.55	340	8.0
1982	8,382	5,243	431.40	800	10.4
1983	8,047	5,756	512.22	1,010	10.7
1984	10,158	6,562	606.34	1,360	13.5
TOTAL	30,671	25,645			

Source: Qi, 1985, pp. 59–62.

Note: na = not available.

*Both sets of figures differ somewhat from table 21.4, owing to different systems of data collection.

the allocation of resources including capital, building materials, labor, and land and thus significantly influence housing development. The State Construction Commission established in 1954, dissolved in 1958, and revived in 1965, controlled a wide range of decisions on national investment programs, including those on new buildings, public utilities, and restoration and alteration of existing buildings; it has now been terminated (Kwok 1973, 82–86). Of the three commissions, the State Planning Commission and the State Economic Commission still remain (*Zhongguo zuzhi yingyiming shouce* 1986, 8–18).

The Ministries of Construction Engineering, Building Materials, and Urban Construction were established, merged, and then subdivided under the State Council (for a summary of changes, see Donnithorne 1967, 517—27). Their general functions in administering basic construction, construction resources, and urban planning and construction had various influences on housing development. The State Housing and Estate Management Bureau was responsible for the allocation and management of public housing stock, resident relocation, and compensation for redevelopment (Kwok 1973, 82–87). All of these ministries and the bureau no longer exist. The Bureau of Building Materials Industry has partially replaced the Ministry of Building Materials. Also, the Ministry of Urban and Rural Construction and Environmental Protection (MURCEP) was established in May 1982 (since 1988 called Ministry of Construction), taking over some functions of the three previous state agencies. It is now the ministry responsible at the state level for, among other things, land use, water supply, building materials, and housing development—rural and urban ("Chengxiang jianshe huanjing baohu bu chengli" 1982, 2).

Design

There are four kinds of design organizations for urban housing development. Ministries constantly engaged in construction usually have their own design organizations. These organizations provide engineering services, primarily to service the ministries' own construction projects, including workers' housing, but they also accept work from the outside. Because of their specialization, their range of design is limited to the functional and technical aspects, and less attention is given to the social and architectural elements.

Municipalities have their own Bureaus of Planning, Architectural Engineering, and Civil Engineering and potentially are more able to provide a full range of designs. However, because of the comparative scarcity of planners and architects, these bureaus are often staffed by technicians with engineering training.

Engineering companies and corporations independent of governmental administration have been established by the central government (*Zhongguo zuzhi yingyiming shouce* 1986, 33–34). Local government has also set up similar organizations. Their functions are to design, provide specifications, and estimate costs. Each corporation specializes in one or several types of projects. Since most construction investments are in industries and infrastructure, only a small portion of them specialize in civic buildings (Chao 1968, 25–27).

Another type of design organization comes from the universities. Relevant departments accept projects from enterprises. Either they are integrated in the curricula as field work or there are special contracts for which the departments receive fees. These institutes are able to provide a comprehensive service because of the variety of specializations available to them within the universities.

Generally, there is a shortage of trained design personnel. Since the existing technicians are dominated by engineers, housing designs tend to be functional and dominated by construction technology. Because of the shortage of design organizations, housing designs normally are a variation of several standardized prototypes. Rural housing designs are left to the rural construction workers, although some efforts have been made to formalize architectural forms for different regions (*Nongcun xingxing zhuzhai tuyang* 1982).

Finance

Financing of rural housing is strictly from rural savings—individual or collective. The rural housing-finance institutions are informal, semi-organized in some communes during the Cultural Revolution. There is no evidence that the Agricultural Bank has any housing-construction loan program.

In urban housing, there is no building society, savings and loan, or other mortgage system. The present system of housing finance relies heavily on the public sector—state or municipalities. There are two programs that use domestic personal savings and foreign and overseas Chinese investment as a supplement to the public financing: commodity housing and joint-venture housing. The People's Construction Bank, a subsidiary of the People's Bank of China, was formed independently specifically to serve investment in construction. Since 1978 it has been financing joint-venture projects, for example, commodity housing development for sales to the overseas Chinese in Shenzhen Special Economic Zone (Chu 1985).[6] From 1984 to 1986 the bank also participated in commodity housing for the domestic sector; as much as U.S. $1.36 billion (5.1 billion RMB) was lent to the various enterprises that participated in commodity housing development (Shi, 1987, 2). This development shows that the state is willing to provide loans to private housing development. However, there is no published information on the application process and the conditions for repaying these loans.

The Chinese government's policy on housing finance attempts to mobilize all possible resources from the state, local government, enterprises, which can be state, collective, or privately owned, and individuals. Interestingly, private investment in urban housing increased to 10.92 percent of the total urban housing investment in 1985, while enterprise investment amounted to 60 percent (Zhu 1987, 17).

Management

Housing management in the rural sector remains in private hands since all housing is owner occupied. Urban private housing is similarly managed. State enterprise housing is allocated, managed, and maintained by the enterprises under the ministries, and municipal-owned units are allocated, managed, and maintained by the Housing Management Bureau under the Municipal Construction Commission (Badcock 1986, 154). The municipal Housing Management Bureau has another management function: to monitor the urban private housing sector.

HOUSING MARKETS AND POLICY ORIENTATIONS

With the exception of some recently completed housing projects for nonlocals and overseas Chinese, the provision and allocation of housing is largely undertaken as a nonprofit venture without housing submarkets. This is true not only for public construction and enterprise but also to a slight extent for commodity housing.

Rural Areas

In the rural sector, housing has been provided privately. Since the rural population has traditional building skills, most of the rural housing is constructed by pooling off-season labor and using indigenous building materials. The rural population constructs and expands housing units for the households' own use. During the Cultural Revolution some communes organized construction teams whose role was to construct rural projects for production and social purposes, such as developing marginal farm land, establishing water conservation, and building roads and public buildings. The construction team could also build housing units when there was a social demand. During the Cultural Revolution (1966–76), under the commune system, the income after subsistence expenditure, state tax, and collective accumulation was distributed to members of the commune according to a work-point system (*Nongcun renmingongshe shengchangdui Kuaiji* 1974, 7). The collective accumulation was used for production investment and social welfare such as education and health (*Remin gongshe caizheng yu caiwu guanli* 1981, 53–78). During the Cultural Revolution (1966–1976), more developed communities would pool their savings for building housing units allocated to the member households (Tang-Ning-Bang 1971, 23–24), a method no longer practiced today.

Because rural housing finance is entirely dependent on personal savings and collective savings, investment in housing is determined by rural income. When families have greater spatial needs (e.g., when sons are planning marriages), they save in order to construct new housing units or expand existing units for the newly formed families. The most commonly used form of housing provision is the self-help method whereby the owners finance and plan, while design and construction are largely left to the construction workers or team. Labor is either organized by the construction team or by pooling relatives, friends, and neighbors.

Since 1978, especially in the rural counties of Guangdong and Fujian, some commodity housing has have been constructed for sale to overseas Chinese. The profit so generated went to the county- or village-level government, which provided the land and resources for construction. Like other private houses constructed by the local people, these houses could be handed down to other family members when the owners were deceased.

Urban Areas

At present, most of new urban housing is still publicly financed. It comes from the state through the ministries that allocated an investment fund to workers' housing, which is built around the production units. The construction and management costs are borne by the ministries, and the housing units are distributed exclusively to members of each ministry.

Another housing form is financed, constructed, and managed by local municipalities. It is built to relocate dwellers of substandard housing and for residents displaced by urban rehabilitation. Before 1978 very little publicly financed urban housing was built for rental purposes, since housing was considered a social service and income subsidy. Construction was largely a consequence of state investment policy. Housing was in the nonproductive sector, thus receiving low developmental priority. Development concentrated on the production sector, specifically in social overhead capital such as infrastructure and production plants. Consequently, state investment in urban housing in the 1950s was the residual of the annual investment from the aggregate allocation to nonhousing sectors. As the national economic growth rate fluctuated, so did the state's housing investment. Moreover, the state budget was calculated and allocated on an annual basis. With the vacillation of proportionate investment in other sectors, state investment in housing and dormitories was low and unpredictable (Kwok 1973, 209). Long-term planning was impossible. Supply was small compared to demand. New urban housing was distributed by the state only to cadres, employees, and workers of the state enterprises according to rank through the various ministries (Chao 1968, 106). Besides, marital status, years of service, and interpersonal relationships also entered into allocation considerations. Interagency intervention in housing allocation was inevitable; for example, some new units were exchanged among different with relevant ministries for necessary resources and amenities (Badcock 1986, 164).

State investment was distributed to the various ministries, which allocated housing investment in relation to its construction investment, which included all construction projects for the ministries. Since ministries were responsible for providing housing for all of their cadres and workers, the new enterprises had to be provided with housing. As a result, new enterprise housing was planned and designed around the new plants as focal points. Social services (including retail) were also provided for the new housing; thus this type of new urban housing project formed a neighborhood development, centered around the enterprise.

In municipalities and cities, the planning department is responsible to develop urban housing for its residents. Investment funds either are allocated by the state or are derived from various taxes, a portion of which is retained by the local government. Construction teams with engineering support were set up by the city government to build construction projects in specific districts of the city. All construction projects within the district had to be executed by the local construction unit. Construction projects by ministries, sources of collective investment, and private enterprises either contracted with the unit within the district or used their own construction units. Since 1978, the local monopoly of construction units has been dismissed, and developers can choose construction units without locational constraints. Many construction teams that have been established by rural enterprises now undertake urban construction projects.

Commodity and Joint-Venture Housing

Since 1978, urban housing provision and allocation has been further complicated by the development of commodity housing. The "commercialization" of housing draws on the success of private housing investment in the rural areas and is one way to reduce housing subsidies and to recoup part of the rapidly rising investment in housing, which according to Lin (1987) amounted to 8.35 percent of the gross national product in 1985 and was still on the rise. At the beginning of the 1980s, the Ministry of Urban and Rural Construction and Environment Protection officially announced that "urban residents should be allowed to buy or build houses . . . to be repaid in a lump sum or by installment over 10–15 years" ("Deng Proposes New Housing Policy," May 16, 1984). In April 1982, a trial program to construct and subsidize the sale of apartment units was launched in four cities: Zhengzhou, Changzhou, Shashi, and Siping. The purchase price, presumably with interest rate built in, was fixed at 30 percent of the construction costs, the other two-thirds was paid by the government or the enterprises (normally, the purchasers' work unit). But even that 30 percent could be paid in installments with 10 percent as a down payment and the remaining 20 percent spread over up to fifteen years. However, if the individual paid his share all at once, an additional 30 percent discount was offered. A standard housing unit in Siping with construction costs about U.S. $5,400 (10,000 RMB) and was thus sold at U.S. $1,600 (about 3,000 RMB).[7] If the purchaser chose to pay immediately instead of by installment, the actual lump sum paid was U.S. $1,100 (about 2,100 RMB) (*Zhongguo baike nianjian* 1982, 667).

This program has now been extended to more than eighty Chinese cities. These apartments were offered to party members and municipal employees in the first round and then to medium and small enterprises. According to one survey of thirty-six medium-size cities, 79.5 percent of the completed commodity housing space was taken up. Of the sold space, 97.7 percent was purchased by enterprises, and only 2.3 percent was bought by individuals ("Fangzu taidi, shoujia piangao, daipi shangpin fang jiya nanxiao" June 29, 1987, 4). Because of the demand for commodity housing in the large cities, particularly in the Special Economic Zones, the sales rate there is much higher.

Besides, many joint-venture housing projects have been launched since 1980 in the Special Economic Zones and the Open Cities. The target clients of these houses and apartments are overseas Chinese and joint-venture corporations (Wong 1982, 54). For these ventures, profit is the sole motive, and earnings are split among the various parties concerned. However, to prevent undue speculation, the apartments purchased must not be resold without the prior approval of the municipal government. This housing submarket is therefore still under strict control, and in the Special Economic Zones its allocative mechanism is constrained. For foreign joint-venture corporations, housing for their managers and workers has to be provided, and units are rented or sold to these corporations. The tenure of foreign ownership is normally less than fifty years; once expired, the house or apartment will be reverted to the municipal government without compensation.

Renewal

Apart from new construction, urban renewal is an important source of urban housing supply. Urban renewal is the responsibility of the city government. In the 1950s, urban renewal was limited to slum clearance. The government was concerned about providing employment for the slum dwellers and preventing health and fire hazards. The method adopted was sites-and-services, whereby, drainage, water, and electricity were provided to the squatters who in 1949 were estimated to number 1 million in Shanghai alone, living in dispersed squatter areas (*Shanghai Panhuqu de bianqian* 1965, 7). There were also some limited efforts in relocating the dwellers of the worst slums into new housing units. Actual examples, however, were few (Kwok 1973, 306–16).

Because of war damages, dilapidated urban infrastructure and services were the most important urban issues in the 1950s; it affected not only urban residents but also economic production. Reconstruction concentrated on engineering projects in supplying the basic infrastructure to all urban residents and production units. For the first decade (1949–1958), infrastructure development was the single item that dominated urban renewal efforts (Chi 1959, 8–9). During the Great Leap Forward years (1958–1961) ambitious renewal plans covering large parts of many large cities were drawn up. Most of these projects were beyond the cities' resources and technical capability, and they remained on the drawing boards (Kwok 1973, 301–6). Systematic renewal of urban housing started only after 1978 when urban housing and social services began to receive national attention.

MAJOR PROBLEMS

In any society, housing is dominated by socioeconomic forces. In China, its development has changed as much as its political and ideological undercurrents. Admittedly, the housing stock in China is relatively small compared to the huge number of people, its quality is poor by standards of advanced countries, and resources available to housing construction and maintenance are scarce. However, to understand the housing problem in its proper perspective, apart from analyzing quantity and quality, the Chinese mode of development and the housing ownership are of particular importance.

Quantity, Quality, and Location

As far as space is concerned, the current standard in rural areas is adequate. With private ownership as the dominant form of tenure, the recent improvement of the rural economy has channeled more resources into housing-construction materials through the market, and both quantity and quality are improving. The only concern is that rural housing is taking up more and more agricultural land, which is counterproductive to the national objective of increasing agricultural production. The siting of newly built houses and the building of multistory houses are important for further expansion of rural housing without reducing agriculturally productive land.

Because urban housing is predominantly nonprivately owned and allocated by nonmarket mechanisms to fit socialist ideology, it presents a fundamental difficulty. The concept of housing as a welfare and income subsidy and as a means to attain social equalities results in heavy investment in housing construction and in the policy of low rentals. The low returns account for the limited resources available for urban housing provision and maintenance. Indeed, the existing low level of rent cannot even cover operation and maintenance, let alone repay the capital in housing construction. As nonowner–occupiers, the renters have no incentive to maintain or improve their houses, further contributing to the rapid deterioration of the housing stock. This system of housing financing has aggravated the shortage and low quality of housing provision.

Housing grants were allocated from the state to the locality, and there was little capital available for the enterprises and the local government. The latest urban economic reform in 1984 has allowed more capital and flexibility in housing-provision for enterprises and local governments, which accounts for the construction boom in the last several years.[8] Yet, existing urban land still presents an enormous problem for housing construction and urban planning since urban land is state owned but allocated by the local government. Once land is allocated to an enterprise or a ministry, the user, though technically not the owner, has absolute right and control over the development of the allocated land. Since the local government is unable to reclaim the use of allocated land, it has no power to redevelop it. Because of the housing shortage, land for existing private housing can be reclaimed for renewal only if housing units are available to relocate the residents. The urban land-use pattern is fixed. Therefore, urban expansion into the urban fringe, where the most productive rural land is found, is the simplest solution since there is the least resistance from the farming communities. Moreover, with low-density rural housing, the relocation of farmers is less of a problem. It is, however, against the policy of increasing agricultural production, and the most fertile and productive farm land is diminishing. An alternative to encroachment on farm land is rebuilding on an existing plot, which is not always compatible with urban planning and the best uses of the land. The current solution is to allow the enterprises to exchange their plots through the municipal government. This method allows the city to negotiate with the major land users to rationalize land use and to reorganize the urban land pattern. Since work units provide employees with access to nearby housing, the success of land-use rationalization depends largely on the willingness of enterprises to be relocated and on the availability of developable sites. The absence of a land market still impedes the development of a rational and efficient exchange system.

Mobility of the rural and urban population was totally restricted in the late 1950s when household registration and food rationing were introduced. Each household registered with the local governmental office, and the monthly food ration could be collected only at the location of the household's registration. A traveling permit had to be obtained from the police station at the place of residence as well as destination. Apart from state population policy, such as the sending of urban youths to rural areas during the Cultural Revolution,[9] there was little population movement between cities, villages, or between cities and the countryside. Since 1978, with the introduction of rural markets in the cities, food grains have become available everywhere. Subsequently, travel restrictions have been relaxed, and the population can now move more freely in response to the availability of jobs. According to recent estimates rural migrants comprise between 10 and 20 percent of the urban population (Goldstein and Goldstein 1987, 23). Since members of mobile households register in the place of residence from which they come, they are not officially counted as urban population. Therefore, the state and the local government are not responsible to provide housing for them. All of the mobile population has to find accommodations in the workplace—building sites for construction workers, production plants for industrial workers, homes for household help, and so on. So far there is no report that this group poses any serious threat to the formal housing sector.

The nonmarket allocation of housing has also deprived people of the possibilities of choosing a residential location and sharing housing expenditures. This in turn has affected the standard of housing and residential satisfaction. In urban China, it is a general practice that both husband and wife work. More often than not, they work for different enterprises at different locations. Only one of the spouses can enjoy the housing benefits provided by the enterprise, and the other has to commute; that is, up to one-half of the urban working population has to travel. This strict housing-distribution process has certain benefits and costs. Usually, community services and facilities are also provided by the enterprises. The proximity of work, residence, and community services fosters a close sense of community, a stable social network, and a mutual support system. Congenial neighborhoods are especially supportive of bringing up children and have other social benefits. Since two parents have two different work locations, these benefits will accrue to only one, and the other is isolated from his or her coworkers. Furthermore, it is almost impossible to choose a midway location or a location convenient to all members of a family. Once households get a dwelling, moving is difficult because of the housing scarcity. Moreover, changing job locations does not necessarily lead to a change of residence. The exchange of housing within the same enterprise or a locational exchange through the Housing Management Bureau is possible but certainly not easily accomplished, for the housing standard has to match one's rank, seniority, and so on. Opportunities for exchange are therefore very limited. In reality, once housing units are distributed, there is practically no further movement.

Affordability and Equity

The percentage of income spent on housing is low, particularly in the urban sector; "low"-income rural households spend a relatively higher percentage of their income while their "higher"-income urban counterparts pay a relatively lower percentage of their income on housing. However, about a quarter of the urban population has inadequate housing.[10] Field surveys indicate that most cities have scattered slum areas. In Shanghai, many pre–1949 squatter areas still exist, although the infrastructure is provided either by the municipal government or through the pooling of residents' own resources. Over time, the infrastructure and the environmental conditions have been improved by a combination of sporadic government action and regular self-help efforts. Residents in these areas are employed, and many have been sent there by the municipal Housing Management Bureau. A partial explanation for this situation is that many of these employees are too poor and their employers have too few resources to provide better housing for their workers. Many of these employers are collective enterprises. Others include money-losing state-owned production and service units. Families with political difficulties, including those being classified as undesirable elements, also live in poor housing, because during the socialist transformation they were driven out from their homes, and in general, they would not be given good jobs or houses. Apart from this group, the present urban population has no problem of affordability, and there is no evidence of a homeless population.

This question of equity, however, does arise. Is it equitable that those in the state-owned sector should be subsidized while the rest are not, for example, as with the rural population that largely has to provide its own accommodations?

If one views the housing subsidy as part of a payment in kind, the problem of housing equity is exacerbated by the inequity of the salary structure, a topic that is beyond the scope of this chapter.

From a different viewpoint, private ownership and public rental housing have created inequality. In the past, the right to live in subsidized housing had been regarded as a privilege; those in the private sector have had to pay higher housing costs. On the other hand, with the latest round of economic reforms, those in the private sector in the countryside have had greater choices in housing with the standard and style of their own desire. In urban areas, except for those already owning private housing, the possibility of owning a house is limited since the only source of private housing is commodity housing. Even with generous subsidies, few urban workers can afford to purchase these units. The emergence of commodity housing since 1984, catering to only the privileged urban groups who can afford to pay one-third of the construction costs, now creates more inequalities in housing. It can be seen that urban commodity housing has actually reinforced existing inequalities rather than reduced it. The high-standard commodity housing in the Special Economic Zones and Open Cities catering to the overseas Chinese have a similar discriminatory function, for the prices of these units are well beyond the means of the local population. Thus only two groups of urbanites at present can enjoy the higher-quality private housing. The high-level cadres in rich units with influence can obtain better housing through the financial support of the work units. The other group is those with overseas relatives, who purchase commodity-housing units for them or through individual savings from overseas remittances.

The process of housing commodification, nevertheless, seems to have passed the point of no return; it has evoked a desire for private property ownership that has long been suppressed by socialist ideology (Lai 1985, 76). It is also officially endorsed. The present thinking is that this process should be accompanied by a policy of housing-subsidy reduction and by increasing rents in the state-owned sector. The immediate target is to balance rent and operating costs.

PROSPECTIVE DEVELOPMENTS

The future development of housing provision depends on the balancing of urban supply to demand, on improving housing resources, and on the general level of development.

Demographic Trends

Responding to the recent economic-reform policies and the relaxation of population-movement control, the agricultural labor force has been shifting to the nonagricultural sector at a high rate. Some have estimated that 200 million people in the agricultural population will move into the nonagricultural sector by the year 2000 (Huang 1985, 18). At present, the mobile population, largely consisting of rural-urban migrants, estimated to be 10 to 20 percent of the urban population, will continue to be mobile because of the outmigration of the surplus rural labor and the attraction of urban economic opportunities and higher standard of urban living.

A second demographic trend is the aging of the population (Coale 1981, 930–34). Population-control measures have reduced the dependent population in the lower age group. As the general standard of living improves, life expectancy increases, and the dependent population in older age groups also increases. The population pyramid is moving toward a bell shape. Therefore, labor productivity will have to increase to support a larger dependent population and to maintain (or improve) the standard of living.

The trend toward smaller families also results from population-control measures. As household size declines, the number of households is likely to increase, thus demanding more housing units. Smaller housing units require higher per capita space standards and per capita utility provisions (bathrooms, kitchens), which are the most costly items in housing construction. Therefore, the per capita cost of the housing supply will increase.

Although projections of the proportion of the future urban population range from 50 percent in the year 2000 ("Population Issue a Great Challenge" 1987, 1) to a few percentage points over the existing level, the demographic trend of increasing urbanization will continue to exert heavy pressures on urban housing provision. The slight improvement in urban overcrowding since 1978 due to the massive addition of newly constructed houses could be masked by the fact that urban household registration has excluded rural-urban migrants.

Privatization of Urban Housing

Although most rural housing is privately supplied and owned, a majority of urban housing is still owned by the state. With the present annual deficit of urban housing at U.S. $0.37 (1.2 RMB) per square meter (see above, "Urban Construction"), and the demographic pressure requiring more urban housing in the future, the state can ill afford to continue to supply urban housing by the same method. As the per capita housing cost is also increasing, the deficit will continue to grow accordingly. With limited public resources available, privatization of ownership is inevitable since it will use private savings as the source of investment. Foreseeing this dilemma, the Chinese have introduced commodity housing. However, this effort is meeting with mixed success, since the rent level of public housing is so low compared to the heavily subsidized state housing that there is no economic incentive for an individual to acquire a housing unit ("Fangzu taidi, shoujia pianqao, dai pi shangpin fang jiya nanxiao" June 29, 1987, 4). Only those individuals with enormous savings potential that have no access to subsidized state or enterprise housing can consider purchasing a commodity housing unit. Those with rich relatives overseas and those with recently accumulated wealth through individual (private) enterprises also belong to this commodity-housing consumer group. The number of individual purchasers, however, compared to the enterprise and ministry buyers, is relatively small.

So far, commodity housing is not lacking ready buyers because it has been sought after by the rich enterprise units. Since enterprises are usually responsible for their workers' housing, housing units are necessary, and good housing is a means to attract capable personnel. The cadres within enterprises—the high-level technical and managerial staff—also desire to live in the newly finished and better-quality commodity housing units both as a reflection of their status and power and as a reward for their contribution to the enterprises. A portion of the retained profits of these enterprises is thus allocated for the purchase of commodity housing. The rent charged for these enterprise-owned units has to be voluntarily adjusted to the normal average rent. Thus they are heavily subsidized by the enterprises. Enterprise-owned and subsidized commodity-housing units are accepted as an interim form of private housing. Since individuals have neither sufficient resources nor much desire for private ownership, enterprises may remain the main buyers of commodity housing for a considerable period.

The most successful example of commodity housing bought by individual buyers is in the Shekou Industrial District within the Shenzhen Special Economic Zone, where the industrial wages are higher than the national average. Workers migrating into Shekou are usually housed by the enterprises that employ them, but only if they are single. Workers with families have two choices—to rent or to purchase housing units from the Shekou Real Estate Company, a corporation under the Ministry of Transport. By heavily subsidizing sales prices and providing a mortgage for the owner–occupiers, Shekou Real Estate Company markets its housing to individual workers with families. The monthly mortgage payment is higher than the monthly rent charged to workers with families, but the differential is relatively small. By reducing the difference between a mortgage payment and rent, it provides an incentive for families to own housing units.

Until 1987, 62 percent of the family workers had purchased their own units (1,310 worker households had owner-occupied units given by Shekou Real Estate Company). To privatize urban housing, it is essential to raise the rent in state housing, thereby narrowing the gap between the existing low rent and the current high cost of housing purchase. This strategy will no doubt create social and political difficulties, but this is unavoidable in the short term.

Increasing the present rent can be made more acceptable if household income improves. Since household income is a function of economic growth, private home ownership is a function of economic growth. Because of the demographic trends toward aging and smaller families, labor productivity has to improve significantly to produce real economic growth.

The demand for private housing is also generally determined by social and political attitudes toward property ownership. The ideology of production commodification is already advocated and widely encouraged in every sector of the economy. This ideology may spill over to property ownership.

To date, commodity housing, apart from that in Shekou, is largely acquired by enterprises and factories. Individual acquisition of commodity housing is infrequent. When the ideology of commodification can be transferred to individuals, when the gap between rental and purchase price can be reduced, and when household real income can be increased, China's private housing market will have the necessary conditions to flourish.

NOTES

1. *Commodity housing* includes all types of housing built not as a form of social welfare but as a commodity for sale or rent, mainly for profit either from the domestic economy or from the foreign-trade-linked economy. For fuller discussion, see the sections "Commodity and Joint-Venture Housing" and "Privatization of Urban Housing."

2. Figures contained in the *Statistical Yearbook of China*, 1986; figures contained in an article by Zhu Yi in *Beijing Review* 30, no. 17 (1987): 16–19; and figures employed by Qi Ming-chui in *The Almanac of China's Urban Economy and Society* (1985, 59–62) do not match one another perhaps because of different definitions and a different system of data collection. For this study, we generally adopted the internally consistent official figures published in the *Statistical Yearbook of China*.

3. This bureau is a unit within the city government. Its functions are to distribute and manage housing, including rent collection, to maintain and exchange city-owned housing within the city, and in some cases to manage, under contract, the ministry's worker housing within the city. It also inspects private housing for standards, safety, structure, and renovation, and collects property tax.

4. *Cadres*, in current Chinese usage, denotes officials and semi-officials in responsible positions in any organization of the party, various levels of government, and state-owned enterprises, normally at the managerial and supervisory levels.

5. Special Economic Zones (SEZs) and Open Cities are products of the open policies since 1978. There are four SEZs, namely, Shenzhen SEZ, Zhuhai SEZ, Shantou SEZ, and Xiamen SEZ. Fourteen coastal cities were declared open since 1983: Dalian, Qinhuangdao, Tianjin, Yantai, Qingdao, Lianyungang, Nantong, Shanghai, Ningbo, Wenzhou, Fuzhou, Guangzhou, Zhanjiang, and Beihai. Various preferential treatments and tax concessions are offered to foreign investors to invest in these zones and cities.

6. *Joint-venture projects* are undertakings in which investment and profits are shared between the Chinese and foreign parties. There are various forms including equity joint ventures and contractual joint ventures.

7. For a housing unit, the standard varies with time. In 1978 the average construction area of a housing unit was about 40 square meters. In the 1980s it increased to about 50 square meters.

8. Building on the success of the rural reforms and the experience gained in the Special Economic Zones and experiments in selected cities, the Third Plenary Session of the Twelfth Central Committee of the Chinese Communist party concluded on October 1984 that system reforms in the urban economic structure should be carried out. One of the most significant elements is to inject more flexibility and independence into the enterprises.

9. For more details, see Bernstein's *Up to the Mountains and Down to the Villages*, 1977.

10. Inadequate housing is largely defined by overcrowding; the standard of overcrowding, however, varies with time. In the past, only those with less than 2–4 square meters per capita were considered overcrowded. Recently, the standard has increased to 4–6 square meters.

REFERENCES

Badcock, Blain. 1986. "Land and Housing Policy in Chinese Urban Development, 1976–1986." *Planning Perspectives*, no. 1:147–70.

Bernstein, Thomas P. 1977. *Up to the Mountains and Down to the Villages: The Transfer of Youth from Urban to Rural China*. New York: Yale University Press.

Chao, Kang. 1968. *The Construction Industry in Communist China*. Chicago: Aldine Publishing Co.

"Chengxiang jianshe huanjing baohu bu chengli (Establishment of the Ministry of Urban and Rural Construction and Environmental Protection)." 1982. *Chengshi jianshe* (Urban Construction), no. 6, p. 2.

Chi, tai. 1959. *Tientsin, the New Capital of Hopeh Province*, U.S. Joint Publications Research Service, 2094–N, New York, December, 1–11.

Chu, David K. Y. 1985. "Population Growth and Related Issues." In *Modernisation in China: The Case of the Shenzhen SEZ*, edited by K. Y. Wong and D. K. Y. Chu, 131–39. Hong Kong: Oxford University Press.

Coale, Ansley J. 1981. "Population Trends, Population Policy, and Population Studies in China." *Population and Development Review* 7, no. 1:85–97.

"Cultural Revolution Victims Win Back Homes." 1984. *China Daily*, October 20, p. 1.

"Deng Proposes New Housing Policy." 1984. *China Daily*, May 16.

Donnithrone, Andrey. 1967. *China's Economic System*. London, Eng.: Allen & Unwin.

"Fangzu taidi, shoujia piangao, daipi shangpin fang jiya nanxiao (Housing Rent Is Too Low, Price Is Too High)." 1987. *Shenzhen tequbao* (Shenzhen Special Economic Zone Daily), June 29, p. 4.

Howe, Christopher. 1968. "The Supply and Administration of Urban Housing in Mainland China: The Case of Shanghai." *The China Quarterly*, no. 33:73–97.

Huang, xiang ming. 1985. "Nonye shengyu renkou di zhuanyi yu jingji fazhan (The Movement of Agricultural Surplus Population and Economic Development)." *Jingji yanjiu* (Economic Research), no. 2, 16–21.

Kwok, R. Ying-wang. 1973. "Urban-Rural Planning and Housing Department in People's Republic of China." Ph.D. dissertation, Columbia University.

———. 1981. "Factors Determining Construction Technology and Building Materials in People's Republic of China." *Habitat International* 5, no. 3–4:332–36.

Lai, C. F. 1985. "Special Economic Zones: the Chinese Road to Socialism." *Environment and Planning: Society and Space*, no. 3:63–84.

Lin, Zhiqun. 1986. "On the Construction Use and Expenditure of Housing." *China City Planning Review* (Zhongguo chengshi guihua) 2, no. 1:43–52.

———. 1987. "Housing Construction in China." *City Planning Review* (Chengshi guihua), no. 6:3–5.

Nongcun remingongshe shengchandui kuaiji (Rural People's Commune: Brigade Accounting). 1974. Guangdong: Remin chupanshe.

Nongcun xingxing zhuzhai tuyang (New Models of Rural Housing). 1982. Guangdong: Keji chupanshe.

"Population Issue a Great Challenge." 1987. *China Daily*, February 2, p. 1.

Qi, Ming-chui. 1985. "China's Urban Housing." In *Zhongguo chengshi jingji shehui nianjian* (The Almanac of China's Urban Economy and Society). Beijing: Zhongguo chengshi jingji shehui chupanshe, 59–62.

Remin gongshe caizhang yu caiwu guanli (The Management of Accounting and Finances in People's Commune). 1981. Zhejiang remin chupanshe.

Shanghai panhuqu de bianqian (Evaluation of Shanghai's Hut District). 1965. Shanghai: Shanghai remin chupanshe.

Shi, ming shen. 1987. "Huan jie shimin zhufang nan, tuidong zhuzhai shangpin hua, gedi gongshang yinhang shiban fangdi chan yewu (To Slow Down the Housing Problem and to Promote Commercial Residential Housing, the Real Estate and Property Market Is Developed)." *Renmin renbao*, March 3, 2.

State Statistical Bureau. Peoples Republic of China. 1986. *Statistical Yearbook of China, 1986*. Hong Kong: Economic Information and Agency.

Tang-Ning-Bang. 1971. *Da-zhai Xing* (Visit to Dazhai). Hong Kong: Chaoyang chupanshe.

Wong, Kwan Yiu. 1982. *Shenzhen Special Economic Zone: China's Experiment in Modernization*. Hong Kong: Hong Kong Geographical Association.

Zhang, Kai Ji. 1979. "Cong Beijing qian san men gao wu zhu zhai tan qi (A Discussion on High-Rise Residential Buildings in Qian San Men, Beijing)." *Jianzhu xuebao* (Architectural Journal), no. 6, 21–29.

Zhong Hwa. 1987. "Too Low Rents Cause Housing Shortage." *China Daily*, March 21, p. 4.

Zhongguo zuzhi yingyiming shouce (English Handbook of Chinese Organizations). 1986. Beijing: Xinhua chupanshe.

Zhu, Yi. 1987. "Housing Prospects for the Year 2000." *Beijing Review* 30, no. 17 (April):16–19.

FURTHER READING

Carlson, Eric. *Housing Finance Development in China: An Overview of Issues and Prospects*. Chicago: International Union of Building Societies and Savings Association, 1986.

———. "China Achieves Record Housing." *Habitat Intl.* 11, no. 4 (1987):47–67.

Casault, Andre, et al. *Open House International*. Special issue on China. 12, no. 1 (1987).

Chang, Gu Yun. "Urban Housing Developing and Policy for the Future." *Ekistics* 54, no. 322 (1987):9–13.

China City Planning Review (Zhongguo chengshi guihua) (in English) 3, no. 2 (December 1986).

Crump, G. Lindsay. "Housing in China." *Journal of Property Management*, 1988.

Fei, Hsiaotung, ed. *Small Towns in China: Functions, Problems, and Prospects*. Beijing: New World Press, 1986.

Fong, Peter K. W. *The Commercialisation of Housing in a Socialist State: An Attempt to Solve China's Urban Housing Problem*. Hong Kong: Centre of Urban Studies and Urban Planning, University of Hong Kong, 1987.

Goldstein, S. M., and W. Parish, eds. *Urban Life in Contemporary China*. Chicago: University of Chicago Press, 1984.

Guang-qi, Dong. "Beijing: Housing and Community Development." *Ekistics* 54, no. 322 (1987):34–39.

Howe, Christopher. 1968. "The Supply and Administration of Urban Housing in Mainland China: The Case of Shanghai." *The China Quarterly*, no. 33:73–97.

———. *Shanghai: Revolution and Development in an Asian Metropolis*. Cambridge: Cambridge University Press, 1981.

Kirby, Richard J. R. *Urbanisation in China: Town and Country in a Developing Economy, 1949–2000 A.D.* London: Crown Helm, 1985.

Kim, Joochul. "China's Current Housing Issues and Policies." *Journal of the American Planning Association* 53, no. 2 (1987):220–26.

Kwok, R. Ying-wang. "Trends of Urban Planning and Development in China." In *Urban Development in Modern China*, edited by L. J. C. Ma, and E. W. Hanten, 147–93. Boulder, Colo.: Westview Press, 1981.

Lalkaka, D. "Urban Housing in China." *Habitat International* 8 (1984):63–73.

Lee, Yok-shiu F. "The Urban Housing Problem in China." *China Quarterly* 115 (1988):387–407.

Leung, C. K. and J. C. H. Chai. *Development and Distribution in China*. Hong Kong: Centre of Asian Studies, University of Hong Kong, 1985.

Ma, L. J. C. "Urban Housing Supply in the People's Republic of China." In *Urban Development in Modern China*, edited by L. J. C. Ma and Edward W. Hauten, 222–59. Boulder, Colo.: Westview Press, 1986.

Mok, B. H. "Grassroots Organizing in China—The Residents Committee as a Linking Mechanism Between the Bureaucracy and the Community." *Community Development Journal* 23, no. 3 (1988):164–69.

Parish, William L., and K. Whyte, Martin. *Village and Family in Contemporary China*. Chicago: University of Chicago Press, 1978.

Philips, D. R., and A. G. O. Yeh. "The Provision of Housing and Social Services in China's Special Economic Zones." *Environment and Planning (C): Government and Policies, 1987* 5 (1986):447–68.

Schmidt, Charles G., and Yuk Lee. "Residential Preferences in China." *Geographical Review* 77, no. 3 (1989):318–28.

Tan, K. C. "Revitalized Small Towns in China." *Geographical Review* 76, no. 2 (1986):138–48.

———. "Small Towns in Chinese Urbanization." *Geographical Review* 76, no. 3 (1986):265–75.

Yao, Zhen. "Housing and Planning." *Planning and Development* 3, no. 1 (1987):15–19.

Ye, Shunzan. "Urbanisation and Housing in China." *Asian Geographer* 2, no. 2 (1982):1–12.

Yeh, Anthony G. O., ed. "Special Issue on Urban Planning in China." *Planning and Development* 3, no. 3 (1987):

Zhongguo baike nianjian, 1982. (China Encyclopaedia Yearbook, 1982). Beijing: Zhongguo dabaikequanshu chupanshe, 1982.

Zhongguo zuzhi yingyiming shouce (English Handbook of Chinese Organizations). 1986. Beijing: Xinhua chupanshe.

Zhao, Guanquian. "On China's Urban Housing Development." *Building in China*, no. 2 (1986):42–48.

22

Japan

KAZUO HAYAKAWA

Notes
References
Further Reading

Japan is located at the eastern-most end of Asia and at the western-most end of the Pacific. It is a long, narrow chain of islands stretching north to south. It comprises 4 major islands and 3,900 adjacent smaller ones, covering 377 thousand square kilometers. Plains and basins account for about 29 percent of Japan's territory; the remaining 71 percent is mountains. Habitable land is scarce, and in 1985 about 76 percent of the population of 120 million lived in urban areas. The population density of Japan far surpasses that of most other countries.

Due to urbanization and industrialization, the urban population has increased rapidly since 1955. It is concentrated along the Pacific seaboard where transportation and industries are most highly developed. Expansion of the Tokyo metropolitan area has been particularly remarkable, mainly because of its political, economical, and international concentration today. Its population was 9,368,000 in 1945, 17,864,000 in 1960, and 30,272,000 in 1985.

Since World War II the Japanese government has been run by the conservative parties except for 1947, when it was controlled by a socialist party. As the conservatives strongly encouraged industries and big enterprises, Japan has achieved fast economic growth, and today it is well known as an "economic giant" in the world. On the other hand, there have been many drawbacks such as low social security levels and poor housing conditions.

In 1983–1987 the Nakasone government embarked on a drastic policy change. Privatization, for example, the sale of the Japan National Railways to the private sector and public lands to real estate companies, caused many serious problems such as rising land prices (figure 22.1) and growing resident displacement. As a result, urban land has become an immediate target of speculation by real estate companies, banks, and big enterprises. Newspapers and television broadcasts are reporting almost daily on these phenomena. Congress opened a special committee for land and housing policy in December 1987. A new housing crisis has emerged, and it is having a deep impact on contemporary Japanese society.

TRENDS IN HOUSING CONDITIONS AND CONSTRUCTION[1]

In 1968 there was an average of 3.9 people per dwelling.[2] By 1988 this number had decreased to 3.2 (see table 22.1). This decline is a reflection of the nuclearization of the family in postwar Japan. However, it not only shows the decline of the extended family system, it also reflects the shrinkage in the size of postwar housing as well as the large-scale movement of the population to the cities. In 1988, on the average, privately owned housing accommodated 3.64 people, whereas small, private rental housing accommodated only 1.26 people to 2.45 people in 1983 (table 22.1).

Figure 22.1
Trends in the National Urban Land Price Index, Japan, 1955–1985

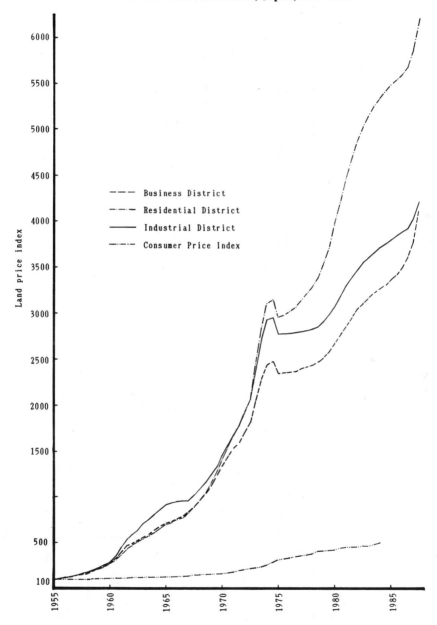

Table 22.1
Housing Conditions, by Tenure, Japan, 1988

	Total	Owned Houses	Rented Houses	Public Rented Houses	Private Rented Houses[1]	Private Rented Houses[2]	Employee houses
People per dwelling	3.20	3.64	2.47	3.14*	2.45*	1.26*	3.10*
People per room	0.66	0.61	0.84	1.00*	0.88*	0.96*	0.88*
Rooms per dwelling	4.87	6.04	2.95	3.14	2.86	1.33	3.50
Area of floor space per dwelling(m²)	89.90	117.29	44.77	46.43	42.46	18.03	54.42

Source: Japan, 1983a, 1988.

[1]Private amenities.
[2]Shared amenities.
*1983 figures.

The average number of people per room has gradually declined, reflecting improvements in postwar housing conditions and declining household size. In 1963 there were 1.16 people per room, but by 1988 this had dropped to 0.66 people. However, the occupancy rate varies greatly with tenure. In public housing the rents are relatively low, leading to higher densities.

The average number of rooms per house has increased rapidly: from 3.82 rooms in 1963 to 4.87 rooms by 1988. Here again, the figures vary with type of tenure. In 1988 there were only 1.33 rooms in private rental housing with shared amenities, compared with 2.86 rooms in private housing with their own amenities (toilet and kitchen) and compared with 6.02 rooms in privately owned homes. But there is no definition of "room" in Japan. Even a space of 3 square meters is counted as a room if people live in it. A kitchen-dining space of more than 5 square meters is also counted as a "room."

The average floor area of privately owned houses has increased rapidly. As of 1988 it had reached 117.3 square meters. However, in all other kinds of housing, the floor area is small, with the average for rental housing having increased only slightly. In public rental housing it was 36.7 square meters in 1963, increasing to 46.4 square meters in 1988, and in private rental housing the floor area has actually decreased. There is thus a significant difference in dwelling size depending on tenure.

In 1988, 8 percent of privately owned houses did not have running water. Many farm houses still use well water. One characteristic of Japanese housing is that even today there is a lack of sewers. Houses without flush toilets number 32.8 percent of the total; 7.6 percent lacked a bathroom; 39.9 percent of all households lacked more than one of the fundamental facilities (flush toilet, kitchen, or bath). In the Tokyo metropolitan area 23.7 percent lacked such facilities.

In 1975 the government for the first time set a "minimum housing standard." However, those not meeting this standard could not legally be prohibited from obtaining a building permit. According to the minimum standard, bedrooms should satisfy the following conditions:

1. A separate bedroom (10 square meters) for a married couple; only one child under five years old can share the room with them.

2. Children six to seventeen years old require a bedroom separate from the parents, 10 square meters for two children and 7.5 square meters for one child, with a maximum of two children per room. A boy and a girl should not share the same room after the age of twelve.

3. Each child eighteen years and over requires a separate bedroom (7.5 square meters).

4. A master bedroom should be at least 10 square meters and other bedrooms 7.5 square meters.

Dining rooms should satisfy the following conditions:

1. A dining-kitchen may be used as a dining place; a kitchen only for a one-person household.
2. The size of a dining room should be at least 7.5 square meters for a two- to four-person household and 10 square meters for households of five or more persons.

Facilities should satisfy the following conditions:

1. A toilet exclusively for the household members
2. A bathroom for each household (excluding one-person households)

In 1988 the percentage of the housing stock below the minimum housing standard in terms of space and density only, was 9.5 percent of the total (table 22.2). Here again, there is a significant difference depending on tenure. Among rented houses it was 1.1 percent, more than five times that of owned houses.

However, if we count houses lacking facilities and houses where major repair is needed as "substandard houses," 28.9 percent of all houses in the country are substandard, and 39.9 percent in Tokyo and 40.3 percent in Osaka are substandard (table 22.2).

In 1941 most housing was in the private rental sector: 89.2 percent in Osaka, 73.3 percent in Tokyo, and 75.9 percent of the housing in the twenty-six remaining cities (Japan 1941). In 1946 with the establishment of the Rent Control Ordinance, the management base of private rental housing supply collapsed. The purchase of private rental houses by renters as well as the outright building of their own house increased. This is considered to be the start of the increase in postwar home ownership. However, the Rent Control Ordinance did not apply to housing built after 1950, when private rental housing did increase again.

In spite of the government's home-ownership oriented policy, the percentage of privately owned housing did not increase because of the high price of lots and houses. Since 1950, the proportion of extremely low quality private rental housing with shared facilities increased, as did those with private amenities. In 1988 small public rental houses made up 7.5 percent of the national housing stock (table 22.3).

Wooden detached houses make up the greater part of Japanese houses today. In 1963 they comprised 72 percent of the total, falling to 62.4 percent by 1988, while apartments during that same period increased from 12.5 to 30.3 percent. In 1988, 94.4 percent of all detached houses were wooden buildings. In general, apartment buildings less than five stories high do not have elevators. In Japan there are no mobile homes.

After World War II, particularly after 1960, there was an extremely rapid concentration of the population in the cities. The urban population increased from 38.1 percent immediately after the war to 76.7 percent by 1985. Thus the demand for housing in cities increased, too, forming a major cause of housing

Table 22.2

Number and Ratio of Households below the Minimum Housing Standard, Japan, 1988

	Total	(a) Under Minimum Space Standard	(b) Lack of Facilities[1]	(c) Major Repairs Needed[2]	(a+b+c) Under Minimum Housing Standard
Total	37,453,800	3,574,700 (9.5 %)	4,261,800 (11.4 %)	1,022,600 (2.7 %)	8,859,100 (23.6 %)
Owned houses	22,980,500	633,600 (2.8)	1,737,800 (7.6)	633,000 (2.8)	2,434,700 (13.2)
Rented houses	13,950,300	2,940,600 (21.1)	2,524,100 (18.1)	389,500 (2.8)	5,854,200 (42.0)
Public rented houses	2,027,700	769,100 (37.9)	353,800 (17.4)	48,300 (2.4)	1,171,200 (57.7)
Private rented houses	9,614,300	1,981,900 (20.6)	1,986,900 (20.7)	298,700 (3.1)	4,267,500 (44.4)
Employee houses	1,539,200	189,500 (12.3)	83,300 (11.9)	42,600 (2.8)	415,400 (24.2)
Tokyo[3]	4,028,600	714,700 (17.7)	806,200 (20.1)	88,300 (2.1)	1,609,200 (39.9)
Osaka[3]	2,650,100	500,600 (18.9)	520,000 (19.6)	48,700 (1.5)	1,069,300 (40.3)

Source: Japan, 1983a, 1988.

Note: (a), (b), and (c) are mutually exclusive.

[1]Exceeding space standard.

[2]Exceeding space and facilities standarc.

[3]1983

Table 22.3
Dwellings, by Tenure, Japan, 1958–1988

Year	Total (x1,000)	Owned Houses	Rented Houses	Public Rented Houses	Private Rented Houses[1]	Private Rented Houses[2]	Employee Houses
1958	17,432	71.2%	28.8%	3.5%		18.5%	6.7%
1963	20,372	64.3	35.7	4.6	15.3	8.8	7.0
1973	28,731	59.2	40.8	6.9	22.1	5.3	6.4
1983	34,705	62.4	37.3	7.6	21.7	2.8	5.2
1988	37.454	61.4	37.2	7.5	24.0	1.7	4.2

Source: Japan, 1983a, 1988.
[1]Private amenities.
[2]Shared amenities.

difficulties in Japan. At the same time, problems such as rapidly decreasing inner-city populations and long distance commuting became serious. For example, the population of Tokyo's central district of Chiyoda-ku dropped from 61,800 in 1980 to 54,200 in 1987.

In 1960 the number of households with elders sixty-five or older was 4,437,200 (22.5 percent of all households). In 1985 it had more than doubled to 9,249,000 (24.3 percent of the total). The trend is the same for elderly one-person households, which increased from 203,200 in 1960 to 1,180,723 in 1988. Meeting the needs of the single elderly is a major issue. Also single-parent households increased, from 1,744,000 in 1970 to 2,403,000 in 1985 (Japan 1986).

THE ROLE OF HOUSING INSTITUTIONS AND ORGANIZATIONS

In Japan housing supply depends by and large on market conditions. The government has almost abandoned public sector housing policy. Instead, it is encouraging private housing developers, housing industries, and real estate companies. People are forced to buy sites and houses, sold as profitable commodities. This is a main circumstance of housing in Japan and the operational background for housing institutions and organizations.

National Government Organizations

The following are national government organizations:

1. Ministry of Construction Housing Bureau. It is in charge of the overall administration of the housing affairs of the national government.
2. Housing and Urban Development Corporation (HUDC). It is responsible for the construction and administration of housing, development and redevelopment, and construction and management of railways and parks.
3. Housing Loan Corporation. It issues long-term low-interest loans to individuals seeking help in housing finance. There are many categories for loans, but generally, individuals can borrow one-half or one-third of the cost, and the rest is loaned by commercial banks. This corporation also makes loans to housing developers.

Local Government Organizations

Among local government organizations, there are forty-seven prefectures and about a thousand cities with local governments. All receive central government funds to prepare, build, and finance housing at the municipal level.

Private Housing Supply and Development Organizations

The private housing supply and development organizations include the following:

1. Urban Developers Association of Japan. This is the real estate organization for Japan's twenty-eight major private railroad companies, which secure land for housing development in the areas along the rail lines.

2. Japan Real Estate Association. This is a special interest organization for the nation's real estate companies with strong lobbying pressure in Parliament.

3. The Housing Industry Association. This is a special interest organization of small- and medium-scale housing-development companies.

4. The Japan High Rise Housing Association. This is a special interest organization for the builders of middle- and upper-middle-class condominiums.

Tenant Associations

Tenant associations are voluntary organizations of renters of private and public housing aimed at protecting the rights of the tenants:

1. The Tenant Association of Japan. This is an organization of renters of private housing. It is now resisting changes in the Rent Act by which landlords could evict tenants because of renovation of their properties.

2. The Japan Public Housing Tenant Association. This organization serves the renters of all public housing provided by local authorities.

3. The Housing and Urban Development Corporation Resident Association. This is an organization of renters of housing built by the HUDC. In the early 1980s the HUDC Tenant Association started the movement against rent increases.

Japan Citizen Association for the Improvement of Housing

The Japan Citizen Association for the Improvement of Housing is a citizens' movement aimed at improving housing conditions and policy. It was established in 1987 on the occasion of the International Year of Shelter for the Homeless (IYSH). It surveys housing demand, holds symposia, comments on housing-related policies, and organizes demonstrations. It is composed of eighteen citizens' groups, including consumer groups, renter unions, and construction- related unions.

Research Organizations

The research organizations include the following:

1. The Japan Architectural Institute. This is an academic association of design professionals, established in 1886, numbering 29,400 members in 1986. The institute publishes magazines and holds conferences.

2. The Japan Housing Council. Established in 1982, this is a national association of lawyers, economists, sociologists, health and welfare professionals, geographers, political scientists, housing-policy experts, architects, urban planners, conservationists,

journalists, councilmen, parliamentarians, and citizens. It studies housing conditions throughout the nation, supports citizen housing movements, and makes proposals on housing policy to local and national governments. In 1987 there were about 2,000 members.

HOUSING MARKETS AND POLICY ORIENTATIONS

In 1987, 1.38 percent of the total national budget, 5.76 of 416.16 billion dollars, was spent on housing, which is a decrease from 5.92 billion dollars or 1.55 percent in 1982. The housing budget and its allocation (table 22.4) reveal that available funds were cut by 20 percent during 1986–1987. Underlying trends indicate decreasing money for public housing and increasing support for redevelopment and subsidization of private initiative, although the overall pattern has remained fairly stable during the past several years.

Publicly Funded Housing

Public Housing by Local Authorities. Public housing is inexpensive rental housing, constructed by local public entities with subsidies from the national Treasury and supplied to low-income people living in cramped quarters. In 1987 the budget was 2.03 billion dollars, 35.2 percent of the housing budget. From 1945 to 1986, approximately 2,623,000 public housing units (6.5 percent of total) were constructed. Construction of public housing decreased yearly from 108,000 (7.2 percent of total new construction) in 1970 to 45,000 (3.2 percent of the total) in 1986.

One of the outstanding features of public housing is that the rent is extremely low compared to private rental housing of the same quality. Public housing is roughly divided into two classes: class no. 1 and class no. 2. The national Treasury subsidizes 50 percent in class no. 1 and 66 percent in class no. 2. Class no. 2 houses are for the people with incomes lower than those in class no. 1, for example, female-headed households, welfare recipients, and the disabled.

Due to the low rents, there are many applicants in the big cities where a majority of the households are dissatisfied with their housing.[3] A pool of possible tenants is made on the basis of (1) whether the applicant's income complies with the standards set and (2) their current housing conditions. The final selection of tenants is determined by public lottery. A limited amount of special public rental housing (class no. 2) is sometimes built for the elderly, one-parent households, and households with disabled people, although they, too, are selected by lottery if there is not enough housing to meet the need. In 1951, 80 percent of all households was eligible for public housing in class no. 1. In 1987 the eligible proportion was limited to 20 percent (figure 22.2). If a tenant's income is within the prescribed income standards at time of occupancy but rises above this level at a later date, it will be his or her duty to vacate the house and immediately

Table 22.4
National Housing Budget, Japan, 1984–1987 (In Million Yen)

	1984	1985	1984/85	1986	1987	1986/87
Housing budget (total)	666,381	712,721	1.07	940,231	748,352	.80
Public housing	284,483	275,949	.97	276,041	264,469	.96
Improvement of blighted areas	83,155	81,492	.98	86,067	79,587	.92
Subsidization of the interest for the Housing Loan Corporation	286,250	341,250	1.19	343,250	343,250	1.00
HUDC	0	0	–	173,926	0	–
Subsidization of the interest for private rental housing	5,009	5,684	1.13	5,714	5,545	.97
Subsidization of the interest for developers when they supply rental housing	2,464	2,510	1.02	2,683	2,792	1.04
Promotion of public facilities such as roads, schools, redevelopment	3,550	4,378	1.23	45,500	45,000	.99
Redevelopment	0	0	0	5,543	6,197	1.12
Improvement of wooden apartments	239	294	1.23	382	420	1.10
Prevention of disasters of houses on slope or cliff	1,231	1,164	.95	1,125	1,092	.97

Source: Economic Planning Agency, 1988.

Figure 22.2
Public Housing Eligibility, by Income Quintile, Japan, 1951–1985

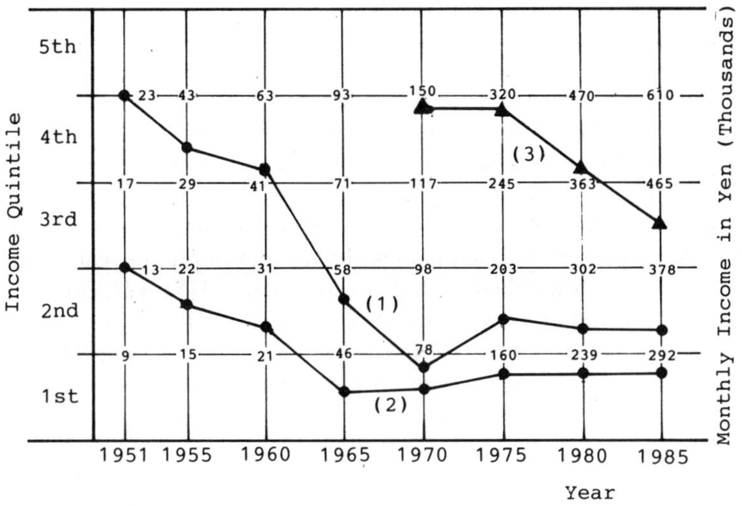

Source: Statistics Bureau, 1951–1986.

Notes: The data are taken from the following: 1951–1961, worker households in all cities; 1962–1985, worker households nationwide.

(1) First class of public housing: one-half of construction costs are subsidized by the central government.
(2) Second class of public housing: two-thirds of construction costs are subsidized by the central government.
(3) Upper-income limit.

turn it over to another low-income household. Local entities may also request increased rent within the range governed by law.

Public Housing by the HUDC. The Housing and Urban Development Corporation constitutes the principal means for carrying out national government housing policies. The HUDC funds consist of (1) government loans, such as the funds operation division: 62.7 percent; post office life insurance: 14.4 percent; and the HUDC fund: 2.8 percent, together comprising nearly 80 percent; (2) loans from private financial institutions, such as commercial life insurance: 13.9 percent; and trust banks: 8.3 percent; (3) investment from the government and local bodies, which was only 0.8 percent in 1984 (Japan 1985).

The HUDC housing units are classified into the following categories:

1. Rental Houses. These are apartment units intended to be rented to middle-income workers. Construction interest is subsidized.
2. Houses for Sale. These are condominium units, sold to the upper middle class. To make them readily available to buy, the price is below market value. It is made more affordable by long-term mortgage loans at low interest rates.

3. Special Rental Houses. These are housing units that the HUDC builds for and sells to individual land investors who then manage them as rental property.

Private Sector

Since the end of World War II more than 34 million private housing units have been built. This figure is approximately 85 percent of all units constructed during that period, indicating the predominance of this type of housing in the postwar era (figure 22.3).

The private sector consists of houses owned by individual landowners, houses sold by developers, and rented houses. Private developers or real estate companies provide detached houses and condominiums. However, private rented houses are generally provided by small landlords. Recently, the government has been encouraging the construction and renovation of privately rented houses with some subsidies to control the quality and the rent level.

Infrastructure

In general, the housing-related infrastructure, including roads, sewers, water, schools, and parks, is provided by the local government, and gas, electricity, and rail service are provided by the private sector. Land-use readjustment by local authorities and private landlords in urban, suburban, and rural areas may help provide an existing infrastructure for land converted to housing usage.

MAJOR PROBLEMS

Quality

As of 1983 the number of housing units in Japan was 10.4 percent above the number of households, so the problem of quantity is basically solved. Now emphasis needs to be placed on quality. This is generally recognized by the government. There is a basic shortage in the exclusive use of flush-toilet, bathroom, and kitchen facilities; there are space and density deficiencies; and there are many very old buildings (table 22.2). So despite the great number of housing units, the problem of quality remains to be solved.

From 1968 to 1983, 21 million new housing units were built. During the same period 11 million units were demolished (Japan 1983a). The main reason was poor quality, resulting from short-term wood construction. Many temples and shrines built of wood in the Eighth Century A.D. still stand, as do many wooden residences built in the seventeenth and eighteenth centuries. However, postwar wooden buildings are of such inferior quality that they do not last long. They age rapidly and are also destroyed by floods, fires, and other natural hazards.

There is also urban planning, which in the process of road construction and urban redevelopment has wiped out many older housing units in a short time.

Figure 22.3
Housing Construction, by Finance Base, Japan, 1945–1986

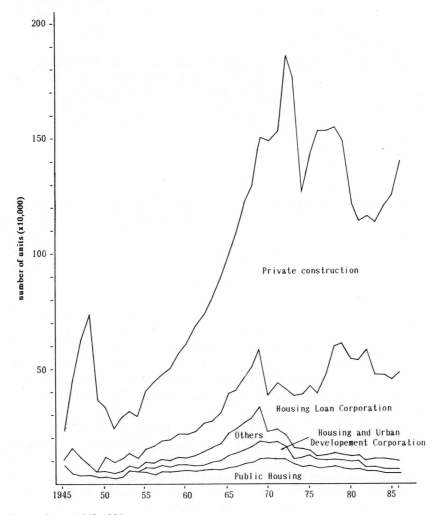

Source: Japan, 1945–1986.

In 1968, 32.8 percent of the lost houses was due to this redevelopment and road construction, increasing to 53.4 percent by 1984 (Japan 1945–1986).

Zoning of land use is not very strictly adhered to. Land use is basically controlled by the market with high-priced land devoted to high-rise commercial, office, and housing uses. Existing housing is easily destroyed, since, characteristically, it is not considered to be of social value.

The size of housing sites has also decreased. In 1988 the percentage of sites with an area under 100 square meters was 20.0 for detached housing and 57.9 for rental houses. This decline in space has contributed to a deterioration in the quality of the housing environment.

Accordingly, the level of satisfaction with housing has decreased from 64.1 percent in 1973 to 47.6 percent in 1983, with the level of those dissatisfied with housing increasing from 35.1 to 51.1 percent in the same period (Japan 1988). The causes include lack of sunlight, loss of good air circulation, noise, rats and roaches, increased distance to work, and general deterioration in the quality of the housing environment.

High Land Prices, Services, and Commuting

The concentration of political, economic, and information functions in large cities drives up the price of urban land. The sale of publicly owned land in the large cities at high prices to real estate companies has further increased land prices overall. There has been an increased demand for office building space in Tokyo, leading to intense competition between real estate firms. Industries with large financial assets lend money to real estate firms through loan agencies. All of this has resulted in extremely sharp increases in land prices (figure 22.2). The use of gangster-related bullying by real estate interests to force the sale of land by urban landowners has often been seen.

Furthermore, urban landowners sell their holdings at inflated prices and buy suburban sites and buildings again at high prices, forcing the price of land there to go up too. This phenomenon began in Tokyo but has now spread to all of the large cities. The high price of land has also increased the rate of land taxes paid by residents to local authorities.

The sudden decline in old-town populations and aging of the population has resulted in confusion in providing and maintaining public services such as buses, hospitals, and schools. Furthermore, crime has tended to increase.

With the use of housing land for commercial and business purposes in the central city, the population there declines, and housing moves to the suburbs, increasing the distance from housing to the workplace.

Lack of Housing for the Elderly

Public housing units have been decreasing yearly because the government has been cutting the budget for public housing. The upper-income limit for those

Table 22.5

Average Monthly Household Income of Owners and Average Monthly Debt Payments for Houses and/or Lots, Japan, 1977–1986 (In Yen))

Year	Average Monthly Income	Average Mortgage	Avg. Payment as % of Income
1977	285,187	27,684	10
1978	383,998	43,474	11
1979	403,700	45,494	11
1980	436,480	48,948	11
1981	452,737	50,339	11
1982	483,635	55,103	11
1983	498,157	59,226	12
1984	519,714	61,853	12
1985	538,983	64,940	12
1986	551,442	65,346	12

Source: Statistics Bureau, 1951–1986.

eligible has been dropping. As a result, there is a tendency for those occupying such housing to be the poor, one-person households; the elderly; or those on welfare. Unemployment and the collapse of the family unit have tended to segregate these people from the rest of society, creating a new social problem.

In general, private landlords do not want to rent to the elderly, especially the single elderly. The reasons for this are said to be that these people have no income, that they will not be able to pay the rent when it is increased, that they might cause fires, that they might die on the premises and the landlord does not want to pay for a funeral, and so on. With the rapid aging of the population, the problem of housing for the elderly is becoming a major social problem.

Elderly people often prefer not to go back home after a hospitalization. Japanese housing is generally small, has uneven floor levels, and has narrow stairways without handrails. This kind of environment is conducive to tripping, falling, drowning in the bath (if there is one), and gas poisoning from exposed leaky gas pipes. All of these incidents are increasing today. In 1985, according to government statistics (Japan 1984), 6,120 people have died due to these kinds of domestic accidents, and another 1.3 million were injured. Among them there were many elderly: 58 percent of the total.

Affordability

From 1950 to 1983 the price of the average house increased 147 times, and average income increased only 25 times. In 1988 the price of housing was 6.7 times income. Although average housing costs are moderate compared to those in many other Western countries, increases have continued in recent years (table 22.5). In the large cities, the average price of housing is eight to ten times the average annual income, making it extremely difficult to buy a house in the city.

The number of people who take loans from the Housing Loan Corporation and who are unable to make payments for more than six months has been

Table 22.6
Average Monthly Household Income of Renters and Average Rent, Japan,
1977–1986 (In Yen)

Year	Average Monthly Income	Average Monthly Rent	Avg. Rent as % of Avg. Income
1977	233,013	18,825	8
1978	247,910	20,592	8
1979	269,177	22,601	8
1980	282,642	24,389	9
1981	296,138	26,766	9
1982	313,339	29,417	9
1983	318,683	30,451	10
1984	337,751	32,961	10
1985	324,590	34,583	10
1986	350,367	37,032	11

Source: Statistics Bureau, 1951–1986.

increasing. From 1979 to 1985 alone, it increased 10.8 times: from 1,382 in 1975 to 14,888 in 1985. Many of them had to move to a small private rental house, and many divorced or even attempted suicide. Causes of requests for extensions included a drop in absolute income, business failure, bankruptcy, and illness. There are no means of protecting households from such tragedies, because there are no legal or administrative systems and no Housing Act to guarantee their housing.

Increases in rent have been great. For instance, according to the HUDC figures, in 1955 average rent was about 38.5 dollars a month for 40 square meters of floor space; in 1985 the rent of newly constructed dwellings in metropolitan areas had increased to more than 796 dollars for 60 square meters, or about 40 percent of the average salary. Nonpayment of rent for three months or more results in eviction from public to private rental housing. These observations notwithstanding, in comparison with other capitalist countries Japanese tenants pay, on average, a moderate, although increasing, proportion of their income on rent (table 22.6).

Equity

Postwar housing policy has been owner oriented. In 1988 public housing represented 8.0 percent of the total housing stock. Construction of public housing dwindled from 108,000 units in 1970 to 45,000 in 1986, and construction of units mortgaged by the Housing Loan Corporation rose from 158,000 in 1970 to 387,000 in 1986. These trends have greatly widened the gap between the quality of housing of those who are socially weak and deprived and those who are not. There are many kinds of inequalities, discrimination, and segregation in housing. For example, figure 22.4 shows home ownership by income class, and figure 22.5 shows home ownership by region.

Figure 22.4
Tenure, by Income, Japan, 1983

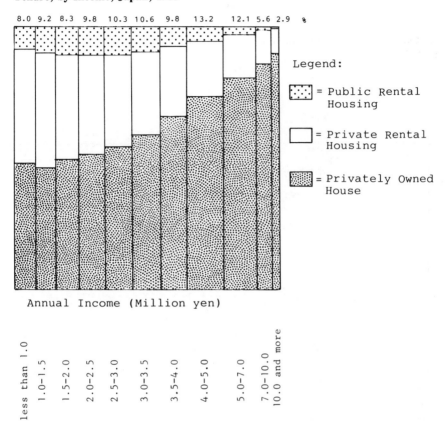

Annual Income (Million yen)

Source: Japan, 1983a.

PROSPECTIVE DEVELOPMENTS

Japan's economic growth has been very successful since it began in 1960. But this success is not yet reflected in the quality of housing for most people. Despite the second largest GNP in the free world, the standards of housing and quality of the urban environment are still extremely low. What is needed is not just improvement in the physical aspects of the problem but also increased awareness of the problem among people, land price controls, and recognition of the housing needs of society's weak and the elderly. However, the central government refuses to see housing policy as a part of social welfare policy. Therefore, there is no clear national housing policy. Japan continues to pursue

Figure 22.5
Average Floor Area and Proportion of Privately Owned Houses, by Prefecture, Japan, 1983

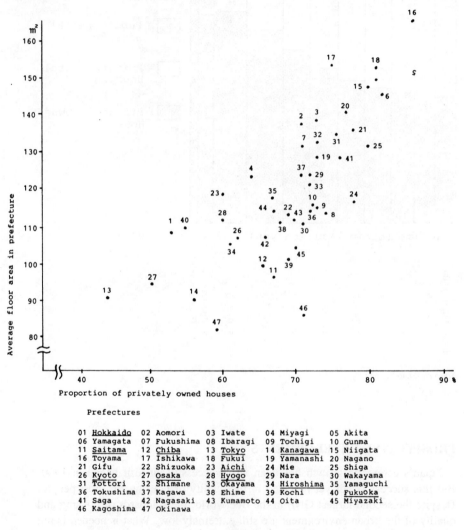

Source: Japan, 1983a.

an owner-oriented housing policy despite the obvious need for a strong renter-oriented policy.

The interests of the real estate industry are abetted by lack of adequate controls on land prices as reflected in the fact that the nation's wealthiest people tend to be the heads of major real estate firms. It appears that the future direction of the central government will be a continuation of the present tendency, which serves its own financial and political interests.

Present national housing policy is unlikely to change if there is no threat of a loss of financial or political support from real estate, land development, or profit-making mortgage or construction interests. Furthermore, many citizens are so accustomed to the "poverty of housing" in which they live that they are not consciously aware of their plight or of their basic rights to live in decent and affordable housing without having to fall into a "loan hell." To improve the situation, the following are necessary:

1. *Central and local government actions*: Both levels of government need to recognize housing as a fundamental and essential human right. They should recognize that it is their responsibility to provide decent and affordable housing for every family. To provide the needed housing, government should (a) strengthen policies related to land price controls as well as implement policies providing public assistance to housing land acquisition by local authorities; (b) for those who cannot afford decent housing, the government should provide low-rental and good-quality public housing. Private rental housing development and construction should be done without destroying either the natural environment or destabilizing the surrounding social environment.

2. *Citizen groups*: Citizen participation in the housing process should be made obligatory. Once citizens understand the scope of the problem, a commitment to participate would arise. Each citizens' group should attempt to go beyond its own special interest and work together with other groups toward comprehensive, fundamental housing-policy reform.

3. *Private developers*: Housing construction and housing development are economic as well as social welfare activities. Private housing developers should be aware that what they build will impact the quality of the surrounding environment. They should also realize that rising land prices decrease housing demand.

Rapid postwar growth gave rise to the prefab industry, which did not provide safe, livable, low-price housing. Instead, it has done little more than provide superficial decorations without making basic improvements in housing quality. From now on, the housing industry should work to fulfill its social responsibility by providing for the housing needs of various life-styles and age groups.

4. *Expert and research groups*: Doctors should recognize that decent housing is fundamental to human health and welfare and make this recognition known to the public. They will need to survey the relationship of housing to health carefully to give their claims a scientific base.

Lawyers and teachers should also recognize the relationship of decent housing to the healthy development of children and to safe and comfortable old age for senior citizens. They must make their voices heard and their force felt in the movement toward reforms in housing policy.

The Japan Housing Council published the first white paper on housing in 1985, and in 1987 it developed a "Charter of Housing." That year also marked the establishment of the Citizen Association for the Improvement of Housing. These new developments help to strengthen the people's role in the provision and improvement of housing.

NOTES

1. The Housing Survey of Japan has been conducted by the Statistics Bureau, Management and Coordination Agency, every five years since 1958. The last one was conducted in 1988.

2. The Housing Survey of Japan defines "dwellings," "number of rooms," and "floor space" as follows:

A *dwelling* is a permanent building or a structurally separate part thereof such as an apartment or an apartment house, which, by the way it has been built, rebuilt, or converted, is intended for habitation by one household. A structurally separate part should be completely partitioned with fixed concrete or wooden walls. A dwelling should have at least one private room, a sink for cooking and a toilet used jointly, and direct access to the street or to a common space within the building.

The total *number of rooms* includes living rooms, bedrooms, dining rooms, guest rooms, and studies. Porches, kitchens, kitchenettes, toilets, bathrooms, passageways, shops, offices, and other rooms used for professional or business purposes are not counted as rooms. However, kitchens of 5 square meters or more (excluding the space of the sink) are included in calculating the number of rooms. Rooms occupied by lodging households are also included.

Floor space refers to the total space of every floor, including the entrance, kitchen, passageways, toilet, bathroom, and other rooms. Also, closets and rooms used for professional or business purposes are included. However, storage space for goods, workshop, garage, and so on, constructed separately from the main part of the dwelling, are excluded. In the case of apartment houses, the passageways, kitchen, toilet, and so on, when used jointly, are also excluded.

3. The percentage of households who said "we have some problem" or "we have to do something about our housing problems" was 35.1 in 1973 and 51.5 in 1988.

REFERENCES

Economic Planning Agency, Japanese Government. 1988. *Economic Survey of Japan.* Tokyo: Ministry of Finance.

Japan. 1941. Ministry of Health and Welfare. *Housing Statistics Survey of Large Cities.* Tokyo.

———. 1945–1986. Ministry of Construction. *Annual Bulletin of Building.* Tokyo: Building Cost Research Association.

———. 1983a. Statistics Bureau, Management and Coordination Agency. *Housing Survey of Japan.* Tokyo: Japan Statistics Association.

————. 1983b. Ministry of Construction. *The Housing Demand Survey*. Tokyo: Japan Housing Association.

————. 1984. Health and Welfare Statistics and Information Department, Minister's Secretariat, Ministry of Health and Welfare. *Vital Statistics 1984 Japan*. Tokyo: Health and Welfare Statistics Association.

————. 1985. Housing and Urban Development Corporation. Tokyo: Public Relations Division, General Affairs Department.

————. 1986. Statistics Bureau, Management and Coordination Agency. *The 1985 Population Census*. Tokyo: Japan Statistics Association.

————. 1988. Statistics Bureau, Management and Coordination Agency. *Housing Survey of Japan*. Tokyo: Japan Statistics Association.

Real Estate Institute of Japan. 1987. *Index of National Land Prices*. Tokyo.

Statistics Bureau. 1951–1986. Prime Minister's Office. *Annual Report on the Family Income and Expenditure Survey*. Tokyo: Japan Statistics Association.

————. 1958, 1963, 1973. Management and Coordination Agency. *Housing Survey of Japan*. Tokyo: Japan Statistics Association.

FURTHER READING

Donnison, David, and Shinya Hoshino. "Formulating the Japanese Housing Problem." *Housing Studies* 3, no. 3 (1988):190–95.

Goldberg, Paul M. "Housing Development in Japan." Alfred P. Sloan School of Management Working Paper. Cambridge, Mass.: Massachusetts Institute of Technology, 1971.

Hayakawa, Kazuo. "Housing and the Quality of Life." *Built Environment* 4, no. 7 (1978):23–26.

————. "Housing Poverty in Japan." *Ekistics* 50, no. 298 (January-February):4–9.

————. "Japan." In *Housing Policy and Practice in Asia*, edited by Seong-Kyu Ha, 117–34. London, New York, and Sydney: Croom Helm, 1987.

Horioka, Charles Yuji. "Saving for Housing Purchase in Japan." *Journal of the Japanese and International Economies* 2, no. 3 (1988):351–84.

————. "Tenure Choice and Housing Demand in Japan." *Journal of Urban Economics* 24, no. 3 (1988):289–309.

Japan. Ministry of Construction. *Annual Bulletin of Building*. Tokyo: Building Cost Research Association, by year.

Kendall, Stephen, and Seiji Sawada. "Changing Patterns in Japanese Housing." *Open House International* (special issue) 12, no. 2:7–19.

Kirwan, R. M. "Fiscal Policy and the Price of Land and Housing in Japan." *Urban Studies* 24, no. 5 (1987):345–60.

Molotch, Harvey, and Serena Vicari. "Three Ways to Build: The Development Process in the United States, Japan, and Italy." *Urban Affairs Quarterly* 24, no. 2 (1988):188–214.

Open House International. Special issue on Japan. Vol. 12, no. 2, 1987.

Sato, Mikio. "Housing Is the Most Backward Aspect of an Economic Superpower." *Japan Quarterly* (April-June 1981):227–33.

Savasdisara, I. "Residents' Satisfaction and Neighbourhood Characteristics in Japanese Urban Communities." *Landscape and Urban Planning* 15, nos. 3, 4 (1988):327–36.

Ueda, Michiko, and David R. Darr. "The Outlook for Housing in Japan to the Year 2000." Research Paper PNW–276. Washington, D.C.: U.S. Department of Agriculture, Forest Service, August 1980.

Witherwick, M. E. "The Japanese Housing Corporation." *Town and Country Planning* 40, no. 11 (November 1972):521—25.

23

Pakistan

JAN VAN DER LINDEN, PETER NIENTIED,
AND SYED IQBAL KALIM

BASIC DEMOGRAPHIC DATA, URBANIZATION, AND INCOME

Since independence, in 1947, Pakistan's population has grown—and continues to grow—fast. Compared with the overall growth of around 3 percent per year, the urban population has increased even much more rapidly. (Table 23.1 gives an impression of Pakistan's population dynamics.)

Compared to two cities having a population of more than 500,000 in 1951, there are now eight such cities. Karachi and Lahore, Pakistan's two primate cities (Qadeer 1983, 75) grew from 400,000 and 800,000 at independence to well over 5 million and 3 million, respectively, by 1981 (Ahmed 1984, 10). Although the official population figure for Karachi in 1981 was 5.1 million, other sources estimated it between 5.5 million and 7.0 million (Nientied et al. 1982, 33).

After independence, many rural settlements were transformed into urban ones, and existing towns and cities expanded enormously. However, the contribution to urbanization caused by administrative measures, such as annexation of surrounding areas, is estimated at a low 8 percent. Much more important is the natural growth of the urban population, contributing 70 percent, while the remaining 22 percent increase of the urban population is caused by rural-urban migration (Asian Development Bank 1984). (Table 23.2 shows the development and distribution of cities and towns.)

Growth rates of towns and cities are uneven. Karachi goes on growing at more than 5 percent per year; Lahore's growth is just over 4 percent, a figure that

Table 23.1
Population Growth, Pakistan, 1951–1981

Year	Total population (in millions)	Rural			Urban		
		N	%	Avg. growth %	N	%	Avg. Growth %
1951	33.7	27.7	82		6.0	18	
				1.8			4.8
1961	42.8	33.2	77		9.6	22	
				3.3			4.7
1972	65.3	48.7	74		16.6	25	
				2.6			4.4
1981	84.2	60.4	72		23.8	28	

Source: Ahmed, 1984.

Table 23.2
Urban Population Distribution, by City Size, Pakistan, 1961–1971

City Size (millions)	No. of cities			Percent of Urban Population			Annual Growth Rate	
	1961	1971	1981	1961	1971	1981	1961-72	1972-81
over 1	2	2	3	33	34	38	5.0	4.2
0.5 - 1	-	4	5	-	16	15	-	3.3
0.2 - 0.5	5	4	4	18	6	5	4.2	6.7
0.1 - 0.2	5	10	16	7	7	10	3.8	4.3
below 0.1	213	82	345	42	36	32	4.5	4.5
Total	225	302	373				4.6	4.4

Source: Government of Pakistan, 1972, 1981.

resembles the pattern of many of the smaller towns. An exceptionally high growth rate was recorded in Islamabad between 1972 and 1981: 12.2 percent, reflecting its special position as the newly created capital, while also a boundary change took place during the intercensus period.

In general, a concentration in the bigger cities is taking place. Of the estimated 30 million urban population, 42 percent is living in four major cities, namely Karachi, Lahore, Faisalabad, and the twin city of Rawalpindi-Islamabad. The contribution to the urban population of smaller towns and cities has decreased relatively. The National Human Settlement Policy Study estimates that by the year 2003 the total population will be 156 million, of which 67 million (42.9 percent) will be urban with an annual growth rate of 4.79 percent (Government of Pakistan 1986).

In 1985 per capita GNP amounted to U.S. $380 per year, implying that, according to World Bank criteria, Pakistan is grouped among the "low-income economies." A substantial proportion of the population has incomes below poverty levels. Figures on this issue are scarce, and their reliability is doubtful. But in 1978, for example, it was estimated that 26 percent of the households in Karachi were under the poverty line (Nederlands Economisch Instituut 1985, 9.3).

The employment situation is far from optimal. In the early eighties, an official estimate put the unemployment figure at 3.5 percent, but hidden unemployment was estimated around 20.0 percent (Nederlands Economisch Instituut 1985, 9.3). Because of the diminishing job opportunities in the Middle East, where large numbers of migrant workers had found jobs during the past fifteen years, the employment situation has deteriorated in recent years.

Table 23.3
Urban Housing Types According to Quality, Pakistan, 1980

Type	N(x 1,000)	%
Walls		
baked bricks/concrete/stone with cement as binding agent	1,512	42.5%
baked bricks/stone with mud as binding agent	1,281	36.1
unbaked bricks	646	18.2
wood	40	1.2
other	72	2.0
Roofs		
reinforced concrete	941	26.5%
girder/beam, wood, tiles etc.	2,201	61.9
other	411	11.6
Total	3,554	100

Source: Government of Pakistan, 1980, p. 29.

TRENDS IN HOUSING CONDITIONS AND CONSTRUCTION, 1945–1985

Housing Conditions

Although both rural and urban housing conditions leave much to be desired, they differ widely from each other in a number of respects. Therefore, in this review of housing conditions, both types are dealt with separately.

Urban Housing. 1. Type and quality: Building materials vary according to region. For instance, in many regions of Pakistan, baked bricks are popular. However, in Karachi they are seldom available, and concrete blocks are the most commonly used material for the construction of solid houses; in the mountainous regions of the Northwest, stone is often used. The 1980 Housing Census Report of Pakistan distinguished housing types according to building material used for the construction of walls and roofs (see table 23.3).

2. Occupancy status: A majority of urban houses (67.7 percent) are owner occupied. Only some 22 percent are rented, and the remaining 10 percent are rent-free accommodations (Government of Pakistan 1980, 29).

3. Numbers of rooms and occupants: The national average number of persons

Table 23.4
Numbers of Rooms and Occupancy Rates of Urban Housing, Pakistan, 1980

No. of Rooms	N (x 1,000)	%	Persons per Housing unit	Persons per Room
1	1,513	42.5	5.8	5.8
2	1,120	31.5	7.1	3.5
3	486	13.6	7.9	2.6
4	231	6.5	8.5	2.1
5	90	2.5	8.8	1.8
over 5	110	4.1	12.5	1.2
Total	3,554	100.7	6.7	3.5

Source: Government of Pakistan, 1980, p. 19.

living in a housing unit was 6.7 in 1981, whereas in 1961 it was only 5.1. The average number of persons per room increased from 3.3 to 3.5 in the same period. The percentage of dwellings with 3.0 or more persons per room, considered overcrowding by the World Bank, has increased from 59 percent in 1960 to about 80 percent in 1980. The urban average is almost 7.0 persons per housing unit, with almost three-fourths of the population living in either one- or two-room units at an average urban density of 4.8 persons per room (table 23.4).

4. Service levels: The 1980 housing survey estimated that 58 percent of Pakistan's urban population had access to piped water (38 percent through house connections and 20 percent through shared arrangements or public standpipes), 33 percent used handpumps, 7 percent used wells, and 1 percent had direct access to surface water (Government of Pakistan 1980, 15).

In all major cities, the water supply is intermittent, with the supply ranging from two to eight hours a day at varying pressure. The resulting periodic underpressure in the water mains leads to the contamination of water, especially since in all major cities and towns, sewerage is inadequate. Network losses through leakage in Karachi are estimated to be about 30–50 percent of the supply (Asian Development Bank 1984, 15).

Of the urbanites, 42 percent are served with sewerage facilities. In many cases, these facilities are open collection systems, from which the untreated sewage is discharged into watercourses or ponds. Population not connected to the sewerage system depends on manual collection of night soil in most of the cases.

Sewage-treatment facilities exist only in Karachi and Islamabad. In the case of Karachi, it covers a minority of the population only; however, oxidation ponds and lagoons are now being built. A large part of the urban sewerage system depends on the soakpit system. This, however, also creates a potential health hazard in areas where water for consumption is drawn from subsurface wells.

Drainage systems, although existing in all of the major urban areas, are unable to prevent periodic flooding in the monsoon season. Besides the regular flooding of parts of the urban centers, especially near the Indus and its tributaries, water logging in urban areas has become a serious problem, also as a result of increased irrigation and the urban water supply, both resulting in high groundwater tables.

Garbage collection and disposal in urban areas is inadequate. Collection services have received much less attention than, for example, the water supply and are poor. In Karachi about 7,500 tons of garbage are generated daily. Only one-third of solid waste generated is properly collected and dumped by the municipal service. Presently, a composting plant has been set up by a private entrepreneur, and garbage is being processed on a small scale. In Lahore, 40 percent of all waste is collected, and in other major urban centers, the figures are similar. As a result, very often drains and sewers get clogged with uncollected refuse.

The supply of electricity and gas has greatly increased during the past few years. By 1970 it was estimated that in Karachi, about 50 percent of the households had an electric supply in their houses (Master Plan Department of the Karachi Development Authority 1974, 217). In 1980, this had increased to 70 percent. The 1980 housing survey reveals that 71 percent of the urban population enjoys a connection to electricity.

Similarly, the gas supply had reached 364,000 Karachi households by 1980 (compared with 64,000 in 1973). In other places as well, gas, one of the few natural resources Pakistan has, is replacing other fuels. The 1980 housing survey shows that 22 percent of the households use gas for cooking, 20 percent use kerosene oil, and 48 percent use wood in urban areas. Since bottled gas is now also available, the number of connections underestimates the actual use of gas for domestic purposes. Gas is three times cheaper compared to conventional fuels like wood or kerosene. However, most of the informal low-income settlements are deprived of gas connections. A limited supply of gas is inhibiting new connections.

Most of the urban services are in the diminishing-return stages, where the unit cost increases with the expansion of the network. Since most provisions for services have to be self-financing, the low-income areas get discriminated against because of their low paying potential.

Rural Housing. 1. Type and quality: The more than 60 million rural dwellers of Pakistan live in or near some 43,000 villages. The Housing Census of 1980 reveals that there are substantial differences in the type and quality of housing in urban and rural areas. Compared with 43 percent of brick or concrete with cement used for outer walls in urban areas, the rural scene has only 5 percent. Similarly, in roofing materials, reinforced concrete roofs in urban areas account for 26 percent, whereas in rural areas this percentage is only 1. This does not necessarily imply that rural houses are of a bad quality. In 1975 it was estimated that about 2 million rural houses (i.e., some 25 percent) were of a very poor quality (Government of Pakistan 1975). Renting housing in rural areas is very rare.

The piped water supply reaches 6 percent of the rural population. Of the households, 52 percent obtain water from hand pumps, and the rest, 42 percent, get it from wells, ponds, streams, or rivers (Government of Pakistan 1980, 15). However, an increasing number of tubewells deliver water of good quality, so some 22 percent of the population has access to safe water (Nederlands Economisch Instituut 1985, 9.2)

Of the rural houses, 16 percent are connected to (mostly open) sewers (Nederlands Economisch Instituut 1985, 9.2). Yet some 90 percent of the rural houses have no latrines or bathrooms (Government of Pakistan 1982, 8). Drainage and garbage-collection services are virtually nonexistent in rural areas. Although the electric supply in the countryside is rapidly increasing, in 1983, 65 percent of the villages in Pakistan were still not connected (Nederlands Economisch Instituut 1985, 9.2).

Construction Output

Since 1947, a sharp increase in construction of housing units has been noticeable, with 44 percent of the total stock constructed after 1971. Of the housing stock, 37 percent was built between 1947 and 1970, and 19 percent was constructed before 1947 (Government of Pakistan 1980, 12). During the fifth Plan Period (1978–1983), 510,000 urban housing units conforming to official standards were provided. Out of this total, the private sector constructed 225,000 units, and the public sector was responsible for the other 285,000 units. This last figure comprises a large component of sites-and-services and renovation, where the public sector only provided, or renovated, the infrastructure, and individual dwellers were responsible for construction. As will become clear in a later part of this chapter, on many of these plots, there can be no question of construction yet. Thus the figure of public construction output appears to be exaggerated.

Officially, the sites and services are intended for low-income groups. As will be explained later, the practice is different. Apart from the sites and services, even officially, the supply of additional housing is almost exclusively geared to the needs of the upper- and middle-income classes. This is especially true for private sector housing. Construction by the public sector also includes a substantial component of housing for government servants.

This total supply of 510,000 housing units matched an estimated 43 percent of the demand only (Nederlands Economisch Instituut 1985, 9.1). The remaining 57 percent of unmet potential demand partially finds accommodations by doubling up in existing housing: the number of persons per housing unit went up from 5.1 in 1961 to 6.7 in 1981 (Ahmed 1983, 48).

Most of the unmet demand, however, found shelter in informal settlements, known as *katchi abadis*. The *katchi abadis* grow very rapidly. For instance, during the seventies Karachi's *katchi abadi* population increased by 7.5 percent per year, whereas the growth rate of Karachi as a whole was just over 5 percent. Only temporary houses are constructed by the dwellers themselves. When they decide to have a semipermanent or permanent house, they engage professionals, such as masons and carpenters, or leave the whole construction to a small, informal contractor (Van der Harst 1983, 61–63).

Government-supplied housing units officially intended for low-income groups—including plots in sites-and-services projects—seldom or never really serve these groups: mostly, they are occupied by middle- or upper-middle-income groups (Nientied 1987, 126–42). On the other hand, the informal housing process is almost fully commercialized. Pure squatting, that is, the noncommercial illegal occupation of land, has become rare in the major cities. Instead, those who cannot afford housing at the official market nowadays cater to their shelter needs by buying plots of land in illegal subdivisions, both of private and government land. Illegal subdivision has, increasingly, become the system through which the low-income groups find housing (see Nientied 1987, 165–175; Van der Linden 1986, 2–7; Qadeer 1983, 190–92).

In rural areas, public housing provision is absent. An overwhelming majority of rural houses are constructed by the inhabitants themselves, sometimes with the assistance of hired local artisans. Of the approximately 20 percent of rural houses built of permanent materials, most have been constructed by local contractors.

ROLE OF HOUSING INSTITUTIONS AND ORGANIZATIONS

Role of the Public Sector

It is difficult to speak of "the" role of "the" public sector. In fact, many public agencies are involved from the federal to the local level. At the local level again, many public agencies, often with ill-defined and overlapping responsibilities and competences, deal with planning, construction, and housing. For Karachi, for instance, T. J. Segaar identified more than sixty government and semigovernment agencies active in these fields (1975, 27).

The principal agencies and their interrelationships can be summarized as follows: The federal structure of government in Pakistan consists of three tiers: national, provincial, and divisional. The divisions are divided into districts and then into *tehsils*. As far as urban development and urban planning are concerned, the federal ministries have the task of preparing general policies. At the provincial level, the main task is planning and financing the projects, whereas administrations in towns deal with the day-to-day running of the programs and projects (World Bank 1984).

At each of the three government levels, certain institutions are involved in the housing policy. At the top, the Environment and Urban Affairs Division

(Ministry of Housing and Works) is responsible for the national policy guidelines. It prepares, for example, the National Human Settlements Policy, Guidelines for Management of Cities (Government of Pakistan 1984a) and a National Reference Manual on Planning and Infrastructure Standards (Government of Pakistan 1984b). In the Five Year Plans, assessment of means and achievements in the field of housing are made.

In the provincial government, the Department of Town Planning, Housing, Local Government, and Rural Development is directly involved with urban housing policy and programs. It is legally entrusted with town planning and urban expansion, apart from the task of supervising local bodies.

At the local level, municipal institutions comprise district councils, metropolitan (or municipal) corporations, and municipal or town committees. These municipal institutions are placed under elected mayors and councils. For cantonment areas, the counterpart authority is the Cantonment Board. Whereas the municipal institutions operate under the local government, the Cantonment Boards are under the federal government. This arrangement hinders coordinated development.

Separate from these local public agencies, local "development authorities" or "improvement trusts" are under the provincial physical planning and housing departments and operate in all large urban centers. They plan and execute development projects. They have very little input from the elected representatives and enjoy considerable leeway in their operations, although officially placed under supervision of the provincial government. A major criticism is that these authorities are unrepresentative, encroach upon the functions and authority of the local municipal corporations, and are not accountable to anyone.

Coordination between the different levels of government is often poor. The same applies to coordination of the activities of different agencies—and often even of departments within agencies—at the local level. This problem is further exacerbated by the existence of a multitude of sectoral agencies, such as the Public Works Department, Cantonment Boards, Port and Airport Trusts, and Pakistan Railways, all of which claim authority over parts of the urban area and over the planning and housing in these areas. The existence of parallel institutions, some of which are governed by federal laws (Cantonment Boards), often nullifies planning efforts by local bodies. The Karachi Development Plan, 1974–1985, recommendations have often been disregarded because of this lacuna.

Planning. There is no shortage of planning for city expansion, especially for the two major cities, Karachi and Lahore. The Development Authorities of both of these cities have planned extensive housing schemes.

In Karachi huge resettlement schemes were planned for squatters in central parts of the city. For this purpose, two satellite townships—Korangi and North Karachi, with planned populations of 400,000 and 200,000, respectively—were envisioned. When, in 1964, 45,000 dwelling units had been constructed (i.e., somewhat less than half of the total planned), this program was discontinued because it could no longer be financed since the cost-recovery system had failed.

One reason for this lies in the location of both projects far from the (then) city and job opportunities. Among other things, because of the high transport costs, many of the "beneficiaries" could not afford living in the new townships and came back again to find illegal shelter in the city proper.

No doubt the houses in the satellite townships eventually became inhabited, but most of the target population was missed, and the substantial subsidies benefited better-off sections of the population.

After 1969, for a long period, the Karachi Development Authority (KDA) limited its role to planning and implementing the development of new urban land in numerous "schemes," among which eventually a few sites-and-services were included. A majority of these schemes, however, are destined for middle- and upper-class housing, to be constructed by private firms. In the period 1945–1980, a total of 43,389 acres were planned or developed in this way.

Only since 1979 has the KDA again been engaged in planning and construction of housing, partially claimed to be public housing for "people of modest means" and for "low-income people" (Moinul 1980, 38) in four- or five-story apartment buildings. A total of 2,470 apartments were constructed between 1979 and 1983; 2,000 apartments were built for low-income groups (cost, U.S. $3,800, calculated at an average exchange rate in the early eighties: U.S. $1.00 = Pak Rs 17), 350 apartments for middle-income households (cost, U.S. $9,000) and 120 for high-income groups (cost, U.S. $13,500). The claim that people of modest means or low-income people could be reached by this form of public housing is dubious since the price of a two-room apartment was U.S. $3,800 in 1981 (Nizami 1981, 35). Considering that 80 percent of the households earn less than U.S. $58 per month (1985) and spend approximately 70 percent of their income on food and clothing, the price of official low-income housing is beyond the reach of these groups (Siddique 1987, 2). The KDA also has planned and constructed a number of independent bungalows for high-income groups. Similar developments are reported from Hyderabad (*Landmark*, April/May, 1981, 63–66).

Planning in Pakistan still suffers from a number of shortcomings. For instance, planning is still basically done from behind the drawing board, it is mostly limited to narrow physical planning only, standards tend to be overly high, and public participation in planning is nonexistent (Nientied and Kalim 1986). Some plans, although applauded and sometimes even approved, never reach the stage of consistent implementation. A notorious example is Karachi's Development Plan, 1974–1985. Although it is outdated, the follow-up was yet to be prepared in 1987. Unfortunately, this does not appear to make much difference. The roots of this problem probably stem from general policies (to which we will turn later).

Land Supply. Impressive as many new urban-housing-scheme cities may be, the supply of land for housing is far short of the demand. It is the poor majority of the population who suffer the most from this situation. The land requirement for the proposed program during the sixth plan is large (54,000 acres). The existing land-acquisition practices will not permit timely availability of land.

Even if other requirements of implementing the program are fully met, the problem of making sufficient land available alone will defeat it (Ahmed 1983, 50). For instance, in Lahore, until 1979, the public bodies had developed 38,844 residential lots, averaging about 1,200 lots per year, whereas—according to Lahore Development Authority's own estimate—about 60,000 housing lots per year were required to meet the city's needs (Qadeer 1983, 86). In Karachi, the KDA claims to have developed 200,000 plots between 1960 and 1980, whereas in 1980 the output was 25,000 plots per year (Shamsuddin 1980, 29). This last figure would in principle cater to about 50 percent of the yearly demand.

Especially the component that is claimed to serve low-income needs, however, is being executed extremely poorly. Allocation procedures discriminate against the poor (World Bank 1984). Second, execution of the schemes often causes deviations from the stated objectives. For instance, the sale of plots is sometimes given to the private sector to handle. Also, the high standards tend to exclude the low-income groups (Nientied 1987, 136–37). A third factor preventing the poor from benefiting from the KDA's housing schemes is the very slow development of the schemes even after the plots have been allotted. When, for instance, water is not provided, nobody can live in the scheme. This implies that only those allottees can benefit who can afford to invest in a plot and subsequently wait for periods up to well over five years before they can start constructing a house. Obviously, the really needy cannot afford this (Nientied 1987, 136–37). Fourth, to overcome financial problems the development authorities have turned into developers. Projects designed for low-income groups are announced before they are physically commenced, and the public is asked to apply for a plot with advance payment. This system is now in vogue in most cities in Pakistan, and the development authorities amass huge sums of money that may be channeled to other projects. In some of the cases the actual development has taken ten to fifteen years (Siddique 1987, 8).

As a result, in the KDA schemes initiated from 1970 onward, comprising a total of 110,470 plots, only some 2,900 were really occupied in 1984, and most plots are in the hands of middle-income groups (Nientied and Van der Linden 1987, 7). In brief, public land supply in no way matches the demand. Besides, it is highly skewed.

In urban areas, a special place is taken by the Cooperative Housing Societies. They get land allocated by the government, in principle to provide plots to their members, who belong to middle- and upper-income groups. They are known, however, for their "history of bad management, incompetence and speculation" (Master Plan Department of the Karachi Development Authority 1974, 200). This was reason for the Development Plan's recommendation to provide no more land to housing societies. This recommendation was not followed, and as J. A. Khan noted, housing societies "are dominated by commercially motivated groups, who secure government land for speculative purposes" (1984, 12). In Karachi alone, they control close to 28,000 acres of land (Nientied 1987, 38).

There is, however, one form of government land supply for the poorer sections of the population that is much more successful. This is posthoc land supply in the shape of legalization (termed *regularization*) of since-long-occupied plots in squatments. This is handled by the Municipal (Metropolitan) Corporations. In Karachi, between 1978 and 1984, in this way 38,000 leases were issued, and another 44,000 applications were being handled in 1984 (Karachi Metropolitan Corporation-NESPAK, 1984, 1.8). Similarly, in Panjab, by 1982, 143 (out of 343) *katchi abadis* had been regularized.

This procedure is perhaps typical of both planning and land supply. The public agency charged with planning and developing residential land (KDA) fails to keep up with the demand; consequently, a large part of the population has no alternative but to use informal or illegal systems to shelter itself. With most of the land in and around cities being public land (especially in Karachi, where almost all the land is owned by the government), illegal occupation or subdivision of land goes unchecked. Government leaders exploit the *fait accompli* situation by announcing wholesale legalization of such squatments. Finally, another public agency, Karachi Metropolitan Corporation (KMC), has to regularize the situation thus created. This implies that planning and land supply—especially for low-income groups—take place post hoc, as an official adaptation to accomplished facts rather than as a supportive and guiding service to the citizens.

Financing. Credit for housing is a serious problem in Pakistan. Commercial banks rarely lend for housing construction. The only agency that gives long-term credit for this purpose is the House Building Finance Corporation (HBFC), a government institution. The HBFC provides credit both to individuals and to local authorities. Its sum total issued was Rs 850 million in 1984. Some 20,000 individuals borrow from the HBFC each year. The corporation has been constrained in its lending operations due to limitations of funds and normal midyear cuts of its original allocations. The corporation's conditions render this institution irrelevant for the low-income sections of the population. For instance, credit never exceeds 50 percent of construction costs (Nederlands Economisch Instituut 1985, 9.6). A recent trend is that a large chunk of the HBFC credit is utilized by private developers who manage to obtain the lion's share of the resources available, thereby further curtailing individual efforts to obtain credit.

Construction. Mass public housing is no longer being constructed after the disappointing results of two such schemes in Karachi (see above) and one in Lahore (Lahore Township, with 10,000 houses). Public construction now comprises quarters built for the personnel of various sectoral agencies and bodies, such as the universities, police, ministries, local bodies, and Pakistan Railways.

Apart from that, in Karachi, for a number of years the KDA has undertaken construction of apartment buildings, which it offers for sale on a purely commercial basis. Under such schemes, 2,470 apartments were delivered between 1979 and 1983. But this is against the policy recommendations of the KDA's

Development Plan of 1974 (Master Plan Department of the Karachi Development
Authority 1974, 196).

Role of the Private and Popular Sectors

Most of the housing units are built by the private and popular sectors. In rural
areas, practically all housing construction is done by these sectors: poor people
build their houses themselves, and the few rich engage a contractor from a nearby
town or city. Most of legal housing in urban areas is constructed by private
formal contractors on land developed, for the major part, by the local development authorities or improvement trusts.

In the past years, private construction companies and contractors have faced
some problems in recruiting sufficient numbers of trained workers, many of
whom had migrated to Middle East countries. Also, prices of building materials
have risen enormously during the past years, and so have—to a much lesser
extent—the costs of labor.

However, the major constraint on the output of the formal sector is that it
builds for middle- and high-income groups only: the planned schemes and formal
building serve a part of the urban population only. Regarding Lahore, M. A.
Qadeer notes

that massive additions to the city's housing stock occurred through private, unplanned
and often unapproved and unregistered home building. People have individually built
homes, cajoled and bribed officials to extend them electricity, water and other community
services. The cumulative result of these individual incremental effects has appeared in
the form of vast neighborhoods . . . (which) have appeared on tracts of land left over by
the expanding city. Contrary to Western practice, the public agencies leapfrog to virgin
lands in the periphery and the private builders do the infilling. (1983, 86)

This is a general pattern. About Karachi, it was noted that "over 12,000 acres
of land . . . lie unutilized in the heart of the city and in other parts of the built-
up area, with public utilities being extended expensively into outlying areas in
response to pressures that are primarily speculative" (Master Plan Department
of the Karachi Development Authority 1974, 21). Also in Karachi, quite a few
of these open spaces were filled by popular housing.

As noted above, instead of earlier spontaneous squatting, the commercial
illegal subdivision of land has now become the dominant system by which the
urban low-income groups house themselves. Construction in these areas is mainly
done by small, informal contractors or by craftsmen working under the owner's
supervision.

No official credit is available for popular housing. This problem is being met
first by incremental, or phased, building. Besides, borrowing from informal
sources is common (e.g., Nientied et al. 1982, 67). One study in the early

seventies regarding low-income areas in Karachi showed that 40 percent of the housing finance came from loans, 32 percent from *bisis* (i.e., informal rotating savings and credit associations), and the rest from savings. Of the households, 50 percent borrowed to build. This borrowing was from relatives, suppliers of building materials, or small contractors (Ahmed 1987, 9). From the midseventies onward, extra earnings from jobs in Middle East countries have constituted an important source of investment in low-income housing.

HOUSING MARKETS AND POLICY ORIENTATIONS

Evolution of a National Housing Policy

Since the first Five Year Plan (1955), housing and physical planning have been treated as distinct sectors of national development. Initially, the emphasis was on institution building, that is, getting all of the institutional (legal, administrative, staff, and so on) arrangements in order, but gradually, a "wide ranging array of policies, programmes and practices have come to characterize public efforts in housing development" (Qadeer 1983, 234).

In the national Five Year Plans, the importance of housing has never been very high and has gradually decreased. In the first Five Year Plan (1955–1960) 10.4 percent of the budget was allocated to physical planning and housing. In the sixth Five Year Plan (1983–1988), this percentage decreased to 5.1. Only 9 percent of this figure was spent on housing, that is, 0.5 percent of the total budget (Government of Pakistan 1983; Nederlands Economisch Instituut 1985).

In the period after independence, coordination of the housing policy was barely institutionalized. In different cities, a multitude of agencies carried out measures to expand the housing stock, but their actions were insufficient. Clearance of "slums" and resettlement of families was one of the measures frequently applied. Naturally, this type of action did not add to the housing stock—on the contrary.

Although a wide range of policies had been implemented, national housing-policy guidelines were lacking. It was only in 1976 when the first proposals were made: a suggested national housing-policy framework entailed "main objectives" and a set of recommendations regarding low-income housing. The chief emphasis was on coordination of institutions. The main objectives were as follows:

1. To set up a coordinated institutional framework relating to housing at three levels of Government, i.e., federal, provincial and local

2. To provide sufficient funds in the National Credit Plan for house construction and to mobilize private savings for investment in housing

3. To prepare proper programmes of housing supply for all income groups, and to give priority to the housing needs of low-income groups

4. To seek active participation of construction companies in the housing programmes

5. To promote research and development in the housing sector (Government of Pakistan 1976, 20)

The specific recommendations regarding low-income housing encompassed terms such as *sites-and-services* and *guided* or *aided self-help*, but upgrading had not been taken up as yet. The framework stressed that policy-making was to be done at the federal and provincial levels, whereas the functions of the local bodies were "survey and planning, execution, management and recovery" (Government of Pakistan 1976, 10). These guidelines of the first National Housing Policy Framework (that only exists in concept) were, in certain respects, trailing the developments at a local scale.

The work of the Physical Planning and Housing Division of the government of Pakistan can be seen as the basis for housing policies in the fifth Five Year Plan (1978–1983) and the sixth Five Year Plan (Shah 1977; see also Shah 1978). In 1977 the Physical Planning and Housing Section of the Planning Division (government of Pakistan) listed the following policy areas to be considered for adoption: slum improvement, low-income housing, planning standards, planning of sites-and-services, housing finance, institutional house building, standardization, prefabrication, and rural housing. The eleven paragraphs contain many technical issues. Matters to which no attention has been paid (this also holds for later documents of the national government) include the inner-city housing problems and rent control, housing as a social need and a social policy, the relation between housing and planning policy in other policy areas (such as employment), and the evaluation of policy and control of implementing agencies by the higher tiers of government.

Salient details of the paragraphs on future policies as developed by the government of Pakistan in 1977–1978 are the following policy guidelines:

Slum improvement
It will not be possible to replace all the substandard housing as well as to meet the additional annual requirements in the short term. Therefore all the existing houses in slums and katchi abadis (substandard urban areas), irrespective of the quality, should be preserved. Slum areas and katchi abadis not occupying land for public purposes, should be regularized to give ownership to residents and to pave way for environmental improvement.

Low income housing
It is neither possible due to financial and physical constraints nor is it desirable in view of the complex estate management problems, for the government to provide constructed houses to satisfy requirements. The public sector should therefore limit its operation to the provision of maximum opportunities for house ownership for all income groups in urban as well as rural areas. This would include the provision of developed land, adequate housing finance, ensuring adequate supply of building materials, providing technical guidance and removing institutional obstacles. The provision of serviced plots for low income groups should be made in socially balanced and self-contained communities.

Planning of sites-and-services
All housing and urban development, including sites-and-services programs for low income groups and environmental upgrading of slums and katchi abadis should be on a self-financing basis. In case of lowest income groups, the cost may be recovered over a longer period with subsidized interest rates. The recoveries from all such schemes should be diverted to a general housing fund so that more schemes can be undertaken without needing additional public sector financing.

The public sector investment in sites and services programmes should be in the form of seed capital to the urban development authorities or to the general housing fund recommended to be created for this purpose. The amount of seed capital may be up to 30% of the total cost which may vary from case to case depending upon the financial condition of the executing agency. The balance of the cost of the schemes should be financed through advance instalments for the plots to be allotted, as well as, ploughing back the recoveries.

Institutional house building
Construction by individual house builders results in considerable waste of time and materials. Institutional house building by semi-public autonomous corporations and construction companies should be encouraged to decrease reliance on the individual house builders and to gain from the economies of scale. It would be necessary to strengthen the capacity for institutional house building by allowing liberal import of machinery and equipment and construction technology. (Shah 1978, 8–10)

It is remarkable that much attention is paid to technical issues such as planning standards. Another point worth noting is that, on the one hand, some main elements of the self-help housing approach are advocated, whereas, on the other hand, it is said that individual building is in fact a waste of time and material. One may also note the economic justification of *katchi abadi* upgrading and sites-and-services schemes.

The chapter on housing of the fifth Five Year Plan of the government of Pakistan contained a housing policy reflecting the work of the Planning Division: sites-and-services would be provided to contribute to an extension of the housing stock, and *katchi abadi* upgrading was proposed to improve the conditions in the ''substandard'' urban residential areas. The sector goals of the fifth Five Year Plan were not achieved. The target ''environmental improvement'' was to provide basic services to a population of 1.33 million in Pakistan. The actual coverage was 500,000 (Government of Pakistan 1983). Similarly, it was proposed to develop 425,000 urban residential plots, 75 percent of which would be designed for and allotted to the lower-income groups (i.e., plots up to 200 square yards). The actual number of plots developed in the fifth Five Year Plan was 285,000 (Government of Pakistan 1983, 454). As we have seen above, very many of these plots did not benefit low-income groups. Against a target of 350,000 houses to be constructed by the private sector, the number actually constructed was only 225,000 (p. 454).

Contrary to the fifth Five Year Plan, where an economic rationale was given for the new approach of sites-and-services and slum improvement, the sixth Five

Year Plan (1983–1988) starts with the premise of a basic dilemma in the housing situation: "those who need housing are far too poor to afford it—either to build it or even rent it—at the market rates; left at the mercy of the market mechanism they will always remain deprived of proper shelter." On the other hand, "society is reluctant to pay in perpetuity the required subsidy for the poor" (Government of Pakistan 1983, 456). To solve this dilemma, a five-points strategy has been evolved to tackle the low-income-housing problem during the sixth plan period.

1. Government will assume a major responsibility for low income housing.
2. 500,000 small size residential plots (60–150 square yards) will be developed in the public sector; this would cost approximately Rs 10,000 million (U.S. $590,000) which will be ultimately recoverable from the beneficiaries. However, the entire amount would not need only a revolving fund to start off the programme by purchase of required land and execution of some preliminary works. In addition to the above, the private sector will be inducted for development of 120,000 small size plots for low income housing. For this purpose, suitable undeveloped land will be allotted to private sector entrepreneurs at reasonable rates.
3. With a view to reducing costs and ensuring ready availability, government will provide needed construction materials at reasonable rates to intending house builders for low income groups.
4. All nucleus housing units (up to 200 square ft covered area) will be financed entirely through interest free loans of Rs 20,000 (U.S. $1200) per family, to be advanced by the House Building Finance Corporation. The programme will start from the year 1983–84 and a separate allocation of Rs 1 billion per year would be made available to HBFC for the purpose.
5. The poor will be allowed to construct houses according to their own design and with their own labour without interference from the concerned building authorities. (Government of Pakistan 1983, 456–57)

On the improvement of slums or *katchi abadis* it is stated that

while total elimination of slums is not feasible in the short term, a phased programme for improvement of such areas in major cities like Karachi, Lahore, Hyderabad, Faisalabad, etc. would be undertaken during the sixth plan; the important element of this programme would be the coverage of about 2 million slum dwellers, and will include provision of basic services such as electricity/water supply, drainage and sanitation, development of proper streets with minimum of realignment etc. Technical guidance will also be provided to the residents for improvement of their substandard houses. For carrying out this programme, during the Plan period, an amount of Rs 530 million (U.S. $31,000,000) has been provided on a matching basis, the balance being provided by the beneficiaries themselves. (Government of Pakistan 1983, 459)

A substantial difference exists between national five-year plans and local practice. The national level provides only some broad guidelines, and it is up to the provincial, and especially the local, government to carry out housing programs according to the five-points strategy. Moreover, even at the national level substantial changes are brought about, such as regular cuts in the allocation to the HBFC.

Two main observations can be made regarding the national strategy. The first regards affordability. It is assumed that small-size residential plots (up to 150 square yards) will reach low-income groups. The point that plots of 150 square yards are unaffordable to those groups is not taken into account. Likewise, interest-free loans go to buyers of nucleus housing units, so that allottees of plots of 120 square yards with a small nucleus house, costing at least Rs 40,000 (U.S. $2350), will be subsidized. Moreover, such allotment will be recorded as an achievement of providing small plots (to the poor) while such housing programs do not reach low-income groups when no additional supportive regulations are defined.

In connection with this, it is striking that again in the sixth Five Year Plan a total of 15,000 government servant units are planned to be constructed, for which Rs 2,040 million (U.S. $120 million) that is, 13 percent of the budget for physical planning and housing, is reserved (compared with 9 percent for housing in general). This somewhat contradicts a policy whereby limited budgets are spread over a maximum number of people.

A second main point is that the Five Year Plan has allocated Rs 530 million (U.S. $31 million) to assist 2 million people in slum areas in Pakistan, that is, 400,000 people annually. This figure is insufficient because, first, the existing housing stock deteriorates quickly (Government of Pakistan 1983), and second, the deficient number of plots to be provided to low-income groups guarantees further growth of *katchi abadis*. A modest amount of money is allocated to provincial governments for the development of small plots, and it is assumed that the development authorities provide most of the plots from their own resources. From the achievements of the earlier plan periods there is no reason to believe that the development authorities will achieve this goal. It can, therefore, be expected that *katchi abadis* will continue to grow faster than the remainder of the cities, and the 1981 census confirms this.

From Policy to Practice: Developments in the Housing Markets; Provision and Allocation at the Local Level

The above review has already implicitly described the housing markets and their development. Perhaps the most striking characteristic is that the housing markets have operated along the lines of the market mechanism under conditions of a continuous and even increasing housing shortage.

Second, government intervention has most of the time responded to the same laws and thus in no way intervened in the operation of the free market. For instance, no measures against speculation have ever been tried, and the leapfrog development of city extensions has been the common way of planning. Recently, the Karachi Development Authority has started constructing upper-class housing, which it offers for sale in advertisements that underline the investment opportunity offered. Large plot developments that officially are destined to serve low-income groups are mismanaged, partially handed over to project developers and construction firms, and end up in the hands of middle-income groups and speculators. Assessments show that 25 percent of the urban population in the high- and middle-income groups received about 64 percent of the resources available for housing and services (Jafri 1987, 31). The development plan recommended an aggressive and efficient system of user charges for public services with clearly identifiable beneficiaries.

In the third place, the informal housing market, which is the only option for some 50 percent of the urban population increase, has almost fully commercialized from the early seventies onward: as explained earlier, ''pure'' squatting has been almost completely replaced by commercial illegal subdivision (Van der Linden 1986, 17). Also in this development, the government is highly involved.

First, and mainly, it keeps on failing to provide an alternative. Second, it turns a blind eye to what the illegal developers do and—at the same time—increasingly prohibits unorganized squatting. Third, many politicians and administrators take a substantial profit from the illegal system, by taking bribes or securing votes. Fourth, even the bureaucratic and legal systems themselves with their cloudy and overlapping responsibilities and unrealistic and sometimes contradictory requirements, enhance the operation of the illegal system (Nientied and Van der Linden 1987).

Through all this, the illegal system has come to resemble the official system ever more, and as a result of this, a growing group of the poorest is now excluded even from illegal housing (Van der Linden 1982).

MAJOR PROBLEMS AND PROSPECTIVE DEVELOPMENTS

The government of Pakistan estimates that the 1983 habitat shortage was around 1.4 million units (Government of Pakistan 1983, 455). Another source estimates the requirement for the sixth plan period at 4,597,000 units, out of which 1,147,000 are urban (Ahmed 1983, 7). Such figures, though, are highly arbitrary, dependent as they are on statistics of dubious reliability and on standards and definitions.

What is clear is, first, the existence of a huge and increasing shortage of housing that meets formal standards. Second, even in the official Five Year Plan, there appears to be a strong bias toward the provision of housing for the less poor and the rich.

The allocation of housing has been skewed throughout the plan periods, and the sixth plan does not appear to deviate significantly from this pattern. As long as large portions of the increasingly small budget allocation are devoted to less than basic items (government servants' housing, commercial housing), this implies that less money, expertise, and—in general—attention is being paid to the basics of housing: a plot and a minimal infrastructure. These basics are precisely the maximum that the majority of the poor can afford. If the choice is between housing of good quality for the few and the maximum opportunity for optimally achievable shelter for the many, clearly, the first option is getting more emphasis in the sixth Five Year Plan and certainly in practice.

We have already reviewed the shortcomings of much planning in Pakistan. More important perhaps is the fact that good planning—which certainly exists—is not backed by the right policies. This probably was the cause of the failure of the sites-and-services program in Karachi, which had been carefully conceptualized and planned (Master Plan Department of the Karachi Development Authority 1974, 184–186) but suffered delays of close to a decade, which was reduced in scale more than ten times, and which had plots that seldom were occupied by the target groups (Islamuddin 1983; Swan et al. 1983; Herbert 1982; Nientied 1987). The most basic cause, however, is perhaps that this—and so many other—programs lacked sufficient backing on the part of the political and administrative power structure.

Take the case of the National Housing Policy. Initially framed in 1972, it has yet to be approved by the government. Meanwhile, drafts continue to be made and changed. The federal Physical Planning Act and the Provincial Physical Planning Act drafted in 1972 have not been finalized as yet, either by the federal or provincial government. Without the requisite local cover to the planning agencies, development plans like that for Karachi can expect to reap few positive results.

In an attempt to explain this situation, it may be noted that the present system entails many benefits to those charged with policy-making and execution. Development strategies such as sites-and-services and built-up units give the bureaucrats a lot of discretion to obtain favors and also chances for misusing government funds. It is an admitted position that at least 30 to 40 percent of the funds are siphoned off by the corrupt and inefficient bureaucracy (Siddique 1987, 21). As noted before, the government is much involved in the illegal housing system, which flourishes more to the extent that official attempts to reduce housing shortages fail. Thus whatever the seriousness of institutional constraints to solving the housing problem, these same constraints enhance the possibilities of bureaucrats to obtain graft and of politicians to manipulate large low-income populations (Van der Linden 1983, 1986, 52–57). At the same time, by the illegal system, the government is relieved—at least temporarily—of the responsibility of providing small plots with basic infrastructure on a mass scale (Nientied and Van der Linden 1985).

Since housing demand is increasing and nothing is being done to enhance equity in the delivery of housing, it is but logical that shortages are badly felt by an increasingly large group of people; shortages are filtering in an upward direction. The clearest examples of this are the poorest who no longer have access even to illegal housing.

As we have argued, the root cause of the insufficient housing supply lies in dominating interest; in other words, the problem is political. In the present situation, this worsening of the habitat conditions is perhaps a major condition for a breakthrough in housing policy, because it is bound to increase political pressure for a solution. Two such concessions have already been made. Through an announcement on July 1, 1978, the president of Pakistan made the first policy statement regarding regularization and improvement of illegal settlements. In Karachi alone, about 362 settlements got de facto legal tenure. The next announcement was made by the prime minister on April 7, 1986, which gave legal status to all irregular settlements that had more than 100 housing units and were in existence on March 23, 1985.

In this regard, it is also of importance that there are now good examples of what can be done. Although previously, low-income housing was almost completely left to the illegal commercial sector and a few scattered Non-Governmental Organizations (NGOs), public agencies have started approaching the problems in a more realistic and equitable way. Examples are an exercise in inner-city redevelopment in Lahore, *katchi abadi* upgrading in Karachi, and sites and services in Hyderabad. No doubt these interventions are scattered, of a somewhat ad hoc nature, and much too small in scale to have a major impact on housing markets. Their impact, however, might well reach far beyond the limits of these individual projects, because they show what good policies and proper execution can achieve. Therefore, by providing a tangible alternative, they may arouse a better awareness of what is wrong and at the same time provide a concrete goal to strive for.

REFERENCES

Ahmed, Shafiq. 1983. "Housing Supply for Pakistan: Sixth Five Year Plan." *Landmark*, April/May, 48–54.

Ahmed, Viqar. 1984. "Managing Urban Development: Focus on Services for the Poor." Paper presented at the National Seminar on Management of Urban Development and Services for the poor, Lahore, September.

———. 1987. "Approaches to Integrated Urban Management." Paper presented at the National Seminar on Urban Development, Management, and Participation for Integrated Development, Islamabad, January.

Asian Development Bank. 1984. *Pakistan Basic Urban Strategy Study*. Manila.

Government of Pakistan. 1972. *Population Census Report of Pakistan*. Islamabad: Population Census Organization.

———. 1975. *Planning Commission: Working Papers for the Development Perspective (1975–1980)*. Vol. 2. Karachi.

———. 1976. *National Housing Policy Framework*. Islamabad: Ministry of Housing and Works.

———. 1980. *Housing Census Report of Pakistan*. Islamabad: Population Census Organization.

———. 1981. *Population Census Report of Pakistan*. Islamabad: Population Census Organization.

———. 1982. *The State of the Environment, Pakistan, 1982*. Islamabad: Environment and Urban Affairs Division.

———. 1983. *The Sixth Five Year Plan (1983–1988)*. Islamabad.

———. 1984a. *Management of Cities Policy*, draft of final report prepared by Pakistan Environmental Planning and Architectural Consultants (PEPAK). Islamabad: Ministry of Housing and Works, Environment and Urban Affairs Division.

———. 1984b. *National Reference Manual on Planning and Infrastructure, Standards Analysis, and Critique*, prepared by Pakistan Environmental Planning and Architectural Consultants (PEPAK). Islamabad: Ministry of Housing and Works.

———. 1986. *National Human Settlement Policy Study*. Islamabad.

Herbert, J. D. 1982. "The Karachi Development Programme, 1974–1985: An Interim Appraisal." In *Urban Planning Practice in Developing Countries*, edited by J. L. Taylor and D. G. Williams. Oxford: Pergamon.

Islamuddin, Siddiqi. 1983. "Implementation of the Metroville I Project in Karachi." In *Between Basti Dwellers and Bureaucrats*, edited by J. W. Schoorl, J. Van der Linden, and K. S. Yap, 103–124. Oxford: Pergamon.

Jafri, T. A. 1987. "Problems of Urban Settlement." Paper presented at the National Seminar on Urban Development, Management, and Participation for Integrated Development, Islamabad, January.

Karachi Metropolitan Corporation-NESPAK. 1984. *Special Development Programme: Katchi Abadis Improvement Scheme*. Project report. Karachi: NESPAK.

Khan, J. A. 1984. "Managing Government Lands in Karachi to Supply Land for Housing." Master's thesis, Asian Institute of Technology. Bangkok.

Master Plan Department of the Karachi Development Authority. 1974. Karachi Development Plan, 1974–1985. Karachi.

Moinul, Arifin. 1980. "Karachi Development Authority, Development Projects 1980–1981." *Landmark*, September, 37–40.

Nederlands Economisch Instituut. 1985. *Habitat en beleid in de programmalanden van het Nederlandse Ontwikkelingssamenwerkingsbeleid*. Rotterdam.

Nientied, P., and S. I. Kalim. 1986. "Policy Constraints on Planning Land for Low-Income Groups in Karachi." *Habitat International* 10, nos. 1–2:79–92.

Nientied, P., E. Meijer, and J. Van der Linden. 1982. *Karachi Squatter Settlement Upgrading: Improvement and Displacement?* Amsterdam: Free University.

Nientied, P., and J. Van der Linden. 1985. "Legal and Illegal Plots Development: A Rationale for Illegal Subdivision of Land in Karachi." *Nagarlok* 17, no. 1:32–45.

———. 1987. "The Government and Illegal Land Supply for Low-Income Groups in Karachi." Paper presented at the Seminar on Habitat and Land Supply, Rotterdam, January.

Nientied, P. J. M. 1987. "Practice and Theory of Urban Policy in the Third World: Low-Income Housing in Karachi." Ph.D. thesis, Free University, Amsterdam.

Nizami, Z. A. 1981. "KDA Meets the Challenge of Growth: A Review of Projects for 1978–1982." *Landmark*, April/May, 29–40.

Qadeer, M. A. 1983. *Lahore: Urban Development in the Third World*. Lahore: Vanguard.

Segaar, T. J. 1975. "Karachi en de basti." Ph.D. thesis, Free University, Amsterdam.

Shah, A. A. 1977. *Housing in Pakistan*. Islamabad: Government of Pakistan Planning and Development Division.

———. 1978. *Country Monograph on Pakistan for the Expert Group Meeting on Human Settlements Technology for the ESCAP Region*. Islamabad: Government of Pakistan Planning Division.

Shamsuddin, S. S. 1980. "Housing: Its Challenges and Response; the Role of KDA." *Landmark*, September, 29–38.

Siddique, T. 1987. "Shelter for the Urban Poor: An Experiment by Hyderabad Development Authority." Hyderabad: Hyderabad Development Authority. Mimeograph.

Swan, P., K. Panchee, and E. A. Wegelin. 1983. *Management of Sites and Services Housing Schemes: The Asian Experience.* Chichester, Eng.: John Wiley.

Van der Harst, J. 1983. "Financing Housing in the Slums of Karachi." In *Between Basti Dwellers and Bureaucrats*, edited by J. W. Schoorl, J. Van der Linden, and K. S. Yap, 61–66.

Van der Linden, J. 1982. "Squatting by Organized Invasion in Karachi: A New Reply to Failing Housing Policy?" *Third World Planning Review* 4, no. 4:400–412.

———. 1983. "Actors in Squatment Upgrading, Their Roles and Interests." In *Between Basti Dwellers and Bureaucrats*, edited by J. W. Schoorl, J. Van der Linden, and K. S. Yap, 249–261. Oxford: Pergamon.

———. 1986. *The Sites and Services Approach Reviewed.* Aldershot, Eng.: Gower.

World Bank. 1984. *Pakistan, Sind Urban Sector Memorandum.* Washington, D.C.

FURTHER READING

Landmark. Periodic publication of Karachi Development Authority and Its Master Plan Department, Karachi.

Shahani, P. K. "The Importance of Housing in the National Economy of Pakistan." *Landmark*, April/May 1983:35–39.

Van der Linden, Jan. "The Squatter's House as a Source of Security in Pakistan." *Ekistics* 286 (1981):44–48.

IX

OCEANIA

24

Australia

TERRY BURKE, PETER W. NEWTON, AND MARYANN WULFF

Australia, with a population of 16 million in 1986, is an advanced capitalist society with a federal system of government. More than 85 percent of Australia's population lives in urbanized areas, particularly in the East, Southeast, and Southwest of the continent. Sydney with 3.4 million residents and Melbourne with 2.9 million are the country's two largest cities. Australia's population density of 2.1 persons per square kilometer is lower than that of any other country having a population of more than 5 million.

The domestic economy is dominated by the finance, service, and manufacturing industries; yet in terms of external trade Australia has an export dependence on agricultural and mineral commodities, making the economy sensitive to world trading conditions. Like many other similar societies, Australia has experienced some economic contraction since the mid–1970s, a contraction exacerbated by the small indigenous market and commodity-based export dependence.

TRENDS IN HOUSING CONDITIONS AND CONSTRUCTION: 1945–1986

Australia emerged from the depression and World War II with an immense backlog of housing needs due to the severe contraction in new housing production since the mid–1930s. Australia also emerged from the war with the main dimensions of its tenure system set in place (Williams 1984). Home ownership in Australia had long been established as the dominant tenure form, and no attempt was made by the government to interfere with this trend. The private rental sector was nearly of the same scale as the owner-occupied sector but was seen by many Australians as a temporary housing phase before moving on to ownership. Minimal residential tenancy legislation and some residual rent control from the war years affected the private rental sector. The third tier of the Australian housing system, public housing, was at that stage very small. This was because government housing commissions had been established in each state just before the war, and little construction had taken place during the war years.

Reflecting a similar sense of idealism that the end of the war bred in Britain, Australian housing and planning authorities evolved a number of well-intentioned housing objectives and urban planning principles in the immediate postwar years. Proposed, for example, was the development of public sector housing to around 10 percent of the total housing stock along with integrated plans for transport, employment, retailing, and community facilities for new public and private housing estates (Allport 1986). Unfortunately, these well-intentioned housing and planning goals were abandoned in the 1950s because of subsequent demographic and economic imperatives.

In the 1950s and 1960s Australia experienced consistently high birth rates, high levels of immigration, and a "marriage boom," all of which led to very rapid household formation. Hence, in addition to the accumulated backlog of households requiring housing, the public and private sectors had to grapple with the immense growth in new housing demand as well. (See table 24.1.)

Between 1947 and 1971 household formation averaged 2.8 percent per annum, considerably faster than that in most developed countries (Hugo 1986). The upturn in household formation immediately after World War II is evident in table 24.1, which shows that the rate of growth in households between 1947 and 1954 was 3.2 percent per annum. Household formation has slowed somewhat since the early 1970s, but the number of households continues to grow much faster than the population. This has led to a considerable decline in the average size of households.

Simultaneous with rapid rates of household formation in the 1950s and 1960s, the Australian economy experienced a long wave of economic growth characterized by extremely low unemployment and relatively low rates of inflation. Confronted with these intense demand pressures, the earlier government programs supporting a relatively large public sector stock of housing and carefully articulated urban planning diminished. This change in policy direction was encouraged and accelerated by private sector housing and building lobbies that were vociferous in their opposition to public housing and interventionist planning (Sandercock 1976). The return to power in the 1950s, both at state and federal levels, of conservative Liberal and Country party governments gave further momentum to a predominantly private market, owner-occupancy housing system.

Since the mid–1960s, the characteristics of the housing system have remained broadly unaltered, although the economic and demographic needs and demands of the Australian population have changed considerably. Particularly since the mid–1970s, there have been major changes in the economic and financial context in which the housing system operates. Because many of the housing problems affecting Australia in the 1980s flow from the tensions between a relatively unchanging housing system and a dynamic and uncertain socioeconomic environment, it is necessary to review the broad dimensions of the socioeconomic environment in which housing provision has taken place in the past decade.

The Changing Context of Housing Provision: 1975–1986

The sacking of the Australian Labor government by the governor general in 1975 not only marked a turning point in Australian politics but was symbolic of the fact that the certainties of the past could not be counted on. This was as true of Australian housing as it was of other sectors of the Australian economy

Table 24.1
Population and Households, Australia, 1947–1986

Year	Population*		Private Households		
	Number (x 1,000)	Average annual growth rate	Number (x 1,000)	Average annual growth rate	Mean Household size
1947	7,579	-	1,874	-	3.75
1954	8,987	2.43	2,343	3.19	3.55
1961	10,508	2.23	2,782	2.45	3.55
1966	11,551	1.89	3,152	2.50	3.47
1971	13,067	2.47	3,671	3.05	3.31
1976	14,033	1.43	4,141	2.41	3.12
1981	14,923	1.23	4,669	2.40	2.98
1986	16,018	1.42	5,187	2.10	2.87

Sources: Australian Bureau of Statistics, 1984c; Australian Bureau of Statistics, 1987.
*Estimated resident population as of June 30 in each census year. This figure adjusts the actual census count for underenumeration and for Australians temporarily overseas on census night.

and society. In the past decade, Australia, like other advanced capitalist societies, has been experiencing a period of economic restructuring. This restructuring has the potential to affect housing provision both indirectly, in that it provides a changed economic climate for housing consumption (by shaping the income and expectations of households), and directly, in that the institutions of housing provision (including financial, land development, building, and planning) are part of the restructuring.

In terms of economic change, the past decade has witnessed a transition from the rapid growth of the preceding decades to one of economic recession. There are several economic indicators of the post–1975 decline in national prosperity. For example, since 1975, the gross domestic product has expanded at an average of only 2.2 percent per year, a rate insufficient to provide jobs for those entering the job market or for those displaced by technological change. Consequently, unemployment in Australia increased less than 2 percent in the early seventies to more than 10 percent a decade later. Inflation, less than 4 percent in 1970, averaged 11.5 percent during the decade 1974–1984 and declined in 1985–1986 to approximately 7 percent (Indecs, 1987). The same period also witnessed growing current-accounts deficits, increasingly financed by an inflow of foreign capital, thereby expanding public and private debt liability. The greater proportion of budget outlays directed to both internal and external debt servicing detracted from the ability to finance government programs, including housing.

The poor performance of the economy helped mold an increased conservatism in government. Since 1975, governments of both major political parties have been committed to cutbacks in public spending, a reduction in taxation, and deregulation of the economy. Ironically, the commitment of Liberal governments of Australia to these economic programs was more at the level of rhetoric than practice. It has been the federal Labor government, in office since 1983, that has initiated most of the policy changes, particularly those with respect to deregulation of the financial system and the opening up of the economy to more competitive international forces.

Before the election in 1983, the Labor government possessed a clearly articulated housing policy: greater funding for housing generally, a commitment to the expansion of public housing, and encouragement of a greater involvement by local government and community groups in housing provision (Paris 1987a). In practice, however, most of these policies have been modified. Although the federal Labor government has provided more funds for public housing than its Liberal predecessors, the significant Labor initiatives to affect housing have tended to be broad economic policies, notably deregulation of the finance system in 1984 and reforms of the taxation system in 1985.

TENURE STATUS

The dominant characteristic of the tenure system in Australia is home ownership. As early as 1911 nearly half of all dwellings in Australia were owner occupied, and this sector continued to expand in the postwar years (see table 24.2). The experience of the 1950s and 1960s, with the emphasis upon private housing provision in the form of the single, detached, owner-occupied house was an extension of housing trends established in the early twentieth century. Home ownership was not a product of the postwar era as some observers of the Australian housing scene imply (Kemeny 1981) but was well established by the late nineteenth century (Hayward 1986). By 1966 owner occupation had reached 71 percent, a figure beyond which it has been unable to progress. In fact, by 1986 there was a slight decline to 69 percent. In 1984 housing costs for outright owners as a percentage of mean weekly income after taxes was 6.7 percent; the comparable figure for purchasers was 19.6 percent (Australian Bureau of Statistics 1984b).

Although the home-ownership sector continued to develop throughout the early decades of the postwar era, the private rental sector declined markedly until the early 1960s but thereafter has remained a stable component of the housing system. For private renters of unfurnished dwellings, housing costs in 1984 accounted for 18.5 percent of after-tax household income (Australian Bureau of Statistics 1984b). The public housing sector grew slightly as a proportion of all tenure types, reaching about 6 percent in the midseventies, declining in the decade until 1981 but thereafter expanding to 7 percent of the housing market in 1986. Public tenants lay out 14.9 percent of their income on housing (Australian Bureau of Statistics 1984b). In recent years, there has been some attempt to develop a fourth tenure sector in the form of cooperatives, but in 1987 this represented a miniscule proportion of the total stock. In addition to the above tenure classifications and largely hidden by official statistics is what Hal Kendig and Chris Paris (1987) called the ''underbelly of Australian housing,'' the estimated several hundred thousand households living in boarding houses, lodging houses, nursing homes, and caravan parks. Also hidden by official statistics is the growing problem of homelessness. Homelessness was ''rediscovered'' in the early 1980s when it became increasingly clear that homelessness was not just a problem of the ''down-and-out'' alcoholic, but of young people moving into independent living and of women and their families forced from the family home (Coopers and Lybrand 1985).

Owner Occupancy

Among advanced capitalist societies, Australia has one of the highest home-ownership rates (Burke et al. 1984). The 70 percent owner-occupancy rate understates the dominance of ownership in the Australian value system, because most of the renters aspire to ownership and see renting as a transition stage before purchasing a home, however unrealistic this aspiration might be. Housing-preference studies indicate that more than 90 percent of Australians desire home ownership (Maddocks 1978). It is little wonder, therefore, that some critics see private ownership as a fetish or an ideology (Kemeny 1981). The dominance of

Table 24.2
Tenure and Dwelling Type, Australia, 1911–1986 (Percentages)

Tenure					Years of Census					
	1911	1947	1954	1966	1971	1976	1981	1986		
Outright owner	45	45	48	n/a	n/a	32	33	39		
Purchaser	4	8	15	n/a	n/a	35	33	31		
All owners/purchasers	49	53	63	71	67	67	71	70		
Public tenant	0	n/a	4	5	6	5	5	7		
Private tenant	45	43	30	21	22	20	20	19		
Not stated	5	4	3	3	6	8	8	4		
TOTAL ('000)	894	1,874	2,343	3,152	3,671	4,141	4,699	5,187		
Private Detached House *%	N/A	86.4	85.6	85.1	83.9	83.8	79.6	78.0		

Source: Australian Bureau of Statistics, Census data, various years.
Note: n/a = not available.

private ownership in Australian society has been linked with class segregation, gender stereotyping, privatization of social values, poor urban planning, and an impediment to economic growth (Kemeny 1978, 1981, 1983; Shelter 1982). The evidence for such assertions, however, is contested. David Hayward (1986) argued, for example, that many of the effects attributed to owner occupancy flow instead from the dominant housing form, the detached house. Recent data suggest, contrary to the experience of other countries, that access to ownership does not have a class bias. Ownership is almost as high among blue-collar workers as professionals and lower-income earners as middle- and upper-income earners (Hayward 1986; Beed et al. 1987).

Yet it is growing increasingly clear that a mono-tenurial system does have its negative implications for certain sections of the population. High entry costs are precluding substantial numbers of special needs groups, including single-income families, sole-parent families, the disabled, and aborigines from the benefits that attach to ownership. For example, 35 percent of sole-parent households are owners compared with 80 percent for married-couple households (Australian Bureau of Statistics 1984b). These benefits include security, capital gain, state subsidy, and decreasing housing costs over time, benefits that flow from the particular form of home-ownership provision in Australia.

Why home ownership is so pervasive is not an easily answered question. Certainly, government subsidies during the past three decades have been important, but these subsidies appear no greater than they are in many other countries, including countries of the United Kingdom and in the United States where, unlike Australia, mortgage interest tax deductibility exists as a major and inequitable form of financial subsidy. One largely unresearched explanation for the dominance of home ownership in Australia is the importance of international migration throughout Australia's history. Almost all of the major postwar migrant groups, with the exception of those from the United Kingdom, have achieved inordinately high levels of owner occupancy (Australian Bureau of Statistics 1984b). Perhaps ownership represents something solid and tangible among all of the other uncertainties that changing one's country represents. With international migration (including both migrants and their offspring) accounting for 60 percent of Australia's postwar population growth, the impact that the housing choices of these groups exert upon the Australian tenure system cannot be overlooked (Department of Immigration and Ethnic Affairs 1985).

One dimension of owner occupancy that appears less important than in other, particularly European, societies is the holiday home. In 1986 census data indicated that holiday homes constituted only 2.5 percent of the total housing stock. One explanation is that Australians, in a society characterized by the detached home in a low-density suburban environment, do not require the breathing space of a holiday home. Moreover, the majority of Australians reside in cities with easy day access to natural amenities, such as coastal beaches, bush terrain, mountains, and rivers.

Private Rental Sector

In the postwar period, the private rental sector has declined from 43 percent to 19 percent of the total housing stock. The steady decline in the 1950s and 1960s was related to the growing affluence of households, enabling many to achieve their preference for ownership. Combined with the effects of substantial direct and indirect government subsidies to the other two tenure sectors, the proportion of the stock either owner occupied or publicly rented grew at the expense of the private rental sector. The stability of the private rental sector since the 1960s is a result of the sustained demand from young, newly forming households. In 1981 persons under age twenty-nine accounted for some 40 percent of rental households. This demand has been further reinforced in recent years by the increased need of low-income households such as single-parent families, youth, and low-income aged for inexpensive accommodations (Hancock and Burke 1983; Paris 1984; Core Consultants et al. 1983).

Although the evidence is often debated, the private rental supply has broadly kept pace with this demand, although there are shortages of adequate and affordable accommodations for lower-income households, particularly in certain regions and in relation to specific dwelling types (Burke 1987d; Paris 1984). Many of the outer suburban areas of the capital cities, traditionally dominated by owner occupancy and detached family homes, are experiencing an increased demand for affordable rental accommodations as a result of social and demographic changes such as youth wishing to move into independent accommodations or recently divorced family members who wish to remain in the same community (Hancock and Burke 1983).

In Australia the relative decline of private rental as a tenure form does not reflect the effects of restrictions on this sector such as residential tenancy legislation or rent controls. By world standards, such controls are minimal and, in the case of rent controls, virtually nonexistent (Core Consultants et al. 1983; Nicholson and Weeks 1984). In fact, residential tenancy reform in the past decade has been one of the most contentious issues with regard to the private rental sector. Some states, namely, those with Labor governments, have made reforms, but security of tenure for tenants remains limited. Effective, vociferous opposition from real estate interests, decrying their loss of rights to control privately owned property, has been the major barrier to widespread reform.

Public Housing

Before World War II, public sector housing was virtually unknown in Australia. The private sector dominated both the ownership and rental sectors of the housing market. But in 1945 the federal government established an organizational mechanism, the Commonwealth State Housing Agreement (CSHA), for determining, in conjunction with the states, national housing policies and to provide appropriate funding arrangements to achieve these policies. Efforts to establish a Commonwealth Housing Commission in the early 1940s failed mainly as a result of strong state opposition to federal control of public housing. Instead, State Housing Commissions were set up with the federal government providing a measure of policy direction and funding. The State Housing Commissions operate within the budget limits and policy course set by the Commonwealth and outlined in successive CSHAs. There have been several CSHAs since 1945, in 1956, 1961, 1966, 1973, 1978, 1981, and most recently, 1984. State governments do allocate funds from their own budgets for funding public housing, and this provides some variability between jurisdictions in housing policy and programs.

The objectives of public housing programs, as outlined in the CSHAs, have altered with the changing economic and social climate. The initial call for public housing after World War II stemmed in large part from a concern with building up the housing stock, which was clearly inadequate given the rapid household formation and the backlog of house construction. Later, in the 1950s, the aim shifted to include provision for adequate housing for the waves of immigrants who were arriving from overseas, many of whom were recruited to help alleviate the labor shortage in Australia. The standard public client during this period was the traditional family of married couple, with employed male head, and dependent children. The housing needs of other groups, such as single-parent families, childless couples, and single persons, regardless of their hardship, went unmet (Burke et al. 1984). Public housing in this period was oriented principally to the low-income working-class family.

By the mid–1970s, the objectives of public housing and indeed the typical client had changed dramatically. The recognition that public housing was not serving the neediest members of the community became clear in a national inquiry into poverty in Australia, which found that a significant proportion of public housing tenants were not poor (Committee of Inquiry into Poverty 1975). Although entry into public housing was means tested, a family could remain permanently in public housing no matter how improved their economic situation became. Indeed, many were encouraged to purchase their rental property. A recognition that State Housing Commissions had been pursuing nonwelfare roles when there were growing numbers of genuinely needy led to some major changes in the objectives of public housing. Market rents rather than rents based on historic costs were introduced for the first time, and in place of the standard working-class family, the typical client was now more likely to be a member of a single-parent family, unemployed, and living primarily on government benefits. After 1975 state housing authorities became increasingly geared to a welfare role (Burke et al. 1984).

As indicated above, a notable feature of Australian public housing policy has been its promotion of home ownership for low-income public tenants. Reflecting the dominance of conservative federal and state governments, various CSHAs from the mid–1950s to the early 1980s have progressively allowed the State

Housing Commissions to sell off their public housing stock to existing tenants. In Victoria, the state where the policy was most aggressively pursued, 51.5 percent of the metropolitan public housing stock had been sold by 1981 (Newton and Wulff 1985). In Australia the scale of conversion from public rental stock to private owner occupancy has been considerably greater, occurred earlier, and was certainly less politically and academically debated than were the privatization policies occurring in Great Britain, the United States, and some other European countries. Because of the privatizing of so much of the public housing stock, state housing authorities in Australia have created many of the negative outcomes predicted by researchers in those overseas countries that more recently embarked on a similar policy (Forrest and Murie 1985; Forrest 1987). Much high-quality and better-located stock has been sold, leaving behind a residual of low-status, often high-rise, dwellings. Moreover, public authorities still have years to wait for purchasers to pay their loans, yet are hard pressed to find public funds to meet the increasing demand for rental rebates to the predominantly welfare tenants left in the wake of privatization. By the 1990s, it may be that Australian public housing authorities will be unable to meet their then current financial commitments, let alone provide for future need.

The 1984 CSHA still promotes home ownership for low-income families but requires that public housing authorities maintain their stock by replacing each dwelling that is sold at market rates. Moreover, eligibility criteria for public housing have been expanded to include all sections of the community including, for example, the increasing number of homeless young people who formerly were not catered to in public housing. Market rents have been abandoned in favor of rents based on historic costs, and, as in previous decades, rental rebates are available for clients unable to meet even the costs of historically based rents. Moreover, there has been some effort to accelerate the rate of public housing purchase or construction with much of the latter characterized by considerable innovation in design and appearance. Although positive, these changes appear inadequate considering that in 1986 the waiting list for public housing stood at 158,000 families nationally, compared with 77,000 in 1979, with waiting periods extending up to several years depending on location and client type. Nevertheless, Australia currently is one of the few countries where both the absolute number and proportion of public housing units are expanding.

Tenure Neutrality

One of the major debates with respect to Australian housing policies since the mid–1970s has been a questioning of the dominance of home ownership. One challenge to the predominance of owner-occupied housing policies came from a broadly liberal-Left grouping of housing interests, including the consumer lobby group Shelter, certain trade unions, and sections of the Australian Labor party. Direction was given to this group by the various antihome-ownership writings of Jim Kemeny (1978, 1981, 1983). Another strand of antihome-ownership policy came from various sections of a reemergent Right that feared that investment in ownership was diverting domestic savings away from more productive sectors of the Australian economy (Stone 1979). The push of the former group was for a reduction of government support for ownership and an increase in support for public and private rental sectors, the sectors where the housing need was perceived to be greater, particularly for groups such as single parents, youth, aborigines, persons alone, and low-income households generally. The push of the latter group, including the Australian Treasury, was for a reduction in assistance for housing generally and an opening up of the housing market to market forces unfettered by subsidies or regulated interest rates that artificially lower the cost of home ownership, raise ownership expectations, and encourage overconsumption of housing.

Both Left and Right positions have been challenged. As previously mentioned, Jim Kemeny has been criticized for exaggerating the effects of home ownership and for ignoring other influences including the structures of provision that underpin the Australian housing sector (Hayward 1986; Kemeny 1987; Berry 1988). He has also been criticized for underestimating the historical desire of working people in Australia for a tenure form that promises security and independence (Paris 1987b). The economic rationalists, on the other hand, have been criticized for narrowly applying neoclassical economic theory to an analysis of the housing market and for oversimplistic assumptions about how the housing market works. They include the debated belief that government tax treatments disproportionately favor the private ownership sector and an inadequate conceptualization of financial deregulation and its impact on both the wider economy and the housing market (Stretton 1987).

State Expenditure Directions and Distributional Implications

Underpinning the debate on tenure neutrality is the question of who benefits and who loses from state expenditures and outlays on housing. In a comprehensive analysis of the state subsidy of housing in Australia, Joe Flood and Judith Yates (1987) have distilled the forms of housing subsidy available to households in each tenure sector. Table 24.3 shows the direct and indirect outlays as well as the per capita and net assistance for each tenure sector. The three forms of subsidy highlighted by the table are as follows:

1. Direct and indirect budget outlays on public housing capital works, home purchase assistance to first-time home buyers on an income-tested basis, rental assistance to low-income private rental tenants, community housing funds to facilitate joint ventures with local government and community groups, and employee housing (housing provided for defense personnel, teachers in remote areas, railway employees, and so forth).

2. State revenue foregone principally via the taxation system including nontaxation of capital gains, mortgage interest deductions, rate and land tax exemptions.

3. Market regulation whereby interest rates are pegged below market levels providing an effective subsidy to borrowers. For example, since 1985 existing home purchases have had their repayments pegged at 13.5 percent, whereas new purchasers for most of this period were paying in excess of 15.0 percent.

Aggregating the various forms of assistance, the data reveal that of the U.S. $202 assistance per capita, U.S. $148 or 73 percent flow to owner occupancy with the result that "homeownership has been largely immune to the effects of government policy and to changes in economic conditions" (Flood and Yates 1987, 87). According to Flood and Yates, private tenants have received little assistance, and much of the home-ownership assistance has been poorly targeted in that income eligibility limits and criteria regulating the value of properties purchased were of a magnitude that the benefits accrued to households on relatively high incomes. Nevertheless, as Hal Kendig and Chris Paris (1987, 50) pointed out, the total amount of support received by the average household through government expenditures is small: "Housing in Australia is primarily a private rather than public responsibility." (Figure 24.1 shows the pattern of Commonwealth government assistance for housing in current and constant prices since 1976–1977.) The increase in government assistance that has occurred has been predominantly in the form of tax advantages rather than outright budget outlays.

Since a sizable proportion of total assistance to owner occupiers in this analysis is in the form of nontaxation of imputed rent, this is a contentious analysis of state housing assistance. Although the taxation of imputed rent is rarely discussed in other countries, in Australia it has remained an ongoing issue because Australia actually had such a tax until 1923. Hugh Stretton (1987) argued that the taxation of imputed rent incorrectly assumes that housing is unproductive capital. If housing were viewed as productive capital, a tax on the imputed rent of residential properties would be no more justifiable than an imputed rent tax on commercial or industrial properties. There has never been any discussion of a tax on the latter. When imputed rent is excluded from the figures in table 24.3, the degree of subsidy to the home-ownership sector is considerably reduced. Another area of contention is the treatment of the private rental sector. Flood and Yates appear to have underestimated the absence of a capital gains tax on the economics of the private rental sector. During the period of rapid dwelling-price inflation that has characterized the Australian property market since the 1970s, the nontaxation of capital gains represents a substantial subsidy to the private rental sector, although recent research suggests that the subsidy may have been captured by the landlord rather than passed on to tenants in the form of lower rents (Bethune and Neutze 1987).

Contrary to the trend in other countries, in Australia the deductibility of mortgage interest as a form of subsidy to homeowners has been progressively removed. As a result, Australia does not confront the costs of automatic creep in tax relief created by this policy. Moreover, the direct-assistance programs to

Table 24.3
Commonwealth Assistance for Housing, by Tenure and Type of Assistance, Australia, 1984–1985

DIRECT ASSISTANCE: BUDGET OUTLAYS (net of repayments or surplus)	Net Assistance $M (US)	Per Capita $ US
Public Tenants		
Acquisition Improvement	345.8	
Rental Assistance	26.0	
TOTAL Public Tenants	371.8	24.02
Private Tenants		
(Rent assistance and rent relief)	169.6	
TOTAL Private Tenants	169.6	10.94
Home Owners (First Home Buyers)		
Home Purchase Assistance	238.3	
Home Deposit Assistance	175.7	
Other	5.2	
TOTAL Home Owners	419.2	27.20
Community Housing	108.0	
Employee Housing	161.1	
General	29.6	
TOTAL Other	298.7	19.17

| | TOTAL BUDGET OUTLAYS | 1259.3 | 81.30 |

INDIRECT ASSISTANCE : TAX EXPENDITURES (Revenue Foregone)

Home Owners
Non taxation of imputed rent	3262	
Non deducatability of mortgage interest	1700	
Mortgage interest deduction	42	
TOTAL Expenditures	1604	102.24

INDIRECT ASSISTANCE : MORTGAGE MARKET REGULATION

Home Owners
| Interest rate regulation | 300 | 18.94 |

TOTAL DIRECT AND INDIRECT HOUSING ASSISTANCE | 3163 | 202.48 |

Source: Calculated from data in Flood and Yates, 1987.
Note: U.S. values calculated at an exchange rate of AUS $1.00 = U.S. $0.72.

Figure 24.1
Direct and Indirect Commonwealth Budget Outlays, Australia, 1976–1977 to 1984–1985

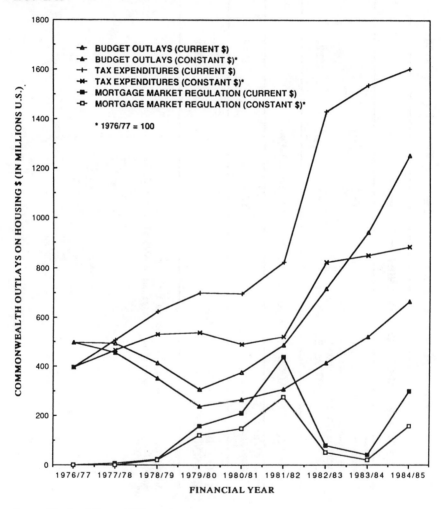

Source: Flood and Yates, 1987.

first-time home buyers are now more closely targeted to those on lower incomes. On the other hand, some adjustments to the tax treatment of housing further modify the picture of housing outlays depicted by Flood and Yates. In 1985 a tax on capital gains (excluding owner-occupied housing) and a taxation depreciation allowance for private landlords were introduced. The former increases indirect subsidies to owner–occupiers, the latter to landlords, although the exact effect of these changes is not estimated.

HOUSING QUALITY

In the immediate postwar years, Australia did not present the same problems of poor-quality housing stock as did many contemporary advanced capitalist nations. Because Australian cities developed primarily on a commercial and financial, rather than an industrial, base (Newton and Johnston 1981; Berry 1983), they never developed on any scale the squalid, cheaply built high-density housing that emerged to accommodate the industrial working class in Britain, Europe, and the Northeast of North America. Although there were certainly substantial pockets of substandard housing in some areas, notably the inner suburbs of Sydney and Melbourne, most of the housing was relatively spacious and adequately equipped relative to world standards of that time. (See table 24.4.)

The average number of persons per room has steadily declined (table 24.4). This has been assisted by a general increase in the average floor area of Australian homes and in the increase in the number of rooms per dwelling. The decline in the average size of families and households has also contributed to Australians' enjoyment of relatively uncrowded living conditions, a situation further reinforced by an increase in the average floor area of newly constructed houses in both the private and public sectors. The major deficiency in housing standards in 1947 was the absence of flush toilets; in addition, there was a significant percentage of households at that time without electricity or bathrooms. These housing problems had largely disappeared by the 1970s. There also has been an increasing trend toward the construction of brick homes and a decline in timber construction (table 24.4).

The general high quality of the housing stock by and large absolved federal and state governments of the need to expend substantial organizational and financial resources on massive urban-renewal programs such as those that took place in the 1960s in many European cities or in the large northeastern cities of the United States. In Australia limited amounts of urban renewal have occurred in selected inner-city pockets: initially, as public ventures in the 1960s and early 1970s (and in Sydney and Melbourne associated with controversial high-rise housing) and, more recently, as market-driven gentrification (Newton and Wulff 1985; Logan 1985).

Table 24.4
Indicators of Housing Conditions, Australia, 1947–1981

INDICATORS	1947	1971	1976	1981
Rooms per dwelling	4.9	5.0	5.5	5.5
People per room	0.77	0.67	0.57	0.54
Overcrowding % of households	-	6.7	2.0	-
Average floor area of houses				
houses (m2) – Private Sector	-	130.0	145.0	159.0
– Public Sector	-	98.0	109.0	105.0
People per dwelling	4.0	3.5	3.3	3.0
Lacking electricity %	16.0	0.6	0.5	n/a
Without Bathroom %	14.1	4.4	1.0	n/a
Without flush toilet %	43.3	10.5	4.4	n/a
Brick/Concrete %	41.1	50.9	58.0	n/a
Timber Construction %	47.4	32.4	26.2	n/a

Source: Australian Bureau of Statistics, Censuses, 1947, 1971, 1976, and 1981.
Note: n/a = not available.

HOUSING CONSTRUCTION, HOUSING TYPE, AND LOCATION

The lesser need relative to other nations to direct resources to inner-city renewal in the 1950s created greater freedom for the government and private sector to direct housing resources to facilitating and subsidizing owner-occupied suburban development. This was mainly achieved in two ways: first, by offering favorable loan conditions for new rather than existing housing; and second, by ensuring through financial regulation adequate funds for new house construction. This direction is reflected in high per capita rates of dwelling construction (table 24.5).

The per capita rates of housing construction have been sustained at relatively high levels throughout the postwar period, with the major form of construction the single-family detached dwelling.

For the period 1955 to 1985, the largest share of total production clearly was taken up by single detached houses, usually on allotments of around 0.1 hectares (figure 24.2). The late 1960s, however, did see a boom in apartment development, partially in the form of inner-city high-rise public housing but mostly in private sector speculative apartments built for the rapidly growing number of young, newly forming households. The inner- and middle-ring suburbs of Melbourne and Sydney received much of the medium-density housing built at that time. Spatially, apartments and medium-density housing were concentrated in the inner-urban areas, whereas detached houses were constructed on greenfield sites in the rapidly sprawling suburbs. Given that apartments and other multiunit dwellings were largely rented, while detached homes were built for owner occupancy, the outcome of this period is that the newly developing suburbs became predominantly owner occupied while the inner urban areas maintained a mix of tenures.

In the late 1960s and early 1970s, growing resident opposition to both private and public sector apartment development eventually resulted in local governments instituting restrictive planning provisions (Archer 1980; Indicative Planning Council 1980). These controls, while not stopping the construction of apartments and medium-density housing forms, certainly have slowed their rate of provision and have been a major obstacle to creating more flexible and diverse housing forms.

Related to the dramatic changes in the economy and political climate after the mid–1970s, the housing sector particularly the private dwellings component, experienced increasing instability (figure 24.2). In terms of new construction, the average annual rate of 4 percent was marginally less than in the previous decade, despite larger numbers of newly forming households. This average, however, disguises increasing cyclical instability, which led to changes in the house-building industry, notably the move to contract rather than speculative housing. The public housing sector experienced greater relative contraction in construction during the late 1970s and early 1980s, in response to cutbacks in

Table 24.5
New Dwelling Commencement per 1,000 Inhabitants, Australia, 1950–1986

Year	Houses Total	Flats Total	Private (All Dwelling Types)	Public (All Dwelling Types)	All Dwellings
1950	8.3	0.3	7.0	1.6	8.6
1954	8.4	0.3	6.8	1.9	8.7
1961	7.1	1.4	7.1	1.4	8.5
1971	7.6	3.2	9.4	1.4	10.8
1976	7.9	2.3	8.9	1.1	10.2
1981	6.6	3.1	9.0	0.7	9.7
1986	5.8	1.8	6.5	1.1	7.6

Source: Calculated from *Monthly Summary of Statistics*, Canberra: Australian Government Publishing Service, various years.

Figure 24.2
Dwelling Commencements, Australia, 1955–1985

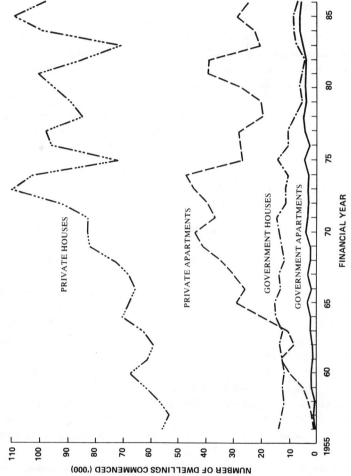

Source: Australian Bureau of Statistics, *Building Statistics*, cat. no. 8705, Australian Government Publishing Service, 1948–1988.

741

Commonwealth funds by federal Liberal governments. With the election of the federal Labor government in 1983 committed to an expanding public sector, public housing starts increased rapidly after years of progressive decline.

At the end of the decade until 1986 the detached house still accounted for some 80 percent of all new starts (figure 24.2). Other residential dwellings such as apartment and villa units temporarily reached 30 percent, previously only achieved in the apartment boom of the late 1960s. By 1986, as a result of three decades of predominantly detached housing production, 84.8 percent of Australians in private households were residing in separate dwellings. Reflecting the low-rise character of Australian cities, less than 2 percent of the dwellings are more than three stories high, and most of them can be found in either Sydney or Melbourne. The dominance of the detached house imparts to Australian cities an urban sprawl that has few parallels in the world. Sydney, the most dense city in Australia, with 1,918 persons per square kilometer, has less than half the density of Washington, D. C. (3,852 persons per square kilometer), and London (4,276 persons per square kilometer) and only one-tenth that of Bombay (Department of Immigration, Local Government and Ethnic Affairs, 1987).

SPECIAL POPULATION GROUPS AND CHANGING PATTERNS OF HOUSEHOLD FORMATION

One of the dominant changes of the past decade has been a growing diversity in family and household composition. Although the rate of household formation has been steady since the midseventies, the types of households being formed differ from earlier decades. The changes in household formation of significance to the housing sector are the very rapid growth of one-parent families, the increase in persons living alone, the tendency of youth to leave the parental home at a much younger age, and the increased numbers of aged persons. Importantly, many among these groups are on low incomes, thereby considerably constrained in their housing options.

Single-parent households in 1984 comprised slightly under 5 percent of all households. This in part reflects a major legislative and normative change in Australia with regard to divorce. The introduction of the Family Law Act in 1976 led to a very sharp rise in the number of divorces between 1977 and 1979, much of this representing a backlog of couples waiting for the act to come into existence. Between 1966 and 1981 the incidence of divorce rose from 3.7 to 12.1 divorces per thousand married persons (Australian Bureau of Statistics 1984a). On average, the head of a single-parent family is younger than that of a married couple family. Although about one-third are homeowners, this compares unfavorably with four-fifths of married-couple families owning or purchasing their homes. Seventy percent of single parents have government benefits as their principal source of income (Australian Bureau of Statistics 1984a). Given the relatively low level of these benefits and the marginal work-force participation of female single parents, 41 percent of single-parent families have incomes classified as below the poverty line when housing costs are taken into account (Rossiter and Vipond 1985). This figure compares with an estimated 11 percent of all families living in poverty after housing. Significantly, most of the poor single-parent households are headed by females, leading many observers to talk in terms of a "feminization of poverty" (Cass 1985).

One-person households also have increased as a percentage of all households, from 8 percent in 1947 to 18 percent in 1981 (Australian Bureau of Statistics 1984a). The most rapidly growing category of one-person household is that headed by persons under thirty years of age (Hugo 1986). Several factors have contributed to the increase in young one-person households: the increasing propensity of young Australians to leave the parental home for a period of independent living (Young 1987), the trend toward postponing (or foregoing) marriage, and the decline in the median age at divorce with persons under the age of thirty years having the highest divorce rates (Australian Bureau of Statistics 1984b). A minority of young households have neither the income nor the social skills to move into independent living, and consequently, the past decade has seen the emergence of a youth housing problem (Hancock and Burke 1983). This problem has manifested itself in the form of youth homelessness, dependence on refuges or other crisis-accommodation centers, and generally unstable living situations.

Australia's elderly enjoy the highest rates of home ownership among the population. Three-quarters of households headed by a person aged sixty-five years or older owned or were purchasing their home in 1981, a figure that is higher than that found either in the United States or Britain (Kendig 1984). The family home is not taken into account when assessing eligibility for the government pension in Australia, and neither is there a capital gains tax on the dwelling, resulting in considerable financial advantages of home ownership for the elderly (Kendig 1984). Recent surveys in Sydney, however, have shown that the majority of elderly homeowners in the study had lived in their homes thirty or more years. Many of these homes were found to be in need of repair. Furthermore, it was found that 30 percent of dwellings had no wash basin in the bathroom, and a similar proportion still had outdoor toilets (Thorne 1986). Many local councils have attempted to assist elderly homeowners in their areas by introducing council-provided home-maintenance and home-help services.

On the whole, the major housing problems of the elderly stem from a lack of economic and social support, rather than from poor housing design or home-maintenance difficulties (Thorne 1986). Australia's low-income elderly experience particular housing disadvantages, especially those who are confined to renting private sector accommodations. Aged tenants in the private sector, commonly less well off than homeowners, face rents that in the early 1980s were already four times that of the rents paid by public tenants (Kendig 1984). With rental costs that often consume half of their government pensions (McWilliam 1986) and the lack of security of tenure associated with private rental accommodations, the plight of many aged renters is serious. Only about one-third of all aged pensioners who rent housing are able to obtain public housing. The waiting list for public housing among the aged is substantial, and the waiting time can be as long as three to four years in some areas (McWilliam 1986). Aged persons in public rental dwellings pay a reduced, or rebated rent, which amounts to between 16 to 20 percent of their income, and also enjoy security of tenure.

The increased longevity of the elderly means that many are remaining in their homes as they become increasingly frail. Both state and local governments provide a range of social and health-related services to the aged, but there are significant variations in the level of provision (Howe et al. 1987). Often the social support and care of these elderly family members who wish to remain in their home, rather than enter a nursing home, become a burden on younger family members (Thorne 1986). Slightly more than two-fifths of elderly Australians also live on their own. A recent survey of elderly persons in Australia revealed that those who live alone draw more substantially on outside support than do those who share their accommodations with others (Kendig 1986).

In general terms, Australia's elderly can be described as a group divided between the "asset rich" (owner–occupiers) and the "asset poor" (aged renters) (Kendig 1986). In recognition of the expansion in the number of aged, many with adequate incomes and a substantial wealth base, private sector developers, and some religious groups have been investing in a "retirement housing market" (Howe 1986). Such responses, however, to the growth of the aged population ignore the plight of the many aged on lower incomes.

One group with recurring housing needs is the Australian aborigine, who comprise about 1.5 percent of the nation's population. Dispossessed of most of their land, deprived of their own unique life-style, and unable to acquire adequate incomes in a society dominated by whites, many aborigines live in housing conditions more akin to those of a Third World country than an affluent advanced Western society (Braddock and Wanganeen 1980). Although many millions of government dollars have been injected into aboriginal housing, the emphasis of state government provision has been on public rental housing. Alan Gray 1987, 34) stated that "the effect of government policy has not worked to the satisfaction of the supposed beneficiaries," and he recommended channeling government money into grants for aboriginal organizations for improving housing on the aboriginal reserves (Gray 1987). Aboriginal housing provision is so intertwined with other issues, including land rights and a long overdue recognition of their cultural identity (which affects housing form and housing use), that resolution of the problem requires a broad policy focus.

THE COST OF HOUSING

One of the key issues in Australian housing provision in the 1980s has been changes in affordability and the implications of these changes on tenure choice for households. (Table 24.6 indicates the trend in housing costs for Melbourne

Table 24.6
Dwelling Prices, Price Index, Sydney, Melbourne, and Australia, 1970–1988 (In U.S. Dollars)

	SYDNEY		MELBOURNE		AUSTRALIA	
Year	Mean Dwelling Price (House & land)	Index Dwelling Price	Mean Dwelling Price (House & land)	Index Dwelling Price	Index Consumer Prices	Index Average Earnings
1970	12,182	100.0	10,113	100.0	100.0	100.0
1971	13,752	112.9	10,620	105.0	105.0	111.1
1972	15,552	127.6	11,860	117.2	112.5	122.4
1973	17,200	141.4	15,341	151.6	127.3	133.4
1974	20,448	168.0	19,926	197.0	148.5	155.0
1975	23,328	191.0	22,709	224.6	167.5	194.4
1976	25,056	205.9	26,942	266.4	191.5	222.2
1977	26,856	220.7	29,772	293.9	210.6	250.0
1978	27,864	228.9	30,469	301.3	227.0	275.0
1979	33,120	271.9	31,016	306.7	249.8	296.0
1980	41,832	343.7	34,040	336.6	273.3	310.0
1981	54,144	444.9	38,751	383.2	301.5	324.2
1982	55,332	454.7	39,803	393.6	335.2	373.8
1983	57,816	475.1	44,091	435.9	373.8	395.5
1984	56,160	460.9	54,299	536.9	399.6	439.4
1985	59,932	491.8	66,319	655.8	416.6	471.4
1986	62,280	511.1	71,640	708.4	451.5	504.9
1987	68,500*	567.2	82,000	811.8	493.8	537.7
1988	124,500*	1029.4	108,000*	1076.4	530.3	571.0

Sources: Sydney–BIS–Shrapnel: *Real Estate Prices 12 months moving medians*; Melbourne: Valuer Generals' Department, *Property Sales Statistics*, 1970–1984; CPI and average weekly earnings: *Monthly Summary of Statistics, Australia,* (Canberra: Australian Bureau of Statistics, various years).

Note: Different methodologies in the construction of Sydney and Melbourne price data limit direct comparisons. U.S. values calculated at AUS $1 = U.S. $0.72.

and Sydney relative to the increase in consumer prices and average incomes.) Dwelling prices in Australia's two largest capital cities, Sydney and Melbourne, have tended to increase more rapidly than the consumer price index (CPI) and average weekly earnings (AWE) throughout much of this period.

The timing of house-price inflation has differed between Sydney and Melbourne. Comparatively little study has been undertaken to explain these cyclical patterns and regional differences, although research by Maurie Daly (1982) provides some indication of the role of foreign capital inflow as a trigger for bursts of inflation in property prices in selected Australian capitals. Furthermore, during a property boom in the mid–1970s, a National Committee of Inquiry identified a range of local bottlenecks that contributed to the general inflation of house prices such as the limited supply of land in some areas and the costs of servicing new residential areas (Report of Committee of Inquiry 1978).

Such increases in house prices, particularly those in 1988, have raised the question of housing affordability for the "average family." In previous decades, many studies of affordability used average earnings for a single-income earner as the measure of income against which house prices were compared (Report of Committee of Inquiry 1978). Against this benchmark, the possibility of home ownership for the single-earner family looks bleak. In contrast to 1972 when, on average, it took a single-income family 4.7 years to save for a deposit on a home, figures for 1983 show that the average savings period has lengthened dramatically to just slightly fewer than 15 years. For a dual-income family, the 1972 average savings period was 2.4 years; by 1983 this had more than doubled to 5.3 years, still three times less than the savings period required for a one-income family (Burke et al. 1985). Two incomes have become increasingly essential to achieving home ownership, and most first-time home-buying households are now dual-income households. Mortgages may now be negotiated on the basis of a two-income family, a possibility precluded in the early 1970s, when the income of the "head" was sole determinant (Wulff 1982). During the years between 1964 and 1985, the labor-force participation rate of females aged twenty to forty-four (the first home-buying age cohort) increased from 32.9 percent to 62.5 percent (Australian Bureau of Statistics 1965, 1986). House prices have come to internalize this second income and the borrowing capacity that this income can command. Terry Burke (1987b) argued that house prices as a ratio of household rather than individual income have varied little over time. Whether trends in house prices indicate a crisis in housing provision is debatable, although households on single incomes certainly face extreme difficulties in achieving home ownership.

As Kendig and Paris (1987) pointed out, the commonly used measures of affordability (house price in relation to income or consumer price index) exclude the crucial factor of interest rates. General inflationary forces since the midseventies combined with the effects of financial deregulation in the 1980s have increased real interest rates dramatically. As a result, by 1988 the average repayment burden for first-time home buyers nationally was 34.7 percent earnings, considerably higher than the 25 percent conventionally considered by Australians as acceptable (Housing Industry Association and Commonwealth Bank of Australia, 1988).

The debate on affordability in the private rental sector has been restricted by the inadequate data that are publicly available. The only official source of information is the rent component of the consumer price index, and this exists in the form of an index rather than actual rent. A recent source is that of median rent of properties advertised for rent in capital city newspapers. Published by the Master Builders Construction and Housing Association (1988) there are unfortunately no historical data for this series. Analysis of classified rent data for Melbourne reveals that private sector rents have not recorded the same degree of increase since 1975 as have house prices; in fact, rents have risen broadly in line with the general price levels and considerably less than average earnings (Burke 1987d). (Table 24.7 shows the rental component of the consumer price index and average weekly earnings for selected years.)

Although rents nationally and in Melbourne have not increased relative to average income, the dilemma confronting the private rental sector is that increasing numbers of those demanding private rental accommodations are forced to live on considerably less than average incomes, for example, families with one-earner, youth, and aged households. Although these rents are relatively less than they were a decade ago, even these levels represent severe economic hardship for such groups.

THE ROLE OF HOUSING INSTITUTIONS AND ORGANIZATIONS: THE SYSTEM OF PROVISION

Planning

In Australia, planning for residential development has largely been facilitative, that is, broadly accommodative to market forces. In the immediate postwar years, particularly with respect to Sydney, the largest city in Australia, the metropolitan plans promised considerable intervention, including designation of greenbelts. But these plans, based on low-growth assumptions, collapsed under the pressures of rapid population growth. Subsequent plans have tended to follow market forces by allocating large areas of fringe land to urban development, almost all, with the exception of the national capital, Canberra, owned by private sector interests. Rarely has planning involved actual state acquisition of land: as a result, the profits or surplus generated by rezoning rural to residential land was appropriated by developers and speculators, not by the state. Moreover, the ability to control land-price inflation through selective release of state land was lost. In the early 1970s the federal Labor government initiated state land councils, but with few exceptions (e.g., South Australia), these acquisitions represented a very small proportion of urban land. Metropolitan planning, a state function

Table 24.7
Rents and Rent Index, Australia and Melbourne, 1971–1988

Year	Consumer Prices Rental Component (Aus)	Comsumer Prices all Commodities	Index Average Earnings	Median Rent (Advertised Properties Melbourne)			
				House $	Index	Flats $	Index
1971	100	100	100	31	100	25	100
1976	175	178	195	55	177	40	160
1981	238	273	326	85	274	65	260
1985	373	378	474	120	387	85	340
1986	403	407	498	130	419	90	360
1987	439	445	530	140	451	95	380
1988	478	478	563	160	515	110	440

Sources: CPI rent component: Australian Bureau of Statistics, unpublished data; median rents, Melbourne: Burke et al. 1987; CPI all commodities and AWE: Australian Bureau of Statistics.

in Australia, has therefore generally facilitated a low-density pattern of suburban development by designating areas on the metropolitan fringe suitable for residential development. Urban consolidation strategies are now in place in the larger Australian cities, encouraging higher density residential development, dual occupancy, and infill; but most of the new household growth continues to be accommodated at the periphery.

Whereas state-government-devised metropolitan planning schemes designate the broad areas for residential development within cities, the various local government bodies within the cities possess the power to grant planning permits for dwellings. Most local governments have chosen to exercise these powers in the form of controls over multiunit and medium-density housing. Many of these controls emerged in the wake of objections by local residents to the apartment-development boom of the sixties. For example, in metropolitan Melbourne, the average number of stories for multiunit housing is two, and only the inner-urban municipalities (comprising eight out of the fifty-six local governments within the Melbourne metropolitan area) will approve more than two stories (Indicative Planning Council 1980), Moreover, although local governments in the state capital cities generally have not excluded multiunit housing completely, they have effectively limited the number that can be constructed to relatively small percentages: for example, in Perth, only 17 percent of land zoned as residential is set aside for medium-density development (Australian Institute of Urban Studies 1983). When other requirements for medium-density development are met such as car spaces, boundary setbacks, minimum open-space and height limits, the proportion of multiunit dwellings that can be built is probably even less.

Housing-preference studies indicate that around 90 percent of Australians want to live in single-family houses rather than multidwelling units (Maddocks 1978), and local government planning controls clearly reinforce this emphasis. But with the increasing price of detached houses on traditional-sized allotments and the predilection of state planning authorities toward higher residential densities, the time has arrived for the development of more innovatively designed "compact" housing, representing a compromise between expressed preferences for a detached form of housing and the reality that costs are inhibiting access to "traditional" detached living for a significant segment of the population. Local government regulations pertaining to minimum lot size limit the diffusion of this housing form widely throughout Australia's metropolitan areas. As a consequence, flexibility of housing provision and consumer choice has been reduced (Paterson, Yenken, and Gunn 1976). In the 1980s a number of state governments attempted to overcome the problem by introducing planning regulations that override local government interests. For example, "dual-occupancy" provisions that give owners the right to put a second dwelling on a site as long as it meets certain health and amenity standards are available in many local government areas. These provisions are by no means universal across Australia and represent only incremental changes to the restrictive planning system.

House Building

The Australian house-construction industry is highly fragmented with slightly fewer than 20,000 private firms involved in house construction in both the public and private sectors. The average number of employees on a regular payroll with house building firms in 1984–1985 was three persons, including working proprietors. In 1984–1985 the average number of dwellings constructed per firm per annum was eight with 85 percent of firms producing less than nine (Australian Bureau of Statistics 1987). The dominance of the industry by very small producers, most of whom have limited capital, architectural, and management resources, creates an industry predisposed toward conservatism of design and form. Nonetheless, comparative studies indicate that Australian house builders, using largely conventional techniques, can reach levels of productivity equal to, or better than, most other countries. The high level of performance already achieved by conventional building techniques in Australia suggests why it has been difficult for industrialized systems such as prefabrication to penetrate here as they have overseas (Blakey 1977).

Until the early 1970s, speculative house building, whereby a builder purchases land, constructs one or many dwellings, and then markets the development, dominated the residential building field. In the long wave of prosperity between 1950 and the early 1970s this scheme produced excellent returns and ensured the attraction and survival of speculative house building. But in the economic recession of 1974 with rising inflation and finance costs, the sensitivity of speculative house building to economic cycles was exposed, and many speculative builders collapsed.

In the most recent decade, project building has emerged as a major form of new residential development. In this building and development form, it is the householder who first acquires a site, arranges the finance, and only then approaches a builder to build a project home, chosen from one "on show" at one of a number of sites or display villages around a city. Much of the financial risk is removed from the house builder, enabling many builders to survive the cyclical downturns of the housing sector.

Housing Design

The detached house, still the dominant dwelling form in terms of overall housing output, has undergone changes in internal and external layout, reflecting not only rising affluence and technological changes in the postwar period but also shifts in family values and life-styles. A drive through a 1940s Australian suburb, followed by one through a mid–1980s area, visibly reveals some major changes in design and construction. In the 1980s, and indeed in most of the postwar era, the typical new dwelling is of solid brick or brick-veneer construction, the latter referring to brick built around a timber frame. This compares with a substantial proportion of timber construction in the prewar era. The contemporary brick dwelling is also much larger than its counterpart three decades ago. A drive through the suburbs—in effect, a drive through time—indicates other changes as well. Because blocks (dwelling sites) were larger in the 1950s and 1960s, dwellings were laid out across the block producing a large front garden and orienting key rooms such as lounge and parents' bedroom to the front of the house (see figure 24.3). Exterior and interior designs were remarkably uniform, producing a monotony of appearance that has prompted considerable criticism of postwar suburban Australia (Boyd 1963). Not visible in a drive through suburbia in the 1940s is the internal layout, characterized by a kitchen with minimal bench space (located at the rear of the house), a combined lounge-dining room spatially cut off from the kitchen, three bedrooms (all lacking built-in cupboard space), and a long hall serving to separate the living room from sleeping areas.

The 1980s dwelling not only occupies a smaller block but also tends to be sited forward on the block, thus deemphasizing the front garden as a focus for the orientation of key rooms. The pride of the new owners is less likely to be a green-lawned front garden than a courtyard or patio at the side or rear of the house opening off the family room. The family room is a recent addition to the Australian home and evolved to accommodate a more casual life-style centered around the television, stereo, and home entertainment. The kitchen, instead of being tucked away at the rear, is now the center of activity in the house, opening to both a formal dining room and family room. Bedrooms are no longer grouped together but are spread along the house with the parents' room at one end (termed the ''parent's retreat'') and childrens' rooms at the other, allowing greater privacy for both. Considerable cupboard space is now built into the house, thereby requiring less free-standing furniture. Two bathrooms per house, one attached to the parent's bedroom, is an increasingly common design characteristic.

There have been several catalysts for the change in design. An increase in the real income of the typical new home buyer has enabled a larger home with additional rooms and amenities. Shifts in family values including a progressive breaking down of gender stereotypes has brought the female out of the smallish kitchen at the rear of the house into a more centrally located kitchen, where cooking and food preparation are now likely to be shared with other family members. A trend toward individualism at the family level is apparent in the separate housing spheres that are now designed for children and adults. Technological developments as well have affected the internal layout of the home: the popularity of television, stereo, and home computers has dictated an adaptation of design to accommodate the conflicting demands of these products. The standard new home now commonly features a family room in addition to the traditional lounge room. Reflecting the cosmopolitan effects of international migration, Australian life-styles are becoming home entertainment and dining

Figure 24.3
Typical Design of an Australian Family Home, 1948, 1980–1985

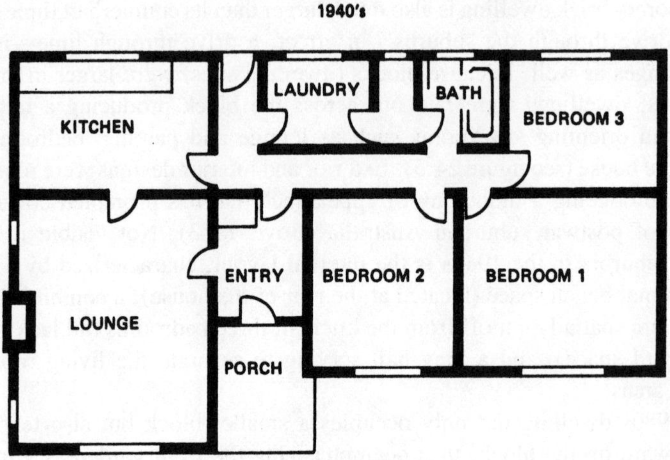

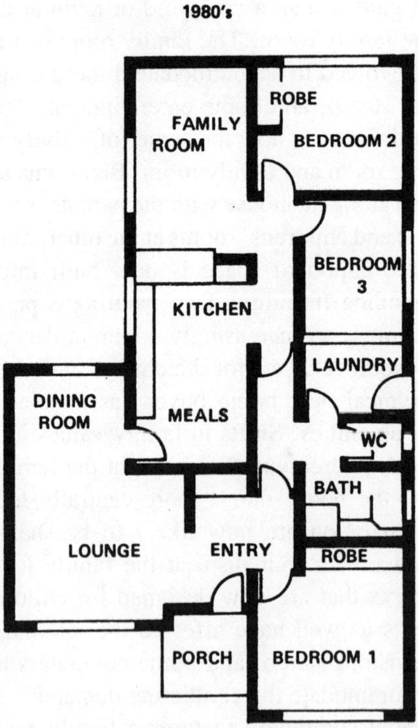

1940's

1980's

Source: Highett Commonwealth Scientific and Industrial Research Organization, Building Research Division.

conscious, and the new consumer requires a home that is consistent with the demands of both formal and informal entertaining.

Although the detached dwelling is still the dominant new housing form, some of the larger building firms and a few State Housing Commissions have produced, since the early 1980s, new types of dwellings targeted at singles, childless families, and sole-parent households. Facilitated in some states by necessary changes in building regulations, such as dual-occupancy provisions, these designs include the duplex, or villa, unit, whereby two small dwellings can be combined on an existing block by sharing a common wall or an intervening garage, and the "mingle," for singles who are sharing an accommodation that has communal living areas but self-contained bed, bath, toilet, and storage areas.

Finance

The Australian housing-finance system for much of the postwar era can be described as a state-regulated, private market deposit financing system; that is, one where the majority of dwellings purchased or constructed have been financed through a variety of deposit-raising institutions, in particular, banks and building societies (Boleat 1985). Until recently, the form and level of housing finance have been strongly regulated by the federal government.

Private banks and building societies, the latter similar to savings and loan associations in the United States, have been the dominant sources of housing finance since the midnineteenth century, although the proportions accounted for by each have fluctuated over the decades (Hill 1959). Other sources of finance in the postwar era included life offices and the Commonwealth government through its war-service loan schemes (loans for veterans). The latter has waned as the number of war veterans seeking application has declined. The decline in life offices, on the other hand, largely reflects a switch in their investment portfolio as the returns on housing became less attractive relative to alternative investment sectors.

The two major forms of postwar regulation of the Australian financial system, particularly with respect to banks and building societies, were interest-rate control and restrictions on the use of asset holding, which ensured that housing would have an adequate share of the depositors' funds. Throughout the 1950s and 1960s this system adequately served not only the needs of the housing sector but also the entire economy. In the 1970s, however, the changing structure of the Australian economy and its relationship to the world economy created a growing tension between the finance requirements of housing and those of other sectors of the economy. The increasingly competitive investment and trading climate required a finance system unfettered by state regulations. Such regulations, it was argued, prevented financial institutions from making the most efficient use of their funds and also inhibited the overall growth of the pool of funds by constraining the ability of financial institutions to use competitive finance instruments (e.g., market rates of interest) to attract funds (*Australian Financial*

Table 24.8
Savings Bank Home-Loan Interest Rates, Australia, 1970–1987

Date	Nominal Interest Rate	Real Interest Rate
30/12/1970	6.9	3.6
1971	7.1	2.0
1972	7.0	-0.9
1973	8.2	0.7
1974	10.4	-3.4
1975	10.3	-7.2
1976	10.3	-3.0
1977	10.3	-3.4
1978	9.4	-0.4
1979	9.4	1.8
1980	11.5	1.6
1981	12.5	3.7
1982	13.5	4.0
1983	11.7	3.2
1984	11.5	7.0
1985	13.5	9.2
1986	15.0	5.2
1987	14.0	5.0

Sources: Nominal Rates Indices: Index, 1987; real rates calculated from consumer price index figures in *Monthly Summary of Statistics* (Canberra: Australian Government Publishing Service, various years).

System Inquiry 1981). Further fuel for deregulation came from those who argued that these regulations artificially subsidized home ownership and created an investment in housing at the expense of other sectors of the economy (*Australian Financial System Inquiry* 1981). That such regulation did subsidize home purchase is indicated in the trend in nominal and real home-loan interest rates (see table 24.8). Real home-loan interest rates in the period before deregulation in 1984 were low and for a number of years in the 1970s were negative.

Following two major inquiries into the financial system (*Australian Financial System Inquiry* 1981, 1984), it was recommended that many of the regulations within the Australian financial system be dismantled. It fell to the new Labor government to implement these recommendations: that is, control on asset holdings was removed in 1984, and the ceiling on housing interest rates was removed in April 1986, although only for new borrowers.

It is difficult to disentangle the effects of financial deregulation on housing consumption and provisions from the effects of other processes affecting the housing market. This problem in itself captures one of the key criticisms of the two inquiries into financial deregulation: a failure to comprehend or analyze the complex and contradictory interlinkages with other components of the economy, including the tax system (Sheehan 1983), As it turned out, financial deregulation was implemented simultaneously with the floating of the Australian exchange rate and major reforms of the Australian tax system, including a number of reforms associated with housing. The latter included a capital gains tax on property transactions (excluding the first home) and the abolition of certain tax benefits for private landlords, one of which, negative gearing, was reinstated two years after being withdrawn in response to effective lobbying by real estate interests. Although it is difficult to disentangle the separate effects of the above changes, the cumulative effect, at least in the period until mid–1987, has arguably been an unhappy one for the Australian housing industry and many housing consumers. Real mortgage interest rates increased, and in June 1989 the real interest rate of 10 percent for new borrowers was markedly higher than experienced during the period 1970 to 1983.

Agents of Exchange: The Real Estate Industry

Often neglected in the analysis of national housing systems is the process of exchange. In Australia, estate agents, the key agents of housing exchange, play a more dominant role than in many other societies. For example, in Melbourne, some 89 percent of households owning or buying houses found their accommodations through an estate agent (Age Market Research 1987). A number of overseas and Australian studies have examined the role of estate agents and have found they have considerable ability to shape housing opportunities for different groups or to mold property values in particular areas (Williams 1976; Palm 1979; Hancock and Burke 1983).

Although the private sale overall is still dominant, auctions have emerged in the past decade as a major form of house sale with an associated contraction in the private sale, the method used in most other countries. Initially emerging in Melbourne, where it now accounts for 25 percent of all residential sales, the auction is now spreading rapidly to other capital cities (Burke 1987a). The process of sale by auction, that is, the public sale of a property to the highest bidder on a nominated day and time, has been the focus for growing criticism: possible abuse through dummy bidders, prices pushed artificially higher than otherwise would be the case, and higher advertising costs than for private sales. Furthermore, auctions deny the purchaser certain rights compared to the private sale situation (specifically, a three-day cooling-off period) and reduce the housing choices for lower-income purchasers. The latter occurs because auctions require finance to be approved before purchase, and finance institutions are reluctant to provide open-ended approval to lower-income earners without first knowing the price and inspecting the dwelling. Finally, by eliminating house-price information before the housing search, auctions considerably weaken the sovereignty of purchasers (Maher 1986; Burke 1987a). Although the evidence concerning these problems is mounting, governments have yet to respond in policy terms.

PROBLEMS AND PROSPECTIVE DEVELOPMENTS

The experience of the Australian housing market in the postwar era, and in particular during the 1970s and 1980s, parallels the experience of the wider Australian economy. Although the majority of Australians have enjoyed a substantial improvement in housing conditions, particularly the most affluent, a growing minority of households have experienced a deterioration in their housing conditions and opportunities. In short, the widening inequalities of Australian society as evidenced by recent wealth-distribution statistics (Raskell 1987) are being paralleled and reinforced by the inequalities of housing provision. The expectations engendered in the early decades of the postwar era of an affordable home of one's own for every household have not been fulfilled. This chapter has outlined the many factors that have brought this situation about, notable rapid family and demographic change, economic and financial restructuring, and a housing system slow to adapt to this changing environment. The following interrelated problems mirror these factors.

Housing Affordability for Special Population Groups

Although private rents relative to average earnings are generally less than they were a decade ago, the rents remain too high for the growing numbers on low income, notably those on government benefits. Growing numbers of single parents, largely females; unemployed youth; single persons; aboriginal families; and the low-income aged are finding it increasingly difficult to acquire secure and affordable private rental accommodations with the result that the waiting list for public housing has risen substantially in the past half-decade.

Owner occupancy is also increasingly less affordable for many households, with the property boom of 1988 greatly accentuating this problem. As dwelling prices, at least in the major cities, have built or "capitalized" into them the additional lending capacities of the second income of a dual income household, single-earner households face major constraints in achieving home ownership. Because many of this group will now remain in the private rental sector, the supply of rental accommodations for even lower income carners will be further restricted. Although existing owner–occupiers experience capital appreciation, security of tenure, declining housing costs, and direct and indirect state subsidies, households in other tenure sectors, notably low-income households in the private rental sector, enjoy no such advantages. The gap between renters and owner-occupiers has widened considerably in recent years. These inequalities resulting from differences in affordability are related less to traditional issues of social class than to different households at varying stages of the family life cycle.

An Emergent Problem of Housing Quality

By the 1990s, a sizable proportion of the nation's housing stock will be more than fifty years old with a significant component constructed in timber. Moreover, some of the inexpensively constructed dwellings of the postwar era, including sizable numbers of both public and private apartments, will also be nearing the end of their life in the absence of substantial maintenance expenditures or renewal. Increasingly, larger amounts of public and private capital will need to be expended on maintenance and repair of existing stock, rather than adding much needed new stock.

A Mismatch between Housing Needs and the Actual Stock

The homogeneity of stock both in terms of tenure and type severely constrains the housing choices of population groups on lower incomes, for whom large owner-occupied housing is not financially feasible, or for groups who require smaller, more-maintenance-free dwellings, such as the aged. In addition, there is a need for special accommodations for those individuals and households who need some element of community support linked to their housing, that is, the disabled, deinstitutionalized persons, or the frail aged living on their own. Special accommodations meeting the cultural needs of the ethnic aged will be increasingly required. Perhaps the most important dimension of the mismatch between need and existing housing stock is evidenced in the public housing sector, where lengthy waiting lists are out of proportion to existing stock or current rates of construction, despite the expansion of the public housing sector since 1982.

These problems have prompted a number of policy responses. The major initiatives in policy in the past decade have come mainly from states with Labor governments, facilitated by appropriate federal government policy changes incorporated into the Commonwealth State Housing Agreements. The housing-policy initiatives include the encouragement of rental housing cooperatives (Burke et al. 1984); changes to the first-time home-buyer subsidy program to target them more effectively (Flood and Yates 1987); experiments with new ways of funding low-income home ownership, such as loans with payments indexed to the rate of inflation, but never exceeding 25 percent of the purchasers' household income (Carter 1987); the spot purchase of existing dwellings for public housing; joint ventures between the public and private sector in small-scale estate provisions; and the "affordable housing" program, a pilot program of the federal government to illustrate how changes in estate design and infrastructure production, accompanied by appropriate planning amendments, can reduce the costs of a dwelling (Burke 1987c). Few of these policy responses are likely to be anything more than incremental and marginal to the lives of well-housed Australians. As discussed in this chapter, the major policy changes affecting housing in the past decade have been nonhousing changes, such as economic deregulation.

Although there is a growing perception of a housing crisis among a number of advanced capitalist countries (Malpass 1986; Hartman 1983), it would be inappropriate to characterize the Australian housing system as such. Most households are extremely well housed whether assessed in terms of measures of housing size, quality, or affordability. But therein lies the dilemma for those who are not. As this chapter has shown, broad demographic and economic processes have increasingly denied a minority of families and individuals adequate housing. For these households, their experience of the housing system is one of crisis. Until the institutions of housing provision in both the public and private sector recognize and respond to this problem, major change is unlikely to occur.

REFERENCES

Age Market Research. 1987. *The Melbourne Home Buyers Survey, 1987*. Melbourne: David Syme & Co.

Allport, Carolyn. 1986. "Women and Suburban Housing: Post War Planning in Sydney, 1943–61." In *Urban Planning in Australia: Critical Readings*, edited by J. McLaughlin and M. Huxley, 233–50. Melbourne: Longman Cheshire.

Archer, Ray. 1980. "The Market for Multi-unit Housing in Sydney and Melbourne." In *Housing Economics*, 172–87. Canberra: Australian Government Publishing Service.

Australian Bureau of Statistics. 1987. *Census of Building and Construction Industry: Australia*. Canberra: Australian Government Publishing Service.

Australian Bureau of Statistics. 1984a. *Family Survey*. Canberra: Australian Government Publishing Service.

————. 1984b. *Household Expenditure Survey*. Canberra: Australian Government Publishing Service.

————. 1965, 1986. *The Labor Force*. Canberra: Australian Government Publishing Service.

————. 1984c. *Social Indicators*. Canberra: Australian Government Publishing Service.

Australian Financial System Inquiry. 1981. "The Campbell Report." Canberra: Australian Government Publishing Service.

————. 1984. "Martin Review." Report of the Reviewing Group. Canberra: Australian Government Publishing Service.

Australian Institute of Urban Studies. 1983. *Housing Policy in the Perth Region: Density and Form*. Project 65. Canberra.

Beed, Terry, Robert Stimson, Chris Paris, and Hugo Graeme. 1987. *Housing Tenure Costs and Policies in Australia*. Project 161. Canberra: Australian Housing Research Council.

Berry, Michael. 1983. "Posing the Housing Question in Australia." In *Urban Political Economy*, edited by L. Sandercock and M. Berry, 91–115. Sydney: Allen & Unwin.

Berry, Mike, 1988. "To Buy or Rent? The Demise of a Dual Tenure Housing Policy in Australia." In *New Houses for Old* edited by R. Howe, 95–122. Melbourne: Victorian Ministry of Housing.

Bethune, Graeme, and Max Neutze. 1987. "Costs of Owner Occupied and Rented Housing." *Housing Studies* 2, no. 4:237–48.

Blakey, F. A. 1977. *An Overview of Australian Housing Construction*. Melbourne: Commonwealth Scientific and Industrial Research Organization, Division of Building.

Boleat, M. 1985. *National Housing Finance Systems: A Comparative Study*. London: Croom Helm.

Boyd, Robin. 1963. *The Australian Ugliness*. Ringwood, Victoria: Penguin.

Braddock, M., and M. Wanganeen. 1980. *Aboriginal Housing Need*. Project no. 90. Canberra: Australian Research Council.

Burke, Terry, David Hayward, and Peter Nisbet. 1985. *Melbourne Housing Indicators*. Melbourne: Estate Agents Board of Victoria.

Burke, Terry. 1987a. "Buying by Auction: Problems and Policy Implications." Paper presented to the Melbourne Urban Studies Group, Royal Melbourne Institute of Technology, Melbourne, April 24.

————. 1987b. "Housing Affordability and the Decline of Home Ownership: Myth or Reality." In *Housing Affordability*, edited by Bruce Judd. Canberra: Royal Australian Institute of Architects.

————. 1987c. "Innovations in Reducing the Cost of Private Housing Provision." Paper prepared for the International Year of Shelter for the Homeless.

————. 1987d. "The Rental Housing Crisis—Myth or Reality." *Shelter: National Housing Action* 3, no. 3:6–10.

Burke, Terry, Linda Hancock, and P. Newton. 1984. *A Roof over Their Heads: Housing and the Family*. Melbourne: Institute of Family Studies.

Carter, Robert, 1987. "Where Will the Money Come From." *Australian Society* (Melbourne), October, 48–53.

Cass, Bettina. 1985. "The Changing Face of Poverty in Australia, 1972–82." *Australian Feminist Studies*, no. 1 (Summer): 67–90.

Committee of Enquiry into Poverty. 1975. *Poverty in Australia*. Canberra: Australian Government Publishing Service.

Coopers and Lybrand and W. D. Scott. *Study into Homelessness and Inadequate Housing*. Canberra: Department of Housing and Construction. 1985.

Core Consultants Pty. Ltd., Terry Burke, and Gim Teh, 1983. *A Review of the Private Rental Housing Market in Victoria and Implication of Tenancy Law Reform*. Melbourne: Ministry of Housing.

Daly, Maurie. 1982. *Sydney Boom, Sydney Bust*. Sydney: Allen & Unwin.

Department of Immigration and Ethnic Affairs. 1985. *Australia's Population Trends and Prospects, 1914*. Canberra: Australian Government Publishing Service.

Flood, Joe, and Judith Yates. 1987. *Housing Subsidies Study*. Project 160. Canberra: Australian Housing Research Council.

Forrest, Ray. 1987. "Privatisation, Marginality, and Council Housing." In *Public Housing: Current Trends and Future Developments*, edited by D. Clapham and J. English, 67–85. London: Croom Helm.

Forrest, Ray, and Alan Murie. 1985. "Restructuring the Welfare State: Privatization of Public Housing in Britain." In *Housing Needs and Policy Approaches: Trends in Thirteen Countries*, edited by W. van Vliet—, E. Huttman, and S. Fava, 97–109. Durham, N.C.: Duke University Press.

Gray, Alan. 1987. "*Need a New House*." Aboriginal Family Demography Study Working Paper no. 4. Canberra: Australian National University.

Hancock, Linda, and Terry Burke. 1983. *Youth Housing Policy*. Canberra: Australian Housing Research Council.

Hartman, C., ed. 1983. *America's Housing Crisis: What Is to Be Done?* Boston: Routledge and Kegan Paul.

Hayward, David. 1986. "The Great Australian Dream Reconsidered: A Review of Kemeny." *Housing Studies* 1, (October): 209–10.

Hill, M. R. 1959. *Housing Finance in Australia, 1945–56*. Melbourne: Melbourne University Press.

Housing Industry Association and Commonwealth Bank of Australia. 1988. *Housing Report*. Canberra.

Howe, A. 1986. "The Retirement Housing Market: Demand, Response, and Responsibilities." In *The Housing and Living Environment for Retired People in Australia*, edited by R. Thorne, 194–212. Sydney, NSW: Hale & Ironmonger.

Howe, Anna, Peter Newton, and Penny Sharwood. 1987. *Ageing in Victoria*. Melbourne: National Research Institute of Gerontology.

Hugo, Graeme. 1986. *Australia's Changing Population*. Melbourne: Oxford University Press.

Indecs. 1987. *State of Play 4*. Sydney: Allen & Unwin.

Indicative Planning Council for the Housing Industry. 1980. *Report on Multiunit Dwelling Development in Australia*. Canberra: Australian Government Publishing Service.

Jansen, J., and W. Temby. 1987. "Changing Access to Home Ownership." *Australian Journal of Regional Studies*, 1:78–102.

Kemeny, Jim. 1978. "Home-Ownership and Privatization in Capitalist Societies: A Cross-Cultural Perspective." In *Paper of International Sociological Association* (ANZ Branch). Brisbane: University of Queensland.

———. 1981. *The Myth of Home Ownership*. London: Routledge and Kegan Paul.

———.1983. *The Great Australian Nightmare*. Melbourne: Georgian House.

———. 1987. "Towards Theorised Housing Studies: A Counter-Critique of the Provision Thesis." *Housing Studies* 2, no. 4 (October): 249–60.

Kendig, Hal. 1982. *The Cumulation of Inequity: Housing in Old Age*. Working paper no. 28, Aging and Family Project. Canberra: Australian National University, Research School of Social Sciences.

———, ed. 1986. *Ageing and Families*. Sydney: Allen & Unwin.

Kendig, Hal, and Chris Paris. 1987. *Towards Fair Shares in Australian Housing*. Canberra: National Committee of Non-Government Organizations International Year of Shelter for the Homeless.

Logan, William. 1985. *The Gentrification in Inner Melbourne: A Political Geography of Inner City Housing*. Brisbane: University of Queensland Press.

Maddocks, Steven. 1978. "Exploring the Housing Attitudes of Future Home Buyers in Four Australian Cities." In *The Cost of Housing*, 59–160. Report of Committee of Inquiry into Housing Costs. Canberra: Australian Government Publishing Service.

Maher, Chris. 1986. "Information and Uncertainty in Urban Property Markets: The Case of Real Estate Auctions." Paper presented at a seminar of the Urban Research Unit, Australian National University, Canberra, September 11.

Malpass, Peter. 1986. *The Housing Crisis*. London: Croom Helm.

McWilliam, J. 1986. "Australian Government Policy: Recent Changes." In *The Housing and Living Environment for Retired People in Australia*, edited by R. Thorne, 134–40. Sydney, NSW: Hale & Ironmonger.

Newton, Peter, and Ron Johnston. 1981. "Melbourne." In *Urban Problems and Planning in the Developed World*, edited by M. Pacioni, 154–81. London: Croom Helm.

Newton, Peter, and Maryann Wulff. 1985. "State Intervention in Urban Housing Markets: Melbourne, 1945–1980." In *Housing Needs and Policy Approaches*, edited by

W. van Vliet—, E. Huttman, and S. Fava, 127–40. Durham, N.C.: Duke University Press.

Nicholson, Judy, and Phillipa Weeks. 1984. "A Survey of Law Governing Private Residential Tenancies in Australia." In *Affordable and Available Housing*, edited by C. Paris, 38–51. Canberra: Australian Institute of Urban Studies.

Palm, R. 1979. "Financial and Real Estate Institutions in the Housing Market: A Study of Recent House Price Changes in the San Francisco Bay Area." In *Geography and the Urban Environment*. Vol. 1, edited by D. Herbert and R. Johnston, 83–124. Chichester: Wiley.

Paris, Chris. 1984. *Affordable and Available Housing*. Canberra: Australian Institute of Urban Studies.

Paris, Chris. 1987a. "Housing under Hawke: Promise and Performance." *Journal of Australian Political Economy*, no. 21 (May):3–24.

———. 1987b. "Housing Issues and Policies in Australia." In *Urban Australia: Planning Issues and Policies*, edited by S. Hamnett and R. Bunker, 79–107. London: Mansell Publishing Limited.

Patterson, John, David Yenken, and Graeme Gunn. 1976. *A Mansion or No Home*. Melbourne: Urban Development Institute of Australia.

Raskell, Peter. 1987. "Whose Got It? Who Needs It?" *Australian Society*, May, 21–24.

Report of Committee of Inquiry. 1978. *The Cost of Housing*. Canberra: Australian Government Publishing Service.

Rossiter, Chris, and Joan Vipond. 1985. "*Housing Tenure—Social Welfare Issues.*" Paper presented at the Fourteenth Conference of Economists, University of New South Wales, Sydney.

Sandercock, Leonie. 1976. *Cities for Sale: Property, Politics, and Urban Planning in Australia*. London: Heinemann.

Sheehan, Peter. 1983. "The Campbell Report: An Overview." In *Economic Papers Special Edition: The Campbell Report*. Melbourne: Economic Society of Australia, April.

Shelter. 1982. *Non-profit Housing. The Only Way Out*. Melbourne.

Stone, John. 1979. Addresses to Australian Institute of Management, Annual Conference, Sydney, September.

Stretton, Hugh. 1987. "Housing Policies, Past and Future." In *Political Essays*, by Hugh Stretton, 109–29. Melbourne: Georgian House.

Thorne, Ros., ed. 1986. *The Housing and Living Environment for Retired People in Australia*. Sydney: Hale & Ironmonger.

Williams, Peter. 1976. "The Role of Institutions in the Inner London Housing Market: The Case of Islington." In *Readings in Urban Analysis*, edited by R. W. Lake (1983), 157–72. New Brunswick: Rutgers University Centre for Urban Policy Research.

Williams, Peter. 1984. "The Politics of Property: Home Ownership in Australia." In *Australian Urban Politics*, edited by J. Halligan and C. Paris 167–92. Melbourne: Longman Cheshire.

Wulff, Maryann. 1982. "The Two-Income Household: Relative Contribution of Earners to Housing Costs." *Urban Studies* 19 (October): 343–50.

Young, Christobel. 1987. "Young People Leaving Home in Australia." Australian Family Project Monograph no. 9. Canberra: Australian National University.

FURTHER READING

Australian Bureau of Statistics. *Directory of Housing Related Statistics*. ABS catalogue no. 1118.0. Australian Bureau of Statistics, 1988.

Badcock, Blair, and D. Cloher. 1979. "An Approach to the Formulation and Implementation of Marginal Housing Policy: The Low-Rent Boarding and Lodging Sector, City of Adelaide." In *Processes Influencing Low Income Housing*, edited by P. W. Newton. Melbourne: Australian Housing Research Council.

Beed, T. W., R. J. Stinson, C. T. Paris, and G. J. Hugo. *Stability and Change in Australian Housing. Final Report*. Project no. 161. Canberra: Australian Housing Research Council, 1988.

Bradbury, Bruce, Chris Rossiter, and Joan Vipond. "Housing and Poverty in Australia." *Urban Studies* 24 nos. 95–102 (1987).

———. *Poverty Before and After Paying Housing Costs*. SWRC report no. 56. Sydney: Social Welfare Research Center, 1988.

Burke, Terry. "The Private Rental Sector: Problems, Prospects, and Policy." *Urban Policy and Planning* 1, no. 4 (December 1983): 2–10.

Butler, G. J., J. Flood, and S. N. Tucker. "Determinants of Housing Expenditure in Australia." *Environment and Planning A* 16 (1984):1099–1113.

Donnison, David. "The Politics of Housing." *Australian Quarterly*, June 1976, 18–31.

Hargreaves, Kaye. *This House Is Not for Sale*. Melbourne: Centre for Urban Research and Action, 1975.

Hugo, Graeme. "Some Demographic Factors Influencing Recent and Future Demand for Housing in Australia." *Australian Quarterly* 51, no. 4 (1979): 4–25.

Indicative Planning Council for the Housing Industry. *Resources Report 1988*. Canberra: Australian Government Publishing Service, 1988.

Kilmartin, Leslie, and David Thorns. *Cities Unlimited*. Sydney: Allen & Unwin, 1978.

King, Ross. "Monopoly Rent, Residential Differentiation and the Second Global Crisis of Capitalism—the Case of Melbourne." *Progress in Planning* 28 (1987): 195–298.

Manning, Ian, and Anthony King. *Income and Housing Costs for Older Australians*. Woden: Department of Social Security, 1988.

Manning, Ian, Anthony King, and Judy Yates. *Housing Futures*. Melbourne: National Institute of Economic and Industry Research, 1988.

Paris, Chris. "Private Rental Housing in Australia." *Environment and Planning A* 16(1984): 1079–98.

Paris, Chris, Peter Williams, and Bob Stimson. "From Public Housing to Welfare Housing." *Australian Journal of Social Issues* 20, no. 2 (1985): 105–17.

Perlgut, D. "The Hidden Housing Policy: Management of Public Housing Estates in Australia." *Australian Journal of Social Issues* 21, no. 3 (1986): 163–71.

Thorns, D. C. "New Solutions to Old Problems: Housing Affordability and Access within Australia and New Zealand." *Environment and Planning* 20, no. 1 (1988): 71–82.

Tucker, S. N. "An Analysis of Housing Subsidy Schemes in Australia." *Urban Studies* 20 (1983): 439–53.

Watson, Sophie, and Lisa Coleman. "Housing, Demographic Change and the Private Rental Sector." *Australian Journal of Social Issues* 21, no. 1 (1986): 16–27.

Appendix A

Journals That Publish Housing Research

Housing studies are undertaken by researchers from many disciplines in many parts of the world. Hence research findings are scattered in a great number of outlets worldwide. The following list is restricted to journals that publish in English and frequently contain articles on housing. Periodicals oriented to the more technical and professional aspects of the design and management of housing have generally been excluded.

Architectural Psychology

Architecture and Behavior/Architecture et Comportement

Architecture and Planning

Australian Planner

Built Environment

Canadian Housing/Habitation Canadienne

Canadian Planner

Cities

Comparative Urban Research

Ekistics

Environmental Psychology

Environment and Behavior

Environment and Planning, Government and Policy

Environment and Planning, Planning and Design

Environment and Planning, Society and Space

Environments

Habitat International

Habitat News

Housing

Housing and Development Reporter

Housing and Society

Housing Finance Review

Housing Studies

International Journal of Urban and Regional Research

Journal of the American Real Estate and Urban Economics Association

Journal of Architectural Education

Journal of Architectural and Planning Research

Journal of Housing

Journal of Housing for the Elderly

Journal of Planning Education and Research

Journal of Planning Literature

Journal of the American Planning Association

Journal of Urban Affairs

Journal of Urban History

Netherlands Journal of Housing and Environmental Research

Open House International

Planning Magazine

Population and Environment

Progressive Architecture

Real Estate Law Journal

Real Estate Review

Roof

Sage Urban Studies Abstracts

Scandinavian Housing and Planning Research

Tijdschrift voor Economische en Sociale Geografie (TESG)

Town Planning Review

Urban Affairs Quarterly

Urban Geography

Urban History Review

Urban Studies

Women and Environments

A very extensive listing of periodical, abstracting bibliographic, and statistical sources on housing can be found in *Ulrich's International Periodical Directory*, 28th ed., 1989– 90, New York: R. R. Bowker.

Appendix B

Organizations and Information Resource Addresses

The following list is limited to organizations, institutes, and agencies in the countries covered in this book and several that are international in orientation.

INTERNATIONAL

Afro-Asian Housing Organization (AAHO)
30 Twenty Six of July Street
Cairo
Egypt

Economic Commission for Europe
Economic and Social Council
Committee on Housing, Building and Planning
Geneva
Switzerland

Environmental Design Research Association (EDRA)
4977 Battery Lane, #413
Bethesda, MD 20814
USA

European Network for Housing Research
POB 785
S–801 29 Gävle
Sweden

Habitat for Humanity International (HFHI)
Habitat and Church Streets
Americus, GA 31709
USA
Telephone: (912) 924–6935

Institute for Housing Studies
P.O. Box 20718/Weena 718
3001 JA Rotterdam/3014 DA Rotterdam
The Netherlands

International Association for Housing Science (IAHS)
P.O. Box 340254
Coral Gables, FL 33134
USA
Telephone: (305) 448–3532

International Association for the Study of People and Their Physical Surroundings
c/o Architectural Psychology Research Unit
Kingston Polytechnic
Knights Park
Lingston-Upon-Thames
Surrey KT1 2QJ
England

International Association for Metropolitan Research and Development
130 Bloor Street West, Suite 1200
Toronto, Ontario
Canada M5S 1N5

International Association of College and University Housing Officers (ACUHO-I)
c/o Rhea Dawn Smith
Central Support Services Office
101 Curl Drive, Suite 140
Columbus, OH 43210
USA
Telephone: (614) 292–0099

International Cooperative Housing Committee of the International Cooperative Alliance
S–116 81 Stockholm
Sweden

International Federation for Housing and Planning (IFHP)
Wassenaarseweg 43
HL–2596 CG The Hague
The Netherlands

International Organization for Housing Finance Institutions (IOHFI)
3 Savile Row
London W1X 1AF
England
Telephone: 1 4370655

International Union of Tenants (IUT)
Postfack 7514
S–103 92 Stockholm
Sweden

Latin American and Asian Low Income Housing Service (SELAVIP)
German Yungue, Numero 3825
Casilla 871
Santiago
Chile

Organization of Cooperative and Non-Profit-Making Housing Enterprises in the Nordic
Countries (NBO)
Fleminggatan 41
Postfack 8310
S–104 20 Stockholm
Sweden

Settlements Information Network Africa
Mazingira Institute
P.O. Box 14550
Nairobi
Kenya

United Nations Center for Human Settlements (HABITAT)

Africa

P.O. Box 30030
Nairobi
Kenya

Asia and the Pacific

Room No. 1004, Block-A (10th floor)
c/o United Nations Building
Rajadamnern Avenue
Bankok 10–200
Thailand

Eastern Europe

Depository Film Library
H–1400 Budapest, PF 83
Hungary

Latin America and the Caribbean

c/o CEPAL—Naciones Unidas
Apartado postal 6–718
Mexico City
Mexico

North America

Information Office for North America
c/o Faculty of Environmental Studies
York University
4700 Keele Street
North York, Ontario M3J 1P3
Canada

Western Asia and All Arabic-Speaking Countries

Regional Information Office for Arab States
P.O. Box 35286
Arman
Jordan

Western Europe

Palais des Nations, Room E–3.1
1211 Geneva 10
Switzerland

United States International Development Cooperation Agency
Agency for International Development
Washington, DC 20523
USA

USAID/RHUDO
P.O. Box 30261
Nairobi
Kenya

Working Group on Housing and the Built Environment
International Sociological Association (ISA)
Secretariat: Willem Van Vliet—
College of Environmental Design/Institute of Behavioral Science
Campus Box 314
University of Colorado
Boulder, CO 80309–0314
USA

World Bank
International Bank for Reconstruction and Development
International Development Association
Washington, DC 20433
USA

AUSTRALIA

Government Agencies

Australian Bureau of Statistics, Canberra
Cameron Offices
Chandler Street
Belconnen Act 2617

Australian Housing Research Council
P.O. Box 111
Dickson Act 2602

Indicative Planning Council for the Housing Industry
Department of Industry, Technology and Commerce
GPO Box 9839
Canberra Act 2608

Private and Community Section

Housing Industry Association
79 Constitution Avenue
Canberra Act 2608

Shelter Australia
P.O. Box 138
Civic Square
Canberra Act 2608

Research Institutes

Centre for Urban and Social Research
Swinburne Institute of Technology
John Street
Hawthorn Vic 3122

Institute of Local Government Studies
Canberra College of Advanced Education
Kirinari Street
Bruce Act 2617

Urban Research Unit
Australian National University
Acton Act 2601

State Housing Authorities

Department of Housing
302 Castlereagh Street
Sydney 2000

Department of Housing and Construction
30 Wakefield Street
Adelaide 5000

Homewest
99 Plain Street
East Perth 6000

South Australian Housing Trust
Kintore Avenue
Adelaide 5000

Victorian Ministry of Housing and Construction
Myer House
250 Elizabeth Street
Melbourne 3000

BRAZIL

Associação Brasileira de Estudos Populacionais (ABEP)
Secretaria Geral
SBS - Ed. BNDES, 14° andar
70076 Brasília - DF

Associação Nacional de Tecnologia do Ambiente Construido (ANTAC)
Instituto de Pesquisas Tecnológitas do Estado de São Paulo - IPT
Divisão de Edificação - Prédio 27 - C. Universitária
05508 São Paulo SP

Banco de Dados do Mestrado em Desenvolvimento Urbano
Universidade Federal de Pernambuco
Cidade Universitaria
Engenho do Mejo
Recife / PE

Caixa Econômica Federal (ex - BNH)
Av. República do Chile 230 / 3° andar
Rio de Janeiro / RJ

Conselho Nacional de Desenvolvimento Urbano
Ministério do Interior
Esplanada dos Ministérios, Projeção 23 - térreo
Brasília / DF

Escola de Arquitetura e Urbanismo
Universidade Federa de Minas Gerais
Rua Paraíba, 697
Bairro dos Funcionários
Belo Horizonte / MG

Faculdade de Arquitetura
Universidade Federal da Bahia
Rua Caetano Moura, 121
Campus da Federação
Salvador / BA

Faculdade de Arquitetura e Urbanismo
Universidade de São Paulo
Rua do Lago, 876
05508 São Paulo - SP

Faculdade de Arquitetura e Urbanismo
Universidade Federal do Rio Grande do Sul
Av. Oswaldo Aranha, s/nº - térreo
Porto Alegre / RS

Financiadora de Estudos e Projetos (FINEP)
Av. Rio Branco 124 / 8º andar
Rio de Janeiro / RJ

Fundação Sistema Estudual de Análise de Dados
Av. Casper Libero, 464
01033 São Paulo - SP

Instituto Brasileiro de Geografia e Estatística (IBGE)
Rua Urussuí, 93 - Térreo
04542 São Paulo - SP

Instituto de Arquitetura e Urbanismo
Universidade de Brasília
Campus Universitário
Asa Norte
Brasília / DF

IPPUR / UFRJ
Edifício da Reitoria S. 543
Cidade Universitária - Ilha do Fundão
21910 Rio de Janeiro - RJ

Núcleo de Estudos Regionais e Urbanos (NERU)
Rua Cajaíba, 144
05025 São Paulo - SP

CANADA

Canadian Home Builders Association
20 Toronto Street, 4th Floor
Toronto, Ontario
Canada M5C 2B8
(416) 364–4135

Canadian Housing Information Centre
Canada Mortgage and Housing Corporation
National Office
682 Montreal Road
Ottawa, Ontario
Canada K1A OP7

Centre for Equality Rights in Accommodation
308 - 229 College Street
Toronto, Ontario
Canada M5T 1R4
(416) 599–9496

Centre for Human Settlements
University of British Columbia
2206 East Mall
Vancouver, British Columbia
Canada V6T 1W5
(604) 228–5254

Centre for Urban and Community Studies
University of Toronto
150 St. George Street
Toronto, Ontario
Canada M5S 1A1
(416) 978–2072

Community Planning Association of Canada
425 Gloucester Street
Ottawa, Ontario
Canada K1R 5E9
(613) 238–7834

Co-operative Housing Foundation of Canada
202 - 275 Bank Street
Ottawa, Ontario
Canada K2P 2L6
Canada K2P 2L6
(613) 238–4644

INRS—Urbanisation
Institut National de la Recherche Scientifique
Université du Quebec
3465, rue Durocher
Montreal, Quebec
Canada H2X 2C6
(514) 842–4191

Institute for Research on Public Policy
3535 Queen Mary Road, Suite 514
Montreal, Quebec
Canada
(514) 342–9121

Institute of Urban Studies
University of Winnipeg
515 Portgage Avenue
Winnipeg, Manitoba
Canada R3B 2E9
(204) 786–9849

Social Planning Council of Metropolitan Toronto
650 Yonge Street, Suite 1000
Toronto, Ontario
Canada M4W 2J4
(416) 961–9831

Urban Development Institute of Canada
151 Slayter Street, Suite 204
Ottawa, Ontario
Canada K1P 5H3
(613) 238–3998

CHINA

The Architectural Society of China
Baiwanzhuang, West District
Beijing
Telephone: 893868

Bureau of Science and Technology
Ministry of Urban and Rural Construction and Environmental Protection (MURCEP)
19, Che Gong Zhuang Street
Beijing
Telephone: 8992567

Centre of Urban and Regional Studies
College of Geoscience
Zhongshan University
Guangzhou 51027
Telephone: 4463000, ext. 677

China Academy of Urban Planning & Design
Baiwanzhuang
Beijing
Telephone: 896902

College of Architecture and Urban Planning
Tongji University
Shanghai
Telephone: 462121

Department of Architecture
Tsinghua University
Beijing
Telephone: 282451, ext. 2109

Shanghai Research Institute of Building Sciences
75 Wan Ping Road, South
Shanghai
Telephone: 380803

COLOMBIA

Directora Ejecutiva
Fedevivienda
AA 57059
Bogota

Ena/Fundemos
AA 2133
Manizales

Program de Estudios de Vivienda en América Latina
Facultad de Arquitectura
Universidad Nacional de Colombia
Medellín

CUBA

Facultad de Arquitectura (School of Architecture)
Instituto Superior Politécnico José Antonio Echeverría
Marianao, Ciudad de La Habana

Instituto de Planificación Física (Institute for Physical Planning)
Lamparilla 65
Habana Vieja
Ciudad de La Habana

Instituto Nacional de la Vivienda (National Housing Institute)
Apartado Postal 6157
Zona 6, Ciudad de La Habana

Union Nacional de Arquitectos e Ingenieros de la Construcción de Cuba (National Union
of Architects and Construction Engineers of Cuba)
Calle Humboldt No. 104 esq. Infanta
Ciudad de La Habana

EGYPT

Central Agency for Public Mobilisation and Statistics (CAPMAS)
Ministry of Planning
Arab Republic of Egypt
Heliopolis, Cairo

Department of Architecture
Cairo University
G12A
Cairo

General Organization for Building, Housing, and Planning Research
Pahrir Street
P.O. Box 1770
Cairo

Ministry of Housing
Kasr El Aini Street
Cairo

Information on housing in Egypt is also available from the following U.S. addresses:

Abt Associates, Inc.
55 Wheeler Road
Cambridge, MA 02138

Aga Khan Award for Architecture
Massachusetts Institute of Technology
77 Massachusetts Avenue
Building 10, Room 390
Cambridge, MA 02139

PADCO
1012 N Street, NW
Washington, DC 20003

United States Agency for International Development (USAID)
ANE-EE
Room 6723
2201 C Street, NW
Washington, DC 20523

FEDERAL REPUBLIC OF GERMANY

Bundesforschungsanstalt für Landeskunde und Raumordnung
Am Michaelshof 8
D 5300 Bonn 2
Städtebau
(research institute run by the federal government)

Bundesministerium für Raumordnung, Bauwesen und Städau
D–5300 Bonn-Bad Godesberg 1
Deichmannsaue
Telephone: 02221/8321
(Federal Department of Housing)

Deutsche Akademie für Städtebau und Landesplanung e.V.
D–8000 München 2
Arcisstrasse 21
Telephone: (089) 28 33 11

Deutscher Mieterbund e. V.
Postfach 41 02 69
D 5000 Köln 41
(interest group organizing renters)

Deutscher Städtetag
Lindenallee 13–17
D 5000 Köln-Marienburg
(local authority association that organizes big municipalities)

Deutscher Verband für Wohnungswesen, Städtebau und Raumordnung e. V.
Simrockstr. 20
5300 Bonn 1
(The Deutscher Verband is organizing interest groups and research and institutes that are active in the field of housing.)

Deutsches Institut für Urbanistik
Strasse des 17. Juni 112
D 1000 Berlin 12
Telephone: (030) 39 10 31
(research institute run by local authorities)

Forschungsgemeinschaft Bauen und Wohnen (FBW)
D–7000 Stuttgart 1
Silberburgstrasse 160
Telephone: (0711) 61 06 19

Gesamtverband gemeinnütziger
Wohnungsunternehmen e. V.
Bismarckstr. 7
D 5000 Köln 1
(interest group organizing not-for-profit housing associations)

Gesellschaft für Wohnungs- und Siedlungswesen e. V. (GEWOS)
D–2000 Hamburg 60
Schwalbenplatz 18
Telephone: (040) 692 02 1
(private research institute)

Informationsverbundzentrum Raum und Bau der Frauenhofer Gesellschaft
D–2000 Stuttgart 1
Silberburgstrasse 119A
Telephone: (0711) 62 39 62

Institut für Stadtforschung
und Strukturpolitik
Schöneberger Ufer 65
D 1000 Berlin 39
(private research institute)

Institut für Wohnen und Umwelt GmbH
D–6100 Darmstadt
Annastrasse 15
Telephone: (06151) 2 69 11

Statistisches Bundesamt
Philipp-Reis-Str. 3
D 6200 Wiesbaden 1
(Federal Statistical Office)

Zentralverband der Deutschen Haus-wohnungs- und Grundeigentümer e.V.
Cecilienalle 45
D 4000 Düsseldorf 30
(interest group organizing landlords)

GHANA

Ghana Cooperative Housing and Builders Association
Cooperative Housing
P.O. Box 8657
Accra—North Accra

Ministry of Works and Housing
Box M.43
Accra

Government organizations formulating housing policies:

Department of Rural Housing and Cottage Industries
P.O. Box 55
Accra

Ministry of Works and Housing
P.O. Box M.43
Accra

Institutions involved in the development of large scale housing estates for the general public:

The Estates Department
Social Security and National Insurance Trust
P.O. Box M149
Accra

REDCO Ltd.
P.O. Box 9753
Accra

State Housing Corporation
P.O. Box 2753
Accra

Tema Development Corporation
P.O. Box 16
Tema

Main financial institutions specializing in the provision of finance for house building:

Bank for Housing and Construction
P.O. Box M 1
Accra

First Ghana Building Society
P.O. Box 2958
Accra

Main research institutions:

Building and Road Research Institute
Council for Scientific and Industrial Research
P.O. Box 40
Kumasi

University of Science & Technology
Department of Housing & Planning Research
Kumasi

A source of information on housing projects funded by foreign sponsors:

Technical Services Centre
Ministry of Works and Housing
P.O. Box M.43
Accra

HUNGARY

Center for Building Information (ETK)
Hársfa u. 21
1074 Budapest

Housing Department
Ministry of Transport, Communications, and Building
DOB utca 75–81
H–1077 Budapest

Hungarian Academy of Sciences
Committee for Urban Studies
Münnich Ferenc u. 47
1051 Budapest

Hungarian Institute for Town and Regional Planning (VATI)
Krisztina krt. 99
H–1016 Budapest

Institute for Building Economy and Organization (EGSZI)
Pf. 267
H–1519 Budapest

Institute of Sociology
Hungarian Academy of Sciences
H–1014 Uri utca 49
Budapest

Központi Statisztikai Hivatal (KSH)
Central Statistical Office
1024 Budapest, II
Keleti Kàroly utca 5/7

Ministry of Internal Affairs
Beloiannisz u. 2–4
1054 Budapest

Town Planning Department of the Technical University of Budapest
Müegyetem rkp. 3
1111 Budapest

ISRAEL

Amidar
Department of Community Work
33 Shaul Hamelekh Boulevard
Tel Aviv

Center for Urban and Regional Studies
Faculty of Architecture and Town Planning
Technion—Israel Institute of Technology
Technion City, Haifa 32000

Center for Urban Studies
The Hebrew University of Jerusalem
Mount Scopus, Jerusalem 91905

Center of Information and Economic Analysis
The Ministry of Construction and Housing
P.O. Box 18110
Jerusalem 91180

National Institute for Building Research
Faculty of Civil Engineering
Technion—Israel Institute of Technology
Technion City, Haifa 32000

ITALY

Associazione nazionale fra gli Istituti Autonomi e Consorzi Case Popolari (ANIACAP)
Palazzo della Civiltà del Lavoro—EUR
00144 Roma

Centre for Social and Economic Research in the Housing and Building Market (CRESME)
Via Lebenico
2 Rome

Centro Ricerche Economiche Sociologiche di Mercato sull'Edilizia (CRESME)
Via Sebenico 2
00198 Roma

(An institute promoted by an association of construction companies, municipalities, banks, and so on. It does research on different aspects of housing and current trends in housing production. It also issues a regular series of research reports and a quarterly, *Cresme Notizie*.)

Comitato per l'Edilizia Residenziale of the Ministry of Public Works (CER)
Porta Pia, Rome

Comitato per le Scienze di Ingegneria e Architettura
Piazzale delle Scienze 7
Rome

Committee for Research and Experimentation on Housing
Higher Council of Public Works
Rome

Directorate-General of Territorial Co-ordination of the Ministry of Public Works
Rome

Instituto Centrale di Statistica (ISTAT)
Via Cesare Balbo 16
00100 Roma

Instituto Nazionale di Urbanistica (INU)
46 via de S. Caterina da Siena
Rome

JAPAN

High-Rise Housing Association of Japan
Shinjuku-Sumitomo Building
Nishi-Shinjuku 2–6–1
Shinjuku Tokyo 160

Housing and Urban Development Corporation (HUDC)
Kudankita 1–14–6
Chiyoda Tokyo 100

Housing Association of Japan
Jutaku-Kaikan Building
Toranomon 2–3–8
Minato Tokyo 105

Housing Council of Japan
c/o Professor K. Hayakawa
Department of Architecture and Environmental Planning
Kobe University
Rokkodai, Nada Kobe 657

Housing Loan Corporation
Koraku 1–4–10
Bunkyo Tokyo 112

Architectural Institute of Japan
Shiba 5–26–20
Minato Tokyo 108

Ministry of Construction
Kasumigaseki 2–1–3
Chiyoda Tokyo 100

Ministry of Health and Welfare
Kasumigaseki 1–2–2
Chiyoda Tokyo 100–45

Public-Housing Tenants' Association of Japan
Nakasatocho 25
Shinjuku Tokyo 162

Real Estate Institute of Japan
Kangin-Fujiya Building
Toranomon 1–3–2
Minato Tokyo 105

Residents Association of the Housing and Urban Development Corporation
Fujimi 1–7–9
Chiyoda Tokyo 102

Tenant Association of Japan
Yoshiko Ueno
Sun-City 21 Building
Togoshi 5–19–13
Shinagawa Tokyo 142

Urban Developers Association of Japan
Nagatacho 2–14–3
Chiyoda Tokyo 10

KENYA

Central Bureau of Statistics
Herufi House
P.O. Box 30266
Nairobi

Government Press
Haille Selassie Avenue
P.O. Box 30128
Nairobi

Housing and Social Services Department
Nairobi City Council
City Hall
P.O. Box 30075
Nairobi

Housing Development Department
Nairobi City Commission
P.O. Box 42074
Nairobi

Housing Finance Company of Kenya Ltd.
Rehani House
Kenyatta Avenue/Koinange Street
P.O. Box 30088
Nairobi

Housing Research and Development Unit
University of Nairobi
P.O. Box 30197
Nairobi

Ministry of Cooperative Development
Housing Unit
P.O. Box 30547
Nairobi

Ministry of Lands and Housing
Department of Housing
P.O. Box 30450
Nairobi

Ministry of Local Government and Physical Planning
Jogoo House A
Harambee Avenue
P.O. Box 30004
Nairobi

National Cooperative Housing Unit
P.O. Box 51693
Nairobi

National Housing Corporation
Aga Khan Walk
P.O. Box 30201
Nairobi

MEXICO

Centro de la Vivienda y Estudios Urbanos (CENVI)
Violeta 27
Copilco el Bajo
CP 04340
Mexico DF

Centro Operacional de Poblamiento y de Vivienda (COPEVI)
Tlaloc 40
Mexico DF

Fideicomiso Fondo de Habitaciones Populares (FONHAPO)
H Suderman 159
CP11560
Mexico DF

Instituto del Fondo Nacional de la Vivienda Para los Trabajadores (INFONAVIT)
Barranca del Muerto 280
CP 01020
Mexico DF

Secretaría de Desarrollo Urbano y Ecología (SEDUE)
Constituyentes 947
CP 01110
Mexico DF

THE NETHERLANDS

Bouwcentrum
Weena 760
3014 DA Rotterdam
Telephone: (010) 430 99 11

Centraal Bureau voor de Statistiek
Prinses Beatrixlaan 428
2273 XZ Voorburg

Centrale Directie Voorlichting en Externe Betrekkingen
(Department for Information and External Relations)
Ministry of Housing, Physical Planning and Environmental Protection
Van Alkemadelaan 85
2597 AC 's-Gravenhage
Telephone: 070 - 264201

Centre for Metropolitan Research
University of Amsterdam
Oude Hoogstraat 24
1012 CE Amsterdam
Telephone: 020 - 5252204

Department of Research in the Directorate of Housing
Ministry of Housing, Physical Planning and Environmental Protection
Boerhaavelaan 5
2713 HA, Zoetermeer
Telephone: (079) 27 91 11

Economic Institute for Building Construction
Cuserstraat 89
1081 CN Amsterdam
Telephone: 020 - 429342

Economisch Instituut voor de Bouwnijverheid
Afdeling Voorlichting
Cronenburg 150
1081 GN Amsterdam

Institute for Geographical Research
University of Utrecht
P.O. Box 80.115
3508 TC Utrecht
Telephone: 030 - 534261

Landelijke Organisatie Belangengroepen Huisvesting
Henri Polaklaan 12^b
1018 CS Amsterdam
Telephone: (020) - 223 505

National Physical Planning Agency (RPD) of the Ministry of Housing, Physical Planning
and Environment
Willem Witsenplein 6
2596 BK Den Haag
Telephone: 070 - 26 42 01

Nederlands Instituut voor Ruimtelijke Ordening en Volkshuisvesting
(Netherlands Institute for Physical Planning and Housing)
Mauritskade 21–23
2514 HD's-Gravenhage
Telephone: 070 - 469652

Research Institute for Policy Sciences and Technology
Delft University of Technology
Thijsseweg 11
2629 JA Delft
Telephone: 015 - 783005

PAKISTAN

(Requires postage paid reply envelope)

Chief, Physical Planning and Housing Section
Planning and Development Division
Secretariat Block P.
Islamabad

Directorate Kotehi Abadig and Evaluation
KMC Head Office
M.A. Jinnah Road
Karachi

Director General
Capital Development Authority (CDA)
Islamabad

Director General
Hyderabad Development Authority (HDA)
Hyderabad

Director General
Karachi Development Authority (KDA)
Karachi

Director General
Lahore Development Authority (LDA)
Lahore

Environmental and Urban Affairs Division
Ministry of Housing and Works
Islamabad

Federal Bureau of Statistics
Sindhi Muslim Housing Society
Karachi

Baharia Complex (NESPAK)
Queens Road
Karachi

Pakistan Environmental Planning and Architectural Consultants (PEPAK)
25 Main Gulberg
Lahore

POLAND

Glowny Urzad Statystyczny (Central Statistical Office)
Warsaw

Instytut Gospodarki Przestrzenia (Institute of Space Economy)
Wydzial Geografii i Studiow Regionalnych
Uniwersytet Warszawaki
ul. Krakowskie Przedmiescie 30
Warsaw

Instytut Ksztaltowania Srodowiska (Institute of Environmental Policies)
ul. Krzywickiego
Warsaw

The following universities have specialized sections dealing with urban sociology and urban social problems:

Institute of Sociology
Catholic University
Lublin

Institute of Sociology
Jagiellonian University
ul. Grodzka 52
Cracow

Institute of Sociology
University of Warsaw
ul. Karowa 18
Warsaw

Information about current research can also be obtained from the following:

Urban Sociology Section
Polish Sociological Association
ul. Nowy Swiat 72
Warsaw

SINGAPORE

Housing and Development Board
National Development Building
Maxwell Road
Singapore 1

SOUTH AFRICA

Central Statistical Service
Private Bag X44
Pretoria 001

Centre for Policy Studies
9 Jubilee Road
Parktown 2193

Department of Constitutional Development and Planning
Private Bag X645
Pretoria 0001

Division of Building Technology
CSIR
P.O. Box 395
Pretoria 001

Human Sciences Research Council
Private Bag x41
Pretoria 001

Indicator Project South Africa
Centre for Social and Development Studies
University of Natal
King George V Avenue
Durban 4001

Planact
Box 93540
Yeoville 2143

South African Institute of Race Relations
Box 31044
Braamfontein 2017

The Urban Foundation
Box 1198
Johannesburg 2000

UNION OF SOVIET SOCIALIST REPUBLICS

All-Union Research Institute for Theory of Architecture and City Planning (VNIITAG)
Kalinin Avenue 5
121019 Moscow

All-Union Research Institute of Industrial Design (VNIITE)
VDNH Exhibition
129223 Moscow

Central Town Planning Research and Design Institute of the State Committee for Civil
Engineering and Architecture (attached to the GOSSTROY of the USSR)
Pr. Vernadskovo 29
Moscow

Department of Typology
Central Research and Experimental Planning Institute of Residential Buildings (TsNIIEP
zhilishcha)
Dmitrovskoye Road 9, Building B
127434 Moscow

Department of Typology of Residential Buildings
Tbilisi Zonal Research & Experimental Planning Institute
(TbilZNIIEP)
Sandro Euli St. 5A
380086 Tbilisi
Georgia

Environmental Psychology Research Unit
Tallinn Pedagogical Institute
Narva mnt. 25
Tallinn 200102
Estonia

State Committee for Building of the Council of Ministers of the USSR (GOSSTROY)
Prospekt Karla Marksa 4
Moscow

State Committee for Civil Engineering and Architecture (attached to the GOSSTROY of
the USSR)
ul. Pushinskaya 24
Moscow

Union of Architects of the USSR
ul. Shchuseva 3
Moscow

UNITED KINGDOM

Bartlett School of Architecture and Planning
University College London (UCL)
22 Gordon Street
London WC1H OQB
Telephone: 01–387 7050

Centre for Housing Research
University of Glasgow
Glasgow G12 8RT
Telephone: (041) 339 88 55

Centre for Housing Studies
University of Salford
Salford M5 4NT

Department of the Environment
2 Marsham Street
London SW1
Telephone: 01–212 34 34

Institute of Housing
9 White Lion Street
Islington
London N1 9XJ

Royal Town Planning Institute (RTPI)
26, Portland Place
London W1N 4BE
Telephone: 01–636 9107

School of Advanced Urban Studies (SAUS)
University of Bristol
Rodney Lodge
Grange Road
Bristol BS8 4EA
Telephone: 74 11 17

Shelter (National Campaign for the Homeless)
88 Old Street
London EC1

University of Birmingham
Centre for Urban and Regional Studies
PO Box 363
Birmingham B15 2TT
Telephone: (021) 472 13 01

Urban and Regional Studies Unit
University of Kent
Canterbury
Kent
Telephone: 0227 66822

UNITED STATES

American Association of Housing Educators (AAHE)
c/o Jo Ann Emmel
Box 3AE
New Mexico State University
Las Cruces, NM 88003
Telephone: (505) 646–3425

American Planning Association (APA)
1776 Massachusetts Avenue, NW
Washington, DC 20036

Association of Local Housing Finance Agencies (ALHFA)
1101 Connecticut Avenue, Suite 700
Washington, DC 20036
Telephone: (202) 857–1197

American Mobile Home Association (AMA)
12929 W. 26th Avenue
Golden, CO 80401
Telephone: (303) 232–6336

Bureau of the Census
U.S. Department of Commerce
Washington, DC 20233

Cooperative Housing Foundation (CHF)
2501 M Street, NW, Suite 450
Washington, DC 20037
Telephone: (202) 887–0700

Council of Large Public Housing Authorities (CLPHA)
Seven Marshall Street
Boston, MA 02108
Telephone: (617) 742–0820

Council for Rural Housing and Development (CRHD)
2300 M Street, NW, 4th Floor
Washington, DC 20037
Telephone: (202) 955–9715

Department of Commerce
National Bureau of Standards
Center for Building Technology
Washington, DC 20234

Department of Housing and Urban Development
451 7th Street, SW
Washington, DC 20410

Enterprise Foundation (EF)
505 American City Building
Columbia, MD 21044

Floating Homes Association (FHA)
710 Waldo Point Harbor
Sausalito, CA 94965
Telephone: (415) 332–5307

F. W. Dodge Division, McGraw-Hill Information Systems Co.
1221 Avenue of the Americas
New York, NY 10020

Housing Assistance Council (HAC)
1025 Vermont Avenue, NW, Suite 606
Washington, DC 20005
Telephone: (202) 842–8600

HUD User (Information Service of the U.S. Department of Housing and Urban Development)
P.O.B. 280
Germantown, MD 20874

Low Income Housing Information Service (LIHIS)
1012 14th Street, NW, #1006
Washington, DC 20005
Telephone: (202) 662–1530

Mortgage Bankers Association of America (MBA)
1125 15th Street, NW
Washington, DC 20005

National Association of Home Builders of the U.S. (NAHB)
15th and M Streets, NW
Washington, DC 20005

National Association of Housing and Redevelopment Officials (NAHRO)
1320 18th Street, NW
Washington, DC 20036
Telephone: (202) 429–2960

National Association of Realtors
777 14th Street, NW
Washington, DC 20005

National Center for Housing Management (NCHM)
1275 K Street, NW
Washington, DC 20005
Telephone: (202) 872–1717

National Coalition for the Homeless (NCH)
1439 Rhode Island Avenue
Washington, DC 20005
Telephone: (202) 659–3310

National Committee Against Discrimination in Housing
1425 H. Street, NW
Washington, DC 20005

National Council of State Housing Agencies (NCSHA)
444 N. Capital Street, Suite 118
Washington, DC 20001
Telephone: (202) 624–7710

National Federation of Housing Counselors (NFHC)
P.O. Box 33755
Washington, DC 20033
Telephone: (202) 797–8308

National Homeowners Association (NHA)
1906 Sunderland Place, SW
Washington, DC 20036
Telephone: (202) 223–1453

National Housing and Rehabilitation Association (NHRA)
1726 18th Street, NW
Washington, DC 20009
Telephone: (202) 328–9171

National Housing Conference (NHC)
1126 16th Street, NW, Suite 211
Washington, DC 20036
Telephone: (202) 223–4844

National Housing Law Project (NHLP)
1950 Addison Street
Berkeley, CA 94704
Telephone: (415) 548–9400

National Institute of Senior Housing (NISH)
c/o National Council on the Aging
600 Maryland Avenue, SW
W. Wing 100
Washington, DC 20024

National Low Income Housing Coalition (NLIHC)
1012 14th Street, NW, #1006
Washington, DC 20005

National Mobile/Manufactured Home Owners Foundation (NMMHOF)
P.O. Box 33
Redmond, WA 98073

National Rural Housing Coalition (NRHC)
201 Massachusetts Avenue, NE, #C–8
Washington, DC 20002

National Shared Housing Resource Center (NSHRC)
6344 Greene Street
Philadelphia, PA 19144

National Tenants Union (NTU)
439 Main Street
Orange, NJ 07050

Public Housing Authorities Directors Association (PHADA)
Hall of the States
444 N. Capitol Street, NW, Suite 614
Washington, DC 20001
Telephone: (202) 624–5445

Shelterforce
439 Main Street
Orange, NJ 07050

United States Congress
House of Representatives
Committee on Banking, Finance, and Urban Affairs
Sub-Committee on Housing and Community Development
Room 2139, Rayburn House Office Building
Washington, DC 20515

Urban Homesteading Assistance Board (UHAB)
40 Prince Street
New York, NY 10012

Urban Institute
2100 M Street, NW
Washington, DC 20036

Urban Land Institute (ULI)
1090 Vermont Avenue, NW
Washington, DC 20005

Name Index

Subject Index

About the Contributors

SETH OPUNI ASIAMA is a senior lecturer in land economy at the University of Science and Technology in Kumasi, Ghana. He specializes in housing research with an emphasis on land factors in Ghana in particular and Africa in general, and he is the author of several publications about these topics.

LARRY S. BOURNE is Professor of Geography and Planning and past Director of the Centre for Urban and Community Studies (1972–1984) at the University of Toronto. His most recent books include *The Geography of Housing* and the edited collections *Internal Structure of the City*, 2d ed.; *Urbanization and Settlement Systems: International Perspectives*; *Progress in Settlement Systems Geography*; and *Urban Systems in Transition*.

TERRY BURKE is a senior lecturer in the Social and Political Studies Department and chair of the Center for Urban and Social Research at Swinburne Institute of Technology in Melbourne. Coauthor of the books *Youth Housing Policy*, *A Roof over Their Heads*, and *Social Theory and the Australian City*, he has also contributed to a number of journals and edited texts. As a consultant to federal, state, and local government authorities, he has prepared documents on the private rental sector, housing needs, youth housing, and local government development controls.

NAOMI CARMON is a faculty member in Architecture and Town Planning and a senior researcher of the Samuel Neaman Institute for Advanced Studies in Science and Technology, both at the Technion-Israel Institute of Technology. She has lectured in Israel, the United States, and Great Britain and has published extensively in the fields of urban sociology, social policy planning and evaluation, housing, and urban renewal. Carmon also has served as a government consultant. Her recent books are *Neighborhood Rehabilitation* (Hebrew) and, as editor, *Neighborhood Policy and Programs*.

LATA CHATTERJEE is Associate Professor of Urban Affairs and City Planning, Boston University. Her research interests are in Third World development and international housing policy. She was on two USAID missions to Egypt that analyzed the problems of land development for low-income housing and the informal housing sector and has published more than thirty articles on Korea, Indonesia, India, Egypt, Nigeria, Ghana, and Brazil as well as editing two books: *Urban Problems and Economic Development* and *Urban and Regional Policy Analysis in Developing Countries*.

DAVID K. Y. CHU has been a lecturer in the Department of Geography at the Chinese University of Hong Kong since 1979. He specializes in the urban and economic geography of China and Hong Kong and is the author of many articles and book chapters as well as editor and coeditor of two books on Shenzhen Special Economic Zones.

DANIEL CZAMANSKI is Associate Professor of Economics in the Faculty of Architecture and Town Planning at the Technion-Israel Institute of Technology. He has published on local public finance and public utility regulation and, more recently, on theoretical models of industrial location in the face of divorce of ownership and management. He is currently exploring future market characteristics of housing markets, evaluating Israel's efforts to settle the Galilee, and preparing an economic development plan for Israel's high-technology region.

JILL HAMBERG is an urban planner whose work in recent years has included writing and consulting on housing and homeless issues and community needs assessments. She has taught at universities in Latin America and in the New York City area. At present, she is completing a doctoral dissertation on Cuban housing and urban planning.

MICHAEL HARLOE is a reader in sociology and Dean of Social Sciences at the University of Essex. He is the author of numerous books and articles based on extensive research in housing and urban studies. His present work includes an international study of innovative housing policies and practices as responses to emerging housing crises and a study of urban change in London and New York. He is also the editor of the *International Journal of Urban and Regional Research*.

TIMOTHY HART is an urban geographer and head of the Environmental Studies Division of the National Institute for Personnel Research of the Human Sciences Research Council in South Africa. His recent research and publications have covered many aspects of low-income housing and housing policy under apartheid, including self-help housing, the privatization of black township housing, housing finance in informal residential areas, and the upgrading of services in black towns.

KAZUO HAYAKAWA has been an architect in the Japan Housing Corporation and Chief Researcher in the Building Research Institute, Ministry of Construction, of the Japanese Government. He is currently Professor of Architecture and Environmental Planning at Kobe University, Japan. He is also the founder and chairman of the Japan Housing Council. His English publications include the articles "Built Environment in Japan," "The Management of Land as an Environmental Resource," and "Housing Poverty in Japan," as well as one chapter, "Japan," in *Housing Practice in Asia*.

J. DAVID HULCHANSKI is Director of the UBC Centre for Human Settlements and Associate Professor of Community and Regional Planning, University of British Columbia, Canada, where he teaches housing policy. He previously taught in the Urban Studies Program at the University of Toronto where he was a research associate with its Centre for Urban and Community Studies. His contributions to the housing literature deal extensively with policy aspects and low-income populations, and his research for federal and provincial governments has focused on housing affordability, rental-subsidy programs, and residential land-use intensification.

WOLFGANG JAEDICKE is a political scientist at the Free University of Berlin. He specializes in social policy, housing policy, and intergovernmental relations. He has done research on local authorities and low income housing. His publications include: "Regulating and Implementing Social Assistance in Germany" (with Kurt Ruhland and Hellmut Wollmann, in *Discretionary Politics*, ed. Douglas E. Ashford (forthcoming); and "Rote Politik im schwarzen Rathaus? Die Bestimmungsfaktoren der wohnungspolitischen Ausgaben bundesdeutscher Grossstädte" (with Hans Grüner und Kurt Ruhland), *Politische Vierteljahresschrift* 29: 42–57.

SYED IQBAL KALIM is a city and regional planner who has research expertise as well as practical experience in the field of low-income housing and planning through posts with the federal and local government in Pakistan and with private consultants. At present, he is with the Karachi Development Authority and teaches urban planning at the Dawood College of Engineering, Karachi. His publications include the chapter "Incorporating Slum Dwellers into Redevelopment Schemes: The Jacob Lines Project in Karachi," in *Land for Housing the Poor*, and the articles "Policy Constraints on Planning for Land for Low-Income Groups in Karachi" and "Redeveloping Karachi's Inner City: The Lines Area Project" (both with Peter Nientied).

R. YIN-WANG KWOK is a professor and director of the Centre of Urban Studies and Urban Planning, University of Hong Kong, and holds visiting professorships at Zhongshan University (Gaungzhou), Tsinghua University (Beijing), and Wuham Academy of Urban Construction (Wuhan) and an advisory professorship at Tongji University (Shanghai). He specializes in urbanization in contemporary China, Third World development and urbanization (Pacific Asia), urban and regional economic development, and the theory of urban planning and design. His recent publications cover urbanization in contemporary China and Hong Kong, urban-planning and urban-design theory, and planning education.

KINUTHIA MACHARIA is a graduate of the University of Nairobi and a Fulbright Fellow. He has just completed his Ph.D. in Urban Sociology at the University of California, Berkeley. His current research is on the social dynamics of the urban informal sector in Nairobi, Kenya. Most of his past research has been on housing in Kenya, some of which has been published in the *International Journal of Urban and Regional Research*. In 1982–1983 he worked as the social sciences program consultant for the East and Southern Africa Regional office for both the Ford Foundation and the International Development Research Center.

PETER MARCUSE, an attorney and planner, practiced law for twenty years in Waterbury, Connecticut, where he served as majority leader of its Board of Alderman, on its Planning Commission, and as first chair of its antipoverty agency. He is a professor of urban planning at Columbia University, and chair of the Housing Committee of Community Board 9 in Manhattan. Marcuse has written extensively on housing policy, housing theory, the history of planning, planning ethics, planning law, and international comparisons of planning and housing issues in the United States and Western Europe and is currently at work on a history of public housing in New York City.

WILLIAM MICHELSON is Professor of Sociology at the University of Toronto, where he is also associated with the Centre for Urban and Community Studies. His research interests concern how people's contexts bear on their lives; this has led to work on such topics as housing, urban children, and maternal employment. His most recent books are *From Sun to Sun: Daily Obligations and Community Structure in the Lives of Employed Women and Their Families* and (coedited with Robert Bechtel and Robert Marans) *Methods for Environmental and Behavioral Research*.

BRONISLAW MISZTAL is Associate Professor of Urban Sociology at Indiana University-Purdue University in Fort Wayne. His research deals with theoretical and political-economic aspects of the production of the built environment, and he is particularly interested in the spontaneity of social processes and state interventionism aimed at controlling such processes. He also studies urban social movements and has published three scholarly books and edited two volumes.

His articles have appeared in *Urban Affairs Quarterly, Politics and Society, Sociology, British Journal of Sociology, Australian and New Zealand Journal of Sociology*, and the *International Journal of Comparative Sociology*.

HENRY W. MORTON is Professor of Political Science at Queens College of the City University of New York. He has written extensively on Soviet urban problems including "Who Gets What, When and How? Housing in the U.S.S.R." and is coeditor of and contributor to *The Contemporary Soviet City*.

PETER W. NEWTON is a principal research scientist in the Commonwealth Scientific and Industrial Research Organisation, Melbourne. He is the author or editor of several recently published books in several arenas of planning: *A Roof over Their Heads: Housing Issues and Families in Australia, The Future of Urban Form: The Impact of New Technology, Microcomputers for Local Government Planning and Management, The Spatial Impact of Technological Change, Resource Communities: Settlement and Workforce Issues*, and *Desktop Planning: Advanced Microcomputer Applications for Physical and Social Infrastructure Planning*.

PETER NIENTIED is a social geographer who has done extensive research on low-income housing and government housing policy in Karachi, Pakistan. As a staff member of the Institute for Housing Studies at Rotterdam, he is presently on assignment as the codirector of the Indian Human Settlements Programme, New Delhi, India. His publications include the article "The Short-Term Impact of Housing Upgrading on Housing Values" and the book *Practice and Theory of Urban Policy in the Third World*.

JOSÉ OSPINA, who helped to found the Bristol Self-Help Community Housing Association, participated in several initiatives within the British housing association movement, and helped to found FEDEVIVIENDA, the National Federation of Popular Housing Organizations. He is now a development worker for Cooperative Housing in South East London and a member of the National Committee of the National Federation of Housing Cooperatives (UK) as well as a representative of FEDEVIVIENDA abroad. He is the author of a number of articles on housing in Colombia that have appeared in *Habitat International, Open Door International, Cities*, and the *Journal of Community Development*. He is also the author of *Housing Ourselves*, a book on community housing in Britain and Colombia.

J. JOHN PALEN is a professor and chair at the Department of Sociology and Anthropology at Virginia Commonwealth University. His most recent urban books are *Gentrification, Displacement, and Neighborhood Revitalization* and *The Urban World* (4th ed.). Palen is particularly interested in revitalization of working-class neighborhoods and housing patterns in Southeast Asia.

HUGO PRIEMUS is a professor in housing at Delft University of Technology, The Netherlands. Since 1985 he also has been managing director of the OTB Research Institute for Policy Sciences and Technology at the same university. He is chair of the Editorial Board of the *Netherlands Journal of Housing and Environmental Research*, and his publications include numerous books and articles about housing markets and housing policy.

CÉLINE SACHS is a consultant in the Strategic Planning and Review Department at the World Bank, Washington, D.C., where she is working on the project "Facing the Urban Challenge: What Strategy for the World Bank?" Her publications include a study of low-income housing policies in São Paulo, "Evolution et limites de la promotion publique de logements populaires à Sao Paulo (1964–1985)." She was the coordinator of the United Nations University/Groupe de Recherches et d'Echanges Technologiques Project "Communication and Urban Self-Reliance Strategies" and is coauthor of the International Foundation for Development Alternatives *Urban Self-Reliance Directory*.

JOHN A. A. SILLINCE teaches at Coventry (Lancaster) Polytechnic, Coventry, England. He has published articles on planning in Spain, English Key settlement policy, bias in local press reporting, attitudes toward nuclear power, and housing and regional policy in Hungary. He is the author of *A Theory of Planning* and is editor of *Housing in Eastern Europe*.

SUZANA PASTERNAK TASCHNER is an architect and professor in the Department of Architecture and Planning at the University of São Paulo, and was director of the Programa de Estudos em Demografia e Urbanização—Demography and Urbanization Studies Program, Conselho Latino Americano de Ciencias Sociais—Latin American Council of Social Sciences, and Financiadora de Estudos e Projetos—Project and Surveys Financing Agency until 1983. She organized the First Squatter Settlement Census in São Paulo and wrote, with Y. Mautner, *Habitação da Pobreza* (Housing for the Poor). She is the author of several articles and chapters about squatter settlements and self-help housing.

ANTONIO TOSI is Professor of Urban Sociology at the Polytechnic of Milan. He has written on comparative urbanization, welfare state and social policies, and housing policies and practices in Italy. He is the author of *Ideologie della casa* (Housing Ideologies) (1978) and co-author of *Modelli di cittá* (Patterns of Cities) (1987). He has consulted with various planning agencies and educational institutions in Italy and abroad. His current research deals with informal sector and self-help housing, theoretical problems in the analysis of housing needs, and comparative housing policies.

JAN VAN DER LINDEN is a social geographer who, since 1971, has been involved in research on low-income housing and housing policy in Karachi,

Pakistan. He is a senior lecturer at the Department of Development Sociology, Free University, Amsterdam. His publications include the book *The Sites and Services Approach Reviewed*, and the article "Sites and services: The Background of Bottlenecks."

WILLEM VAN VLIET— is a sociologist in the College of Environmental Design and a research associate in the Institute of Behavioral Science at the University of Colorado. His research interests concern international housing policies and practices, the political-economic context of planning, and the housing and community requirements of special population groups. He has contributed widely to journals and books and recently edited *Housing Markets and Policies under Fiscal Austerity* (Greenwood 1987) and *Women, Housing and Community*.

PETER M. WARD is a lecturer in Geography at the University of Cambridge, England, and a fellow of Fitzwilliam College. He is sometimes adviser to the United Nations Centre for Human Settlements and to the World Health Organization and has extensive advisory experience in Mexico. His principal research interests lie in social welfare provision, urban land development, self-help housing, community action, and local leadership structures. He has written extensively on these topics and among his principal publications are *Self-help Housing: A Critique* (editor), *Housing, the State, and the Poor: Policy and Practice in Latin American Cities* (with Alan Gilbert), *Welfare Politics in Mexico, Leadership and Self-Help Housing* (with Sylvia Chant), and *Corruption, Development, and Inequality* (editor).

HELLMUT WOLLMANN is Professor of Political Science at the Free University in Berlin. He is author and editor of numerous articles and books including *Kommunale Wohnungspolitik* (with Hans-Georg Lange and Adalbert Evers), *Lokale Beschäftigungspolitik* (with Hans E. Maier), *Die zweite Stadt* (with Bernhard Blanke and Adalbert Evers), and *Dezentrale Technologiepolitik* (with Jochen Hucke).

MARYANN WULFF is a fellow with the Australian Institute of Family Studies. Previously, she was on the academic staff of Cornell University and Swinburne Institute of Technology in Australia. She has prepared a number of papers for international journals, books, and conferences on housing costs, housing satisfaction, and public housing policy. She is currently working on a monograph on low-income families and their housing options.